MW00810876

CHURCH HISTORY: THE BASICS

AN ABRIDGED EDITION OF
THE CHURCH FROM AGE TO AGE

GENERAL EDITOR: EDWARD A. ENGELBRECHT

ROBERT G. CLOUSE

KARL H. DANNENFELDT

MARIANKA S. FOUSEK

WALTER OETTING

K. DETLEV SCHULZ

ROY A. SUELFLOW

CARL A. VOLZ

Concordia
Publishing House

Library of Congress Cataloging-in-Publication Data

Names: Engelbrecht, Edward, editor. | Clouse, Robert G., 1931-
Title: Church history : the basics / General Editor, Edward A. Engelbrecht;
  Associate Editor, Laura L. Lane ; Robert G. Clouse, Karl H. Dannenfeldt,
  Edward A. Engelbrecht, Marianka S. Fousek, Walter Oetting, K. Detlev
  Schulz, Roy A. Suelflow, Carl A. Volz ; Foreword by Paul L. Maier.
Description: St. Louis, MO : Concordia Publishing House, 2016. | Includes
  index. | Description based on print version record and CIP data provided
  by publisher; resource not viewed.
Identifiers: LCCN 2015035287 (print) | LCCN 2015034632 (ebook) | ISBN
  9780758652720 () | ISBN 9780758652713
Subjects: LCSH: Church history.
Classification: LCC BR145.3 (print) | LCC BR145.3 .C482 2016 (ebook) | DDC
  270--dc23
LC record available at http://lccn.loc.gov/2015035287

1 2 3 4 5 6 7 8 9 10   25 24 23 22 21 20 19 18 17 16

Contents

Foreword

Christianity is the greatest success story in the history of the world. No other religion or institution or government comes even close to the number of its adherents, with some two and a quarter billion in the present generation alone. It has exerted a greater influence, changed more lives, educated more people, fostered more progress in the arts and sciences, inspired loftier achievements in culture, and had a more powerful role in helping the helpless than any other institution on earth. In the past two thousand years, it has indeed proven to be the greatest movement ever.

The organized expression of Christianity is the Church—that wondrous collective of Roman Catholics, Eastern Orthodox, Protestants of every variety, and groups that defy any category—a mighty miscellany of those who confess Christ as Savior. That the Church should have sprouted from the seedbed of Judaism through the life and teachings of one man and be transmitted by His twelve followers and their followers seems inconceivable. That this movement even survived beggars belief, since the most powerful empire in the world tried every means available to eradicate it. Judaism, its parent, largely disowned its own offspring. A welter of competing pagan religions all hated the Christian movement and tried to suppress it.

Nay, more. Not only did the Church have to struggle for survival against external foes, but internal enemies as well: heretics, who, like opportunistic bacteria, preyed upon the wounded body of the Church before its own defenses—the New Testament canon and the Creed—had been fully developed to separate truth from error. By all rules of historical precedent, then, Christianity should have shared the fate of countless extinct sects in the ancient world, the butt of jokes about a peculiar breed of people who believed that their founder was the Son of God when in fact He was a crucified criminal.

That Christianity not only survived but thrived is miraculous and itself a proof of God's existence. The incredible saga of how this happened, and how the Church grew and spread, is the substance of this book. It will not, however, be a prolonged glory story. Alas, "the Holy Christian Church" has always been composed of saints who are sinners as well. There will be disappointing chapters as sad counterpoints to the successes and triumphs, since scrupulous honesty has been the absolute mandate in these pages.

Clearly, this book has a huge story to tell. It may be helpful to offer, at the outset, a menu for the literary feast to follow. This is not to "give away the plot," as it were, but to offer something of an appetizer that may help the reader more easily digest two thousand years of Christian history. In this volume, seven distinct eras appear—seven, not because of any biblical significance, but because it accords well with the way historians often divide the past two millennia.

The Early Church (to AD 250) deals with the all-important beginnings of Christianity: Jesus; Paul; the apostles and their mission journeys; the testimony of the Church Fathers; the early defenders and defamers of the faith; how the New Testament canon, the Creed, and church government were established; and especially the horror of the Roman persecutions.

The Church in a Changing World (250 to 600) tells how the persecutions were finally halted after the extraordinary conversion of Constantine, the first Roman emperor to convert to Christianity, and how the faith went on to conquer Rome itself. Although the empire declined and fell to Germanic invaders, they, in turn, were conquered by Christ through Christian missionaries. As dark ages blanketed Europe, the Church and its priests and monks, as the only educated class, saved civilization in the West, while Christians of Asia and Africa continued to thrive until suppressed by *dhimma* status under Islam.

The Church of the Middle Ages (600 to 1400) deals with Medieval Europe when the Church and its papacy were challenged by their own successes as *the* dominant forces in Western civilization, much as the patriarchs of Constantinople were in Eastern Orthodoxy. This was the era of powerful popes and soaring cathedrals, yet also a time when too close a link between Church and state led to doctrinal error and moral corruption. And in 632, with the death of the Muslim prophet Muhammad, Christianity had to face—and still faces—its greatest confrontation ever in Islam. Christendom was also weakened by the Great Schism—the huge split between the Eastern and Western Churches, as well as the failure of the Crusades and the fall of Constantinople to the Muslim Turks in 1453.

The Church of the Renaissance and Reformation (1300 to 1600) was impacted by these two very diverse movements. The Renaissance ("rebirth") emerged in Italy already in the fourteenth century. It did not bring on more culture but a change in culture from a totally religious worldview to a secular alternative. A great constellation of scholars, artists, sculptors, and authors pioneered the new learning, and popes patronized them in hopes of saving the Renaissance for the Church. What happened instead was the secularization of the papacy, as well as moral and theological crises in the Church that demanded reform.

Reforms had indeed been attempted by Peter Waldo in France, John Wycliffe in England, Jan Hus in Bohemia, and Savanarola in Italy. All had failed, with the reformers themselves often burned at the stake. It was left to Martin Luther—the providential person at the perfect time—to inaugurate the Protestant Reformation, which transformed much of northern Europe and the future itself.

The Church in the Age of Orthodoxy and the Enlightenment (1600 to 1800) followed the religious wars of the seventeenth century. This bloodshed showed Christendom at its worst. Although the Thirty Years' War finally ended in 1648 for a battered Germany, religious hatred and persecution continued in Europe for many years. Positions became entrenched and a stolid form of orthodoxy grew dominant, provoking a reaction to this faith of the head with a faith of the heart called Pietism in Germany and Methodism in England. The Enlightenment of the eighteenth century, however, became a powerful secularist challenge to all branches of Christianity. While some leaders of the Enlightenment such as Isaac Newton remained Christian, others such as François Voltaire ridiculed the faith.

Christian Churches in Modern Times (1800 to World War I) presents three revolutions that rocked the world: American, French, and Latin American. Napoleon tried to redraw the map of Europe but failed. All branches of Christendom were impacted by these events and also by the many political and social uprisings that punctuated the nineteenth century. Even more so than previously, the Church now had to meet a fourfold ideological challenge from rationalism, the theory of organic evolution, materialist philosophy, and biblical higher criticism. Christian reaction to these ranged from militant denial to accommodation, and the debate continues to this day. But this was also the time of intense missionary activity across the world and a response to Matthew 28 not seen since the earliest missionaries from Rome and Constantinople Christianized the rest of Europe.

The Spread of Global Christianity (The World Wars to the Present) describes the mission outreach of Christendom, restarted so strongly in the nineteenth century. This outreach has continued and even accelerated to the present day because the Church has capitalized on the communications revolution. Much as the printing press made the Reformation possible, so, too, radio, television, the Internet, and other technological gifts have transformed the way Christians spread the Gospel. The worldwide response has been phenomenal, especially in

Africa and the southern hemisphere. A strong ecumenical movement
is also contributing toward at least a partial fulfillment of Jesus' prayer
"that they might all be one."

These, then, are some of the headlines in the story of Christianity. On the pages
that follow come the delicious details. These pages will easily engage readers while
offering them totally trustworthy information that avoids the usual denominational
and parochial approach in favor of a truly global perspective. Our Founder did not
limit His missionary mandate to Europe and America. "All nations" were His target,
and that prophetic instruction—which must have seemed totally impossible at the
time—is actually being fulfilled before our eyes. How could this miracle ever have
happened in fact?

Read on . . .

—Paul L. Maier, PhD
The Russell H. Seibert Em. Professor of Ancient History
Western Michigan University

From the Editors

The history of God's people covers thousands of years. Through Moses and the prophets, God recorded the events and people important to the "Church" of Israel. And through the pens of those who walked and talked with our Savior, we have the history of Jesus' time on earth and the founding of the Christian Church. Within the first centuries of the missionary activity of Paul and Peter and the other apostles, numerous writers had recorded the activities of local churches and leaders as well as the doctrinal deliberations of church councils and the mergers and schisms that human beings have experienced as Christians.

Exploring the Church in history provides us the opportunity to learn from past events and discover ways to further the spread of the Gospel worldwide. From the 1960s to the 1990s, Concordia Publishing House offered its Church in History series as a popular presentation of the nearly two thousand years of people and events that have formed our definition of "Church." In 2011, with *The Church from Age to Age* we completely revised the series, uniting content of the six volumes into one book, adding new content, and updating the presentation to bring readers into the twenty-first century. In this newly abridged history, we wanted to provide a smaller, lower cost volume for a new readership. We focused on presenting the historical narrative, summarizing information in charts to save space. Below, we provide the following biographical sketches for the writers.

- **Dr. Robert G. Clouse** is professor emeritus of history at Indiana State University. He was a founding member of the Conference on Faith and History, served on the editorial board of the *Brethren Encyclopedia*, and was a contributing editor of the *New Twentieth Century Encyclopedia of Religious Knowledge*.

- **Dr. Karl H. Dannenfeldt** † served as professor of history at Arizona State University, the American editor of *Archiv für Reformationsgeschichte*, a committee member for the American Society of Church History, and president and officer for the American Society of Reformation Research.

- **Edward A. Engelbrecht** (STM) served as general editor for *The Lutheran Study Bible* (2009) and *Lutheran Bible Companion* (2014).

- **Dr. Marianka S. Fousek** is an independent historian who served as a professor at Miami University and other schools. She also served as a council member for the American Society of Church History.

• **Walter Oetting** † (MA) served as professor of Church history at Concordia Seminary. He died young, just after completing his book for the Church in History series, which was reissued in 1992 due to continuing interest in the book as an introductory text.

• **Dr. K. Detlev Schulz** is associate professor and chairman for the department of pastoral ministry and mission at Concordia Theological Seminary, serves as the PhD supervisor of the missiology program, and is dean of the graduate school. He grew up in Africa, studied in Europe and the United States, and served as a missionary in Botswana.

• **Dr. Roy A. Suelflow** † served as a missionary in China, Japan, and Taiwan. He also served as a seminary professor and mission director in East Asia. He later taught church history at Concordia Seminary and served as associate editor for the *Concordia Historical Institute Quarterly*.

• **Dr. Carl A. Volz** † served as professor of church history at Luther Seminary and as an editor for *Dialog: A Journal of Theology*. In 1997, the American Academy of Parish Clergy selected his book, *The Medieval Church*, as one of the ten best books of that year.

This general history of the Church presents themes, persons, and events in historical and chronological order. The content is arranged by the different eras that historians commonly use as well as by geography as needed. The writers commended themselves to the work through their ability to present matters in a readable, fair, and straightforward way.

CHAPTER ONE

The Early Church

FROM THE APOSTLES TO AD 250

We begin our study of the Church from age to age by considering the events in the Christian communities after the period that is described by the literature of the New Testament. Basically, this section analyzes the last decades of the first century through the first decades of the third century. The last specifically historical material included in the New Testament is the Acts of the Apostles, which reaches about AD 60; however, the composition of some of the New Testament documents falls after that time period. We have attempted to pick up the story where these materials leave off.

Because of challenges in describing any new movement, we have treated early Christianity topically rather than purely chronologically or geographically. The themes discussed take up issues that still confront the Church in our own generation, questions concerning mission work, modes of worship, polity of congregations and synods, the Church's effort to speak the Gospel in terms relevant and meaningful, the orientation of the Church toward society, and the relationship of Christianity to the state. We have endeavored to limit value judgments and applications to the minimum. Such judgments are something the reader must make for himself, either alone or in discussion with others.

Jesus Christ. Christianity is a faith—a faith that is based on the activity of God in history. The writer to the Hebrews began his letter, "Long ago, at many times and in many ways, God spoke to our fathers by the prophets, but in these last days He has spoken to us by His Son." This was God's unique intervention into history for the salvation of man. Jesus was born at Bethlehem in Judea during the reign of Caesar Augustus. He was executed during the reign of Tiberius some thirty years later. His crime in the eyes of the Romans was apparently that He called Himself a king. The grave did not hold Jesus. He arose "on the third day" and appeared to His followers. This was the foundation of the Christian faith.

Jesus spent His life working in one province of the Roman Empire, a "world-wide" state covering the area surrounding the Mediterranean Sea. He lived during a crucial period of this empire's history. Caesar Augustus's reign was the beginning of the imperial period. As Rome slowly encompassed the Mediterranean, the old city-state governmental and social structures broke down, and Italy was plunged into a century of civil and social war. It was Augustus who brought peace and justice out of this chaos. And it was precisely at this time—a long-sought-after period of peace—that Jesus taught.

Peter characterized Jesus' activities in the short phrase "He went about doing good" (Acts 10:38). If Jesus went about visiting the socially disinherited as well as people of influence, He also taught whoever was willing to listen. Jesus' language was not learned but rather evidenced the quality of abandon. He did not generally quote other sources as authority, and when He did, He had no scruples about suggesting that Moses said certain things only because the people would not have accepted the whole counsel of God. One poet has characterized His language as "gigant-esque." Jesus could call His followers "the salt of the earth" (Matthew 5:13) and refer to Himself as "the door" (John 10:9). He told the man whose eye caused him to sin to "tear it out" (Matthew 5:29). He reproved people who were so concerned with the speck in their neighbor's eye that they didn't see the log protruding out of their own; He rebuked teachers whose lives seemed as pure as the whitewash on a tomb but whose true, inner qualities could better be likened to "dead people's bones" (Matthew 23:27).

It wasn't merely the way Jesus said things that struck people but also what He said. Mark summarized His preaching: "The time is fulfilled, and the kingdom of God is at hand; repent and believe in the gospel" (Mark 1:15). "Repent!" Jesus insisted that the people to whom He was speaking were hiding from God's presence. Instead of listening to what God had really said—"Love the Lord your God with all your heart and with all your soul and with all your mind. . . . You shall love your neighbor as yourself" (Matthew 22:37, 39)—they were following the rules by which they interpreted this Law of God to suit their own convenience. They defined the meaning of "love" and of "neighbor" to the point where they could claim to be doing the Law. Jesus distinguished between what the people had been taught and what God had actually commanded. He called them from hiding behind their own systems of morality into the living presence of God with the word "Repent." But at the same time, He announced that the kingdom of God was present in His person. The prophets had said that in His own time God would descend and reign among men. This reign, Jesus claimed, was being inaugurated in Himself. This is the Gospel, the Good News, to which Mark referred.

Jesus' disciples spread this message of "Repent and believe in the Gospel" wherever they went in the Roman Empire and beyond, always insisting that they behold "His glory, glory as of the only Son from the Father, full of grace and truth" (John 1:14). The letters of Paul, Peter, John, and James breathed this message. They confidently preached "there is forgiveness with God" since Jesus Christ fought the forces of darkness and won! "In Christ God was reconciling the world to Himself, not counting their trespasses against them" (2 Corinthians 5:19). It was the message of victory over death through the resurrection of Jesus Christ from the dead that summarized their mission to men. Easter was *the* great feast day of the early Christians because it was on this day that they celebrated their victory over death.

Jews and Gentiles. Christianity spread over the Roman Empire from the cities of Jerusalem and Antioch. To one who looked at it from the outside, the Church in Jerusalem appeared like merely another sect within Judaism. Yet the Christians differed fundamentally from their Jewish brethren, even though they were themselves Jews, when they accepted Jesus as the Messiah (the Christ) and taught that salvation would not come through doing the Law but had already come in Jesus, the Christ, as the fulfillment of God's gracious promise.

Believing that they represented authentic Judaism, the earliest Christians closely related their lives to the religious lives of their neighbors. The Christians were under the jurisdiction of the Jewish Sanhedrin. When Peter and John preached in Jerusalem, they were forced to defend themselves before the religious and civil courts of the Jews. Many of the early Christians continued to worship in the synagogue and were faithful to some of the ceremonial laws of Judaism; they fasted twice a week, attended temple and synagogue, observed dietetic regulations, practiced circumcision, and in many cases probably continued to observe the Sabbath.

The gap between Christian and non-Christian Jew was widened with the persecution of the Christians in Jerusalem by the anti-Christian Jews. It was in this persecution, probably in the year 36, that we hear of the first Christian martyr, Stephen. As a result of this persecution, it seems that a number of Christians fled from Jerusalem and settled in the Greek city of Antioch, where Christianity was preached to the uncircumcised.

The city of Antioch was very important for the spread of the Christian Gospel. Its population was made up of people from many lands. Since the successors of Alexander the Great sent Jews there when they refused to comply with pagan religious regulations, there was a large Jewish settlement in Antioch by the time of our Lord. There were also many proselytes in this city, Greeks who had been fully converted to Judaism, as well as the so-called "God-fearers," or "devout men" (Acts 10:2), Greeks who accepted the God of the Jews but not the ceremonial laws of Judaism. The Greek-speaking Jews, or "Hellenists" (Acts 6:1), and the Gentiles who worshiped with them in the synagogues in Antioch provided the fertile ground for the Christian appeal outside the confines of strict Judaism. As a result, both circumcised and uncircumcised Christians worshiped and ate together for the first time.

Since this type of integrated church represented a new turn for Christianity, the Church in Jerusalem sent Barnabas to check on these activities. Barnabas was a Christian Jew from Cyprus and so fit well into the environment of Antioch. He also encouraged Paul, a Jewish convert to Christianity from Greek Tarsus, to help in the work at Antioch (Acts 11:19–26).

Preaching the Gospel to the Gentiles was continued especially through the work of the apostle Paul. Commissioned by the congregation in Antioch, Paul and Barnabas carried the Christian Gospel through Asia Minor. Dividing into two teams, Barnabas took John Mark with him to his home in Cyprus, where they continued their efforts; Paul, accompanied by Silas, covered the same territory again in Asia Minor but then went on into Greece. Paul was ultimately able to reach Rome. Because he did not require his converts to become Jews before they became Christians, Paul aroused the displeasure of some Jewish Christians in the Church at Jerusalem (Acts 15:1–5).

To settle this question, a number of the early Christian leaders met in Jerusalem. They agreed that Christianity was more than a sect in Judaism but assumed that the followers of Jesus would remain loyal to the revealed Word of God—the Torah (Acts 15:6ff.). Observing the Sabbath, circumcision, and the food laws was not demanded of all followers of Jesus Christ. Gentile Christians were merely required to refrain from strangled meat, food offered to idols (cf. 1 Corinthians 10:25ff.), blood, and unchastity (Acts 15:28–29). But it was not decided at Jerusalem how a Christian who had come out of the Jewish tradition should act in a congregation that was predominantly Greek. Would it be possible for a Jewish Christian to forsake Jewish regulations if he lived among Greeks who did not know this heritage? This continued to cause discussion in the Early Church. It seems that Peter and Paul, for example, had difficulty with this issue (Galatians 2:11–16). It was Paul's position that Christians must forbear one another (Romans 14:1–15:6; 1 Corinthians 8:1–9:27).

The leader of the Church in Jerusalem was James, the brother of our Lord. Attempting to mediate between Paul, the missionary among the Gentiles, and those zealots in the Church at Jerusalem, who insisted that all the Gentiles converted to Christianity be circumcised, James did not insist on the full acceptance of all the traditions of Judaism. But at the same time, he advocated that the Church avert any break between herself and the ancient people of God (Acts 21:18ff.). James was a blend of Jewish piety and of the belief that Jesus is the Messiah.

These were the years in which the Jewish rebellion against the Romans, which culminated in the destruction of Jerusalem in the year 70, was gaining momentum. Since the day when the Jews were able to win back their freedom from the Seleucids under the leadership of the Maccabees in the middle of the second century BC, only to lose it again to the Roman Pompey in the middle of the sixties BC, the Zealots especially continued to propagandize and terrorize in the hope of freedom from foreign domination. When the Roman governor died in 62 and the new governor had not yet arrived, the Sanhedrin in Jerusalem took power. Venting their zeal on the small Christian group, they accused James of blasphemy and demanded that he go before the people and tell them that Jesus was not the Messiah. Instead of disclaiming his belief, he confessed that Jesus was indeed the Anointed of God. As a result of this "blasphemy," James was thrown from a cliff and stoned to death. Because the Christians in Jerusalem sensed the fearful events about to take place and because the Jewish authorities were less and less tolerant of their activities, the Christians fled from Jerusalem to the Gentile city of Pella in the years 62–70.

When these Christians fled to the east of the Jordan, they established communities of faith that did not remain in contact with the congregations established by Paul and other missionaries. These communities existed in isolated areas into the fifth century.

Since most of them were Jewish Christians, they developed a form of Christianity that attempted to preserve much of the ritual of Judaism as part of their faith. Accepting the "Judaizing" position as more or less the correct one in opposition to Paul, they continued to follow certain Jewish practices, such as circumcision and the Sabbath observance. They did, however, celebrate the Eucharist on Sunday and accept Jesus as the promised Messiah, but they claimed that He was born in a natural way, receiving divine power in His Baptism. Our Lord's Baptism and His resurrection played most important roles in their theology. One of these communities took the name "Nazarenes" (Matthew 2:23; Acts 24:5). This was a name given early to the followers of Jesus. Another group called themselves "Ebionites," a word meaning "poor," which they presumably applied to themselves after the words of Jesus in the Sermon on the Mount: "Blessed are the poor in spirit."

Into All the World. No one knows who established the churches in Rome, Alexandria, Carthage, or Lyons, but there were many traditions about the origin of these congregations among the early Christians.

Early Christian leaders, such as Bishop Irenaeus of Lyons, credited Peter and Paul with the founding of the Church in Rome. This is a tradition that doesn't square with the fact that Paul wrote to the Roman Christians before he was in Rome himself and that when he came to Rome for the first time he was met by the "brethren" (Romans 1:10; Acts 28:15–28). The best explanation of the origin of the Christian community in Rome is that Jewish Christians traveling in the area and settling there founded it.

This congregation became the uniquely honored church in Christendom by the beginning of the second century. A number of reasons are given to explain this. It was the first church to suffer persecution by the Roman government. Nero (64) and probably Domitian (95) persecuted Christians there. Clement, a presbyter-bishop in Rome c. 95, assumed that both Peter and Paul were martyred there during these persecutions. These two facts, together with the imperial position of Rome and the reputation for charity and hospitality that the congregation possessed, help to explain why it was revered as preeminent very early in the Church.

There was a saying that "all roads lead to Rome." When trouble arose in Corinth, one of the presbyter-bishops in Rome, probably Clement (c. 95), wrote to that church, as Paul had previously, suggesting that they return to the Rule of Obedience. Ignatius, bishop of Antioch (c. 110), was taken to Rome to be martyred. Many

Christian intellectuals from various parts of the world, men such as Justin Martyr, Marcion, and Valentine, spent some time in Rome as teachers. This church was a "vast multitude" already at the beginning of the second century. By the middle of the third century, the Roman Church had one bishop, forty-six elders, seven deacons, as many subdeacons, forty-two acolytes, fifty-two readers, exorcists, doorkeepers, and over fifteen thousand widows and poor persons under its care.

The beginnings of the Church in Egypt are lost in the mist of time. Early Christians believed that Mark or Barnabas founded the Church in Alexandria. The limited evidence we have concerning Christianity there in the second century indicates that it was in part an attempt to find a philosophical basis for combining various religious traditions.

This type of religious thought was common in Egypt among the Jews. According to tradition, Ptolemy, the ruler of Egypt 285–247 BC, had the Hebrew Scriptures translated into Greek in order that they might become part of the overall religious life of the Egyptians. This version is called the *Septuagint*. The Alexandrian Jew Philo felt he could bring the Hebrew prophets and the Greek philosophers into conformity by finding the supposed "hidden" meaning in the Old Testament. This type of interpretation is called allegory.

Among the Christians, Valentine (c. 135) tried to get behind the words of Scripture to the "spiritual" meaning. What the Scriptures really taught, he claimed, was a form of religion that was quite compatible with the other religions of Egypt. He suggested, for example, that there is only one God, but this one God has no name. Ultimately, then, the many names applied to divine beings do not refer to many gods but are simply names by which the one God is worshiped. The Valentinian Gnostics portrayed Christ as a Savior sent from the hitherto unknown God to bring saving knowledge to men about God. Since the word for knowledge in Greek is *gnosis,* this variance from Christianity is called Gnosticism.

About 180, a teacher by the name of Pantaenus came to Alexandria. He had been a Stoic philosopher before he was converted to Christianity. The school that flourished under Pantaenus in Egypt, one of the most famous Christian schools in the Early Church, also illustrates the syncretistic nature of Christianity in Egypt. It was basically a school to instruct the young and old, educated and uneducated, in the Christian Gospel. But attached to this school, though not identical with it, was a course of instruction that went all the way from basic grammar to the highest speculations in Christian philosophy. Geography, archaeology, astronomy, and medicine may also have been studied here. This school was open to any interested pagan, even if he or she was not interested in becoming a Christian. Here, a long succession of theologians taught that true philosophy would ultimately lead to the Christian faith and that all the arts and sciences were valuable to the believer as tools to elucidate the Christian Gospel. The disciple of Pantaenus was Clement, the successor of Clement was Origen, and Origen was the teacher of many of the bishops from that part of the world who were at the Council of Nicaea in 325. These individuals can be credited with bringing Egyptian Christianity into the mainstream of the Christian tradition.

Of the Church's origin in Carthage in Africa and Lyons in southern France we know even less. It is probable that Christians either from Ephesus in Asia Minor or from Rome were the first to bring Christianity to Carthage in northern Africa. Tertullian, a presbyter there toward the end of the second century, is the first Christian whom we know by name in that church. But by this time, there were so many Christians in North Africa that Tertullian could threaten the local Roman ruler with rebellion if he continued to persecute Christians.

We first hear about the Church at Lyons around 170 through the writings of Irenaeus, a bishop in that church. By this time, there were many Christians in this area and more than one congregation. When Emperor Marcus Aurelius persecuted this church c. 170, there were some fifty martyrs.

Toward the end of the second century and in the beginning of the third, the Church also continued its eastward spread. Around 160, we hear of a teacher by the name of Tatian in Edessa in eastern Syria. Tatian was known for his *Diatessaron,* in which he attempted to combine the Four Gospels into one account. It remained the standard reading in the worship of the Church in that part of the world into the fifth century.

The most famous missionary in this early period of the Church's history was Gregory Thaumaturgus. Gregory was born around 213 at Neocaesarea in Pontus. He studied under Origen at Caesarea in Palestine, where he was converted to the Christian faith. While bishop of Neocaesarea, he did mission work in Cappadocia, where he converted many pagans to Christianity, among them Macrina, the grandmother of the great fourth-century theologians Gregory of Nyssa and Basil of Caesarea. Many stories were told concerning his ability to work miracles. At daybreak, men, women, and children suffering from demon possession and disease would gather at his door. As he healed these people, he would talk to them about the Gospel, advise them about their troubles, and discuss with them various religious problems. Gregory of Nyssa wrote that it was "above all for this that he drew many numbers to hear his preaching. . . . His discourse would astonish their hearing, and the wonders he performed would astonish their sight."

By the year 250, Christianity had spread to the limits of the known world. We hear legends about it in England, but know little more. We hear about it in areas to the east of Armenia, even in India and China, but know almost nothing about it. Two facts, however, become clear. First, the Church spread rapidly over a wide geographical area, increasing phenomenally in numbers at the same time. Second, this work was done by ordinary Christians. We know of no missionary societies; we hear nothing of organized effort. Wherever Christians went doing their regular tasks, the pagan saw a different kind of individual and heard about "the Savior." The spread of Christianity followed the trade routes. In the Middle Ages, we hear of many individuals such as Patrick in Ireland and Ansgar in Scandinavia; outside of Gregory, we know few missionaries of the Early Church by name.

When the early Christians themselves recount how they learned of the Gospel, they usually confess that their faith was the result of casual contact with that "way of life." Gregory the missionary claimed that there were many influences in his conversion, but especially the influence of his teacher Origen. Gregory also came to study in Caesarea and happened to find a Christian teacher. Minucius Felix described how Octavius told Caecilius about his Christianity in casual conversation. Justin Martyr was accosted by an old man along the seashore who explained the Old Testament to him. Justin recalled that he was converted to the faith when he saw people willing to die for it in the arena. The pagan Celsus scoffed at the workers in wool and leather, the rustic and ignorant persons who spread Christianity. The work was not done by people who called themselves missionaries but by rank-and-file members. The least among men, even the unknown, are indeed the greatest in the kingdom of heaven.

WORSHIP

If you had asked, "Where is the Church?" in any important city of the ancient world where Christianity had penetrated in the first century, you would have been directed to a group of worshiping people gathered in a house. There was no special building or other tangible wealth with which to associate "church," only people! A pagan critic of Christianity, Celsus (c. 170), reproached the Christians for their lack of "temples" and "images." Origen simply replied that all of this was unnecessary for true religion, and Christians could worship their God anywhere.

When Justin Martyr (c. 150) was executed because of his Christian faith, the Roman official asked him to reveal the homes where the Christians worshiped since that was common Christian practice. In Jerusalem, the first Christians worshiped in the house of John Mark (Acts 12:12). Paul often referred to the worship that took place in the homes of various individuals (1 Corinthians 16:19; Romans 16:5; Colossians 4:15). These places received no other consecration than the worship and teaching that took place there.

Christians sometimes used synagogues, centers of Jewish communities all over the Roman world. Jesus Himself went to the synagogue in Nazareth "as was His custom" (Luke 4:16). Paul usually began his preaching in these centers (Acts 13:5, 14, 42, 43). Peter and John also attended the temple in Jerusalem for afternoon prayers (Acts 3:1).

In Rome, Christians sometimes worshiped in burial caves under the city called catacombs. These catacombs were natural caves that intersect the area on which Rome is built. It is estimated that there are 550 miles of these caves under Rome today. The Christians found these to be natural places for burial. In the East, the tombs were usually cut into rock. These caves were an obvious substitute. The bodies of the dead were placed in cavities along the tunnel walls and especially in shelflike openings in the large chambers. The largest chambers held about fifty people. The tunnels from chamber to chamber were very narrow—perhaps three feet wide. For this reason, it is improbable that Christians used these caves for regular worship at any time. It is certain, however, that specific ceremonies, especially celebrations of the Eucharist, were held by small groups in connection with the burial and remembrance of the dead.

The first traces of special places for worship occur in the writings of Clement of Alexandria (c. 200), who pointed out that "church" could refer both to the worshiping group and to a special building (*Stromateis*, VII, 29). Not until the middle of the third century did Christians begin to build special buildings for worship in great numbers. It is probable that this building began under the protection of the Persian Empire to encourage the Christians to be loyal to them rather than to Rome. In the third century, Persia or the regional ruler at Palmyra controlled much of Asia Minor and Syria. The first archaeological evidence of a church building proper dates from about 256 in Dura-Europos, a town on the Euphrates River. About the same time, a church building was erected in the city of Antioch, which was also under Persian domination. After the year 300, many church buildings, generally in the East, were destroyed in the persecution under Diocletian.

The early Christians were not particularly interested in religious art either. As late as 315, the council meeting at Elvira in Spain legislated against pictures in churches "lest the paintings on the wall be worshiped and adored." Interpreting the First Commandment to mean that any representation of God is idolatry and/or blasphemy, early Christian writers generally condemned any artistic representation of the deity and limited themselves to decorative art, such as geometric designs. It is interesting, however, that notwithstanding these many condemnations, the Christians in Rome filled their burial catacombs with extensive religious art, including human figures. Usually of flat lines with no architectural feeling or sense of sensuous beauty, the figures symbolized the faith and hope of Christians as expressed in the words: "According to [God's] great mercy, He has caused us to be born again to a living hope through the resurrection of Jesus Christ from the dead, to an inheritance that is imperishable, undefiled, and unfading, kept in heaven for you" (1 Peter 1:3–4). The paintings of the catacombs depict events from both the Old and New Testaments and testify to the intervention of God in history for the salvation of man. The stories of Jonah, Noah's ark, Daniel in the lions' den, the near sacrifice of Isaac, the raising of Lazarus, and the Good Shepherd were among the favorites.

There was more than one liturgy, or form of worship, in the Early Church. Individual areas had their own liturgies, and the liturgy in any given area changed from one period to the next. There is an obvious accumulation as the liturgy grows in form and depth. The chart on "Worship in the Early Church" summarizes key elements and concerns in early Christian beliefs and practices.

WORSHIP IN THE EARLY CHURCH		
	BELIEFS	PRACTICES
FORMS AND REGULATIONS	Based on apostolic practice.	Had both set forms and spontaneity.
SUNDAY	Day of Christ's resurrection.	Gathered for reading, preaching, and Eucharist.
BAPTISM	Trinitarian instruction. Holy Spirit given in Baptism. Dying and rising with Christ. Forgiveness of past sins. Born again.	Examined for purity of life before Baptism. Exorcisms. Rite of anointing, prayer, fasting, immersion, or sometimes by pouring water. Infant Baptism practiced by at least AD 200.
READING AND RESPONSE	Old Testament and apostolic writings regarded as God's Word. Old Testament read as fulfilled in Christ.	Regular readings from the Old Testament and apostolic "memoirs" and letters. Preaching, singing, prayers in a Jewish style.
EUCHARIST	Lord's Supper as joyful thanks to God and highest form of worship. Eating and drinking the body and blood of the incarnate Christ without explaining how.	Kiss of peace between members. Agape or love feast meal along with Eucharist. Prayer including words of Christ instituting the Eucharist. Emphasized worthy participation.

The worship of the Early Church was not as fixed and formal as it was later to become. But it did not lack forms either. Many parts of the traditional liturgical framework are not found in the documents from this period. The Eucharistic liturgy contained no Confession and Absolution, and there is no explicit reference to the Kyrie, the Creed, or the Our Father. Prayers, hymns, and responses, slowly accumulated by the worshiping communities all over the world, give us the many ingredients of worship that are known in Christendom today.

ORGANIZATION

The administrative structure of the Early Church grew out of her "liturgy," which included not merely worship of God but also service to men in works of love (2 Corinthians 9:12; Philippians 2:17, 30). Especially in the earliest years of the Church's life, there was no single preconceived plan of organization. The patterns differed from one region to another. Christians organized to overcome difficulties and to meet the challenges of their time. But there was an unmistakable trend toward uniformity. While patterns are vaguely discernible in the period when the literature of the New Testament was written, by 250, all the churches were ruled by a bishop, who was assisted by elders. The chart on "Church Offices" summarizes various offices, functions, and some developments.

CHURCH OFFICES		
	CALLINGS AND FUNCTIONS	NOTES
ELDERS (PRES- BYTERS); PASTORS	Discipline, teaching, and leading in worship. Early on, the office of bishop was not well distinguished from the office of elder.	Continued from synagogue practice. Office for respected older men. Some congregations may have had "teachers" or "prophets" instead.
BISHOPS	Oversee a congregation (second century). Referred to as "father" and overseer of a region in the third century. Ordained by other bishops.	Some believed the office of ruling bishop was an apostolic practice. Role emphasized for unity of doctrine and practice.
OTHER MINISTRIES	Deacons, subdeacons, acolytes, doorkeepers, widows and virgins, exorcists, confessors, and readers.	Assisted the elders and bishops with Communion, ministry to the sick and the poor, praying and caring for the sick, and public reading of Scripture. Confessors were persons honored for suffering persecution.
PRIEST- HOOD OF ALL	Laymen participated in Eucharistic offering. Holiness of life. Some served as teachers. Could baptize.	Laymen first distinguished at end of first century. They consented to appointment of their leaders.

Further Developments. Early sources reveal very little of anything analogous to modern supracongregational organizations; each congregation was an autonomous unit. There was, of course, communication between various churches, but no administrative unity. However, when a city congregation became too large, it split into two or more churches, headed by elders but remaining under the rule of the original bishop. The rural churches around the city were likewise under the bishop's spiritual jurisdiction. A development away from local autonomy became inevitable and imperative as soon as inter- and intracongregational strife occurred and schism threatened. The emergence of factions ready to name their own bishops, of heresy, and of differences in dealing with gross sins necessitated the use of arbiters from the outside to adjudicate difficulties. The matter of uniformity in observing the Feast of the Resurrection was another problem requiring decisions above the local level. Generally, Easter was celebrated on the same day of the week, Sunday, the day of the resurrection. In part of the Church, however, Easter was celebrated in accordance with the Jewish Passover observance on a particular day of the month, the 14th of *Nisan*, regardless of the day of the week. Such disunity was considered scandalous. Gnostic and Montanist assertions that they represented authentic Christianity, especially their claims to knowledge or revelation not accessible to all believers, also caused division in the churches. For the adjudication of such larger problems, bishops of various cities in a geographical area began to meet in conferences, or councils, as they came to be called.

In the course of the second century, the bishops of provincial capitals, or metropolises, in the East, following the pattern of imperial administration, acquired jurisdiction over the bishops of the towns within their provinces. They received the status of "metropolitans." In the West, the jurisdiction of the "metropolitan" developed only later. Bishops, however, never settled issues in a dictatorial manner but through council. At first, such councils were gatherings of all the bishops in a given area together with their presbyters, deacons, and some laymen. A council to represent the *whole* Church, that is, a universal (or ecumenical) council, was not known until 325, the time of the First Council at Nicaea in Asia Minor.

With the rapid expansion of the Church and a growing number of problems, the tendency developed to look to some individual with final authority. Before the fourth century, the Roman Church was honored as the place where Peter and Paul worked and died, but it had no power of judgment recognized by the Church as a whole. However, a third-century Roman bishop did claim to be *the* guardian of the true tradition, and Victor, the bishop of Rome (198), excommunicated those who did not agree with his position on the dating of Easter. A heathen Roman emperor, Aurelian (c. 270), suggested that church disputes might be settled by turning them over to the judgment of Rome. But no Roman bishop in this early period claimed to have any jurisdiction outside of his province because of some authority derived from Peter. This is a later development.

Indeed, there were many indications that the Roman bishop was rebuked whenever he interfered in the activities of other bishops. When Victor attempted to force all of the churches to conform to Rome's dating in the celebration of Easter, Irenaeus reminded him that this was not the manner in which such difficulties were settled. Tertullian rebuked Callistus, bishop of Rome in the years after Victor, for "immodesty" when he claimed to have certain exclusive powers from Peter to remit sins. Even Cyprian, who held that Jesus Himself made Peter a symbol of ecclesiastical unity by giving the keys to him individually, did not acknowledge the right of Rome to interfere in other areas to keep ecclesiastical peace. Cyprian also had no qualms about accusing bishop Stephen, his counterpart in Rome, of improper and unapostolic practice in not rebaptizing converts to the Roman Church from a heretical group. Firmilian, a bishop in Cappadocia, called Stephen a "Judas" in the Church for this practice.

The Roman Church was highly honored in the Early Church, but this does not change the fact that organizationally, this church had no more right to interfere in the affairs of another church than any other bishop in Christendom. *Each* was to be responsible for all. This was the position of Irenaeus, Tertullian, Cyprian, and perhaps, when all is said and done, also of Rome.

The New Testament concept of the Church as one and holy (*una sancta*; see Ephesians 4:4–6; 5:27) continued to have a strong influence on the thinking of the Early Church. This unity among the various churches in Christendom was assumed, however, rather than organized. There was no administrative structure to which one could point in order to show "unity." It was taken for granted that all except the heretics believed the same things and that they were doing the same work. They communicated with one another when difficulties arose; individuals traveled from one church to another as teachers; but there was no organization beyond this.

If there was any visible symbol of unity, it was epitomized in the figure of the bishop associated with other bishops. Cyprian in his conference essay *On the Unity of the Catholic Church* insisted that there is only one Church. This Church is found where the bishop is. Ignatius had said this earlier, but he was speaking about the individual congregation. Cyprian applied this to the Church at large. That is, he said that a group can call itself "Church" only if it has a bishop who has been properly ordained and who is in unity with the other bishops of the Church. There is, therefore, only one Church. All who were not part of this empirical reality were not considered Church. Cyprian allowed that they were at most "dead branches." He compared this Church to Noah's ark, outside of which no one could be saved.

Apostolic Teaching

Many bishops and teachers in the Early Church were the students of the apostles. In the early second century, the bishop of Hierapolis in Asia Minor, a certain Papias, had been a hearer of a disciple of the apostle John. Polycarp, who later became bishop of Smyrna, was a pupil of John himself. This Polycarp was in turn the teacher of Irenaeus (170), the bishop of the congregation in Lyons in Gaul. Irenaeus wrote about the hours he spent listening to Polycarp reminisce about John.

In this way, the teachings of the apostles were passed down by word of mouth from generation to generation. This "handing down" was called "tradition." When Irenaeus debated with the Gnostics about who was teaching the apostolic doctrine, he pointed to his clear relationship to John. He insisted, furthermore, that there was such a tradition of apostolic teaching in other churches.

Early Christian teachers pointed not only to oral tradition but also to the fact that the writings of the apostles existed in the same churches that they had established. These writings were called the written tradition. They contained the same teaching that had been handed down orally. Tertullian (195) told the heretics who opposed him to check these writings of the apostles, which were called "Scripture" and were honored together with the Old Testament as the Word of God.

"Scripture" referred, however, first of all, to the Old Testament. In the period under our survey, the books that are called "apocryphal" or "deutero-canonical" were quoted as part of the Old Testament. These are books that originated in Jewish communities outside Palestine, especially in Alexandria. They were probably not in the Old Testament used by the Jews in Palestine, where Hebrew was still studied. Most of them were written in Greek and included in the Septuagint, a Greek translation of the Old Testament from the second or third centuries BC, also originating in Egypt. The Old Testament in this Greek form was read in worship.

Various apostolic "memoirs" of Christ were also read in worship. Gospel accounts other than our traditional four (such as *The Gospel of the Hebrews*) were circulated, but by the year 200 only our four were commonly read in worship, as Irenaeus described them and their apostolic origins.

Various other writings, such as letters of the apostles and "Acts" describing their ministry, were also read in services. Little concern is evident at first to limit the variety of these readings; it was only by the middle of the fourth century that there was almost universal agreement on what books were part of the New Testament.

It was as a result of conflict with the claims of Montanist and Gnostic heresies that the Church Fathers, the classical writers and teachers of the Early Church, came to grips with the question of exactly what formed the legitimate basis of teaching.

Montanism spread from Asia Minor (c. 150) with the claim that it possessed revelation from the Holy Spirit demanding purer ethical conduct and separation from communities of Christians less pure.

There were many types of *Gnosticism.* Essentially, Gnostics reacted negatively to the natural world in which they lived, claiming that it was the product of an evil demon. The ideal world is above all this. To reach this ideal world, the soul must be enlightened by a savior sent from the true God to ignite a spark that exists in certain selected individuals by giving them an experience (*gnosis*) of heavenly reality. Since the physical creation is evil, this savior cannot be "man" in any natural sense. For this reason, the Docetists (from the Greek *dokeo,* "to seem"), an early group who claimed that Jesus only *seemed* to be human, are sometimes classified as Gnostics. But because of the number and variety of the dualistic groups, Docetists were not necessarily Gnostics. Disdaining material creation, a Gnostic either abstained from sexual relationships or engaged in every debauchery because he believed the body irrelevant to the life of the spirit.

An extensive cache of Gnostic writings was found in 1945 at Nag Hammadi in Egypt, giving us in hitherto unknown quantities firsthand evidence of what the Gnostics wrote. Such writings as *The Gospel of Truth* and *The Gospel of Thomas* were among the important finds. This discovery is easily as important for the study of early Christianity as the Dead Sea Scrolls.

Gnostics who claimed to be Christians were marked by their rejection of the God of the Old Testament. These Gnostics claimed that the God whom Jesus Christ called His "Father" was not the God who was described in the Old Testament. Marcion, the son of a Christian bishop in Pontus, traveled to Rome before the middle of the second century and expounded this new theology there. In a writing called the *Antitheses,* he contrasted the God acting in the Old Testament with Jesus' description of His Father. The contrasts revolved around the claim that in the Old Testament, God (Yahweh) is "just," a God of the Law; while the God described by Jesus is "loving," the God of the Gospel. Though Marcion had perhaps the deepest appreciation of God's free grace in Jesus Christ of anyone in his day, he stressed "justification by grace" to the point of denying that a loving God could at the same time be just. He found it necessary in support of his thesis to "use the scissors," as Tertullian wrote, on those parts of the New Testament that were not compatible with his thinking. Having rejected the Old Testament as irrelevant for the Christian religion, Marcion accepted the Gospel of Luke and Paul's letters, but only after he had cut out those sections where either Jesus or Paul referred to Yahweh as God.

Gnostics claimed that their writings were the authoritative interpretation of what Jesus really meant to say. They claimed to have a "secret tradition" passed down from Peter and Paul—a tradition they could not establish and also one that no one else ever heard of—that confirmed their "Gospel." The Christian Fathers pointed to the churches that the apostles established, emphasizing that if there were any "secret" doctrine, the disciples surely would have imparted it to the shepherds they appointed over their congregations. Irenaeus and Tertullian also pointed to the accepted writings of the apostles, showing how they disagreed with the teachings of the Gnostics. This conflict was very important because it forced Christians to recognize more precisely which of the writings used in the Church were actually apostolic and authoritative.

The teachings of the apostles, passed down orally and in their writings, were summarized in the Rules of Faith. These Rules, like creeds, verbalized in brief form what was taught by the Church all over the world. Unlike creeds, however, these summaries were not used in the Eucharistic liturgy nor composed specifically to condemn heretical positions but were, rather, summaries of what was taught to the catechumens entering the Church. These Rules also differed from the later universal creeds in that they were not recited in precisely the same way, with exactly the same words, in every area of the Church. It is possible to read the Rule in Irenaeus, Tertullian, and Origen, but the words are nowhere alike.

This was the message of the Early Church. It was called the Apostolic Rule, since the Fathers believed that it summarized the teaching handed down from the apostles. Any new teaching was measured by this Rule.

Jesus, Messiah and Savior. The major emphasis in the theology of the Early Church was that Jesus Christ is the Savior from sin and death. In the Acts of the Apostles, the sermons of Peter and Paul illustrate the centrality of "Jesus is the Christ" in the message of earliest Christianity: "Let all the house of Israel therefore know for certain that God has made him both Lord and Christ, this Jesus whom you crucified" (Acts 2:36). As various controversies beset the Church and as Christians attempted to communicate their faith to others, this message of salvation too often took a seemingly secondary position. The Gospel does not shine through with the same brilliance in Clement of Rome as it does in Paul, even though they were writing to the same congregation with many of the same problems. The apologists in the second century were more concerned to defend the Christian belief in one God than they were to impress the message of salvation. In some of the Apologies, the saving Word of Jesus Christ is hardly discussed. This was certainly unusual, but the fact that it happened illustrates the point. On the other hand, these instances must be weighed against other evidence that indicates that the message "Jesus is Savior" did remain central.

This centrality is illustrated by the writings of Irenaeus (c. 200), bishop of Lyons in southern Gaul. In his works *Demonstration of Apostolic Preaching* and *Against Heresies*, he presented a brilliant interpretation of the atonement, in which the centrality of Jesus Christ both in history and in the individual relationship between God and man is obvious. His view is summarized in the word *recapitulation*, or "summing up." The Greek word for it, which can also mean "uniting," was used by Paul when he wrote that God has made "known to us the mystery of His will, according to His purpose, which He set forth in Christ as a plan for the fullness of time, to unite all things in Him, things in heaven and things on earth" (Ephesians 1:9–10). Irenaeus taught that Jesus summed up in Himself the entire history of mankind—as all men are in Adam by birth, they are in Christ by rebirth. Christ is the Head of God's new creation, the Church. It is God's purpose ultimately to unite all men under Christ.

When God created Adam "in His image," according to Irenaeus, God meant that man, unlike the animals and angels, was to contemplate His glory and goodness. But God did not create Adam with the fully developed ability to do this. Only Christ is fully the Image of God. Adam was created to develop "into the fullness of the image." Genesis does not record that Adam was "the image" but rather that he was made "in the image." In Paradise, therefore, Adam was not fully developed spiritually. Irenaeus did not mean to say that Adam was imperfect, but rather that he was innocent like a child, not knowing the difference between good and evil.

Irenaeus felt that the devil took advantage of Adam's innocence just as an adult can take advantage of a child. God planned that Adam should ultimately be "like God." But the devil interrupted this spiritual development by tempting Adam to presumption—the presumption of being "like God" and of "knowing good and evil" without spiritual struggle. Adam's disobedience meant that he turned his thoughts in upon himself instead of continuing in the contemplation of God. No longer able to grow in the knowledge of God, Adam was cast out of Paradise. Repeating the phrase of Paul, "in Adam all die" (1 Corinthians 15:22), Irenaeus discussed Adam as a historical figure but also as the representative of mankind.

In order to rescue mankind from this plight, Christ, "the Image," became a man and recapitulated all that man experiences: childhood, manhood, temptation, and death. But there is one important difference. Christ reversed what happened to man. Man's life is one of defeat by evil forces. When Christ became a man, He was not defeated by evil but gained the victory over it because of His perfect obedience to the will of God. The history of the First Adam recorded in Genesis is reversed by the story of the Second Adam in the Gospel (1 Corinthians 15:22; Romans 5:17–21).

Irenaeus also discussed the temptation of Christ as part of this recapitulation. The devil took Jesus to a high mountain and tempted Him to be like God just as Adam had been tempted. But unlike Adam, Jesus was not a spiritual infant; He was fully developed spiritually. Indeed, He was "the Image." Where Adam was disobedient to God's plan for his spiritual growth, Jesus reversed this by obediently answering the devil, "You shall worship the Lord your God, and Him only . . ." (Luke 4:8). Finally, Jesus also experienced death. But He experienced it voluntarily in order to go the whole way with man. Here is where the reversal of the human situation really comes through. Since our Lord experienced death because He was perfectly obedient rather than disobedient, death could not hold Him. He victoriously triumphed over death.

Jesus was then all that man was. But because He was also "the Image" of God, divine in every sense of the term, He did not succumb to temptation but was victorious over it. This began a new era for man. We divide history into BC and AD to illustrate in part that whereas "in Adam all died," in Christ "all are made alive." For Irenaeus, these "alive" people made up the Church. Entering the Church through Baptism, each individual is incorporated into Christ and is thus restored to his original innocence and allowed once again to grow into the image of God.

Monotheism and Trinity. Early Christianity faced a polytheistic society, not a secular society. Gods abounded. All the Christian teachers who wrote "apologies" for Christianity to engage the pagan mind emphasized that Christianity taught monotheism. The Christians pointed to the teaching of Greek philosophy that there was only one source of being, that changelessness is one and simple rather than multiple and complex like the changeable. The Christians rehearsed the Epicurean criticisms of the traditional myths about the gods, adding their invective to the scoffing already common and echoing the Old Testament emphasis that "God is one" (Athenagoras, *Plea*, 5–8).

But it was not this simple. Christians also taught that Jesus was the Son of God. For this reason, pagans and Jews insisted that Christianity was in fact polytheism. It was necessary, therefore, for Christians to show just how Jesus was related to the Father in order to substantiate their claims to monotheism. Apart from Gnosticism and Montanism, the other heresies in the Early Church arose from the attempts to describe this relationship. There were certain aspects about which all agreed. The general Christian practice was to baptize in the name of the Father, Son, and Spirit. Still, they insisted that there was only one God. They taught that Jesus was the Savior of men and therefore had to be divine. But assuming all this, how is the relationship of the Godhead to Jesus Christ described? This was perhaps the most perplexing question that Christians faced in this early period. It did not receive an official solution until 451.

One of the first solutions to be offered was that by Justin Martyr. He was a philosopher turned Christian who worked with the *logos* idea as described in the Gospel of John: "In the beginning was the Word [*logos*], and the Word was with God, and the Word was God." He taught that this *logos* was "generated"—a word meaning "to come out of" as a branch comes out of a tree—out of the Father before time began. This generation, he said, did not involve any diminution of the essence of the Father, nor was there any division that took place. He compared the relationship to that of the sun to its rays; the one comes out of the other, but the rays never decrease the light of the sun. When he debated with Trypho, a Jew, about the meaning of the Old Testament, he suggested that the many divine appearances in the Old Testament to the patriarchs were not by angels but rather by the *logos*. Justin was able to preserve the identity of the *logos* as well as its relationship to the Father, but the fact that he spoke of it as the "other" divine being disturbed many Christians.

In fear of constructions like Justin's, the "Monarchians" opposed this "logos speculation," as they called it, with an emphasis on the oneness of God (monarchians). So Praxeas, a teacher in Rome c. 190, taught that the Son was a mere "mode" or "form" that the Father became for a space of years in order to redeem man, only to discard it when the work was finished. Praxeas denied the essential "threeness" of God by insisting that there was no Father when there was a Son, and conversely, there was no Son either in the period before the incarnation or after the ascension—only the Father. This forced him into the position, as Tertullian suggested, of "crucifying the Father." Since the Gospels clearly state that it was the Son who died, and that the Son had a relationship to His Father, Praxeas's solution was not accepted.

Paul of Samosata, bishop of Antioch c. 270, is the classical example of another type of monarchianism. He taught that since God cannot change, He certainly could not become a man. Paul explained what happened in Jesus by insisting that He was born and grew up as any other individual, but was later selected by God to become the Christ at His Baptism when the voice spoke from heaven, "This is My beloved Son. . . ." In these words, God poured out on Jesus a special "power" to remain perfect and "adopted" Him to be the "firstborn" of God's new creation—the Church. Paul preserved the oneness of God with this solution, but in the process made Jesus little more than a unique man.

Both Praxeas and Paul of Samosata were excommunicated by local councils. But their errors forced the Church to develop refutations on the basis of the apostolic writings. The answers given in this period were not adequate, but they evidence a concern to be loyal to the apostolic witness. It is also true that sometimes the answers of this period are inadequate specifically because they were attempting to be loyal to the Scriptures. Sayings of our Lord such as "I and the Father are one" and "the Father is greater than I" posed a problem of interpretation, especially since the verses of Scriptures were read in isolation rather than in larger sections.

In addition to the scriptural approach, the Fathers also attempted to give their answers a systematic, or logical, cast. This involved the Church in the philosophical thought patterns of the time. Christians used words, for example, not just from the Bible but also from the philosophical classroom to express what they wanted to say. There was little concern to give formal logical expression to questions relating to the Godhead by the writers of the New Testament or even by the earliest Christian writers not included in the New Testament. They simply stated certain basic, but unsystematized, facts about Jesus and the Father. Ignatius, for example, wrote that Jesus was "flesh yet spiritual, born yet unborn, God incarnate, true life in true death, sprung from Mary but also from God, subject to suffering and later beyond it" (*To the Ephesians*, 7). These statements were made but not explained. The first Fathers to answer the Monarchians by trying to explain the true relationship between the Father and the Son were Tertullian in Carthage and Origen in Alexandria.

Tertullian's treatise *Against Praxeas* was the first attempt to systematize the Church's understanding of the apostolic witness. He suggested that there is only one God (one monarch), one divine "substance," but that the one God consisted of three "persons." The word *person* is from the Latin word *persona*, which originally meant a mask worn by an actor, then the role portrayed by the actor, and finally an individual. By speaking of three "persons" in the divine substance, Tertullian did not mean that God had three different personalities. Tertullian asserted that the three persons had but one purpose. He compared the Godhead to the Roman government, which at that time had three heads, Septimius Severus and his two associates. He wrote, "A unity that derives from itself a trinity is not destroyed but administered by it" (*Against Praxeas*, 3). According to Tertullian, each of the individuals has full executive powers and exists simultaneously, yet the three accomplish one action. They are therefore one in unity.

Origen was more speculative than the jurist Tertullian, but he relied no less on Scripture to prove each point he made. Indeed, Origen left a greater number of biblical commentaries than any other Early Father and is often, though perhaps improperly, called the first Christian exegete. In his attempt to explain the triune nature of God, he insisted that there are three distinct entities in the Godhead, distinct but not separate. All three of these entities (*hypostaseis*) exist eternally. Justin and Tertullian merely suggested that the Son is generated from the Father, as light is from the sun, without getting involved in the problem of sequence, but Origen noted that if the Father is always the Father, there must always be a Son. Accordingly, he spoke of the Son as eternally generated.

Neither the position of Tertullian nor that of Origen was popular in their day. They were accused of being too philosophical in their analysis of Scripture. Both were accused of tritheism by their opponents in the Church. But it is ultimately their formulations that form the basis for the settlement of the problem in the fourth century—our Nicene Creed.

Salvation. The early teachers agreed with Irenaeus that salvation has its source in God and in the victory of Christ. But they stressed that ultimately each individual is responsible for either his salvation or damnation. Tertullian wrote that God does not choose to save an individual out of free grace, but rather because the individual has proved his worthiness. He also emphasized that after the grace of God has been accepted, one must continue to cooperate with God to attain ultimate salvation. Man is judged and saved by his response to God's grace in Christ.

This stress on human responsibility for salvation or damnation can perhaps be explained by analyzing two of the situations that faced the Early Church.

There was a prevailing stress on morality in early Christian writings because the converts who came into the churches came with ethical standards far below those of God's Law. In Roman society, humility was scorned, and boasting with pride was the mark of the real man. Enlightened self-interest was the highest norm for the pagan rather than selfless concern for the needy brother. Revenge was the basic law of human relationships. Early Christian teachers could not assume that a man was married to only one woman or that he was not keeping a number of mistresses. The Roman world took homosexuality lightly. For these reasons, the apologists stressed how Christians were different from their pagan neighbors because they followed God's Law rather than any human regulations and whims. Tertullian wrote many tracts for the times, and most of them deal with ethical and disciplinary matters.

A second and perhaps more important reason for early Christianity's stress on man's responsibility for his own salvation was the fact that the prevailing philosophies of the day tended to blame "cosmic structure" or "involuntary tendencies" and even "divine decrees" rather than man himself for his predicament. This thinking was also especially common among the Gnostics, who claimed that every event in human history was predetermined. The world was created and governed by invisible powers who controlled everything that took place on earth, including every human action. They pointed out that an individual is not born by choice and that his race, social status, and mental qualities are all predetermined. This invisible plan that maps out the quality of man's desires beforehand also operates in the area of the spirit. Evil powers control the spiritual destiny of everyone except the "few" who are mysteriously chosen by a higher power to be saved, without any willed action on their part. The Gnostics taught that both salvation and damnation are beyond human control.

Because of the prevailing immorality and denial of human responsibility, the early Christian teachers stressed the accountability of each man for his actions as well as for his salvation. Whenever the Early Fathers discussed man's salvation, this was usually the context.

The emphasis on responsibility led to a number of accents in their thinking. First, if man is responsible for his life before God, he must have "free will" to exercise choice. They opposed the Gnostics who denied free will. Second, the Fathers avoided any suggestion that man's relationship to Adam so corrupted the human will that it had no power to choose the good. They allowed that as the result of Adam's sin all men have a tendency to evil and must necessarily die. But they said no more. They insisted that even though all men are born "in Adam," they have the ability to choose between right and wrong. There were a number of theories current about the precise nature of mankind's relationship to Adam's sin, but they all stressed that each individual is responsible for his own guilt.

Third, early Christian teachers would not allow either philosopher or heretic to blame God as Creator for man's plight. The Gnostics claimed that man's dilemma was the result of certain weaknesses in creation itself. Christians, on the other hand, taught that creation is good and that only man is responsible for his condition. The corruption that prevails in life is not from creation but from man's perverted use of creation.

These concerns are the context of the statements of the Fathers on salvation. Sometimes, in their concern to preserve the integrity of both God and man, they seem to ignore God's grace. This is not the case. Unlike Paul, however, who emphasized that man is declared just by God's grace for Christ's sake, the early Christians usually stressed "salvation" as the end product of God's grace and man's response.

Resurrection. The early Christians looked for the culmination of the reign of God in Christ's return to raise all men from the dead and in the establishment of the kingdom of the saints. The early writings, prayers, artwork, and tracts emphasized the sure character of this hope. Perhaps it was Paul himself who best summarized this firm conviction when he wrote, "But in fact Christ has been raised from the dead, the firstfruits of those who have fallen asleep" (1 Corinthians 15:20). In the ancient world, there were many myths about the gods' dying and rising from the dead to give immortal life to man, but none of these was based on historical fact. Peter also wrote that we have been "born again to a living hope" (1 Peter 1:3). Personal life beyond death was one area where most pagans were never sure. They had many ideas about immortality, but they were rather vague. The Roman thinker Cicero, mourning the death of his daughter, wanted so much to be sure about her fate, but he had only a vague hope. Paul wrote that if Christians had no more than this, "we are of all people most to be pitied" (1 Corinthians 15:19). Peter affirmed, "We have a sure hope" because it is based on the certainty of God's promise given in the resurrection of Jesus Christ from the dead. God does not lie!

In the face of strong Gnostic tendencies to deny the redeemability of the material creation since it was not produced by the true God, the emphasis of Christian teaching shifted in the second century from the joyous affirmation of a certain hope to a constant reiteration of the fact that it is the created body that will be resurrected. Responding to philosophies that assumed merely the immortality of the soul and argued the impossibility of a decayed corpse being restored to life, the Christians stressed the resurrection of the body and produced many rational arguments to demonstrate the ability of God to perform this miracle (see *1 Clement*, 22–26). In this discussion, however, the Christians make it clear that they meant no more than that the identical body that had died would be resurrected. They were not concerned to affirm that the body would bear the same characteristics that it does now. This insistence on identity is especially obvious when the apologists claimed that Christians, more than other people, were law-abiding since they knew that precisely the same body that commits the sin must answer for it before the divine judge. When Origen pointed out that Christians teach the "resurrection of the body" rather than the "resurrection of the flesh," he was making the point that by bodily resurrection, Christians do not teach that every aspect of the flesh will be the same, including the injuries and defects, but rather emphasize that the *same* body, though in a glorified form, will be resurrected. Origen encountered great difficulty and misunderstanding as a result of this distinction, but the debate illustrates the early Christian concern with identity and no more. It is precisely what God created that is redeemed and resurrected. Later, this is summarized in the words "I believe in the resurrection of the body."

It is unfortunate, perhaps, that the belief in resurrection should be the last item of the chapter. Actually, it is among "the first things" that early Christians confessed. Everything the early Christians believed and did resulted in great part from their conviction that God won the decisive victory in Jesus Christ and through this action would bring men to glory.

CHURCH AND SOCIETY

The early Christian attitudes toward society cannot be understood apart from their views concerning the end of all things. Most primitive Christians believed that they were living in the last times and expected the *Parousia*, the triumphant return of Jesus, the culmination of all prophecy concerning the Kingdom, the visible reign of the Messiah, to take place in the immediate future. This did not happen. Jesus Himself had warned in His parables that they should not expect Him to return too quickly (see especially Matthew 24–25). Both Peter and Paul were forced to explain the delay to the early communities (2 Peter 3; 1 Thessalonians 5).

End Times. After the period of the New Testament, Christians began to think of the "last things" as taking place primarily in the more distant future. They continued to repeat the old phrases about the end being near, but they didn't expect an immediate return of Christ. Indeed, in some cases, they formulated intricate and imaginative timetables showing that there were still many years before Christ could return. These early Christian theorists, perhaps getting their ideas from Jewish apocalyptic speculations, believed that the world had to exist for six thousand years. This calculation was based on the theory that each of the six days of creation equaled one thousand years. Claiming to have a special ability to interpret the Old Testament, a Christian writer who called himself Barnabas wrote, "Observe what 'He ended in six days' means. It means that in six thousand years the Lord will bring all things to an end, for a day with God is as a thousand years" (*Barnabas*, 15). Hippolytus, writing some time later, claimed that fifty-five hundred of these years had already elapsed before the coming of Christ. Since he lived in the first decades of the second century, he could not have expected Christ to return in his own lifetime.

While few early Christians went so far as to say that the world would last just six thousand years, many of the Early Fathers did believe that when Christ returned, He would reign here on earth for "a thousand years." Papias claimed to have heard this from a disciple of John. Justin Martyr insisted this was the belief of all orthodox Christians.

To list all the early Christians who believed as did Justin and Papias would include most of the important names. There were those Christians, however, who did not accept this interpretation of the New Testament. Some went so far as to deny any historical occasion when *all* would be resurrected and judged at once. They reacted rather violently to these computing Christians. One of the most important in this number was the Alexandrian theologian Origen. He taught that judgment comes for each person when he is confronted by the Holy Spirit in his lifetime. If he refuses God's grace, he is judged. On the other hand, if he accepts God's grace in Christ, he is "born again to eternal life." All bodies will be resurrected individually to live eternally with God. It was not until the time of Augustine in the late fourth century that any synthesis of these views took place.

Whether Christians were waiting for the immediate return of Christ, merely looking forward to reigning with Him in the new Jerusalem someday, or simply hoping to be united with Him after death, they agreed that the present order of creation would be completely destroyed by fire. For this reason, they had little interest in the improvement of society as such.

Modern Christians are often critical of the achievements of early Christianity in society because it didn't reconstruct society along Christian lines, especially when it gained control in the fourth century. The Christians then had no intention of doing this. The achievements credited to Christianity in this area, and there are many, are merely a by-product of their concern to live according to the will of God by loving others as they loved themselves. No other explanation is needed. Even to suggest that they couldn't change the institution of slavery assumes that they wanted to. They had no interest in what we today term "economic injustice," but they did care for the poor. Even military service gets amazingly little attention from the Church Fathers of this period. It has been suggested that they were opportunistic by not being critical of the existing social order. Perhaps. We would rather suggest that they had their eyes fixed on what Augustine called "the eternal city."

Discipline. The strict disciplinary procedures in the early Christian communities demonstrate their prevailing concern to not become engulfed by the corruption of the pagan society surrounding them. The Church protected each individual within the group from "being turned aside" through a strong emphasis on holy living and through confession of gross deviations before the congregation or its leaders. Once admitted into the Church through Baptism, the Christian was expected to avoid all sin. If he became guilty of grave sin, he was expected to confess it and prove his sorrow by becoming a public penitent. The status of such a penitent was somewhat analogous to that of a catechumen. Temporarily placed outside the community of the faithful, he was refused the Holy Eucharist. During this period of exclusion, he was to indicate his repentance by abstaining from all pleasure, such as ornate dress and sexual intercourse. Tertullian describes how penitents dressed differently, prayed, fasted, and pleaded for the elders and congregation to intercede on their behalf. The penance assigned to a person was gauged according to the character of the sin. The actual decision was made by the individual bishop. It is not until the Middle Ages that this process is standardized through the Irish Penitentials. Only after a protracted period of such penance was the penitent allowed to participate in the Eucharist through a public "reconciliation," which consisted of a prayer and the "laying on of hands" by the bishop.

One of the most difficult problems the Church faced in the third century was determining which grave sin could be granted the privilege of such "repentance" and the number of times this should be allowed. This became especially acute when dealing with the members who had "lapsed" or fallen off during persecution.

In the early persecutions, individuals who confessed to being Christians were simply executed. They were called "martyrs," that is, "witnesses." In the third century, however, there were so many Christians that to kill them would have decimated the population. Since the Roman government could not afford to practice this sort of thing, the Christians were tortured until they denied Christ by saying "Caesar is Lord" instead of "Christ is Lord." If a Christian sustained this persecution without denying Christ, he was called a "confessor." Such an individual was ranked with the presbyters, evidently endowed with a special gift of the Spirit for the witness he had borne. If a believer under torture did what the Romans demanded, he was classed among the "lapsed." Could the Church accept the subsequent repentance of those who had lapsed? At first, it seemed beyond the Church's powers to restore lapsed members to a participation in the holy things of God, which they seemed to have spurned (see Hebrews 3:7–19). They had, some asserted, committed the "sin against the Holy Spirit" (see Matthew 12:31, 32). Since the Romans often tortured an individual to deny more than once, the question also arose how many times denial could be forgiven if it was to be forgiven at all.

A number of positions were taken on this question. The strict position was exemplified by the schismatic Montanists and Novatians (200–235), who classified falling away as the sin against the Spirit and refused the Eucharist to those repenting, even on their deathbed. The Novatians separated themselves from other Christians who had decided to receive the lapsed who repented of their action. The Gnostic Christians, on the other extreme, distinguished denial by the mouth from denial in the heart and took such lapsing rather lightly. The Church as a whole finally took the middle position of granting the lapsed the possibility of "repentance," sometimes once, sometimes twice, but always under severe restrictions. They feared that greater lenience would encourage Christians not to take such lapses seriously and tempt them to try to take advantage of God's grace. The seriousness with which the Christian communities dealt with the lapsed illustrates the attitude of the Early Church toward gross sins.

Separation. That the Christians were aloof from pagan society is illustrated by their attitude toward Roman entertainment. The arena, circus, and theater seem to have been avoided completely. The theaters were infamous to the Christian mind because they portrayed immorality among gods and men. Gossip had it that only women of light virtue played in these productions. The Romans also had a custom of substituting criminals where the script demanded that a killing take place. Indeed,

Nero forced Christians to play various mythological roles both to amuse the crowds and also as a form of public execution.

Perhaps the worst form of amusement among the Romans was the gladiatorial combat. This was big business. At one point in the second century, over half the days in the year were taken up with such shows in the arena. They were free to the populace and became so common that mere races and other forms of athletics were too tame for the people. Roman officials vied with each other to put on the biggest and the best show for the people. It was a way to keep the government popular with the masses. Entrepreneurs trained men to fight in these shows. Often, they were captives who had no choice. Not until the third century were laws passed forbidding anyone to force a slave into the arena. In these gladiatorial combats, the crowd took sides. Often, the winner of one bout would be pitted against other winners until only one or two were left from a field of men. As many as two hundred pairs would fight a day. If a free man won such a round, he could earn enough to spend the rest of his life in ease. This type of combat was also used by the Roman government to execute criminals.

The Christian attitude toward such amusements is illustrated by Tertullian's tract *On Shows*. He warned the newly baptized of the danger involved: "It is not by being merely in the world that we fall from faith, but by touching and tainting ourselves with the world's sins. To go to the circus or the theater as a spectator is no different from sacrificing in the temple of Serapis" (*On Shows*, 8). Admitting there was no divine command forbidding attendance, Tertullian quoted Psalm 1, "Blessed is the man who walks not in the counsel of the wicked." His main reason for forbidding this activity, however, was the idolatry associated with it. He pointed out that the gladiatorial combats and the races were dedicated to the gods. Recalling that Christians did not eat food offered to idols, he continued: "If we keep our throats and bellies free from defilement, how much more should we withhold our nobler parts, our ears and eyes, from such enjoyments. This idolatry does not merely pass through the body, but is digested by our very souls and spirits. God has a right to claim purity here even more than in our body" (*On Shows*, 13). "From the sky to the sty" was the way he curtly cut off all further debate and pleaded for complete separation: "Would that we did not even inhabit the same world with such people! While that wish cannot be realized, we are separated from the worldly. The world is God's, but the worldly is the devil's" (*On Shows*, 25, 15).

Tertullian's statements were often in the extreme. But the attitude he represented was rather common. Athenagoras put it just as clearly, "We see little difference between watching a man being put to death and killing him. We have given up such spectacles" (*Plea*, 35). Tatian was perhaps the most bitter about the theater, "They carouse in affected manner going through many indecent movements; your sons and daughters behold them giving lessons in adultery on the stage" (*Oration*, 23).

This separateness is also illustrated in the early Christian attitude toward military and civil service. Such service was of course the pride of the Roman citizen.

The classical mind considered the well-organized state as the highest condition of well-being. This did not mean that the individual was unimportant—they were most concerned with the individual's cultural development—but the concerns of the individual were subordinated to those of society. The important "virtues" and "duties" were political in character.

It seems that some Christians may have served in the military prior to the end of the second century, but they were apparently individuals who had been in either civil or military service prior to their conversion. Tertullian (c. 200) argued from the fact that there were Christians in government work: "We are a new group but have already penetrated all areas of imperial life—cities, islands, villages, towns, marketplaces, even the camp, tribes, palace, senate, the law-court. There is nothing left for you but your temples" (*Apology*, 37). To show that Christians were really good citizens, he pleaded: "We live in the world with you. We do not forsake forum . . . or bath . . . or workshop, or inn, or market, or any other place of commerce. We sail with you, fight with you, farm with you. . . ." (*Apology*, 42).

By the end of the second century, however, the Fathers, including Tertullian, opposed such service. It is quite possible that Christians were not drafted before this time since they were generally from the noncitizen classes before Caracalla (212) lowered the property requirements for citizenship. From *The Apostolic Tradition* (200), we gather that Hippolytus reluctantly allowed an individual to remain a soldier if he was converted in the army, but he did not allow an individual to join the army after his Baptism. Tertullian contended that Christians were not useful to the army because they would rather be killed than kill. He also questioned whether a Christian could serve both God and the government, given the immoral practices of civil servants of that time.

Origen in another part of Africa took the same position. To Celsus's charge that Christians avoided these responsibilities out of fear or lack of patriotism, Origen asserted that Christians perform greater service to the state when they serve as officials in the church and especially when they pray for the government. When Origen was asked what would happen if the majority of people in the world were Christian, he deduced that there would obviously be no more war. In any case, Origen agreed with Tertullian that nothing is more alien to the Christian than politics and military service. It is difficult to say how strong the opposite opinion on this subject was during this period. It was certainly not as ably presented, if presented at all.

Slavery and Charity. Christian writers from this period exhibit little concern about the institution of slavery. When they do speak of it, it is in terms of loving all men as brothers. This expressed itself mainly in the treatment of slaves but also in either setting them free or buying their freedom.

Slavery was an accepted part of the Roman political and economic system. Slaves were usually captured enemy soldiers, and in the centuries before Christ, an owner had absolute control over them. They could be sold, lent, given, bequeathed, or killed. In the second century after Christ, legislation made the institution more humane. Allowed to share in the growing wealth of the empire, many slaves accumulated enough wealth to purchase their freedom. Laws were passed forbidding the use of slaves in the public games, easing manumission of slaves no longer needed or sick, making the murder of a slave a crime like any other murder, and giving the slave a right to bring grievances before a court of law.

The Stoic philosophers were in the forefront of this movement for humane treatment. Cicero differed from the ancient Greek philosopher Aristotle by insisting that all men are equal since they have the ability to differentiate right from wrong. Seneca, a Roman contemporary of Christ, taught that slaves had the same nature as their master because they could develop in virtue. The slave should realize, Seneca thought, that bondage was merely external, and the master should treat a slave more like a servant.

Actually, the Christian Fathers said little more than this, but they put it into practice by urging the Christian master to treat a slave as his brother. Aristides wrote: "Slaves, male and female, are encouraged to be instructed in Christianity on account of the love their masters have for them. When this happens, they are called brethren without any distinction" (*Apology*, 15). When Euelpistes, a slave in the imperial household, was brought before the tribunal of Rusticus with Justin Martyr, he explained that although he was a slave, as a Christian he received freedom in Christ. No slave was allowed to accept Baptism without an attestation of character from his owner if the latter was a Christian; but once the slave was baptized, he could become even a clergyman. At least one ex-slave, Callistus, became bishop of Rome (c. 220).

That Christians owned slaves is obvious from the records we have, but they encouraged manumission. Congregations set aside funds to purchase the freedom of slaves (Ignatius, *To Polycarp*, 4). There was a special ceremony for manumission in Christian communities. The master led the slave to the altar, where the document of emancipation was read. After the bishop pronounced the blessing, the ex-slave was received as a free brother by the congregation. The early Christians were warned to stay away from public meetings unless they attended to purchase the freedom of a slave. One individual freed some 1,250 slaves on the day of his Baptism, and this is not the only recorded incident of this kind.

The works of charity that Christians accomplished in the Roman Empire continue to be one of the greatest stars in the Church's crown. Even the pagans noticed this. Lucian, who is known more for his satire than his appreciation, wrote that all Christians regarded one another as brethren.

The classical world had little concern for the sick and poor. Plato suggested that allowing the poor to die shortened their misery. Cicero allowed help only to those who would receive such charity to improve themselves. There is a hint of this same attitude in some Christian literature. The Didachist exhorted the Christian to allow the gift to "burn in the hand" until he knows to whom he is giving it (*Didache*, 1:6). The position of Hermas, however, seems to be the more normal. He wrote that it is in the attitude of the giver that God finds pleasure, not in how the gift is used.

From the beginning, Christians shared their wealth. There is no suggestion, except in Acts, that wealth be redistributed or that poverty is an injustice, but a common fund was set up in each congregation to which all contributed as they could for the benefit of the poor. The original practice in the Jerusalem community continued to exercise an influence: "Now the full number of those who believed were of one heart and soul, and no one said that any of the things that belonged to him was his own, but they had everything in common. . . . There was not a needy person among them, for as many as were owners of lands or houses sold them and brought the proceeds . . . and laid it at the apostles' feet, and it was distributed to each as any had need" (Acts 4:32–35). This, however, was unique in early Christianity; the rest of the Church did not follow this example. The example they followed was one of *continuing* to share their wealth with those less fortunate. Justin Martyr informs the emperor that "we who once took pleasure in the means of increasing our wealth and property now bring what we have into a common fund and share with everyone in need" (*1 Apology*, 14).

Christians practiced this charity both among themselves and toward others. Aristides informed the emperor, "He who has gives to him who has not without grudging, and when they see a stranger they bring him to their dwellings and rejoice over him as a true brother" (*Apology*, 15). Hospitality to strangers was important in a day when inns were not desirable places. Ancient society did not provide care for orphans but allowed them to be raised for prostitution or other disreputable occupations. Christians made these unfortunates the object of their concern. Since the only hospitals in existence were private or associated with religious cults, Christians also took care of the sick. During plagues in Carthage and Alexandria around the middle of the third century, the Christians cared for the suffering even after the pagans had abandoned them.

Marriage and Sex. The Christians' attitude toward sexual morality and their interpretation of the nature of marriage was radical. Pagan philosophers and religious teachers talked about moral purity, but they did not regard sexual immorality with the same degree of seriousness as did the Christian teachers; the family stability and moral discipline of ancient Rome were giving way to decadence.

It is perhaps important to pause here for a moment to emphasize the ascetic character of early Christianity and to point out that this asceticism did not deny the original goodness or redeemability of the physical. In the face of Gnostic assertions that the body is evil since it is part of the physical creation, the Christians taught that it was not the body itself that was evil, but rather the irrational and selfish will within man that failed to curb his lusts and passions. Early Christian asceticism then is not a Gnostic negation of creation but rather an attempt to give God's creation back to Him in a good and holy state, not perverted by the will of man. The Church's attitude toward sex is an illustration of it.

Monogamy was the rule among the Romans. Adultery, or sexual union with the wife of another Roman citizen, was severely punished. Yet, although allowed only one wife, a married Roman was free to have sexual intercourse with a mistress, a prostitute, or even with his male and female slaves. The wife did not have these privileges. While divorce was not common among the Romans at the time of early Christianity, Seneca noted that it was still a significant problem.

Christians were much more severe in their demands for marital faithfulness. Any coition outside of marriage was considered a grave sin. Many felt that after Baptism, adultery could be forgiven only once if at all. Early Christian teachers suggested that the purpose of sexual intercourse was merely to produce children. They contrasted their attitude with that of the pagan, who undertook it "to satisfy his lust." Monogamy in the Early Church meant that a man was to have only one wife at a time, but many also believed that he was to make only one such contract in his lifetime.

Christian teachers regularly quoted the words that Jesus addressed to His disciples and with which He forbade divorce except for fornication (Matthew 19:9). But they insisted that the permission to divorce here meant merely separation since there is no permission to remarry. They also quoted Paul to the effect that widows do better to remain unmarried (1 Corinthians 7:8–9). These attitudes occur in the earliest literature outside of the New Testament. Polycarp (115) wrote about widows who were "pledged to the Lord," and Ignatius greeted "the virgins enrolled with the widows." Hermas in Rome (c. 100) stressed that believers ought not automatically seek divorce for adultery since spouses might be able to help each other overcome evil. Hermas did not treat adultery lightly, for he was not sure that it is even forgivable after Baptism; but he encouraged the injured party to show Christian love even here and discouraged second marriage in any case (*Mandate*, 4:4). Rejoicing that "those who once rejoiced in fornication now delight in continence alone" and that "many men and women now in their sixties and seventies, disciples of Christ from their youth, have preserved their purity," Justin Martyr suggested, "Those who make second marriages according to human law are sinners in the sight of our Teacher."

Some early Christians, especially those with tendencies toward Gnosticism or Montanism, were even more severe. Tatian condemned the marriage relationship itself as destructive of prayer life. In a letter to his wife, Tertullian caustically questioned whether their marriage was really for the best. He calls their sexual relation a "voluptuous disgrace" and suggests that it certainly ought not to be repeated. The death of a spouse is God's call to continence for the other (*To Wife*, 2:2; 1:7). He noted that in the old dispensation under Adam, men were encouraged to marry, but in the new covenant, we follow the example of Christ who did not marry (*On Monogamy*, 7–11). Such extremists in an earlier period seem to have prompted the censure of Paul, "In later times some will depart from the faith by devoting themselves to deceitful spirits . . . who forbid marriage" (1 Timothy 4:1, 3).

Clement of Alexandria's appreciation of both celibacy and marriage as gifts from God, as well as his willingness to allow second marriage if necessary, is more representative of early Christianity. The early Christians universally taught that the first purpose of marriage was to have children. The Romans had the custom of exposing children they did not desire. A letter from the period of our Lord written by a pagan in Egypt shows the cold, matter-of-fact character of this custom when it directs: "When you give birth to your child, if it is a boy, let it live; if it is a girl, expose it." The philosopher Seneca explained, "We destroy monstrous offspring; if they are born feeble or ill-formed, we drown them. It is not wrath but reason that separates the useless from the healthy." In the face of this attitude, Christians insisted that they did not marry except to bring up children; if they didn't desire children, they abstained from sex.

The Church Fathers revealed another purpose of marriage, that of mutual spiritual support, when they condemned mixed marriages. Tertullian wrote about this to his wife: "How can I paint the happiness in a marriage that the church ratifies, the celebration of Communion confirms, the benediction seals. . . ? What a union! . . . They pray together, fast together, instruct, exhort, and support each other. . . . They share each other's tribulation, persecution, and revival. . . . They delight to visit the sick, help the needy, give alms freely. . . . Christ rejoices when He hears and sees this" (*To Wife*, 2:8). It is this ideal of marriage that led Tertullian to question whether a mixed marriage ought even be contemplated. He asked whether a heathen would allow his wife to attend night meetings, participate in the slandered Supper of the Lord, take care of the sick in the poorest hovels, kiss the chains of martyrs in prison, rise in the night for prayer, or show hospitality to strange brethren.

Early Christianity did not attempt to change any social or economic structures. Therefore, the Church cannot be scorned for having effected so few changes in them. No voice was raised against the institution of slavery. Wars continued to be fought; Christians even participated. What was revolutionary about the social outlook of the early Christians was their adherence to God's will that they love their fellow men rather than selfishly entangle themselves in the things of this world. There was a necessary tension here. They avoided any pagan activities that would tend to betray their moral code. But at the same time, the early Christians worked hard, gave much, and treated all men of whatever station as "brothers."

The Christians looked for the end of the age and as a result were not interested in social structures, but they were at the same time deeply committed to the welfare of their fellow men. An eschatological involvement!

CHURCH AND STATE

Christianity entered a world in which it was taken for granted that the state dominated religious activities. Prior to the advent of Christianity, the Romans made no distinction between the life of the state and the religious life of the people. The Romans felt that the gods had given them empire, peace, and prosperity as a result of their being pleased with the worship they received from the Romans. Cicero admitted that it was because the Romans surpassed all others in piety that the gods had protected and prospered the empire. Horace insisted that the Romans owed their empire to their submission to the gods and attributed the ills of Rome to the neglect of the temples. The maintenance of this covenant was the responsibility of the state. The priests appointed by the Senate carried out the ritual worship under the direction of the *pontifex maximus*. The people had little to do with this worship except on festivals. The citizen, however, was expected to do nothing that would displease the gods of Rome. In his home and on his farm, every Roman had altars dedicated to the traditional gods of Rome. This family worship took the form of various rites that had to be carefully carried out.

Since the oversight was in the hands of the Senate, only gods whose cult was allowed by the Senate could legally be worshiped. Whenever the Roman armies incorporated a new area into the Roman state, the Senate would add the statues of the gods of that territory to the Pantheon. As the empire expanded, people from all over the Mediterranean moved to Rome, bringing the worship of their own gods with them. Since these gods had not received the official sanction of the Senate, they were designated as "private" gods. Worshiped by the people rather than by officially appointed priests, they were not related to the most ancient religious traditions of the Roman people. The cults were often of the "mystery" type.

The *mystery religions* emphasized the assurance of personal immortality through personal relationship with deity. This experience took place when the initiate into the cult was allowed to view the mystery of death and the restoration to life presented in dramatic form. The ritual drama was the "mystery." The most popular of the deities involved in the mystery cults were Isis and Osiris from Egypt, Attis and Cybele from Asia Minor, and Demeter from Greece. The dramas differed in particulars, but essentially each recounted the "mystery" of how the deity suffered death, was forced to reside in Hades for a time, but ultimately triumphed over death through a resurrection. The myths reenacted here originally concerned the annual death and rebirth in nature. The gods were involved in the recurring advent of winter and birth of spring. Only later were the myths viewed as the key to an eternal life for human beings. After an individual had witnessed this drama, he was a "knowing one." The ritual connected with this initiation included washings, eating the flesh of slain animals, and, in some mysteries, participating in various orgiastic activities such as wild dancing, being drenched in blood, mutilating oneself, and sexual license.

The Roman government carefully watched these cults to prevent any citizen from participating in immorality. The immoral rites of Cybele were permitted in Rome, but no Roman was allowed to participate. The police were often called to break up gatherings for the worship of Dionysus, the god of wine, because of the immoral practices involved. The Roman government was also concerned about the possibility that these foreign cults might be a breeding ground for sedition since they were very popular with the disinherited in Rome.

It was not tolerance that caused Rome to allow these forms of worship but rather the popular demand for them. Indeed, just before Christianity began to be popular in Rome, the government attempted to reestablish its control of popular religious life by introducing a new cult to preserve the religious traditions of Rome through the worship of "the spirit of Rome" in the person of the emperor. "Deity" was usually not defined philosophically, but was seen as that which gives good things. Since Rome brought peace and justice, it was honored and praised or worshiped. But what was the symbol of imperial Rome? The person of the emperor was the obvious choice. Hence, the emperor cult. The Romans gave to the emperor honor and praise as the incarnation of all that made Rome great and all that Rome did for the world. The names of most of the traditional gods of Rome were attached in one way or another to this cult. Generally speaking, however, the emperors did not think of themselves as gods walking on the earth. Rather, they participated in deity to the degree that their wills determined the course of peoples' lives through their office. This cult became rather popular, even though the people were not expected to participate in these rites before the third century.

Since Christianity was not the official religion of any state with which the Romans came into contact and was therefore considered a private and unofficial cult, it developed as an institution entirely separate from the state.

Conflict and Martyrdom. The attitude of Roman society toward Christians was one of suspicion. Since Christianity began in Palestine and many of the early Christians were Jews, the Roman populace simply transferred to the Church their detestation of the Jew. The Christians could show no image of their God and denied the existence of the gods. The Romans deduced from this that they were "atheists." When Christians spoke of eating the "body" and drinking the "blood" of the "Son," the Romans gossiped that they were butchering babies and consuming their flesh and blood. This was the rumor among the Romans. The good qualities of the Christians were lost in this mire of suspicion and gossip. Suetonius suggested that the Christians were "superstitious," a word associated with witchcraft. Tacitus called them "haters of the human race" because they didn't worship any known or knowable god and practiced immoral rites.

It was only natural that Nero should play on the suspicions of the people and blame the fire in Rome (64) on Christians. We do not know who started that blaze. Nero, however, made the mistake of rebuilding the burned part of the city and constructing many beautiful temples. The people suspected that he was building temples to placate the wrath of the gods for his having destroyed part of their city. To turn suspicion from himself, he picked a small foreign group in Rome (that everyone suspected of the most horrible crimes and hated for their aloofness from most social activities), blamed them for the fire, and encouraged against them the wrath of the populace. Even Tacitus thought the punishment severe: "Besides being put to death they were made to serve as objects of amusement; they were clad in the hides of beasts and torn to death by dogs; some were crucified, others set on fire to serve to illuminate the night when daylight failed" (*Annales*, XV, 44). Most Romans regarded such execution of criminals as routine. Peter and Paul probably lost their lives in this persecution.

Following the pattern of Nero's day, persecution spread to other areas of the empire at the turn of the century. John was exiled to the island of Patmos. The grandchildren of Jude were called to Rome by Domitian to determine whether his suspicions were true. Ignatius, bishop of Antioch, and Polycarp, bishop of Smyrna, were martyred in the midst of celebrating and cheering mobs. In Lyons, about fifty Christians were mobbed.

There were no empirewide, centrally directed persecutions until the third century. Before this time, persecution was sporadic and local. The government usually acted when encouraged by the mob. Officials did not seek out Christians. Only if an individual was accused of being "Christian" was he liable to police action. It was assumed that if he confessed to "the name," he was guilty of all the actions that gossip credited to Christianity. For this reason, Peter wrote, "If anyone suffers as a *Christian*, let him not be ashamed, but let him glorify God in that name" (1 Peter 4:16, emphasis added).

The courage of Christians who faced diabolical tortures earned the admiration of both Roman and fellow Christian. Tertullian wrote, "The blood of Christians is seed" (*Apology*, 50), indicating that many were converted who witnessed the death of these "athletes of God." The term *martyr* meant "witness" in Greek. Originally, any Christian who suffered for the faith, whether he was or was not executed, was spoken of as a "martyr" or "confessor." The memory of these martyrs who went all the way with Christ was honored in the churches. They were the highest expression of Christian selflessness. And more, they symbolized the belief that a true confessor or prophet must suffer, as Jesus said: "Whoever does not take his cross and follow Me is not worthy of Me. Whoever finds his life will lose it, and whoever loses his life for My sake will find it" (Matthew 10:38–39). Irenaeus thought of Jesus as the Master Martyr. Origen wrote: "As we behold the martyrs coming forth from every church to be brought before the tribunal, we see in each the Lord Himself condemned." When Ignatius heard that the Christians in Rome hoped to prevent his execution, he wrote that they should not interfere with his martyrdom.

Shrines developed around the relics of martyrs. The places where they lived or were buried, articles they used, and their bones were held in high honor and became centers of devotion. The anniversaries of the local martyrs' deaths were celebrated by the Christian communities as these heroes' heavenly "birthdays." Since early Christians believed that martyrs had a special status "with the Lord" (see Revelation 6:9–11), their lives and prayers served as intercession for those still on earth. While seeking martyrdom was generally discouraged, the high regard in which it was held is indicated by the fact that it was called a second baptism.

Christian Attitudes toward the State. To explain their position, some Christians in the second century wrote apologies (*apologia* meaning "defense") to the emperor in which they declared that they were not atheists, immoral, or unpatriotic. Justin admitted that Christians did not worship the gods, but he insisted that this did not mean that they were atheists. He explained that there is only one God, and this is the God Christians worship. Since the Christians were suspected of disloyalty to the state because they spoke of Jesus as "Lord," a title assumed by the emperor, Justin also attempted to show that when Christians talked about a kingdom of Christ, they were not necessarily disloyal to the empire (2 *Apology*, 11). It is important to note, however, that the millennialistic teaching of early Christianity certainly gave cause, unjust though it was, to these suspicions. Tertullian pointed out that Christians refused to worship the emperor because he was not God, but he insisted that Christians were loyal to the emperor.

Aristides also defended Christians against the charge of immorality: "Wherefore they do not commit adultery nor fornication, nor bear false witness, nor embezzle what is held in pledge, nor covet what is not theirs. . . . And their women, O Emperor, are pure as virgins, and their daughters are modest; and their men keep themselves from every unlawful union and from all uncleanness" (*Apology*, 15). Theophilus claimed that on the basis of such evidence, the Christians were actually the empire's best citizens (*To Autolycus*, 9–15). Both Justin and Tertullian included descriptions of Christian worship to prove that it was not immoral.

EARLY CHRISTIAN VIEWS OF GOVERNMENT		
VIEWS	AGREEMENT	DISSENT
Government Divine and Human Institution	Paul (Romans 13); Irenaeus: God established government to reward good and punish evil.	Tatian: Mankind originally created without government. Tertullian; Hippolytus: Empire not divinely blessed. Origen: government is for non-Christians.
Obedience Necessary	Justin, Tatian, Tertullian, Hippolytus, etc., taught obedience to government.	Origen: non-Christians might properly rebel against tyranny, though Christians owed love even to tyrants.
Pay Taxes	Tertullian: Christians loyal in paying taxes.	Tatian: Pay, but taxes are a form of slavery.
Separation of Church and State	No such political view at this time.	Melito: Christianity is separate but should work with the state as a divine institution.
Divine Law	Obey laws of the state when they agree with divine Law.	Disobey when laws conflict with God's Law (Acts 5:29).

These apologists pleaded for toleration of Christians. They justified this in a number of ways. Athenagoras suggested that Christians were like any other philosophical group and should be accepted as such (*Plea*, 2). Justin Martyr appealed to the generally accepted idea that Rome stood for justice, insisting that to allow mobs to control legal procedures was not justice. Certainly, the emperor could not allow Christians to be executed without a fair trial in which all the evidence was laid out.

Justin seems rather sure that a fair trial would exonerate the Christians (*1 Apology*, 4, 7). But these earlier apologists requested toleration only for themselves. They did not argue from a basic principle of "rights." Tertullian was the first to demand freedom to worship for all individuals on the basis of a fundamental human right. He contended that it was a privilege of nature to worship God as one pleased. He did not urge that the state withdraw from the religious life of the community but merely suggested that it ought not to attempt to control *how* an individual worshiped God (*To Scapula*, 2). This was not an uncommon idea among pagans in the fourth century; it is rather interesting coming from a Christian.

CHAPTER TWO

The Church in a Changing World

EVENTS AND TRENDS FROM 250 TO 600

Our own era is marked by revolutions and dramatic changes among the nations in the areas of culture, social mores, worldviews, philosophy, technology, and our whole way of life. The Church is caught up in the midst of the swirl.

When we consider the period of this section, the years between AD 250 and 600, we see that the society and the Church of those days underwent similar earth-shaking changes. That era of tremendous upheavals necessitated adjustments as great as ours. Around 250, the Church saw the first systematic persecution of Christians by the Roman Empire, which had begun to feel threatened by the spiritual challenge of the growing Christian movement. In the early fourth century, almost overnight, came a period of imperial favor for the Church and a wide acceptance of Christianity by society. Within less than a century came the collapse of the Roman world in the West under the impact of barbarian invasions. The Church then entered an entirely new and unfamiliar world, which it undertook to win for its faith. The years around 600 saw chaos-driven Western Christendom obtain the history-making leadership of Gregory the Great, who is considered the last great "Father" of the Ancient Church and a founder of the medieval papacy.

Our aim is to probe the life and thought of the Church in the changing world of this era. How did the Church fare in these periods of persecution or seductive favor? Did its devotion, thought, and leadership grow, or did these become stale and irrelevant with the advance of time? How much real influence did Christianity exercise on society? How did the Church adjust to the disappearance of the familiar Roman world and to the chaos and new societies that succeeded the Roman order? Did this era of changes produce any significant developments that endure to this day?

Ordeal by Fire. The first period of the great changes started in the mid-third century and lasted for almost seventy-five years. It brought fierce, intermittent, empirewide persecutions of Christians. It was for the Christian community, grown large and soft by the security it had enjoyed for most of the preceding half century, a trial by fire.

The first great persecution began in 250, when the new emperor Decius launched a new policy requiring all citizens to sacrifice to the pagan gods and to have a certified statement (a *libellus*) of their compliance with the edict. The Roman Empire had suffered serious setbacks in the preceding years. It was generally believed that the ancient gods were revenging themselves on the empire for its lax policy toward the Christians, who refused to worship the gods and who influenced others to neglect their civic duty toward them as the divine patrons of the empire. Many Christians could not bring themselves to face the fierce penalties and so either performed the required ritual or at least secured the *libellus* from friendly or bribed officials. The leaders of the Church naturally considered such acts a repudiation of the baptismal vow, by which the baptized had foresworn all pagan gods and bound themselves only to the one God. The fallen, or *lapsed*, Christians were barred from the Church's Communion until they showed sufficient penitence and received reconciliation from the Christian community, the household of God.

The number of the "lapsed" was alarming. As many as 80 percent of some congregations' members were classed among the public "penitents" once the rugged-but-brief first wave of the great persecutions was over. Other waves followed. The last universal and greatest persecution took place under Emperor Diocletian in 303–4. He ordered all Christian churches to be destroyed, Christian sacred books and vessels confiscated, and all Christian clergy imprisoned. Finally, all citizens were required to sacrifice to the gods or face death. The persecutions tested the Church's mettle, restored it to its unique calling within society, and renewed its spiritual vigor. The Church was being prepared for a role of leadership in Roman society, a role that fell to it with the final victory of Constantine when he became the sole ruler of the Roman Empire in the autumn of 324.

Surprising Victory. The definitive end of the persecutions and Christianity's sudden rise to imperial favor and prominence in Roman life came as a surprise to the Church. From its beginning, the Church had been a small and often suspect minority.

Constantine was a military leader. He turned to the Christians' God for aid in battle, and when he won, he became devoted to the Christian Church. There is the famous story of his vision of the cross and the words "By this sign conquer" inscribed on the midday sun. Another story tells of a dream in which Constantine was told to put the XP (Chi-Rho) monogram on the shields of his soldiers to secure victory.

We may have doubts about the depth of Constantine's understanding of the Christian faith and of his conversion, but the emperor was after all a military man, for whom victory in battle was crucial. Although he never became a man of peace, his legislation as emperor testifies to his Christianity.

He forbade the branding of prisoners on the face "because man is made in the image of God." He directed all prisons to let the inmates out into the open air each day, so that a day may not pass without their having seen the salutary sun. Constantine also assigned a large portion of the government's revenues to the support of the philanthropic work maintained by the Church (a work which was not being undertaken by any other organization or agency; the Church was a pioneer in the works of mercy). He built magnificent, large churches, exempted the clergy from taxes, and made Christian clergymen paid civil servants of the empire.

His support of the Church was a mixed blessing. It radically altered the status of the Christian in society and the life and makeup of the Christian community. It became easy to become a Christian and advantageous to enter the clergy. However, the meaning and cost of discipleship became all too often obscured, and many people entered the ranks and offices of the Church without conviction.

The Marriage of Faith and Culture. Constantine must have hoped that the empirewide Christian Church would become the cement that would unite the badly cracking empire and give it a sense of common purpose and dedication. The Roman Empire had become too huge and heterogeneous to have such a unity of itself. It contained many annexed and conquered provinces, and its population and army included more and more immigrants from the nomadic Gothic (that is, Germanic) tribes, who were pressing in on the empire from several directions. To stem the inflow of immigrants, the imperial officials sometimes refused them permission to settle on Roman land, an action that evoked successive Gothic invasions of the empire. To guard the security of its frontiers, the state needed inner unity in its population and army. There was nothing corresponding to the American school system, with its Americanizing effect on immigrants, to unite the empire. The cult of the emperor, designed to develop a common loyalty in the empire, had failed in its purpose.

The Christian Church was the only institution that might perhaps weld the people into one. Thus, the emperors initiated the marriage of Church and society. We use the image of marriage purposefully, for marriage means union and not identity, and it involves give-and-take, adjustments, crises, and storms.

Society was not immediately Christianized, of course, nor was Christianity the state religion under Constantine. Christians were then only a substantial minority. It was not until the end of the fourth century, under Emperor Theodosius, that the Church became the state church and that laws were issued against public pagan worship. Pagans still continued to hold high positions in the empire until the mid-sixth century, when Emperor Justinian outlawed paganism. Jews were protected by imperial law, even if they were not always free from molestation. Yet Christianity was obviously the imperially favored religion, and a harmony and cooperation between Church and state was the envisioned ideal. More and more, people poured into the Church. The Church had an opportunity to influence the society; it became wide open to the existing culture, with its riches and its problems.

The fourth century was the "Golden Age" of Christian antiquity. The accumulated learning, arts, and skills of the Greco-Roman and ancient Near East civilizations were now absorbed by the Church without fear of heathen contamination. The pagan culture ceased to appear dangerous. Most of the best minds embraced the faith that had been considered vulgar and low-class by the educated classes only a short while before. The result was a flourishing of Christian literature and theology, of skillful preaching, and of the arts connected with Christian worship and devotion.

The Christianization of a whole society and its culture was a difficult and long-term task. Many of the existing cultural and social forms and customs had to be adapted, and they transformed only very gradually. The Church engaged in a vigorous teaching activity, not only in preaching but also in the preparation of candidates for their Baptism. But the former rigorous screening of these catechumens fell into disuse. The Church now rejoiced at having the opportunity to reach the multitude.

There was a parallel growth of Christian ranks outside the Roman circles. However, while Christianity within the empire spread by and large simply by "contagion," it was often brought by specific individuals to the nations outside the Roman confines. There were, however, no "missionary societies." Since, in contrast to the population of the Roman Empire, most of these peoples had a strong sense of their corporate unity, whole tribes and kingdoms accepted Christian Baptism. The majority of the Gothic peoples (in and outside the empire), several Arab tribes, the kingdoms of Armenia, Georgia, and Ethiopia, as well as the Franks, the Irish, the Scots, and finally the English, had become or were to become Christian between the end of the third and the end of the sixth centuries. (Christianity also penetrated from Christianized Syria into Mesopotamia and Persia even though it was not favored by the Sassanite rulers, the great rivals of the Roman emperors.) The traditions and folklore of the baptized peoples were also "baptized" in the process. A most striking example of this is the introduction of Christmas into the Church's calendar. It was typical of the fusion of formerly pagan customs with Christian celebrations. The early Christians considered the celebration of Jesus' birthday unnecessary or even inappropriate. No one knew when Jesus was born. It was not customary to celebrate people's birthdays. The emperors' birthdays may be feted, but Jesus was not an emperor, Origen (third century) curtly said.

December 25 (in the West) and January 6 (in the East) were popular holidays in honor of the birth (return) of the sun. Eastertime roughly coincided with spring fertility rites. Some scholars hold that when the Church wanted to win the masses in the fourth century, it was good psychology to transform the pagan feast days into Christian festivities. This common argument remains unproven. However, it is the case that some illogical customs associated with the Christian holy days, such as Easter eggs and bunnies, likely have pagan origins.

Not only *harmless* pagan traditions found their way into the Church. Some pagan ideas were irreconcilable with Christian teaching and values, giving the Church a hard struggle or actually a new face.

The fourth to the sixth centuries were marked by violent theological debates and by conflicts between bishops and emperor. The great theological question of the time dealt with the relationship of the transcendent God to the world and to human existence. Much of Greek and Oriental philosophical thought made an absolute separation between the infinite and the finite, between the spiritual and the earthly. If there was such an infinite chasm between these spheres, how could God create the world or have any relationship with it? How could men know God? How could the infinite God enter history or human existence and redeem it? Who, then, was Jesus Christ and what did He accomplish? These questions affected the heart of the Christian faith; they were fought over bitterly, with a Greek philosophical thoroughness that sometimes seems pointless to the practical Western mind.

Although these controversies often appear to have been only wrangles over words, ultimate questions were at stake. They also often involved open conflict between the Church's leaders and government officials who wanted to achieve peace and unity in Church and empire by means of compromise. The emperor considered himself responsible for his entire realm, and in his mind, theological matters were not separable from it. Recalcitrant bishops were usually deposed and exiled, but the emperors were only temporarily successful in imposing their will on the Church's creeds. At other times, emperor and bishop faced each other over questions of imperial policy and practice in the social realm. The Church was by no means separate from the state, and although the Church did not wish a separation, the truly great bishops, whether in the East or West, were no puppets of the imperial court. The fourth to the sixth centuries provide a rather fascinating history of church-state relations.

Among the most dangerous results of the marriage of Church and society in the fourth century was the transmission of the easygoing ways and values of society into the Church. Power, ease, and comfort changed the Church from an elite minority into a comfortable, all-inclusive Church that could no longer be distinguished from the rest of society. Discipline and self-sacrifice were not its marks. Its life had ceased to be an inspiration and challenge to men.

It is against this background that we must understand the rise and attraction of Christian monasticism. The fourth century ascetic movement arose as a protest against the loss of the heroic nature of the Church. The early hermits and monks wanted to obey Jesus' demand to "sell all" and "follow" Him on His hard and lonely way. They wished to bear His cross and follow in the footsteps of the martyrs who bore witness to their Master by their rejection and agony. Wonderful as it was that society no longer wanted to suppress the Christian faith and even wished to embrace it, the change in social status robbed the Church of its heroic character and blunted the sharp edge of the Gospel for the multitude and the highborn who were now entering it. The men and women who were enthralled by the monastic ideal in this period knew the cost of Christian discipleship and wanted to pay it. Since the age of the martyrs was in the past, the hermits and monks became the new heroes of Christendom. They were a constant challenge to the superficially Christian society.

How great was the actual Christian influence on Roman society and government? Although it is difficult to assess such a complex matter, the influence seems disappointing. It was impossible to really convert a whole ancient culture and a totalitarian system of government within a few generations. By the turn of the fourth century, the imperial government had indeed become totalitarian out of the fear of collapse before the onslaught of continued invasions and mutinies. Nevertheless, the Church did have an important role and considerable influence within the given limits.

The most striking example of the Christian influence was the introduction of the seven-day week into Roman society and from there eventually into other parts of the world. The system of dividing time into weeks, with one day as a holiday, was completely unknown outside Jewish and Christian circles. When Constantine and his successors made Sunday an official day of rest, it was a tremendous boon to the working man, and it provided a new rhythm of life in society. Under Christian influence, concubinage for a married man was forbidden, adultery and rape became more severely punished, divorce was made less easy, and infanticide became illegal (but not the abandonment of infants; a Roman father had the right to dispose of his newborn children). The immensely popular and bloody spectacle of gladiatorial contests in the circus shows was discontinued but not until well over one hundred years after Constantine's conversion. The lot of slaves and prisoners became somewhat humanized during the first one hundred years of the rule of Christian emperors. In the sale of slaves, it was forbidden to separate the members of a family (a regular practice in modern Christian America until the middle of the nineteenth century), and the freeing of slaves was made easier. Jailers were forbidden to starve prisoners and were commanded to bring them to the baths once a week. But the torture of prisoners suspected of any antisocial activities was a regular feature of the system. It should be noted that even prior to the Christian impact, reforms in the status of slaves had been effected as a result of Stoic philosophical influence on emperors. It is sometimes difficult to distinguish between Stoic and Christian influence in the framing of more humanitarian laws.

Landed aristocrats were quite free to do as they pleased with the farmers on their estates. While the slaves there received better status, the peasants became bound to the soil and were almost slaves in their standing. The institution of serfdom was beginning to emerge, and neither the government nor the Church was particularly effective in checking the oppression by the wealthy.

On the whole, the Church was not an effective agent of social reform. Originally a small voluntary brotherhood awaiting the end of this world with its injustices, it was not prepared to reform an empire. The Church was not a group of plotting social revolutionaries. It probably would have taken a revolution to shake up the structures of the entrenched society. It took the barbarians to do that. Except in time of war, barbarian customs and laws were less savage than those of the late Roman Empire, corrupted as it was by wealth, power, and fear. Still, the bishops were able to be a saving or chastening influence in many individual instances. Bishops could intercede with the authorities on behalf of accused or threatened individuals or cities, and in the ancient world, the intercession of respected persons counted heavily. So Bishop Flavian averted a major disaster from the city of Antioch, whose population expected fearful reprisals for their rioting and smashing of the emperor's statues when an increase in the already oppressive taxation had been announced. Bishop Ambrose of Milan for a while persuaded Emperor Theodosius not to wreak bloody revenge on the population of Thessalonica for its riots against the imperial troops stationed there. When the emperor in hot temper changed his mind and had seven thousand unsuspecting Thessalonians massacred in the circus, to which they had been invited by subterfuge, Ambrose announced he would not give the emperor Communion until he had submitted himself to public penance—and the emperor complied.

Perhaps what the Church lacked was more men like Ambrose, though unfortunately he did not use his skill and power always for the benefit of justice. A better balance of power in the empire was what the welfare of the society needed. If all power had not been concentrated in the hands of the emperor and of the extremely rich, Christian social teaching could have made the Church more effective. Or, would a greater emphasis on a biblical understanding of social justice in the Christian training of the emperors' and aristocrats' children have done the job? Would the parents have kept such disconcerting tutors?

In the sphere of philanthropy, the Church did make a genuinely pioneering impact on its society. The Church was able to introduce the principle of compassion for the weak (pity for the weak was scorned by pagan philosophy) and a sense of the dignity of the less fortunate members of society. In the Christian understanding, the rich bestowing gifts on the underprivileged were not considered to be generous benefactors but to be following simple justice (this, by the way, was a part of the Christian's Jewish heritage) and to be doing themselves actually a favor, for the poor were considered specially close to Christ. The intercessions by the poor for their donors were respected as having special weight with God. Thus the commonly accepted practice and notion of intercession was reversed; here, the poor were the powerful intercessors and therefore benefactors of the disadvantaged rich. The wealthy may have their money, but the poor have their prayers. This tipped the balance.

In addition to the Church's care for needy individuals and its encouraging generosity and interest on the part of the wealthy Christians in this work, the Church (richly endowed by imperial and private monies and wills, the latter especially bequeathing large tracts of fertile land to the Church) pioneered in the development of institutions and professional staff for the care of the sick, especially the lepers, the insane, the homeless, the poverty-stricken, and the travelers. These works of the Church provide the foundation of all modern institutions of this nature. The Church's influence of instilling a compassionate attitude in the minds of the people toward the less fortunate may have been the most revolutionary principle introduced into civilization, even if its full effect has been felt only in modern times and often in secular guise.

The Church exhorted slave owners and other men with legal powers over people to be humane. In the case of slavery, the Church encouraged the freeing of slaves and accepted slaves as important officeholders in the Church. Slaves were certainly not segregated from freemen in church. Nevertheless, the Church did not seriously try to reform the structure of society and its laws. Instead of trying to change the system, earnest Christians simply tended to shrink from being in a position that would involve them in unchristian actions, at least during the earlier part of the era under our survey. During the third and fourth centuries, it was not at all clear to Christians whether they could be soldiers or magistrates (which involved judicial responsibilities) with good conscience. Although Christians were usually allowed to remain or become soldiers during peacetime, they were not allowed to shed blood or torture anyone, even when under orders. The same held true for Christians in the position of judges. Given the harsh laws of the era and the common practice of judicial torture, it is easy to see why Christians would initially avoid the office. If a Christian as a magistrate or soldier became responsible for the torture or death of a man, he was to abstain from Communion and undergo the prolonged penance customary for grave sins. In the fifth and sixth centuries, when society became almost wholly Christianized on the surface, it became inevitable and acceptable that Christians should assume all the burdens of law-and-order enforcement, including the use of violence on behalf of the safety of the empire, as long as the war could be considered morally justified and was conducted without barbarism.

It is hard for us to see why Christians in influential positions did not try to change the laws more radically, though of course the ability to reform the rules of war has eluded us to this day. The resignation of the Church to the brutalities of the Roman legal system, with all its inequalities and with slavery and torture as a part of it, seems to have come from an unquestioning identification of the "world" with the society they knew. They had no illusions about the nature of the "fallen" world, and since they knew no social system other than their own, they assumed that such aberrations as legal inequalities, torture, and capital punishment were as much an inevitable, even if a deeply deplorable, part of the fallen world as were social inequalities, sickness, and death. Their realism about the world made them accept the use of external, often brutal, force and restraint (laws) as a means of curbing violence and chaos in the world.

Now that the Christians assumed responsibility for their world (which the *early* Christians, a small minority which felt quite apart from it, really did not and did not need to do), they became its reluctant guardians and defenders against external attacks. They assumed one could do little to alter the basically oppressive nature and the social inequalities of the secular community. This was why the clergy merely tried to ameliorate the situation by attempting to shape a more humane conscience among men. They confined themselves to this instead of attacking the basic structure or at least some of the laws of the socially stratified and totalitarian Roman Empire in its later period. It is of course an unanswerable question whether the Christians could have succeeded, had they attempted it. For one thing, the Church's marriage with society tied its hands and also made it accustomed to its ways. For another, the empire was anything but a democracy.

A New Society. The world in which the Church found security by Constantine's victory did not last long. Early in the fifth century, Roman power in the western part of the empire collapsed under the assault of invading Germanic tribes. In 410, the Visigoths under Alaric sacked Rome. In 429, the Vandals crossed the Strait of Gibraltar and flooded Roman North Africa, only to return to sack Rome in 455. The emperor, however, continued to reside in Constantinople, the "new Rome" built by

Constantine on the strategic site of old Byzantium on the Strait of Bosporus as the imperial residence and headquarters of the empire. The empire was able to hold its own in the East, but the West was for all practical purposes lost to the barbarians. Germanic chieftains and kings, together with able bishops, replaced the imperial rule and administration there.

It fell to the lot of Christian bishops to restore order out of the chaos and to maintain a measure of safety and well-being for their people. It was often the bishops who led the defense of their towns and negotiated the peace with the barbarians. It was the bishops and monks who carried on the educational and feeding activities formerly provided by the government (the latter as the Roman counterpart to modern food-assistance programs). They preserved and passed on whatever could be salvaged of Roman order and civilization, worked for a peaceful coexistence between the old population and the new settlers, and exerted themselves for the extension of the orthodox Christian faith in the new kingdoms. The greatest leadership in these respects was provided by some of the bishops of Rome.

Most of the barbarians (so-called because of the unintelligibility of their speech to the Greco-Romans, to whom their words sounded just as so many "bar, bars") did not wish to destroy the Roman Christian civilization, for which they held the highest admiration. They hoped to reap its benefits. They were driven into the Roman Empire by their flight from the savage Huns, who had displaced them from the East. Thus, the efforts to extend to them the Roman Christian culture and faith were not in vain, and in time, a synthesis of the two worlds—Latin Christian and barbarian—emerged. It was the making of the new Christian Europe.

East-West Cleavage. The barbarian takeover in the West naturally created a deep wedge between the eastern and western parts of the empire and thus between Eastern and Western Christendom. The Latin-speaking West always had a somewhat different mentality and type of civilization than the Greek-speaking East. Broadly speaking, the West (the Romans proper) was more practical-minded than the more philosophically and mystically inclined Greek East. The West, except for a few great metropolitan centers like Rome and Milan in Italy and Carthage in North Africa, was also more rural in character than the urban civilization of the Greco-Roman East. Culture was more refined and more advanced in the East; the West had imported Eastern culture and imitated it. The Roman higher classes were educated by Greek masters and learned the Greek language. The great intellectual centers—the universities and libraries—were in the East, where the arts and commerce also flourished. The East provided the Church with its greatest theological teachers.

The barbarian seizure of the West stopped the interchange and communication between the East and the West. The Westerners no longer learned Greek; they were happy if they could maintain (or learn) even a simplified Latin in their lands. The imperially maintained city schools disappeared, and the cities themselves almost did too. The barbarians were a rural folk, and the Roman cities were devastated. It was only the old Roman landowning families and the bishops and monasteries who preserved (or copied) the remainders of the Roman libraries and learning. The cultural impoverishment of the West and its separation from the Greek East created an estrangement between the churches of the East and West. The lack of contacts between them and the development of different conditions and traditions in the East and West led to misunderstandings, suspicions, and schisms between Eastern and Western Christendom. The real division between the Eastern Orthodox and Western Christians stems from this period, resulting in two different Christian histories.

Both Church and state and their mutual relationship developed along different lines in western Europe and in the Orthodox Byzantine Empire, as the eastern part of the empire came to be called (from Byzantium, the old name of Constantinople). The patriarch-bishop of Constantinople could never develop a very strong or independent position for his office. He was curtailed by the proximity of a powerful emperor and was hemmed in by the other great patriarchates of the East, especially by Antioch and Alexandria. The tragic history of John Chrysostom, who dared to criticize the conduct of the empress and of unworthy bishops and who was ruined by them and by the intrigues of the jealous patriarch of Alexandria, is a glaring example. Thus, Byzantine Christendom never developed anything parallel to the power and authority of the pope in the West.

The patriarch-bishop of the West, the pope of Rome, had no real rival counterparts in the West. His bishopric inherited both the ancient glory of the Church in Rome, with its claim to a link with the apostle Peter, and much of the prestige and responsibilities of imperial Rome after the emperor had left for the East. With the emperor far away, the Roman patriarch could usually act independently of the emperor. Most of the smaller bishops and other clergy, as well as the population, looked to him for leadership and help. The various barbarian chieftains and kings recognized the prestigious nature of his venerable office. Moreover, the papal office was occupied by several remarkable men, culminating in Gregory the Great at the end of our period. The Western Church and society for several centuries found their natural leaders in the Roman popes.

The old Roman population had a hard time accepting the collapse of its world. The end of "eternal Rome" seemed an impossibility and the greatest imaginable calamity. It was fortunate that the Church was able to divorce itself from the old order and perceive a providential design in the history of the times. Augustine, who died during the Vandal siege of his African city Hippo in 430, bequeathed to Western Christians in his *City of God* an interpretation of history, which helped them and succeeding generations to see the transitoriness and corruption of every social order and yet the role each has in divine providence. He pointed out that the Church, the agent of the "City of God," must operate within every city of man and yet distinguish itself from it, functioning as its light. Thus, the Latin Church accepted the new order of things and set out to win the new societies and shape them. Its success was not a little due to the prestige of Christian Rome among the barbarians and to the influence of the popes, bishops, monks, and prominent Christian wives who made the orthodox

Christian faith attractive to the heretical (Arian) or heathen barbarians. Missionary monks, such as Patrick, Columba, and Augustine of Canterbury, and their disciples converted Ireland, Scotland, and England in the fifth and sixth centuries.

The close of our age was marked by a clarification and definition of the Church's creedal standards. The canon of the Bible had largely been settled by then, and the orthodox creed regarding the person of Christ had been defined. The Church developed a great reverence for the "Fathers," its great teachers and the writers of the past, and for the councils of Christian antiquity. The age of creative theological work in the West gave way to the age of preserving and of handing on the great tradition to succeeding generations. This was the beginning of the early Middle Ages, when the Eastern world and Church guarded, developed, and eventually passed on to others their Byzantine-Greek culture and orthodoxy, while the Latin Church began to be shaped by and to shape the new nations that replaced the old world of the western Roman Empire.

WORSHIP, DEVOTION, AND ART

The central act of the assembled Christian community was the Eucharist, or Holy Communion, celebrated by the Ancient Church every Sunday and on all festival days. The primary form and spirit of this service was that of thanksgiving (the literal meaning of the Greek word *eucharistia*) and of a joyous celebration. It was a great thanksgiving for the creative and redemptive work of God in Christ, a celebration of Christ's life-giving presence among His people, a communion of the entire Church on earth with the Church in heaven, and a pledge of the great reunion of all the faithful at the eternal banquet of God.

Ancient Christians prayed standing or kneeling prostrate. The most common form and the only one thought fitting for Sundays and feast days was standing, a posture of free men and of exaltation. This was the general custom of all ancient worshipers. Their eyes, arms, and hands were raised toward heaven and their thoughts to God. They were not introverts probing their inner selves in prayer. The sign of the cross was used frequently from early times. It was a tangible way of realigning oneself with Christ, who on the cross triumphed over the powers of evil, and of recalling one's baptismal seal.

With the advent of Christian emperors, Christian assemblies became huge. Large and magnificent churches were built to house them. Christ was now thought of as the heavenly Emperor, the Ruler of all (*Pantokrator* in Greek), and His assembly on earth as reflecting the glory of His heavenly court. A splendid liturgical ceremony developed, especially in the East, patterned after the formalities of the imperial court. In imitation of the imperial ceremonies, incense found its way into the liturgy. Originally, it had been a token of the divine honors paid to gods and deified kings. Large choirs, often antiphonal double choirs answering one another in music, enhanced the beauty of the service. A sense of awe and mystery came to predominate both in the liturgy and in the building.

WORSHIP AND DEVOTION		
	BELIEFS	PRACTICES
THE LITURGY	The "public work" of worshipers. Centered on God's Word.	Procession. Responsive prayer led by deacon. Simple responses from congregation. Readings and homily. Attended by catechumens.
EUCHARIST	Joyous thanks for redemption. Central act of the community. Bread and wine as figures, which became Christ's body and blood through consecration.	Weekly. Catechumens dismissed. Kiss of peace. Consecration. Distribution. Converted masses feared unworthy reception. Bishop or presbyter led service.
BAPTISM	Admitted to membership. Bestowed the Holy Spirit. Forgiveness of sins.	Catechumens renounced Satan and the flesh. Anointed with oil. Baptized nude on Easter Eve or Pentecost. People postponed Baptism for fear of apostasy. Mass Baptism of tribal people.
PENITENCE	Church is a new humanity and creation, the Body of Christ filled with the Holy Spirit. Must be holy.	The lapsed made confession, were severely disciplined, prayed, fasted, gave alms. Formally reconciled. Mass conversions nearly ended public penitence.
OTHER SERVICES	Weddings were civil though could be blessed. Anointing for healing. Eucharist for healing and a time to remember those who died.	Regular morning and evening services and hours of prayer, especially in monastic communities. Matins and Vespers entered parish life.
CALENDAR	Participation in Jesus' death, resurrection, and gift of the Spirit. Later viewed more as historical commemoration.	Easter to Pentecost as Christian Passover. Later added Passion season of Lent. Jewish holidays replaced over centuries. Saints days added.
DEVOTION TO SAINTS	Martyrs and heroes of the Church. Mary termed "mother of God" in fifth century.	Eventually viewed as intercessors who understood human suffering.

Christian Art. The early Christians met for their services almost always in private houses. Sometimes when a house was donated for the exclusive use of the Christian community, they transformed the interior of the building, adapting it for its new function as a meeting place for Christians. Because the persecution of Christians involved a wholesale destruction of church property in AD 303–4, only one example of such a house-church has survived.

DEVELOPING ARTISTIC FORMS		
	ART	NOTES
SYMBOLIC PAINTINGS	Representation of biblical stories.	House-church at Dura-Europos (AD 256).
CATACOMB ART	Simple line drawings; adaptations of pagan and Old Testament figures; early symbols for Christ, the Church, Eucharist.	Cemeteries in Rome, Naples, Sicily, France, Greece, and the Near East.
BASILICAS	Adaptations of Roman public buildings after Christianity legalized.	Included narthex (porch), nave (sanctuary), and apse (semicircular space) at the front.
MOSAICS	Bright stones and cubes of glass set in the floors of basilicas.	Professionally designed.

FAITH AND TEACHING

The center of Christian life was the faith that Jesus Christ provided a new life and gave power over evil and death. Those who joined the early Christian community through Baptism found their lives transformed and the power over evil and death broken. Thus, the teaching of the Ancient Church was based not only on Holy Scripture but also on the experience of deliverance, or salvation, which Christ brought to mankind. The core of Christian theology was Christology. Its basis was soteriology, *soteria* meaning "salvation," or "deliverance," in Greek.

This explains the puzzling fact that the theological struggles in the fourth and fifth centuries, the centuries that worked out the great creeds of Christendom, were largely Christological. This was the question theologians as well as the people asked: "Who was and is this Christ who brought us a new life, who brought us from darkness into light, the Christ whom we worship?" Theology at this time was also a consuming concern of the laymen, educated and uneducated, not just of the clergy. One of their concerns may be stated thus: "We worship but one God, and yet our worship is Christ-centered. How do we reconcile the apparent contradiction? Do we worship two divine beings, after all?" The ancient theologians wrestled with this problem because they knew that the community's life of prayer is the yardstick of its belief. Christian worship finds its focus in two acts, Baptism and Communion, both centered in Christ. One is the beginning of the life in Christ and the other its nurture. What are the implications of this for theology?

Redemption. The early Christians viewed Baptism as the birth to a new life and the Eucharist mainly as the means of sustaining it. We can see from this that redemption was understood primarily as the victory of life over the powers of destruction and darkness. In his youthful writing *On the Incarnation*, Athanasius, the great theological teacher of the fourth century, explained that since life and the power over death are inherent in God alone, Jesus Christ, who lived a life victorious over death and gives a new life to people, must be God Himself present and active in the midst of men. In Him, God and man, so long and so tragically separated by mankind's defiance or ignorance of God, are marvelously joined, and mankind is plugged in to the source of life again. This is the deepest meaning of the incarnation, God's becoming "flesh" (*caro* in Latin), or man. What no man and no creature at all could accomplish, namely, the bridging of the wide gulf between man and God, God Himself undertook to accomplish by His becoming man in Jesus Christ.

The gulf between man and God has given rise to all the tragedies in mankind's history: man's enslavement to evil and his ultimate defeat by death. Therefore, the union between God and man in Jesus brings also victory over the powers of evil and annuls the finality of death. Death is no longer the final word for man. *Christus victor:* Christ is victorious. The victorious Christ is the final word. For in Jesus' death, the divine life inherent in Him overcame the powers of death as the rising sun vanquishes darkness. The process was already begun in Jesus' conflict with the powers of evil during His life. The victory was made manifest in Jesus' resurrection and became also the experience of the men and women who were instructed in the Christian faith and joined the Christian community. In Baptism, they were united to God in Christ and filled with His Spirit. They lived a new life, and their union with God and their brothers was weekly renewed by their taking part in the banquet of Jesus Christ, the Holy Communion. All the world witnessed the power and life of God at work in this community. The power of the resurrection was already evident in the healings that took place in the Christian Church and in the martyrs' bold defiance of death. And since Christians had thus already a part in the divine life, as they were united to Him who triumphed over death, they, too, would be victorious over ultimate death. "Who, then, can this life-giving, triumphant Christ be but God Himself in the flesh of man?" they asked. This is how the Christian community saw it.

Christ as the victorious and reigning King was the central image of Jesus the Redeemer during this age as well as in the early Middle Ages. This is why the early crucifixes, once they appear on the scene (the first centuries did not produce crosses or crucifixes at all), have Jesus *reigning* from the cross, not hanging on it as a helpless, defeated victim. Other intriguing illustrations of the ancient Christian understanding of redemption are the "icons of the resurrection," produced in the early Middle Ages and still made in Eastern Christendom. The actual resurrection is not their subject; they instead portray Jesus' victorious "Descent into Hades [Hell]," His "Harrowing of Hell." The ancient pictures try to say in symbolic language what the theologians were saying in their teaching: *Jesus' death and resurrection are inseparable*, and in Jesus' death the resurrection was already in the making. The power and hold of death were broken by Christ's entering the realm of death (hades); He was thus able to release men from the hold of death. The icons picture the gates of hades thrown wide open. They show Christ with the victorious banner of the cross and the dead, often headed by Adam and Eve, as finally free. Death or Satan is seen languishing under Christ's trampling foot. Jesus' own rising from the tomb is not portrayed;

ancient Christian art shied away from realistic or naturalistic representations. The idea represented in these icons is also contained in the somewhat puzzling clause in the Apostles' Creed: "He descended into hell"—to *conquer* it. Early medieval hymns are a telling expression that Jesus' apparent defeat, His death, was, paradoxically, a victor's feat.

This victorious faith proved the main attraction of Christianity during the era of its greatest expansion, its first thousand years.

Christ, the Revelation of God. To ancient Christians, Christ was first of all the Redeemer of men, but He was also the Revealer of God. It was their conviction that in Him the mind and will of God, His very being, are revealed, that is, unveiled. The mystery of God's mind and being is so great that it transcends all human minds; man's reason cannot penetrate or explore it. The infinite and wholly transcendent God must come to man's aid if man is to know him. The knowledge of God can come only through God's self-disclosure. This is the biblical assumption. No one but God's own mind knows God's mind. It follows that if Christ brings the knowledge of God to men, He must be, in some mysterious way, the mind of God Himself, the Mind, or *Logos* in Greek, by which God made the world and by which He ever reveals Himself to men. He is the wisdom of God that never changes and is from everlasting (Proverbs 8:22–30). This is what the Gospel of John says, especially in its prologue (John 1:1–18).

The word that this prologue uses in the Greek text is *Logos*, which can be trans-lated as both "Mind" and "Word." It seems that both meanings are intended here; it is usually used by the ancient Greek Christian writers in this double meaning. God created the world by His *Logos*, and by it He enlightens all men. This *Logos* became incarnate in Jesus Christ, who is *the* self-expression of God.

The word *Logos* was a useful term for ancient theology, for it played an impor-tant role in Greek philosophy as well as in the Old Testament. To those trained in philosophy, it meant before all else the Mind, the rational Principle inherent and discernible in the universe, the divine Intelligence that forms and governs the har-monious cosmos as well as all rational creatures. This concept was a bridge to the biblical understanding of God, the Creator, who governs His world and reveals His will to men. The Hebrew Bible spoke of God's Word as the instrument of God's creation (God *said* . . . and it was so) and revelation, for when He *speaks* He reveals something of Himself and His will. His Word is His self-expression. When the Old Testament was translated into Greek, the translators made use of the term *Logos* to speak of God's Word. Thus, a synthesis between the Hebrew and Greek worlds was created; the Bible now could speak to the Greeks. The Christian theologians who spoke of Jesus as the *Logos* of God could strike a familiar chord for both Jews and Gentiles and so communicate what the Church meant by Jesus as the Revealer of God in terms meaningful to their world.

Christ and God. The Ecumenical Creeds, the heritage of the greater part of Christendom, were hammered out in the heat of controversies about the relationship of Christ to God and to man. The Nicene Creed was shaped by the Arian contro-versy.

Arius was a presbyter in Alexandria in the early fourth century. For centuries, Alexandria had been a center of Greek philosophical learning. Already before the Christian era, the Jews who had settled there thought more often in philosophical than in biblical categories or, rather, subconsciously read Greek philosophical con-cepts into the Bible. The pioneer of this process was Philo. The Greek-influenced Jewish thinkers were not aware of the profound differences between the philosophi-cal and biblical approaches to reality. The Greek-educated Christians continued in this tradition in varying degrees. Arius is its extreme product.

Arius taught that God is so transcendent that He Himself could not create the world or be in any way accessible. He saw an infinite gulf between God and all else, a gulf unbridgeable from either side. The idea of a chasm between the infinite and the finite and of the inferiority of everything finite was of Greek and Oriental philosophical origin. It had led the Gnostics to deny any connection between the High God and the world. Although Arius was not a Gnostic—he did not teach that matter was contemptible—he had a certain kinship with the Gnostics. Arius used the Greek philosophical-Christian tradition that God created the world by means of the divine *Logos* (John 1:3) and claimed that God first created a being called "Logos" or "Son of God" in order that this divine yet inferior and created spirit might make the world, which God could not make without losing His deity. The servant-spirit created the world and eventually became incarnate in Jesus Christ. It was also this "Logos" that granted the divine revelations men received.

The last doctrine named above could be perfectly orthodox, for in the Christian tradition it was the *Logos*, or Word of God, which was the means of all revelation. But the relationship of the *Logos* to God was completely different in traditional Christian teaching from that expressed in the teaching of Arius. Arius denied any interior or essential relationship between God and the *Logos*. The agent of creation and of revelation was, according to him, not God's own *Logos* (Mind and Word) or Son *properly* so called, but something exterior to God and only *called* "Logos" or "Son." He was a separate being, divine or semidivine, but not something essential to the being of God or an expression of God. For God's own mind cannot come into contact with the world, according to Arius. Therefore, it can neither make it nor reveal itself to it. Even God's agent of creation cannot come into real contact with Him, cannot know Him. God is essentially beyond reach.

Arius ended up without knowing anything about the love of God that leads God into a relationship with the world and to dwell in it. As Gregory of Nyssa, the greatest theological mind of the Greek-speaking East, later pointed out, the incarna-tion is not a loss of God's greatness; it *shows* the greatness of God, who was willing to stoop so low in order to save men. Besides, there is nothing inherently inferior about the world, which God saw as "very good," according to the Bible (Genesis 1:31). Arius also ended up with two divine beings, one superior, one inferior, for to

Arius the Father and the Son were not essentially one. With one foot, Arius was still in the polytheistic world of ancient thought, and his ideas gave no difficulties to new converts from paganism, accustomed as they were to a multiplicity of gods and demi-gods. To Athanasius, who was then a young deacon in the Church of Alexandria, the greatest problem with Arius's doctrine consisted in its threat to the security of salvation. For, if it was not the true God who became man in Jesus Christ, how could men receive divine life from Him? The Arian issue rocked the Church.

Arius's doctrine became rather popular. He even composed popular musical hits to instill his teaching among the common people. Almost simultaneous with Constantine's rise to the imperial throne and the Church's rise to imperial favor, the Christian Church faced the danger of an imminent split over the Arian doctrine. Alarmed, Emperor Constantine immediately summoned a worldwide conference of Christian bishops, called the First Ecumenical Council, or Synod, to Nicaea (Iznik in today's Turkey), near his imperial residence in Nicomedia. This council, meeting in AD 325, was an important watershed in the history of the Church. It was the first time an emperor called a Christian council. It was also the first gathering of Christian leaders beyond their regional boundaries. Before the legalization of the Church, Christians could hardly undertake such a conference. There had been no organized body that could represent the whole Church. Now the Christian churches could deliberate and agree on policies and principles of common interest to all.

The Nicene Council agreed on a creed for all the churches, the famous First Ecumenical Creed of Nicaea. Up to then, each city or region had its own version of the baptismal creed. The various creeds followed a basically common pattern, a pattern best known to us from the Apostles' Creed. The Nicene Creed, in an expanded form, has remained as the one truly ecumenical Christian creed to this day.

The creed accepted at Nicaea kept the usual structure of the ancient Christian creeds, narrating the events of creation and redemption. What the council added was a precise metaphysical explanation of the relationship between Jesus Christ and God. It took a stand against the Arian position that the world was made and saved by someone different from God. The council said that the world was made and redeemed by God by means of His Son, who is an expression of God. Its creed affirmed the unity between the *Logos* and God. The crucial anti-Arian affirmations in the Nicene Creed are as follows: "We believe in one God . . . Maker of all things visible and invisible, and in . . . Jesus Christ, begotten uniquely of the Father, that is, of the substance of the Father, God of God, Light of Light, true God of true God, begotten, not made, of one being [essence, or substance] with the Father, through whom all things came into being . . . who for us men and for our salvation came down and was incarnate, becoming man."

The Nicene Creed was originally in the plural. It expressed the corporate faith of the Church. It insisted that the Son of God is the "true God," "of one being with the true God," and not another being separate from God. The relationship of the divine Son to His Father is seen like that of a light (flame) lit from a light; they are not different from each other, although one is generated from the other. The Father is the source of the Light, which is Christ. The Son is not a creature, someone made by God, as Arius had claimed, but is "begotten," or "generated," by the Father, though not in a physical manner. The difference between God's creature and God's Son is analogous to the difference between an artist's sculpture and his child; only the latter is of the "substance" of the father, bearing his life in him. The phrase "of one being [of the same substance] with the Father" was considered the most crucial in the argument with the Arians, who wanted "of similar being" [substance] or "of like being" in its stead. The Nicene Creed affirmed the identity of the Father and the Son's essence, or of the underlying reality behind the Father and the Son, for the Son is an expression of the Father. He is the Word "through whom all things came into being."

We should notice the soteriological climax of the affirmations about the true divinity of Christ: ". . . who for us men and for our salvation . . . was made man." It is because of this that the foregoing is important. The Nicene theologians were not concerned with some abstruse speculations about matters that had no connection with the human situation. The eternal status of the Messiah was important to them because men needed such a great Redeemer if they were to be delivered from their alienation from God and from their consequent captivity by the forces of evil and death.

The struggle with Arianism was by no means ended by the Nicene Council's acceptance of the anti-Arian creedal formulation. The Arian forces soon recovered. More than fifty years of warfare followed between the Arian and Nicene parties. Since the unity of the empire was threatened by the splitting of the Church, the emperors and their imperial politics became deeply involved in the struggle. The principal means of coercion used by pro-Arian and anti-Arian bishops, councils, and especially by emperors, who simply wanted peace at any price, were excommunication, deposition from ecclesiastical office, and the sending of bishops into exile by the emperor. Athanasius, who became bishop of Alexandria shortly after the Council of Nicaea and was Nicaea's chief theological defender, was excommunicated, deposed, exiled, and then again restored many times during his long, battle-filled life (he died in 373). He spent most of his career in exile or even in hiding. Many attempts at compromise between the Arian and Nicene theologians were framed, but none of them worked out. The Nicaean side finally won the empire by a combination of hard theological work, shrewd politics, and the arrival of the theologically well-informed, pro-Nicene Theodosius upon the imperial throne in 380. He summoned an "ecumenical council" to Constantinople the next year, and this council reaffirmed the Nicene formula that the Son is "of one being with the Father," or "of the same substance as the Father." It was this council that apparently adopted the Nicene faith in its present creedal form, as used in the liturgy and confessional books of Christian churches all over the world.

The Holy Spirit. The original Nicene Creed was reserved about the Holy Spirit since the status of the Holy Spirit was not at stake in the early stage of the Arian controversy. Thus the Creed simply said, "And [we believe] in the Holy Spirit." As the century proceeded, the situation changed. It became necessary to think through and state the relationship of the Spirit to God after some stated that the Holy Spirit is simply a supreme angelic creature. Athanasius wrote that if the Holy Spirit has the power to join men to God, as Christians believed happened in Baptism, then the Holy Spirit has to be the Spirit of God Himself. Such a task, he reasoned, could no more be accomplished by a creature than could man's redemption. Basil the Great, the leader of the Nicene party after Athanasius, picked up the thread where Athanasius had left off and pointed out that in the liturgy, the yardstick of the Church's beliefs, the Spirit is invoked and adored in the same breath as God the Father and God the Son. Since the Church worships only God, the Holy Spirit must belong to God as intimately as does Jesus Christ. Or else, why do Christians baptize "in the name of the Father and the Son and the Holy Spirit"?

Because of this controversy, the Council of Constantinople added a paragraph about the Holy Spirit to the Creed. Yet in comparison with the lengthy and complex Christological part of the Creed, the wording about the Holy Spirit is reserved and modest; it does not attempt to define or explain the Spirit. The divine nature of the Holy Spirit is stated in the Creed, just as in the New Testament, only indirectly: by the references to the divine origin and work of the Holy Spirit and by the references to the Church's worship. In a way, all the affirmations in the Creed are statements about the work of the Holy Spirit. The stress on the activity of the Spirit, rather than on who or what the Spirit is, was not only biblical, but it also reflected the experience of the Christian community, which was very conscious of the animating Breath of God in its midst. In the ancient era, Christians were much more aware of the role of the Spirit than Christians in a later era, especially later in the West.

The Triune God. As is apparent from the above, the Church Fathers were struggling with the mystery of the triune God, the one God who was known to the faithful as the Father in heaven, Jesus Christ the Redeemer, and the Holy Spirit. The anti-Arians fought first for the essential unity of the three. However, the distinctness of the Father and the Son and the Spirit also had to be maintained in order to be true to the Gospel record, which portrays Jesus as praying to the Father and promising His disciples to send them the Spirit. To express the divine unity, the Church Fathers spoke of the oneness of "being" (essence, or substance) shared by the divine Trinity.

To express the distinctness of the three, the theologians were driven to use perhaps more misleading terms, since no adequate words were available. Basil spoke of the three *hypostases*, a rather ambiguous and untranslatable word for that which exists in its own right and does not have a borrowed existence. The Latins either used the Greek word or spoke of the three "persons" of the Trinity.

It must be remembered, however, that the word *persona* in ancient Latin did not have the same connotation that the word *person* has acquired for us today. The word *person* was not conceived psychologically. Thus, when the Fathers speak of the three "persons" of the Trinity, they do not mean that there are three different personalities in God. Ancient philosophy was not concerned with the uniqueness of each individual but rather with that which the different individuals of the same species share in common, for example, what makes all men "human," or what makes tables "tables." The discovery of personality came only later, under Augustine, and was a result of Christian influence. But the new concept of "personhood" was not applied to the three "persons" of the divine Trinity.

Thus, while the Father, the Son, and the Spirit are distinct, they share the same divine nature and are one God. There is no adequate human vocabulary for the triune character of God. From the human perspective, it has to remain a paradox. Augustine, in his monumental work *On the Trinity* in the early fifth century, finds an analogy for the triuneness of God in the triuneness of the human personality, composed of "memory," "intelligence," and "will." As man is made in the image of God, his inner being reflects in an imperfect way the Holy Trinity. If it were not for his fall, man's faculties and actions would be as perfectly integrated as the being and the work of the Holy Trinity, for God is no split personality. The triunity of God transcends the comprehension of man. It is a mystery apprehended only by faith.

The Person of Christ. The fourth-century theologians wrestled primarily with the question of Christ's relationship to the Father. In the fifth and sixth centuries (as also in the seventh), theological struggles concentrated on the relationship of the divine and human in Christ's person, that is, on Christology. At stake here were the reality of Christ's humanity, the unity of His person, and the redemptive significance of both. Can one say that God the Word was born as human beings are? That He suffered privations, was limited in His knowledge, and died? How can the eternal and all-powerful God be born, have any weaknesses, and die? Isn't this contradicting the nature of God?

Several different answers were given. They were strongly influenced by the regional traditions of the different theologians. The theological school (tradition) of Alexandria in Egypt was characterized by Athanasius's stress on the saving significance of the full deity of Jesus Christ. The rival theological school of Antioch in Syria was preoccupied with the reality of Christ's humanity as the condition for His being able to redeem humanity. The West held to Tertullian's (turn of third century) balanced stress on both aspects of Christ and did not indulge in much speculation on the subject.

The controversy started in the East already in the second half of the fourth century. An Alexandrian theologian named Apollinaris could not see how Christ could have both the Divine Mind and a human mind if He was one person, sinless, and a true Savior. Apollinaris concluded that Jesus was human as far as His flesh was concerned, but that in Him the Divine Mind (the *Logos*) replaced the fallible and sin-bent mind of men. The *Logos* even acted as the life-giving principle in Christ's flesh, forming one (divine-human) nature with it. This fusion of the *Logos* with the flesh made Christ's body life-giving. (We should note Apollinaris's characteristically

Alexandrine use of the word "nature," by which was meant one entity or what we might call one "person." This is not how the word was used in Antioch.)

But was Christ, then, actually human when He lacked what makes man "man": the human mind? So asked the Cappadocian Church Father Gregory of Nyssa. The Church, in a series of councils culminating with the Second Ecumenical Council (held in 381 at Constantinople) condemned Apollinaris's attempt to solve the Christological problem as creating an inhuman Christ. Apollinarianism was untrue to the Gospel record, which portrays Jesus as "*growing* in wisdom" (the Divine Mind certainly doesn't need to grow!), struggling with temptations, ignorant of the hour of the Kingdom's triumph, and crying on the cross, "My God, My God, why have You forsaken Me?"

It was not only faithfulness to the biblical record that was at issue. The redemption of man as man was at stake, as the Cappadocian theologians pointed out. For if man's salvation depends on God-and-man-becoming-one and if Jesus is not fully man, then man is not redeemed. The incarnation means that God assumed the entire human nature, including the mind of man. Since the emperor wanted an orthodox and united imperial church, Apollinarianism was outlawed by Theodosius. This did not mean, of course, that this kind of thinking simply died out. The controversy stimulated the Church's leaders to think through some thorny questions. It took several centuries to tackle them. The Christological controversies finally resulted in a split of the Church, a split that has lasted to this day.

The Antiochene school, as was already said, bent in the other direction of the Alexandrine. It was its great merit to insist on the importance and fullness of Jesus' humanity. It did not succeed at first to unite His humanity with His divinity in a satisfactory manner. The best-known but tragic product of the Antiochene Christological tradition was Nestorius, who became the imperial court preacher and patriarch of Constantinople in the first part of the fifth century. His Antiochene background, his coveted patriarchal rank, and his way of expressing his deep concerns made him almost an immediate object of attack by the Alexandrines. Alexandria was not only the chief rival of Antioch but also of Constantinople, which was considered the "New Rome" and therefore given higher ecclesiastical honor than the more ancient patriarchate of Alexandria.

For Nestorius, as for all Antiochene theologians, it was extremely important to keep the human and divine natures in Christ clearly distinct and not assign divine attributes to the former and human attributes to the latter. This was, however, customary both in the language of ordinary Christian piety and in the Alexandrine theology. So people spoke of Jesus' mother as the "mother of God." To Nestorius, this was outrageous, for how could God, who is without beginning, have a mother? His complaint seemed a justifiable one to ears unaccustomed to this title. But to popular piety, Nestorius's storming against this usage seemed blasphemy. To the Alexandrines, it was a clear sign that the new patriarch of Constantinople was, as could be expected, a heretic. For, wasn't Mary the mother of the Word-become-flesh? Nestorius would say that Mary was the mother of the man Jesus, but that it was nonsense to say that *God* was a small babe or that He, who is by nature immortal, died.

Cyril, the patriarch of Alexandria, challenged Nestorius as dividing Christ into two separate entities and denying the incarnation. While Nestorius did not mean to deny the incarnation, he could not, it seems, accept some of the basic consequences of this doctrine. In any case, his language certainly cast doubts on it. Reared in the Antiochene tradition, he was anxious to maintain the doctrine of the "impassibility of God," that is: God could not be subject to suffering (*passio* in Latin) or change. Speaking of God as subject to human experiences like birth and death was to him untrue to the nature of God. Yet if God became man, as Cyril pointed out, then it could and had to be said that He had a human mother, that He grew, and that He died, for this belongs to becoming man. Cyril and his school were anxious to maintain the unity of Christ's being. They said that in the incarnation, the divine and human natures became so indivisibly united that they came to form one divine-human nature. To avoid splitting Christ into two entities and to maintain His integrity as a person, they liked to speak of the "one nature of the Incarnate God the Word," a complete union of the divine and human natures. These could be distinguished, at best, only in abstraction, they held, for Christ always acted as one person. To attribute His birth and death, for example, only to His humanity and His supernatural powers only to His deity would be to destroy the meaning of the incarnation, the redemptive significance of the divine-human union in Christ, and the life-giving quality of the Eucharist, where the faithful received not just the body of a human Jesus.

The debate was conducted in a spirit of deepest distrust, hostility, and misunderstanding. Cyril, with his "one-nature" talk, sounded to Nestorius like an Apollinarian. He felt that in the Alexandrine theology, which attributed human characteristics to God and divine to the man Jesus, the Deity lost its real divinity and at the same time Christ's true humanity was destroyed. Cyril himself, on the other hand, was sure that Nestorius did not believe in Christ's deity, and he accused him of dividing Christ into two persons by his insisting on the "two natures" (divine and human) of Christ. He charged Nestorius with teaching that there were actually two Christs. The two schools of thought read different meanings into each other's terminology, and the fighting theologians often used hasty or intemperate language.

The controversies that arose were not only theological but also personal and political, as we have indicated. Regional and personal rivalries and the grossest of politics were involved. Thanks to Cyril's ruthless maneuvers, Nestorius lost his patriarchal position, was condemned by church councils, and was exiled by Emperor Theodosius II.

Once his offensive rival was out of the way, Cyril and the Antiochene school came quickly to a mutual clarification of thought and language, arriving at an agreement called the Symbol of Union of 431. The Antiochenes were now willing to accept the title "mother of God" (*Theotokos* in Greek) for Jesus' mother, and Cyril the expression the "two natures" as applying to the incarnate Lord. While the agreement was a great milestone in theological understanding, its binding force remained only as long as Cyril was alive (he died in 444). His more extreme partisans never really recognized it, being horrified by the "two natures" formula especially. To them, it was an unworthy compromise, denying the complete union of the divine and human in Christ and, perhaps no less important, their distinct and treasured Alexandrine heritage. While Cyril himself came through the controversy to a greater appreciation of the importance of Jesus' humanity, some of his devoted disciples actually did lose from sight the fullness of Christ's humanity in their insistence on only the "one nature" of Christ. The result was a Christ in whom the human nature tended to be taken over by the divine. The "Monophysite" (from the Greek *monos*, "alone," and *physis*, "nature") Christ became in reality often only half-human. This, however, was characteristic of popular piety also in churches that did not hold to the "one nature" doctrine. Hebrews 2:16–17 was not too well absorbed by the mainstream of Christianity: "For surely it is not angels that He helps, but He helps the offspring of Abraham. Therefore He had to be made like His brothers in every respect, so that He might become a merciful and faithful high priest in the service of God, to make propitiation for the sins of the people" (Hebrews 2:16–17).

Cyril's successor, the ruthless patriarch Dioscorus of Alexandria, succeeded in having the Symbol of Union annulled by what came to be known as the "Robber Council" of 449, ratified by the emperor but not recognized by the Roman pope. Yet a sudden change on the imperial throne (Theodosius fell off his horse and died) and the papal pressure for a fairer handling of the issues led to the summoning of the Fourth Ecumenical Council in 451. It met, for the convenience of the emperor, in Chalcedon and has gone down in history as rivaling only Nicaea in importance.

The Council, acting under heavy imperial and papal pressures, approved "the letters of Cyril to Nestorius" and rejected both the Monophysite and Nestorian formulas. It accepted a doctrinal formulary called the "Tome of Leo," which had been sent by Pope Leo as a definition of the traditional faith of the Church regarding the relationship of the divine and human natures in Christ. The Council tried to unite the different factions of Christendom by taking and uniting the best from all the three sides involved in the controversy (Antioch, Alexandria, and the West). The creedal definition formulated at Chalcedon incorporated fragments from Cyril, the Symbol of Union (which had originated in Antioch), and Leo. Chalcedon affirmed the abiding reality of both the divine and human natures in Christ and the perfect union of the two in His person. It stated that on account of this it is possible, orthodox, and even necessary to say that Mary became the "mother of God" since God became man and men have mothers and also that God, while by nature immortal, could as *man* actually die. Moreover, the Lord Christ possessed not only the Divine Mind as God but also a truly human mind ("the rational soul") as man. He became in all things like His brothers except for sin. His two natures had to be kept distinct (for example, God as *God* did not die); yet they always acted in union with one another.

How the divine and human attributes such as power and weakness, which contradict each other, coexisted without canceling each other out was not explained. The mystery of the two natures of the one Christ was stated and left unresolved. It would have been a vain exercise had the Council attempted to resolve it. For the Chalcedonian formula that Christ is *fully* God and *fully* man" cannot but remain an apparent contradiction, a paradox, a mystery found true only by faith. In this, it corresponds to the paradox of the triunity of God.

The great merit of the Chalcedonian Council was that it acknowledged both the genuineness and fullness of Christ's humanity and its indivisible union with His deity. It saw the mysterious union as the basis of the salvation of mankind. The council's attempt at synthesis, however, did not heal the schisms and misunderstandings that rent the Church with regard to the Christological question. The heavy hand of the imperial court that steered the council and attempted to enforce, even by police measures, the Chalcedonian decisions, the semantic confusion over expressions like "two natures," popular emotion and conservatism involved in religion, regional loyalties, and the lack of any outstanding theological leaders in the Chalcedonian camp in the East all worked to undo the seeming accomplishment of the council.

In time, the school of Antioch seemed to have used up its light, and now the Monophysites provided the theological leadership. Most of the Monophysites, including their leaders, were actually perhaps no less orthodox than those who accepted the Chalcedonian definition. The picture was one of resentment and defensiveness rather than of deep theological differences. The imperial forces tried in vain to impose Chalcedonian "orthodoxy" on a discontented and aroused populace. For a century or so, the fight continued within the officially one church of the empire of the East. The West had no trouble accepting Chalcedon. In the mid-sixth century, however, the Monophysites, following the lead of Jacob Baradaeus and hence nicknamed "Jacobites," seceded from the imperial Byzantine, or "Greek-Orthodox," Church and formed their own independent, regional churches. Most Christians in Egypt and Ethiopia (the "Coptic," or "Egyptian," Christians), vast numbers in Palestine and Syria, the Syrian-planted "Mar Thomas" Church in South India, and the indigenous Church of Armenia became officially Monophysite, though considering themselves Catholic and Orthodox. On the other hand, the "Nestorians" had been pushed out of the empire and spread as a separate church into Syrian regions beyond the imperial frontiers: to the empire of Persia and eventually to China and India.

Although ecumenical contact has been made in recent times, the tragic schism has not been healed. It weakened the Christian presence in the East considerably. It was even one of the major causes of the rapid surrender of Syrian, Palestinian, and Egyptian cities to the Islamic Arabic invaders in the seventh century, for there was little love for the dictatorial, "heretical" Byzantine government in these disaffected regions of the empire. The Muslims promised freedom to *all* Christians.

A significant accompaniment to and result of the Christological controversies was the high status accorded to Mary, the "mother of God." Devotion to "Mother

Mary" was already strong by 400. Both the Monophysite and the Chalcedonian theologies encouraged its growth. Where the divinity of Christ tended to swallow up Jesus' humanity, as in circles with Monophysite tendencies, there the "Holy Mother" became the human mediator between the majestic Lord Christ and the human family. This was not confined to circles that were officially Monophysite, for the humanity of Christ tended to get lost to the sight of even "orthodox" believers, as we have seen.

The Chalcedonian theology, with its stress on Jesus' mother as the guarantor and bearer of Christ's humanity, likewise encouraged devotion to her. She became the link between man and God, because it was through her that God assumed human stature. She was thus made to be of saving significance to Christians, for had it not been for her, there would have been no incarnation and therefore no redemption. Churches started to be named in her honor at the height of the Christological controversies in the early fifth century. It should be remembered that her importance in Christian devotion, however late it may have developed, was most intimately linked with the development of classical Christology and soteriology. Thus, we end on the same note as we began: Christian theology and devotion are at their core Christological and soteriological, and they are inseparable from each other. Indeed, the devotion to the "mother of God" and to her infant Son toppled Nestorius from his pulpit, for the faithful were enraged to hear that God could not be called a babe in the arms of mother Mary. The formula that Christ is "fully God and fully man" prevailed.

Norms of Doctrine. What were the norms by which a theological position was judged and considered orthodox and normative? From our discussion so far, several norms have emerged. First, we pointed out that there was the norm given by the community's life of prayer—the *lex orandi lex credendi* principle. A theology had to be in harmony with the Church's worship and devotion. Second, though not secondarily, the Church's teaching had to conform to the basic creedal tradition of the Church and the experience of faith. Third, but certainly not third in importance, doctrine had to rest on scriptural support and on clear, unambiguous passages in their *literal* meaning, concerning which there was a unanimity among the Church's teachers.

A precise and definitive delimitation of the canon of Scripture—the determination of what belonged to it and what did not—did not occur until the sixteenth century, the time of the Reformation. The bulk of the New Testament books had been agreed upon already by around AD 200, but uncertainty about a few of the epistles and about the Book of Revelation remained for some time. By the sixth century, most Christian churches used the same New Testament as we do today. The Old Testament in Greek was very naturally taken over from the Greek synagogue at the start of the Church's mission among the Greek-speaking population. This version of the Old Testament, as well as the Latin translations based on it, included books that were not in the Hebrew (and later in the Protestant) canon: the so-called apocryphal books. In the sixteenth century, the Protestant reformers ruled that only the books from the Hebrew Scriptures belonged to the canonical Old Testament. The Counter-Reformation Council of Trent ruled that the Apocrypha belong to the canon and that they are binding for doctrine.

Three bases were used to determine whether a book should be included in the New Testament: its apostolicity, its orthodoxy, and its universal acceptance by Christian churches for use in public worship. Apostolicity meant that a book had to have direct or indirect apostolic origin in order to qualify for the New Testament. This was an important reason why the Epistle to the Hebrews and the Revelation of John, among others, had a hard time getting into the canon, for their apostolic origin was questioned by many. However, also the orthodoxy of these books had been questioned, since Hebrews stated that there was no forgiveness for a voluntary falling away from the faith (10:26–31), and yet the Church admitted renegades to repentance. Revelation seemed to teach bewildering things about the return of Christ to the earth (Revelation 20:1–10).

It is interesting to note that inspiration was not among the criteria that decided the canonicity of a book. Of course, a book had to be inspired by God to be included in the Bible. Yet there were many other books that were considered inspired by God in a general sense but were not in the canon. They were thought useful for private reading and edification, but were not considered "canonical." A book belonged to the canon if it was used in public worship and for determining the Church's doctrine. The word *canon* means a yardstick, or a ruler, in Greek. The canon of Scripture was to serve as a yardstick of the Church's teaching. Thus, Scripture had to have a *delimited* scope, while inspired literature could be unlimited. A canonical book could not have a private character, but it had to be universally known and recognized by all Christians. Since Scripture served as an authoritative basis for distinguishing between true and false teaching, its contents had to have a public character.

The Bible could be interpreted by at least three different methods: the literal, the typological, and the allegorical. The last two were especially used for the Old Testament, to show its abiding relevance. Typology saw various Old Testament events and figures, such as the liberation from Egypt, the Passover, and Moses, as types or figures of man's deliverance and life in Christ, which they foreshadowed. We noted this in the discussion on Christian art. Allegory saw symbolic spiritual significance in the seemingly mundane or dated details of biblical events and laws. The allegorical interpretation flourished especially in the theological school of Alexandria, where it had already been applied to the Old Testament and to Greek myths before the Christian era. Both the typological and the allegorical interpretations were already occasionally present in the New Testament, as in 1 Corinthians 10:1–6 and 9:8–11. The literal, historical interpretation was cultivated in the school of Antioch. Its greatest product in the art of preaching was John Chrysostom.

Since Scripture lends itself in many places to varied interpretations, it was felt that the Church could not use only Scripture. This is why the Church's basic and universal creedal tradition and its formulation in the ecumenical councils served as a guide to interpreting Scripture where it appeared obscure, ambiguous, or as containing contradictions. Thus the Church's living tradition of faith and worship was regarded as checking a possibly imbalanced, provincial, arbitrary, or subjective interpretation of the Church's Holy Scriptures. Vincent of Lerins taught that *catholic* was something believed everywhere, always and by all.

By *tradition*, we mean the heritage of faith and worship passed on from one generation to another, which creates the link binding all generations into an organic, spiritual unity and giving the community its identity. Such a tradition in the Ancient Church was never set over and against Scripture, but was seen as identical with the faith of the Scriptures themselves. As we have seen, it was also not set against development. But growth in theology had to be harmonized with the ancient heritage.

STRUCTURE, LEADERSHIP, AND SERVICE

Like any community, the ancient Christian Church was composed of different categories of members, depending on their responsibilities and corresponding burdens and honors. One group was the people, *laos* in Greek, from which come our words *lay* and *laity*. The others were the leaders, or clergy, from the Greek *clews*, which means elected or selected. The apostolic Church, of course, did not sharply distinguish between laity and clergy, except to observe that certain ones among them were set aside for the ministry of the Word.

DEVELOPMENTS IN LEADERSHIP AND SERVICE		
	BELIEFS	NOTES
LAITY	Baptized laypersons were "offerers," who had a priestly role before God to pray and participate in the Eucharist.	The laity gave consent to the selection of their bishop and other leaders, though this elective role was lost overtime.
SEVENFOLD ORDER	Offices had different degrees of dignity with bishop as the highest.	Offices included presbyters, deacons, subdeacons, lectors, acolytes, exorcists, and doorkeepers.
PARISH AND BISHOP	God's colony (Greek *paroikia*) planted in the world. Presided over by a bishop, successor to the apostles who also had a judicial role.	Centered in a city but came to include surrounding villages where the bishop would appoint presbyters. A collection of parishes became a diocese.
CHURCH AUTHORITY	Leading communities and bishops exercised influence over smaller ones. Christian emperor as protector and supervisor.	Bishops gathered for synods and councils, which came to possess legislative authority in canons ("rulings").
ROMAN AUTHORITY	Jesus gave primacy to Peter. Had the double apostolic foundation of Peter and Paul.	Rome remained orthodox throughout early controversies, which enhanced its authority.

PHYSICIANS OF THE SOUL	Care required sensitivity and insight regarding sins of the flock. A pastor needed the power of the Spirit for discernment.	The Pastoral Rule of Roman bishop Gregory the Great became a standard guide for bishops.
CHRISTIAN OUTREACH	Pagan shrines were reconsecrated to Christ and the saints. Don't change customs too quickly.	Gregory the Great sent Augustine to southern England; Celtic Christians worked in the north.

Early Christian missionaries preserved as much as possible of the native cultures. If the Christian Church in its work with the barbarians at the beginning of the Middle Ages had been less wise and less elastic, we might never have seen a Christian Europe come out of the debris of the western Roman Empire. At best, it would have been a culture deprived of the different folk traditions that mark today's European nations. Many a ghost tale today still reveals its heathen origin.

MONASTICISM, THE NEW LEAVEN

How did monasticism start? Why and when did Christian men and women start withdrawing from civilization and their own parishes to become monks and nuns, or in the case of men, even hermits? What led to the creation of religious orders? In view of the important role the monastic movement has played in the shaping of Christendom, it is essential to understand its history.

The Early Church was an elite minority, separate and distinguishable from the rest of society. Its standards and values conflicted with the world it considered vain, rotten, and doomed. Early Christians eagerly awaited a speedy end of the present age and its replacement by the glorious age in the world to come. The hostility and persecutions they met confirmed them in their separateness from society and kept their ranks disciplined and screened. When the awaited end did not come and Christians were more tolerated, it was inevitable that most of them would come to terms with the world, especially as their ranks swelled and Christianity became popular. Security, comfort, and success in the eyes of the world were less scorned by the Church, and a large degree of conformity to society followed. When the masses started to pour into the Church in the fourth century as a result of Constantine's conversion and changes in imperial policies toward Christians, it became harder to distinguish Christians from the common run of people. The changed character of the Church called forth a movement of protest in the form of a withdrawal from civilization and parish and of a severe asceticism on the part of many earnest Christians. These were the first Christian hermits and ascetics, men and women who were repelled by the Church's compromise with the world.

The root of monastic withdrawal was an ascetic understanding of the call of Christ, which was seen as a summons to a life of self-control and self-denial. Discipleship in the New Testament was often understood as the denial of self and as the forsaking of security and family that tie men down and keep them from giving their whole selves to the spreading of the Good News of God's coming kingdom. Not all who believed in Christ were expected to become disciples in this sense, but it was thought that the core of Jesus' disciples was a group of men who had forsaken all and given themselves to a life of daring adventure. Paul was in some respects an ascetic of this type. He urged others to become untrammeled from the cares of this troubled passing age and to be free for the "work of the Lord." This to him involved a life of celibacy when possible (1 Corinthians 7:9–17, 25–26, 29–32).

Each of the early Christian communities had its own ascetics: men and women who had deliberately remained unmarried or widowed ("virgins" and "widows" were official categories on the rolls of the Church), kept a minimum of personal property for themselves, and dedicated themselves to a life of prayer and the care of the needy in the community. As long as the rest of the congregation of Christians remained separate from society and persecutions still made witnessing for the faith in prison or in the arena as a martyr a distinct possibility, the ascetics remained one with their home communities.

However, when Christianity became popular and conformed to the world, the ascetics became estranged from the Christian mainstream. Many of them came to feel that living within the parish necessarily entailed a wholesale compromise with society and was inevitably distracting from a life of devotion, self-denial, and contemplation. Since they saw the transformation of the Church as a victory for the demonic forces and, in accordance with tradition, believed that the home of the demons was the desert, the Christian ascetics retreated into the wilderness to fight the powers of evil on their home front. Voluntary, hard physical labor, the surrender of all the comforts of civilization and home, and manful wrestling with all the temptations that come to a man in his loneliness were considered a new form of martyrdom, a witness to and a union with the Lord's suffering, by which He triumphed over the world. With the martyrs gone, the monks were now the "athletes" of God.

The first Christian monk was the Egyptian Anthony, who sold his inheritance, gave the money to the poor, and withdrew into the sands of Egypt at the turn of the fourth century. He did return to the city during the Diocletian persecution and again later to lend his support to Athanasius in his fight with the forces of Arianism, which shows that he was not one who wished to escape unpleasant confrontations. But otherwise, he was a hermit, the founder of an anchorite monasticism, that is, a life in solitude. The immediate inspiration for Anthony's drastic action was his hearing the lesson about Jesus' encounter with the rich young man (Matthew 19:16–22): "If you would be perfect, go, sell what you possess and give to the poor, and you will have treasure in heaven; and come, follow Me." These words moved countless other men to leave everything behind and "follow Jesus" in a life of ascetic abandonment of property and home. Anthony was followed by countless admirers—men who wished his counsel or who desired to imitate him—so that he had to withdraw deeper and deeper into the desert to attain the desired (and dreaded) solitude. He is known for his vivid temptations in the form of lurid visions, though this type of temptation seems typical for and invited by his style of life.

Shortly after the start of the anchorite movement, Pachomius started a community (coenobite) monasticism in Egypt. Coenobite monasticism is a Christian communism, at the opposite pole of the extreme individualism of the anchorites. Here, persons subjected themselves to a communal ascetic discipline, with hard labor and self-mortification such as fasting and very sparse meals undertaken in common under the direction of Pachomius, their leader. Complete solidarity with the community, soldier-like obedience, and suppression of all self-assertion were seen by these earnest Christians as necessary parts of the taking up of one's cross. Here is the origin of monasteries and also of female cloisters, for this type of monastic life was a possibility also for women. The communities were directed by an abbot (from *abba*, the Aramaic affectionate term for "father") or an abbess.

A third type of monasticism appeared in the wilderness of Judea in the fifth century: a compromise between the extremes of the solitary life on the one hand and the completely communal life on the other. The monks here did not live together but close to one another and to their spiritual father. They met for meals and prayers in common but spent much time by themselves. This satisfied the individualist who could not have adjusted well to life in a commune but who was not quite ready for complete solitude and desired spiritual guidance from a desert father known and revered for his wisdom and holiness. The arrangement served as spiritual preparation for many a future hermit.

The Radicals. The Egyptian and Syrian deserts were famous for their hermits, who were the greatest heroes of the people. The life apart from the community appeared as the greatest sacrifice and surely meant deep holiness. The wrestlers with the demons of the desert came to take the place of the martyrs of old. Villagers and city dwellers sought out the hermits to receive guidance and counsel in their perplexities. Their hermits' sayings and experiences became famous, passed on from mouth to mouth. Most of the monks were simple, uneducated laymen. Their type of life made them the people's philosophers. Their stories and sayings are sometimes shocking to us by their negation of what seems natural and human, especially in the sphere of food and human sexuality. From early times, Christian ascetics were intent to live the life of angels instead of flesh-and-blood mortals, thus anticipating already here and now existence in the age of the resurrection (Matthew 22:30). Their stringent fasts were believed to foster chastity.

Yet, alongside the strange and inhuman rigor, there is a strand in their stories that is very understanding, very wise, and very human. The true ascetic saint was extremely approachable and had a fatherly attitude to his spiritual children. He was no stranger to human weakness, and his fierceness toward himself was coupled with compassion rather than with intolerance toward others. Since his struggle with Satan was interior, the monk's gaze went inward: he became very introspective and preoccupied with his sins and temptations. The constant self-analysis of monks, this new phenomenon in the history of Christianity, made them also analysts and counselors of others. They developed the custom of confessing their sins and temptations to their spiritual fathers and became popular confessors themselves.

The early monks were radicals. Their self-mortification, especially of the anchorites who devised their own ascetic exercises, were extreme and often bizarre. Some seemed intent on a slow suicide and self-torture, with their long fasts and vigils and other more ingenious self-punishments. Some monks, while seeking to flee the world, only succeeded in attracting its attention. The famous Simeon Stylites did not live in a desert but on the top of a pillar to get away from impertinent pilgrims who would not leave him alone. Whatever misgivings we might have about this, he considered his action an important witness to detachment from the world, a world that admired him for it. The radical protesters against the Church's accommodation to the world were not only an interesting sociological phenomenon, but they also would have been fascinating objects of psychiatric analysis. Their steeling themselves against all feelings of pleasure and pain made them strikingly similar to the Indian fakirs.

Was there any Indian influence on the monastic movement in the Near and Middle East? The most extravagant feats of asceticism were found in Syria and Mesopotamia.

Anyone acquainted with the Bible can discern non-Christian elements in the attitudes of the ascetics toward the body and the bodily functions and joys. The biblical understanding of creation involves a great appreciation of the physical aspects of existence. Jesus was criticized for liking to eat and drink in contrast to the ascetic John the Baptist. He was even called "a glutton and a drunkard" (Matthew 11:19). Jesus did not stress the importance of self-control and the danger of passions. The emphasis on restraint and self-control and on the presumed superiority of mind over body was, however, characteristic of philosophies popular in the Greek-influenced world. While there were different philosophical parties, most men lived by a synthesis of elements from the various philosophies, and these all worked to foster an ascetic attitude in life.

Platonic philosophy bequeathed its emphasis on the superiority of the spiritual realm over the "misleading" world of senses. Socrates taught that the body was a prison house of the soul. The Cynics, of whom the most famous was Diogenes, who lived naked in a barrel, taught that men should be free from all the cares of the world, especially from the conventions of society, and should develop an utter self-sufficiency by divesting themselves of all that was not absolutely necessary in life. The Epicureans preached the pure pleasures of the spirit. The Stoics emphasized the importance of rational self-control, frugality, and moderation, pointing out the harmful nature of passion and desire. Stoic philosophy and its way of life intended to enable a man to take all privations and losses in stride. The ascetic discipline was to enable man to be unaffected by what he has or does not have.

All this shows that Christian ascetics were really philosophers more than saints, or rather that they held to a Greek-philosophical interpretation of holiness without knowing it. Philosophical ideas and ideals had so penetrated the spiritual climate of the late-Roman Empire that one simply took them for granted. In this way, they became part and parcel of Christianity.

The extremes of Christian asceticism, however, cannot be attributed directly to the influence of Greek philosophy, which extolled moderation as the golden mean. Was the extremism then a result of the intense temperament of the people, or was there an Indian influence? Both probably played a role, though documentation is difficult. However, Mani, a Mesopotamian religious reformer who founded the popular Manichean movement, acknowledged his debt to Buddha, among others, which clearly shows that Mesopotamia was not immune to Indian thought. The areas where Christianity became popular absorbed and cultivated a host of Eastern or Eastern-influenced philosophical and religious ideas and practices. All of them, like Gnosticism and Manicheanism, pitched the spiritual against the physical and cultivated a contempt for the latter. Leaders of the church fought both Gnosticism and Manicheanism as well as the extremes of asceticism. Nevertheless, the suspicion and low view of the body made their way undetected into Christian mentality. Nobody seemed to notice that this was a subtle infiltration of foreign elements into Christian asceticism and into the mainstream of Christianity. To this day, much of Christianity remains affected by it.

Jerome. While it was the East that gave birth to monasticism and witnessed the flowering of some of its bizarre forms, the West developed its own monastic heroes and "fakirs." The most famous of the Western ascetic radicals was Jerome, considered one of the four great fathers of the Western Church, the other three being Ambrose, Augustine, and Gregory. Jerome was born in Italy in the mid-fourth century and received a superior education in Latin classical literature. He loved his classics and could not part with them when he settled as a monk in Palestine's Bethlehem. He brought his entire library into his cave, a "luxury" and a comfort over which he never had an easy conscience.

He was a prodigious writer, not original in his thoughts but masterful in his style. He is famous for the revision of the Latin Bible, the Latin biblical commentaries, and his witty and biting letters. He undertook the revision of the Latin Bible at the initiative of Pope Damasus because the old Latin translation was not reliable. Its Old Testament was not based on the original Hebrew but on the old Greek version called the Septuagint. Jerome's presence in the East, where he became acquainted with Hebrew and Greek manuscripts and with Eastern (Jewish and Christian) biblical scholarship, enabled him to arrive at a good knowledge and understanding of the best available Hebrew and Greek manuscripts and thus to produce a more accurate translation of the Bible for Latin-speaking Christians. He was also able to put together valuable biblical commentaries for them. Biblical and theological scholarship was not as developed in the West as it was in the more cultured and more Christian-ized East.

The Bible Jerome produced is known as the Vulgate because it was written in "vulgar" Latin, that is, in the common language of the people (*vulgus*). Its style was nonclassical, just as most of the New Testament had been written in a very common, lowbrow Greek. The Vulgate gradually became the standard and only authoritative Bible of the West. Even Martin Luther normally read and quoted from the Bible in this version, although he had mastered Greek and Hebrew and produced his own German translation from these languages. Until very recently, all Roman Catholic translations of the Bible into modern languages had to be based on the Vulgate. Even though modern scholars base their work primarily on Greek and Hebrew biblical manuscripts, the Vulgate is still a valuable source for them. The reason is that Jerome had at his disposal some important older manuscripts that are no longer available.

When Jerome, to his great surprise, found that the Hebrew Old Testament did not contain all the books to which Christians were accustomed from their Greek and Latin versions of the Old Testament, he nicknamed these books "Apocrypha," that is, "hidden" or "puzzling" in their origin. He included them in his translation since they were used in the Church's worship. These apocryphal books form the difference between Catholic and Protestant canons of Scripture. The Protestant Reformers rec-ognized only the "original sources," that is, only the Hebrew text of the Old Testa-ment and the Greek text of the New, as having binding authority.

Jerome was a devotee not only of literature and scholarship but also of the strin-gent ascetic life, especially of celibacy. Monasticism had not yet taken root in the West, and Jerome did everything in his power to foster it, or at least to cultivate asceticism within families. He used for this his powerful pen. Jerome carried on a voluminous correspondence with men and women in the West. His letters to ladies of high rank in Rome, among whom he had many admirers and friends, encouraged them to scorn and forsake the pleasures of family and social life, to become nuns in Palestine if possible, and to train their daughters as ascetics. He pointed out with vivid sarcasm the annoyances of married life, in which he could see nothing but a pointless burden and from which he would have liked to save his lady friends and their innocent daughters. Marriage had only one positive role, as far as he could see: to produce virgins.

The letters make for fascinating and often hilarious reading. However, his asceti-cism was not primarily based on a contempt of marriage—he simply was a satirist and his remarks about marriage have to be read with this part of his personality in mind—but on a *mystical* view of voluntary Christian virginity. The Christian virgin was married to Christ, and how could any earthly union compete with that? The concept of a mystical marriage between God or Christ and His people is of course biblical. In the Bible, however, it is the *community* that is "betrothed" to God or His Christ. Christian mysticism, beginning with Origen in the early third century, applied the analogy also to the union of the individual soul with God. This became a very strong element in Christian asceticism, where it came to be assumed that the heavenly union replaces the earthly instead of existing alongside it. The elevated status of female Christian martyrs and of virgin women (as well as women's scholarly potentialities, in Jerome's view) gave the woman a new, high status in Christianity. She did not exist just for the sake of man nor was she dependent on him. She was not necessarily the "weaker sex." It is needless to say how damaging these ascetic views were for the status of marriage, no matter how much the Church stressed that marriage was a creation of God sanctified by Christ.

Jerome was highly respected and admired by many people in the West, for they were so proud of having at last one great Western ascetic, brilliant writer, and erudite scholar. He was therefore very influential in spreading monastic ideas in Rome, although its bishops were conservative, given to common sense, and therefore suspicious of this new and extravagant movement flourishing in the East. Yet it was Gaul that produced the first Western monks. The hero of Gaul was Martin, a soldier who tore his winter mantle in two to cover a shivering beggar and then in a dream learned that he had really clothed Christ in this poor brother. Martin founded a monastic community and also fostered monasticism when he later became the bishop of Tours. The asceticism of early Gallic monasticism was severe. It was influenced by Eastern radicals and itself became the inspirer of the all-important Celtic (Gaelic) monasticism of the Irish.

Monastic Reformers. The excesses of asceticism and the extreme individualism of the anchorite monastic movement east of Egypt (Pachomius's community monasticism did not spread there) did not stay uncriticized, even among men favoring monasticism.

In the troubled times and upheavals of an age that saw a new world being born, Benedictine monasteries were veritable havens of peace, civilization, and stability. They attracted many by the quiet, humane, purposeful, and noble life they offered. Monasticism provided also an important role for women, for in monastic communities, women were autonomous and could develop their initiative and potential for learning and leadership. In several cases, women became founders and heads (abbesses) of double monasteries, for men and women. Female religious communities compensated in part for the rather unfortunate absence of the deaconess and "widows" from the church's parish ministry at the end of the Middle Ages. The monastic movement may actually have caused the disappearance of the services of deaconesses and "widows" because it swept the congregation's ascetics away into the retreat of hermitages and monasteries.

REFORMERS AND PIONEERS IN MONASTICISM AND CHRISTIAN OUTREACH		
REFORMERS	VALUES	CONTRIBUTIONS
Basil of Caesarea (330–79). Great Father of Eastern Church.	Community, moderation, obedience, and service to larger church. Freedom from worldly cares.	Basil's Rules. Led by superior and educated monks. Novitiate (probation) before lifelong vows of poverty, chastity, obedience.
Evagrius of Pontus (346–99). Mystic.	Contemplation of visible world, invisible, and climax in mystery of God.	Listed principal or root sins from which all others grew. Greatest prayer contemplates God.
Patrick of Ireland (fifth century). Monk and bishop.	Severe monasticism. Voluntary foreign service in mission monastery.	Monks' penitential system brought to the parishes. Preserved classics for West.
Benedict of Nursia (c. 480–c. 550). Founder of Monte Cassino, Western pattern.	Discipline in community. "Prayer and work." No private possessions.	Benedictine Rule, with democratic element. Sanctified view of labor. Shorter prayers.

It is difficult to stress enough the importance of the monastic movement for Christendom. Its asceticism may have had a harmful effect on the understanding of the true Christian life, interpreting it as a life removed from an active involvement in the "world" and "rising above" the natural joys and instincts, especially those of the sexual relationship, as if they were not good gifts of God. Nevertheless, once Christianity had become the religion of the majority, and the Christian way of life had lost its original and distinctive character, the Church needed a separate corps of men and women who would give up the values and ambitions of society, bear witness to the challenge of the Gospel to leave everything and follow Christ, keep the centrality and art of prayer and meditation before the eyes of Christians, and stand out as an example of the solidarity that marks the true Christian community. Though monasticism was not originally intended to serve the Church and the world (as we might understand the following of Christ to involve), it did become a valuable agency for the service of Christ in the world, transforming the world it scorned and renewing the Church life it fled. It functioned as salt and leaven in the dough of Christendom.

AUGUSTINE, THE GREAT TEACHER OF THE WEST

The truly great original thinkers of the Church in the first centuries were all Easterners. The only partial exception was the North African Tertullian, the father of Latin theology, at the turn of the third century. Yet the last towering ancient theologian was a Westerner, again a North African, Aurelius Augustine, bishop of Hippo in today's Algeria. He was born in the mid-fourth century, the century of the development of a Roman Christian culture. He died in 430 during the Vandal siege of Hippo. It was the end of an era: the time of the collapse of Roman rule over the

West. Augustine was a brilliant heir of the harvest of his era, the harvest of a rich classical and Christian culture. He was a dynamic and creative thinker and writer, and his influence is stamped on the thought of Western Christendom to the present. Both Roman Catholicism and Protestantism are at their deepest level Augustinian.

Although his mother, Monica, attempted to rear Augustine as a Christian, he spurned the Church and the Bible as a young man because he thought that Christianity was just for the simple. It was only after a tortuous intellectual and moral quest—he was a Manichean for nine or ten years and then became a deep skeptic—that he became a Christian and embraced Baptism in his early thirties. He was deeply steeped in the Latin classics and was a professor of rhetoric, a study that was essential to a law or civil service career.

On the basis of his remorseful *Confessions*, written many years after, he is generally considered to have led a wild youth. This judgment is, however, grossly exaggerating the matter. He went through his adolescent problems, but at seventeen, he settled down to live with a woman whom he deeply loved and to whom he remained faithful for the next fourteen years, until his mother broke up their household and arranged for a socially advantageous marriage. Imperial and social laws made marriage of middle-class citizens with people of lower rank an impossibility. So society and the Church considered common-law marriages acceptable and moral as long as faithfulness was maintained. This certainly was Augustine's case. He had not been a profligate. His stern judgment on his sexual past was certainly due to the influence of Manicheanism and of Platonic philosophy, neither of which had any appreciation of man's psychosomatic nature. Both considered the sexual impulse a bar to attaining a truly spiritual or philosophical existence.

While teaching in Milan, Augustine was much impressed by its bishop, Ambrose. Ambrose's sermons aroused Augustine's interest by their oratorical skill, intelligence, philosophical orientation, and their resort to an allegorical interpretation of the Old Testament wherever given passages seemed offensive or irrelevant. In Ambrose and his Neoplatonic circle, Augustine at last found a Christianity worthy of his intellectual respect. Augustine was converted both to Neoplatonic philosophy and to Christianity. He saw little difference between them at the time. Under this influence, Augustine decided to embrace a philosophical-Christian life in ascetic retreat from society. He was baptized and returned to his native town in Africa, forming a semimonastic philosophical community around him in which he hoped to spend the rest of his life in contemplation. Contrary to all his plans and wishes, he was forced to become presbyter in the nearby city of Hippo. Five years later, he became bishop of Hippo. His ecclesiastical responsibilities involved him in the life and thought of the Church, especially in the thought of the Bible, and made him a theologian. He became a prodigious writer and campaigner in all the theological and ecclesiastical issues of the day and soon became the intellectual leader not only of Roman Africa but also of the entire Latin-speaking Christendom.

Apart from his numerous expositions of Scripture and his huge work *On the Trinity*, which stressed the oneness of the triune God, Augustine's writings concentrated for the most part on current controversies. His earliest writings as a Christian show how deeply affected he was by Neoplatonic philosophy.

AUGUSTINE ON THREE MAJOR CONTROVERSIES		
	ISSUES	OUTCOMES
ANTI-MAN-ICHEAN WRITINGS	Mani contended that evil is eternal, a godlike being that matches God. Mankind imprisoned in the flesh. Conception was a tragedy. Emphasized reason.	Augustine affirmed goodness of bodily life, created by God. Evil not eternal but the absence of good. Emphasized revelation, need for God's teaching through the Church.
DONATIST SCHISM	Persecuted clergy "handed over" Christian books for destruction. Known as *traditores*. Donatus and other North African Christians separated from these tainted clergy and would not recognize their ministry.	Augustine condemned Donatists' pride and lack of charity. Church is not pure but a mixed body. Only God knows the true Body of Christ. Sacraments are valid despite sins of the clergy. Government became involved in controversy, pressured Donatists.
PELAGIAN CONTRO-VERSY	Pelagius, a British monk, emphasized holiness and ability to fulfill God's laws. Mankind free in reason and will.	Augustine taught mankind was torn by knowing right and failing to do it. Human nature corrupt by fall into sin. Needed grace, empowering gift of the Spirit. Came to emphasize predestination.

The most famous of Augustine's works are his *Confessions*, the first spiritual autobiography, and his *City of God*, a monumental series of reflections on human social existence and human history. Augustine's *Confessions*, impassionedly written in the form of a prolonged prayer examining the underlying motives in his life up to his conversion, is poetry in prose. As to content, it is an introspective self-analysis. As pointed out earlier, its brooding introspection and the preoccupation with the depths of the human psyche blazed, for better and for worse, a new trail in the development of Western culture.

The writing of the *City of God* was prompted by the fall of "Eternal Rome" into the hand of barbarians in 410 and by the cry of dismay it raised on the part of pagans and Christians alike. When Christians wondered why God had "forsaken" Christian Rome, pagans retorted that the ancient gods had forsaken Rome as a punishment for its defection to the Christian God. Rome, they said, began to decline as soon as Christians began to multiply and the cult of the gods became neglected. Augustine wrote to give to both bewildered Christians and embittered pagans a better perspective on history and empires. All history is a story of violence and disasters, conquests and defeats—the fruit of men's fear and self-love. The Roman Empire, in spite of the ancient Roman virtues and its present Christian faith, is no exception in the history of nations. Augustine's views helped to make men open to the purposes of God that lay hidden in the uncertain future. Augustine provided the Western Church, on the threshold of a new age, with a philosophy of realism, flexibility, and hope with which to face and conquer the new future.

ASIAN AND EAST AFRICAN CHRISTIANITY

In this section, we will survey the persons and events leading to the separation of early Christians and the history of Christians in Asia and East Africa after the separation. An introduction to the common history of Eastern and Western churches will appear first, followed by their stories from east to west, an order that will also provide a roughly chronological account of their separation from the Christians in the Roman Empire.

An Asian Religion. Christianity is a religion native to Asia, which spread to East Africa and to other regions almost immediately (Acts 2:5–11; 8:26–40). Yet the broad and enduring history of Christians in these regions has sometimes received little consideration among Western Church historians.

Christianity had reached Rome by the middle of the first century AD, and within a few centuries, it had become so closely associated with the Roman Empire that Western Church historians made that relationship their primary concern. The remoteness of the Upper Nile, the eastern border with the Sassanid (Persian) Empire, and breaches of fellowship caused by doctrinal developments all served to distance Asian and East African Christians from their Western brethren. Finally, in the seventh century, the Arab conquests guaranteed only limited contact between Eastern and Western Christian leaders as the boundaries of empire and religion restricted travel and trade.

Amid all these changes, Asian and East African Christians prospered, developing a rich history of missionary activity, literature, and churchly organization. While Western Christians struggled to recover from the Germanic invasions and the collapse of classical civilization, Eastern Christians were translating Euclid and Aristotle into Arabic and were carrying the message about Christ ever further into Asia and Africa.

The story of Asian and East African Christianity covers events that correspond to the early and medieval eras described by Western Christian historians, especially the events after the Council of Ephesus (431), when doctrinal developments contributed to divisions. The history of Asian and East African Christians will be described by its major cultural groups: East Syrians, West Syrians, Armenians, Copts (Egyptians), and Ethiopians, whose Ethiopian Orthodox Church is the largest of these ancient churches to survive to our day.

Relating East to West. Since the history in this section will encompass roughly twelve centuries and the vast territory of Afro-Asia, a sketch of the region and its common events will assist the reader in relating the different Christian groups to one another. Five important centers of activity arose among early Christians:

1. Edessa/Nisibis in northern Mesopotamia, on the eastern border of the Roman Empire, where the Christians spoke Aramaic

2. Antioch, on the eastern shore of the Mediterranean, where the Christians spoke Aramaic and Greek

3. Alexandria, on the Nile Delta, where the Christians spoke Greek and Coptic

4. Constantinople (Byzantium), the East Roman capital, on the waterway between the Mediterranean and the Black Sea, where the Christians spoke Greek

5. Rome, the ancient heart of the empire, where the Christians spoke Latin

In ancient times, Roman imperial administration held these distant regions together. Administrators could usually communicate in Greek because of the earlier Hellenistic empires of Alexander the Great, the Seleucids of Asia, and the Ptolemies of Egypt, which bound the ancient Persian territories to the West.

In 293, Emperor Diocletian established a "tetrarchy," a system with four rulers under himself as Augustus. Two rulers served in the eastern half of the empire, two in the western half. This guaranteed that imperial leadership would be readily available to all corners of the empire's vast territory. Unfortunately, the four rulers fought with one another after Diocletian's death. Constantine I (312–37) won out and issued an edict of toleration in 313, providing freedom of religion for citizens of the empire. Christianity soon went from a persecuted minority to a preferred minority, receiving masses of converts. Although a variety of theological positions arose in the Early Church, readers should bear in mind the common faith all these churches professed in the creed drafted at the Council of Nicaea in 325.

In 330, Emperor Constantine I established Constantinople (Byzantium) as his capital. He had moved the capital eastward to the point where the European and Asian continents divide. This made the capital more central so that he could manage both ends of the empire. But this change also more or less divided the empire under two administrative capitals: old Rome and the "new Rome," Constantinople. The division naturally created rivalry between East and West and invited leaders from the major cities to take sides against one another.

Early Syrian Christianity. According to Acts 2:5–11, when Peter addressed the temple crowd on Pentecost, he began by listing Jews and proselytes from the East: Parthians, Medes, Elamites, and residents of Mesopotamia. A myriad of Israelites had populated these regions because of the Assyrian and Babylonian exiles in the eighth and the sixth centuries BC. The report in Acts concludes with the Baptism and faith of such persons, who would return home with the message of Christ after the festival (Acts 2:37–41). In Galatians 1:17 and 21, the apostle Paul wrote that he visited Damascus, Arabia, Syria, and Cilicia after his conversion. Acts describes Antioch—the Roman Empire's gateway to Syria and the East—as a center of early mission activity (Acts 11:19–30; 13:1–3). However, the story of the Book of Acts turns to the West, following Paul's missionary efforts into Asia Minor and Europe, though it might just as easily have turned to the East, where people spoke Aramaic, the native language of Jesus and many Jews. The Aramaic dialect of the people near Edessa came to dominate these regions north and east of Israel, where the Gospel was received early (though only legendary accounts about how this occurred have survived). The dialect came to be known as "Syriac."

One of the earliest Christian documents—and the earliest collection of Christian poetry and hymns, the Odes of Solomon—demonstrates the vitality of these Syrian Christians in the second century AD. Not long after the Council of Nicaea, the first Syriac Church Father, Aphrahat, busied himself with teaching and with writing his "Demonstrations" (composed 337–45). One of the greatest early poets of Christianity, Ephrem (c. 306–73), wrote in Syriac while serving as a deacon in Nisibis and Edessa, which became the most important centers of Syrian Christianity until the rise of Baghdad.

Council of Ephesus. The story of Syriac Christianity is closely tied to the early ecumenical councils, in which theological and imperial decisions greatly affected the thought and fellowship of Syriac Christians.

Nestorius, who came from Germanicia (east of Cilicia), lived as a monk at Antioch, where he may have studied under Theodore of Mopsuestia (c. 350–428). Nestorius became well-known as an excellent preacher. In 428, Emperor Theodosius asked Nestorius to serve as the bishop of Constantinople, the capital of the Eastern Roman Empire. Nestorius gladly accepted but soon found himself embroiled in a controversy over the two natures of Christ after one of his priests, Anastasius, preached a chapel sermon against the use of the term *Theotokos* ("God-bearer"), which the Christians of Constantinople used to describe the Virgin Mary. In 430, Celestine I of Rome (d. 432) and Cyril of Alexandria (d. 444), two influential bishops, condemned Nestorius's teaching. Rabbula of Edessa (d. 435), an influential theologian among the Syrian Christians, likewise condemned Nestorius as well as the teachings of Theodore of Mopsuestia, who had influenced Nestorius. At Ephesus in 431, a general council condemned Nestorius's teaching. He was exiled, first to Antioch and finally to Upper Egypt, where he died among the Copts. These imperial decisions did much to alienate Nestorius's countrymen. Although "Nestorianism" was suppressed in imperial regions, it flourished beyond the eastern border of the empire in the Sassanid regions of modern Iraq and Iran, where the "Church of the East" would carry on an independent existence and far-reaching missionary activities.

The Church of the East. With Nestorius in exile, East Syrian Christians began to focus on their heartland and let go of concerns with and connections to Antioch and imperial Christianity. Ibas, bishop of Edessa beginning in 435, remained sympathetic toward Nestorius and had great respect for Theodore of Mopsuestia, whose works Ibas translated from Greek to Syriac. As a consequence, the Council of Ephesus deposed Ibas in 449, a move designed to eliminate all perceived Nestorian influence. However, the Council of Chalcedon reinstated Ibas in 451, preserving relations between imperial Christianity and East Syrian Christians at that time. But the next bishop of Edessa (457–471), Nonnus, preferred monophysite views against Nestorian views, which increased local tensions.

The School of Edessa flourished despite the Roman Empire's suppression of Nestorianism because it was difficult for the empire to enforce its concerns on the frontier. The head of the school of Edessa was Narsai (c. 399–503), who may have led the school as early as 437. When Emperor Zeno (474–91) ordered the closing of the school, Narsai fled imperial territory. Bar Saumas of Nisibis (d. before 486) welcomed Narsai, inviting him to reestablish the educational center there. Thus, the Nestorians simply moved their educational center approximately 150 miles eastward into Sassanid territory, where they were able to continue undisturbed.

The School of Nisibis flourished under the leadership of Narsai and Bar Saumas, becoming a renowned center of learning for centuries. Narsai wrote extensively on the Bible and authored numerous sermons and hymns. As a consequence, he was known as the "Harp of the Spirit."

A noteworthy student of Narsai and the School of Nisibis was Abraham of Kashkar (491/2–586). Abraham not only studied at Nisibis but also spent time in Egypt among Coptic monks. Abraham instituted important monastic reforms among the Nestorians. These reforms spread through the work of his successors, especially Babai the Great (d. 628). Babai wrote a systematic treatise on Christology, which became the doctrinal standard for the Church of the East and was embodied in its liturgical tradition.

Missionary Expansion. The spread of Syrian missionaries is one of the more amazing aspects of their heritage. They spread quickly along the eastern trade routes. Although legendary accounts state that the apostle Thomas reached India in the first century and established Aramaic-speaking churches there, it is historically certain that Syriac-speaking congregations existed in Malabar, in southwest India, from the sixth century. Known as Mar Thoma (St. Thomas) churches, they received their bishops from the Church of the East.

The year 635 marks a significant moment in Christian missionary efforts. In that year, Tai-Tsung (627–50), a Chinese ruler, welcomed a Nestorian missionary, as reported on the Si-ngnan-fu monument. A-lo-pen, a Persian monk, presented the Scripture to the Chinese ruler, who was impressed with its teaching and urged its use throughout his kingdom. Monasteries were built, and Christianity became well established in western and middle China.

At nearly the same time that the Nestorians established themselves in China, Arab armies crossed the western border of the Sassanid Empire. They took control of Mesopotamia in 636/7. The Nestorians welcomed this change, having suffered persecution from the Zoroastrian Sassanids over the centuries. By 657, the entire Sassanid Empire had fallen to the Arabs.

Amid these changes arose Isaac, a Nestorian monk who was consecrated as bishop of Nineveh in approximately 676. Isaac's role as bishop was short-lived, but the example of his life and the influence of his writings were widely received among fellow Nestorians, who translated his works into numerous languages.

In the eighth century, the 'Abbasid caliphate rebuilt Baghdad, which was near the location of Seleucia-Ctesiphon, the old Sassanid capital. The caliph (Arabic "successor" who ruled after Muhammad) settled there in 763, and the new capital also became the home of a thriving Nestorian community.

The height of Nestorian achievement perhaps took place under Timothy I, patriarch of Baghdad (779–823). Although he began his service under controversy, Timothy renewed the strength of his church. Not only was the mission in China expanded, but also a Turkish king converted to Christianity and requested that Timothy send him a metropolitan bishop to minister to his people. Timothy also corresponded with Caliph al-Maheli to defend the Christian faith. He likewise left a record of Nestorian synods from 790 to 805.

Caliph al Ma'mun founded the "House of Wisdom" in Baghdad, where most of the scholars were Nestorian Christians who preserved and translated the works of classical antiquity into Syriac and Arabic. The Nestorians' learning commended them also to positions within the government. The most notable scholar of this school was Hunayn ben Ishaq (809–73), who produced voluminous translations. The caliphs paid him handsomely for his efforts, and his son inherited his enviable position of service.

Opposition and Decline. In the ninth century, the policies of Chinese Emperor Wu-tsung (840–46) marked a change in opportunities for the Nestorians. He ordered that the Christian priests and monks must return to ordinary secular life and service. Also in the ninth century, Caliph al-Mu'Tasim (833–42) brought Turkish bodyguards into his palace. The Turkish ambitions for power soon outstripped those of the Arabs, and the Turks rose to power.

As Muslims benefited from the training they received from their Nestorian teachers, they began to take positions of leadership in government that had previously belonged to Christians. The Christians became unnecessary to their rulers and fell further and further out of power. From 945 to 1258, the Arab Empire was also breaking up into smaller and smaller regional kingdoms, which increased the number and intensity of rivalries.

When the Mongols invaded in 1220–60, they were at first favorable toward Christians. Hulagu Khan, who conquered Baghdad in 1258, ended the 'Abbasid caliphate. Hulagu's wife was a Christian, and it appeared at first that the Christians would find enduring security under their new rulers. However, in 1295, Mahmud Ghazan killed his brother to become sole ruler. Ghazan converted to Islam, and from that point the decline of Christianity in the East progressed steadily. For example, at the city of Maraghah, hundreds of thousands of Christians were massacred.

Later, the Turkish leader Timur Lane (1396–1405) took control from his Mongol lord and proceeded to conquer region by region with devastating results. He killed all who opposed him, whether Christian or Muslim. However, Christian communities suffered most of all and nearly disappeared. Positions of church leadership were left vacant for decades. Successive Turkish leadership led to similar consequences. The Church of the East survived in only the more remote regions.

***Dhimma* Status.** Before turning to the story of West Syrian Christianity, it is important to understand more about Christian and Muslim relations.

Historical descriptions of Islam and its relationship to Christianity sometimes note that Muslim rulers were generally tolerant of their Christian subjects so long as they kept the law and paid their taxes. To understand the matter more fully, it is important to understand the *dhimma* (Arabic: "protected") status and how it developed over the centuries.

Muslims introduced the *dhimma* status in the seventh century, following the Arab conquests. It granted certain protections to "peoples of the Book," that is, to Jews, Christians, and perhaps others who were expected to pay general tribute (Arabic: *kharaj*) as well as a poll tax (Arabic: *jizya*). The poll tax was to make up for the fact that able-bodied Christians and Jews did not serve in the caliph's military.

The idea of a "protected" status can be somewhat misleading. It did not simply imply that Islamic rulers and subjects had responsibility to one another. It included the idea that the Christians and Jews were inferior persons, like dependent children. For the Muslims, the inferiority was confirmed by the fact that the Christians and Jews adhered to what Muhammad regarded as inferior religions.

Standards of *dhimma* status were codified in Sharia law during the eighth and ninth centuries. The list of standards varied from ruler to ruler and from place to place. They could prohibit the following types of activities:

- striking a Muslim
- converting a Muslim
- interfering with the conversion of others to Islam
- public displays of non-Muslim religions
- teaching polemically from the Qur'an
- repairing or building new religious buildings
- interfering with confiscation of property for Muslim purposes
- dressing like a Muslim
- selling alcohol to a Muslim
- riding horses

Enforcement of these and similar standards would guarantee the decline of competing religions. Later rulers would appeal to the "covenant of 'Umar," which described a legendary agreement between Caliph 'Umar and Sophronius, patriarch of Jerusalem, wherein a Christian leader readily agreed to *dhimma* status for his people. Assemblies of bishops, abbots, and perhaps other representatives held elections to choose Christian leaders. Muslim rulers had to approve those who were elected, which guaranteed that Christian leaders would be eager to work with their Muslim rulers.

Violence against Christians. During the Arab conquests, violence between Christians and Muslims was, of course, common. Atrocities occurred on both sides. But after the conquest and imposition of *dhimma* status, the violence subsided.

About three hundred years after Charles Martel and the Franks halted the advance of Islam into Europe (732), Muslim and Christian tensions in Spain increased again. Muslims had also pressed into the islands of the Mediterranean and into southern Italy. Christian leaders needed to defend themselves. This time, the Christians began to push the Muslims back, signaling a change in momentum as European kingdoms gained strength.

Another historic change took place in 1009 when al-Hakim, a Shi'ah caliph, became a persecutor of Christians, Jews, and Sunni Muslims in his realm. The violence of this persecution was far different from anything that a Muslim leader had enacted before. Gregory Bar Hebraeus described the circumstances in his *Chronography*. Caliph al-Hakim destroyed the Church of the Holy Sepulchre in Jerusalem and confiscated its furniture. He destroyed thousands of other churches and enforced a stricter *dhimma* status on Christians and Jews, even persecuting Sunni Muslims. He forced Christians to convert to Islam, and those who would not convert were urged to leave his realm. Driving Christians out of his territory toward Rome naturally provoked European involvement. The changes horrified Christians in Europe, though al-Hakim later relented from his harshness and allowed forced converts to return to their earlier faiths.

In 1076, when the Seljuk Turks conquered the Holy Land, they killed approximately three thousand Christians and harassed Christian pilgrims who came to pray at the holy sites. This new violence and interference with long-standing pilgrimages alarmed the Europeans again, who also were receiving requests for aid from Eastern Romans and from Armenians. Instability caused by the provincial divisions of the 'Abbasid caliphate, the Mongol invasion, and the Turkish invasions had devastating consequences for the Christians living under Islam. Rulers and regimes often combined political or military motives with religious motives. Christians, too, responded with violence. But from the eighth century to the close of the medieval period, Christians experienced greater suffering, which clearly led to decline in Asian and Egyptian churches.

West Syrians and Chalcedon. Having described the division of the East Syrians and the general consequences of Muslim rule, we may return to the earlier, parallel history of the West Syrian Christians.

Just as the East Syrian churches distinguished themselves because they dissented from a general council, the West Syrian churches likewise distinguished themselves following a general council. In fact, decisions and events in 451 resulted in the alienation of Syriac as well as Coptic Christians. Leaders on all sides of the issues felt that others were dealing unjustly with them.

The Council of Chalcedon was called to deal with the teaching of Eutyches, a monastic leader at Constantinople who sharply opposed the teaching of Nestorius. Eutyches emphasized that Christ had only one nature after the incarnation. The council condemned his teaching as contrary to Scripture and exiled Eutyches.

As with the condemnation of Nestorius, the condemnation of Eutyches did not settle the matter for all Christians in the empire. Some believed that the Chalcedonian teaching came too close to the teachings of Nestorius. The leaders among these dissenting theologians were the Coptic bishop Timothy Aelurus (d. 477) and Severus, the bishop of Antioch (c. 465–538). Their teaching came from Cyril of Alexandria, who had unfortunately used the Greek terms for "nature" (*physis*) and "substance" (*hypostasis*) without careful distinction. These circumstances contributed to misunderstandings following Chalcedon as theologians continued to debate about the relationship between the divine and human natures of Christ after His incarnation.

In 482, Acacius of Constantinople (471–89) and Peter Mongos of Alexandria (d. 490) issued the *Henoticon*, a document intended to unite the Chalcedonians and those who disagreed with them. Emperor Zeno supported their efforts, but the bishop of Rome, Felix III, rejected the *Henoticon*. This resulted in a breach of fellowship between Rome and Constantinople, known as the Acacian Schism (482–519). Emperor Justin I (518–27) resolved the Acacian Schism for many imperial regions. But on the borders of the empire, Syriac Christians, Armenians, and Copts retained their beliefs from Cyril's theology and continued to use confessions of faith that differed from those used by imperial Christians.

Melchites, Jacobites, and Maronites. In the aftermath of the Council of Chalcedon, Christians in the Eastern Roman Empire grew increasingly distinct from one another. Those who held to the Chalcedonian formulas became known as "Melchites," from the Syriac term for "imperial," whether they were found in Syria or in Egypt. The Melchites were often of Greek descent or spoke Greek. They were concentrated near the Mediterranean coast, closer to the heart of the empire. The different groups typically lived alongside one another but had separate churches and church leaders. However, Jerusalem became the only major city with one patriarch, who was Melchite.

Some Melchite leaders persecuted those who did not accept the decisions of Chalcedon. Their measures could be quite extreme. *The Chronicle of Zuqnin* describes a deadly persecution by the Melchite bishop of Amid, Abraham Bar Kayli, who would force people to take Communion consecrated at a Chalcedonian service. In one case, a priest named Cyrus refused. The handle of a whip was forced into Cyrus's mouth so that the elements of the Sacrament could be fed to him. Cyrus spat them out, which then became an excuse for Bar Kayli to have him burned. The chronicle indicates that the emperor was not fully aware of the extreme measures some of the Melchites were taking to gain absolute control of their region and that Bar Kayli was fearful that the emperor would find out what he had done.

Theodora I, the wife of Emperor Justinian I (527–65), advocated on behalf of the non-Chalcedonian Christians. She convinced her husband to attempt reconciliation with them. These efforts ultimately failed. But they prevented imperial Christians from conducting more severe persecutions or purges of the non-Chalcedonian Christians in Syria such as the persecutions that had taken place against non-Chalcedonians in Egypt, which will be described later in the chapter.

Among the Syriac-speaking Christians who held non-Chalcedonian views, there emerged a number of important leaders. For example, Bishop Philoxenus of Mabbug (c. 440–523) wrote noteworthy treatises on the Christian life as well as commentaries on the Bible. Yet another West Syrian figure, and perhaps the most important, was Jacob Baradaeus (c. 500–578), who had close contacts with Empress Theodora at Constantinople. In approximately 542, Jacob was appointed as the bishop of the important Syrian city of Edessa. At this time, Emperor Justinian I was in the process of suppressing non-Chalcedonian leaders by imprisoning them or sending them into exile. Jacob dressed himself in shabby clothes and set out to visit the non-Chalcedonian churches, ordaining new bishops as he traveled and encouraging the congregations with his teaching. Accounts describe him traveling virtually everywhere accessible in the Eastern Roman Empire, including islands and even Constantinople itself. As a result of Jacob's remarkable efforts, the majority of West Syrian Christians came to call themselves "Jacobites."

Another West Syrian group is the Maronites, who trace their roots to the fifth century Maro, a monastic leader and priest whose efforts were recognized by John Chrysostom and Theodoret of Cyrrhus. The Maronites became a clearly distinct group during the reunion efforts between Chalcedonian and non-Chalcedonian Christians in the seventh century. The Maronites agreed that Christ was God and man who had "one will" (called *monothelitism*) after His incarnation. This view was rejected at the Third General Council of Constantinople.

Medieval writers also mention a John Maro, who served as bishop to the Maronites from 685 to 707. He provided crucial leadership to his people during the Arab conquest, leading them into the security of the Lebanon Mountains.

Before the seventh-century Arab conquests, the Jacobites were an underground movement, resisting imperial persecution. The Arabs did not concern themselves with distinctions among the various Christian groups within the territory they conquered. All groups were subject to the taxes and restrictions on non-Muslims. These new circumstances suited the Jacobites better than what they were experiencing under the Chalcedonian Christians of the empire. As a consequence, the Jacobites welcomed Muslim rule. They soon began to prosper through missionary efforts among the Melchite Christians to the west and Nestorian Christians to the east, moving into Persia and Mesopotamia.

The first important Jacobite leader of this era was Marutha, metropolitan of Tekrit. From 629 to 649, he served as "Maphrian of the East," a Syriac title for the head clergyman of the Persian region. Marutha witnessed the Arab conquest and guided his people to a peaceful transition under the new rulers.

The next important Jacobite leader of this era was Jacob of Edessa (633–708). Jacob was a prolific scholar of theological and philosophical topics. He enacted revisions of the Peshitta Old Testament and the Syriac liturgy. He also wrote numerous biblical commentaries. Jacob helped to reform the monasteries and encouraged more rigorous discipline.

Bishop Severus Sebokht (d. 667) was famous for his knowledge of Greek philosophy, math, and astronomy in addition to theology. He made the monastery of Kenneshre the center of Jacobite education.

Dionysius of Tellmahre (817–45), while managing a controversy about "the heavenly bread," traveled to visit and pacify troubled congregations. During this effort, he intervened with Muslim rulers to prevent the destruction of religious institutions in Edessa. He also interceded for the Bashmuric Copts, who had rebelled against Arab rule, though his efforts failed to spare bloodshed. Dionysius wrote a collection of *Annals*, which describe this troubled period.

After this, Jacobite Christianity entered a period of decline brought about by changes in Muslim rule. New groups were wrestling for power, such as the Turks and Turcomen of central Asia. As a consequence, Christians suffered. The Melchites were more numerous in the regions conquered by the crusaders, where their patriarchs were driven out and Latin patriarchs introduced. The Crusades also added to the woes of Syriac Christians because the Muslims feared a Christian revolt and conquest of their territories.

Jacobite Renewal. In the twelfth century, conditions improved for the Jacobites, in part because of the leadership of three important figures.

Dionysius Bar Salibi (d. 1171) served as bishop of Mar'ash (Germanicia) and Amid. He wrote extensive commentaries on the Old and New Testaments. He also wrote a compendium of theology and a treatise against heresies.

At age 31, Michael the Syrian (1126–99), a monastic leader, was appointed the Jacobite patriarch at Antioch. Michael wrote an important chronicle, tracing history to the year 1194/5, including comment on the Arab general Saladin (c. 1138–93) and the Third Crusade (1189–92). Michael was troubled by the betrayal of his colleague Theodore Bar Wahbun. Theodore represented Michael at a conference with Byzantine leaders. In an effort to seize leadership among the Jacobites, Theodore accused Michael of Chalcedonian teachings, which caused trouble with Jacobite leaders. Theodore's effort failed, but he became a rival patriarch at Amid in 1180 and among the Armenians until he died in 1193. As an author, Michael's chronicle was a remarkable contribution, which included extensive lists of church leaders in eastern regions.

The last of the great Jacobite writers was Gregory Bar Hebraeus (1226–86), who became a bishop in 1264 and lived at the monastery of Mar Mattai near modern Mosul. He wrote extensively on theology, the Bible, science, and Aristotelian philosophy. His *Chronography*, written in three parts, traced the history of the world down to his own time. He witnessed the invasion of the Mongols, which ultimately led to the decline of his churches.

Armenian Christianity. The story of Armenian Christianity takes us back again to the earliest years of the Church. That Christianity took root early in Armenia is beyond question. The great Early Church historian Eusebius of Caesarea noted that Dionysius of Alexandra (d. c. 264) wrote a treatise to the Armenians, whose bishop was Meruzanes (*Church History* 4:56). This shows that Christians were in Armenia in the second century. The Armenians themselves teach that the apostles Thaddaeus and Bartholomew preached to them in the first century, though others regard these accounts as legend.

The great flowering of Armenian Christianity took place in the fourth century under the leadership of Gregory the Illuminator (c. 240–332). Gregory was from the Armenian royal family. He was exiled at an early age and became a Christian while in Cappadocia. When Gregory returned from Cappadocia, his teaching converted King Tiridates (c. 238–314) to Christianity. Tiridates then made Christianity the official religion—the first nation ever to adopt Christianity as the religion of the state. The metropolitan of Caesarea in Cappadocia consecrated Gregory as bishop. Gregory's son, Aristakes, represented the Armenians at the Council of Nicaea (325), having been consecrated as bishop by his father. Armenian church leadership centered in Ashtishat, where members of the royal family would consult the clergy in matters of dispute.

An important early council was called at Ashtishat in 365 by Bishop Nerses (353–73), the great-great-grandson of Gregory the Illuminator. Nerses identified and changed various pagan habits that prevailed among the Armenians. Thus, Christianity was firmly established throughout the nation by the middle of the fourth century.

Unfortunately, trouble soon followed when King Pap sought to overturn Nerses's reforms. Since the king was concerned about outside influences, he chose a bishop from a different noble family and had Nerses's successor consecrated by Armenian church leaders rather than the metropolitan of Caesarea. In this way, Armenian church leadership became independent from imperial church leadership. When a member of Gregory's family—Sahak I (387–439)—again became bishop, he did not restore the breach with Caesarea but maintained Armenian independence.

In 396, Sahak I ordained as a priest Mesrop, who had served as Sahak's secretary. Mesrop (d. 440) was commissioned with defending the people against heretical teaching. After visiting churches throughout the country, Mesrop decided that it was necessary to put the Bible into the Armenian language, since the people did not understand the Greek and Syriac that the government officials and clergy used. King Vramshapooh supported Mesrop's efforts.

Mesrop crafted an alphabet; translation began in 404 and was completed by 433. The Old Testament was based on the Septuagint with reference to Syriac manuscripts. The Liturgy of St. Basil and other worship resources were likewise rendered in Armenian. So both the Bible and liturgical texts were issued in standardized forms in the middle of the fifth century, bringing greater unity to both church and state.

While the Armenian Church made important advances in the fifth century, it also faced the challenge of attacks from Persian Sassanids, who sought to spread Zoroastrianism and to conquer the Armenian people. This great struggle prevented the Armenians from meaningful participation in the great councils of 431, 449, and 451, when the churches of the Roman Empire debated and worked through the early Christological controversies. However, after the Sassanids were turned back, Catholicos Babguen (490–516) summoned a regional council of Armenian, Georgian, and Caspio-Albanian bishops at Dwin in 506. This council affirmed the anti-Nestorian decisions of the 431 Council of Ephesus but did not approve of the teaching of the 451 Council of Chalcedon. In this way, the Armenians became firmly non-Chalcedonian.

When the Arabs conquered the Middle East, Armenia became a vassal state to the caliph. The Armenians grew content with Arab rule and continued to reject Roman interference in their churchly matters. For example, the Synod of Manzikert (726) was held jointly with West Syrian bishops and again rejected Chalcedonian teaching. The leader of this synod was Armenian Catholicos Hovhannes Otzun the Philosopher, who was recognized as a capable theologian. Hovhannes secured amiable treatment from Caliph 'Umor II (717–20) when he demonstrated his piety by wearing a goat-hair tunic under his sumptuous vestments. He requested religious freedom for his people and exemption of the clergy from taxes, conditions that the caliph granted.

Catholicos Zaccharias, in 862, again rejected efforts from Photius of Constantinople (858–67), who sought to reunite the Armenians with the Church of Constantinople. The Synod of Shiragavan confirmed Zaccharias's decision.

Relations with the Arabs did not remain completely peaceful. Armenian church leaders had to plead to the caliphs on behalf of their people as local conflicts caused Arab leaders to exploit or injure the Armenians. For example, Arabs captured Dwin during the patriarchate of Hovhannes V (898–929). During these conflicts, the seat of church leadership moved from place to place, as necessary. The rise of the Saljuk Turks in the eleventh century brought still greater challenges and threats.

The East Roman emperors also pushed into the area as they found opportunity. In 1071, at the Battle of Manzikert, the Turks defeated Emperor Romanus Diogenes (1068–72) and took full control of Armenia, which suffered increasing division. Armenian leaders and people became dispersed from one another as the Turks settled among them.

The Crusades. Before the Crusades started, the Armenians had reached out to Western leaders for help against the Turks by sending a bishop to meet with Gregory VII (1073–85). Gregory had attempted reconciliations with Eastern churches and a unified campaign against the Turks, which were not realized. However, Urban II proclaimed the First Crusade in 1095.

During the catholicate of Constantine I (1221–67), Armenian church leaders sought a united resistance from Latin, Greek, and Syrian Christians against the Seljuk Turks. But such an effort was never accomplished. A negotiated union with the western Roman Church was proposed. A portion of the Armenians agreed to the union, but most would not accept Chalcedonian teaching. Although negotiations occurred again throughout the next few centuries, the majority of Armenians remained non-Chalcedonian.

Unlike many other Asian and North African Christian groups, the Armenians found encouragement in the crusaders from the West. In fact, the daughters of the Armenian nobility and leaders of the Crusades intermarried. However, the relationship between the two powers was not without turmoil. For example, in 1219, Philip of Antioch married Isabel, an Armenian princess. Philip was poised to become an Armenian king—if he would convert to the Armenian confession. When Philip did not fulfill his obligations, the Armenians removed him from power, and he was killed. Isabel was then given in marriage to an Armenian.

At the close of the medieval period, the warlord Timur Lane and the Turks dominated the Armenians, who maintained their profession of Christianity in the face of great suffering. This remains a matter of great pride for the Armenians today.

Early Coptic Christianity. Archaeologists have discovered Egyptian papyri that date from the early second century and contain portions of the Greek New Testament. They confirm that Christians entered Egypt at a very early date. According to Eusebius of Caesarea, Mark founded the Christian churches of Egypt (*Church History* 2:16). Alexandria, which had been a center of Judaism, soon arose as a leading Christian community. It remained so throughout the ancient and Arabic periods, though the Arab conquest (AD 642) limited Alexandrian Christians' contact and influence with churches in Europe.

Egypt was the home of great Christian thinkers whose views competed with early Gnosticism and Greek philosophy. Clement of Alexandria (c. 150–215) and Origen (c. 185–254) taught at the city's catechetical school, which encouraged allegorical interpretation, an approach that spread widely and characterized the Alexandrian school of thought. Bishops Athanasius (c. 296–373) and Cyril (d. 444) were among the most famous leaders of the Early Church. They were vigorous defenders of doctrine at the early ecumenical councils, where they provided pivotal influence in the composition of creedal statements.

Christians of Alexandria spread into the upper valley of the Nile, in part because of imperial persecutions. The Upper Nile and desert regions provided natural havens. It was also in these regions that early monasticism flourished. Antony (c. 251–356) and Pachomius (c. 290–346) drew many Egyptian Christians into the wilderness to practice quiet, meditative lives in isolation or in community (cenobite monasticism). The devotion of these early monks and their practices amazed persons of this era. Their practices soon spread to other regions of the ancient world. Shenoute (d. c. 450), abbot of Athribis, composed letters and sermons in the language of ancient Egypt: Coptic (from the Greek for "Egypt"). Coptic Christians prepared their own translation of the New Testament into the various dialects of Egypt (Sahidic, Bohairic, Fayumic, and Akhmimic). Coptic remained in use for approximately one thousand years until increasing use of Arabic displaced the various dialects.

Following the patriarchate of Cyril of Alexandria (d. 444), Dioscorus I became bishop and used his influence to support the doctrinal views of Eutyches, a monk of Constantinople, at a Council in Ephesus (449). Eutyches had been in trouble with authorities for vigorously opposing the idea that Christ had two natures after His incarnation. Eutyches's view, ultimately known as *monophysitism* (Greek for "only one nature"), was upheld by Dioscorus and others at the council. The majority also supported the primacy of Alexandria over other bishoprics, which brought speedy response from other church leaders, who came to regard the Synod of Ephesus as a "robber council" (*Latrocinium*). Dioscorus was deposed and exiled by the ecumenical Council of Chalcedon (451), but he was ultimately honored as a saint by his fellow churchmen in Egypt.

This dispute over the natures of Christ and churchly authority led to a formal break between churches of the Roman Empire and churches of Egypt. Following the Council of Chalcedon, Proterius (452–57), a man favored by imperial leadership, was appointed bishop of Alexandria by brutal imperial action. The Copts appointed their own bishop, Timothy Aelurus (d. 477). From that point onward, Christians in Lower Egypt were divided into imperial and local parties.

Imperial Era. Christians who were loyal to the empire (commonly known as "Melchites" from the Syriac term for "imperial") continued to dominate Lower Egypt. They were of Greek descent, in contrast to the local Coptic Christians who opposed the imperial decisions.

In 457, Proterius was murdered while imperial leadership was occupied with the invasion of the Vandals in North Africa. Angry Copts dragged Proterius's body through the streets and burned it, adding further insult. Timothy Aelurus was now sole bishop of the region, able to strengthen the hold of Egyptian views and interests. However, Emperor Zeno (474–91) soon appointed a new bishop, Timothy Salophaciolus (460), since Roman rulers could not afford to lose control of Egypt, which was the chief source of grain in the empire. When Timothy Aelurus died, the Copts elected Peter Mongos (d. 490) as bishop.

In 482, Peter Mongos and Acacius of Constantinople (471–89) sought a peaceful settlement to the schism with a document titled the *Henoticon* (Greek for "union"). The theology of this document reached back to pre-Chalcedonian formulas, and it affirmed the decisions of the earlier ecumenical councils. Broader tensions between Bishop Felix III of Rome (483–92) and Acacius of Constantinople hindered official progress on the document and led to the Acacian Schism between Rome and Constantinople (482–519). Bishops of Constantinople approved the document, which broadened the opportunity for non-Chalcedonian teaching in the Eastern empire. However, under the leadership of Emperor Justin I (518–27), relations between Rome and Constantinople were mended, and Chalcedonian orthodoxy ultimately prevailed in imperial regions, though non-Chalcedonian views persisted in Egypt.

Roman Emperor Heraclius (610–41) sought to strengthen his position in Egypt and to suppress non-Chalcedonian views by the appointment of a new Alexandrian bishop: Cyrus, who was serving as bishop of Phasis. With imperial approval, Cyrus tyrannized the Copts from 631 to 642. The Coptic patriarch, Benjamin I (623–62), had to stay in the remote monastery of Thebaid to escape Cyrus's brutality. Unfortunately, many Coptic leaders and monks did not escape the imperial persecution.

The Arab Conquest. The collapse of the imperial forces before the Arabs in 640–41 shocked the people of Egypt. In 642, Alexandria surrendered to the invaders and accepted their status as a subject people. However, the Muslim conquerors endeared themselves to the native population when they allowed the return of their bishop, Benjamin I, who had been forced into hiding during Cyrus's leadership of Alexandria. The Arabs were not interested in the Christians' theological disputes, only in the political advantages the situation afforded and in the opportunity to draw taxes from the Christians (both general tribute and a poll tax). By granting the Melchite Christians and the Copts the same status, the Arabs secured a stability that suited their interests. Under this new arrangement, the Copts paid fewer taxes to Arabs than they had to the Romans.

Increases in taxes by later rulers, however, led to discontent among the Copts. Rebellions between 739 and 773 led to brutal suppression, as did the later Bashmuric uprising around 830. Over time, the tax policy, which became increasingly burdensome, led to conversions of convenience to Islam. In 869, the last 'Abbasid governor demanded a lump sum of tribute from Patriarch Sanutians (859–80) to cover all the clergy and monks. A patriarchal delegation to Baghdad helped secure exemption for religious leaders.

In 969, the Fatimids invaded Egypt. They established Cairo as an imperial center. Caliph al-Mu'izz (952–75) showed special kindness to the Copts, as did his son, who married a Christian. Al-'Aziz appointed Christians to important positions. Unfortunately, these kindnesses finally ended in brutal attacks upon Christians. The next caliph, al-Hakim (996–1021), brutally persecuted Christians, Jews, and Sunni Muslims.

When the crusaders took control of the Holy Land in the eleventh century, Muslim hostilities generally increased against Christians. During the time of Cyril II (1078–92), the Muslim ruler, Badr al-Jamali, requested that the Coptic patriarchate move from Alexandria to Cairo. This would keep the patriarch close and away from the coast, where the crusaders might land and take control of the Christian leader. On suspicion that the Copts were planning to rebel, Saladin, the Muslim general, had the Alexandrian Cathedral of St. Mark destroyed. Unfortunately, the Eastern Christians did not always receive ideal treatment from the crusaders when compared with the treatment they received from the Muslims.

After the First Crusades, the Copts experienced sometimes more, sometimes less persecution and suppression from the Ayyubid rulers (1169–1250). During this time, the Coptic language fell into greater disuse, except as a liturgical language. However, attempts to preserve Coptic resulted in unique literary output.

The years of Mamluk and Turkish rule were likewise difficult, and the survival of the Copts in the face of centuries of Muslim dominance is remarkable.

Ethiopian Christianity. After the account of the Ethiopian eunuch in Acts 8, which was noted and affirmed by Irenaeus and Eusebius of Caesarea (*Against Heresies* III.12.8; *Church History* II.2.13), there is virtual silence about the progress of Christianity in Ethiopia. The next report describes the missionary activity of Frumentius (c. 300–380) and of Aedesius, Syrians from Tyre, who reached Ethiopia in the fourth century (Rufinus, *Church History* 1.9). These two men befriended the Ethiopian ruler, who adopted Christianity for himself, opening the way for the conversion of his people. Athanasius of Alexandria consecrated Frumentius as the first bishop of the Ethiopians (c. 347), which established a long-term relationship with the Coptic Christians to the north. General confirmation of the change to Christianity is known from inscriptions and from coins minted under Ezana, king of Axum.

Once again, there is a period of silence about the history of the Ethiopian Christians until reports about nine monks from the Greek region of the Roman Empire. These men introduced Pachomian-style monasticism to the Ethiopians around 480. Numerous monasteries attribute their founding to these "Nine Saints." (For example, the monastery of Debro Damo was attributed to Apa Michael Aragawi.) Later, kings in the sixth century spread Christianity through successful military campaigns in Yemen. Portions of the Bible were likely translated into Ethiopic at this time.

The coming of Islam in the seventh century likely cut off the Ethiopian Christians from interaction with Coptic and imperial representatives. Inscriptional evidence shows that Muslims reached the interior of the country by 1006. Yet the Ethiopian highlands provided an effective barrier against Muslim conquest. Almost nothing is known about the next six hundred years, until the Zagwe dynasty appeared (1137–1270). During this period, the famous rock-hewn churches were created, an accomplishment attributed to King Lalibela (1190–1225). In 1270, a Solomonic Dynasty was established, attributing its origins to the descendents of King Solomon and the queen of Sheba. Their story is recorded in *The Glory of Kings*.

In 1441 and 1442, Ethiopian monks from Jerusalem traveled to Italy to witness the Council of Florence (1438–45), where representatives discussed possible reunifications of Eastern and Western churches, though these efforts did not bear immediate fruit.

CHAPTER THREE

The Church of the Middle Ages
GROWTH AND CHANGE FROM 600 TO 1400

For many people, the term "medieval" carries with it romantic associations of a remote age characterized by knights in armor, lordly princes, and imposing castles, all supported by exploited serfs who were forced to till the rocky soil. For many contemporaries, the term has also become identified with that which seems archaic, irrelevant, impractical, or even benighted.

Before embarking on a description of the Church of the Middle Ages, it may be helpful to discuss some presuppositions often harbored by the average modern reader concerning this period. First, one sometimes encounters the notion that the Medieval Church (and society as well) was a static, monolithic institution that remained unchanged for nearly a thousand years. The assumption is often made that people lived and thought exactly the same in 600 as in 1400. The present study will attempt to show that the Church in these centuries was dynamic, ever changing, and in constant flux.

Second, modern man often sees the Medieval Church as something existing apart from the political and economic world of its time—but at the same time as an institution that possessed unlimited power and a monopoly control over men's thoughts. The role of the clergy is often stressed to the point where craftsmen, merchants, serfs, and kings were largely directed by the Church, which stood outside of society and manipulated it. In reality, the Church was inextricably a part of the society in which it lived, and for centuries, popes, bishops, and priests were actually dominated by princes and subject to lay control.

The third modern myth concerning the Medieval Church suggests that it devoted itself to turning men's minds away from the present world to a supernatural, future life in heaven. Those who foster this view often claim that the medieval man's lot in life was so burdensome he had no choice but to take refuge in the hope of future bliss. In reality, the Church of this period was probably no more "future oriented" than the Church of any other age.

These three presuppositions regarding the Medieval Church are largely the result of Renaissance humanism. That is, historians of the sixteenth and seventeenth centuries tended to repudiate the millennium that preceded them in order to return to the patterns of civilization of Greece and Rome. This attitude also affected some theologians, who tended to glorify the Ancient Church as a kind of golden age of Christianity. In order to make antiquity appear more desirable, they tended to color the Middle Ages extremely dark, so that into modern times the very term "medieval"

90 /

has retained overtones of static traditionalism and unrefined barbarity, which the facts of history do not bear out.

It may not be misrepresenting modern men to say that the Medieval Church is often interpreted according to one's religious attitude—whether Protestant, Roman Catholic, or secular humanist. The Protestant registers disapproval of the Medieval Church because he believes it departed from the alleged purity of the patristic age, and it was therefore necessary for a Reformation to purge the Church of corruption and malpractice. In so doing, he tends to cast the reformers in a heroic stance, battling against dark and malevolent forces. The Roman Catholic may tend to look upon this period as a golden age, an "age of faith," when men revered the Church and followed her unchanging laws. The secularist objects to the supposed otherworldliness of the Medieval Church and its authoritarianism, both of which seem to be contrary to the modern age of science and democracy. All three views—Protestant, Roman Catholic, and secularist—are based upon a kind of mythical Medieval Church that actually never existed. It is a purpose of this section to present the Church as it developed, with the hope that the reader will be able to assess its true nature with sympathetic understanding.

It is difficult to defend any single set of dates for the beginning and end of the Middle Ages, and historians have rarely agreed on determining its limits. This study begins with AD 600 because by this time, the West was relatively stable politically, the first wave of barbarian invaders had ceased, and Western Europe was beginning to develop its own unique culture. On the other hand, by AD 1400, the most distinctly medieval traits had either died or were in the process of radical change. Feudalism had already given way to capitalism, and new national states were emerging from older tribes and kingdoms. The Church in the fourteenth century was entering a new stage of ferment, which would ultimately result in the Reformation.

Between the years 600 and 1400, Western Christianity was concentrated in the lands bordered by the Atlantic on the west; the Vistula, Theiss, and Adriatic on the east; the Mediterranean on the south; and the Baltic on the north. At the beginning of this period, however, Christianity was largely confined to the Mediterranean basin. This chapter is the story of the expansion of Christianity northward, setting the stage for the drama of the Medieval Church.

The Setting. Christianity was born into a politically stable world during the time of the *Pax Romana*. For over three centuries, the Church developed within the confines of the Roman Empire. Although Christian missionaries occasionally crossed the boundaries of the empire to evangelize the barbarian tribes, the Church in the West remained largely centered in the Mediterranean basin.

By the year 600, this situation had changed. The unity of the empire had been shattered by the influx of German tribes, who had crossed the Rhine and were in the process of establishing themselves as independent states: the Burgundians in the Rhone Valley, the Visigoths in Spain and southern France, and the Vandals in North Africa. Italy had already come under the domination of the Lombards thirty years before, though the Eastern Roman Empire (Byzantium) still controlled southern Italy and Sicily. All of these tribes had been converted to Arianism, a heretical form of Christianity, and when they settled among the orthodox Roman inhabitants, a religious dimension was added to the frictions that naturally arose between them.

The Franks dominated France and the low countries. Although they had adopted orthodox Christianity under Clovis (about AD 496), it had been more in the nature of a political conversion than an espousal of the Christian faith and way of life. To the north of the Franks lived the fierce Saxon tribes, who were still devotees of Teutonic nature religions. To the east, extending through modern Russia, lay the kingdom of the Slavs and Avars, who likewise worshiped their tribal gods. Orthodox Christianity was strongest south of the Danube and in the eastern provinces stretching through Asia Minor, Syria, and Egypt and to the borders of Persia.

The isles of Great Britain had been invaded by the Picts, Scots, and Angles during the fifth century. By the year 600, these tribes had sorted themselves out into seven small kingdoms known collectively as the Heptarchy. Although Christianity had made an appearance in Britain by the year 300, the invaders had forced the Christians to flee to western England, where they maintained a separate existence.

Despite the fact that barbarian hordes had threatened the unity of the West, no one at this time considered the empire either to be divided or to have "fallen." Since 476, there had been only one emperor, and he lived in Constantinople. He was acknowledged as the supreme ruler from Britain to Persia, although this homage was often merely token. The emperor's "presence" in the West was through a representative known as the exarch, who resided in Ravenna.

The Conversion of Great Britain. We are fortunate to have a full account of the early English Church from the Venerable Bede, who wrote during the eighth century. He reports that in 596, Gregory the Great sent the monk Augustine with forty companions to reconvert England after seeing angelic-faced "Angles" for sale as slaves in a Roman market.

Augustine and his companions arrived in Kent early in 597, where they were given a cordial reception by King Ethelbert and his Christian wife, Queen Bertha. The missionary was invited to an audience held in the open because the king feared magical trickery indoors. Soon afterward, Ethelbert was converted, and at Christmastime, ten thousand of his followers were also baptized. Augustine established the monastery of St. Peter and St. Paul at Canterbury to serve as a center of evangelistic activities, and eventually it became the mother church of all England. Inasmuch as the mission had been under the auspices of Pope Gregory, the new converts came under the primacy of Rome, using its liturgy and following its practices. But Gregory did not insist on this.

Gregory also permitted Augustine to adapt the old pagan customs to Christian uses, such as the heathen Yule and the practice of sacrifices. The latter were henceforth to be permitted only "in praise of the true God." The correspondence between Gregory and Augustine reveals a great deal about early Christian mission methods and attitudes. In his instructions to Augustine, Gregory sets down the rules for the distribution of the Church's funds, which became normative for the Medieval Church.

It is significant that fully one-fourth of all revenues was to be used for the poor, and when one takes into consideration that the bishop's "hospitality" likewise included relief of the destitute, it appears that fully one-third of the church's income was theoretically to be used for social work.

Augustine was confronted with more than the problem of evangelizing the pagans. When he arrived in England, he also found remnants of the older Celtic Church, which had managed to survive the invasions of the fifth century. The Celtic bishops were suspicious of the newcomers from Rome, especially since their liturgy and customs differed from the old English. For instance, they disagreed on the date of Easter, on the manner of the tonsure (the cut of hair indicating a man was in holy orders), and in church organization. Furthermore, the Celtic bishops were not at all enthusiastic about Augustine's mission work among the Anglo-Saxons, who had so long oppressed them.

Bede tells a story that reveals something of the spirit of those times. The Celtic bishops asked an old monk whether they should submit to Augustine or not. The monk replied, "Yes, if he is a man of God." "How can we tell?" they asked. "If he is gentle and humble of heart," the monk answered. They asked how that could be determined. "Arrange it so that Augustine and his men arrive first at your meeting place. If he stands up when you arrive, it will prove that he is a servant of Christ. In that case, do as he bids you." Unfortunately, Augustine failed to rise as he greeted the Celts, and they refused to accept his leadership. In fact, mutual hostility continued for at least another century, and the Welsh Christians refused to pray in the same churches as the Latins or eat meals with them.

About 630, King Edwin of Northumbria, the land north of the Humber River, married a Christian girl from Kent. She brought with her the monk Paulinus, who converted the king's court and introduced Christianity into the north country, establishing a second center of Christianity at York, which subsequently became England's second archepiscopal see.

But the real missionary of the north was Aiden, who established a monastery on Lindisfarne, an island on the east coast of Scotland. Aiden had come from Iona, the center of Celtic Christianity, so that much of northern England and Scotland began to follow the old English customs instead of the Latin forms more recently introduced by Augustine in the south. In 664, a conference was held at the monastery of Whitby on the Northumbrian coast, at which representatives of the two sides met to discuss and resolve their differences.

The meeting was chaired by the Northumbrian king, Oswald. Abbot Colman, Aiden's successor at Lindisfarne, defended the Celtic practices, and Abbot Wilfrid of Ripon supported the Roman usages. The king was to judge the outcome. The two sides debated at some length, until finally Wilfrid appealed to the primacy of

Peter and to Matthew 16:19 ("I will give you the keys of the kingdom of heaven") in support of the Roman practices. Whether this is accurate it is impossible to judge, but the Synod of Whitby did establish the Roman usages in the island. By 700, England was nominally Christian and followed the Latin customs. Shortly after this synod, the pope sent Theodore of Tarsus as archbishop of Canterbury to organize the church by establishing dioceses and consecrating bishops. To him belongs the credit for bringing order and discipline to the English Church, although Celtic Christianity maintained its independence from Rome for centuries, notably in Wales and Scotland.

The origins of Christianity in Ireland are uncertain, but Patrick of Armagh (d. 461) is credited with establishing the Church among the Irish clans. He was born in England about 389, son of a deacon and grandson of a presbyter. At age 16, he was carried off during a raid by some pirates and sold to a devotee of druidism in Ireland. Here, for seven years he tended swine, which, a biographer informs us, became exceptionally good breeders. After being reunited with his parents, Patrick went off to Gaul, where he spent fifteen years with Germanus of Auxerre, learning theology and secular literature. He was consecrated a bishop and returned to Ireland to preach.

The accounts of his missionary activities, mostly written years later, are filled with legends and miracles. According to his own account, Patrick baptized thousands, ordained many priests, and preached throughout the island. He followed a dual method in his approach to the pagan: aiming at the conversion of the heads of clans and establishing numerous monasteries. Patrick established himself in the See of Armagh, which became the mother church for Ireland. Since towns or urban centers were practically nonexistent, Christianity radiated from monastic centers, which in turn became the administrative centers of the Church. Therefore, in Ireland it was the abbot, not the bishop, who guided the central administration, which was based on tribal and clannish units instead of dioceses. The pope was referred to as the "abbot of Rome," and occasionally Christ was called "the great abbot of God."

Irish monasticism was characterized by a severity that rivaled that of the Egyptian desert. It is here that we first find the practice of private Confession and Absolution and the emergence of a penitential system. Irish Christianity was also marked by a strong individualism, having considerably weaker ties with Rome than the English Church had. During the sixth and seventh centuries, the Irish monasteries became centers of learning and repositories of culture, giving the island ever after the title "isle of saints and scholars."

From Ireland, monks carried the faith to Scotland. In 563, an Irishman, Columba, together with twelve companions, established a monastery on Iona, a small (six square miles) island off the west coast of Scotland. During the thirty-four years that he labored at Iona, Columba and his disciples established over one hundred churches and monasteries in Scotland and northern England. The oldest literary composition from Scotland, the *Altus Prosater* (the Great Creator), has been attributed to

Columba. It speaks of creation, sin, and judgment and is arranged so that each line begins with the succeeding letter of the alphabet.

In 635, some monks from Iona laid the foundations for the famous monastery at Lindisfarne, which became a second center of Celtic mission activities. Iona continued to flourish until the dissolution of the monasteries by Henry VIII in the sixteenth century.

The Continent. By the fifth century, Christianity in Gaul was well over three hundred years old, but the Church had fallen on evil days. Clovis, the leader of the Franks, had been given Christian Baptism, together with three thousand of his men, by the bishop of Rheims. They succeeded in baptizing most of the barbarian tribes between Paris and the Pyrenees. Under the Merovingians, as the descendants of Clovis are known to history, Christianity expanded, but the secular princes thoroughly dominated the Church. Christianity was often but a thin veneer covering a still vital Teutonic paganism. When the Merovingians exchanged their old German gods for Christ, they were simply following an old Roman custom of adopting the religion of the ruler without experiencing a moral or intellectual conversion.

The most important historian of this period, Gregory of Tours (d. 594), describes the late sixth century in the prologue to his *History of the Franks*. Gregory noted how avaricious laymen with the help of the king established themselves as abbots and bishops and how the gross manners of the nobility undermined Christian morality throughout the land.

Columban. This was the situation in Gaul when on a summer's day in 575, a shipload of Irish monks landed near Mont Saint-Michel. Their leader was Columban, a physical giant and a moral rigorist who was determined to revive the Gallican Church by preaching, moral example, disputation, and occasionally through feats of strength. Columban and his companions were the first wave of hundreds of Irish and English monks who were to cross the channel during the next two centuries to do mission work on the Continent. The inspiration for this activity came from a principle of the monastic vocation, which was unique to the Celts, the *peregrinatio pro Christo*, voluntary exile for the purpose of spreading the Gospel. The theory seems to have been akin to the Early Church's idea of "white martyrdom," as contrasted with blood martyrdom. Since the state was no longer persecuting the Christians, it behooved those who sought to test their faith to seek out other dangerous situations that demanded courage and privation. One of the best opportunities for heroic faith was presented by the challenge of multitudes who were still living in the clutches of paganism. It was here, in the vast stretches of European forests and marshes, that many missionary-monks succumbed to martyrdom in the pursuit of their apostolate.

Columban established a monastic house of Luxeuil in Gaul, which served as a center for the revival of Christianity and the conversion of the pagans. The Celts encountered considerable hostility from the neighboring bishops, not only because their mission was a judgment upon the existing church, but also because they followed the Celtic assumption that the abbot was superior to any bishop. The Irish also asserted their independence from episcopal control by observing a different date for Easter than that of the Gallican Church. In fact, Columban took it upon himself to write to Pope Gregory the Great in imperious terms.

Columban's rigorism can be seen reflected especially in the rule he laid down for his monks. Whoever failed to make the sign of the cross over his spoon at dinner was punished with six strokes of the lash, and whoever did not kneel to receive a blessing when entering or leaving the monastery received twelve strokes. There were likewise punishments for failure to say grace at table, and remarks that detracted from the abbot were classified with homicide. In 603, the Gallican bishops called a council to discipline Columban, but when he appeared, he fearlessly lectured the assembled prelates on their vices. He went too far, however, when he threatened the king with excommunication and denounced the vicious life of Queen Brunhilde, calling her a new Jezebel. She expelled him from Gaul, but he succeeded in jumping ship, traversing the length of Gaul, and founding a new monastery on Lake Constance, which became known as St. Gall after Gall, who accompanied him. After three years, Columban left there and established another monastery at Bobbio in Lombardy, where he died in 615. Altogether, this heroic saint established over forty monasteries, which served as mission centers in Europe.

The first territory to be evangelized outside the old Roman boundaries on the Continent was Belgium, Holland, and the coasts of the North Sea inhabited by the Frisians. About 690, an Anglo-Saxon who had spent twelve years in an Irish monastery arrived on the shores of Frisia with eleven companions. He was Willibrord, known to history as the "Apostle of Frisia." Three years later, he traveled to Rome to secure papal authorization and support for his work, and shortly after this visit, he was consecrated an archbishop, with Utrecht as his center of operations. Thus Willibrord inaugurated that alliance between the papacy and Anglo-Saxon mission endeavors, which would closely bind the continental church to the authority of the Roman See. Willibrord was also supported in his work by Pepin, king of the Franks, who was not above using Christianity as an instrument for Frankish expansion.

Boniface. The best known and most successful Anglo-Saxon missionary was Winfrid of Nursling, later known as Boniface, who for thirty years consolidated the existing churches and pushed the frontiers of Christianity north to Scandinavia. He was born in Wessex about 680 and from age 5 was reared in English monasteries. In 716, he went to Frisia to assist Willibrord for a short time. He worked closely with the popes, maintaining a regular and detailed correspondence with Rome. In 722, he was consecrated bishop and in 732 archbishop, having as his sphere of operation that part of Germany east of the Rhine and north of the Danube. Pope Gregory II had outlined Boniface's mission of teaching.

Five years later, Boniface received a letter from the bishop of Winchester, advising him on the proper approach to the pagans. The bishop warned against arguing with the pagans about their gods, as this would merely antagonize them. Rather, the missionary should frequently remind them of the works of the Christian God, the universality of the faith, and the omnipotence of the Creator. On at least one occasion, Boniface took more direct action by cutting down the Oak of Jupiter at Geismar.

Like other Anglo-Saxons before him, Boniface was supported by the Carolingian rulers who tended to identify Christian Baptism with acknowledgment of Frankish control. For several years, Boniface traveled under the safe conduct of Charles Martel. It was this identification of Christianity with a political system that caused the faith to be resisted in some quarters.

Boniface used monks as his missionaries, though he began the practice of using women evangelists as well, and he established more than sixty monastic houses in Germany. The most famous of these was at Fulda, established in 743 as the mother-house of Germany, where Boniface's tomb remains to this day. In 747, he established an archepiscopal see at Mainz, which became the center of German Christianity. After 741, he undertook a thorough reform of the Franco-German Church by holding a series of five councils in which laymen participated alongside bishops. In 751, he anointed Pepin the Short, father of Charlemagne, as king of the Franks, thus inaugurating the long line of Carolingian kings who would dominate European affairs for two centuries. Already in his midseventies, he decided to return to Frisia to continue evangelism there. While waiting for some converts to arrive to receive confirmation, he was set upon by some pagans and murdered, thus sealing his lifelong labors with "red martyrdom."

Saxony and Scandinavia. The conversion of the Saxons was associated with Frankish imperialism more than any other missionary enterprise on the Continent. In 772, Charlemagne undertook a campaign against the Saxons in order to "win them for Christ" by force of arms and through the destruction of their idols. Missionaries were sent into Westphalia to begin the work of evangelism, and hostages were taken from the Saxons to ensure their safety. Two of the monks sent to preach were Willehad and Sturmio. In 777 at Paderborn, most of the Saxon chieftains submitted to Charlemagne, and the sign of their submission was the reception of Christian Baptism. One leader, Widukind, was absent, and he became the center of Saxon resistance to Charlemagne and Christianity. For the next eight years, Widukind and his men raided Frankish territory, penetrating as far as the left bank of the Rhine, while Charlemagne was engaged elsewhere in defense of his kingdom. In 782, the king of the Franks lost all restraint when he beheaded forty-five hundred Saxons for being traitors and murderers. Finally in 785, Widukind's resistance was broken, and the Saxon received Christian Baptism. It was about this time that Charlemagne took his revenge by promulgating the bloody Capitulary [ordinance] on Saxony.

But this repressive measure was not without its critics. Alcuin, Charlemagne's chief counselor, wrote to Charlemagne's chamberlain that if the sweet Gospel of Christ were preached with as much vigor as Charlemagne's laws were enforced, perhaps the Saxons would be more easily converted. Apparently, Alcuin's admonitions were heeded, since the king very shortly repealed or mitigated the Capitulary on the Saxons. Thus the way was opened for the last great apostle to Saxony: Liudger [Ludger] (d. 809), a pupil of Alcuin, who became the bishop of Münster. Two of his disciples, Adalhard and Wala, founded the monastery of New Corbie, which served as a missionary center for Saxony as Fulda had for northern Germany.

The conversion of the Saxons paved the way for the evangelization of Scandinavia, which was inaugurated through a fortuitous diplomatic negotiation. King Harald [Harold] of Denmark sought the aid of Louis the Pious, son of Charlemagne, in his contest for the Danish throne. Louis suggested that aid would be assured if Harald would espouse the Christian faith, and in May of 826 Bishop Ebbo of Rheims baptized the Danish king, his family, and four hundred warriors. The way was thus opened for Ansgar, a monk of New Corbie, to begin preaching the Gospel in Denmark and Sweden. In 831, the pope created Hamburg an archepiscopal see to serve as a center for Scandinavian missions, and Ansgar became its first archbishop. Several years later, the new center was destroyed by Norse pirates, and in 848 Pope Nicholas I established Hamburg-Bremen as a united archdiocese for the work of missions to the north. Ansgar, who continued his work until his death in 865, has become known to historians as the "Apostle of the North." The eradication of paganism in Sweden took much longer than in the rest of Scandinavia. In the twelfth century, the Cistercian monks took a lead in the work, and it was not until 1164 that Sweden received its first metropolitan see when Pope Alexander III conferred this dignity on Uppsala.

The conversion of Denmark was facilitated when the German emperor Otto I defeated Harald, king of the Danes, in the middle of the tenth century. The conversion of Norway came about from its close ties with England rather than from the Continent. King Haakon the Good (938–61), who was raised and educated as a Christian at the Anglo-Saxon court, was unsuccessful in his attempts to convert the Norsemen, but King Olaf Tryggvesson (995–1000), who was baptized in England, and King Olaf Haroldsson (St. Olaf, 1014–30) did much to spread Christianity in Norway. Tryggvesson, according to the chronicler, first elicited a promise from his men to follow him in whatever he did. Then he announced that he would become a Christian and punish those who did not follow him into the new faith. This same king, perhaps inspired by the example of Boniface, convinced a large number of doubters on one occasion when he pushed over a statue of the god Thor without suffering any reprisals from the impotent statue. Christianity became even more firmly rooted in the north when Canute of Denmark, a staunch Christian and supporter of the papacy, was sole ruler of Norway, Denmark, and England (1016–30). Lund, the center of Christian missions in Norway, became an independent archbishopric in 1104. Iceland received Christianity from Norway during the time Tryggvesson was king. The missionary who is given credit for this work is Dankbrand of Bremen. He succeeded in winning over a number of pagans to Christian Baptism, but his most important convert was the king of Iceland, who made it a law that one had to become a Christian.

Missions to the East. During the course of the eighth century, Christian expansion to the East closely followed the victorious armies of Charlemagne, although the real task of evangelization was left to later Carolingians. In 805, Charlemagne conquered the Czechs, and in 845, fourteen Czech chieftains were baptized in Regensburg at the court of Charlemagne's grandson. The Avars were conquered by Charles in 796 and accepted the faith, but they became absorbed by their Slavic neighbors and by the ninth century had lost their identity.

Of great interest to missiologists is the conversion of Moravia and Bohemia by two celebrated brothers, Cyril and Methodius. Frankish missionaries had ventured into these territories already during the eighth century but with little success. In 863, King Ratislav of Moravia petitioned the Eastern emperor for missionaries to preach the Gospel, and he was sent Cyril and Methodius. They had grown up in Thessalonica and were familiar with the Slavic customs and language. Cyril invented an alphabet (today called Cyrillic, the ancestor of modern Russian) and translated portions of the Bible and liturgy into Slavonic. After four years of fruitful activity in Moravia, they were summoned to Rome by the pope, who sanctioned their liturgy and ordained them bishops. This incident illustrates that in the ninth century, Christendom was still considered a unity, and the East acknowledged the preeminence of the papacy. Cyril died in 869, but Methodius returned to become the first archbishop of Moravia. From there, Christianity spread into Bohemia. In the work of these two brothers, we see some marked differences in approach between the Eastern and Western missionaries. Cyril and Methodius developed a new language and liturgy as teaching devices. The faith was presented to the people not as a foreign element but rather as something indigenous to their culture. We also know that the Eastern missionaries were far more concerned with presenting dogma to the pagans than were the Westerners. On the debit side, the Eastern missionaries were sent by their ruler and were under his tutelage, whereas in the West they maintained a sense of independence from political control (though they used the political arm when it suited their purposes).

Bulgaria was evangelized at the same time as Moravia and Bohemia. King Boris received Christian Baptism about 865, after his kingdom had been conquered by the Eastern emperor. In order to assert his independence from Eastern control, he suggested to the pope that Bulgaria follow the Latin forms of Christianity, provided the pope would establish a patriarchal see in Bulgaria equal in dignity to Constantinople. The pope refused to do this, and Bulgaria reverted to the Eastern customs. In 870, a Bulgar archbishop was consecrated by the Eastern patriarch, and by 900 the kingdom was at least nominally Christian. Bulgaria became the center of missions to the Slavs.

The Saxonian emperors of Germany (919–1024) promoted the eastward expansion of Christianity as a means of extending their territorial control. Some historians see in this policy the beginnings of the German "drive to the East," which has played a large part in European history. Otto I (936–73) first spread Christianity, and with it

German influence, into Denmark, where he founded three new bishoprics. Pushing to the East, he organized five "marches" (frontier states) along the Slavic border, at the same time establishing six new bishoprics, including Magdeburg and Brandenburg. In 968, the first Polish bishopric was erected by Otto at Posen. Although the first bishops there were German, the Poles succeeded in maintaining their ecclesiastical independence by resisting Otto's efforts to make Posen subject to Magdeburg. Hungary was evangelized by German missionaries sent by Otto II (973–83), who negotiated a treaty with Duke Geisa permitting missionaries to enter the territory. Geisa's son was the famous Stephen (997–1038), who became the founder of Christian Hungary. Thus the Eastward thrust of Christianity owed much to the initiative of the German Saxon princes, who like Charlemagne combined conversion with colonization.

Russia derived its faith from Constantinople and the Greeks. During the middle of the ninth century, Scandinavian "Vikings" settled around Kiev, which subsequently became their capital and the center of Russian Christianity. It was these Norsemen who organized and controlled this territory, and one version of the name Russia derives from the Slavic name for the Scandinavians, Ruotsi. About the year 987, King Vladimir, in order to derive the benefits of a superior Greek culture, married the sister of the Eastern emperor and allowed himself to be baptized. He together with his men forcibly rooted out the worship of idols, and they introduced into Russia the Slavonic Bible and liturgy, which had come to them from Cyril via Moravia and Bulgaria. The Russian Church was therefore closely allied with Byzantine Christianity, but it retained its own language, customs, and rites.

Islam and Spain. While Christianity was slowly spreading from its Mediterranean cradle to the less hospitable areas of Russia, Europe, and Britain, more spectacular events were taking place farther south and east. There lived in Mecca, a city in Arabia, a caravan trader named Muhammad who claimed to have revelations from God. He began to preach the doctrines of resurrection, monotheism, and justice toward the poor. He also taught that God, or Allah, had manifested himself through great religious leaders in the past, including Jesus of Nazareth. Allah's final and complete manifestation had come in Muhammad. In 622, he was expelled from Mecca, partly because of his lofty social ethics, and he went to Medina (the City of the Prophet). This event, known as the *Hegira*, is usually taken as the starting point of Islam. Muhammad died in Medina in 632.

Thirty years after the *Hegira*, a collection of Muhammad's sayings called the Qur'an ("recitation") was made; this became the bible of the religion. Muhammad's followers were known as Muslims, meaning "he who submits himself utterly to God," and the religion was called Islam. The five pillars of the faith are the profession of faith (there is no god but Allah, and Muhammad is his prophet); a ritual prayer; almsgiving; the fast of the month of Ramadan; and a pilgrimage to Mecca, the holy city of the Muslims. They developed the idea of the *jihad*, or "holy war," to spread the faith. Paradise was depicted in highly materialistic, even sensual, terms. A believer who fell in battle contending for the faith was said to enter heaven directly and enjoy privileged rewards. Part of Islam's attractiveness lay in its stringent morality, its discipline, and its simplicity. Muhammad borrowed a great deal from Judaism and Christianity in his preaching, and this syncretism probably commended the faith to dissidents from the other religions.

The rapid spread of Islam was breathtaking. The Arab army, impelled by religious idealism, swept everything before it. Damascus fell in 635, Jerusalem in 638, Alexandria in 643, and by 711, all of North Africa had capitulated. The Muslims also swept northward to Constantinople and seemed destined to conquer the very capital of Eastern Christianity when they were defeated before the walls of the city in 718 by Emperor Leo III (the Isaurian). Thereafter, Constantinople served as a bulwark against Islam for Christian Europe until she fell to the Turks in 1453 and the Muslims continued as far as Vienna (1529).

To what can we attribute the rapid decline of Christianity in the lands of Tertullian, Cyprian, Origen, Athanasius, and a host of noble martyrs? Although the Bedouin armies were well organized and formidable, a large part of the answer lies in the religious and political particularism of Egypt and North Africa. Nominally, these areas were part of the Eastern Roman Empire, but they never felt especially loyal to Byzantium, which was oppressive and interfering in its control. In some cases, the North Africans looked upon the Muslims as deliverers instead of conquerors. The North African Church had also become alienated from both Rome and Constantinople. During the sixth century, when Eastern Christianity had been torn by a number of theological dissensions over the nature of Christ, the emperors had tried to impose a uniform orthodox dogma on the empire. The Africans, ever jealous of their independence, resented such interference. When the Muslims conquered a town, they often permitted the Christians a great deal of latitude in belief, granting them the toleration that had been denied by the Christian emperors. Furthermore, the African Church was itself torn by internal strife, offering weak opposition when confronted by Islam. Christianity died out, and by 1050 there were only five bishops left in all of Africa, their flocks comprising foreign merchants and Christian prisoners.

The fall of Spain followed that of Africa, but it was even more rapid. In 711, the Muslim general Tarik crossed the straits of Jebel—whence the modern Gibraltar (Jebel-Tarik). Within nine years, the Muslims dominated the peninsula, and they continued northward into France until they were stopped by Charles Martel in 732 at the Battle of Tours. Three reasons are often suggested for the demise of Christian Spain. Like their coreligionists in Africa, the Christians of Spain could think of nothing else than fighting each other on points of doctrine, while Islam used one side against the other. The Spanish Church was also closely identified with the state, that is, the ruling Visigoths. When the state fell, the Church fell with it. It is also a fact that the Jews had been oppressed by the Christians through forced conversions and Baptisms, and they tended to side with the Muslims. But Christianity was not eclipsed altogether. Pockets of resistance remained to form the nucleus of reconquest. The Spanish Church developed its own liturgy and customs, which have been given the name Mozarabic, and throughout much of the medieval period the Muslims, Jews, and Christians in Spain lived side by side in relative harmony. Spain was the door through which classical influences entered Europe to inspire the renaissance of the twelfth century, a reawakening that owed much to the culture of Islam. But the Christians continued to resist the infidels. One heroic figure in the reconquest of Spain is the famous El Cid (Ruy Diaz de Bivar), who in the late eleventh century played a conspicuous part in pushing the Muslims out of Castille. Not until 1492, when Ferdinand and Isabella finally expelled the Muslims from Granada, was Spain again nominally Christian. From the seventh to the eleventh centuries the Mediterranean was controlled by the Muslims. They displaced the Byzantines in southern Italy; the islands of Sicily, Sardinia, and Corsica likewise succumbed to their control. This situation prevailed until the early twelfth century, when the Norsemen established themselves in southern Italy.

Mission Methods. When Christian missionaries ventured into pagan territory, they first established a self-sufficient monastic community, planted crops, acquired herds, and built buildings. Using the monastery as their home base, they traveled wide stretches of territory, contacting pagans wherever they could be found. Their numbers were usually small. Among the Benedictines and the Irish, twelve men were required to found a monastery. One can trace the activities of the Anglo-Saxon missionaries on the Continent by noting the monastic houses they established. The missionaries remained in close contact with their motherhouse, never wandering too far from their center. This was true of Willibrord, Liudger, Willibald, and Wynnebald; provisions were made for their return to the monastery to report on their activities. The lists of missionaries at Salzburg gives evidence that they also had adopted a system of rotation.

What was the content of missionary preaching? After a group of pagans had been assembled, they were addressed in their native tongue. A primary objective was undermining the pagan religion by demonstrating its impotence through a comparison with Christianity. The missionaries do not seem to have spent much time expounding Christian theology on the assumption that this could wait until after Baptism. Alcuin deplored this lack and suggested that Christianity might be more readily accepted if doctrine were taught first. This omission did not hold in the East, where Cyril, Methodius, and their disciples spent much time indoctrinating their converts in the Trinity, Christology, and the Church. In the West, the attacks against idolatry were sometimes accompanied by actual destruction: witness Boniface at the oak of Geismar and Tryggvesson's toppling of Thor. The missionaries also painted heaven and hell in vivid colors for their impressionable hearers.

The missionary endeavor was certainly assisted by the strong arm of the state, which at least created a situation favorable to evangelism. We must be careful not to judge these kings too harshly. They were genuine Christians convinced that God had given them material power to carry on the spread of Christianity. They looked upon the Church as the City of God, as an island surrounded by a sea of pagans. It was their responsibility to bring more and more pagans into the fold by whatever means. They were convinced that their position was that of a wise father, who at times had to use force for the good of the child. Their brand of evangelistic imperialism should not be equated with the more cynical type pursued during the nineteenth century. The missionaries could not depend upon continued support from the state in any case, because eventually the armies of occupation would have to be withdrawn for service elsewhere, and the evangelist was invariably left on his own.

With very few exceptions, the missionaries sought the conversion of the king and aristocracy first, since the chieftains usually determined the religious beliefs of the people. But we cannot help deploring the tactics used by many kings who imposed faith upon their people by force. Occasionally, we find Christians offering outright bribes to the pagans.

The moral examples and Christian integrity of the missionaries also impressed the pagans. Almost all the biographers of these pioneer evangelists stress the fact that the pagans were won over by their charity, patience, mercy, and superior way of life. Willibrord helped beggars. Boniface and Gregory braved warfare, pestilence, and famine with the people rather than flee to safer territory. Liudger ate with paupers as well as with the rich. Willibrord restrained his followers from killing a man who had just made an attempt on his life. It is clear that many of the missionaries cultivated a close personal bond with their converts, and multitudes flocked to their tombs after death.

By the beginning of the twelfth century, Christianity had triumphed over paganism in most of Europe, at least to the extent that in many minds, Christendom and Europe were synonymous.

The Church in Feudal Society

Feudalism is a comprehensive term used to describe the European structure of society roughly between 900 and 1200. It was never planned coherently nor did medieval men think in terms of a broad feudal theory. The word itself was not coined until the nineteenth century.

Basically, feudalism was derived from two distinct traditions—Roman and Germanic—involving personal and economic bonds. The personal element came from the late Roman practice of patronage, whereby an aristocrat surrounded himself with clients who served him while he in turn saw to their needs. A similar tradition was known among the Germans, whose leaders were attended by a circle of warriors called the *Gefolge* (or *comitatus*). In both cases, the bond between leader and follower was expressed through a personal oath of loyalty. When the fusion of cultures took place in the early Middle Ages, one institution passed over into the other, and the personal bond between a wealthy or powerful lord and his retainers became a fixed practice known as *vassalage,* which was entered into by the ceremony of *homage.* The

Church superimposed the oath of *fidelitas* (fealty), wherein the vassal swore on the Gospels, relics, or sacred objects to observe the terms of the contract.

The second basic ingredient of feudalism was the economic bond stemming from the Roman system of land tenure known as *precarium*. In the late empire, the tax burdens and other obligations of small landowners became so crushing that many of them deeded their land to large estate owners who then assumed their debts. The farmer retained the use of his land, but at his death it usually became the possession of the estate owner. Although the Germans had no comparable institution, their kings and war leaders often rewarded their followers by distributing large tracts of land to them, and in return, the user of the land was bound to supply the king with warriors or rent. The actual plot of land was at first called a *precaria*, but later it was known as a benefice, and when it became hereditable, a *fief*. It was a lease of land for a definite period of time in return for rent or services. The ceremony through which a man was given use of a fief was known as *investiture*. When the economic bond represented by the fief combined with the personal oath of loyalty in vassalage, Europe was well on its way toward feudalism. Charles Martel, grandfather of Charlemagne, is generally credited with effecting this combination. In the 720s, he confiscated large tracts of ecclesiastical lands to distribute among his dependent warriors, enabling them to raise more troops and defray their expenses. Charles demanded a pledge of personal loyalty as a precondition for receiving the use of the land.

Entering into a state of vassalage did not involve loss of prestige or social standing. Lords and vassals belonged to the same class of landed nobility. Most lords were also vassals. Such relationships often became quite complex, since one lord could be another's vassal on one piece of land, but their position might be reversed on a second holding. For instance, the king of England, who also happened to be the duke of Normandy in France, was a vassal of the king of France in Normandy, but he was his equal as king in England. On the other hand, the king of France might be England's vassal on other lands. Some princes held dozens of estates scattered throughout Europe, each involving a different set of loyalties and feudal contracts. A vassal was bound to fight for his lord, but when a man had many lords and they were fighting with one another, it became difficult for the vassal to choose whom to serve. The introduction of a *liege lord,* the one to whom a vassal owed first *allegiance,* served partially to clarify a man's loyalties in such circumstances. Such complexities were the source of endless litigation and frequent warfare among the feudal nobility.

Theoretically, the king stood at the apex of the feudal pyramid, but in actual practice the king's vassals were often more powerful than he. By 1000, the process of decentralization in France had progressed to the point where the king held only a small portion of land around Paris. William the Conqueror, who invaded England from Normandy in 1066, imposed a strongly centralized feudalism there. The Germanies also had strong kingship for most of the Middle Ages, but during the fourteenth century the cities and local princes asserted themselves, and by Luther's day there were over three hundred semiautonomous units that made up Germany.

It is clear that feudalism could function only so long as wealth was reckoned on the basis of land. By 1200, however, a commercial revolution had taken place, accompanied by the rise of many cities. With the increasing availability of money, it was no longer necessary to hold land in order to maintain oneself, and feudalism was on its way out. Together with the growth of capitalism, Europe witnessed a rising tide of nationalism and the emergence of strongly centralized national states. By 1300, England, Spain, and France were conscious of themselves as political units under the rule of strong monarchs.

Churches and the clergy, by holding lands under various forms of tenure, became a part of the feudal system. There was no alternative, for holding land was the sole means of support under this economy, but each "holding" carried with it the obligation of rent or service to each lord. Thus the Church became enmeshed, both as lord and vassal, in the feudal complex.

When a bishop or monastery functioned as a lord, there was often involved the management of thousands of acres of property farmed by many serfs on widely scattered manors. This meant that entire towns, forests, roads, waterways, fairs, and other economic assets would be under the supervision of clergymen. It also meant that the ecclesiastical lord was under obligation to protect the property and see to its improvement. In some cases, the more gifted clergy would rise to these administrative posts, leaving the lesser-talented men to serve the spiritual needs of the people.

Ecclesiastical lords were also vassals under obligation of service to other lords. This relationship resulted in count-bishops going to battle, having in their entourage numerous clergy-knights. Although canon law forbade the shedding of blood by a clergyman, the law was not always observed. Some scholars claim the use of the mace (a kind of club) helped salve the consciences of those clerics who at least wished to observe the letter of the law.

Abuses crept into the Church when kings or princes rewarded their secular vassals by bestowing church property on them. In a number of instances unworthy lords actually moved into monasteries with their families and friends, bringing serious disorder into the observances of the house.

Churches also accumulated land that carried no other obligations than prayer for those who gave it. Such holdings were called *immunities* since they were literally immune from most outside interference, or as a thirteenth-century historian described them, "lands in which the king's writ did not run." Naturally, acquisitive instincts prompted some churches to extend their properties, but others received great wealth in spite of themselves. A popular practice, especially among the elderly, was to deed property to a church or monastery with the understanding that the church would care for them in their old age and pray for them after death, when the property would become a permanent holding of the church. This practice, the medieval equivalent of social security, had the added advantage of prayers for the repose of the benefactors. Another source of land grants was the troubled consciences of princes who thereby hoped for clemency in eternity.

Theoretically, every church or monastery was under the jurisdiction of the local bishop, but in actual fact a large number of them were completely controlled by lay lords. Princes often built chapels on their property or in their castles, reserving to themselves the right to appoint the priest, often one of their own serfs, and to enjoy the revenues. These were called *proprietary* churches (*eigenkirchen*). It was shrewd business for a lay lord to found ecclesiastical establishments, for they returned to the owner considerable income with the added benefit of a reputation for piety. Monasteries likewise erected chapels and appointed priests, a practice that usually was detrimental to the local parish church.

The Papacy. The theoretical basis for papal power lay in the claims of the bishop of Rome to be the vicar of Christ on earth. This was based on Rome's interpretation of Christ's words to Peter (Matthew 16:13–19) and was given powerful expression by Innocent I (409–17), Leo I (440–61), and Gregory I (590–604). The theory of papal primacy was not fully realized in actual fact, however, until the pontificate of Innocent III (1198–1216).

Although the theory of papal infallibility had not yet become an article of faith, popes were the final authorities in matters of dogma and discipline. To rebel against them was tantamount to rebellion against God. They retained the sole right of creating cardinals, ratifying the election of bishops, authenticating relics, canonizing saints, and of absolving grave sins.

From the 300s until 1309, the popes lived at the palace of the Lateran in Rome, which had been given to the Church by Constantine. The pope's cathedral church (his seat of authority as bishop of Rome) has always remained the Lateran basilica, known today as St. John Lateran, one of Rome's four major churches.

Bishops. The actual day-by-day government of churches on the local level was carried on by bishops, whose jurisdiction extended throughout a territorial unit known as the *diocese*. The boundaries of these episcopal territories usually conformed to those of the old Roman provinces from the time of Diocletian (AD 284–305), and often to those of the Roman *civitas* or city-state. Indeed, during the period of economic decline that followed the fall of Rome, it was often the presence of the bishop and his household alone that kept the towns alive. The bishop's throne (*cathedra*) gave to the church where it was located the name *cathedral*. An administrative staff grew up around the bishop, which resembled the papal curia on a smaller scale. Priests assigned to the cathedral to assist the bishop were called canons, and by the high Middle Ages they were usually organized in a *chapter*, which observed a semi-monastic rule. The archdeacon was their leader, and it was a rare bishop who did not experience tension between himself and this influential official.

THE MEDIEVAL PAPACY	
555–752 EAST AND WEST UNIFIED	Popes accepted imperial tutelage. Chosen by churchmen and nobles. Ratified election with the Eastern emperor.
752–1059 WEST INDE-PENDENT	Papacy crowned Western emperor, Charlemagne. Church and state tensions developing.
1059–1415 ELECTION BY CARDINALS	Nicholas II seeks to remove secular influence from papal elections. From 1179, a two-thirds majority of cardinals elect the pope.
KEY TERMS	
ANTIPOPE	Disputed elections led to some popes who were not widely approved.
CURIA	Court of cardinals.
CONSISTORY	Counsel meeting of the pope with his cardinals.
LEGATES	Papal representatives.
INTERDICT	Disciplinary exclusion of Christians from the Sacraments; could apply to individuals or whole nations.
EXCOMMUNICATION	Removal of a Christian from Church life and, in medieval era, from society in general.

In the Early Church, bishops were elected by the clergy and people of a diocese. During the tenth century, the cathedral canons gained control of episcopal elections, but the king's "consent to elect" (*concessio regalis*) was required. The consecration of a bishop took place following his confirmation by the archbishop, who claimed the right to judge his suitability. The *Decretum* of Burchard of Worms (c. 1012) stated that bishops should be "elected by the clergy, asked for by the people, and conse-crated by the metropolitan (archbishop)." Popes claimed the right of intervention in all episcopal elections. With all these vested interests at stake, it is not surprising that there were numerous contested elections in the Middle Ages.

At his consecration, the bishop received the symbols of his office: the pastoral staff, the ring, and (after 1100) the mitre, a shield-shaped headdress.

The bishop's primary responsibility was the supervision of all churches, monas-teries, revenues, and ecclesiastical justice within the diocese. In order to do this most effectively, he was required to conduct visitations to every ecclesiastical establish-ment under his care once every three years. We possess a number of records of such visitations, which record weaknesses and misdeeds.

Bishops engaged in a multitude of responsibilities. They baptized, preached, heard confessions, aided the poor and oppressed, founded and supervised welfare agencies, and acted as arbitrators between individuals, cities, lords, and even kings. They maintained a court, administered the physical properties of the diocese, en-gaged in wide correspondence, attended church councils, advised monarchs, and oc-casionally wrote devotional and theological treatises. In addition to this, bishops held land that required feudal services, such as leading knights in warfare, collecting taxes, and giving counsel.

Standing between the bishop and the pope was the archbishop or metropolitan, who was simply the bishop of an important city and whose jurisdiction included those dioceses in proximity to his own. His territory was called a province. Usually, the popes exercised their authority through archbishops, who were in some cases also permanent papal legates (such as the archbishop of Canterbury).

From the eleventh century, all bishops and archbishops were required to make periodic visits to Rome to report on their stewardship.

The Parish. The basic unit of ecclesiastical organization was the parish, which was often coterminous with a manor and was served by a priest. Most parishes in the Middle Ages were rural, since towns were neither large nor numerous. The priest himself was often a son of the manor who knew intimately the people he served (and vice versa).

The parish priest was directly responsible for the spiritual welfare of the mass of Christians. He was authorized by the bishop to administer all the sacraments of the Church except ordination and confirmation. Up to 1100, his education was usually shallow, derived either from another parish priest or from a monastery nearby. In the high Middle Ages his opportunities were enhanced by the growth of universities in the towns. Priests who lived in towns enjoyed a greater variety of service and chances for advancement. In the larger churches where there were many priests, they often lived a semimonastic life according to a rule, usually that of Augustine. These priestly communities were called *collegia*, hence the churches came to be known as collegiate churches, though they had nothing to do at this time with colleges in the modern sense of the word. Our contemporary term *college* derives from the fact that many early universities grew out of collegiate churches.

The priests who served cathedral churches as canons and those who lived in a collegiate chapter were supported by endowments of income-producing land called *prebends*. It was a scandal of the late Middle Ages that many canons went about collecting the rights to several prebends, from which income they hired other priests called *vicars* to fulfill the parish duties that were required. The Church finally enacted a regulation that stipulated that every priest must spend at least one-third of each year in residence at his parish.

Unfortunately, many of the records of this period reflect only the violations of canon law and Christian ethics. To reconstruct history from episcopal visitation diaries is like writing an account of society solely from police court records.

At first, the parish church was a small frame building, but after 1200, stone came into general use. The land around the church, including its cemetery, was considered sacred ground, and all acts of violence within these precincts were forbidden. From this arose the right of sanctuary, or asylum, whereby a person in danger of physical harm by another could flee to the church, hoping that his persecutor would respect the custom. Churches normally did not have pews, and people stood for the liturgy.

Church buildings also served as social centers for the parish. Children played in its cool interior, and secular business was often conducted there. Dances were held in the churchyard and many churches laid a *choraria*, or dancing pavement, at the main entrance. Occasionally, one reads of grain being stored and animals lodged in churches. It was not a lack of reverence that prompted such use of sacred buildings but rather the consciousness that God was very close to man and was his friend. It was only in the late Middle Ages that God became more remote and His home became a place of awe, fear, and silence.

Finance. In addition to the gifts of the faithful, the papacy received income (called *census*) from its considerable estates in Italy. From the time of Gregory I (590–604), these holdings had continued to grow so that by the high Middle Ages, the papacy was the feudal lord of almost one-third of Italy. Peter's pence was contributed annually by the Christian monarchs of England, Poland, Hungary, and Scandinavia. The popes also received fees for *exemption,* that is, the right of monasteries, churches, and religious orders to be released from the jurisdiction of bishops in order to come directly under papal authority (such as Cluny, the Premonstratensians, Cistercians, Knights Templars, and Knights Hospitallers of St. John of Jerusalem). Since the pope was far away, exempt institutions usually enjoyed greater freedom than did those who came directly under the local bishop's supervision. High church officials paid fees for the confirmation of their appointments, and archbishops paid to receive the *pallium,* a circular band of white wool worn on the shoulder, which was their insignia of office. In the late Middle Ages, newly consecrated bishops were required to pay the *annate,* a sum equivalent to one year's revenue from their diocese. Finally, there were fees to be paid for papal documents, charters, and the use of papal courts. In many cases, the papal fees represented parallel customs in the feudal system. For instance, the annate was an extension of the feudal *relief,* wherein the heir paid a sum of money to the lord for the confirmation of his inheritance.

As capitalism accelerated during the fourteenth and fifteenth centuries, old landed institutions throughout Europe experienced a period of inflation and tight money. Popes and kings went to great lengths to secure revenues by levying extraordinary taxes. It was at this time popes introduced the practice of *provisions* and expectancies, which for a fee guaranteed a prospective officeholder the right to succeed a prelate who was still living. Reformers had legitimate cause for their criticism of a church too much preoccupied with finance.

The lower echelons of the Church had four principle sources of income: tithes, perquisites, donations, and benefices. Every Christian was expected to contribute one-tenth (a *tithe*) of his income, whether in money or in kind, to the Church. This was often difficult to collect and disputes arose as to the obligation of carriage. Priests had to go about the parish and gather together whatever grain, animals, cloth, or other goods the parishioners were willing to give and store it in the tithe-barn. On one occasion, we read of a priest who was beaten when he attempted to collect the tithe, and one was murdered in 1226. Perquisites were gifts to the priest for special pastoral services, which at first were voluntary, but in time they became fixed charges. Donations, usually obits (payments of masses for the dead), were gifts to the local church prompted by sincere piety, and benefices included all properties that were held by each church. Bishops and abbots often possessed considerable revenue-producing real estate.

According to canon law, the parish income was to be divided four ways: to the bishop, the poor, the upkeep of the church, the support of the priest. However, since many parish churches were controlled by lay lords, the priest was often not free to determine the disposal of his income.

At first glance, it would appear that churchmen lived in opulence supported by the sacrifices of the faithful, but this was hardly the case and was certainly not true of the lower clergy. In some cases, as with tithes, it was almost impossible to collect the amount due. Furthermore, as with proprietary churches, lay lords appropriated church revenues, from which they paid the priest a very small salary. When an abbot or a bishop died, the king was entitled to receive his income until a successor was elected. Often, kings would prolong such vacancies. William II of England (1087–1100) enjoyed the income from Canterbury for four years. By the twelfth century, the tithe had become an article of trade. Laymen gained the rights to receive tithes, and they sold these rights on the open market. Clergymen were also guilty of abusing the system. Some accumulated a number of church offices (called *pluralism*) and, with the income thus derived, hired poorly educated priests to discharge their responsibilities. Many clerics never set foot in the parishes from which they derived their support. Papal bulls and church councils that sought to correct these evils were usually ineffective; in practice, the papacy itself was among the worst offenders.

Courts, Canon Law, Councils. Emperor Constantine I (312–37) conferred judiciary rights upon bishops when he decreed, "If anyone desires to transfer his case to the Christian law and to accept its judgment, he shall be permitted, even if the case has already been before the judge." The decision of the bishop was final. During the period of barbarian invasions of Europe, the bishop's court was often the only institution for justice available. By 1100, a very large percentage of the population came under the jurisdiction of ecclesiastical courts and law.

The lowest church court was that of the dean, who was a priest exercising the oversight of ten parishes, usually in an area about the size of a county. He held a monthly court (*Kalends*), which also had disciplinary and educational functions. The next highest court was that of the bishop (or the archdeacon), from which appeals could be taken to the papal court in Rome. Part of the secret of Rome's primacy in the West lay in the judicious use of courts by the popes. Ever since 343, the appellate jurisdiction of the papacy had been acknowledged, and throughout the Middle Ages, thousands of litigants flocked to Rome as the court of omnicompetence. Popes also sent personal representatives called judge-delegates throughout Europe to hear special cases.

Ecclesiastical courts claimed jurisdiction in all cases touching persons in holy orders (priest, deacon, subdeacon, acolyte, exorcist, lector, doorkeeper), including virtually all students, crusaders, and household servants of churchmen. Cases heard in these courts were those involving violation of oaths (which under feudalism included all breaches of contract), orphans, widows, marital problems, physical injury to churches or clergy, and a host of infractions of moral law. On occasion, churchmen insisted on transferring cases from civil to ecclesiastical courts "by reason of sin" (*ratione peccati*), claiming that inasmuch as a sin had been committed, the matter should be heard by the Church. Had this logic been followed consistently, there would have been little need for civil courts whatsoever.

One reason for the popularity of church courts was that they tended more toward clemency than did the civil courts. This was because the Church took into account intentions, motivation, and mitigating circumstances, whereas the civil laws were more rigid. This also meant that many a cleric went free of punishment for an offense that would have brought a fine, imprisonment, or death to a layman.

The means whereby a verdict was determined varied. Usually both parties, plaintiff and defendant, began by taking a solemn oath upon the Bible or on sacred relics. In an age of profound faith, even superstition, the solemnity of the oath itself often served to bring a confession from the guilty party. The defendant, who was considered guilty until proved innocent, could "purge" himself by offering character witnesses on his behalf. After hearing the evidence, the judge, assisted by peers of the litigants (usually twelve), rendered his verdict. Appeals to a higher court had to be made within ten days. Although use of the ordeal was condemned by the Church, it nevertheless found its way into the system. It took a great variety of forms, such as walking several paces carrying hot irons or retrieving stones from the bottom of a cauldron of boiling oil. If the wounds healed without infection, the party was judged innocent. One curious ordeal was throwing the defendant into a lake. Water, being pure, was said to expel impurities. If the man floated, he was guilty. If he sank, he was innocent. A common ordeal was trial by battle, or judicial combat, where the accuser and the accused fought each other, with the loser considered guilty. The theory behind all ordeals was that God would intervene directly to keep the innocent from harm. But churchmen consistently denounced ordeals. Pope Nicholas I in 867 and Stephen V in 887 declared them to be a form of blasphemy. Ordeals were finally abolished by the Fourth Lateran Council (Canon 18), which forbade priests to participate in them.

The legal code of the Church that governed litigation was called canon law. This body of law grew very gradually. At first, it included all the canons of the most important councils of the Early Church. To this was added the decrees of influential bishops, letters and pronouncements of popes, and important decisions of church courts. By the twelfth century, this mass of material had grown unwieldy, so Gratian, a monk of Bologna, collected, refined, and published a systematic treatment of canon law. His work, *Decretum Gratiani*, became the basis for subsequent elaborations undertaken by Raymond of Penaforte in 1234 (called *Corpus iuris canonici*), Boniface VIII in 1298 (*Liber sextus*), Clement V in 1314 (*Clementinae*), and John XXII in 1320 (*Extravagentes*). In 1500, this material was systematically arranged and published as the *Corpus juris canonici*, which remained the official exposition of canon law until it was revised in 1917.

Church councils had served as deliberative organs of the Church ever since the assembly at Jerusalem (Acts 15) in the first century. When the decrees of a council were accepted by the universal Church, or when its delegates were considered representative of all Christendom, it was called an *ecumenical* council. The first eight such councils were held in the East but were concurred in by the West as well. Beginning with the First Lateran Council in 1123, the next nine councils to the time of the Reformation were Western affairs. They varied considerably in significance and numbers; in 1215, over 3,000 clerics of all nationalities met in Rome, but in 1245, only 140 French and English bishops met in Lyons. During the Middle Ages, the theory developed that only the pope possessed the right of convening an ecumenical council, and only his ratification gave its decisions authority in the Church.

One of the most important medieval councils was the Fourth Lateran Council, called by Innocent III in 1215. Altogether, seventy canons were enacted. Here for the first time, the doctrine of transubstantiation was officially declared dogma. Every Christian was required to receive the Eucharist at least once annually; dioceses were not to remain vacant more than three months; a lectureship in theology was ordered to be established in every cathedral school; fees for pastoral acts were forbidden; bishops were reminded of their duty to preach; ordeals were abolished; and clergy were ordered to wear distinctive garb so as to prevent them from frequenting taverns and engaging in other undignified behavior. The council ordered archbishops to convene an annual provincial council for the correction of abuses, and official papal investigators were appointed for every diocese to ensure the enforcement of moral and theological discipline.

Besides the infrequent ecumenical councils, there were annual diocesan synods and numerous meetings of prelates, which did not rank as general councils.

Monasticism. The origins of Christian asceticism are as old as Christianity itself, but its organization along communal lines did not occur until the fourth century. Although it was essentially a unique way of worshiping God, early monasticism was also predominantly a lay movement protesting the secularization of Christianity following the conversion of Constantine. At that time, it was largely confined to Egypt and Syria. Athanasius is credited with introducing communal religious life to the West when he visited Rome in 340, bringing with him two monks and his influential *Life of St. Anthony*, the "father of monks." For the next two hundred years, Western monasticism largely followed the Egyptian pattern, characterized by rigorous austerities, corporal punishments, a daily recitation of the entire psalter, and individualism. This brand of religious life was especially fixed among the Irish. During this time, numerous rules for monks appeared in the West, although all of them generally followed the Egyptian pattern.

Primarily, Western monasticism was shaped by Benedict of Nursia, who felt that earlier monks had gone to extremes in solitude and solo displays of extravagant piety. In 529, he founded a monastery at Monte Casino, north of Naples, and as a guide for his monks, he drew up a comprehensive set of regulations known as the Rule of St. Benedict. In time, monks came to be known as *regular* clergy (because they lived by the *regula*, or rule) as distinct from the *secular* clergy (who lived in the *saeculum* or world).

Benedict's Rule, which he called simply "a school for beginners in the service of the Lord, which I hope to establish on laws not too difficult or grievous" (Prologue), had the merits of moderation coupled with flexibility, so that it was easily adaptable to many situations. For the last thousand years up to modern times, this rule has formed the basis for almost all Western monastic orders. Benedict suggested that the psalter should be recited over a week's time instead of daily, as before. He insisted on balanced meals, even allowing up to 1½ pints of wine daily. (They were Italian monks!) He permitted the use of heavy clothing in winter (Egyptian rules had no provisions for winter), and he forbade any ascetic practices that might be injurious to health.

During the "Benedictine centuries" (600–1100), Europe was a society composed of cells in which the estate, village, and manor were units. The monastery was an expression of this decentralization in the ecclesiastical sphere. Each one contained everything necessary for the maintenance of life: fields, cattle, barns, craftsmen's workshops, winepresses, dormitories, library, refectory, and herb garden (for the infirmary); dominating the entire complex was the abbey church.

The monk's day was spent performing three main duties. The "work of God" (*opus Dei*) was foremost; this involved worship in the church seven times. A total of 3½ hours was spent in communal worship. Monks received the Eucharist daily and, until the thirteenth century, under both kinds. The "spiritual reading" (*lectio divina*) was directed toward the spiritual growth of the monk, although in time the celebrated monastic intellectual activities developed as a result of this reading. About 4½ hours were spent in this daily occupation. Finally, Benedict required about 6½ hours of manual labor (*opus manuum*) of his monks. Most scholars are agreed that this aspect of the rule constituted a revolution in European attitudes, for it elevated the idea of manual labor as a virtue, which in late Roman times had been performed mainly by slaves.

The monk's schedule varied according to the season of the year, since it was regulated by the sun and influenced by fast days and seasons of the Church Year. A typical monastic day might include devotion, labor, meals, and naps from 2 a.m. to 6:30 p.m. In winter, the monks enjoyed nine hours of uninterrupted sleep, but there were longer services and less work and reading. In summer, they had about seven hours of sleep, but they enjoyed a two-hour siesta at noon.

The rule demanded of every monk a twofold vow: that of "stability" (*stabilitas loci*), which required of him permanent residence at the monastery of his entrance to the order, and "conversion of life" (*conversatio morum*). In addition to this, it was understood that he would follow the three "evangelical counsels" of poverty, celibacy, and obedience to the abbot. The *chapter* of monks (all monks gathered for official business) elected the abbot for life, who was then solely responsible for the welfare of the house. He in turn chose a *prior* to be his chief assistant in addition to a *cellarer*, who was in charge of the temporal affairs of the house, and *deans*, each of whom was in charge of ten monks. The chapter had only a negative function. It could veto a suggestion by the abbot, but it could not initiate action the abbot opposed. By the twelfth century, this had changed, however, and most chapters possessed considerable powers of legislation. One reason for this was that very few abbots lived in the monastic cloister anymore. Instead, they had their own ménage within the monastic compound.

At first, all monasteries were diocesan establishments and were under the jurisdiction of the bishop, which meant that all religious houses could expect official episcopal visitations regularly. The rule permitted bishops to interfere in monastic elections. Added to this source of potential friction was the fact that the rule permitted the *sanior pars* (more sensible group) to prevail in an election even though it might be a minority. Furthermore, abbots were also state officials since most monasteries held land from the king and owed him feudal services, so the crown insisted on its rights in the choice of abbots. It is not surprising to find many contested abbatial elections during the Middle Ages.

When Benedict wrote his rule in 529, it was intended only for his own monastery. The rule did not become generally accepted until the Council of Aachen in 817, where Louis the Pious, son of Charlemagne, decreed that henceforth this rule alone would be permitted in the empire. This was done at the insistence of Benedict of Aniane (d. 821), an influential adviser of the emperor.

Benedictine monasticism underwent many changes during the Middle Ages through reinterpretations of the rule. Two of the most significant developments are the establishment of Cluny in 910 and of Citeaux in 1098. Cluny sought to accomplish three things: (a) emphasize worship [cultic] to the virtual exclusion of reading and labor, (b) organize the monasteries into a coherent system with vertical and horizontal relationships to each other, and (c) free the Church and especially the papacy from the control of lay lords. During the tenth and eleventh centuries, the Cluniac Order represented everything that was vital and progressive in Christianity. The Cistercian Order came into being as a reaction to the secularization of the Church that followed the rise of capitalism in the eleventh century. These monks sought to return to the simplicity of Benedict's Rule and to the ideals of poverty and isolation.

One of the best-known contributions of monasticism to culture is the preservation of Christian and pagan classics. The *scriptorium* became an important adjunct to the library, where monks copied and thereby perpetuated the works of Virgil,

Priscian, Ovid, Donatus, Cicero, and Latin translations of the Greeks. Next to the Bible, their most popular Christian authors included Augustine, Boethius, Origen, Jerome, and Pseudo-Dionysius.

By the high Middle Ages, a distinction had arisen between ascetics who were considered *contemplatives* and *actives*. The latter insisted that the best way to serve God was by serving one's neighbor, whereas the former emphasized prayer and worship. Much twelfth-century monastic literature deals with the tensions between these two groups, the contemplatives identifying themselves with Mary, sister of Lazarus (Luke 10:38–42), and the actives with Martha.

The monastery became a familiar feature of the medieval countryside. It employed numerous servants, was usually lord of several manors, served as a social welfare agency, experimented in agriculture and breeding, and through its schools educated most of Europe's leaders for several centuries.

The Church Year. Medieval society was permeated with a Christian atmosphere fostered by the liturgical cycle of festivals, fasts, and saint days. Both church and state calculated time according to the Church calendar. (For example, in England, the king met with parliament at Christmas, Easter, and Pentecost.)

FESTIVE CYCLE	
FEASTS/FASTS	NOTES
ADVENT	Four Sundays herald the coming of Christ.
CHRISTMAS	Midnight Mass. Crèche introduced by Francis of Assisi (1223).
EPIPHANY	January 6. Candle Mass commemorating purification of Mary, February 2.
ASH WEDNES-DAY/LENT	Fasting begins; reception of ashes as signs of penitence. Wooden crosses, black robes.
HOLY WEEK	Maundy Thursday Communion. Reception of the excommunicated and penitent. Good Friday. New supply of holy oil from bishop.
EASTER	Jubilant celebration of the resurrection.
ASCENSION	Forty days after Easter; festive.
PENTECOST	Birth of the Church and gift of the Spirit. Close of festive cycle.

All work and secular activities were prohibited on major festivals, which tended to increase in number. A council at Oxford in 1222 mentions fifty-five, which together with Sundays added up to 107 days on which no work was done. With the increasing secularization of society during the thirteenth century, the number of days of obligation tended to decrease.

The observance of the Church Year fostered a sense of solidarity among medieval men, for they were conscious of the fact that no matter where they traveled or what their station in life, virtually every Western Christian was united in the same worship and rites on any given day. This gave meaning and reality to the concept of Christendom.

The Christian Leaven. After the downfall of the Roman Empire, the Church was the only institution in the West capable of filling the political and moral vacuum. It brought society under the civilizing influence of Christian ethics, provided leaders for government, and ameliorated the evils brought on by the conquering barbarian tribes.

The Church was exclusively responsible for the care of widows, orphans, the sick, the destitute, and the aged. She ransomed captives, cared for prisoners, and taught children. All of these activities were the direct responsibility of the bishops, who according to canon law were required to spend one-fourth of their revenues for charity. Following the dissolution of the monasteries as a result of the Reformation, many of these welfare activities either ceased to exist or were taken over by the state.

As moral guardians of society, popes and bishops did not hesitate to employ spiritual force (notably excommunication) to bring immoral and rapacious princes to heel. Although prelates sometimes abused this prerogative in order to foster their political interests, in general, they brought a beneficent influence to an age of coarseness and brutality. Three notable institutions served to mitigate the evils of feudal warfare: the Peace of God, the Truce of God, and chivalry.

The complexities of feudalism promoted private warfare, and it was usually the innocent who suffered most. Toward the end of the tenth century "a league of the friends of peace" was established by a series of church councils and supported by clergy and laity. Violators of the peace were liable to the interdict. The Church went further and recruited volunteers for a militia to defend the peace, which in effect supported the concept of just wars. The principle was that the strong were honor-bound to defend the weak against unjust aggression.

The Truce of God was first introduced in 1027; this forbade warfare during specified periods of time. At first, it ran from the ninth hour on Saturday to the first hour on Monday. Soon it was extended to include Friday. Then, it covered entire periods of the Church Year (Advent and Lent) plus a number of feast days. Although the idea was originally promoted according to dioceses, the first three Lateran councils (1123, 1139, 1179) prescribed the truce for the entire Church.

Chivalry was also instituted for the preservation of law and order. In effect it was an absorption of knighthood by the Church, in which the knight swore to uphold Christian ideals. His investiture was surrounded with Christian symbolism. In actual practice, of course, few knights succeeded in living up to this ideal, but it served to hold before them a standard of moral conduct.

At no time in the history of the West was Christianity's influence so pronounced as during the age between the decline of Rome and the beginning of the Renaissance.

TEACHING

The nature of theology from the fifth to the eleventh century was primarily that of preserving the traditions of the past. During these centuries, when barbarian invaders were unsettling the West, society assumed the characteristics of a rugged frontier, and Christian thought in greater or lesser degree was more derivative than it was creative. No single individual exerted a more profound influence on the theology of these centuries than Augustine of Hippo (d. 430), through whose writings the wealth of patristic thought was transmitted to the West.

MEDIEVAL THEMES OF AUGUSTINE'S THEOLOGY	
GRACE	Sinful mankind needed God's grace. John Cassian's semi-Pelagianism opposed Augustine's "pessimism." Council of Orange (529) supported Augustine's view but did not condemn all aspects of Cassian's view.
NEOPLATANISM	Provided terms of Augustine's theology: tended to stress unity of God; all truth spiritual; visible church a pale reflection of true, invisible Church. Heavenly focus.
BODY AND SOUL	Soul eternal; body good. Government needed to curb sinful nature.

The Medieval Church inherited Augustine's teaching on sin, grace, the soul, the Trinity, and government. Also, its understanding of the Sacraments, Church, ministry, salvation, scriptural interpretation, and practically every other aspect of theology was ultimately in debt to him. Later medieval controversies (for example, the Eucharist, predestination) arose because of ambiguities within Augustine's own writings to which each side could appeal.

Latin Transmitters. Sharing Augustine's role as a teacher of medieval Christianity are four significant churchmen of the sixth and seventh centuries: Boethius (d. 524), Cassiodorus (d. 580), Gregory I (d. 604), and Isidore (d. 636). Because they serve as a bridge between the patristic age and the Middle Ages, they are often referred to as the Latin transmitters.

The influence of Boethius on the eleventh and twelfth centuries is second only to that of Augustine. Practically everything these centuries knew of Aristotle came by way of Boethius's translations of his logical works, and it was Boethius who first applied Aristotelian methods to theological problems, a method that found its fruition in scholasticism. It is ironic that his *The Consolation of Philosophy*, the favorite philosophical treatise of the Middle Ages, contains few uniquely Christian ideas, but his work on the Trinity and on the Catholic faith stamp him as a genuine Christian father. One of his primary concerns was the relation of man's free will to divine foreknowledge, which he answered by stating that God sees all things concurrently and eternally, while man is bound by his nature to see events through a succession of time.

Boethius's pupil Cassiodorus wrote a treatise explaining his educational program for the residents of a monastery he established at Vivarium. This work, *The Institutes on Divine and Secular Letters*, compares the growth in knowledge of Scripture to a ladder. Cassiodorus insisted that a thorough grounding in secular literature must precede the study of Scripture, and he outlined the course of study required before his monks were permitted to pursue theology. This course constituted the seven liberal arts divided into the *trivium* and the *quadrivium*. The first dealt with grammar, rhetoric, and logic, which had to do with the ordering of experience and giving expression to what was known. The second comprised the four sciences of arithmetic, astronomy, geometry, and music, which focused on the acquisition of knowledge. These liberal arts formed the basis of learning throughout the Middle Ages up to modern times.

Cassiodorus also wrote the *Tripartite History*, a compilation of three earlier histories of the Church by Socrates, Sozomen, and Theodoret, which became the standard Church history of the medieval period. The monastery at Vivarium was the first in the West to adopt a program of preserving classical and patristic learning, and unlike other religious communities, Cassiodorus sought out scholars and literary men to become monks. In the centuries following his death almost all the monastic houses in the West followed the example of Vivarium and became repositories of culture and education.

Gregory I (the Great) was the primary source for the medieval practices of saint worship, veneration of relics, the doctrine of purgatory, and the notion of demons and angels who intervene directly in human affairs. His longest work, *Moralia in Iob*, expounds in great fullness the allegorical method of scriptural interpretation by which theologians were enabled to draw surprising conclusions from the Bible. He also wrote four books of *Dialogues*, which form a collection of miracles, visions, and prophecies. His handbook on the duties of a priest, *The Pastoral Rule*, was the basis of clerical education during most of the Middle Ages and became for the secular clergy what Benedict's Rule was for the monks. From the eighth century, virtually every European monastery contained at least one of Gregory's works.

Isidore of Seville composed the *Etymologies* based on the principle that the nature of all things could be explained by a study on the origins of names. It is an encyclopedia of the knowledge of his time, including miscellaneous material on law, theology, medicine, man, the Church, animals, politics, architecture, agriculture, military science, navigation, and other subjects. Since his etymological explanations, like those of ancient grammarians and rhetors, are often based only on the sound of the word, he frequently gives the most astonishing interpretations. Thus *apis* (bee) is explained as *sine pedibus* (without feet), and *amicus* (friend) is derived from *hamus* (hook). This work remained a standard book of education until the thirteenth century.

In addition to these Latin writers, an anonymous sixth-century Greek author exerted considerable influence on the medieval West. Since his works were mistakenly attributed to Dionysius the Areopagite, whom Paul converted in Athens (Acts 17:34), he has come to be known as Pseudo-Dionysius. This author aimed at a synthesis between Neoplatonism and Christianity, stressing the intimate union between God and the soul and the gradual deification of man. The relationship between God and the world was established through a hierarchy of graded beings.

Pseudo-Dionysius provided the charter for Christian mysticism, and his works were studied and commented on by practically every significant Christian writer from the twelfth century on.

Carolingian Controversies. During the two centuries from Gregory the Great to the time of Charlemagne, the Christian West, besieged by Islam on the south and preoccupied with civil wars, showed little appetite or competence for theological discussion. In most cases, Baptism alone represented the maximum requirement for the name Christian, regardless of faith or life. Charlemagne's celebrated revival of learning, however, also spurred reflection on Christian dogma, and a number of doctrinal controversies marked the late eighth and early ninth centuries.

CONTROVERSIES		DEVELOPMENTS
ARIANISM	Promoted anew in Spain by Felix of Urgel and Elipandus.	Alcuin emphasized the divinity of Christ, present to bless in the Eucharist. Sacrament venerated.
FILIOQUE ("AND THE SON")	Since Arians questioned dignity of the Son, Catholics affirmed that the Spirit proceeded from the Son.	"And the Son" added to creed by 589 Toledo Council. Later caused controversy with Eastern Church.
PREDESTINATION	Gottschalk taught predestination of the damned and the saved. Hincmar of Rheims stressed free will and priestly role in salvation.	Synod of Mainz (848) condemned and imprisoned Gottschalk. Semi-Pelagian views renewed.
EUCHARIST	Paschasius Radbertus of Corbie wrote that Christians received the actual body and blood of Christ. Ratramnus argued for spiritual presence.	Culminated in Berengar-Lanfranc controversy. Council of Vercelli (1050) condemned Ratramnus and Berengar.
MYSTICISM	John Scotus Erigena emphasized soul's upward journey through contemplation. Pantheism.	Views condemned at Vercelli (1050) and Paris (1210) though mysticism flourished.

The tenth century was devoid of significant theological activity as Europe was besieged by Norsemen, Magyars, and Saracens. The papacy sank to its nadir at the hands of Roman factions. Gerbert of Aurillac, who was Pope Sylvester II from 999 to 1003, is a notable exception. He instituted reforms to purge the Church of simony and concubinage, actively promoted mission work in Hungary and Poland, and was an early proponent of the use of dialectics in theology. His revival of interest in Boethius and Aristotle had a direct bearing on the birth of scholasticism.

Beginnings of Scholasticism (1000–1200). With the eleventh century, we move into a new world as compared with the previous five hundred years. Europe, no longer on the defensive, began to expand and colonize. The rise of commerce undermined the feudalistic self-sufficient economy, and a newly emerging middle class populated the growing cities. Whereas in earlier centuries the monastic schools had dominated theological education, it was now the urban cathedral schools that took the lead. Between 1050 and 1200, every cathedral had a school; in influential centers, these in turn became universities. The Church was also influenced by the general expansion of intellectual and cultural frontiers, and this became most evident in the growing importance of dialectic.

Earlier Fathers had maintained that reason was the handmaid of faith and that the truths of Christianity were the only legitimate objects for intellectual reflection. The eleventh- and twelfth-century theologians, on the other hand, often viewed the rational process as increasingly independent of the faith. The new dialectic took the form of posing a problem as a question (*quaestio*), then arguments were presented for and against (*disputatio*), and finally a tentative solution was proposed (*sententia*). This, in short, is the method known as scholasticism. It was essentially the application of reason to revelation with the object of harmonizing the two. It took place within the context of the faith. The main single impetus to the growth of rational inquiry at this time was the discovery of Aristotle's works on logic and a corresponding revival of Boethian studies. (Boethius was a Roman philosopher and interpreter of Aristotle.)

Theologians from Chartres were most illustrious in the twelfth century. The cathedral center was founded in 990 by Fulbert (a student of Gerbert). Fulbert, like earlier medieval masters, usually permitted the authority of Scripture and the Church to prevail over reason.

By 1050, Berengar of Tours allowed no such restrictions on reason. As we have seen, his use of dialectic prompted him to reject the traditional interpretation of the Eucharist. Thus for the first time since the patristic age, the Church was beset by numerous doctrinal controversies that threatened its very unity. For the remainder of the Middle Ages, the use of logic undergirded heresy and orthodoxy alike. There was considerable opposition to the use of dialectic. One of its most outspoken critics was Peter Damian (d. 1072), who looked upon it as "worldly, beastly, and devilish."

The school of Bec in Normandy sought to follow a middle ground between the two extremes. Anselm (d. 1109), its most illustrious son, suggested the proper use of reason in his celebrated *Proslogion*, "I believe in order to understand" (*credo ut intelligam*). Stated in another way, he maintained that faith is in search of understanding (*fides quarens intellectum*). His treatise, *Cur Deus Homo?* (Why the God-Man?) is a major document in Christian theology. Up to his time, a popular conception was that man was saved because God, in Christ, had made a payment to Satan. Basing his theology on Paul, Anselm showed that in the Christian scheme of redemption, satisfaction was owing to God, not Satan. He taught that God had created man in order to fill the vacancy left by the fallen angels, but by falling into sin himself, man had thwarted God's purposes. Man was now required to satisfy God's justice either through holiness of life or by suffering eternal damnation. This situation also placed God in a dilemma. He could not simply forgive man's sin, for this would violate justice, and He could not punish man forever, for this would violate mercy and thwart His original plan. But if His original plan was thwarted, it would prove God to be less than all-powerful. The solution lay in sending His Son as God and man, who was able to render the satisfaction man owed to God. Anselm elaborated a juridical satisfaction explanation of the Atonement, with the death of Christ as His most important single act. The influence of this interpretation of Christ's death on the medieval mind may be seen in the increasing use of the crucifix after the twelfth century.

By 1150, almost all theologians accepted the use of dialectic in theology, but a new issue arose among the dialecticians—the problem of universals. Universals were general concepts representing the common elements belonging to things of the same species. Thus "humanity" belonged to all people, "goodness" belonged to the good angels, "brightness" to all light. The question was, do universals exist apart from their objects; that is, could there be "humanity" apart from people (*universalia ante rem*)? Or did universals exist in things (*in re*)? Or were they merely names describing the collective quality of things (*post rem*)? The question posed serious ramifications for theology. For instance, could the Church exist without people, as an invisible entity in the mind of God? Was there such a thing as an evil principle existing in nature? Could God exist apart from His manifestations in nature? Those who held to the reality of universals apart from things, following Plato, were called Realists. Those who took the position that universals were merely words describing things, following Aristotle, were called Nominalists. The extremists in the latter group were inclined to believe only that which could be seen and touched. Obviously, Nominalism tended to question the accepted traditions of the Church, and much of the remainder of medieval theology can be interpreted as a struggle between the two extremes.

Peter Abelard (d. 1142) was undoubtedly the most brilliant twelfth-century theologian. He espoused a modified form of Nominalism, which led him to cast doubt upon ancient Christian formulations. He expressed his ideas on the Trinity in terms bordering on tritheism, and as to the atonement, he believed the chief value of Christ's work was to provide men with an example of holiness. His book *Sic et Non* (Yes and No) was a compilation of contradictory statements from the Scriptures and the Fathers on a large number of issues with a view toward arriving at the truth, a methodology that exercised a decisive influence on the scholastic method. Unlike Anselm, Abelard maintained, "I know in order that I may believe" (*intelligo ut credam*). His teachings were condemned at Soissons in 1121, but he resumed his teaching career at Paris in the 1130s. Four years later, several propositions from his writings were condemned at the Council of Sens. Although his speculation (and no doubt his personality) led him to a life of controversy, he considered himself a faithful Christian. When he died in a Cluniac monastery, he was reconciled to the Church.

Peter Lombard (d. 1160) used Abelard's methods, but the end product, his *Four Books of Sentences*, was more orthodox. These books dealt with God, creation, the incarnation and redemption, and the sacraments. He was one of the first to fix the number of sacraments at seven in order to distinguish them from the lesser sacramentals. Like Abelard, he collected conflicting quotations from the Fathers on questions of dogma and then resolved them by dialectic. The *Sentences* became the standard theological textbook of the Middle Ages, and by 1200, a commentary on them was one of the requirements for all students who wished to become masters of theology.

Carolingian theologians (Alcuin, Agobard of Lyons, Theodulph of Orleans) had opposed Arianism by stressing the divine nature of Christ. Similarly, the use of dialectic in the twelfth century had produced Christian thinkers that stressed reason to the detriment of faith. A reaction against both of these extremes came about with a renewed interest in the human nature of Christ and in personal religious experience as contrasted with knowledge. This movement is commonly referred to as mysticism.

Bernard of Clairvaux (d. 1153) was a guiding spirit of the twelfth century. Although he counseled kings and popes, strenuously upheld orthodoxy against Abelard, and was a tireless preacher, his fame as a theologian rests on his classical expression of the new piety. Whereas others had worshiped Christ as a king and transcendent God, Bernard devoted himself to Jesus the man in His humility, suffering, and obedience. He maintained that if the believer meditated on Christ's holiness and God's wrath, he would become aware of his sinfulness. But then as he gazed upon God's mercy, he became certain of His forgiveness, and in response he imitated the life of Christ. The goal of the mystical life was the complete surrender of the will of the individual to the will of God. Bernard placed such great emphasis on the grace of God that he became known as *Augustinus redivivus* (Augustine revived). He is traditionally cited as the author of the well-known hymn "O Sacred Head, Now Wounded," which reflects his devotion to Christ's suffering and the deep emotion it evoked.

Along with Clairvaux, a center of mysticism emerged in the abbey of St. Victor at Paris. The Victorines, Hugh (d. 1141), Richard (d. 1173), and Walter (d. 1180), combined mystical speculation with their attempts to give faith a rational foundation.

The Thirteenth Century. This century is the fruition of the twelfth. It is the age of comprehensive doctrinal systems known as *summae theologicae*. It witnessed the emergence of great universities that developed from the cathedral schools. It saw the recovery of Aristotle, first through the tainted versions of Arab translators, then through the work of William of Moerbeke, archbishop of Corinth. It was the age that marked the zenith of cathedral building and Gothic architecture. In a sense, this century was the watershed of the Middle Ages.

The Church was the matrix from which the modern university developed, but from the very beginning, the scholars sought freedom from the control of the episcopal chancellors. In effect, a university (*studium generale* was its technical name) was simply a guild of masters and students, a *universitas magistrorum et scholarium*, organized along the same lines as trade guilds. At Paris, studies were divided into four faculties, each under the jurisdiction of a dean: theology, law, medicine, and arts. Teaching was done by the *lectio*, in which the text of Scripture or a Church Father was read; the *quaestio*, which was the master's commentary on the text; and the *disputatio*, in which all present discussed the thesis. Students were under the direct supervision of a master who personally followed their progress. A *collegia* referred to fraternities of students, which handled matters of room and board. The baccalaureate degree, corresponding to the status of journeyman in the trade guilds, entitled a student to teach without abandoning his own studies. The master's degree *(licentia docendi*, license to teach) was conferred after the student had successfully produced his own "masterpiece" (just as in the guilds) by defending a thesis or dissertation in the presence of the assembled masters. It entitled him to become a master and to open his own school wherever he desired. The doctorate was of late origin and was honorary. Medieval universities were centered largely around individual masters of renown rather than courses of instruction. Whereas theology tended to dominate education north of the Alps, Italian schools, especially Bologna (law) and Salerno (medicine), were oriented toward secular studies. Because students in law and medicine were usually mature men, the Italian schools were generally controlled by the students. Their oversight could be harsh. At the beginning of a term, an instructor was required to place a down payment with the student officers, who would deduct fines whenever the teacher was late for lectures or slipshod in his work. Another regulation protected the master from beatings by students who had failed, a rule that apparently was found to be necessary. In Paris, where three-fourths of the students were in their teens studying the arts, the masters controlled the academic policies.

The four great masterpieces of Gothic architecture were completed in the thirteenth century: Paris (1260), Chartres (1260), Amiens (1270), Rheims (1300). The cathedral is the embodiment of an epoch that began with the reawakening of Europe in the eleventh century, when a Burgundian chronicler noted that "a white mantle of churches" covered the world. The Church taught the faithful through art and architecture as well as words; a synod at Arras in 1025 urged scenes from the Bible to be represented on church walls. The cathedral was a great stone book that taught the illiterates basic Bible stories and truths by means of sculpture and stained glass windows. It also provided the masses with an opportunity of expressing the new piety that mysticism supported—not unmixed with the incentive of human pride in outbuilding the neighboring towns with this symbol of grandeur.

Thomas Aquinas. The culmination of scholasticism was reached in the writings of Thomas Aquinas (d. 1274), Dominican philosopher and theologian, *doctor angelicus*, self-styled "dumb ox." Although Aristotle was the most formative influence on his thought, Thomas insisted that philosophy had its limitations. He sought to use reason to support the probabilities of Christian dogma and to refute heretics, but basically, he believed that matters of faith lay outside the province of reason and beyond it.

A catalog of his writings would fill several pages, but those by which he is most remembered are the *Summa contra Gentiles*, designed as a handbook for missionaries containing his defense of natural theology against the Arabians, and the *Summa theologica*, the latest of his works and the capstone of medieval theology. In 1879, the papal bull *Aeterni Patris* required the study of Aquinas by all students of theology in the Roman Catholic Church.

Whereas Aquinas followed in the scholastic tradition, a contemporary of his, the Franciscan theologian Bonaventure (d. 1274), represented the Augustinian and mystical strand of thought. Bonaventure, like Bernard of Clairvaux, was suspicious of the use of reason. He believed the goal of the Christian should lie in the contemplation of God and the submission of one's will to the faith of the Church as received through tradition.

Skeptics vs. Authority. The fourteenth century, a period of social upheaval aggravated by the Hundred Years' War, stood in stark contrast to the thirteenth. Old ways were challenged, and a spirit of individualism characterized by skepticism undermined practically every institution—whether ecclesiastical, political, or economic. Significantly, not a single major cathedral dates from this time. The Avignon Captivity of the papacy reduced its prestige, and the Church's incessant need for revenue further alienated the people. This critical attitude is reflected in the theology of the time.

AUTHORITY: REASON AND REVELATION	
DUNS SCOTUS (D. 1308)	Oxford theologian. Attacked Aquinas's views combining reason and revelation, which limited God. First to teach immaculate conception of Mary.
WILLIAM OF OCCAM (D. 1347)	Franciscan. Advocated nominalism, opposed realism of Aquinas, and questioned Fathers. Placed authority of the Bible above reason and Church. Men could please God through merit.
JOHN (MASTER) ECKHART (D. 1327)	Dominican. Soul was meeting place of God and creation. Divine spark within for contemplation and exercises to experience union with God.
JOHN TAULER (D. 1361)	Dominican. Mystical union with God for practical purpose of love and self-sacrifice.
DEVOTIONAL WRITERS	Thomas à Kempis (d. 1471) wrote *Imitation of Christ*. Unknown writer produced *Theologia Deutsch*. Popular, practical mystical views.

Although theologians in the late mystical tradition were highly individualistic, they shared a common interest in fostering a personal relationship with God. They often opposed, or were indifferent to, traditional ecclesiastical structures. These, they maintained, more often hindered than helped to sustain sound Christian faith. They tended to be suspicious of human productions—institutions, society, and wisdom.

The Common Man. While philosopher-theologians were speculating about God in the heady atmosphere of the schools, what was the nature of the average Christian's faith during these years?

Medieval folk piety was influenced to a large degree by stories taken from the Bible. Both testaments were mined to provide fitting subjects for art and sermon illustrations. The lives of Christ and the apostles were most popular. In the monasteries, one-third of the day was devoted to the study of Scripture, and in the parish schools, the Bible was often the only textbook. This does not mean that every man was an accomplished exegete, for his interest in Scripture was usually limited to the moral of a story or to its basic human interest. The Bible was so interpreted that any given text was said to have no less than four different meanings. The epistles of Paul and the more difficult theological sections were relatively ignored outside the schools, but the Gospels, Proverbs, Psalms, Kings, and Song of Solomon were well known and loved.

The medieval man, feeling a need for intermediaries between himself and God, centered much of his piety on the veneration of saints, whose lives vied in importance with those of Christ and the apostles. Every aspect of daily life, every diocese, province, and church came under their protection. Sailors and fishermen addressed prayers to St. Nicholas; St. Genevieve cured fever; St. Blaise was known to relieve toothache; St. Hubert guarded against madness; and St. Jude was the saint of last resort. Each season was under saintly protection: spring, St. Mark and St. George; summer, St. John the Baptist; autumn, St. Martin; winter, St. John the Evangelist. Each parish church was placed under the protection of a saint from whom it then derived its name. St. John's church, for instance, was considered literally to be the possession of St. John, and any violators of its precincts would be answerable directly to the saint. The martyrdoms of the saints replaced the deeds of the warriors as subjects for wandering minstrels. Modern scholars have amassed a collection of stories that include more than twenty-five thousand saints venerated in the Middle Ages.

Beginning in the twelfth century, there was a special interest given to the humanity of Christ and His suffering and to the Virgin Mary. The former was no doubt fostered in part by the theology of Anselm and Bernard, while devotion to the blessed Virgin was the ecclesiastical side of the honor being given to women in general through chivalry, although Mary had always been given high honor since the Council of Ephesus (431), which had declared her to be the mother of God.

The cult of saints fostered an intensive preoccupation with their relics. Though Augustine in the fifth century had cautioned against the practice, nevertheless by 787 a church council approved it. The Crusades especially set off a wave of relic hunting. Pieces of bone, fingers, hair, and teeth of saints flooded the West, and magnificent reliquaries fashioned to house them were often carried in procession. Naturally, authentication in most instances was impossible. Nevertheless, no less an eminence than King Louis IX of France built Sainte-Chapelle to receive Christ's crown of thorns, and the first crusaders were spurred on to victory through the discovery of the lance that had pierced His side. Relics were credited with miracle-working powers. Oaths were customarily taken on them much as they are solemnized with the use of a Bible in modern times.

Though saint veneration was often a veneer covering crass superstition, a carryover from Teutonic paganism, it also served the salutary purpose of providing examples of Christian morality, fortitude, and love in action. It symbolized men's belief in the doctrine of the communion of saints and the Church Triumphant. While some critics of this age point to its other-worldly preoccupation, perhaps it is more accurate to say that heaven became terrestrial, with angels and saints crossing freely back and forth. This worldview, so alien to modern man, was not without its benefits.

Veneration of saints led to another medieval phenomenon, the pilgrimage. Shrines of saints were everywhere, and it was a rare person who had not taken the pilgrim's staff in hand at least once in his lifetime. The three most popular attractions were Jerusalem, Rome, and Compostella in northern Spain, but there were others. The tomb of St. Thomas à Becket at Canterbury, the shrine of the Magi at Cologne, the tomb of Martin of Tours, and the sanctuary of the archangel at Mont Saint-Michel all attracted thousands of visitors each year. Pilgrimages were a leveling force in society, as serfs jostled with princes, bishops with laymen, craftsmen with laborers, with no preference given to status. They also served to relieve the tedium of a rustic existence by providing the stimulation that travel brings, and a pilgrim who returned to his German farm after having traveled to Jerusalem was never quite the same again.

The Christian life was sustained through the use of the sacraments. Their number remained flexible during most of the Middle Ages, since there was no official definition of the nature of a sacrament. Hugh of St. Victor enumerated as many as thirty. Peter Lombard listed the seven that have become traditional, though the Church did not officially agree to this until the Council of Florence in 1439.

Baptism was conferred upon the newborn child. Under Charlemagne, the baptistery gave way to the font, and Baptism by immersion was replaced by pouring. The rite was accompanied by the use of symbols—the candle, white gown, salt, and oil. When the child grew to adolescence, he repeated the act of faith his godparents had spoken for him. This was *confirmation*, which was from early times reserved for the bishop or his representative. *Holy orders* (ordination) was the rite by which a man entered the office of the priesthood. The path led through a series of suborders, culminating in the diaconate and finally the priesthood itself. Only a bishop could ordain. *Matrimony* was the sacrament by which the Church elevated and hallowed the marriage bond. Despite the dignity attached to this sacrament by the Church, recent studies have shown that there were more common-law liaisons in the Middle Ages than properly ratified marriages, especially among the lower classes. At the hour of death, the Church fortified the faithful with the sacrament of *extreme unction*, accompanied by prayers and litanies for the departing soul. These five sacraments were nonrepeatable, but the remaining two, *penance* and the *Eucharist*, were to be used continuously to sustain Christian life and faith.

Penance was the most popular sacrament, consisting of private confession to a priest, who pronounced the absolution and enjoined an act of piety that allowed the penitent to prove his remorse over his sin. Many times, the penitent failed to understand the act of penance in this light and considered it reparation for sin, an abuse that tended to obscure the Augustinian teaching of grace and encouraged the semi-Pelagianism, which was endemic in popular thinking.

The *Eucharist*, wherein the communicant received Christ's body and blood, was most often understood in grossly materialistic terms. This interpretation led to a fear of the Sacrament and in turn to its infrequent reception. Coupled with this tendency went the emphasis on the Eucharist as a sacrifice (to the exclusion of Communion), and the liturgy became a drama enacted by the priest instead of a channel of grace for the faithful. By the thirteenth century, infrequent Communion was so widespread as to call forth a decree of the Lateran Council of 1215, making at least an annual Communion obligatory for every Christian. The custom of receiving the Sacrament under both kinds (bread and wine) by all the communicants was general until the twelfth century. By 1300, the wine was usually taken only by the celebrating priest. The use of the unleavened host instead of bread is usually attributed to Charlemagne. The Corpus Christi festival instituted in 1246 accelerated the custom of adoring the host, either as it was carried in procession or displayed in the monstrance on the altar. The mystics of the late Middle Ages, stressing personal communion with God as they did, revived the concept of the Eucharist as Communion.

Charlemagne decreed that the Roman liturgy be used throughout his empire, although variations were permitted in different localities. The order of worship remained relatively unchanged in its main outline, but there were modifications reflecting shifts in theological emphasis. Louis IX began the custom of genuflecting during the *et incarnatus* of the Creed, and the elevation of the host was added as a protest against Berengarius's denial of the real presence. Vestments, chants, and ceremony all varied in time and place. The stations of the cross were added by the Franciscans, and the rosary was an innovation of the Dominicans.

The Sunday Mass was the main act of corporate worship in which the people found spiritual edification, but occasionally the behavior of priest and people was less than exemplary. Cats, dogs, and hawks were taken into churches, and numerous sermons are extant that admonish the hearers to cease chattering and listen.

The liturgy was drama, and it gave rise to dramatic art. An extension of the liturgy was the mystery play, a dramatization of an event from the Bible—perhaps an incident from the life of Christ or a missionary journey of Paul. From these dramas, there developed the morality play, in which abstract virtues and vices were personified and made into living characters. The miracle play depicted the life of a saint or other post-biblical character. All of these served to teach virtue in an entertaining way.

A revival of preaching occurred during the twelfth century, encouraged in part by the evangelical example of Bernard. Collections of sermons were made for those priests who were deficient in the art. Honorius of Autun (d. 1130) maintained that preaching was the primary responsibility of the priest but that the sermon should not be too long; it must entertain as well as edify, and it must avoid rhetoric that detracts from its contents.

Thousands of hymns are extant from the Middle Ages. Honorius of Autun urged that every service begin with *Veni Creator Spiritus* ("Come Holy Ghost"). One of the most loved of all medieval hymns was the *Stabat Mater Dolorosa*, dedicated to the Virgin Mary. From the eleventh century comes "Kyrie, O Christ Our King," and Venetius Fortunatus's "The Royal Banners Forward Go" is a sixth-century Good Friday favorite. Rabanus Maurus composed the solemn dirge "Day of Wrath, Day of Mourning."

Superstition, ignorance, and abuses existed, yet from birth to death the medieval man lived in the conviction that in some way, his life was tending toward union with God because of Christ. He was supported in his belief by the ministrations of the Church, and though his life was hard and often miserable according to modern standards, he could find serenity and stability in the practice of his faith.

CHURCH AND STATE

The possibility of tension between Church and state was inherent in the very nature of Christianity. The followers of Christ were encouraged to separate themselves from the world while they lived in the world. In the early centuries the Church developed its own structure of government, which stood apart from but yet was based on the Roman political system, and church laws were sometimes at variance with those of the state. The persecuted Church believed that God ought to be obeyed rather than man, although Paul's warning "Let every person be subject to the governing authorities" (Romans 13:1) was generally respected by the Early Church.

The conversion of Constantine (312) dramatically altered the situation. Because of imperial patronage and support, the Church's position was reversed, and from a persecuted minority it changed rapidly to a dominant majority in society. In 392, Emperor Theodosius declared Christianity the only legal religion in the empire. The Church's success during the fourth century sharpened the debate between churchmen and secular rulers over their respective roles in society. The Church in the East tended to acquiesce in imperial domination, whereas churchmen in the West either held to a strict separation of the two institutions or in some cases believed the Church should dominate the state. The theocratic idea in the West was accelerated by the removal of the imperial capital to Constantinople in 330, leaving no effective check on ecclesiastical pretensions to power. But the removal accelerated the growth of caesaropapism in the Eastern Church.

The medieval struggle between the popes and kings was more than a conflict of personal ambition. It was an attempt to reconcile the spiritual claims of the Church with the temporal—the doctrine of redemption with that of creation. Both parties in the struggle relied heavily on biblical material to buttress their position. Those who contended for a strict separation of Church and state relied on such passages as "Render to Caesar things that are Caesar's, and to God the things that are God's" (Luke 20:25) and reminded their opponents that Christ Himself had said that His kingdom was not of this world (John 18:36). Most important for the development of the papacy were Christ's words to Peter, "You are Peter, and on this rock I will build My church, and the gates of hell shall not prevail against it. I will give you the keys of the kingdom of heaven, and whatever you bind on earth shall be bound in heaven" (Matthew 16:18–19). Although medieval writers unanimously agreed that the powers Christ conferred on Peter were transmitted to the popes, they disagreed about the nature of these powers and their role in temporal government. From the eleventh century on, the "two swords" theory was popular on both sides. Derived from Luke 22:38, "'Look, Lord, here are two swords,' and He said to them, 'It is enough,'" the controversialists used this slender basis for supporting either a separation of powers or the primacy of one over the other.

Papal Theory. The popes contended that the secular order was inferior to the spiritual and must therefore be ruled by it. Following the thought of Augustine, almost all the papal theorists believed in the essentially negative role of government. That is, earthly rulers were established primarily to curb the results of man's sinful nature, to punish evildoers, and to maintain order. Since the existence of the state was a consequence of sin, it followed that the state was inferior to the Church, which was God's dispenser of forgiveness on earth. Pope Gelasius I (494) maintained a separation of the two powers. He pointed to Melchizedek (Genesis 14:18) as a symbol of the union of the powers of kings and priests. Since Christ was "the new Melchizedek," He united priestly and royal powers in Himself. However, after the ascension, the two powers were to be separated to better serve different functions.

Isidore of Seville (d. 636) taught that Christ gave the rulership to kings in order to guard the Church. The king's function was to assist the Church and its leaders in the maintenance of justice. It was naturally up to the churchmen to determine the nature of justice since this involved an ethical dimension, and the king was to carry out the wishes of the Church as its auxiliary.

Pope Gregory I (d. 604) was responsible for introducing a theory that gained considerable popularity in the Middle Ages. He believed that terrestrial society was modeled on a celestial pattern. Just as heaven followed a hierarchical order with God at the apex, so also the earth was to be governed by God's vicar, the pope, at the top. It was God's will that the higher should always rule over the lower. To rebel against this rule brought nothing but sin and chaos. Other theorists supported papal primacy on the dualistic conception of man consisting of body and soul. The soul, it was held, being that which is spiritual, was naturally superior to the body. Therefore the popes and priests who were concerned with matters of the soul were considered superior to kings who dealt only with the physical. The sacrament of ordination, which conferred special powers on the priesthood to celebrate the Eucharist and thereby bring God to earth, also tended to set apart the clergy from the laity.

One of the most influential documents supporting papal claims in the Middle Ages was the forged Donation of Constantine. It was fabricated in the Frankish empire sometime during the eighth century in order to support the claims of the Church against the state and in particular to strengthen the position of the pope.

In it, Emperor Constantine purported to give to Pope Sylvester I the rulership over all of Italy and the West, in addition to Antioch, Constantinople, Alexandria, and Jerusalem. Lorenzo Valla (d. 1457) is credited with proving this document a forgery.

A second influential collection of documents, falsely attributed to Isidore of Seville, comes from the ninth century and contains sixty forged decretals plus more than one hundred falsified papal letters. The general tenor of the Pseudo-Isidorian Decretals is calculated to support the clergy over the laity, ecclesiastical freedom from lay jurisdiction, and the primacy of the pope within the Church.

It is significant that the authors of these famous forgeries did not invent a new ideology of papal primacy. They simply gave support to theories that were already current, and the popularity of the views they set forth was due to the receptiveness of the soil.

Kingship in the West. Opposed to the concept of papal-clerical superiority was that of royal theocracy, the idea that kings derived their authority directly from God without the mediation of the pope. The origins of this veneration of the sovereign prince derive from ancient conceptions of divine kingship, from Germanic tribal ideas, and especially from biblical precedent (the examples of David, Solomon, and Paul's Letter to the Romans were often cited). The king was considered sacred, and royal consecration was included among the sacraments in the early Middle Ages. Kings were said to possess miracle-working powers. They typified Christ, and just as He ruled in heaven, kings claimed the right to rule on earth. So supporters of royal supremacy used the Christological argument, as did the papalists, but they turned it around. For example, Hugh of Fleury suggested that bishops should be subordinate to the king as the Son is to the Father.

So long as large segments of the West remained outside of Christianity, the inevitable conflict between these opposing ideologies was postponed. By the eleventh century, however, Christian evangelism had succeeded to the point where Europe was practically synonymous with Christendom in the West. The Holy Roman emperors claimed jurisdiction over the same territory and people as did the popes, and the stage was set for a gigantic struggle that ultimately affected every Western institution. At the heart of the conflict lay the concept of the unity of society. The problem lay in identifying the ultimate ruler.

The Carolingians. Clovis and his descendants, known to history as the Merovingians, ruled in Gaul and the surrounding territories from 481 to 751. During the last century of their reign, the government was largely in the hands of the mayors of the palace, royal officials who maintained order for the incompetent kings. In 751, Pepin, the last mayor of the palace, asked the pope a famous question. Who should rule: the man who has the right but is incompetent or the man who actually has the power? Pope Zachary replied that the competent one should rule. The last Merovingian was summarily deposed; Pepin was crowned and anointed by Archbishop Boniface, apostle to the Germans; and three years later, Pope Stephen III personally repeated the coronation. In this way, the Carolingian dynasty came to power, but the precedent for papal permission and consecration had been established; this was to influence subsequent church-state relations for centuries.

In 756, Pepin conquered a large area of central Italy from the Lombards and bequeathed it to the papacy—a gift known as the Donation of Pepin, which greatly enhanced the pope's position as a temporal ruler. Many scholars maintain that the Donation of Constantine was forged at this time in order to provide a precedent of legality for Pepin's otherwise presumptuous action.

In 768, Pepin's son Charles (Charlemagne) succeeded him as king of the Franks. Charlemagne is perhaps the best example of royal theocracy available to us from the Middle Ages. He supervised practically every aspect of ecclesiastical life with special attention to the reform of the Frankish Church. He personally convened no less than thirty-three church councils. All elections of bishops were conducted canonically by the clergy and people of the dioceses—but always in the presence of the king's representative. He directed the clergy to wear distinctive dress to set them apart in society, thus making it difficult for them to violate decorum under the cloak of anonymity. In church architecture, he encouraged the use of baptismal fonts instead of baptisteries, and he fostered the use of Gregorian chant in the liturgy.

Charlemagne also claimed supreme authority in matters of Christian dogma; at the Council of Frankfurt in 794, he issued the *Libri Carolini*, which rejected the Byzantine Church's position on the use of images in worship. The decrees that were most far-reaching had to do with education, in which he established that every parish was to provide a school for all of the children of the church regardless of class. In 802, he passed legislation for the education of the clergy. Charlemagne also standardized the text of the Apostles' Creed, made the Vulgate (Jerome's fifth-century Latin version) the official translation of the Bible, established twenty-one archbishoprics in the kingdom, and promoted the use of the Benedictine Rule in all monasteries. Most churchmen acquiesced in the strong initiative taken by their ruler.

The revival of letters that has become known as the Carolingian Renaissance was due not only to Charlemagne's forceful personality but also to the men who surrounded him, notably the educator Alcuin of York, the biographer Einhard, the theologian Theodulph of Orleans, and the historian Paul the Deacon.

During Christmas Day Mass in 800, Pope Leo crowned Charlemagne in St. Peter's Basilica in Rome, an event that was to have profound repercussions in Christendom. Since 476, the West had acknowledged only one emperor, the one in Constantinople. But in 754, his representative in the West was ousted by the Lombards and his territory was given to the pope in the Donation of Pepin. Now in 800, a woman (Irene) sat on the Eastern throne, one whom the West declared to be a tyrant and usurper. Although the meaning of Charlemagne's coronation has been sharply debated practically from the moment it occurred, these observations can be made:

1. His coronation continued and strengthened the concept of the Roman Empire. Medieval men did not believe the empire had "fallen." They tended to identify the empire with the fourth kingdom in the vision of Daniel (Daniel 2:40–45), and being convinced that after the fall of Rome the world would end, they attempted to postpone such a catastrophe by prolonging the concept of the Roman Empire. The institution continued, at least in name, until Napoleon declared it a fiction in 1806.

2. His coronation strengthened the concept of unity in Western Christianity. There was now an office superior to that of any king, and its authority was derived from God. At the same time, all the antipapal political forces found their embodiment in this office, and the popes were faced with a powerful rival.

3. The coronation in effect repudiated the authority of the Eastern emperors, which intensified the tensions between East and West.

4. The fact that it was the pope who crowned the emperor was used to prove the superiority of popes over kings. Charlemagne's biographer notes that the emperor was not pleased with this aspect of his coronation. Some years later, Charlemagne had his son and successor, Louis the Pious, crown himself by taking the crown from the altar.

Following the death of Charlemagne, the empire rapidly disintegrated. Rivalry among the claimants to the throne resulted in civil wars, and the situation was further aggravated by a dearth of strong personalities. Men with such characteristic names as Louis the Pious, Charles the Simple, Charles the Fat, Louis the Child, and Louis the Stammerer made futile attempts to regain imperial stability. At Verdun in 843, the empire was divided into three areas, from which partition many historians date the beginnings of modern France, Germany, and Italy. Yet the concept of empire remained, awaiting only the circumstances and personality to revive its ancient glory.

During these years (800–1000), Europe was ravaged by invasions from the north, east, and south. In 846, Norsemen from Scandinavia sacked Paris. Not long afterward, they swept around the Iberian peninsula into the Mediterranean, establishing a kingdom in Sicily and Naples, which was to last a thousand years. Other Norsemen ravaged Britain, and a famous expedition of "Vikings" under Leif Erickson even ventured to the coasts of North America. In 911, a large area of France was given to the invaders; it retains the name Normandy. The Magyars from the East threatened to overrun Austria until they were defeated in 955 and settled down to create the foundations of modern Hungary. The Saracens, who had overrun North Africa and Spain during the seventh and eighth centuries, still menaced Mediterranean commerce. They occupied all of southern Italy until the Norse dislodged them in the tenth century, and they remained in Spain until 1493.

During these troublous times, neither kings nor popes were in a position to assert themselves. The papacy became a pawn of warring factions of Roman nobility, and kings were unable to arrest the acceleration of feudalism, by which their vassals increased in power at the expense of royal authority. The Carolingian dynasty came to an inglorious end in Germany in 911 and in France in 987.

One exception to this melancholy chapter in papal history was Nicholas I (858–67), an energetic and high-minded pope who believed that the Roman Church was the epitome of all Christendom, East and West. From this point of view, it was logical for him to intervene in a disputed election of the Eastern patriarch, and in the West, he reduced the independence of bishops by placing them more firmly under his own control. On the basis of his pastoral authority, the pope denounced the divorce and remarriage of King Lothair of Lorraine and succeeded in persuading the prince to take back his lawful wife. This incident prompted considerable literary activity over the jurisdictional limitations of papal and royal power.

Investiture Controversy. The Carolingian dynasty in Germany was succeeded by a line of rulers stemming from Saxony, who governed from 911 to 1024. The most illustrious representative of this family, Otto I (936–73, "The Great"), succeeded in defeating the Magyars and in imposing a centralized government on the several duchies that constituted Germany. In 962, he invaded Italy in order to defend Pope John XII against a military coalition, and in return, the pope crowned Otto emperor, thus again giving reality to the theory of empire, which had lain dormant for some years. Shortly thereafter Otto deposed the pope and had one of his own choosing elected. The newly crowned emperor also revived Charlemagne's attitude toward the Church by claiming to be society's supreme protector, with the pope's primary responsibility limited to the discharge of spiritual duties and support of the emperor.

This royal theocratic attitude continued under the next dynasty, that of the Salian-Franconians, who ruled in Germany from 1024 to 1125. In 1046, King Henry III, a deeply religious ruler, called a church council that deposed the pope for simony. The next five popes were all from Germany and were elected under the tutelage of the emperor. This imperial patronage was a blessing for the papacy in that it removed the holy office from the control of warring Roman factions and placed men of high caliber and integrity in Peter's chair. But the blessing was clouded by the loss of papal independence even in matters that were primarily spiritual. By the eleventh century, almost every important church was an imperial church, and most bishops were imperial appointees who owed their position to the emperor's favor. The proprietary church system, whereby a lay lord controlled the revenues and life of a church on his land, was everywhere the rule. In 1050, there were seventy-seven dioceses in France, of which the king controlled twenty-five. Other nobles controlled the rest. Under these circumstances, it was impossible for churchmen to discharge their responsibilities conscientiously. Indeed, many leading prelates took their secular duties as counts or royal administrators far more seriously than they did their spiritual functions.

Henry III died in 1056, succeeded by his infant son, Henry IV. During his minority, a radical change in attitude toward the imperial authority appeared among a group of reformers who advised the last German pope until the modern era, Leo IX (1049–54). They questioned the propriety and the right of any lay ruler, particularly the emperor, to exercise influence in clerical appointments. Humbert of Silva Candida was a forceful proponent of ecclesiastical freedom. Peter Damian, another reformer, stressed the separation of priesthood and kingship, both of which were needed. In 1059, Pope Nicholas II issued the famous election decree, which declared that henceforth popes should be elected by the college of cardinals, thus effectively excluding lay and imperial influence. In the same year, he concluded an alliance with the Normans of southern Italy, an act of defiance against the emperor whose predecessors had for three centuries served as Rome's "defenders."

The issue between Church and state came to a head during the pontificate of Gregory VII (1073–85), also known as Hildebrand. The real problem was jurisdictional. Who had the right to appoint the hierarchy? And who selected the emperors? What was the proper relationship between spiritual and temporal powers? The act by which a vassal received his land or office from his lord was called *investiture*. When kings and princes conferred the temporalities (lands and buildings) on bishops, they also gave them the rights of spiritual office by means of the ring and pastoral staff. The pope questioned the right of laymen to influence clerical appointments, especially the practice of laymen bestowing spiritual authority on bishops, and the dispute has become known to history as the Investiture Controversy.

Gregory launched his attack against lay investiture in 1075. The penalty for ignoring his decree was automatic excommunication. In the same year, the pope wrote an aide-memoir for his private use, which was not intended to be seen by others. But it got out somehow. The document, *Dictatus Papae*, made extravagant claims for papal primacy, including the first explicit claim that a pope could depose an emperor. King Henry IV in Germany (not yet crowned emperor) ignored the papal decree on lay investiture and appointed a bishop for Milan. After being admonished for this by Gregory, the king summoned a council of German bishops, which denounced the pope and refused to recognize him as legitimate. Gregory responded by deposing the king from office and excommunicating him. This act released all of Henry's subjects from their oath of allegiance to him. The turbulent princes of Germany, who were never happy under a strong king, used this occasion as a legitimate excuse for revolt, and Henry was forced to agree that a council be held in Augsburg during February of 1077 to determine his future role in Germany.

In January 1077, the pope, en route to the Augsburg council, was resting at the castle of Canossa in northern Italy when the most dramatic episode of the controversy occurred. King Henry appeared outside the castle as a penitent, begging the pope's pardon. Gregory was now on the defensive. As chief pastor of Christendom, he could not refuse absolution to a penitent sinner, even though the king's display of sorrow may have been motivated by shrewd politics. The pope absolved him, but the deposition from office remained in force.

After Canossa many of Henry's vassals again supported him, but his enemies elected a new king, Rudolph of Swabia. Germany was ravaged by civil war while the pope took three years to decide between the claimants to the throne. In 1080, he declared in favor of Rudolph and repeated the excommunication against Henry, but this time, it had little effect in Germany. Rudolph was defeated and killed, and Henry summoned a council of German bishops, which elected a counter-pope, Guibert (Clement III). The German armies marched to Rome and besieged it for three years.

Finally in 1084, the imperial troops succeeded in breaking through to St. Peter's, and they consecrated Guibert as pope. Meanwhile, Gregory summoned his erstwhile Norman allies from southern Italy. Under the leadership of Robert Guiscard, they marched on Rome, but the imperial troops had already fled, so the Norman "defenders" looted the city, razed it by fire, and withdrew to the south with Gregory as their captive. He died a few months later (May 1085). His last words were "I have loved justice and hated iniquity, therefore I die an exile."

The conflict between Henry IV and Gregory VII stimulated a war of propaganda between theorists on both sides. One of Henry's staunchest supporters was a lawyer from Ravenna, Peter Crassus, who defended royal prerogatives in terms of Roman law. Manegold of Lautenbach was a papal theorist who formulated a contract theory of government.

The introduction of Roman legal precedent into European political thought was perhaps the most far-reaching result of the controversy over investiture. It generally served the interests of the secular rulers. Up to the eleventh century, medieval kings had relied heavily on clerical advisers, but after the investiture controversy, they tended to look to the newly emerging class of lawyers for counsel. This change helped to secularize the state and to accelerate the growth of nationalism.

Henry V (1106–25) continued the struggle with the papacy, but by this time, the First Crusade had diverted Europe's attention to a new field of endeavor. Indeed, the pope's call for the crusade hinted that it would serve as a "safety-valve." The Gregorian epoch came to a close with the Concordat of Worms between Calixtus II and Henry V (September 1122), in which the emperor agreed to the canonical election of bishops and to the investiture of spiritual authority (ring and staff) by the archbishop. However, the king was permitted to be present at the election and to invest the bishop with the temporalities of his office. In effect, the kings still controlled the choice of bishops, for without income from the lands that they held from the king, the bishops were unable to maintain themselves.

Regional Rulers	Developments
ALFRED OF WESSEX (849–99)	England. Defeated the Norse. Reformed Church and monasticism. Treaty required Baptism of the Norse. Translated Christian treatises into English.
HUGH CAPET (941–96)	France. Capetian dynasty lasted until 1328. Peaceful relations with papacy.
WILLIAM THE CON-QUEROR (1028–87)	Invaded England. Ended Anglo-Saxon dynasty. Separated civil and church courts. Held right to approve church decisions in his realm. Adviser was Lanfrance, archbishop of Canterbury.
WILLIAM II (1056–1100)	England. Ignored rights of the Church. Left archbishopric vacant four years until he appointed Anselm of Bec, who ended up fleeing from William II.
HENRY II PLANTAGENET (1133–89)	England. Church regained independence during civil war (1135–54). Great king. Ruled from Ireland to Pyrenees. Struggle with archbishop Thomas à Becket, who advocated for Church's rights. Thomas murdered by Henry's knights.
FREDERICK I BAR-BAROSSA (1122–90)	Germany. First Hohenstaufen ruler over "Holy Roman Empire." Rescued pope from Italian factions; appointed king. Revival of Roman law. Power struggle with papacy over north Italy. Installed antipope but finally recognized Pope Alexander III.
JOHN LACKLAND (1166–1216)	England. Struggled with Pope Innocent III over archbishop of Canterbury. England under interdict (1208); John excommunicated (1212). Signed Magna Carta in 1215, making king subject to law.
FREDERICK II (1194–1250)	Germany. Civil war ended when he took throne. Gifted, educated ruler; religious skeptic. Excommunicated twice. Struggled constantly over northern Italian states and with popes.
LOUIS IX (1214–70)	France. Strong ruler. Held that in national emergency the king could confiscate church treasure if necessary. Austere in private life. Emphasized justice for all. Declared a saint in 1297.
PHILIP IV (1268–1314)	France. Taxed clergy for war with England. Boniface VIII declared such taxes unjust but changed his mind after Philip imposed an embargo. Arrested a bishop, which led to bull "Unam Sanctam," declaring all people subject to the pope. Dispute ultimately led to antipopes and lasting division.

Innocent III. In 1198, the greatest of all medieval popes ascended Peter's throne as Innocent III. The young, thirty-seven-year-old pontiff sought to free the papal states from all outside interference, to combat heresy, and to extend Christianity by fighting the Muslims. His most dramatic activity, however, lay in his attempts to bring secular governments under the guidance of his office. By his decretal *Venerabilem*, he claimed the right to decide between the pretenders to the German throne. In a dispute between King Philip of France and King John of England, the pope intervened on behalf of John. When the French king protested unwarranted interference by the pope, Innocent replied that King Philip had sinned. Likewise, the papal interdict of England in 1208 was based on Innocent's theocratic worldview. In reality, he was declaring no new papal theories, but he was in a better position in history to bring practice into line with theory than were his predecessors. His policies have called forth more debates among historians than those of most other medieval popes.

EAST AND WEST

While Europe was under siege by barbarian invaders during much of the early medieval period, causing the political transformation referred to commonly as the "fall" of Rome, the empire continued in the East as a stable institution for more than a thousand years. The Eastern empire at one time or another comprised Asia Minor (its heartland), the Balkan peninsula, Syria, Palestine, Egypt, and parts of North Africa. Modern scholars have labeled this civilization by using the name of the old Greek town Byzantium, on the site of which Constantine built Constantinople, but the "Byzantines" always referred to themselves as Romans. Latin continued to be the official language until the sixth century, when it was replaced by Greek. The Roman Empire was never officially divided between East and West, but Diocletian's and Constantine's creation of a second capital at Constantinople in AD 330 tended to polarize loyalties around two administrative centers. From the death of Theodosius in 395 until 476, there were always two emperors: one at Milan (later at Ravenna) and the other at Constantinople. When the imperial insignia were transferred from Rome to the East in 476 (the event often associated with Rome's fall), the empire was still considered to be united under the Eastern ruler.

The last great effort to realize this unity in actual fact was made by Justinian (527–65), who sought to reconquer North Africa, Sicily, and Italy from the Vandals and the Goths who had taken control of these territories. Although Justinian's generals, Belisarius and Narses, were initially successful, Italy fell prey to the Lombards after the emperor's death. Within a few years, all of North Africa was lost to the Arabian Muslims. From the sixth century on, therefore, the West tended to pursue its own course, although lip service continued to be given to the ideal of empire with the Eastern monarch acknowledged as the supreme ruler in Christendom. Until the coming of Charlemagne, popes sought the confirmation of their election from the ruler in Constantinople, and Western kings (e.g., Clovis, Alaric, Pepin) took pride in their status as consuls, thus deriving their legitimacy from the Eastern emperor.

Justinian was also active in promoting Christianity, in making Constantinople a capital worthy of the empire, and in codifying Roman law. Justinian's building program was crowned by the erection of Santa [or Hagia] Sophia, the Church of Holy Wisdom (i.e., Christ), one of the most perfect examples of Byzantine architecture. Its chief feature is its enormous dome, over 120 feet across and 180 feet high.

For centuries, this was the largest church in Christendom, surpassing in size all the churches of Europe and providing the nerve center for Orthodox (Byzantine) Christianity. In 1453, it was converted by the Turks into a mosque, and in modern times it serves as a museum.

Justinian commissioned a group of lawyers to systematize all existing Roman law: precedents, significant cases, and commentaries. The completed work was the *Corpus Juris Civilis* (or "Justinian Code"), which from the twelfth century provided the basis for all Western European legal systems, canon as well as civil. The code was especially influential in establishing a legal precedent for the divine rights of monarchy, a concept that materially assisted the centralization of the Western states in the late Middle Ages.

During the sixth and seventh centuries, the Eastern Church was torn by controversies over the person of Christ. When the Council of Chalcedon (451) determined that Christ was one person in two natures, it condemned those who insisted on overemphasizing His divine nature (Monophysites—literally, one nature) and those who went to the opposite extreme, stressing His duality (Nestorians). In 551, Justinian condemned three alleged Nestorian writers (an issue therefore named the "three chapters" controversy) in the hope of conciliating the Monophysites. In 553, the Fifth Ecumenical Council, convened by Justinian, ratified his earlier condemnation of the Nestorians. When the pope in Rome condemned this council, the Eastern Church removed his name from the diptychs (lists of people for whom the churches prayed), and the pope eventually acquiesced in the conciliar decisions.

The Monophysite controversy was not settled, however, and in 638, Emperor Heraclius issued a compromise statement ("Ekthesis"), in which he declared that the two natures of Christ were united in one will (monothelitism). The pope refused to agree to this statement; he excommunicated the Eastern patriarch. But in 653, the emperor had another pope, Martin I, arrested and brought to Constantinople as a prisoner, where he died after suffering many indignities. He is the last pope who is revered as a martyr. The Sixth Ecumenical Council, held at Constantinople in 681 but presided over by papal envoys, condemned monothelitism and reaffirmed the Chalcedonian formulation. Ten years later, another council was held in the East in order to complete the Fifth and Sixth Ecumenical Councils by adding disciplinary canons. This council (called the Trullan Synod or Quinisext) was rejected by the pope because it made claims of authority for the patriarch of Constantinople equal to those of the bishop of Rome.

By the end of the seventh century, these theological controversies had resulted in the formation of several Eastern churches that opposed the theology of Constantinople. There was the Church of Armenia, which had never accepted the decisions of Chalcedon. The Armenians, furthermore, were politically the subjects of Persia, and to emphasize their patriotism, they repudiated the Eastern empire by embracing the Monophysite position. The Syrian Monophysites also became a separate body under the leadership of Jacob Baradaeus, from whom they are known as Jacobites. The

Egyptians were also inclined toward Monophysitism, and the Coptic Church there was organized in opposition to the Byzantine Church. A political factor also entered into this situation, because the Egyptians resented Byzantine political controls, and the theological argument over the nature of Christ served to lay bare submerged feelings of exasperated nationalism. They referred derisively to the Greeks who lived among them as "Melchites" (followers of the emperor).

On the opposite side of the Christological question stood the Nestorians, who had also been condemned by Chalcedon. The Christians living in Persia generally espoused Nestorianism, which, because it was condemned as heretical by Byzantium, had the added advantage of reassuring the Persian government of the Christians' loyalty. The Church in Persia was highly organized, having its own patriarch, metropolitans, and bishops. Its intellectual center was the monastery at Nisibis. The Nestorians of Persia established a church in Malabar in India, and by the fourteenth century, they had carried Christianity across Asia as far as Beijing.

Scattered among these Eastern independent churches were small groups of Christians who rejected both the authority of Byzantium and that of their national church, choosing instead to follow Rome. These are known as Uniat churches. In 1950, the total number of Uniats was estimated at over eight million members. Thus throughout her history, the Byzantine Church lived in tension between the Latins of the West and the nationalist dissenting churches to the East. The endemic theological warfare among the Christians in the East helps to explain the astonishing speed with which the armies of Islam were able to subdue them shortly after the death of Muhammad.

After Justinian, "the last of the Roman emperors," Byzantium was threatened by invasion from two sides: to the south and east were the Arabs and Persians; to the north lay the Slavs and Bulgars. The task of defending the empire for the next five hundred years fell primarily to four dynasties: the Heraclids, the Isaurians, the Amorians, and the Macedonians.

Under Basil II (976–1025), Byzantium reached the height of its influence and extent. He accomplished his aims through an almost-ascetical regimen. Basil defeated the Egyptians, pushed the Arabs back into Arabia, and recovered practically the entire Balkan peninsula, for which feat he was styled *Bulgaroctonos*, the Bulgar-slayer. At his death, the empire extended from the Danube to the Upper Tigris and west to Sicily. Perhaps the most far-reaching event during his reign was the conversion of Russia to Christianity, a circumstance brought about by the fortuitous marriage of his sister, Anna, to Vladimir, prince of Kiev.

But the empire soon fell on evil days. The Arabian caliphate was itself taken captive by migrants from central Asia, the fierce Seljuk Turks. In 1071, they defeated a Byzantine army at Manzikert, capturing the emperor himself. Shortly thereafter, they established their capital at Iconium in the heart of Asia Minor. It was this threat that led to Byzantium's appeal for help from the Franks, resulting in the First Crusade.

Part of the legacy of old Rome to Byzantium was the supremacy of the emperor in matters of religion as well as state. Constantine himself had called the first ecumenical council, and each of the six subsequent ecumenical councils was convened by emperors who often injected their own ideas into the proceedings and promulgated the ecclesiastical canons as imperial law. This typically Byzantine concentration of complete civil as well as religious power in the hands of the emperor has been labeled caesaropapism by modern Western historians, although the term itself was unknown to the Byzantines. The difference in point of view between the East and the West on the issue of church-state relations can be traced back at least as far as Augustine and Eusebius. Where Augustine saw their relationship as one of tension between the "city of God" and the "city of man," with the former possessing a moral superiority, Eusebius tended to see the state as the protector of the Church and the emperor as God's vicar on earth, His "image," to whom the Church owed support and gratitude. However, emperor and patriarch were to work in harmony for the welfare of the whole, as expressed by the ninth-century emperor Leo VI. In actual practice, the emperors believed that they were also personally responsible for the supervision of the Church. For example, Leo III identified himself with the role of Peter. Throughout their history, the Byzantines believed that the emperor derived his authority directly from God, hence his titles "Christos Kyriou" ("anointed by the Lord") and "living icon of Christ." They alone of the laity were privileged to enter the sanctuary of the church, to preach, to commune themselves in the same manner as priests, and to convene church councils. Emperors believed that they were bound to rule on earth according to the divine model in heaven, with themselves assuming the role of God. They defended the faith, converted the pagans, and punished heretics. But imperial control of the Church was not absolute, for in the last analysis, it was still the ecumenical council that defined dogma and exercised church discipline. Emperors maintained almost unlimited administrative control over the Church and enjoyed liturgical privileges, but in matters of teaching, every imperial attempt to revise traditional dogma failed. On the whole, imperial control worked smoothly, and only a few energetic patriarchs chafed under the system.

The patriarch, standing at the apex of the Byzantine hierarchy, was assisted by metropolitans who were set over ecclesiastical provinces, each of which was subdivided into bishoprics. Although most parish priests were married, bishops were required to be celibate, and most of them were chosen from the monasteries. During the fourth century, the patriarch of Constantinople claimed precedence over all other Eastern churches because he resided in the capital. The three ancient patriarchates of Jerusalem, Antioch, and Alexandria resisted his pretensions, as did the pope in Rome, but the Muslim conquests of the older churches during the seventh century left the patriarch of Constantinople as the sole leader of the Eastern churches. His authority never became as centralized as that of the papacy in the West, but he governed the churches as "first among equals," leaving each of the metropolitans and bishops largely in control of their own jurisdictions.

Monasticism attracted many to its ranks. The ascetic life in a religious community was considered to be a superior style of Christianity; by the eighth century, tens of thousands of men and women lived as monastics. Eastern monasticism tended to follow the eremitical and isolationist examples of early Egyptian fathers; unlike those in the West, the monks usually did not become involved in the life of the institutional church (with the exception of those who became bishops). Mount Athos in Greece, isolated on a narrow peninsula in the Aegean, was well populated with hermits dwelling in caves and other ascetics living in inaccessible spots. To this day, twenty monasteries and two hundred hermitages of Mount Athos continue to function under the jurisdiction of the patriarch exactly as they did ten centuries ago. Byzantine monks never separated into orders but remained under the single rule of Basil of Caesarea (d. 379).

Byzantine worship was surrounded with rich ceremony and conducted in churches decorated with mosaics and frescoes representing Christ and the saints. The liturgy of the Eucharist, usually that of John Chrysostom or Basil, was celebrated as a timeless event, an appearance (epiphany) of Christ in which the congregation experienced the actual event of the Supper, not as it was or will be but as it is forever. The services began with the "Little Entrance" and the singing of the Trisagion, followed by the lessons and sermon. Then came the "Great Entrance," in which the celebrants carried around the church the bread and wine that were to be consecrated while the choirs sang and the people responded to the exalted entry of Christ Himself. The Nicene Creed and the commemoration of the living and dead followed. Then came the consecration of the elements themselves, in which the *epiklesis*, or prayer for the Holy Spirit, was central. (In the West, the words of Christ ("take, eat," etc.) came to be considered the heart of the liturgy.) Most of the liturgical action took place at the altar, which was closed off from the worshipers by the *iconostasis*, the icon screen. All communicants received both wine and leavened bread. Although the Eastern Church was never much concerned with fixing a definite number of sacraments, it observed the same rites as had become familiar in the West. Children were baptized as infants, usually by immersion, and chrismation (anointing) was administered immediately after Baptism. The Eucharist was given to all who had received chrismation, including the children, and penance was available for those who were troubled by their sins.

Throughout Byzantine Christianity, there was an emphasis on the incarnation of Christ and the mysteries attending the relationship between Christ's human and divine natures. (In the West, the tendency was to emphasize His crucifixion as being of central significance.) Although the Council of Chalcedon had settled the Christological controversy, Eastern Christians still tended to stress the divine nature of Christ over the human. This "divinizing" of Christ can be seen most clearly in the iconographic figure of the *Christos Pantokrator*, the All-Ruler, whose portrait was placed in the highest part of the church. Such was the emphasis on Christ's deity that historians have sometimes claimed the *Pantokrator* was the First Person of the

Trinity in the guise of the Second Person. Because Christ was viewed more as God than as man, the Byzantines required intermediaries to bridge the chasm between sinners and God. The Virgin Mary served to function in this role together with the saints. The Eastern Church tended to distrust the physical, and its rites, sacraments, liturgy, and art all assisted to transport the believer out of the material world into the presence of the divine. Easter was celebrated with greater solemnity than it was in the West as the event that liberated Christ from the boundaries of His human form. This particular emphasis has prompted some critics to disparage the Byzantine ethos as mystical, but at the same time it has inspired some of the world's most uplifting art, architecture, and liturgical forms.

The decisions of the first seven ecumenical councils, along with the Scriptures, were considered the basis of the Orthodox faith. (Note: "Orthodox" in its restricted sense has from earliest times applied to those churches in communion with that of Constantinople.) In addition, the Nicene Creed as revised at Constantinople (381) was accepted as the only authoritative creedal statement, and as such enjoyed wider acceptance than any other creed. The Apostles' Creed, though its roots were buried deep in antiquity, did not achieve a fixed form until the eighth century, and the East-erners rejected it as a novelty. After the eighth century, Eastern theologians tended to look upon dogma as a fixed body of teaching that was to be safeguarded and handed on but was incapable of change or progress.

The greatest Orthodox theologian, whose authority remains decisive in Eastern churches to this day, was John of Damascus (d. 749). His contributions were more in the nature of method than in originality of thought. His major work, *The Fount of Knowledge*, was in three parts: an appreciation of the philosophy of Aristotle to elucidate Christian dogma, a description of one hundred heresies, and an exposition of the Orthodox faith *(De Orthodoxa Fide)* with special reference to the two natures of Christ. John taught the divine maternity of Mary, her exemption from original sin, and her bodily assumption into heaven. He also emphasized the real presence of the body and blood of Christ in the Eucharist almost to the exclusion of the earthly elements. His Easter hymns include the widely known "Come, Ye Faithful, Raise the Strain" and "The Day of Resurrection." Thomas Aquinas relied on the Damascene for his methodology.

While Western Christianity was in its deepest humiliation, the Eastern Church was enjoying its greatest strength. Byzantine culture, the creation of the Church, was in full flower, and Constantinople combined the intellectual glory of ancient Athens with the military might of old Rome. The Western crusaders, coming from their feudal, rustic, provincial enclaves, stood in amazement at the glory of the East. Of all the cities of the medieval world, modern man would have felt more congenial in the urbane and sophisticated society of Constantinople than in the struggling prairie towns of the West. Permeating all the institutions of society was the influ-ence of the Church.

Controversies with the West. Tensions between the Eastern and Western Churches are traceable at least as far back as the Second Ecumenical Council (381), when Constantinople claimed the primacy of honor after Rome, "because Constantinople is the New Rome" (Canon 3). This assertion was repeated at Chalcedon in 451 (Canon 28), but both times, Rome rejected the implication that she owed her primacy in the West to mere association with the old capital and not on the theological basis of apostolic foundation by Peter. During the Christological controversies of the East in the sixth and seventh centuries, the relationship between the churches was often aggravated.

EAST-WEST CONTROVERSIES	
MONOPHYSITES (638)	Christological controversy. Name means "one nature." Addressed at Chalcedon (451) and Constantinople (553) but unresolved. Emperor Heraclius issued compromise statement, "Ekthesis," declaring Christ had one will. Pope excommunicated the Eastern patriarch. Emperor had pope arrested.
ICONOCLASTS (726–84)	Eastern conflict affected the West. Emperor Leo III declared all images to be idols. Ordered destruction. Persecution of iconodules ("idol worshipers"). Nicaea Council (787) reversed Leo's decision, though controversy continued.
PHOTIUS/FILIOQUE (858–86)	Dispute over whether Ignatius or Photius was the patriarch. Brought to prominence the addition of "and the Son" (filioque) to Nicene Creed, a disputed difference between East and West.
GREAT SCHISM (1054)	Patriarch Michael Cerularius published accusation of four errors against Latin Christians (unleavened Eucharist, Saturday fasts, meat from strangled animals, forbidding Alleluia in Lent). The filioque and priestly celibacy were also disputed. Papal legates published anathema against Cerularius; patriarch excommunicated pope.

Crusades. For centuries the East Romans had managed to maintain an uneasy truce with the Muslims, but in 1055 Baghdad was occupied by the militant Seljuk Turks who were determined to push westward as far as possible. In 1071, the Byzantines were routed at the battle of Manzikert, and the same year saw the occupation of Jerusalem by these new Muslim intruders. Emperor Michael VII appealed to Pope Gregory VII for help, but he was too deeply embroiled in the investiture controversy with Henry IV of Germany to provide assistance. During the next quarter century the Turks pushed on to Nicaea, which lay at the very gates of Constantinople itself, and again a plea went out for help. Pope Urban II responded with his famous call for the First Crusade at the Council of Clermont in 1095, which appealed for Christians to rescue fellow Christians. The pope also shrewdly reminded his listeners that the land "flows with milk and honey like another paradise of delights" and that France, suffering from famine that year, was "too narrow for your population." The response was enthusiastic and instantaneous. The crowd shouted, "Deus vult" ("It is God's will"), which became their battle cry, and many tore strips from their clothing to place upon themselves the sign of the cross: the badge of a crusader.

Such was the enthusiasm of the people that many of them refused to wait for the campaign to organize, and about fifty thousand peasants, including entire families with small children, followed the leadership of two bizarre characters: Walter the Penniless and Peter the Hermit. As they proceeded through Germany, they inquired at each town whether it might be Jerusalem. As they went, they also ravaged the countryside, incurring the hostility of the residents. Their vendetta against the infidel found expression in the massacre of thousands of Jews in Speyer, Mainz, Worms, and Cologne. In Bulgaria, the disorganized crusaders were mercilessly attacked; upon arriving at Nicaea, the remnant was exterminated by the Turks.

The main van under the leadership of several French princes arrived at Constantinople in 1096. The residents of the city looked with some amusement on this band of unlikely warriors, mostly drawn from French farms. The Franks were overwhelmed by the glitter of the city, its churches, statues, wide streets, fountains, and the accumulated culture of centuries. Finally, they moved on; in June 1097, they invested Nicaea and recaptured it from the Turks. The Muslims insisted on surrendering to the emperor rather than fall into the hands of the Franks. From there, the crusaders pushed on toward Antioch. Baldwin, one of the leaders, managed to slip over to Edessa near the headwaters of the Euphrates River, where he married the daughter of the prince of Edessa and succeeded his father-in-law to the throne. This County of Edessa became one of the four crusader states. Antioch was besieged from October 1097 to June 1098, when it fell to the crusaders. No sooner had they taken it than the Turks in turn besieged them. The fortuitous discovery of the lance that had pierced Christ's side gave them the courage to sally forth and rout the besiegers. Bohemond of Tarento and his followers decided to stay in Antioch and so established the second crusader state, the Principality of Antioch. Only a remnant finally arrived in Jerusalem and captured it in July 1099, taking the holy city amidst carnage and destruction. A chronicler of the crusade, Fulcher of Chartres, maintained that ten thousand Turks were killed. Baldwin of Edessa was elected "Protector of the Holy Sepulchre," and on Christmas Day 1100, the new Latin Kingdom of Jerusalem came into being. A few years later, the County of Tripoli on the coast was established as the fourth crusader state. Collectively, these territories were known in Europe as "Outremer," the land "beyond the seas," and for two centuries they were Christendom's eastern perimeter. However, the crusaders had succeeded only in establishing themselves along a narrow strip of Palestinian coastline. Inland, the Turks were still masters, and they provided a constant threat to the new Latin states.

In order to meet this threat and to protect the many pilgrims who now flocked to Palestine, two religious orders came into being. The Knights Templar (so called after Solomon's temple) were founded in 1118 by Hugo of Payens to defend Jerusalem against a recapture by the Muslims. In 1128, Bernard of Clairvaux gave them a form of the Cistercian Rule. They were in effect soldier-monks who took the same vows as monks with the additional obligation of fighting for Christianity, thus combining in themselves the twin medieval ideals of knightly chivalry and monasticism. The Knights Hospitaller were organized to defend pilgrims and to tend those who became sick. A third order, that of the Teutonic Knights, was founded in 1189. During the late Middle Ages, this order was primarily responsible for the evangelization and organization of Prussia.

Once the crusaders had settled down in the East, the inevitable process of cultural assimilation began. They were attracted to the more leisurely style of life of the "infidel." They adopted flowing silk robes, became fond of steam baths, wore turbans, and through social contacts and intermarriage learned to know and admire their erstwhile enemy. When later crusaders arrived in Palestine, they were shocked and chagrined at the indifference toward the Turk displayed by the earlier campaigners, and more often than once the first-generation warriors sided with the Muslims against their zealous cousins who arrived some years later.

Europe was galvanized into the Second Crusade when Edessa fell in 1144. Two monarchs participated: Louis VII of France and Conrad III of Germany; Bernard of Clairvaux's rhetoric popularized it. Despite such impressive support, it accomplished nothing except the capture of Lisbon in Portugal by some German sailors who seized this opportunity of fighting Muslims nearer home.

In 1187, a powerful Saracen leader, Saladin, recaptured Jerusalem, and Europe's three strongest monarchs were moved to lead the forces of counteraction. Frederick Barbarossa drowned en route to the Holy Land, Philip II of France became disgusted at the indifference of the first generation crusaders and returned home, and Richard I ("The Lionhearted") of England managed to negotiate a truce that permitted pilgrims to visit the holy places unmolested.

After this crusade, Europe tired of these ventures. The West itself was expanding internally and intellectually, and the emergence of a new urban culture closer to home diverted the Latins' attention. In fact, no crusade ever equaled the popular support (and results) achieved in the First Crusade. All subsequent campaigns were for the purpose of reestablishing territories gained in the initial effort of 1098.

Byzantium gained little from the crusades except a brief respite from Turkish attack. The behavior of the Franks in Asia Minor led some Byzantines to wonder whether the Turks themselves might not be more desirable as neighbors, but the Franks in turn had reason to complain of the duplicity of Byzantium. The most tragic of all crusades for its long-term effect was the Fourth. Innocent III succeeded in gathering an army to recapture the holy places of Palestine, but the Venetians, whose ships were to transport the army, convinced the Latins to divert their course to Constantinople, which in 1204 they pillaged for three days. They forced the Byzantines to accept a Latin patriarch and to observe Latin rites until 1261, when the Greeks finally drove them out.

In 1229, the colorful Frederick II succeeded in negotiating a truce with the Sultan whereby Jerusalem, Bethlehem, and Nazareth would be open to Christian pilgrims. This, the most successful "crusade" after the first, was undertaken by an excommunicated king without shedding a drop of blood.

Two attempts at recovering the holy places were undertaken by King Louis IX of France. Both in 1248 and in 1270, he sought to defeat the Muslims by attacking Egypt, the seat of their power at the time. In the first venture, he was taken captive; in the second, he died of dysentery at Tunis.

In 1291, the forces of Islam took Acre, the last stronghold of the Christians in the Holy Land, and the period of the crusades was over.

Few can discount the significance of the crusades in bringing the West into contact with civilizations of the East. They stimulated commerce, broadened intellectual horizons, served as an outlet for surplus population, gave peasants status, provided land for the landless, and were a primary stimulant in leading Europe out of feudalism. Although they attracted rogues and adventurers whose conduct belied the ideals of the cross for which they contended, there were also innumerable simple folk who believed it was God's will that the Holy Land be rescued from the infidels. In this sense, the crusades were an expression of profound albeit misguided faith. The cost was high, not only in lives and bloodshed but also in the fragmentation of the Church. Following the notorious Fourth Crusade, any rapprochement between Byzantium and the West was impossible. Weakened by this disaster, Constantinople fell to the Ottoman Turks in 1453, and Eastern Christianity to this day bears the scars of this unhappy event.

DISSENT AND REFORM

Christianity has always carried within itself the dynamic of reform. It is clear that Christ and the apostles insisted on a new standard of behavior for converts to the faith. This lofty ethical ideal has continually called men to a reexamination of their personal morality and to a reform when it was necessary. This has also been true of the Church as an institution, especially when its practices have appeared to be in flagrant violation of Christian ideals. The process of continual reform has also been evident in the area of teaching, and each generation of believers has sought to assure itself that the dogma of the Church truly reflects the apostolic witness of the New Testament. When teaching appeared to be inconsistent with orthodox Christian tradition, reforms were called for. Dissenters and reformers were by no means uniformly orthodox themselves, however; occasionally, the Church found it necessary to reject the reforms themselves as innovations contrary to the Gospel (e.g., Joachim of Fiore, the Albigensians). The Medieval Church was *ecclesia semper reformanda* (the Church always to be reformed), both in areas of life and faith.

One institution of reform was the church council, where bishops and other leaders met to discuss the affairs of a diocese, province, nation, or, on rare occasions, of the entire Church. We have already discussed the Council of Orange in 529 (p. 117

[Table: "Medieval Themes of Augustine's Theology"]), which rejected Pelagian ideas and restored Augustine's doctrine of grace. Pepin, father of Charlemagne, convened numerous councils to reform and organize the Church. Charlemagne called no less than thirty-three councils to deal with the problem of clerical discipline. Priests were admonished to teach the people, hear confessions, visit the sick, and preach. If they were unable to prepare sermons, the government supplied them with copies prepared by scholars, which priests were to memorize and deliver in the language of the people. A significant council was held at Kiersey in 853, which reaffirmed the Augustinian doctrine of grace.

Perhaps the best-known medieval councils were those four held in the Lateran Palace in Rome that rank as ecumenical. The First Lateran Council (1123) not only confirmed the Concordat of Worms, which ended the Investiture Controversy, but its twenty-two canons also covered all the social and religious problems of the day. They especially legislated against the control of the Church by lay princes, and the horrors of war were mitigated by the Truce of God, which declared that Mondays, Tuesdays, and Wednesdays between Trinity and Advent were the only lawful days for fighting. The Second Lateran Council (1139) issued numerous canons on organization, but two have to do with belief. Canon 22 instructs bishops to tell their people that outward acts of penance without a corresponding inward repentance are hypocrisy, and Canon 23 condemns those who reject the Eucharist, infant Baptism, priesthood, and marriage; these it calls heretics who are on the road to hell. The Third Lateran Council (1179) declared that a two-thirds majority of the cardinals constituted a valid papal election, but, perhaps more important, it ordered that each bishop should appoint a scholar to teach gratis those clerics of the diocese and poor students who wanted an education. By thus establishing the office of *scholasticus*, this council elevated the general competence of parish priests. The fourth (1215) was the most important of the Lateran councils. In the reform of canon law, this council is second in importance only to Trent among the twenty general councils. Its seventy canons include a statement of belief drawn up against the heresies of the time (Albigensianism and pantheism), a declaration that bishops who permit scandals in the Church are to lose their office forever, and a decree that clergy are to be soberly dressed, their garments neither too long or too short, fastened to the neck—not of red or green cloth. Clerical participation in ordeals was prohibited, since the Church considered them to be pagan. This council also set forth the inquisitorial procedures to put down heresy; if the accused heretic did not renounce his error, he was excommunicated. The council declared that Christians should receive the Eucharist at least every Easter, which seems to indicate that many were receiving Communion less than once each year. Canon 21 of the Fourth Lateran Council emphasized that private confession must remain private.

Canonical visitation by bishops and abbots was another institution for reform in the Church. Each bishop (sometimes abbots for religious orders) was required to visit every parish church and other ecclesiastical establishments in his diocese at least once every three years and to keep a record of his findings. In each place, he inquired into the conduct of the services, the spiritual life of the pastor and people, the physical condition of the properties, and the financial situation. The records of these visitations list only such items as required reform. When all was found to be in order, a simple notation was made to this effect. Some critics of the Medieval Church have relied heavily on these accounts in writing their histories, with the inevitable result of presenting a distorted picture of medieval society based, in effect, on police court records. The very existence of such records indicates that many prelates discharged their pastoral responsibilities with diligence and evangelical concern.

Religious Orders. Part of the historic genius of Christianity has been its ability to create new forms of life and ministry in response to the needs of the time. Cluny was such a creation. During the two centuries of anarchy and dissolution that followed the death of Charlemagne in 814, the Church suffered from the control of self-seeking princes. The papacy, far from exercising a beneficent influence on the Church, reached its nadir during the tenth century. Reformation was not to be expected from this quarter. The monks of Cluny recognized that a prior condition for reform was the dissociation of the Church from control by the state, and it was to this task that the Order of Cluny addressed itself. Rather than seek the Christian ideal by fleeing from the world, it infused the ideal into the world. The order was founded in 910 by Berno of Baume, and by the mid-twelfth century there were 314 monasteries under Cluny's supervision with more than 1,500 affiliates. The document that brought this order into being is significant, for it established the right of the Church to exist independently of king or prince (*existens sine rege et principe*). Cluny also fostered a reform within monasticism itself, recalling the monks to the discipline of worshiping God.

But Cluny's very success proved its undoing; two centuries after its foundation, it was in need of reform. By the end of the eleventh century, Europe was emerging from agrarian feudalism into an age of commercial expansion. With the influx of wealth came a corresponding decline in the values that had been attached to poverty and simplicity. Once again, renewal came from the cloister, this time from the Cistercian Order founded in 1098 in Burgundy. These monks recalled the Church to her pilgrim ideal of being in the world but not of the world. They symbolically underscored this ideal by founding their houses in remote spots—in marshes, swamps, deep forests, and isolated valleys. In doing this, they tended to expand the internal frontiers of Europe by creating more arable land. But their role in society was only secondary to their effect on the Church. Every Cistercian house became a missionary center. The "white monks," by their frugality and simplicity, were a living denunciation of the materialism of the twelfth century.

Ninth-century England witnessed an almost total eclipse of ordered Christian life as the marauding Danes swept everything before them. Monasteries were plundered and burned, churches were destroyed, and the eastern half of the island seemed doomed to revert to primitive paganism. Through the efforts of Alfred, king of Wessex, a truce was signed that permitted the rebuilding of the Church. Once again, the task of reform fell to the monks, notably the houses of Abingdon, Westbury, and Glastonbury under the leadership of Oswald, Ethelwold, and Dunstan. From a meeting of the English church leaders at Winchester in 970, there emerged the *Regularis Concordia*, a lengthy reform document that thereafter continued to influence the relationship between Church and state to the time of Henry VIII. All three of these monks were also bishops, and they were instrumental in restoring an ordered scheme of Christian life to England.

Twelfth Century. The urban and commercial renaissance of the twelfth century was but one facet of a general revival of society. These years also witnessed a rebirth of arts and letters that rivals that of the better-known sixteenth-century renaissance. Like its later counterpart, the intellectual ferment stimulated critical reappraisals of Christian faith and life.

Perhaps the most famous dissenters of this century were the Waldensians whom we know through the observations of their opponents. Accounts show that the Waldensians rejected clerical and papal authority and hoped to return to a simpler form of Christianity that stressed preaching, reading the Bible in the vernacular, and a minimum of ecclesiastical organization. They also rejected purgatory, veneration of saints, and the dietary regulations governing fasts. The episcopate, threatened by this attack, considered them heretical. An appeal for recognition at the Third Lateran Council (1179) failed, and in 1184, they were placed under the ban by the pope. The Waldensians then organized themselves as a separate body, largely centered in southern France, having their own clergy and style of life. Under the Inquisition, they were attacked together with the Albigensians, but unlike the latter, their organization has continued to the present.

While the Waldensians represented a genuine reform movement stemming from Christianity itself, a group known as the Albigensians (from their chief city, Albi, in southern France) took its inspiration from non-Christian sources, principally the ancient heresy of Manichaeism. They believed that there were two eternal principles, of good and of evil. Everything in this world that is material, including man's body, is evil, and only that which was nonmaterial was considered good. Not only did this dualism deny the ultimate supremacy of God, since the principle of evil (i.e., Satan) was coeternal with Him, but it also excluded God from the world of matter and of man. Thus, it denied Christ's incarnation, the reality of His death, and the resurrection of the body. The Albigensians (also called Cathari—the pure ones) condemned marriage and the use of meat, milk, eggs, and other animal produce and recommended a form of austerity (*endura*) that, if followed rigorously, would have led to suicide. The new sect was divided into the "perfect," who attempted to observe all the rules in their fullness, and the "believers," who were less severe in their habits. Obviously, they were anticlerical and hostile to the Church. It is a disputed question whether they should be included among dissenters and reformers of the Church or whether they stood outside the Church altogether. Their attacks on ecclesiastical wealth and clerical hypocrisy, however, gained for them the support and sympathy of many orthodox Christians.

The Albigensians were condemned by several councils, culminating in a general excommunication by the Fourth Lateran Council. Innocent III attempted to reconcile them to the Church by sending several Cistercian missionaries to southern France, and Dominic later visited the area, but when a papal emissary was murdered by the Cathari in 1208, the pope preached a crusade against them. It was in opposition to the Albigensians that the famous medieval inquisition was developed. After twenty years of almost uninterrupted warfare, the Albigensians were crushed, but at the cost of much bloodshed accompanied by gross acts of perfidy on both sides; southern France took centuries to recover from the ravages of the crusade.

The latter half of the twelfth century witnessed the growth of pantheism, which was implicit in the tradition of the school of Chartres. Two main exponents of this heresy, Amaury of Bene and David of Dinant, were condemned at Paris in 1210 and again at the Fourth Lateran Council together with some of Aristotle's works, which were becoming popular among the Paris theologians.

Joachim of Fiore (d. 1202) shared the pantheism of Amaury and David in that he believed God was actively present in nature as well as in history. He divided the history of the world into three epochs, according to the Trinity. The first age of the world, that of the Father, corresponded to the Old Testament and was an age of fear under the Law. The second, that of the Son, was the age of the Church under grace, the New Testament, which was to last forty-two generations. The third, the age of the Spirit, was to begin about 1260 and would be an age of love in which all men would dwell together in peace. Although Joachim never pressed his third age to the point of anticlericalism, his ideas inspired the later Spiritual Franciscans and Fraticelli to stress the role of spiritual men as opposed to the clergy. The Fourth Lateran Council condemned his ideas on the Trinity, and in 1265, his central teachings were condemned by Alexander IV.

The Friars. Europe underwent a socioeconomic crisis with the further development of commerce and the rise of cities. The multitudes flocking to the new urban centers found freedom from direct feudal obligations and opportunities for personal advancement. However, the Church of the Middle Ages, like most other institutions of the time, was based on an agrarian economy. Neither the monastery of the twelfth century nor the rural parish any longer exercised the influence they had enjoyed in earlier ages. The Church was also losing its struggle for the minds of the educated, who crowded around teachers in the emerging universities. At this critical juncture in its history, the Church received help from the new religious orders, notably the Franciscans and the Dominicans. Preaching and pastoral care had fallen to a pitifully low estate among the secular clergy, and the universities tended to foster a secular gospel that called into question truths that had been held to be absolute for nearly a millennium. The clergy and hierarchy were embroiled in a struggle with powerful nobles and kings to keep a firm hold on their landed estates. The papacy, too, was involved in an unhappy conflict with the rulers of the young national states, a struggle that resulted in the Great Schism. The friars represented a new form of ministry to deal with the situation.

Francis of Assisi (d. 1226), son of a wealthy merchant, became dissatisfied with his aimless life of leisure and during a serious illness determined to devote the rest of his life to the service of the poor. During a trip to Rome, he exchanged his clothes with a beggar and spent the day begging for alms. This experience confirmed him in his resolve. Although his father disowned him, Francis succeeded in gathering a number of like-minded friends who took the name "friars minor," or little brothers (OFM—*ordo fratres minores*). From the color of their habit, they have also become known as greyfriars. Pope Innocent III confirmed the new order in 1209 to 1210. The brothers devoted themselves to serving the poor and dispossessed in the ghettos of the new urban centers in addition to reviving the art of preaching. In 1212, Franciscan ideals were espoused by a noble lady of Assisi, Clare, who became the founder of the St. Clares, or female branch of the Franciscans. Foreign mission work was also part of the Franciscan agenda, and the founder himself traveled through Spain, Egypt, and eastern Europe evangelizing the Muslims. The Franciscans were not so much reformers as innovators, creating a new force in the Church to minister to the spiritual and physical needs of a new society.

Dominic of Guzman (d. 1221), founder of the Order of Friars Preachers (OP—*ordo praedicatorum*), or blackfriars, was a native of Old Castille in Spain. For many years, he labored in Albigensian territories, striving to recall the heretical sect to the Church through the arts of preaching and persuasion. In 1216, he received papal sanction for the new order, which henceforth devoted itself to serving the intellectual needs of the Church. Dominican houses were established at all the major university centers of Europe, and Dominican preachers were everywhere in demand.

Because of their popularity, the friars were not always welcomed by parish priests. Clearly one reason for this was the fact that the friars generally outshone the priests in the art of preaching, in pastoral counseling via the confessional, and in piety. The secular clergy were forced into a more diligent exercise of their pastoral functions by the wholesome competition provided in the energetic and competent work of the friars.

The Dominicans were entrusted with the work of the Papal Inquisition, which began under Gregory IX in 1232. Inquisitors were dispatched throughout the Church, summoning all who were suspected of heresy to appear before a jury of clergy and laity. Those who confessed were assigned a penance. Those who remained obstinate in the face of certain proof were excommunicated. In some instances, they were handed over to the state for punishment, which in extreme cases could include confiscation of property, imprisonment, or even death. The notorious Spanish Inquisition bore a different stamp. This was primarily an instrument of the state and not of the Church. On numerous occasions, the Spanish authorities completely ignored papal pleas for clemency. Hundreds of orthodox bishops were killed by state officials, and the Jesuit order (founded 1540) was especially harassed because of its opposition to the Inquisition.

The friars enjoyed immediate popularity. In the second half of the thirteenth century, the Franciscans had twenty-five thousand members and eleven hundred houses. By 1303, the Dominicans numbered ten thousand friars and six hundred priories. The new orders provided a necessary leaven for the interior life of the Church.

Fourteenth Century. The fourteenth century witnessed Europe in transition. The medieval ideal of unity as expressed in the Holy Roman Empire gave way to nationalism, and strong monarchs replaced the weak titular kings of the feudal age. Democratic theories were reflected in the emergence of representative institutions: parliament in England, the cortes in Spain, the estates-general in France. However, Germany was fragmented into more than three hundred autonomous states. The revival of classicism with its emphasis on the individual paved the way for the principle of private judgment over secular and ecclesiastical authority. It was a time of trouble. The Hundred Years' War between France and England erupted in 1328 after years of preliminary sparring; the Black Death in 1348 carried off half of Europe's population; and scores of peasant revolts (one count lists seventy-eight) sparked by the tensions between declining feudalism and nascent capitalism contributed to the general unrest.

During most of this century (1309–77), the papal residence was at Avignon in southern France, where the pontiffs practically became wards of the king. This Babylonian Captivity, as it came to be called, resulted from the power struggle between King Philip IV of France and Pope Boniface VIII. Clement V (1305–14), the first of the Avignon popes, was forced by the king to condemn the Order of the Knights Templar, whereupon the king confiscated their assets. Clement was also plagued by the heresies of the Beghards and Beguines, who maintained that freedom in the Gospel meant freedom from all moral restraint.

As a result of emerging capitalism, princes, both secular and ecclesiastical, felt a great need for money to support their enterprises. The conflict between king and pope in France was sparked by the issue of taxation, and the war between France and England was primarily an economic affair. The Avignon popes, pressed as they were for capital, supported and strengthened some questionable financial institutions; the *annates*, in which the first year's income of a newly appointed bishop went to the pope (thus encouraging the frequent transfer of bishops); *reservations*, in which the revenues from vacant dioceses reverted to the pope so long as the vacancy existed; *expectancies*, in which, for a fee, a person was promised the right to succeed to an ecclesiastical office following the incumbent's death; *commendation*, by which, for a fee, a bishop was permitted to receive the revenues from a vacant diocese. Obviously, this system was subject to gross abuse, and Petrarch (d. 1374) denounced the papacy in scathing terms.

Churchly preoccupation with wealth also precipitated a crisis among the Franciscans. Already during the lifetime of Francis, a dispute had arisen over the possession of wealth. A group calling themselves the Spiritual Franciscans insisted on a return to the austerity required by their rule. By the fourteenth century, the struggle had become bitter; in 1317, Pope John XXII condemned those who insisted on a return to "evangelical poverty" (these were also known as the Fratricelli) and burned four intransigents as heretics. Louis of Bavaria, however, was sympathetic to their cause and sheltered them in his territory. William of Occam became their literary champion. The Fratricelli were also suspect because the works of Joachim of Fiore were influential among them.

The Avignon popes, by their claims to the loyalties (and revenues) of all Christians, brought on a crisis of authority since the monarchs of Europe were simultaneously making the same claims. A vigorous debate ensued as to the nature and origins of papal and regal authority. Perhaps the greatest of all the works on political theory written at this time was *On the Power of King and Pope* by the French Dominican John of Paris. He argued that civil government had its origins in man's nature, while the priesthood was to guide man to the world to come. In both areas, civil and ecclesiastical, the rulers were responsible to the community, and the best government was one in which people participated through duly chosen representatives. Authority derived from the community.

Another famous writer of this time, Dante (d. 1321), wrote "On Monarchy," in which he advocated a universal monarchy and the papacy existing side by side, but the two spheres of equal authority were to be clearly delineated.

Marsiglio of Padua (d. 1342) wrote one of the most challenging works of the late Middle Ages in his *The Defender of Peace*. He declared that the state is supreme and that it derives its authority from the people; the Church is a human institution and should come under state jurisdiction. Marsiglio further declared that Peter never possessed a primacy transferable to the popes and that all general councils should include laymen as well as clergy. *Defender* was condemned in 1327, and its excommunicated author spent the rest of his life in Munich under the protection of Louis of Bavaria. The Franciscan, William of Occam (d. 1347), did not go so far as Marsiglio in placing the Church under the state, yet in a series of antipapal tracts, he advocated a separation of Church and state that denied all temporal power to the papacy. He believed that popes could err and fall into heresy, and he distinguished between the whole Church as genus with the Roman Church as species. He also declared that a general council (which should include women) was the supreme authority in the Church. Both Occam and Marsiglio exercised considerable influence on the conciliarists of the following century.

The English monarchs were especially suspicious of the papacy during its French captivity. The kings of England believed, not without reason, that the popes sided with the French in the Hundred Years' War and that many church revenues being sent to Avignon were actually being used in the war effort against England. Several statutes were passed by parliament forbidding English monies to be sent overseas and establishing a fine for appeals to non-English (i.e., papal) courts. Some scholars detect the seeds of the English Reformation in these attitudes, which antedate the disestablishment of Henry VIII by two centuries. Louis of Bavaria (d. 1347) provided a second center of opposition to the Avignon popes by offering shelter to the literary opponents of the papacy.

During these years of turmoil, many efforts were made to return the papacy to Rome. Catherine of Siena (d. 1380) is especially famous for her letters to the popes, denouncing the style of life at Avignon and pleading for a return to Rome. Finally in 1377, Gregory XI (1370–1378) entered Rome, and the Babylonian Captivity was ended.

But a worse fate was in store for the Church. When the pope died the next year, the cardinals, threatened by the Romans to elect an Italian, chose Urban VI, the autocratic and overbearing bishop of Bari. The French cardinals, who constituted a majority in the College of Cardinals, left Rome and met in the country away from the tumult. There they deposed Urban, insisting that the election had been held under duress, and they chose Clement VII, who promptly reestablished the papacy at Avignon. Since Urban refused to abdicate, the Western Church was now divided in its loyalties between two popes, thus inaugurating the Great Schism, which lasted until 1417.

In contrast to the turmoil of the late fourteenth century stands the quiet mystical contemplation of Julian of Norwich (d. after 1416) in her *Revelations of Divine Love*.

Conciliarism. It was this intolerable situation that called forth advocates of reform of the Church "in head and members" by means of a general council. The conciliarists (those who saw the only solution to the impasse as calling a general council) drew heavily upon the ideas of John of Paris, Marsiglio, and Occam. The center of the movement was the University of Paris.

A year after the schism began, Conrad of Gelnhausen (d. 1390), a German master in Paris, began the movement by appealing to the French and German kings to convene a council. His fellow countryman, Henry of Langenstein (d. 1397) wrote "A Letter on Behalf of a Council of Peace," in which he rehearsed the rise of the papacy to prominence in the Church. He concluded that the power of the papacy derived from the bishops and the faithful.

In 1381, the University of Paris faculty unanimously adopted a resolution calling for a general council. Peter d'Ailly was a prominent leader of this school. His "Treatise on the Reformation of the Church" followed the thought of Occam. He believed that bishops and priests received their authority directly from Christ and not through the mediation of the pope and that both popes and councils were fallible. Jean Gerson followed d'Ailly as chancellor of the university, and though he supported conciliarism, he did not reject the primacy of the pope in the Church. In his work *On Unity*, he declared that the unity of the Church was so important that nothing should hinder it. Popes may be deposed and even imprisoned, but the College of Cardinals was not to elect a pope unless he would be universally acknowledged. The papacy, he said, was permanent, but individual popes could be controlled by councils.

Some years after the schism had actually ended, Nicolas of Cusa (d. 1464), a German cardinal, wrote a famous work *On Catholic Concord*. He outlined a program for the reform of the Church, noting the supremacy of the general councils. However, in later years, Nicolas modified his views somewhat, and he became a strong supporter of the papacy.

In 1409, the College of Cardinals finally succeeded in calling a general council in Pisa, which deposed the popes at Rome and Avignon and elected Alexander V to succeed them. Neither of the deposed popes acknowledged the validity of the council, so there were now three popes claiming the allegiance of Christendom.

The schism was finally healed by the Council of Constance (1414–18), which succeeded in deposing or ignoring all three pontiffs. Martin V was elected true pope (1417). A second issue of the council was the reform of the Church. The newly elected pope was made to promise reforms in the areas of reservations, *annates*, expectancies, simony, and all other abuses that had come to be associated with the late Medieval Church. The council also condemned over two hundred propositions of John Wycliffe and ordered his body to be exhumed from consecrated ground. The Bohemian priest John Hus, after arriving under the promise of safety by the emperor, was declared a heretic and burned at the stake. Although the schism had been healed, the council's treatment of Wycliffe and Hus, together with its failure to effect genuine reforms, made the Reformation of the sixteenth century inevitable.

Wycliffe and Hus. John Wycliffe (d. 1384), who had spent some years as a master at Oxford University and the last two decades of his life as a parish vicar, gained a reputation not only in philosophy but also in political affairs. Shortly after the outbreak of the papal schism, he set forth ideas that were sharply critical of the papacy. He declared that the true Church of Christ was that which reflected true Christian morality. Since the conduct of both popes, in his estimation, was in glaring contrast to this test, he pronounced them "limbs of Lucifer" in addition to labeling them antichrists. He attacked the doctrine of transubstantiation by observing that there can be no substance without observable accidents. He taught that the Bible alone was the source of all authority in the Church and that it should be read by all the faithful. To this end, he began to translate it into English. Membership in the true Church, Christ's mystical Body, was by divine predestination alone, a result of God's grace. Therefore pious works—veneration of saints, pilgrimages, indulgences—had no relation to salvation whatever. Wycliffe's followers, who came to be called Lollards, went preaching throughout England, attacking clerical celibacy, indulgences, and transubstantiation. Although Wycliffe himself escaped censure during his lifetime, the Lollards were severely persecuted.

Whereas Wycliffe's reform movement did not gain the support of most Englishmen, that of John Hus (d. 1415) in Bohemia became closely identified with Czech nationalism. Historians agree that Wycliffe's writings exerted considerable influence on the Bohemian Church. Hus himself admitted in 1411 that he and his friends had been reading Wycliffe's books for over twenty years. Ties between the two countries were strengthened by the marriage of Richard II of England to Anne of Luxemburg, sister of the Bohemian king.

Early in his career at the University of Prague, Hus stoutly maintained his orthodoxy on the doctrine of transubstantiation, the Mass, and indulgences. However, when Antipope John XXIII launched a campaign to raise money by means of indulgences, Hus became critical of the papacy and the church. With Wycliffe, he declared that the true Church of Christ was not identical with the Roman Church. He went on to say that popes have often contradicted one another, that clerics who lead ungodly lives are not worthy of support, and he demanded that the state take the initiative in effecting a moral reform.

In 1412, Hus was excommunicated, and he fled Prague. Emperor Sigismund prevailed upon him to appear before the Council of Constance to explain his views and be released from the ban. Hus, believing that he was innocent of heresy and that a general council would certainly exonerate him, agreed to the proposal and went to Constance. There, he was promptly imprisoned even before his hearing. At his trial, it was his affinities with Wycliffe that ultimately condemned him. He was burned at the stake, a common form of death for heretics since churchmen were forbidden by canon law to shed blood.

But Bohemia was not reconciled. Fifteen years of civil war ensued in which two parties emerged: the moderate Calixtines, who wished to remain in the Roman Church but insisted on free preaching, Communion in both kinds, reform of morals, and reduction of the wealth of the clergy; and the extreme Taborites, who wanted to break away from Rome. Both parties united against the military arms of the Roman faction, and in 1434, peace was attained through compromise. Both Roman and Hussite Christians were permitted to exist side by side. The Moravian Brethren (*Unitas Fratrum*) are today in direct continuation of the followers of John Hus.

EPILOGUE ON THE CHURCH OF THE MIDDLE AGES

At the beginning of the fifteenth century, the Church was in trouble. In the East, the Turks were overrunning Asia Minor; in 1453, Constantinople fell to the Muslims, in whose hands it remains to this day. In the West, the forces of secularism were undermining an already discredited church. But the weakness of Christianity was more apparent than real. The voices for reform found a responsive echo in the multitudes of the faithful who shared their concern. As so often had happened in the past, reform finally did come, but it brought both bane and blessing. The Church of the twenty-first century still lives in the shadow of the problems of authority, Church and state, and the nature of dogma bequeathed to it by the late Middle Ages.

CHAPTER FOUR

The Church of the Renaissance and Reformation

DECLINE AND REFORM FROM 1300 TO 1600

These three centuries witnessed dramatic and substantial changes within the Christian Church, for these were the centuries of the Renaissance and Reformation. Here, told all too briefly, are the stories of the Babylonian Captivity, the Schism and the Conciliar Movement, the Renaissance papacy, the spirit of reform among the mystics and the humanists, and finally the Reformation in its various aspects.

It was an age of great personalities whose impact on history and institutions is still being felt. It was a time of courageous religious heroes, of sainted martyrs, and of great cultural and intellectual giants. It was the time when the Christian Church began to be confronted by corrupting secularism, growing nationalism, and telling criticism. The attempt of the Church to directly influence the whole life of society became untenable, and the clergy found their activities confined more and more to spiritual functions. The secular state and an urban culture, new developments of this age, had a profound impact in changing the Medieval Church.

It was a period during which the Church experienced decline and then revitalization. The unity of the Medieval Church was shattered, but the diversity that arose did not mean disruption. The Christian Church was reformed and strengthened by the struggle that went on among its members during these centuries that ushered in the modern world.

All the denunciations and complaints occasioned by the varied abuses, corruption, wealth, and immorality among the clergy, as well as their commanding secular power and offices, are summed up by the word *anticlericalism*. With the rise of national states and strong monarchs, anticlericalism was often motivated by feelings of nationalism and resentment at the great tax-free wealth of the church, the loss of money to Rome, and papal interference in the politics and economy of the national state. With the increase of a humanistically educated laity, frequent attacks were made on the ignorance of the clergy. Humanists from Italy and later from northern Europe called for a reform from within the Church and used their training and knowledge to pen bitter satires and other works of condemnation. Preachers of reform thundered dire warnings from their pulpits, and everywhere shocked Christians prayed for reform and sought to live pious lives despite the poor example of the clergy.

CAUSES OF CHANGE AND REFORM		
	EVENTS	CONSEQUENCES
Changing Feudalism (c. 1300)	Northern Italian cities developed money economies and populous towns. These changes spread to other areas.	Ended the rural and agrarian economy and social patterns. Church leaders gained greater wealth. Monarchs raised taxes.
The Babylonian Captivity (1309–77)	Troubles in Rome led Pope Clement V to move the papacy to Avignon, France.	Other states saw the papacy as subservient to French rule. Needing money, the papacy became more worldly. Increased secularization.
The Great Schism (1378)	Pope Urban VI attempted to reform cardinals, who had become greedy, worldly. Cardinals declared the election of Urban VI invalid and elected Clement VII.	Each pope excommunicated the other. With a pope at Rome and a pope at Avignon, Europe was split into two parties. Confusion, doubts, and fears followed.
The Conciliar Movement	A series of councils attempted to end disputes (Pisa, 1409; Constance, 1414; Pavia, 1423; Basel, 1431; Ferrara/Florence, 1437).	Council decisions at first led to three popes and ultimately proved less effective than hoped. The papacy reasserted its power.
The Renaissance Papacy (1417–1521)	Beginning with scholarly Nicholas V, popes became more interested in classical learning, the arts, and securing their wealth and power.	Patronage, deep corruption, and even military campaigns dominated papal interests. Undermined credibility of spiritual leaders (anticlericalism).

John Wycliffe. More subversive and more direct than previous attacks were the anticlerical and theological arguments pronounced by John Wycliffe. This English reformer was born about 1320 and became a renowned professor of theology at Oxford. With the papacy residing at Avignon and under French influence, anticlericalism ran strong in fourteenth-century England. In this atmosphere, Wycliffe wrote English and Latin tracts and treatises containing statements and views on the Church that clearly foreshadow some of the expressions of later Protestant reformers. He advocated that the hierarchy, from pope to priest, be judged by the most rigid biblical standards. Since the secularized clergy were faithless stewards, they should be deprived of their power and property by the lay authorities, to whom God had given dominion over temporal matters. The Church had been given dominion only in spiritual matters, and a corrupt clergy loses claim even to this. Like Luther later, Wycliffe undermined the spiritual power and authority of the priesthood. He also recommended marriage of the clergy. He denied the theory of transubstantiation in the Eucharist, considered auricular confession unnecessary, rejected indulgences, and exalted the Bible, "the law of God," as the infallible and final authority in the Church. He recommended the formation of an English Church independent of the pope, whom he repeatedly called the Antichrist. With the help of two assistants,

Wycliffe translated the Scriptures into English. Although he was condemned by the pope for his views, the protection afforded by the powerful son of King Edward III, John of Gaunt, enabled Wycliffe to escape death at the stake. He died a natural death late in 1384. His teachings, however, continued to be spread among the people through the Lollards, or "poor priests."

John Hus. Bohemian students at Oxford took Wycliffe's writings home with them to Prague, where they found ready acceptance. The soil had been prepared by the reform preachers and the literature of the Bohemian *devotio moderna* ("new devotion"), a reform movement that emphasized frequent Communion and a thoroughgoing moral reform among Christians. The reform movement thus begun found a new leader in John Hus of the University of Prague, who was deeply influenced by Wycliffe's works. He did not accept Wycliffe's denial of traditional doctrine but denounced the traffic in indulgences, image worship, immorality among the hierarchy, simony, greed, and impious popes whom he considered antichrists. Despite opposition, excommunication, and a summons to Rome, Hus continued as an enormously popular preacher and writer. Under safe-conduct from Emperor Sigismund, Hus dared to appear before the Council of Constance. There he was falsely accused of heresy, imprisoned, condemned, and finally burned at the stake on July 6, 1415.

The death of the martyred Hus created a national revolt in Bohemia. Under the formulation called the Four Articles of Prague (1420), the Hussites demanded the giving of both bread and wine to laymen, or Communion "in both kinds"; the punishment of simony; the liberty to preach God's Word without ecclesiastical hindrance; and the end of the wealth and secular power of the clergy. The chalice became the symbol of Hussitism, and the moderate Hussites became known as Utraquists (both kinds). Most of the Utraquists, however, ultimately became Lutherans, and Luther liked to call himself a Hussite. The more radical Hussites, the Taborites, insisted on even more thoroughgoing reforms of ecclesiastical practices on the basis of the Bible, "the law of God." They practiced a type of Christian and democratic communism.

Savonarola. In Italy, the voice of warning and condemnation was that of a Florentine Dominican, Girolamo Savonarola (1452–98). This eloquent preacher chilled vast audiences with his impassioned denunciations of the external abuses of his time. The corruption and immorality of the clergy and the papacy, the luxury and greed of the citizens, and the tyranny of the Medici were all denounced in inflammatory sermons by this precursor of the Reformation. Like the Old Testament prophets, he foretold the ruin of sinful Italy and the invasion of the French armies as God's avengers. When the Medici were driven from Florence (1494), Savonarola governed the republic that was proclaimed. The dissolute pope, Alexander VI, summoned him to Rome and ordered him to stop preaching. Neither of these orders was obeyed, and the friar continued his uncompromising attacks on the corruption exhibited by the pope and clergy. Finally, seized by his enemies, Savonarola and two of his followers were tortured, condemned as heretics and false prophets, hanged, and burned (May 23, 1498). When this spirited insurrectionist died, Luther was fourteen years old.

Mysticism. The new spirit of reform was very evident in the work of the mystics, who stirred the Christians of northern and central Europe with their widespread preaching and voluminous devotional literature. These mystics of the fourteenth and later centuries emphasized personal piety and direct access to God. They thus created a religious climate that was to favor the later Protestant reformers. The mystics stressed the emotional religious experience rather than the intellectual and a life in imitation of Christ. They preached and wrote in the vernacular and thus influenced multitudes of Christians who longed for a simple religion along apostolic ideals. Their teachings centered on the *devotio moderna*, or "new devotion."

The *devotio moderna* received its greatest and finest expression in the *Imitation of Christ*, a work most probably written by Thomas à Kempis (d. 1471). As a devotional booklet, it stressed humility, passiveness, and contemplation, while showing little concern for the systematic theology of the Church. Strongly ethical and moral in tone, the *Imitation* was a manual for the truly Christian life. It sought to prepare the reader's soul for the purity necessary for union with God. The reading and study of Scriptures was enjoined as essential for the preparation of the inner spirit.

Christian Humanism. While the mystics sought an emotional religious experience, the Christian humanists used a more intellectual approach in expressing their new spirit of reform. With but few exceptions, Italian humanists did not concern themselves greatly with the Gospel. However, when humanism spread to the areas north of the Alps in the late fifteenth century, a Christian and reformist concern became more evident. Turning away from scholasticism, these humanists sought the true meaning of the sources of Christianity. Many of the northern humanists made excellent use of their knowledge of history and of Greek, Latin, and Hebrew to make the texts of the Bible and the Church Fathers clearer. In the light of a better philological understanding of the actual words used in the early Christian literature, new interpretations of the texts were made. This Christian humanism, as it has been called, sought to bring about a moral and educational reform from within the Church.

Desiderius Erasmus of Rotterdam (1469–1536) was the most significant Christian humanist. Through brilliant satire and ridicule, this international scholar hoped to effect a change in the ignorance, greed, and immorality of the clergy and the laity. In his popular *Praise of Folly*, he castigated the follies and stupid activities of mankind, but the clergy especially were held up to ridicule. Numerous and learned as his writings were, Erasmus's greatest scholarly achievement lay in his editing of early Christian texts. In 1502, he edited and published the first edition of Lorenzo Valla's critical revision of the Latin text of the New Testament. In 1516, he published his own very influential Greek and Latin edition of the New Testament, which bore ample evidence of his humanistic training. He expressed the hope that the Scriptures would be translated into all languages so that everyone would know the sacred words firsthand. In 1516 also appeared his critical edition of Jerome. This was followed later by editions of Augustine, Basil, Ambrose, and other Early Church writers. All these texts were to be used by the reformers. It is no wonder that even in his lifetime, Erasmus was said to have "laid the egg that Luther hatched."

MARTIN LUTHER

In 1513, Niccolò Machiavelli prophetically wrote that Christianity had strayed far from its founding principles and would soon face chastisement. Four years later, Europeans were made aware that the agent of that chastisement was the Augustinian monk of Wittenberg named Martin Luther.

Early Years and Entry into the Monastery. Martin Luther was born on November 10, 1483, in the town of Eisleben, Thuringia, a region in central Germany. His father, of peasant origin, was a miner with high ambitions for his son. Luther's education at home and at schools in Mansfeld, Magdeburg, and Eisenach was in the usual medieval tradition except for his training for one year at Magdeburg, where he was taught by teachers humanistically educated in the schools of the Brethren of the Common Life. In 1501, he entered the renowned University of Erfurt; there he studied the liberal arts and received his bachelor of arts degree late in 1502. His master of arts degree was obtained in February 1505.

In his theological training at Erfurt, Luther was much influenced by the Occamism of his professors, by the emphasis they placed on the Scriptures, and by their attacks on the Aristotelianism of Scholasticism. Luther began the study of law, a parental decision. Then, while returning from a visit to his parents early in July 1505, he was so frightened by a thunderbolt that struck close to him that he called in terror to the patron saint of the miners, "Help, dear Anne, I will become a monk!" Although his friends tried to dissuade him, Luther entered the Black Cloister of the strict Hermits, or Eremites, of St. Augustine at Erfurt on July 17. The entry into the monastery was probably the culmination of an inner struggle he had been experiencing for some time.

In September 1506, Luther professed the irrevocable vows of chastity, obedience, and poverty. He became a priest the next spring and celebrated his first Mass with awe. In the fall of 1508, Luther was transferred to the Augustinian monastery at Wittenberg to teach at the university recently founded there by Frederick the Wise, the elector of Saxony. While there, Luther also continued his theological studies. Recalled to Erfurt late in 1509, his teaching there was interrupted during the winter of 1510–11 by a trip to Rome on business of the order. Later, at Wittenberg, he received his doctorate (1512), the funds being supplied by the elector. He then succeeded John von Staupitz, vicar of the Augustinian order, as lecturer in biblical theology.

Inner Struggle. It was during these years of graduate study and teaching that Luther experienced the inner struggle that was profoundly to affect the history of the Christian Church. The Occamism of his training had stressed God's absolute will in the acts of salvation or damnation and yet admitted that there was a possibility that man could contribute to his salvation by his own will. The sensitive and devout Luther could never reach confidence in the sufficiency of his own love for God because of his despair at the awful justice (righteousness) of a stern and demanding God. He feared that he fell short of the perfection that God demanded, because his own love of God did not merit God's love for him. He wondered whether he didn't belong to those predestined to damnation. He imposed upon himself the most rigorous discipline. He read widely among the medieval theological writers and noted their divergence from Scripture. He sought aid and comfort from the sympathetic Staupitz, who was not only his superior but also his father confessor. All to no avail: Brother Martin's sense of sin and unworthiness was too strong. His entire religious background had stressed Christ as the Judge, not the Savior, of the world.

The Great Discovery. At Wittenberg, instead of resorting to the customary discussions of the traditional commentaries on it, Luther lectured on the various books of the Bible themselves. His own notes, where extant, and those of his students show a new spirit and a growing, bold dependence on the Scriptures alone and an abandonment of the widespread allegorical approach. His fresh approach won him great popularity as a teacher.

Luther's lecture notes reveal the depth of his inner struggle, which centered on the problem of justification, or of God's righteousness, or justice. *Justitia* is the Latin term for the justice of God by which He judges men, either in righteous wrath or in saving mercy.

It was probably in 1514 while he was studying the meaning of Romans 1:17, "For in it [in the Gospel] the righteousness of God is revealed from faith for faith, as it is written, 'The righteous shall live by faith,'" that Luther experienced his historic discovery. He felt as though he "had entered Paradise through widely opened doors" when he suddenly realized that God loves sinners and judges the believer in mercy, acquitting him from his sin and imputing to him by pure grace the righteousness of Christ. That is, God justifies the believer for Christ's sake and by faith alone. Man's moral deeds play no role in it. Faith, that is, trust in God, is the "receiving hand" that enables man to accept God's mercy; it is the instrument of his justification. Although unacceptable in himself, he is now "righteous" in God's sight and saved. Faith simultaneously leads the Christian to a life of gratitude for God's unmerited love.

In the light of this discovery, which Luther found in the writings of Paul, the entire late medieval concept of God had to be reexamined and, along with this, all that was called Christianity. The Gospel, which shows God's mercy through Christ, became the center of Luther's new theology, a theology that was drastically to change so much of the Christian Church of his day. Yet, so far, Luther was unaware that his new understanding of the Gospel would revolutionize and split the Church.

Many of the staff and students at the university were won to Luther's new theology, and the Augustinian's reputation went far beyond the little university town of Wittenberg. Luther, firmly convinced of the truth of his views, also gradually became more critical of his own Scholastic theological inheritance, many of the traditional Christian practices, and clerical leadership. Already in 1516, he preached against the abuses in the indulgence traffic, which subordinated repentance in life to penance, or satisfaction, which, in turn, was taken care of by the purchase of an indulgence letter. It was his concern for the dangers that lay in the use of indulgences that thrust Luther into full visibility in 1517.

The Indulgence Controversy. In 1513, Prince Albert of Brandenburg, a young man without theological training, was named archbishop of Magdeburg and bishop of Halberstadt. Since this involved pluralism, the illegal holding of more than one position in the hierarchy, and since Albert was only twenty-three, not yet thirty as required by canon law, Pope Leo X granted the necessary dispensations to Albert for a good sum of money. The ambitious Albert then also obtained from the pope the more important position of archbishop of Mainz, primate of Germany. A large fee of over 23,000 ducats was required by the papal court for this arrangement. Money to pay part of this fee was borrowed by Albert from the Fugger banking house. To help the new archbishop raise the required funds, Leo X proclaimed an indulgence to be offered to those who contributed to the rebuilding of St. Peter's Basilica in Rome. The papal agreement called for Albert to sell the indulgences in his three ecclesiastical territories and in Brandenburg. When expenses had been paid, one half of the proceeds was to go to Albert's debt with the Fuggers and the other half to Leo.

The archbishop carefully instructed his indulgence agents so as to secure the greatest number of sales. Among these agents was an unscrupulous Dominican friar named John Tetzel, a veteran salesman who employed extravagant language in his sales talk. Tetzel, according to contemporary accounts, was well versed in sales psychology and was credited with using the questionable ditty "As soon as the money clinks in the chest, the soul flits [from purgatory] into heavenly rest" to stress the efficacy of his wares.

The elector of Saxony had not permitted the sale of this indulgence in his lands because he was concerned about any competition to his own remunerative, indulgence-granting collection of relics housed in the Castle Church at Wittenberg. But Brandenburg was not far distant from Wittenberg, and some of the citizens secured indulgences from Tetzel. Luther, as father confessor in the town church, soon became aware of and disturbed by the effect Tetzel was having on the penitential practices of his parishioners, who in place of repentance substituted the indulgence letter.

The Ninety-five Theses. In February 1517, Luther preached a sermon against the false security felt by the holders of indulgence letters. He found indulgences opposed to his new theology that grace alone and no satisfaction on man's part can bring salvation. He decided to open the whole matter to an academic debate. Late in October, "out of love and zeal for the elucidation of the truth," he drew up ninety-five theses, or propositions, dealing with penance and indulgences in general, all of which he was prepared to debate at Wittenberg or through correspondence. On October 31, Luther nailed his printed Latin theses to the door of the Castle Church, the bulletin board of the university. The date was important, for November 1 was All Saints' Day, and on this festival, the elector's large collection of relics was displayed in the church. Visitors who venerated these relics and made the appropriate prayers received indulgences. Luther even respectfully sent a copy of his theses to Archbishop Albert.

The theses were not intended as a protest against the Church, and yet with them the Reformation started. The first two theses set the tone: "When our Lord and Master Jesus Christ said, 'Repent,' he willed the entire life of believers to be one of repentance. This word cannot be understood as referring to the sacrament of penance, that is, confession and satisfaction as administered by the clergy." The indulgence cannot take the place of the penance, the repentance required of the sinner. In other theses, he questioned the pope's power to remit all penalties and wondered why the pope did not use his own wealth to build St. Peter's instead of the money collected from the poor. If the pope could "empty purgatory" for money, why did he not do it out of charity? Luther did not reject papal indulgences at this time, but rather he warned of the dangerous misunderstandings and the extravagant claims for papal power current among the purchasers and preachers of indulgences.

The effect of the theses was astonishing. They were translated into German and soon circulated everywhere. The Dominicans lined up with Tetzel against Luther and his fellow Augustinians. No wonder the unsuspecting Leo X referred to the controversy in Germany as a "monks' squabble." A pamphlet war began, a medium of controversy that was to expand immensely. In October 1518, at the Diet of Augsburg, Luther appeared before the Cardinal Cajetan, the papal legate who had been ordered to declare the monk a heretic and summon him to Rome. Luther thought that the cardinal was as fit to deal with the case on theological grounds "as an ass was to play a harp." Luther refused to recant his views, and an interview brought no reconciliation.

The Leipzig Debate. Luther's next public debate took place at Leipzig in July 1519. Johann Eck, professor of theology at Ingolstadt, was his able opponent. The meeting had originally been planned as a debate with Andreas Karlstadt, a colleague of Luther, although it was obvious to all that Luther was really the opponent. The basic point of contention was Luther's assertion that the papacy was of recent and human origin. Luther studied the medieval papal decretals, or epistles, in preparation for the debate, and this only convinced him that the papacy was the Antichrist, that is, an institution opposed to the true Christian doctrine. Eck cited ancient authorities, now regarded by all as false documents, in support of the divine origin and thus the primacy of the Roman papacy. Luther doubted the validity of these statements, and in this, he was far ahead of his time. Luther was more familiar with Scripture than Eck, but the latter knew the medieval theological traditions better than Luther. Eck very cleverly forced Luther to declare that John Hus, a condemned heretic, had held views that were "plainly Christian and evangelical" and that the general councils of the Church, taught to be infallible, had often erred and "contradicted each other."

The Leipzig Debate settled nothing, of course, but Luther had been pushed farther along in his opposition to the Roman Church. In June 1520, a bull of excommunication against Luther was issued at Rome. It ordered him to recant or appear in Rome within sixty days. On December 10, Luther publicly burned the bull, an act that was a dramatic closing to a year that had seen Luther's maturing views find expression in three famous and revolutionary tracts.

The Treatises of 1520. Luther's *To the Christian Nobility of the German Nation* was a patriot's appeal to the German princes to throw off the bonds that subjected them to Rome. Luther denied that there was any distinction between the laity and the clergy. Every Christian was a member of "the priesthood of all believers" through Baptism. All Christians were responsible for the spiritual welfare of their neighbors and should carry out reforms so that the true faith could flourish. Luther also declared that every Christian had the essential right to read and interpret God's Word. In the priesthood of all believers and in the right of interpretation, Luther was not a religious individualist who felt that everyone should preach, give the Sacraments, and so on, but rather that each Christian had this potential if properly trained and appointed to the office of the ministry. He thus destroyed the unscriptural medieval distinction between the clergy and laity.

In other parts of *To the Christian Nobility*, Luther asserted that Christian laymen and especially the princes should exercise their Christian duty and power by calling a council to reform the Church. He also fiercely denounced the worldliness of the clergy, the drain of money from Germany, and the corruption in Rome. He suggested the formation of a German national church and strongly proposed that the clergy should be permitted to marry so as to eliminate the immorality that so often marked clerical celibacy. He further advocated educational, social, and moral reform. He called for the suppression of the mendicant orders and for the elimination of canon law.

Luther replied to the bull of excommunication by issuing a second revolutionary treatise on October 6, 1520, entitled *The Babylonian Captivity of the Church*, written in Latin and intended for theologians. Here, Luther attacked the entire sacramental and sacerdotal system of the Roman Church, which he felt had held Christian souls captive for over a thousand years. Only three sacraments—Baptism, the Lord's Supper, and possibly penance—met the requirements of having promises of Christ attached to them and so were the only real sacraments. The other four sacraments of the Roman Church—confirmation, matrimony, the anointing of the sick, and ordination—however worthwhile, were not sacraments conferring salvation and were not from Scripture.

To Luther, Baptism was really a continual process of "the drowning of the old man" and the coming forth of the "new man" in Christ throughout life. It was an agreement by which God promises forgiveness of sins to the penitent Christian all life long. This lifelong effect and significance of Baptism had been forgotten in late medieval Christendom. Luther, unlike some of his more radical contemporaries, upheld the Baptism of infants.

In the Lord's Supper, Luther rejected the late medieval doctrine of transubstantiation, whereby the substance of the bread and wine were taught to be transformed into the body and blood of Christ. He did, however, take the Words of Institution literally, asserting that Christ was received by the communicant in the physical elements of this Sacrament that, like Baptism, was a covenant (promise, or testament) of God. He denounced the late medieval practice of withholding the cup from the laity, and most important, he denied that the Mass (Eucharist) was a meritorious action, a sacrifice or offering of Christ by the officiating priest. Christ's death on the cross was the one sufficient sacrifice for the sins of all ages. Man can do nothing and needs to do nothing to "merit" God's grace and favor. Throughout this manifesto, which raised cries of horror from his opponents, Luther emphasized the role of faith in salvation and the priesthood of all believers.

As for the sacrament of penance, Luther felt that, strictly speaking, this was not really a sacrament because it lacked an essential visible symbol. The rite had been much abused, for current practice had removed from it the most important elements of repentance and the unconditional nature of God's forgiveness, or absolution, and had stressed instead the church-imposed satisfaction, in which no faith was required.

Late in 1520, Luther wrote a conciliatory letter to Leo X and accompanied it with a calm and edifying pamphlet entitled *The Freedom of a Christian*. The reformer considered this work a summary of Christian life. He began with a paradox: The Christian man is through faith a free lord and subject to no one; the Christian is the most dutiful servant of all and subject to everyone. That is, the Christian is freed by God's grace from guilt and the need for perfect fulfillment of God's Law. However, the believing, regenerate Christian wants to and is obliged to do good works that aid his neighbor. He has no vested interest in doing them, as he isn't earning his way to heaven by them. He cannot *help* but love his fellowman: "Good works do not make a good man, but a good man does good works; evil works do not make a wicked man, but a wicked man does evil works. . . . As Christ also says: 'A good tree cannot bear evil fruit, nor can a bad tree bear good fruit.'" A Christian, loving God and his fellow man, will strive for social improvement by participating actively in community life.

The Diet of Worms. The new Holy Roman Emperor, Charles V, summoned his first diet to meet at Worms early in 1521. Yielding to the demands of electors and the people, he granted Luther a letter of safe-conduct for a hearing before the diet, something the reformer had long requested. The trip from Wittenberg to the city on the upper Rhine River was a triumphal march, and sympathetic crowds came to see and hear the defiant monk. On April 17, Luther appeared before the assembled nobles, clergy, and representatives of the free cities. When asked to identify certain books as his and to recant the heresies in them, he acknowledged his authorship of the books but asked for time to consider the second demand. When the allotted twenty-four-hour delay was over, Luther again appeared before the diet. When asked to recant, Luther pointed out that no simple answer was possible, as he had written on a variety of things, some of which were truly Christian and in defense of the Word of God. He asked to be corrected on the basis of Scriptures. Then, after being asked for a clear and simple answer, Luther made his historic response: "Unless

I am convinced of error by the testimony of Scripture or by clear reason . . . I cannot and will not recant anything, for it is neither safe nor honest to act against one's conscience. God help me. Amen." Still defiant and uncompromising, Luther left Worms on April 26. In the Thuringian forest, by previous arrangement, men of Frederick the Wise spirited the soon-to-be-outlawed monk away to the seclusion and safety of the Wartburg Castle near Eisenach.

The Edict of Worms. When the emperor had gained from the diet a promise of aid against his enemy Francis I of France and after many representatives of the states had left, Charles submitted and secured the passage of the Edict of Worms, which falsely charged that Luther had written books in which "he destroys, overturns and abuses the number, arrangement and use of the seven sacraments . . . and in astonishing ways shamefully pollutes the indissoluble bonds of holy matrimony. . . . He desires also to adapt our customs and practice in the administration of the most holy sacrament of the holy Eucharist to the habit and custom of the condemned Bohemians. . . . He not only holds the priestly office and order in contempt, but also urges secular and lay persons to bathe their hands in the blood of priests; and he uses scurrilous and shameful words against the chief priest of our Christian faith, the successor of St. Peter and true vicar of Christ on earth. . . . Indeed, he writes nothing which does not arouse and promote sedition, discord, war, murder, robbery and arson, and tend toward the complete downfall of the Christian faith." Since Luther was accused of all these and many other things, the emperor declared that Luther should hereafter "be held and esteemed by each and all of us as a limb cut off from the Church of God, an obstinate schismatic and manifest heretic." Everyone was to refuse Luther "hospitality, lodging, food, or drink." Luther was to be placed in custody and held for punishment. The break with the past was definitive.

Wartburg and Wittenberg. Luther relieved the boredom of his seclusion at the Wartburg by study and voluminous writing. He wrote a series of sermons so as to give some direction and unity to the preaching of the "new theology" being done under the name of "Lutheranism." Late in 1521, he submitted for publication the Latin work *On Monastic Vows*, in which he attacked the monastic system and the vows taken by the regular clergy. He left it up to the individual whether to leave the monastery or not. He felt that monastic vows were unscriptural and that they rested on the false assumption that there was a special religious vocation, or calling, for certain Christians. Rather, Luther extended the concept of a divine calling to *all* worthwhile occupations. Even the common laborer could exemplify the Gospel in his work.

Luther's greatest literary contribution to the Reformation during his stay at the Wartburg was the translation of the entire New Testament from the Greek to German. His translation, accomplished in only three months, demonstrated his gift for languages and showed that he fully understood the message and the spirit of Scriptures. Its great genius was that it made the New Testament speak in the plain and natural language of the people. It did not read like a translation. There had been numerous German translations before Luther's, but these had not been from the

Greek and tended to be wooden and stilted. The translation appeared in September 1522 and was immediately a best seller and an effective medium for the spread of a more biblical piety among its thousands of readers.

Luther's stay at the Wartburg was disturbed by news from Wittenberg, where his zealous and overenthusiastic associates were pushing the Reformation toward impulsive radicalism. As the violence increased and the spirit of reform took forms alien to Luther's thinking, he left the security of the Wartburg and returned to Wittenberg. On March 9, 1522, he began a series of eight sermons in the town church in which he preached moderation and restraint and the abandonment of reform through force. The preaching of God's Word would achieve the reform. Luther always stressed that matters of the spirit can never be forced on anyone. He pointed out that besides the fundamentals of religion, there were many marginal things concerning which man could make a choice. Images, ceremonies, symbols, vestments, festivals, fasts, and other outward customs could be useful in devotion, provided they were not worshiped or regarded as binding the conscience. The Christian was free with regard to them and only had to avoid offending his "weaker brother." There was no iconoclasm in the Lutheran Reformation, and conservatism of this kind was to mark Luther's views for the rest of his life.

LUTHER'S CHANGES TO DOCTRINE AND PRACTICE	
BAPTISM	In 1523, Luther began to simplify rites, starting with Baptism. Revised service renounced the devil and confessed the Creed as central acts.
CONFIRMATION	First rejected by Luther since he did not regard it as a sacrament. Later reintroduced with an emphasis on teaching doctrine.
COMMUNION	1523 Form of the Mass shows Luther's conservatism. Only removed what conflicted with evangelical doctrine. Focused on Christ's Words of Institution. Laity received both the body and blood of Christ. Private masses abolished. 1526 German order.
MARRIAGE	Emphasized high dignity of marriage, though not a sacrament. Announced marriages from the pulpit. Legal aspect belonged to the State. Church was to pray and bless.
HYMNODY	First hymnal published in 1524. Taught doctrine through hymns and treasured music. Lutheran Church became known as the "singing church."

Although much work was still to be done in rebuilding the structure of a reformed Christian Church, the firm doctrinal and liturgical foundation had already been laid by Luther. He had begun his attack on abuses as a loyal son of the Church with no intention of creating separate institutional forms. Yet the Reformation of Luther was not a reform of externals, and so it struck at the very heart of medieval doctrine, practices, and institutions. For, when seen in the light of his new Gospel-based theology, much of the vast superstructure that the Medieval Church had erected on the foundations of early Christianity had to be cleared away. Luther thus rejected the traditions of purgatory, the cult of saints and relics, Mariolatry, the meritoriousness of pilgrimages and fasts, the primacy of the pope, the Mass as a sacrifice, a majority of the seven sacraments, monasticism, celibacy of the clergy, the distinction of the clergy as a separate "spiritual estate," and many other practices and beliefs that in his view had no basis in Scripture and hindered and obscured the true message of the Gospel. And that message centered on salvation as effected by Jesus Christ alone. In his search for the basic doctrines of the pristine Church of the early Christian centuries, Luther reaffirmed Paul's teaching of justification by faith alone instead of by faith *and* good works. By placing the Bible in the vernacular in the hands of all, he emphasized the biblical basis of Christianity and suggested that all tradition must be in harmony with Scripture. In his revision of the service, he properly stressed the glad tidings of God's love, the heart of his theology. Since the hierarchy of his day was not ready for such radical changes, Luther had to be expelled from the Roman Church, and thus an independent evangelical church had to come into being.

LUTHERANISM

Although the Diet of Worms had placed Luther under the imperial ban and in danger of execution, neither the pope nor the emperor was in any position to proceed against Luther and enforce the edict. Popular unrest had been increased by the action at Worms, and many German nationalists felt that Luther must be protected. Many, like Frederick the Wise, wanted a fair treatment for the professor of Wittenberg even though they may not have accepted his new theology. Also, despite the ferment within his Empire, Charles V had begun in 1521 the first of his four wars with France. He was too deeply involved with political matters to execute the Edict of Worms and destroy the widening number of Luther's followers.

Polemical Literature. The Edict of Worms did not prevent the energetic Luther from advancing the cause of his evangelical reform whenever and wherever he could. He and his supporters engaged in a pamphlet war with those who were attacking him with violent and abusive language—and often with little understanding of his theological views. Polemical literature was exchanged with many, and all these numerous works, often written in the vernacular, helped spread the new theology to an eager and ever-wider audience. Indeed, it is difficult to exaggerate the importance of printing for the spread of the Reformation.

Instructional Literature. More constructive for the cause of the Reformation was the instructional literature that flowed from the pen of the busy Luther. There was a desperate need to give some theological unity to the reform movement by such writings and to instruct the numerous preachers, often self-called and unlearned, who were arising in response to their interpretation of the "priesthood of all believers." Luther himself published a number of sermonettes, but most important for the emerging Lutheran Church was the publication of the entire Scriptures in Luther's German translation and of the two catechisms of 1529. The reformer had completed the translation of the New Testament while at the Wartburg, and this was published in September 1522. It is estimated that 200,000 copies were sold in the first twelve years. Work was then begun on the more difficult and longer Old Testament, the German translation of which began to appear serially from 1523 on. The complete German Bible, including the Apocrypha, appeared in 1534 with 124 woodcut illustrations. This great prose work had a tremendous effect on the later development of the German language. It made readily available the all-sufficient source of the faith of the evangelical movement.

Another instructional work resulted from an official church inspection, a so-called visitation, of the churches in Saxony in 1528. Luther saw such "deplorable destitution" and ignorance that he was constrained to prepare a simple catechism as an aid to the pastors and heads of families for the Christian instruction of their congregations or households. He found that the common people, especially in the villages, knew nothing at all of Christian doctrines and that many pastors were quite unfit and incompetent to teach. Yet all were called Christians, had been baptized, and enjoyed the use of the Sacraments, although they knew neither the Lord's Prayer, the Creed, nor the Ten Commandments. Using questions and answers, Luther presented the fundamentals of Christianity in the Small Catechism in a simple and easily understandable way. It was intended that after preliminary instruction in the contents of the Small Catechism, the pastors would impart to their congregations a "richer and fuller knowledge" by using the Large Catechism he also prepared. The value of the German Bible and the two catechisms in spreading the Gospel, the good news of God's unmerited love, which was the heart of the new theology, is immeasurable.

Separation from the Knights and Humanists. After the Diet of Worms, it became necessary for the Reformation to assume its own character and to separate itself from those discontented elements who had different goals and did not really belong in the movement, though they had their usefulness as temporary allies. The earliest separation was from the German knights. This decadent class of feudal society was feeling acutely their loss of prestige as military men, of income in the face of rising prices and an urban economy, and of political power to rising absolutism. During the early years of the Reformation, the knights, strongly nationalistic, hailed Luther as a German patriot who, like themselves, was fighting for liberty from a restrictive and unreasonable foreign (Roman) authority. But the first attempt to use the Reformation in support of social and political reorganization ended in complete failure as the princes everywhere in the German states strengthened their position over the knights.

Another and more serious separation that occurred soon after Worms was from the humanists. Long before the rise of Luther to prominence, northern humanists had appealed for a religious reformation. Although strongly anticlerical, they had hoped for reform from within the constituted lines of ecclesiastical authority. Luther felt a great debt to these humanists who had prepared the way for the Reformation and, by their philological studies and their emphasis on going back to the "sources" of Christianity, had opened up the literature of the Early Christian Church. As long as Luther attacked the abuses in the externals of religion, such as the indulgence traffic, the humanists supported his bold stand. After the Diet of Worms, however, and with the further development of the new theology to a definite break with Roman Catholicism, many of the humanists deserted Luther. They were reformers but not revolutionaries. Moreover, the humanism that stressed the dignity and essential goodness of man could not really fit into a Christianity that emphasized the total depravity of man and his absolute dependence on God's grace.

The separation of humanism from the Reformation is best seen in the case of Erasmus, who was at first sympathetic to Luther's desire for reform. However, the violence of the attacks on medieval dogma and on the hierarchy by the fiery and energetic monk of Wittenberg was against his gentle nature, and he disapproved of the schism within Christianity that he saw would result. At last, yielding to pressure from both sides, he abandoned his neutral position and wrote his *Discourse on Free Will* against Luther's theological position. In this work, Erasmus, averse to dogma, approached the problem of man's ability to act on his own as a humanist. Although he did not completely understand Luther's theological distinctions regarding the subject, he concluded that the denial of the existence of free will on man's part was a dangerous doctrine and incompatible with reason. "I prefer," he wrote, "the opinion of those who attribute something to free will, but a great deal to grace." Without the free will to choose the good, he felt man would be relieved of all moral responsibility.

In reply to the moderate discussion of the problem by Erasmus, Luther published his *Bondage of the Will* in 1525. Here, he condemned Erasmus for his rationalist skepticism, vacillation, and inconsistencies. He presented his views again that "the will, having lost its freedom [with original sin], is compulsively bound to the service of sin, and cannot will anything good." Man is either driven by Satan or led by the Spirit of God, and he is saved solely by grace, through faith. Christian doctrine is not based on rational deduction, but on God's revelation in Scripture. By 1525, the separation was complete.

Philip Melanchthon. While many of the humanists found it more congenial to their spirit to remain in communion with Rome, a number assisted in the development of Lutheranism. The most significant contribution by a humanist was made by Philip Melanchthon (1497–1560). This brilliant young classical scholar came to Wittenberg in 1518 to teach Greek at the university. He entered into a warm and lasting association with Luther, to whom he was deeply devoted. He assisted the reformer in many ways, including the translation of the Bible into German. In 1521, he published the first edition of his *Loci communes,* or "Common (Scriptural) Passages"; a German translation and revisions appeared later. This apt and systematic formulation of evangelical beliefs based on the chief passages of Scripture was to become basic to the Lutheran movement. Luther, the stormy petrel, and Melanchthon, the quiet scholar, worked well together, although the humanistic scholar often tended to compromise with opposing camps. When Luther died in 1546, Melanchthon acquired the role of leadership in Lutheranism, a task for which he was not fully suited.

Peasants' Revolt. Within a few years after Worms, Luther was forced to show that his reform was religious in nature and that it was not to be identified with the schemes of social revolutionaries. The complaints of the peasants—new oppressive taxes, the introduction of Roman law in the place of the customary feudal law, unjustifiable payments and services to the feudal lords, rising prices, economic monopolies, inferior political and social status, and so on—were of long standing, and the peasants had revolted before. However, the general tensions and ferment in Germany, the new evangelism with its misinterpreted "liberty" of the Christian man, and the obstinacy of the powerful princes, who refused to give any concessions to the peasants, created a situation that erupted in violence. Luther, quite naturally, was hailed as a fighter for freedom, and the peasants erroneously identified his cause with political, economic, and social change. Although some groups espoused the more moderate *Twelve Articles* drawn up as a program at Memmingen early in 1525, in general the revolt was a leaderless and programless uprising. It grew more violent as time went on and the demands of the peasants were not met. The destruction of monasteries and castles was great, but eventually the princes, with the aid of German troops released by the emperor's victory at Pavia in February, suppressed the revolt, generally with great cruelty. The position of the peasant was debased and that of the princes enhanced.

Luther, of peasant stock himself, sympathized with the lot of the peasants and criticized the lords for their oppression. Yet he feared anarchy and was basically a conservative. When the *Twelve Articles* were sent to Luther and others for arbitration, Luther wrote an *Admonition to Peace in Response to the Twelve Articles*. He felt that the social and spiritual realms were entirely separate; they were "two kingdoms." A Christian prince or any duly appointed magistrate should govern with justice, but Christian subjects should rather suffer injustice than take justice in their hands. The powers that be have their authority from God. When the revolt increased in violence, Luther wrote an inordinately outspoken and virulent pamphlet, *Against the Thievish, Murderous Hordes of Peasants* (May 1525), in which he called upon the princes to use their God-given authority and put down the anarchistic rebels with all the cruelty necessary. Later, he wrote several more tracts explaining his views on rebellion and condemning those who continued to repress the peasants.

The Peasants' Revolt and its cruel suppression had heavy consequences for the Reformation, for the disheartened peasantry turned from Lutheranism to the more radical sects. Lutheranism ceased to be a popular movement. Many princes were likewise estranged from it or hardened against it because the revolt seemed to confirm their fears that a change in religion could only result in unrest, anarchy, and chaos. Lutheranism and rebellion seemed synonymous to them. Luther's own prestige as a leader of the people suffered, for his attitude alienated the lower classes. Luther himself, equally conservative in nonreligious as well as religious matters, distrusted the peasants thereafter and relied more and more on the authorities for support and leadership in the Reformation churches. The Lutheran churches became "territorial," or governed by the authorities of the different territories and cities. The people and the local congregation ceased to have anything to say in church government.

Luther Marries. It was also in 1525, on June 13, that Luther, then forty-one, married Katharina von Bora, twenty-six, an escaped nun. The decision to follow his own advice that clergy should marry was unexpected even by himself. It caused consternation among his friends, including Melanchthon, and scandalized his enemies. The motives that led Luther into marriage are not well documented. He probably felt that his anticelibacy writings would gain force only if he himself followed his conclusion. He certainly needed a helpmate to take care of the needs of his busy life and to maintain a well-ordered homelife. Undoubtedly, he also was sorry for "Katie," who had deserted the cloister in response to his condemnation of the monastic vow of celibacy and who had previously expressed her willingness to marry him. The union was a happy one and produced six children, two of whom died young. Luther's marriage decisively settled the question about marriage of the evangelical clergy, and the Protestant parsonage was to become a great influence in the Protestant churches and cultures.

The Diets at Speyer and "Protestants." While Lutheranism spread and grew strong, the political authorities in Germany did little, and Charles was much too busy waging war against France to visit his empire. In the diets held at Nürnberg in the period 1522–24, the princes showed their fear of a popular revolt if they attempted to enforce the Edict of Worms, which had banned Luther and his supporters. Instead, they called for a general church council and for reform of the Roman Catholic hierarchy. At the Diet of Speyer in 1526, with the emperor still absent, the strength of the Lutheran princes present resulted in a call for a national church council to be held in Germany. It was also decided by a recess, or concluding act, that as far as the enforcement of the Edict of Worms was concerned, each German ruler should so "live, govern and carry himself as he hopes and trusts to answer to God and his imperial majesty." This compromise meant mutual toleration and territorial control of religion. But three years later, when the diet again assembled at Speyer, the Roman Catholics held a firm majority over the disorganized Lutheran princes. Following the demands of the still absent emperor, the estates acquiesced to his illegal abolition of the recess of 1526.

Meanwhile, when the aims of the emperor were becoming all too clear, the elector of Saxony, the margrave of Brandenburg, the duke of Lüneberg, the landgrave of Hesse, and the prince of Anhalt, along with the representatives of fourteen free cities, some of them Zwinglian, presented a strong written protest. In this document, the signers protested that what had been unanimously agreed upon at the Diet of Speyer in 1526 could not legally be rescinded even by majority vote. While pledging political obedience to the emperor, they asserted that in those matters that "concern the glory of God and the welfare and salvation of souls," they were pledged in Baptism to hold God's Word above temporal authorities. They also felt that they must state their grievances and "protest [witness] and testify openly before God" and all men that if these grievances were not accepted by the emperor, they would all "consider null and void the entire transaction and the intended decree" as being "against God, his holy Word, all our soul's salvation and good conscience," as well as the recess of Speyer. By this brave and religiously oriented pledge, the "protesting" estates unwittingly bequeathed the name *Protestant* to all who left the Roman Catholic Church.

The Augsburg Confession. The emperor ignored the "protest" and called for a diet to meet at Augsburg in 1530. The Protestant princes now feared suppression by force and sought to unite in a political and military union, but the theological differences between them could not be overcome. It was in these troubled times, some suppose, that Luther wrote his great hymn "A Mighty Fortress Is Our God." Charles arrived at Augsburg—his first visit to Germany since 1521—and the atmosphere was decidedly unfavorable for Protestantism. On June 25, the Lutherans read to the diet a confession prepared by Melanchthon, which presented the basis of their faith and their views on such controversial practices as clerical celibacy, monastic vows, and the giving of the cup to the laity. The Lutherans tried to show in this document that they were not innovators, but faithful to the ancient faith of the whole Church. An attempt by Melanchthon to win over the traditionalists was very evident in this Augsburg Confession and in the discussions that followed. Despite the conciliatory tone of the confession, the "Catholics," which term was now becoming the exclusive name for the papal adherents, contemptuously rejected the Lutheran confession as well as the more radical confessions prepared by four South German cities. However, the Lutherans did not swerve from their confession, and the Augsburg Confession became the standard of Lutheran doctrine everywhere.

It was soon evident that the religious issue was to be determined by the use of force, and the Lutherans and other Protestants united in the League of Schmalkalden. Confronted by a stronger opposition than before, the emperor and the Catholic princes could do nothing to coerce the Protestants. In 1532, the Peace of Nürnberg was negotiated as a truce until a general council would be held. Charles V was busy with his wars and negotiations, and religious colloquies between the Catholics and the Protestants accomplished nothing except to give the latter more time to expand.

Luther's Death. Luther died on February 18, 1546, at sixty-two. This great man of God had in his lifetime wrought a tremendous change in the Christian Church through his courage, his creative mind, his preaching and writing ability, his own deep faith, and his personality. Despite frequent illness and great demands and pressures, Luther had restored the Gospel to the hands and hearts of the people, had overthrown doctrines and practices contrary to Scripture, and had restored the Pauline teaching of justification by faith alone. It was his tragic role at this juncture of history to destroy the unity of the Medieval Church, a role that was largely forced on him by the opposition. Rome had not yet awakened to the need for a genuine reform of Christendom, and when the awakening came, the lines of division had already become hardened.

War and Peace. By 1546, Charles was at peace with France, and within a few months of Luther's death, he began a war against the Schmalkaldic League. Although the Protestants had superior forces, they lacked leadership and unity. Wittenberg fell on May 19, 1547, and the league soon collapsed. The victorious Charles did not demand, however, that the conquered Protestants return to Roman Catholicism; he still hoped to secure religious unity through negotiation and a truce.

The final formulation of a religious settlement was made at the Diet of Augsburg in 1555. The Religious Peace of Augsburg concerned only the Catholics and the followers of the Augsburg Confession, the Lutherans. Its provisions excluded the Calvinists, the Zwinglians, and the Anabaptists. These confessions were barred and were to remain illegal in the empire until 1648. The peace officially recognized the principle that religious unity within the political community was necessary for its solidarity; the princes and the free cities had to choose between Roman Catholicism and Lutheranism. All subjects within a principality were required to conform to the official religion or emigrate. Religious minorities in the free cities were to be tolerated, though not given official status. Thus the religion of the government determined the religion of the subject—*cuius regio, eius religio* ("whose region, his religion"). The religious peace also provided for an "ecclesiastical reservation": if a Catholic spiritual ruler of an ecclesiastical territory, like a diocese, should become a Lutheran, he was to be deposed and his territory would remain Catholic under his successor. Thus no new ecclesiastical lands were to become Protestant, but all such church estates confiscated by the Protestants before 1552 were to remain in the hands of the new owners. Despite the limitations and the later violations of these provisions, peace was maintained on this basis for more than half a century.

Territorial Confessions. The Peace of Augsburg (1555) meant that the Lutheran princes assumed episcopal (bishoplike) authority over their territories and administered church affairs through consistories, or tribunals, made up of both clergy and laymen of high status. Instead of the Church being supreme over the state as was so often the case in medieval Christendom, the Lutheran churches were now organized under state superintendents, officials of the government. Separate territorial confessions resulted. With the strong guidance of Luther gone, the Lutheran theologians in Germany became partisans of different factions. This tore German Lutheranism apart. Conflicts within Lutheranism and conflicts between Lutheranism and the growing Calvinism greatly weakened the position of Protestantism before the forces of the Counter-Reformation. An end to the bitter theological bickering was finally achieved with the Formula of Concord in 1580, which laid the basis for unity of doctrine in the Lutheran Church in Germany and clearly differentiated the Lutherans from the Calvinists.

LUTHERANISM OUTSIDE THE HOLY ROMAN EMPIRE	
DENMARK	King Frederick I (1523–33), aided by Hans Tausen, separated the Danish Church from Rome. A 1536 national assembly made Lutheranism the state church with the king as head. Ordinances and state church law approved by Luther. Augsburg Confession adopted.
NORWAY	Under Danish rule, followed Danish example. Progress slower since Bible and religious literature was in Danish, not Norwegian.
SWEDEN	Revolted against Denmark (1521). Gustavus Vasa elected king (1523). Olavus Petri, who studied at Wittenberg, introduced Lutheran reforms. Translated New Testament into Swedish (1526). Diet of Västerås separated nation from Church of Rome.
BALTIC STATES	German population welcomed Reformation, supported by Order of Teutonic Knights. Andreas Knöpken led reform in Riga. Diet of Wolmar declared for the Reformation (1554).
POLAND	Strong Lutheran, Calvinist, and Unitarian groups developed and persisted into the seventeenth century.
BOHEMIA	Home of Hus. German speakers welcomed Reformation. Czech Hussites and Lutherans had good relations.
HUNGARY AND TRANSYLVANIA	Germans and Slovaks welcomed Reformation. Early leader, Mátyás Dévay, studied at Wittenberg. New Testament translated into Magyar.

ZWINGLI AND THE RADICAL REFORMATION

Considering the extent of the desire for reform in the Christian Church in the early sixteenth century, it was to be expected that other leaders besides Luther and new varieties of Protestantism would appear independent of the German Reformation emanating from Wittenberg. The second major reform movement was to be the work of a German-Swiss named Zwingli and was to center in Zurich.

Ulrich Zwingli. He was born in the Swiss village of Wildhaus on January 1, 1484. He was thus only two months younger than Luther. After receiving a good humanistic education at the universities of Vienna and Basel, he was ordained a priest and took a pastorate at Glarus. During his ten years at Glarus, he continued his humanistic studies, corresponded with his idol Erasmus, and even enjoyed for a time a papal pension as a reward for supporting pro-papal political activities. Twice, he acted as chaplain for Swiss mercenary troops campaigning in Italy. In 1516, he removed to Einsiedeln and, although he had been critical of corruption in the Church before, it is here that he began, as a reforming humanist, his attacks on indulgences and other abuses. Then in December 1518, he was called as preacher and pastor to the Great Minster (cathedral) of Zurich, where he took up his new duties on his thirty-fifth birthday, January 1, 1519.

It was not long before Zwingli started his Reformation in this thriving city, which was also a center of biblical humanism. He immediately began an ambitious series of vigorous sermons on the books of the New Testament, though with emphasis and interpretation more Erasmian than Pauline. Early in 1519, with the support of his bishop, he secured the recall of an indulgence seller. Later that year, after Zwingli had recovered from the plague, an illness that provoked a great deal of introspection and soul-searching, his reforming activities increased. Taking encouragement from Luther's open demands for reform, Zwingli preached against the Lenten fast, monasticism, purgatory, and sacerdotal celibacy as unscriptural. Then on January 25, 1523, in a public disputation that was to be the first of three, Zwingli defended sixty-seven theses, or propositions, he had drawn up. These, unlike Luther's, covered a wide range of topics. They stressed the importance of the Gospel and the sufficiency of Christ's atonement for salvation, and they attacked celibacy, the Mass as a sacrifice, purgatory, food restrictions, and other externals not sanctioned in the New Testament. Zwingli condemned the Roman Catholic hierarchy for their negligence and warned them of the consequences.

Changes at Zurich. With the full support of the city council for the innovations, the Reformation at Zurich accelerated. Images were destroyed by iconoclastic enthusiasts, the monastic houses were dissolved, and priests married. Zwingli himself married Anna Reinhard, his companion of many years.

The last Mass was celebrated in Zurich on Wednesday of Holy Week in 1525, after which the altars and sacristies were stripped. This was not done without the disapproval of some, for "what pleased one man well did not please his neighbour." Zwingli then introduced a new order of service. On Maundy Thursday, the young people who desired to partake of the Lord's Supper placed themselves on the "floor of the nave between the choir and the entrance, males to the right and females to the left." Upon completion of the sermon, unleavened bread and wine, in "trenchers and beakers . . . of wood, that no pomp come back," were placed on a table set on the floor of the nave. After the Words of Institution were recited "openly and intelligibly, in German," the bread was carried on large wooden platters from person to person so that each communicant could "break off a bit or a mouthful with his hand and eat it." In the same way, the wine was distributed "and no one shall move from his place." The custom of going up to the altar to commune was thus discontinued, and sitting at Communion received an indirect start. After "open and clear" words of praise and thanksgiving, the congregation responded with an "Amen." On Good Friday, the middle-aged worshipers communed in a similar manner, "men and women apart." On Easter Sunday, the elder participants partook of the Lord's Supper. This order of the Communion service was to be followed at Easter, Pentecost, autumn, and Christmas. On ordinary Sundays, a preaching service, without liturgy or singing, was held.

Later, when it was observed that the people were not attending services but wandering "hither and thither during sermon-time, on the bridges, down the alleys, by the gates and alongside the moats," the city council ordered in the summer of 1531 that "every man shall strictly observe the mandate to go to Church on Sundays and Holy-days." To obtain better supervision, it was also ordained that "the preachers in all the three churches shall begin to preach at one and the same time, convenient to all."

Zwingli Compared with Luther. Many of Zwingli's doctrines and practices were similar to those of Luther; yet there were also marked differences. The Zurich reformer accepted the basic creeds of Christianity, and with Luther he emphasized the unique and all-sufficient role of Christ's atoning death and of faith for salvation. Like the reformer of Wittenberg, Zwingli relied solely on Scripture and rejected papal and conciliar authority, sacerdotal celibacy, purgatory, the possibility of human merit before God, the veneration of images and saints, and monasticism. In Zurich, too, the need was felt for a Bible in the language of the people, and Leo Jud translated the Scriptures into the Swiss-German dialect (1534). Unlike the Lutheran Reformation, however, the movement at Zurich was strongly legalistic and iconoclastic. The Bible was the unique source not only of doctrine but also of all church practice there. The externals of the religious life were not left free but had to be prescribed in the New Testament or done away with. With the great emphasis on the intellectual exposition of the Word through instruction and the sermon and because of the lack of available hymns in the vernacular, music in worship was at an end. The service on an ordinary Sunday was not based on the Mass, and the people played no active part in it.

Zwingli had no feeling for the Sacraments as the Means of Grace. The Spirit did not use physical means in Zwingli's understanding, so heavily influenced by his humanistic-philosophical training. The Sacraments, separated from faith, are simply signs of spiritual realities existing independently from them. So the bread and wine of the Eucharist were not the body and blood of Christ, but only symbols commemorating Christ's Passion. They expressed the fellowship of Christians and indicated that the recipient was a member of a Christian society. To Zwingli, Baptism meant little more than initiation of the Christian into membership in a religious society. Because of this, he was quite willing to have infants baptized. The divergence from Luther's sacramental theology prevented the two reformers from reaching an accord when they met at the Marburg Colloquy in 1529.

Zwingli's Death. From Zurich, a town now virtually a theocracy because of the close association of church and state, the Zwinglian Reformation spread to Bern, Basel, and other Swiss cantons. Opposing them were the Catholic cantons, which resisted the spread of the new doctrines and Zwingli's attempts at political leadership in the Swiss confederation. In 1529, on the burning of a missionary from Zurich in the Catholic canton of Schwyz, Zurich and her allies declared war. No battle occurred, however, and the First Peace of Kappel was negotiated between the opponents. It was decreed that since "no man ought to be forced in matter of faith . . . neither side shall make war upon nor chastise the other for its faith." The districts that had abolished the Mass and done away with images were not to be punished. This constitutes the first gleam of tolerance in the darkness of traditional religious intolerance.

The peace was only a truce, for in 1531, the Protestant allies sought to compel the Catholic cantons to permit the preaching of reformed doctrines in their territories. When this was refused, an economic blockade was instituted by the Protestant league, an act that led to war. The Catholic army of eight thousand men met the Protestant army of only fifteen hundred at Kappel on October 11, 1531. Zwingli accompanied his forces as chaplain, and he was among the five hundred Zurichers killed in the defeat. Luther considered Zwingli's death an example of God's rightful judgment of those who take the sword to defend the Gospel.

In the Second Peace of Kappel, the Swiss cantons were divided along religious lines. Zurich and her allies, in return for freedom to practice their form of worship, agreed to allow the Catholic cantons, seven in number, to abide without dispute. Heinrich Bullinger succeeded Zwingli, and in 1536, he and others drew up the First Helvetic (Swiss) Confession. In 1566, the Zwinglians united with the Calvinists on the basis of one confession, the Second (revised) Helvetic Confession, in the Reformed Church.

The Radical Reformation. The Marburg Colloquy of Luther and Zwingli was not the only demonstration that the Reformation was not to be a homogeneous movement. Despite their initial approval of Luther, many others besides Zwingli soon found that for various reasons they must desert the Wittenberg reformer. In their unbounded enthusiasm for the new evangelical movement, they envisioned more radical changes than the conservative Luther allowed and thus were disappointed in the Lutheran Reformation and even with the more radical happenings at Zurich. Despite a multiplicity of views as to how to restore a true and pure Christianity, all the radicals opposed the close association of church and state that was identifiable in the major churches of their day. Usually, these dissidents wanted to free the Christian Church of the medieval accretion of ecclesiastical traditions and magisterial (civil) power and to restore, resurrect, or re-create the kind of Church that had existed in primitive Christianity. Just how this was to be done was widely debated, but often the scheme included community ownership of property. Because these heterogeneous groups held views of the Church that were more radical than those of Luther and the other major reformers, they have been labeled "the left wing of the Reformation."

Anabaptism. The word *Anabaptism* comes from Greek and means "to baptize again." As a general term, it was applied to all those who did not accept infant Baptism as scriptural and thus rebaptized adults. Baptism to them, as to Zwingli, was not a Means of Grace. In their view, Baptism was a sign of faith and repentance, and only an adult was capable of believing and of feeling need for the newness of life. Although there were great variances among them, the Anabaptists were Zwinglian in their interpretation of the Lord's Supper. Whereas the other reformers saw themselves standing within the ongoing life stream of historic Christianity, the Anabaptists felt they were starting all over again. The Medieval Church to them had lost all continuity with the apostolic life and spirit.

Most of the Anabaptists were extremely literal in their interpretation of the Bible, and there was also a tendency among them to stress the words of the Book of Revelation, which they felt especially applied to their times, the end time of the world. Strongly moral and ethical, they lived exemplary lives marked by simplicity, sobriety, and humility. Most of them repudiated oaths, war, capital punishment, and the union of church and state as found in the political world about them. It was primarily because of their views on these political issues and because of their appeal to the oppressed classes of society that they were persecuted as radical revolutionaries. The cruel punishments visited upon them by Lutheran, Zwinglian, Calvinist, and Catholic public authorities alike only convinced the Anabaptists of the validity of their tenets, for to them the mark of the true Christian Church was suffering and persecution. Strongly apocalyptic, they suffered and awaited the coming of Christ.

Persecution. The Anabaptists first arose in Zwingli's own circle of disciples when a group of like-minded humanists and clerics banded together to press for the establishment of a truly apostolic Church. Two of the early leaders were Conrad Grebel and Felix Manz of Zurich. Both were martyred. Naturally, their rejection of infant Baptism and especially their disassociation from the secular and worldly state and society soon clashed with the opinion of Zwingli, who saw a very close association between the state and the church and who thought in terms of a Christian commonwealth, a Christian society. Early in 1525, the Zurich Council decreed Baptism for children or exile for their families. Those deported spread their faith wherever they went, for all Anabaptists were zealous in their missionary activities. Sterner action was soon necessary, and in March 1526, the Zurich Council forbade adult rebaptism among the Anabaptists and ordered punishment by drowning. By the time of Zwingli's death, the number of Anabaptists in Switzerland was negligible. But the movement had spread throughout the German states, to the horror of the Lutherans and Catholics. In 1528, Emperor Charles V made rebaptism punishable by death; in 1529, the Diet of Speyer decreed death for unrepentant Anabaptists. Although Luther himself was opposed to compulsion in matters of faith, Catholic and Lutheran magistrates united in carrying out this mandate, and many Anabaptists were cruelly executed.

The Münster Episode. The Anabaptists were quietists for the most part, but in 1534 some radical Anabaptists succeeded in taking over the city of Münster in Westphalia when John of Leiden and John Matthys, two Anabaptist leaders, came from the Lowlands to aid the discontented elements in the city and to lead the citizens to a victory over the forces of the bishop to whom the city was subject. Once in control of the city council, the Anabaptists drove out all who refused rebaptism. They then sought to establish a communistic New Jerusalem of truly baptized believers with the young John of Leiden ruling as "King of Zion" over the elect. Besieged, the city was put on a war economy while the confiscated wealth and luxuries were distributed to all. Because of the numerical superiority of women, polygamy was introduced. The "king" took several wives. Many Anabaptists throughout Europe prayed for the success of the Münster experiment, and some sought unsuccessfully to bring relief to the besieged city. As the danger of revolt in other areas increased, authorities in the empire aided the besieging forces. The starving defenders could not hold out much longer, and the city was taken through treachery. Most of the male defenders were slaughtered with the severity considered necessary to wipe out such a threat to the established social order. John of Leiden was cruelly tortured before being killed.

The Münster episode, besides giving Anabaptism an offensive name and intensifying persecution, led the scattered and despised remnants to renounce all forms of violence and extremism and to live quiet, simple, and inoffensive lives. They became uncompromising pacifists. Menno Simons patiently organized his followers in the Lowlands and North Germany into groups later known as Mennonites; Jacob Hutter in Moravia similarly organized the Hutterite communities. Their descendants still maintain disciplined, austere, and pious pacifist communities in America and elsewhere.

Although not as prominent in theology, organization, and number as the other Christian Churches of that day, the groups within the Radical Reformation movement did contribute much to the sharpening of theological studies and argumentation in the Reformation period. By breaking with the commonly held view of the *corpus Christianum*, or the unity between the Church and society, they influenced Western institutions and life.

JOHN CALVIN

Although his name was to be associated most closely with a Swiss city, John Calvin was born on July 10, 1509, at Noyon in northern France. His father, Gerard, was a notary and served as secretary to the local bishop. At fourteen, the young John, already religiously inclined, entered the ancient and famous University of Paris. Calvin soon showed himself to be an eager, serious, and able student of theology. In 1528, he received his master of arts degree and, on the command of his father, turned to the study of law. He also undertook the study of Greek and was strongly influenced by humanism. In 1532, he published, at his own expense, a humanistic and learned commentary on Seneca's *On Clemency*, a work on political ethics. In it, he gave evidence of the humanistic and analytical methods of examination and explanation that he was to follow successfully in his later exposition of Scripture.

The *Institutes*. Meanwhile, Calvin had been influenced by Reformation thought, although the date of his "sudden conversion" is not known. Then in 1533, Calvin's name was associated with Nicholas Cop, the rector of the University of Paris, who was charged with heresy. Calvin fled first to Noyon, later to Saintonge, and in 1534, he visited the aged humanist Jacques Lefèvre d'Étaples at Nérac. Emboldened by his contact with this courageous reformer, Calvin decided not to accept Roman ordination but to dedicate himself to the task of reform. He became convinced that there could be no genuine reform within the institutional church as it then existed. In 1534, he experienced two brief periods of imprisonment; the persecution of Protestants in France was taking a more serious turn. The next year, Calvin appeared in the Protestant Swiss town of Basel. Here, in March 1536, he published his very influential book, *Institutes of the Christian Religion*. It was intended as an expanded catechism. This Latin edition of 1536, consisting of only six chapters and explaining the Decalogue, the Apostles' Creed, the Lord's Prayer, the Sacraments, and church government, was to be greatly enlarged in the second edition (Strasbourg, 1539) and then translated by Calvin into dignified French (Geneva, 1541).

Rightly considered as a "classical statement of Protestant theology," this work of Calvin is very comprehensive and systematic in its treatment of the whole range of Christian theology. The work shows Calvin's legal training as well as his deep piety. Theologically, the *Institutes* is filled with an awed awareness of the majesty and sovereign power of the almighty God. The Scripture contained for him the all-sufficient, authoritative truth upon which the Church rests as well as the entire pattern of its life.

Calvin Compared with Luther. Calvin was deeply influenced by Luther, and there were many similarities between the Wittenberg reformer's fully developed theology and that of Calvin. Both were much indebted to Augustine in their assertions that man is morally helpless and entirely dependent on God's grace for salvation. Both accepted Scripture as the sole source of Christian doctrine, and both discarded as unscriptural purgatory, the papacy, Mariolatry, the cult of the saints and of relics, the Mass as a sacrifice, monasticism, the celibacy of clergy, and many other medieval developments. Both stressed that any useful secular work is a "calling" from God. Both accepted as true sacraments only those sacred actions that had an explicit "promise of Christ" attached to them: Baptism and the Lord's Supper. Man was saved only by God's grace through faith; good works were ineffective for salvation.

Despite these similarities, there were also fundamental differences in the theology and practice of the two reformers. Calvin's theology was much more legalistic than Luther's. The latter stressed the God of love as portrayed in the New Testament, a God who so loved the world that He sent His only-begotten Son to redeem mankind. Calvin was more influenced by the Old Testament in his vision of God as the Lawgiver who demanded obedience to His divine precepts. Luther was quite conservative in retaining such customary things as candles, ceremonials, images, altars, vestments, instrumental music, and chanting as aids in creating an atmosphere conducive to the worship of God; Calvin severely rejected everything that did not have express New Testament sanction. It has been said—somewhat unjustly, for Calvin himself desired a rich Communion liturgy—that a Calvinist church consisted of "four bare walls and a sermon." In his effort to explain the Lord's Supper, Calvin, like Luther, believed there is a real partaking of Christ's body and blood in its celebration; unlike Luther, he did not regard them as present in the bread and wine, nor did he accept the ubiquity of Christ's glorified body. To Calvin, Christ's body is in heaven, and only the devout communicant spiritually partakes of it through the work of the Holy Spirit. This mystery is such that it is to be experienced rather than explained.

As far as the relation between church and state was concerned, both Luther and Calvin held that the pure doctrine of Scripture must be maintained by public authority. Both reformers felt that God had instituted the temporal power of the state and that resistance to rulers was morally wrong. To Luther, however, the state was strictly a worldly power that could in no way coerce the conscience or soul of a subject. Calvin was opposed to the principle of a union of church and state because he felt that the church authorities should set the standards of orthodoxy and discipline for enforcement by the secular powers. This led to the theocracy at Geneva.

Luther felt strongly that secular authority was God given and God ordained, but he showed no preference for any particular form of government. Since the secular authorities were a "divine order," all men must obey the rules. Calvin, too, considered the office of the magistrate one of the most honored of vocations. He condemned the cruel and impious rulers of all times and warned of the Lord's vengeance upon them. Since private individuals could only suffer and obey such rulers, he urged action by a constituted magistracy "to restrain the willfulness of kings" who "violently fall upon and assault the lowly common folk." He felt that an aristocracy (rule of the best) "or a system compounded of aristocracy and democracy, far excels all others."

Predestination Emphasized. Much more than Luther, Calvin placed special importance on the traditionally orthodox belief in predestination. Calvin went beyond the view of Augustine in asserting a double predestination, in which God had not only selected some for eternal life but had also damned all the rest to everlasting damnation. God had from all eternity *willed* the salvation of some and the damnation of others irrespective of merit; He had not used just His foreknowledge of a man's faith or goodness in making these elections because God's knowledge is not a passive knowing but coincides with His will. Calvin himself called the damnation of some by God's decree "dreadful" but certain, unchangeable, and not to be questioned by puny mortals. Many readers of Calvin's works were repelled by this concept of predestination, for it seemed to make God the author of sin, but to Calvin, this example of God's judgments and undeserved mercy was an appalling mystery beyond man's limited understanding.

Since every Christian wanted to know if he was one of those elected to salvation, there developed in Calvinism a tendency to look for possible signs of such selection. Calvin felt that those who publicly professed their faith, partook of the Sacraments, and lived a godly life met the test. However, no one could judge the election status of others, he taught. It was also generally felt that the elect would have within themselves not only the inner "witness of the Spirit" and a strong desire to do good, but also an urge to reform the wicked and remove any opportunity for sinning.

Calvinism was therefore to be marked by a degree of zealousness and reforming activity, much of it preventive, unknown to other Protestant groups.

Calvin Comes to Geneva. In 1536, Calvin went to Ferrara, Italy, for a brief time and then returned to France during a period of amnesty. Intending to go to Strasbourg, Calvin was detoured by war to Geneva, a Swiss commercial city of about twelve thousand inhabitants. A few years before Calvin's arrival, Geneva had turned to Protestantism through the preaching and activities of Guillaume Farel, a provocative, red-bearded, and venturesome evangelist. Although Calvin intended to stay only overnight in Geneva, Farel heard of his arrival and persuaded the author of the *Institutes* to stay by calling upon God to condemn Calvin if he did not devote himself to the work of reform in Geneva. Calvin accepted that as a divine call and, except for a short interlude at Strasbourg, remained in Geneva until his death in 1564.

The Strasbourg Interlude. Calvin and Farel set up a system of instruction and pressed for a close relation between citizenship and church membership, the latter based on a creedal test. All citizens were to be subject to a strict religious-moral discipline, delineated by the clergy. In a showdown between the ministers' demands and the city council's support of the more lenient discipline of the nearby city of Bern, Calvin and his associates were forced by the city's General Council to leave Geneva in April 1538. The reformer accepted the call of the Protestant leaders of Strasbourg to come to their city and take charge of the congregation of French refugees there.

This free city on the Rhine had been influenced very early by the writings of Luther and had soon become an important center of reforming activity and a refuge for religious exiles of all kinds. Most influential among the Strasbourg reformers was Martin Bucer (1491–1551), who preached and wrote there from 1523 to 1549. This indefatigable humanist worked hard to harmonize the theological differences between Luther and Zwingli at Marburg and on later occasions. Bucer firmly believed that the magistrates should promote reform and supervise the Church so as to achieve a moral community. He had very definite ideas about liturgical reform, church discipline, predestination, and education. Since Calvin was a close friend of Bucer and closely associated with him during a highly formative period of Calvin's life, the influence of the Strasbourg reformer on the later theology and ecclesiastical polity of Calvin was great.

For three busy and fruitful years, Calvin resided in Strasbourg. Under Bucer's influence, he compiled a book of French psalm paraphrases set to music for singing in the services. He also introduced a disciplinary system and a new order of service in his parish. Calvin published his *Commentary on Romans* and a revised edition of his *Institutes*. In August 1540, he married one of his parishioners, but his family life was not as significant and comforting for him as for Luther and Bucer. His wife was sickly and died quite early.

The *Ecclesiastical Ordinances*. Late in 1540, Calvin was recalled by Geneva, and in September of the following year, he reentered that city. He immediately set about drafting a new ecclesiastical polity, the famous *Ecclesiastical Ordinances of the Church of Geneva*. The civil government approved a modified version, which did not grant all that Calvin requested but which did place the administration of church discipline in the hands of church officials supported by the state, instead of in the hands of the city council. The document, basic to all later Calvinistic organization, names four divinely sanctioned ministries "instituted by our Lord for the government of his Church." These were pastors, teachers, elders, and deacons.

The pastors, selected on the basis of a test and with the approval of the city government, were to "proclaim the Word of God, to instruct, admonish, exhort and censure, both in public and private, to administer the sacraments and to enjoin brotherly corrections along with the elders and colleagues." The ministers of Geneva and the nearby villages held weekly discussions. In each of the three parish churches, there were three services on Sunday and a preaching service on Monday, Wednesday, and Friday mornings. The weekday services were later held daily. Catechism classes for youth were held at noon on Sunday in every parish, and at sixteen, the young people, baptized in infancy, made their own profession of faith. Communion was celebrated in all three parish churches four times a year: on Christmas, Easter, Pentecost, and the first Sunday in September.

The teachers, or "doctors," were to instruct "the faithful in true doctrine, in order that the purity of the Gospel be not corrupted either by ignorance or by evil opinions." Since instruction in theology was profitable only if the languages and humanities were studied first, "a college should be instituted for instructing children to prepare them for the ministry as well as for civil government." A school for boys was to be set up, but the girls were to have "their school apart, as has hitherto been the case." This stress on education became normative for all Calvinism.

The twelve elders, "men of good and honest life, without reproach and beyond suspicion, and above all fearing God and possessing spiritual prudence," were chosen from and by the city officials. The elders were to exercise "oversight of the life of everyone, to admonish amicably those whom they see to be erring or to be living a disordered life, and, where it is required, to enjoin fraternal corrections themselves and along with others." If necessary, offenders were turned over to the city magistrates for punishment.

The deacons, divided into procurators and hospitallers, were to "receive, dispense and hold goods for the poor, not only daily alms, but also possessions, rents and pensions," and to "tend and care for the sick and administer allowances to the poor."

New Order of Service. In 1542, Geneva adopted with slight modification the new order of service that Calvin had introduced in the French parish at Strasbourg. Its Communion part, contrary to Calvin's wishes, was not to be celebrated every Sunday but only four times a year. Unlike Luther, who basically retained most of the old Mass and cut out only its objectionable parts, Calvin wrote a new liturgy, retaining only some of the structure and elements of the traditional Mass. In his service, he attempted to restore the worship as he felt it had been in the Ancient Christian Church. The focal point of the service was the preaching of the Word. On the Sundays when Communion was to be celebrated, the intercessory prayer with a lengthy paraphrase of the Lord's Prayer led to the Communion rite. A consecration prayer, mostly of Calvin's own composition, was followed by the Words of Institution. In the accompanying exhortation, the minister restricted the Communion to the faithful, a feature that later came to be known as "the fencing of the tables."

In the exhortation, Calvin's theological view of the Lord's Supper is given in that Christ wishes "to make us partakers of his own body and blood, in order that we may possess him entirely in such a manner that he may live in us, and we in him. And although we see only bread and wine, yet let us not doubt that he accomplishes spiritually in our souls all that he shows us externally by these visible signs; in other words, that he is heavenly bread, to feed us and nourish us into life eternal." Christ is not in "these earthly and corruptible elements which we see with the eye, and touch with the hand," but our souls must be "raised above all terrestrial objects, and carried as high as heaven, to enter the kingdom of God where he dwells." The people were to regard the bread and wine as "signs and evidence, spiritually seeking the reality where the Word of God promises that we shall find it."

Rites and Ceremonies. The Rite of Baptism as inaugurated by Calvin differed from that of the Lutheran Church. Since Calvin held that "assurance of salvation does not depend upon participation in the sacraments, as if justification consisted in it," Baptism became in the Calvinistic, or Reformed, Church only "a token of our union with Christ." All the "alien hodgepodge" and "theatrical pomp" were discarded. It was of no importance to Calvin "whether the person being baptized should be wholly immersed, and whether thrice or once, whether he should only be sprinkled with poured water." He left that up to the practice of the locality, but he did point out that "the rite of immersion was observed in the ancient church." Baptism of the children of believers, as heirs of God's covenant with the fathers, was retained. It was to be administered only by the clergy, and since it was not necessary for the salvation of a person whose eternal fate had been determined by God, emergency Baptism at the home of the infant was not permitted. Under no circumstances should a woman ever administer the rite. The ceremony was confined to the Church, before the assembly of believers, to stress the child's membership in the covenant people. No sponsors were required, and no profession of faith was made for the infant.

Confirmation, according to Calvin, should really be a "catechizing, in which children or those near adolescence would give an account of their faith before the church." This procedure became the general practice in the Reformed Church.

The Rite of Communion as adopted by the Reformed Church followed the pattern established by Calvin. The communicants were to announce their intention to commune a week before the celebration so that no unconfirmed child, uninstructed stranger, or newcomer would approach the Table "to his own condemnation." The

Communion tables were placed beside the pulpit, and there was to be no "large number of vessels." Only a minister or a deacon could give the chalice, and the minister himself received the bread and wine first. Then, "in becoming order the believers should partake of the most holy banquet, the ministers breaking the bread and giving the cup." Since Calvin, like Luther, had a deep feeling of the fellowship of Christians in the Lord's Supper, private masses with no congregation present were repudiated.

As for marriage, Calvin felt that the banns should be published in the Church for three Sundays prior to the wedding. Marriages could be performed on any day except a Communion Sunday. In the actual ceremony, the couple to be married came forward to the Holy Table at the commencement of the sermon. Before the assembled congregation, after exhortation from Scripture, the bridegroom and bride were married by separately expressing their intention of accepting each other according to God's Word in holy matrimony. The ceremony was concluded with prayer.

The Consistory. The Genevan Consistory, composed of six pastors and twelve elders, met every Thursday with one of the four city syndics, or officers of the city government, presiding. Although the elders outnumbered the clergy, Calvin's all-pervasive influence and indomitable will were very evident. These alone enabled the consistory to win out in its constant struggle with the city government over the right of the ecclesiastical establishment to control discipline as well as doctrine. For, although the consistory at first confined its disciplinary activity to matters of public morality, it soon extended its functions and control more widely. All sorts of rules and regulations were instituted to make Geneva a saintly city. Church attendance was required of all, and Sunday was decreed a day of worship and strict rest. The keeping of Christmas was forbidden as a pagan and Roman Catholic festival. Attendance at secular theatrical productions was forbidden, as were dancing, playing cards, and the singing of bawdy songs. An attempt to close the taverns failed, but they were carefully regulated. Objectionable names were not to be given at Baptism, and thus there developed the Calvinistic practice of using only biblical names. Types of clothing and luxuries were regulated.

Using methods that reflected the spirit of the medieval inquisition, the vigilant consistory gave its judgments. Capital crimes included blasphemy, heresy, witchcraft, and adultery. All who openly opposed the ecclesiastical system and its police in any way were banished. Between 1542 and 1546, records reveal, fifty-eight people were executed and seventy-six banished from Geneva. To the serious and zealous John Knox, Geneva was "the most perfect school of Christ that ever was on earth since the days of the apostles."

During the last decade of Calvin's life, the consistory and the city magistrates collaborated well. Ecclesiastical discipline was tightened, and the international prestige of the reformer grew immensely. Calvinism itself spread, especially after the establishment in 1559 of the Genevan Academy (today the University of Geneva) and through the training of refugees who later returned to their homelands. Under the able leadership of Theodore Beza, the humanist who was to be Calvin's successor, and staffed with brilliant instructors, many of whom were refugees, the academy made Geneva the intellectual and missionary center for Calvinism. At the time of Calvin's death (1564), there were twelve hundred junior students in the school and three hundred in the higher levels, all receiving their education free of cost. Many of the advanced students were from foreign countries. These returned to their native lands imbued with Calvinistic theology and spirit.

Calvin's Concept of Vocation. The activistic, aggressive, and dynamic spirit of Calvinism can be attributed in part to Calvin's views on predestination, but his concept of vocation was also important. To Calvin, every Christian acknowledging the role of God through faith also accepted thereby grave responsibilities. No matter what his duties or tasks, the Christian must have a deep sense of dedicated service to God and to his neighbor, also created in the image of God. A layman's work was really not a secular calling; he was doing God's work and was acting as a steward of God with his earthly possessions. Calvin expressed his concept of vocation with these words: "The Lord bids each one of us in all life's actions to look to his calling. . . . He has appointed duties for every man in his particular way of life. And that no one may thoughtlessly transgress his limits, he has named these various kinds of living 'callings.' " Even the very humble tasks were precious in God's sight, and every vocation was hallowed. No vocation was without its troubles, but God would guide those He called. In his views on vocation, Calvin thus took a position similar to that of Luther.

Calvinism and Capitalism. Calvin's views on the Christian vocation, or "calling," and his permission to demand interest on loans of money, limited by equity and charity, have led to a great deal of discussion and controversy as to the role of Calvin and Calvinism in modern capitalism. Some writers, like the German sociologist Max Weber, have advanced the thesis that the "spirit of capitalism" was a kind of by-product of the Calvinist ethic of work and vocation. Some authors have accepted this view, others have modified the thesis as an oversimplification, and still others have rejected it entirely. Calvin himself certainly insisted on diligence and frugality and condemned the lazy and wasteful man. Writing on stewardship, he pointed out that all Christians should remember "by whom such reckoning is required." He warned against being overly ambitious: "For no one, impelled by his own rashness, will attempt more than his calling will permit, because he will know that it is not lawful to exceed its bounds. A man of obscure station will lead a private life ungrudgingly so as not to leave the rank in which he has been placed by God." Calvin constantly referred to the more miserable condition of the godly who suffered while the wicked flourished. He rejected economic individualism and advocated altruism. In general, it might be said that there was a greater affinity between Calvinism and business than was the case with Lutheranism. And the cradle of Calvinism was in an urban commercial setting, the city of Geneva. However, the relationship of Calvinism to modern capitalism should not be overemphasized.

THE SPREAD OF CALVINISM	
SWITZERLAND	Geneva became a center of international Protestantism. The Second Helvetic Confession (1566) united Zwinglians and Calvinists.
PALATINATE	A modified and milder Calvinism, based on the Heidelberg Catechism (1563), replaced the Lutheran Confessions.
FRANCE	Protestants favored and persecuted by King Francis I (1515–47). Calvin's *Institutes* in French (1541) spread Calvinism. Persecuted French Protestants, known as Huguenots, gained military strength. War with Catholics began in 1562. St. Bartholomew's Day Massacre (August 24, 1572) saw thousands of Huguenots killed. The 1598 Edict of Nantes protected Huguenots; revoked in 1685.
LOW COUNTRIES	First Lutheran martyrs here in 1523. Protestants persecuted but also spread. Emperor Philip II offended by Catholics and Protestants. William of Orange (1533–84) organized resistance to Philip II; Spanish troops expelled. Pacification of Ghent (1576) united Dutch provinces. Northern provinces were Calvinists; southern were Catholic. Truce in 1609.
POLAND	Calvinists had early success but were displaced by Catholic Counter-Reformation.
ENGLAND AND SCOTLAND	Swiss reform influenced Cranmer. English exiles and refugees came under Calvinist influence on the Continent, and then returned to England. Changing dynamics due to roles of kings and queens.
NORTH AMERICA	Huguenot, English, and other Calvinists from around Europe emigrated to New England and other American and Canadian colonies, leading to Calvinistic Congregationalists and Baptists.

THE ENGLISH AND SCOTTISH REFORMATIONS

The Reformation in England had been long in preparation. In the fourteenth century, waves of anticlericalism had swept the country, Wycliffe had thundered his warnings against the papacy, and the statutes of Provisors and Praemunire had drastically curtailed papal jurisdiction over England. Papal control over the English Church became even weaker when the strong Tudor dynasty came to power in 1485 after the War of the Roses. Nationalism had grown during the Hundred Years' War with France, and such feeling came in conflict with the international sway of the papacy. The people of England readily accepted the English translation of the New Testament by William Tyndale, and Luther's works were widely distributed and debated in England. Yet it is doubtful whether England would have made a complete break with the papacy if Henry VIII had not encountered difficulties in securing an annulment of his marriage to the Spanish royal princess Catherine of Aragon.

Henry VIII and Reform. Henry, well trained in theology and of unquestioned orthodoxy, was perturbed that his marriage with Catherine had produced no male heirs but only a princess named Mary. Since Catherine had been his brother's widow, their marriage had been possible only by papal dispensation as contrary to canon law and certain portions of Scripture (Leviticus 20:21). Henry thought God had evidently not blessed the union. A male heir seemed absolutely necessary to perpetuate the dynasty. In 1527, after eighteen years of marriage, Henry requested an annulment from Pope Clement VII. Because the pope feared reprisals from Catherine's powerful Spanish family, he hesitated. Henry decided to take the matter in his own hands. In 1529, he summoned Parliament, and during the ensuing six years this "Reformation Parliament" carried out his plans to sever the English Church from Rome. In 1531, the king secured from the clergy recognition as the "Protector and Supreme Head of the English Church and Clergy . . . as far as the law of Christ allows." Parliament next moved against the payment of annates to the pope and by the Act in Restraint of Appeals removed the pope's spiritual jurisdiction over England. In 1533, Henry secured a dissolution of his marriage to Catherine from Thomas Cranmer, archbishop of Canterbury and primate of the English Church. The king then married Anne Boleyn, a union that also failed to produce the desired male heir. Their only child was the princess Elizabeth. When the pope excommunicated Henry and declared the marriage of Henry and Anne invalid, and thus their child illegitimate, papal revenues from England were cut off completely. In the Act of Supremacy (1534), Parliament confirmed the king as the supreme head of the Church of England. It became treasonable to deny the king this position and title. John Fisher, bishop of Rochester, and Sir Thomas More, the author of the famous *Utopia*, were executed for not accepting the king as head of the church. In general, however, the substitution of the king for the pope created little disturbance.

The Dissolution of the Monasteries. The supremacy of the king was first exercised in the dissolution of the monasteries of England on the pretext of corruption. The dissolution, a real break with the ecclesiastical past, provided the crown with considerable much-needed money and at the same time eliminated possible centers of pro-papal feelings. The dispossession of all the monks and friars was carried out with efficiency and little suffering. In 1536, those houses having an annual income of less than two hundred pounds were declared dissolved by Parliament so the money could be put to different use. In the following years, the larger monasteries shared the same fate. Many of the monastic properties were given away by the king or sold at bargain prices to the local gentry, who thus became strong supporters of the king's antipapal policies.

In all the actions taken by Henry and Parliament, political, economic, and national motives had been uppermost. The king was not anti-Catholic; he still considered himself a good Christian in the Catholic tradition and had not instituted any changes in doctrine or services. Lutheran influence was spreading in England, however, and the appearance in 1535 of the Bible in the translation of Miles Coverdale led to open discussion of the issues. By the king's order, an English Bible was placed in every parish church, available for reading by laymen. But Henry was not attracted to Luther's views. In order to secure unity in religion, Parliament, under Henry's guidance, enacted the Act of Six Articles (1539). This reaffirmed the traditional tenets of transubstantiation, celibacy, private masses, auricular confession, and Communion under one element. Persecution of those suspected of Protestantism followed.

Edward VI and Cranmer. Henry VIII died early in 1547 and was succeeded by the young Edward VI, his son by Jane Seymour, his third wife. The Council of Regency was predominantly Protestant, and Edward was educated by Protestant tutors. Under the regency of the moderate Protestant Edward Seymour, duke of Somerset, England began to move along the road of doctrinal and liturgical change. The Act of Six Articles and the statutes against heresy were repealed. In 1549, an Act of Uniformity required the use of the Book of Common Prayer in the churches of England. This book, largely the work of Archbishop Thomas Cranmer, provided new services in place of the customary Latin Mass and the monastic "hours." It was written in beautiful English and drew much on the traditional services as purged by the Lutheran reformers. However, Cranmer, unlike the Lutheran reformers, did not merely translate and purge the old Latin texts. He was a creative liturgical writer himself. His phrasing allowed for considerable latitude of interpretation. The services centered on the Psalms, Scripture readings, and appointed collects in an attempt to return to the ancient services of the Christian Church in a condensed, simplified, and purified form. In the Lord's Supper, both the bread and the wine were given to the communicants.

The English Reformation was deliberately conservative and conciliating thus far, but under the growing influence of Bucer and the Swiss, iconoclasm now began in England. Altars and images were removed from the churches. Marriage of the clergy was legalized. When the duke of Northumberland overthrew Somerset in 1549, Protestantism moved more rapidly toward the Reformed types. This was aided by the arrival in England of a number of religious refugees from the Continent. The revised Book of Common Prayer of Edward VI, again produced by Cranmer and made compulsory by the Second Act of Uniformity (1552), was more Zwinglian in tone. Vestments were abolished, and the Lord's Supper was to be received primarily "in remembrance." It was stressed that the Mass was not a sacrifice, since Christ by His death on the cross had made a sufficient sacrifice. Congregational participation was limited to the litany; there was no singing of hymns. In the six years of Edward's reign, England moved gently and with no Catholic martyrs from Catholicism to Reformed Protestantism. However, the English Reformation, imposed as it was from above, was suddenly brought to a halt by the death of Edward in July 1553.

Mary Tudor and the Catholic Reaction. By law, Edward's successor was Mary Tudor, the daughter of Henry and Catherine of Aragon. Mary was passionately Roman Catholic, and Parliament acceded to her wishes by repealing almost all of the religious statutes that had been passed since 1529. It would not restore the confiscated church lands, now in the possession of many of its members, or recognize the supremacy of the pope. As her demands increased and when she even married Philip of Spain, the heir to the throne of a country that was fast becoming England's major enemy, Mary's popularity declined rapidly. Persecutions of Protestants began in 1555, after Parliament had revived the heresy laws. The martyrs burned at the stake numbered about three hundred and were drawn from all classes of society. The most prominent of the victims were the Protestant bishops Latimer, Ridley, and Hooper, and Archbishop Cranmer. Mary's persecutions won her the nickname "Bloody Mary." Many others, the Marian exiles, fled to the Continent and settled as colonists in Geneva, Frankfurt am Main, Strasbourg, and elsewhere. On the Continent, they came more strongly under the growing influence of Calvinism. Mary died in 1558, her plans for a complete restoration of the pre-1529 religious establishment frustrated by the opposition of Parliament and the people of England.

The Elizabethan Settlement. Mary Tudor was followed by her twenty-five-year-old half-sister Elizabeth I, daughter of Henry VIII and Anne Boleyn. Elizabeth's primary concern in her domestic and foreign policies was national unity under a strong monarch. Theological considerations were secondary. Religious differences were for a time tolerated. The Marian exiles returned home. Calvinism came to be a growing influence. The new queen was not identified with any religious group, though she did like the vestments and drama of the Roman Catholic ritual. Yet she was naturally opposed to the papacy that had declared her illegitimate. Unlike her predecessor, Elizabeth moved cautiously, recognizing that the vast majority of the common people were still Roman Catholic but that the middle class and many prominent persons were Protestant in sympathy. She appointed moderate Protestants as officials. In order to secure a Protestant clergy, Parliament passed in 1559 an Act of Supremacy that revived many of the Reformation statutes of Henry VIII and Edward VI. This act, among others, gave the queen the title of the "only supreme governor of this realm . . . as well in all spiritual or ecclesiastical things or causes, as temporal," avoiding the more offensive term "Supreme Head of the Church." All clergy, judges, and high officials had to swear that they accepted the subordinate position of the church to the crown; those who refused to take the oath were deprived of their offices. The somewhat Zwinglian Book of Common Prayer (1552) was slightly revised to include more Catholic passages and ambiguous phrases, and this Elizabethan Book of Common Prayer was to be followed by all. Absence from religious service was punishable by fine. Elizabeth insisted on the retention of certain Catholic usages, as the wearing of white surplices by the clergy and their being called "priests." The traditional role of the bishops in confirmation and ordination was carefully preserved.

So conservative and cautious was Elizabeth in her religious policy that the popes hesitated for a long time in denouncing her. In 1570, however, Pius V excommunicated the "Pretended Queen of England and those heretics adhering to her." The bull also declared that Englishmen did not owe obedience to her and the present laws of England.

Central to the Elizabethan Settlement in religion are the moderate Thirty-nine Articles, enacted by Parliament in 1571. Showing less conservatism than Lutheranism and leaving room for individual interpretation, these articles have remained the authoritative statement of Anglican doctrine ever since. They recognize only two sacraments and define the Lord's Supper in a Calvinistic manner. The articles enjoin infant Baptism and adherence to the Apostles', Nicene, and Athanasian creeds. According to the articles, general councils are to be called only by order of the rulers, as in the early Christian centuries. All councils can err. Marriage of the clergy is permitted.

Anglican Rites. The Anglican Rite of Baptism was administered on the Sunday or holy day immediately following birth. It was performed in English in the presence of the congregation "that the congregation there present may testify the receiving of them that be newly Baptized into the number of Christ's Church, as also because in the Baptism of Infants every man present may be put in remembrance of his own profession made to God in his Baptism." The rite was held after the last lesson during the morning or evening prayer service. After prayers, the godparents, on behalf of the infant, renounced the devil and all his works and professed belief in the articles of the Apostles' Creed. Baptism was performed in the name of the Trinity by dipping the child into the water "so it be discreetly and warily done." If the child was weak, it was considered sufficient "to pour water upon it." Sprinkling did not become common in England until after 1600. Provisions were made for private Baptism at home in cases of emergency. Besides water and the role of the sponsors, the only remnant of the traditional ceremony was the signing of the cross on the child's forehead immediately after immersion.

Baptized children were admitted to the Rite of Confirmation as soon as they could recite in English the articles of faith, the Lord's Prayer, and the Ten Commandments. They also had to be able to answer correctly such catechetical questions as the bishop or his appointee should ask them. Instruction in the faith was given by the parish priest, curate, or vicar every Sunday and holy day for one-half hour. The priest then informed the bishop of the names of those who were ready for presentation by a godfather or godmother. The rite included prayers and the "imposition of hands" by the bishop. Confirmation was now a prerequisite for Communion.

Holy Communion was envisioned as the normal Sunday service. The eucharistic liturgy was stern, stately, and penitential in character and thus in marked contrast with the more joyous Mass of the Lutheran Reformation. Regulations required that every parishioner should receive Communion at least three times a year, of which Easter was to be one. After the reading of the collect and the traditional Scripture lessons, exhortations, and prayers, the minister made a general confession of sins before the kneeling congregation and pronounced a general absolution. The bread and the wine were distributed as the communicants knelt before the Communion Table, which was covered with a "fair white linen cloth." The bread used in the Sacrament was to be such "as is usual to be eaten at the Table with other meats, but the best and purest wheat bread, that conveniently may be gotten." The use of eucharistic vestments was permitted, but they were generally replaced by the black cassock and simple white surplice. Any bread and wine that remained after the service was given to the curate of the parish for his own use.

Opposition to the Settlement. Many Englishmen were dissatisfied with the Elizabethan Settlement. The conservatives, while often antipapal for nationalist reasons, disapproved of the doctrinal changes. On the other hand, many Protestants thought that the settlement, basically a compromise for unity's sake, was too conservative and too close to Roman Catholicism. The returning Marian exiles, numbering over five hundred, especially attacked the settlement. These nonconforming Calvinists were called Puritans, for they wanted to "purify" the Anglican Church of the "vestiges of popery" that remained in ritual and in the episcopal church government. As opposition grew and as pro-papal plots aimed at deposing Elizabeth occurred, the government took stern action with stringent laws against treason, for religious and political convictions were inextricably intertwined. During the last twenty years of Elizabeth's reign, more than two hundred Roman Catholics were executed, chiefly for treason. As the Puritans grew in strength and as their literature became more abusive, Parliament passed the Act against Seditious Sectaries (1593). Those over the age of sixteen who did not attend services given according to the laws of England were to be imprisoned. Many fled to Holland. However, by the end of Elizabeth's rule in 1603, Roman Catholics and Puritans were still strong enough to cause difficulties for the Anglican government in the seventeenth century.

Protestantism Comes to Scotland. The Puritans found more sympathy for their views in the land to the north of England, for Calvinism had become firmly established in Scotland, then independent from the English. Here, too, there had been a long preparation for the advent of Protestantism. The moral and spiritual state of the clergy was worse in Scotland than elsewhere. Dissatisfaction with the wealthy hierarchy and dissolute clergy was strong among the independent-minded Scots, and Wycliffe's views had found sympathetic understanding. Despite official prohibition and suppression, Luther's works were widely read and his ideas preached. Protestantism found strong support among the barons, and religious differences became part of the struggle of the nobility against a combination of crown and hierarchy. King James V died in 1542, leaving his week-old daughter, Mary Stuart, as queen of Scots. There was a brief period during which Protestantism was favored by the regency, but the country soon came under the control of Cardinal David Beaton, who followed a pro-French and anti-English policy. The young Mary was sent to France to be raised by the Guises, a powerful and conservative Catholic family. The cardinal's repression of the growing Protestant and pro-English movement, especially his execution of the courageous preacher George Wishart, led to his own murder at St. Andrews in May 1546.

John Knox. The little band of armed conspirators, secure in the castle of St. Andrews, received as their chaplain a refugee priest named John Knox. This thirty-two-year-old disciple of Wishart had at times protected his teacher with a two-handed sword, and now he became an implacable fighter for Calvinism. When the arrival of a French fleet forced the group in the castle to surrender, Knox and his companions were made galley slaves. Released early in 1549, Knox went to England and began his real work as a reformer under Edward VI. Again his work was interrupted, this time by the accession of Mary Tudor in 1554. Knox fled to Frankfurt and then went to Geneva, where he spent some time with Calvin; he also stayed with Bullinger at Zurich. After a short visit to England, where he married, and to Scotland, where he preached for nine months, Knox returned to Geneva, the "perfect school of Christ," to minister to other English-speaking refugees. During his absence, a few Scottish noblemen, later called the Lords of the Congregation, formed in 1557 the first Scottish Covenant. In this covenant, they committed their lives and fortunes "to establish and maintain the Word of God" in Scotland. In 1558, Mary Stuart married Francis, the dauphin who was soon to be king of France; in the same year, Mary Tudor died and was succeeded by Elizabeth. The Marian refugees now returned to England, and Knox would have gone there also. But Elizabeth was offended by his violent political tract, *The First Blast of the Trumpet against the Monstrous Regiment of Women*, which Knox had directed against the governments of Mary Tudor and Mary of Guise, the wife of the former James V and then the regent of Scotland.

Calvinism Triumphs. Knox returned to his homeland, where he led the forces of Calvinism against the regent, who was attempting to repress the Reformation. All Europe awaited the outcome of this contest, for it was not an internal affair alone; it involved not only the future of Scotland but of Protestant England and Roman Catholic France as well. European Protestantism hung in the balance, for Mary Stuart was now queen of France and threatened to tie Scotland to Catholic France and thus isolate Protestant England. However, the arrival of an English fleet and army led to the surrender of the French troops in Scotland. The regent, Mary of Guise, had died in June 1560. Emboldened by victory, the Scottish Parliament ratified in the same year the twenty-five articles of the Calvinist Confession of Faith prepared by Knox and his associates. They also cut Scotland's ties with Rome, annulled previous anti-Protestant acts, and condemned the Mass. A Book of Discipline was also prepared, and although it was not approved by Parliament, its proposals for the government of the Scottish Church were accepted by the General Assembly of the Church. This work provided a constitution and disciplinary rules for the Reformed Church of Scotland. The government of the church was organized on the principle of democratic assemblies, beginning with the parish church and extending upward through the synods to the General Assembly. Representative leadership in church government was developed through the elected and ordained elders, or presbyters. The endeavor was to follow the New Testament pattern of church government and worship. The Scottish Church with its Presbyterian system thus differed from the Anglican episcopal Church with its bishops and more "Catholic" forms of worship. This difference was to be a source of conflict between the two nations in the seventeenth century. The principle of popular (representative) leadership in Scotland, however, meant that the church there had a much greater impact on the lives of the people. The English clergy, often drawn from the ranks of the younger sons of the nobility and not too well educated for the ministry, were also less popular and less respected than their Scottish counterparts.

The Reformed Church of Scotland had no sooner been established in 1560 than it was confronted by the return of the Catholic Mary Stuart in August 1561. Her husband, Francis II of France, had died in 1560 at the age of sixteen. Both Elizabeth of England and the Scots, most of whom were now Calvinists, feared that the French-educated queen would attempt to use force and the support of her Guise relatives in France to bring her land back to Catholicism and place it under the influence of France. In that country, the wars between the crown and the Huguenots were beginning. However, the shrewd and self-confident young queen did not follow the advice of her counselors to use French troops to repress Protestantism in her realm. Instead, she tried persuasion and dissimulation and held a series of conferences with Knox and his colleagues. Nothing was accomplished by these means, for the fiery Knox could not be persuaded or intimidated. The General Assembly continued to meet without the permission of Mary. In 1567, Mary's husband, Lord Darnley, was murdered. The queen then hastily married the unscrupulous Earl of Bothwell, but the Scottish nobles refused to allow him to become king. Instead, Mary was deposed, and her infant son was crowned as James VI. Parliament declared that all future kings must swear to maintain Protestantism in Scotland. It also recognized the authority of the General Assembly of the Church of Scotland. Mary fled to England, where she was eventually executed for complicity in plots to overthrow Elizabeth.

England and Scotland Compared. While both England and Scotland rejected Roman Catholicism, the Reformations that resulted took different forms. The English Reformation was an act of state in which the monarch and Parliament held final authority in discipline and doctrine. The episcopal form of church government and more traditional forms of worship were retained. The Anglican Church was a compromise between the extremes of continental Protestantism and Roman Catholicism. The definition of the compromise took long to evolve. On the other hand, the Scottish Reformation was a more radical and quicker break with the past. The Scottish nobles, with the support of the people, brought into being a church firmly based on Calvinism, with a representative church government, independent of secular authorities, replacing the episcopal hierarchy. Scottish ministers were mostly sons of God-fearing and Bible-reading commoners and were highly respected for their learning. The Presbyterian worship services, based on the Genevan services, became known for their austere simplicity and the singing of Psalms and other Scripture in vernacular paraphrase. Both ministers and services were somewhat in contrast to what was the rule in the Church of England.

The Catholic Reformation and Counter-Reformation

Long before the Protestant Reformation, there had been pious men and women in the Christian Church who, either as individuals or by banding together with kindred spirits, had sought to reform the Church from within. Even Luther, it must be remembered, had started out as a loyal son of the Church with no intention of breaking with the Church of his day. The authorities, however, had excommunicated the reformer and placed him and his followers among the unorthodox. This brought about the separation. But there were many other reformers and reform movements that were never pushed beyond the established boundaries of orthodoxy, although at times they narrowly skirted the edge.

The mystics of the fourteenth and fifteenth centuries sought to reform the Church by making their own lives models of piety, devotion, charity, and contemplation. There were other groups, including the Christian humanists, who long before Luther protested against the effects of secularism, wealth, and politics on the hierarchy and life of the whole Church. The councils that had met during the first half of the fifteenth century had sought, with negligible results, to achieve reform. If all these reforming groups, and the councils especially, had been successful in achieving a viable reform in "head and members," Luther's name might never have been known beyond the circle of his family and friends.

Reformers in Spain. An effective Catholic Reformation began in Spain about the time Luther was born. The reform was led by Cardinal Francisco Jiménez de Cisneros (d. 1517). His movement was devoted primarily toward an educational reform along humanistic lines. Erasmian Christian humanism was very influential among Spanish intellectuals; but with the spread of Protestantism, with its direct link with humanism, the works and ideals of Erasmus were condemned by the Inquisition. Prominent Spanish Erasmians in the early sixteenth century were Juan de Valdes and Juan de Vives. The other influential element in the Spanish reform was mysticism, and Teresa of Avila is the most noted figure.

New Italian Orders. With the corruption and abuse so evident in troubled Italy, a vigorous Catholic Reformation arose there in the early sixteenth century. As in the Middle Ages, the reform movement was spearheaded by religious orders. About 1517, the Oratory of Divine Love was founded in Rome. Composed of both laity and clergy, many of them illustrious men, this order put new life into Italian Christianity through its members' devotions and charity among the poor. Affiliated groups sprang up throughout Italy. In 1524, papal sanction was given to the Theatines, an order of devout priests who combined preaching and works of charity in their parishes with a life governed by the requirements of a monastic rule. This order spread beyond the territories of Italy. Another group devoted to the restoration of piety and morality in Italy was the austere Capuchin order, a reformed Franciscan order.

The Jesuits. While these orders did much good work in revitalizing Christian life in Italy and elsewhere, they were not intended or designed to fight Protestantism. This was to be the great task assigned to the Society of Jesus, or the Jesuits. The founder of this influential order was a Spanish nobleman, Ignatius of Loyola, who was born in 1491. His right leg was broken by a French cannonball during the defense of the city of Pamplona (1521), an injury that was to make him permanently lame. During the long period of recovery, his reading and meditation led him to renounce his old way of life and to resolve to become a soldier for Christ and the Church. He then wrote the plan of his famous book, *Spiritual Exercises*, which, when completed, reflected his own religious experiences. This handbook offered detailed instructions through which the reader would develop inner peace, self-control, and discipline and finally surrender his will and being to God and the Church. Thus, thoroughly disciplined by meditations and spiritual exercises, the man was ready to submit himself completely to the Church.

Ignatius's desire to convert the Muslims in Palestine was frustrated by the Franciscans there. He thereupon decided to prepare himself for his missionary task by acquiring a better education. At the universities of Alcalá and Salamanca he ran into trouble with the Inquisition because of his unauthorized preaching activities. In 1528, Ignatius entered the College of Montaigu in Paris, a college that John Calvin had just left. By the time Ignatius left Paris in 1535, this small (five feet two inches), deformed, but enthusiastic man had attracted nine faithful disciples, including Francis Xavier, Diego Laynez, and Alfonso Salmeron. Unable to go to Palestine because of war, the group went to Rome to offer their services to the pope. In 1540, papal approval for their new order was gained from Paul III.

Besides the usual monastic vows, the constitution of the new order called for a special vow of complete obedience to the pope. The Jesuits, as they came to be called, practiced only moderate asceticism, for nothing was to interfere with their efficiency. Instead of establishing religious communities like the monastic orders, the Jesuits became very active in the affairs of the world. The upper classes, not the masses, were the object of their efforts and attention. The military character of the organization, the discipline, and the subordination of the individual's will to that of his superior all contributed to the achievement of the society's goals.

Under the skillful generalship of Ignatius, trained Jesuits were sent throughout Europe and made a valiant effort to retain Roman Catholics in the church, to stir up new life and zeal in it, and to bring those already separated back into the fold. They won approval of the rulers by their tact, manners, absolute devotion, self-denial, resourcefulness, and learning. Popular as confessors to rulers and men of high influence, they did not hesitate to use their influence in matters of state. In existing universities and in their own excellent schools and colleges, they trained the youth so thoroughly in Roman Catholicism that that faith was, as a rule, forever retained by their students. The order soon grew in size, power, and wealth. As obedient shock troops of the papacy, they were sent from one danger area to another. As zealous crusaders for the Church, and with the powerful support of the Hapsburg rulers, they recovered much territory from Protestantism in southern Germany and in Austria,

Hungary, Bohemia, and Poland. In North and South America, Jesuits explored the wilderness and made converts among Native Americans. Francis Xavier spent eleven years in India and the Far East converting Muslims, Hindus, and Buddhists. No single force proved so advantageous to the Roman Catholic Church in revitalizing its own ranks and in turning the tide of Protestantism as did the Society of Jesus.

Reform of the Papacy. The popes gradually assumed a position of leadership in the Catholic Reformation. It was a slow and painful process, for no matter how much disposed toward reform a pope personally might be, he had to overcome the massive resistance of members of the Curia, the cardinals, and other prelates who profited from the rampant corruption. The Renaissance popes, Leo X (1513–21), Adrian VI (1522), and Clement VII (1523–34), either were tolerant of abuses or could not overcome the deadweight of the entrenched corruption and abuse.

With the aged Paul III (1534–49), the Catholic Reformation gradually showed a new spirit and entered into what might be called the Counter (Protestant) Reformation stage. Paul III was a paradoxical figure. In his personal life, the pope was notoriously immoral. Frank in his nepotism, he elevated two of his nephews to the cardinalate at fourteen and sixteen. On the other hand, confronted by a vigorous and spreading Protestantism that was feeding on the people's discontent with the corruption and abuses in the Church, Paul III appointed a commission of nine cardinals to consider the matter of reform and present a plan for action. Their *Consilium* (*Advice*) was presented in 1538. In no uncertain terms, this remarkable document condemned, among others, papal absolutism, simony, the ordination of incompetent and immoral youths, abuses in the bestowal of benefices and bishoprics, pluralities, nonresident bishops, neglect of duties by the cardinals, the teaching of impiety at the universities, evils in monasticism, and the deceptions practiced on the simple folk. The clandestine publication of this report was hailed by the Protestants as completely supporting the charges of Luther and the other reformers. So strong and candid were its denunciations, the report was later placed on the Index of Prohibited Books, a catalog of books that Roman Catholics were forbidden to read.

The Roman Inquisition. After the failure of an attempt to reconcile Protestantism and Roman Catholicism at a conference at Ratisbonn in 1541, the new spirit of reform led Paul III to establish in 1542 the Roman Inquisition. This was based on the model of the notorious but efficient Spanish Inquisition. Six cardinals, led by the rigid and zealous Giovanni Caraffa, were named Inquisitors General with wide jurisdiction. The Inquisition moved against the lowly and those in high offices, including several cardinals. Many Italians with leanings toward Protestantism fled, and the evangelical movement was all but eliminated in Italy. Although it was originally intended that the Roman Inquisition should function throughout Roman Catholic Europe, such widespread activity was dependent on the support of the secular powers. This support was not forthcoming, and the Roman Inquisition was limited to Italy.

The Council of Trent. Luther, Charles V, and many others had repeatedly called for a general council to decide the religious issues that were splitting Europe. The agitation increased as reluctant popes toyed with the idea. The popes remembered only too well the attacks on papal absolutism in the period of conciliarism. The recurring wars and political maneuvering also produced delays.

DECISIONS OF THE COUNCIL OF TRENT (1545–47; 1551–52; 1562–63)	
SCRIPTURE	Scripture and tradition given equal weight. Vulgate adopted as standard.
JUSTIFICATION	Rejected justification by faith alone. Faith and good works necessary. Indulgences retained, though office of indulgence seller was eliminated.
SACRAMENTS	Seven sacraments. Transubstantiation upheld.
BISHOPS	Neglect condemned. Instruction, preaching, and visitation expected.
CLERGY	Seminaries in each diocese; examination before ordination or appointment. Periodic synods ordered. Moderation, simplicity, industry, morality, and frugality prescribed. Concubinage forbidden.
LITURGY AND PREACHING	Monastic preachers restricted. Liturgy made uniform.
THE INDEX	Approved Inquisition practice of listing prohibited books. New list made in 1564.

The Council of Trent was an important landmark in the history of Christianity. The dogmas and practices of Roman Catholicism were so carefully defined that only a few additions have been made in the succeeding centuries. Far from achieving a basis for unity and reconciliation within Christendom, the decrees of the Council of Trent made such a hope more unlikely. By defining dogma, removing abuse and corruption, and strengthening the central authority of the popes, the Roman Catholic Church was enabled to present a united and firm front in its defensive and countermeasures against Protestantism.

A Strengthened Roman Catholic Church. By means of reformed and reforming popes, the creation of new and active religious orders, the work of the Roman Inquisition, and by the dogmatic and disciplinary decisions of the Council of Trent, a new and greatly strengthened Roman Catholic Church emerged in the last quarter of the sixteenth century. It was in a much more favorable position than before to combat the non–Roman Catholic part of a divided Christendom. The authority of the papacy was firmly established over the Church's administration, and under papal leadership, the worst abuses and corruption were corrected. Nepotism and simony were ended, the indulgence seller disappeared, and the confessional box was introduced, with a screen separating the confessor and the priest in an effort to prevent dangers resulting from confessional intimacy. The institutions within the Roman

Church and the personnel of these organizations took on a new life. In its encounter with the Reformation, Catholicism came to grips with basic issues and showed little tendency to change the traditional interpretations and practice. Indeed, the preservation of a conservative orthodoxy was guaranteed by placing the right of interpretation of Scriptures and tradition in the hands of the pope. Yet new vitality and spirituality were engendered everywhere, and the new forces in Catholicism were able to stop and even roll back the advancing tide of Protestantism. At the same time, the definitive statements on Roman Catholic doctrine meant an increase in tensions and animosities between the now clearly divided elements in Christendom.

THE CHURCH IN THE SEVENTEENTH CENTURY

In the three centuries following 1300, the Christian Church was dramatically changed. By the beginning of the seventeenth century, Orthodox Christianity of the eastern Mediterranean area and in the Balkans had long been under the control of the Muslim Turks with the patriarch of Constantinople a subject of the sultan. In the West the unity that had characterized the late Medieval Church was shattered for all time. The West was now divided into two opposing religious camps—Roman Catholic and Protestant. Roman Catholicism was predominant in the Italian states, Spain, Austria, France, Portugal, Ireland, Hungary, Poland, southern Germany, and the Spanish Lowlands. Various forms of Protestantism, often hostile to one another, held ascendancy in Bohemia, northern Germany, the Scandinavian countries, the United Provinces, some of the Swiss cantons, England, and Scotland. Strong Protestant minorities could be found in Austria, Poland, Hungary, and France.

In addition to being reduced in number of adherents, the Roman Catholic Church in 1600 differed markedly in character from its parental, late medieval institution. The pope, to be sure, still held the same position of authority in the Church as in the fourteenth century. However, the exercise of his spiritual authority was somewhat restricted by a strengthened episcopacy. His political power was very much limited by the powerful rulers of the new national states, a number of whom were now Protestant. Papal claims of universal dominance were no longer recognized except in the interpretation of doctrine. Even that claim was acceptable only to Roman Catholics. The Roman Catholic clergy was much revitalized by the forces of the Catholic Counter-Reformation and by the confrontation with Protestantism. The new orders, especially the Jesuits, had deepened and reformed the religious life of Catholicism, while the canons and decrees of the Council of Trent had established firm discipline and had clearly defined the criteria of orthodoxy. The most obvious abuses and corruption within the hierarchy had been corrected. Monasticism had become, in general, less ascetic and more activist in missions.

PROTESTANTISM IN 1600	
BIBLE	All Protestants based their beliefs and practices on the Bible.
VARIETY	Differences in interpretation of the Bible, its application, and dependence on reason resulted in Lutheranism, Calvinism, Anabaptism, and Anglicanism.
REJECTED DOCTRINES AND PRACTICES	All Protestants rejected the papacy, the requirement of clerical celibacy, purgatory, monasticism, salvation through faith and good works, the majority of the medieval sacraments, and many other facets of traditional Christianity that they felt were medieval additions not based on Scripture.
LITURGY	Adopted simplified rites. Lutherans and Anglicans were more conservative.
MINISTRY	Public ministers appointed to duties shared by all Christians. Ministers were poorly paid. Married. Preaching emphasized as well as increased education in the Bible.
EDUCATION	Protestants saw need for increased education at all levels of society. Melanchthon instrumental in German education. Universities at first declined due to controversies, and then expanded while emphasizing conservatism and conformity. Local rulers as overseers of education.

Toleration. The Reformation era was not an age of religious toleration. Protestants as well as Roman Catholics persecuted and even executed those whom they considered heretics and blasphemers. While Roman Catholic authorities relied on canon law and the decrees of the Council of Trent, Protestants used the Bible as the guide for their persecutions. The resuscitated ancient Roman law was the basis for the repudiation and persecution of anti-Trinitarians and Anabaptists. Calvin burned Servetus, but banishment was the more usual punishment in Protestant lands. However, despite the intolerance, forces were at work in the sixteenth century that were eventually to lead to religious liberty. The very existence of so many rival factions often meant that no one group was strong enough to force its will on the rest. But only in later centuries did the idea develop that variance in religious views neither weakened the unity of the state nor lead to the corruption of society.

Democracy. The system of government in which all the citizens of a state participate in matters of local or national policy, and in which these citizens have equal and inalienable rights, is a fairly modern development. The democracy of today is the result of a long and slow growth that goes back to Old Testament times. From the Hebrews and from early Christianity came the concepts of the dignity of each human being, the equality of all men before God, and the right and duty to disobey and criticize unjust rulers. But the principles of democracy were seldom evident in the ecclesiastical and feudal civilization of the Middle Ages.

While political and even social democracy are not at all characteristic of the sixteenth century, Protestantism did give impetus to the growth of democracy. Luther's concept of the priesthood of all believers was an attack on the authoritarian hierarchical system and encouraged individual responsibility and freedom of decision.

Calvinism originated in republican Geneva and soon was in open opposition to ty-rannical forms of government everywhere, linked as these were to the forces oppos-ing the Reformation. Calvinism also emphasized the rule of law, both biblical and constitutional. The Anabaptists suffered terrible persecutions because of their passion for freedom of faith and thought. They and the Bohemian Brethren alone demanded the separation of church and state, but their views gained no widespread support.

The Arts. Of all the arts, music was most influenced by the reform movements of the sixteenth century. Zwingli, although himself a musician, abolished music from the church service. However, by the late sixteenth century, congregational singing had been reintroduced at Zurich. Luther loved music, including polyphony, and was himself an able musician. Under his influence, there developed the great Lutheran chorales that enhanced the service. The greater part of the liturgy was also sung by the congregation, and the Lutheran Church became "the singing church." Calvin restricted church music somewhat, but he recognized that "if the singing be tem-pered to that gravity which is fitting in the sight of God and the angels, it both lends dignity and grace to sacred actions and has the greatest value in kindling our hearts to a true zeal and eagerness to pray" (*Institutes* III.xx.32). Calvinistic psalm-singing reached great heights of beauty and solemnity. The Anglican Church also produced considerable church music, although the English hymn is a later development. The Roman Catholic Church continued its use of trained choirs to sing the Latin music of the High Mass.

The content of visual arts embodies the life and thoughts of the people and art-ists who create it. The changes in economy, political life, and religion in the period under consideration naturally were reflected in architecture, painting, and sculpture. The Gothic art of the high Middle Ages had given way to the revival of classical forms of ancient Greece and Rome, reflecting the full life of the Renaissance indi-vidual and the secular spirit of the age. St. Peter's Basilica in Rome is an outstanding example of Renaissance ecclesiastical building. When the Reformation began in the sixteenth century, Renaissance art forms were already declining in grandeur because of excessive ornamentation and lavish decoration.

While many of the great Gothic churches in predominantly Protestant lands came to house reformed services, the new liturgical concepts usually demanded a dif-ferent type of building. To Roman Catholics, the church building was truly the house of God with the divine presence direct and tangible in the consecrated elements of the Eucharist and in the signs and symbols of the sacramental mysteries. The focus of the building was therefore the altar. To the Protestants, the church was more of a meeting place for the congregation and for instruction in the Word of God during the services. The pulpit and lectern thus received a place of equal prominence with the Communion Table or altar. Where iconoclasm prevailed, as in the Calvinistic Reformed Church, there was frequently an excessive plainness and lack of artistry in the churches. Lutheranism and Anglicanism retained the use of sculptured and painted objects as long as they were conducive to evangelical faith and not the subjects of superstitious veneration.

Revitalization of the Church. By 1600, the unity that had existed in the Western Christian Church of 1300 had been disrupted. The new diversity led to mutual suspicion and the attempt to use arms to resolve religious differences. Although largely political in nature, both the Thirty Years' War in Germany (1618–48) and the civil war in England (1642–60) arose out of religious tensions.

While the disunity in Christendom brought about by the Protestant Reformation is often deplored, the break in the external structure of the Christian Church in the West was accompanied by an internal revitalization of the spirit. Out of the upheaval of the sixteenth century came a strengthening of religious life in the various components of Christianity. The worst abuses and the widespread corruption that had characterized the lax Church of the Renaissance were eliminated, and a more vigorous discipline was instituted within the many branches of the Church.

CHAPTER FIVE

The Church in the Age of Orthodoxy and the Enlightenment

CONSOLIDATION AND CHALLENGE FROM 1600 TO 1800

Beginning with the post-Reformation emphasis on orthodoxy and extending through the rise of modern science, this period culminated in attempts to apply the scientific outlook to society during the eighteenth-century revolutions. Though some Christian leaders of this period (e.g., Johann Gerhard, Philipp Jakob Spener, and John Wesley) are not as well known as some leaders of preceding ages (e.g., Augustine, Martin Luther, and John Calvin), many thought patterns and movements surfaced, and many problems developed that have continued into our time.

The modern state system grew during the two centuries from 1600 to 1800. The last important European religious conflict, the Thirty Years' War, saw a shift in loyalty from religion to politics and became in essence the "first world war." When the struggle ended in 1648 with the Peace of Westphalia, absolute dynastic monarchies were clearly to be the supreme institutions in western Europe. The state became more important than religion as a focus for the loyalty of its citizens. In France and certain areas of the Holy Roman Empire, this led to a decline in religious toleration; in the Reformed states of the Netherlands and in England, there was more freedom. At first glance, the shift away from bitter religious struggles to a more secular approach might be viewed as a wholly positive step, but with the advent of the American and French revolutions of the eighteenth century, society was faced with a new source of bigotry and intolerance, namely, the nation-state.

The seventeenth and eighteenth centuries also were a time of the expansion of Europe and the rise of Western civilization to a position of global leadership. From the sixth to the sixteenth centuries, there were four major world cultures: India, the Middle East, China, and Western Europe, all in relative balance. During certain periods one or the other dominated, but not as the West has done since the sixteenth century. Beginning with the voyages of exploration in the fifteenth and sixteenth centuries and continuing to the imperialism of the nineteenth and twentieth centuries, Western civilization has overwhelmed the other cultures. Western political arrangements, technology, and science have developed a lifestyle copied by many world leaders. During the period covered by this section, Europeans colonized distant lands and engaged in much missionary activity. As a result, many natives in the colonies became Christians.

The Political Situation. In the early seventeenth century, Europe was divided into several states whose relations were strained not only by dynastic ambitions but also by differences in religion. France, the Netherlands, and England controlled the Channel and the Atlantic approaches to the Baltic and North Seas.

CHURCHES AND STATES IN SEVENTEENTH-CENTURY EUROPE		
	STATE	CHURCH
FRANCE	Strongest, with large population and resources.	Leading Roman Catholic power.
ENGLAND	Influential due to sound organization.	The Anglican Church became a leader among Protestants.
NETHERLANDS	A commercial and colonial power. Legislative government.	Calvinism became the state religion; later adopted toleration.
SPAIN	Declining power, losing possessions, and separating from the Holy Roman Empire.	Spain became the leading power of the Catholic, or Counter, Reformation.
HOLY ROMAN EMPIRE	A loose federation of principalities that never achieved the unity of France or England.	Lutheranism and Calvinism prevailed but suffered in the Thirty Years' War.
SWEDEN	Able rulers leading a small population with limited resources.	Lutheran and unified.
RUSSIA	Russian czars ruling a vast peasant, agrarian state. Moscow as the "third Rome" after collapse of Constantinople to the Turks.	Poorly educated Eastern Orthodox priests preserved the message of the church in ritual form.

Europe, America, and the Orient. While dynastic and religious changes were taking place in sixteenth- and seventeenth-century Europe, the Christian faith was carried far abroad by colonists and missionaries. Beginning with the voyages of Columbus (1451–1506; first voyage 1492), explorers and adventurers laid claim to vast areas of the Americas for Spain and Portugal. The Spanish claimed the lion's share of the new hemisphere, including Mexico, Peru, Central America, and the West Indies, and established settlements in Colombia, Panama, California, New Mexico, Chile, and the area of the River Plate (*Rio de la Plata*). The expansions into America resembled early medieval missionary work in pagan Germany. Soldiers, called conquistadors, were accompanied by Roman Catholic missionaries who established churches and schools. Many of the troops that came to conquer such empires as the Aztec and the Incan were the scum of Spanish society, and they were often encouraged by fanaticism and a desire for plunder reminiscent of the worst of the medieval crusades. But the friars who came to preach and teach were often very noble. Among them was Bartolome de Las Casas (1474–1566). For over forty years, Las Casas preached to the Spanish that the American Indians were human beings and should be treated with kindness and consideration. Toribio Alfonso de Mogrovejo y Robles

(1538–1606), second archbishop of Lima, Peru (c. 1578/80–1606), and called "apostle of Peru," is said to have confirmed many hundreds of thousands. Mass Baptisms resulted in "converts" who had very little knowledge of Christianity.

In an attempt to deal with problems caused by contact between American Indians and Europeans, separate villages were established for Christian American Indians. These "reductions" were a Roman Catholic form of the later reservations established by the United States. In Brazil, Peru/Mexico, and Paraguay, these settlements offered the natives a better way of life. By the early seventeenth century in Paraguay, for example, there were thirty clerical estates or reductions, each with a church, hospital, convent, and a school where the brightest children could learn Latin. Governed by clerics, these communities offered their residents an eight-hour workday, compulsory divine services, and various recreational activities.

Most of the natives of South and Central America did not live on reservations but attended parish churches modeled after those of Spain and Portugal. Under control of distant bishops, these churches remained untouched by the Counter-Reformation.

As the Spaniards led the way in evangelizing the Americas, the Portuguese expanded in the Orient. Though they encountered more advanced civilizations and stronger religions than those in the New World, the Portuguese brought civil control and Christianity to Goa, Malacca, and Macao. By 1620, the Spanish had an archbishop, a Dominican university, and two thousand baptized converts in the Philippines. Roman Catholic successes here raised expectations among the missionaries that other victories would follow.

Francis Xavier (1506–52), one of the founders of the Society of Jesus (Jesuits), was appointed papal representative to the East Indies. He arrived at Goa in 1542 and later went to Malacca and Japan. Before he was forced to leave Japan he had established a Christian community of over two thousand members. He died while trying to enter China. Though he mastered none of the languages he encountered, he felt at home among Hindus, Muslims, and Buddhists. He appealed to the masses. Working under protection of the government, he gathered people by ringing a hand bell. Then, speaking through interpreters, he recited the Apostles' Creed, the Ten Commandments, the Ave Maria, and the Lord's Prayer. After weeks or months of this, he baptized those who had memorized these statements and professed faith in God. He then moved on to another place but left some followers behind to carry on the work.

Christian missionaries in the Orient faced strong competing religions. Often, they found that Christian worship was welcome in the temples, but that Hindu and Buddhist rites would continue to be observed. The traditional attitude of Christians had been that idols must be destroyed and non-Christian worship suppressed. But in India and China, this exclusive outlook was modified as a result of the toleration, holiness, and asceticism of the Asian religions. In the policy of accommodation, as it came to be called, the Jesuits led the way with a gentle approach to the beliefs and traditions of Asia, holding that such procedure would aid the presentation of the Gospel. They tried to sort out the customs of the Japanese, Chinese, or American Indians and determine which were merely social and civil and which were incompatible with Christianity. The Italians Matteo Ricci (1552–1610) and Robert de Nobili (1577–1656) were among the better known Jesuit exponents of missionary adaptation.

Trained in science at the Roman College, Ricci spent the years 1572–82 at Goa and Cochin before going to China. In typical evangelistic fashion, he began his work by showing clocks, astronomical instruments, maps, and books. He then spent hours in discussion on the agreement between Confucianism and Christianity. Hundreds of thousands of copies of his dialogue between a Chinese scholar and a European priest were distributed to the Chinese. By the year of his death, there were over two thousand Christians in China. As the seventeenth century progressed, the work of adaptation to ancient custom begun by Ricci was undermined and destroyed as a result of the "affair of the rites." In a series of decisions, the papacy declared that it was wrong to value the Confucian tradition too highly and to pay undue reverence to one's ancestors. The Chinese emperor was upset by what he regarded as an insult to the customs of his people and forced Christian missions from his country.

Nobili was a nephew of Cardinal Bellarmine and related to Pope Julius III. He was sent as missionary to India in 1604, arrived in Goa in 1605, and worked especially in Madura. He dressed and lived like a *sannyasi* (Hindu ascetic). The Christian community that resulted from his work is said to have numbered over 100,000.

Japan seemed to offer an opportunity to repeat the success that Christian missionaries had enjoyed in the Philippines. By 1614, there were at least 300,000 Christians in Japan. The rapid conversion to Christianity was halted by fear that the priests would help the Westerners to take over the government. In a series of horrible persecutions marked by savage tortures, the Christian Church in Japan was destroyed. A decree of 1638 closed the land to foreigners, and by the end of the century, few Christians were left in Japan. The fate of the Japanese Church illustrates the problems of early Christian missions in the Orient. Despite impressive initial gains, the work of winning south and east Asia to Christ did not prosper as did similar efforts in the Americas. The Philippines are the only Roman Catholic land in east Asia.

Theological Controversies. At the same time that missionaries were carrying the Gospel far abroad, their fellow churchmen in Europe were trying to define Christianity precisely. Doctrinal quarrels were often intertwined with political struggles and led to conflict between various groups such as Arminians and Reformed (Calvinists), Lutherans and Reformed, and Roman Catholics and Protestants. The conflict between the Arminians and the strict Calvinists centered in the Netherlands. The Arminian party was named for Jacobus Arminius (1560–1609), a Dutch Calvinist theologian who was trained at Leiden and Geneva before he became pastor at Amsterdam. John Calvin (1509–64), Theodore Beza (1519–1605), and other leaders of the Reformed scholastic movement developed the Dutch Calvinism that Arminius studied. These men emphasized biblical literalism (the tendency to adopt literal interpretations), predestination, and Presbyterian church government. Arminius, reacting against this system, proclaimed that God's offer of grace was universal and that individuals possessed the freedom to respond to God in faith.

ARMINIAN VERSUS REFORMED		
	EVENTS	OUTCOMES
JACOBUS ARMINIUS (1560–1609)	Dispute with Franciscus Gomarus (1563–1641). Defined predestination differently.	Arminius sought reconciliation through a national synod but died before the meeting ended.
THE REMONSTRANCE (ARMINIAN) DOCUMENT (1610)	Five points: (1) eternal decree of salvation refers to believers; (2) Christ died for all; (3) can do no good until born again by Holy Spirit; (4) grace is not irresistible; (5) one can fall from grace.	Many in Netherlands, including theologians Simon Episcopius, Jan Uytenbogaert, Hugo Grotius, and statesman Jan van Oldenbarneveldt, agreed with Arminius.
CONDEMNATION AT SYNOD OF DORDRECHT (1618–19)	Five points: (1) total depravity; (2) unconditional election; (3) limited atonement; (4) irresistible grace; (5) perseverance of the saints in grace.	Classic Calvinist positions founded. Remonstrants serving churches were dismissed.
POLITICS	Calvinist Maurice of Nassau (1567–1625) and Jan van Oldenbarneveldt (1547–1619) took opposing sides.	Maurice imprisoned, exiled, or killed leading Arminians. After Maurice's death, they were allowed to return to Netherlands. Toleration advanced.

England provided the most fertile soil for the growth of Arminianism. Many Laudians (followers of William Laud [1573–1645], a high churchman who became archbishop of Canterbury 1633) accepted the more liberal view and passed the teaching on to the latitudinarians (i.e., those tolerant of variations in doctrine). During the eighteenth century, the Unitarians were Arminians, as was the great evangelist John Wesley. Through Wesley's Methodism, Arminianism has come down to our time as an important theology.

Just as the Reformed were confronted with the problem of Arminianism, so the Lutherans had to deal with a number of controversies during the later Reformation era. As in the earlier stages of the Reformation, theological and political problems were intertwined. The Peace of Augsburg (1555), which settled the first period of the religious war within the Holy Roman Empire, gave too little political and legal security to the German Protestants. It was concluded with the understanding that a final settlement of the problems would be made at a later time. But when the theologians representing the Lutherans and the Roman Catholics met at Worms in 1557, the divisions among the Protestants encouraged the Catholics to postpone a settlement.

LUTHERAN VERSUS REFORMED		
	EVENTS	OUTCOMES
SPREAD OF CALVINISM	Frederick III (1515–76) introduced Calvinism in the Palatinate; though he claimed to be Lutheran, he used an altered Augsburg Confession.	Other German princes and theologians followed Frederick's example, leading to religious confusion in Germany.
PHILIPPIST LUTHERANS	Philip Melanchthon created altered versions of the Augsburg Confession. He and his followers were developing different views from Luther on some doctrines.	From Wittenberg, Philippists tried to conciliate with Calvin's views of the Lord's Supper and with Romanist ceremonies.
GNESIO (TRUE)- LUTHERANS	Matthias Flacius Illyricus (1520–75) taught at the University of Jena and wrote *Magdeburg Centuries*, a Church history. He rejected Melanchthon's new views.	The Flacians attacked the Philippists for making concessions to other groups. Jena became a center of conservative Lutheranism.
CHIEF CONTROVERSY: THE LORD'S SUPPER	John Calvin tried to harmonize Luther's and Zwingli's views on the Lord's Supper. Lutheran Joachim Westphal (1510–74) rejected Calvin's spiritual interpretation of Christ's presence.	Melanchthon wrote empathetically to Calvin but refused to engage in the debate. He never broke publicly from Luther's doctrine of the Sacrament.
FORMULA OF CONCORD (1580)	Jacob Andreae (1528–90) and others sought to preserve Lutheranism from the extremes in the controversies. They wanted to retain Luther's doctrine. Centered in Leipzig, Rostock, Marburg, and Tuebingen.	Lutherans adopted the Formula of Concord. This settled interpretations of the Augsburg Confession and brought peace to the Lutheran Church.

The Formula of Concord allowed systematization of doctrine within Lutheranism, using the Loci method developed by Melanchthon. This method flowered in the work of Johann Gerhard (1582–1637). His *Loci communes theologici* is an outstanding statement of Lutheran orthodoxy.

The Reformed theologians and princes of Germany had tried but failed at Frankfurt in 1577 to unite on the basis of a kind of Reformed formula of concord. The Heidelberg Catechism of 1563 continued as the main doctrinal statement of German Calvinism. The University of Heidelberg was the intellectual center of the movement that came to include such territories and cities as Nassau, Bremen, Anhalt, Hesse-Kassel, Cleves, Julich, and Berg. An important milestone in the spread of the Reformed faith in Germany was the conversion of Elector John Sigismund of Brandenburg (1572–1619; elector 1608–19) from Lutheranism to Calvinism in 1613. Conflict between the Lutherans and the Reformed kept the Protestant forces divided and enabled the Counter-Reformation to make impressive gains.

In the mid-sixteenth century, Roman Catholicism seemed to be a dying faith. In Germany, for example, by 1555, nine-tenths of the people and nearly all of the secular princes had become Protestants. The rulers of many other parts of Europe, it appeared, might become the heads of newly established national churches similar to the Church of England under Henry VIII (1491–1547; king 1509–47). But as a result of the Counter-Reformation, this did not happen.

ROMAN CATHOLIC VERSUS PROTESTANT		
	EVENTS	OUTCOMES
COUNCIL OF TRENT (1545–63)	Established teachings of Roman Catholicism, which allowed renewed opposition to Protestantism.	Index of Prohibited Books, Inquisition courts, new schools for priests, and religious orders.
JESUITS	Jesuits worked closely with loyal Catholic kings in Poland and established several colleges.	Nobles and peasants were pressured to renounce Protestantism. Educational institutions fell to the Jesuits.
HOLY ROMAN EMPIRE DIVIDED	The Peace of Augsburg (1555) was strained. Conflict divided the empire. Protestantism lost its drive after 1565.	Superstition, immorality, and social injustice continued to flourish. Protestants did not cooperate well with one another.
DIET AT REGENSBURG (RATISBON) AND EVANGELICAL UNION	The imperial diet did not resolve Protestant-Catholic tensions. German Reformed and Lutheran princes tried to further cooperation with one another.	Maximilian I (1573–1651) and others formed the Catholic League (1609) to rival the Protestants.

The Thirty Years' War. Though each side felt that war was inevitable, the outbreak of the Thirty Years' War surprised both. Before tracing the course of the conflict, it is helpful to have some general characteristics of the war in mind.

By the time the fighting was over, most European states, including France, Spain, Sweden, Denmark, Bohemia, and the various principalities of Germany, were involved. The war can be divided into four main phrases: Bohemian (1618–25), Danish (1625–29), Swedish (1630–35), and French (1635–48). The length of the hostilities and the hundreds of thousands of soldiers involved in the conflict devastated the areas where the fighting took place. The turmoil began as a religious conflict, but during the final phases, it was primarily a political contest. The Catholic Bourbon house of France, frightened by the growth of Hapsburg power, sent troops and money to support the Protestant cause. The political, dynastic side of the struggle led to the Peace of Westphalia, which ended the war. The settlement is, in a sense, the first modern international peace treaty, a precursor of the Congress of Vienna (1814–15) and the Treaty of Versailles (1919).

The Thirty Years' War began in Bohemia. The king of this Slavic land, which is part of the modern Czech Republic, was one of the seven electors who chose the Holy Roman Emperor. The king of Bohemia was elected to his position by the nobility, and for nearly a century, a Catholic Hapsburg had been chosen. But by the early seventeenth century, many Bohemians were Protestants. Bohemia had been a trouble spot for the Roman Catholic Church since the time of the reformer John Hus (c. 1369–1415). In the seventeenth century, the most militant Bohemian Protestants were the Calvinists. The Reformed Church and its allies in Bohemia feared the extension of Hapsburg power and the strengthening of the Catholic Church. Their fears seemed confirmed when Ferdinand II (1578–1637), who was trained to be anti-Protestant, became king of Bohemia in 1617. Despite promises to the contrary, Ferdinand began to persecute Protestants.

The first open act of Bohemian rebellion was the "defenestration of Prague." On May 23, 1618, two Catholic representatives of the king and their secretary were thrown from a window in the Hradschin Castle but were not seriously injured. Jubilant Catholics hailed the incident as a miracle; Protestants pointed out that the men had landed on a manure pile. After the incident, the Bohemian representative assembly, the estates, met to elect a different king. Ferdinand was deposed, and in 1619, Frederick V (1596–1632; elector of the Palatinate 1610–23) became king of Bohemia. He was a handsome young Calvinist prince, active in the Evangelical Union. Statistically, he might have become Holy Roman Emperor, since Protestants now controlled four of the seven votes. But actually Frederick ruled Bohemia for such a brief time that he has gone down in history as the "winter king." In war with the Hapsburgs, he did not receive the aid he expected from the international Calvinist community and the Evangelical Union. Ferdinand, on the other hand, received assistance from Spain, the papacy, Bavaria, and the Catholic League. In November 1620, at the Battle of the White Mountain, west of Prague, the count of Tilly, commanding the forces of the Catholic League, crushed Frederick's troops, and the "winter king" was forced to flee.

Jesuits soon arrived in Bohemia to force Catholicism on the people. Refusing to knuckle under, 150,000 fled from Bohemia. The old Protestant nobility was eliminated when its lands were seized and given to loyal Catholic Hapsburg supporters. Ferdinand followed up this victory by conquering the Palatinate and forcing Frederick into exile.

The sweeping Catholic victory led other Protestant princes of Germany to support Christian IV (1577–1648; king of Denmark and Norway 1588–1648), who began the second phase of the war. As duke of Holstein, the king of Denmark was also a prince of the empire. He had built his power and wealth by controlling the entry to the Baltic Sea, and now he wished to aid the German Protestants while gaining more territory for himself. The Dutch and the English gave him economic aid for a campaign. The emperor, needing additional support to meet the Danish challenge, struck a bargain with Albrecht von Wallenstein (1583–1634), a strange, sinister, mercenary soldier of boundless ambition. Wallenstein, who had gotten rich from lands seized from Bohemian Protestants, agreed to furnish an army of twenty thousand at no cost to the empire. In his campaign against the Danes, he showed himself to be an excellent general, forcing Christian to withdraw from the war by 1629.

The Hapsburg Catholic tide was now at its height, and it looked as though forcible conversion would be the order of the day for most German Protestants. Protestant losses were many and great, but none more symbolic or longer lasting than the loss of the Palatinate library. Bavarian troops who conquered this area seized the library of Heidelberg, a treasure of manuscripts and books, and shipped it to Rome, where it remains. The Edict of Restitution (1629) decreed the restoration of all lands that Protestants had taken since 1552. It not only upset the Protestant princes, who regarded it as a warrant for their destruction, but Catholic rulers also felt that Ferdinand was using it to increase Hapsburg control over Germany. In addition, the princes feared Wallenstein and demanded that his army be dissolved. Ferdinand tried to allay their suspicions by dismissing Wallenstein and disbanding his army.

If the Edict of Restitution had been fully enforced, Protestantism in Germany would have been destroyed. Problems with the German Catholic princes hampered Ferdinand, but the death blow to his dreams came when Gustavus Adolphus (1594–1632; king of Sweden 1611–32) invaded Germany in 1630. A brilliant soldier, statesman, and devout Lutheran, Gustavus was one of the most influential rulers in early modern times. Before his invasion of Germany, he defeated the Danes, the Russians, and the Poles. He entered the Thirty Years' War not only to save Protestantism but also to ensure Swedish control of the Baltic Sea. The changing character of the war is indicated by this, that part of the money financing the Swedish expedition came from the Catholic king of France on advice of Cardinal Richelieu. At first, the German Protestant princes were frightened by the Swedish armies, but after the sack of Magdeburg, they supported them. Gustavus defeated the count of Tilly at the Battle of Leipzig (or Breitenfeld, six miles north-northwest of Leipzig) in 1631 and at Rain (near the confluence of the Lech and the Danube) in 1632. These victories enabled him to restore freedom to Protestants in south and southwest Germany. Ferdinand recalled Wallenstein to counter the Swedish menace in the Battle of Luetzen (southwest of Leipzig) in 1632. The Protestants won, but Gustavus was killed in action. The Swedish army remained in Germany, but its influence declined. When Wallenstein decided to assume political power, the emperor dismissed him and had him murdered.

Despite an attempted settlement in 1635, the war was kept alive by the French. Hiring mercenaries at first and later mobilizing a French army, they were determined to reduce Hapsburg power. The war lost nearly all religious significance as it became a dynastic struggle. Superior resources, coupled with the leadership of brilliant generals, caused the tide to turn in France's favor. The Hapsburgs were defeated so decisively that Spain sank to the status of a second-rate power, while France took its place as the leading European state.

By 1648, the war was settled in a series of treaties known as the Peace of Westphalia. The settlement was a victory for Protestantism and the German princes and a defeat for Catholicism and the Hapsburgs. Some of the terms of the settlement include the confirmation of the Peace of Augsburg, with the addition of Calvinism to Lutheranism and Catholicism as a religious option for a prince. The treaty allowed Protestants to keep all the lands they had taken from the Roman Catholic Church after 1624. It also recognized the sovereignty of some 350 princedoms, cities, and bishoprics and demanded that the emperor secure their consent before making laws, raising taxes, recruiting soldiers, or making war or peace. Since these petty units argued continually, agreement on most issues was virtually impossible. The independence granted these states made the unification of Germany under a single ruler nearly hopeless. Other significant provisions of the peace included recognition of the Netherlands and Switzerland as independent states, approval of Hapsburg control over Bohemia, restoration of part of the Palatinate to Frederick's heir, the granting of electoral dignity to the Duke of Bavaria (thus making eight electors), and extension of the territories of Brandenburg to compensate for land ceded to Sweden.

The war left Germany so exhausted that recovery took almost a century. Most of the armies had lived off the land. The soldiers, mostly mercenaries, had had no pity on the civilians, had sacked cities and pillaged the countryside, and for amusement had raped, burned, and tortured. Disease and famine helped to reduce the population drastically. A malaise settled on the land, making it easy for France to keep it divided.

The Peace of Westphalia did settle long-standing religious differences. Catholics and Protestants realized that they must live together since neither was strong enough to destroy the other. Forced compromise provided opportunity for toleration. At the time, some did not appreciate this and called for renewed war. Angered by concessions to Protestants, Pope Innocent X (1574–1655; pope 1644–55) declared the anti-Catholic clauses of the treaty invalid. Among the Protestants, the exiled Bohemian Brethren demanded that fighting continue until their homeland was restored to them. Neither group gained much of a hearing—a sign that the religious wars in Europe had ended.

The English Revolution and the Cause of Toleration. One of the few major European countries not directly involved in the Thirty Years' War was England. Internal troubles so occupied the attention of the English that Continental involvement was not possible. The seventeenth century began with the death of Elizabeth I and the accession to the throne of a new family, the Stuarts, in the person of James I (1566–1625; James VI of Scotland 1567–1625; James I of Great Britain 1603–25). He was highly educated, intellectual, and the author of several works, including *The True Laws of Free Monarchies*. But he was naive about English affairs. The Tudor dynasty before him had been despotic, but they cultivated popularity with the people. James tried to follow in their footsteps, but his authoritarianism upset the English. The major problem facing him was the struggle with Parliament, which, though it was not a democratic institution, was a powerful group, representing (in the House of Commons) rich town merchants and the leading country families. The conflict that James began was to last through four Stuart reigns and transform England into a constitutional monarchy with the House of Commons, rather than the king, as the real ruler of the land. Underlying the struggle were different philosophies of government. The theory of the divine right of kings was that God had placed the sovereign on the throne as His representative and that anyone who resisted the king was acting against God. Parliament, on the other hand, supported the historic rights of Englishmen and held that control over one's person and property was not to be taken away without the consent of the individual involved (secured either directly or indirectly). The courts of common law helped Parliament protect the rights of the common man and check the king's power.

The Stuarts and Parliament clashed over religion, economics, and rights. The literature of the period is marked by frequent mention of *religion* as the cause for the struggle. The House of Commons was taken over by the Puritan party, a group within the Church of England that demanded simpler church services and a more pronounced Protestant theology. Anticipating a Protestant attitude on the part of the Scottish Calvinist king, the Puritans, in April 1603, gave James the Millenary Petition (named from the Latin for "a thousand"; its authors claimed one thousand signatures for it). It asked him to stop offensive customs, such as making the sign of the cross in Baptism, wearing certain vestments, and using a ring for marriage. The petition also asked that clerical marriage be allowed and that ecclesiastical abuses be eliminated. In 1604, James met with the Puritans at Hampton Court. His sole concession was that a new translation of the Bible be undertaken. The King James Version appeared in 1611 and has had a profound effect on English and American culture. Puritans fought a running battle with James in Parliament. They wanted him to intervene on the Protestant side in the Thirty Years' War, and they wanted Charles, his son, to marry a Protestant princess. They failed in both.

James argued with the Protestants but did not favor Roman Catholics. The Jesuits encouraged attempts to assassinate him. The most famous attempt was the Gunpowder Plot of 1605, in which conspirators led by Guy Fawkes (1570–1606) tried to blow up the king and Parliament. Many Catholics were executed. An oath of allegiance was required of those who were not taken into custody. The English were haunted also by specters of the "Black Legend," a term associated by Protestants especially with the anti-Protestantism of Philip II (1527–98; king of Spain 1556–98).

The reign of Charles I (1600–49; king 1625–49) saw the religious strife intensify. James was a Calvinist. Charles was an Arminian. The latter's reign was marked by a division in the church as a result of growing Arminianism among the clergy. In 1633, Charles appointed William Laud (1573–1645) archbishop of Canterbury with instructions to enforce a universal liturgy even if it meant driving the Puritans from the Church. In some respects, such as doctrinal matters, Laud was more tolerant than the Puritans, but he sought complete outward uniformity of worship. It was a matter of supreme importance to him that the Communion table be placed at the east end of every church and that all should bow when the name of Jesus was mentioned. Using the Court of High Commission and the Court of Star Chamber (where royal power prevailed), he vigorously enforced severe sentences on nonconformists. Over twenty thousand Puritans emigrated to New England while Laud was in power.

Economics also divided the monarchy and Parliament. The House of Commons was part of the revenue-collecting system of the English kings. Lacking patience to work with Parliament, both James and Charles tried to raise money on their own through forced loans, ship money, forest fines, knighthood, and the granting of monopolies. The people hated these taxes, many of which were based on old laws that had not been enforced for years.

The issue of *rights* took several forms. Problems involved free speech in Parliament, resistance to forced loans, and arbitrary imprisonment. In order to secure revenues, Charles I in 1628 signed the Petition of Right, which safeguarded Englishmen from arbitrary taxes and illegal imprisonment as well as other royal abuses. But Charles dismissed Parliament and for eleven years ignored this document.

By 1640, Charles was at war with the Scots and desperate for money to secure an army. He therefore summoned an assembly, called the Long Parliament (1640–53; dated by some to 1660), which became a rallying point for opposition to royal absolutism. Puritan forces in Parliament joined the Scots (1643), and England was plunged into a civil war. A little known member of Parliament, Oliver Cromwell (1599–1658), showed himself to be a military genius in leading the rebel forces (called "Roundheads" because they wore their hair cut short) to victory over the royalists (the "Cavaliers"). The king was captured and executed in 1649. The nation then came under the control of Cromwell, who became Lord Protector in 1653. A church settlement to replace the Anglican establishment was attempted by the Westminster Assembly (1643–48/49; met irregularly thereafter until 1652/53), but the Presbyterianism agreed upon by the clerical representatives in attendance was not enforced. Fragmentation of the Puritan position led Cromwell to be more tolerant. National life during the Commonwealth (1649–60) was heavily influenced by Calvinist Puritanism. The Christmas festival was abolished, the marriage ceremony was made a civil act, and plays were forbidden.

When Cromwell died, a desire for stability led Parliament to invite the son of Charles I to return as king. Charles II (1630–85; king 1660–85) had spent many years in exile in France, where he had come to admire the absolutism and Catholicism of Louis XIV (1638–1715; king 1643–1715). Neither of these qualities were to endear him to the English people. He kept the "Cavalier Parliament," elected in 1661 and overwhelmingly royalist, in session until 1679. It passed a series of acts called the Clarendon Code, which provided legal basis for persecution of Puritans. Over two thousand clergymen lost their pulpits, and over five thousand persons were jailed as a result of these laws. Other provisions excluded Puritans from posts in city governments. In 1670, in the secret Treaty of Dover, Charles promised Louis XIV to restore Catholicism to England as soon as possible in return for French subsidy. But when he tried to do this in 1673 by allowing freedom of worship in private homes, Parliament reacted so violently that he abandoned the plan and remained Anglican until his deathbed confession of Roman Catholicism.

James II (1633–1701; king of England, Scotland, and Ireland 1685–88), successor of Charles II, tried more openly to restore Catholicism. He appointed Papists to command the army and to teach at universities. To win support among the dissenters (Puritans), he included them in his first Declaration of Liberty of Conscience (1687; he issued a second in 1688). But when seven Anglican bishops were charged with treason for not supporting the Declaration, they were found not guilty. Tories (Anglicans) and Whigs (Puritans) united against the king and offered the throne of England to William (1650–1702; prince of Orange, France; stadtholder of Holland 1672–1702; king of England 1689–1702) and Mary (daughter of James II; 1662–94; married William 1677; queen of England, Scotland, and Ireland 1689–94) in 1689. James fled to France, and William and Mary took the throne without opposition. This came to be called the Glorious Revolution. Later in 1689, Parliament passed the Toleration Act and the Bill of Rights, which guaranteed civil rights and parliamentary supremacy and extended freedom of worship to all except Unitarians, Roman Catholics, and Jews. A provision in the Toleration Act stated that only Anglicans could serve in the government and the army, but even this restriction could be lifted by the dispensing acts. Even limited toleration was a great step forward in the history of human freedom.

The new English parliamentary government found justification in the political writings of John Locke (1632–1704). His *Two Treatises of Government* argue that government is a contract between a ruler and the citizens and that revolution is justified if the contract is broken by arbitrarily denying the people their natural rights to life, liberty, and property. He also claimed that the most effective form of government is based on a representative system. In one of the ironies of history, Locke's apology for the revolution of 1688 was later used by American colonists in 1776 in revolt against the British.

THEOLOGY AND CULTURE IN THE AGE OF ORTHODOXY

A long period of controversy followed the rediscovery of the Gospel by the sixteenth-century Protestant reformers. The quarrels that resulted from the breakup of the Medieval Church led to definition of the Protestant position. The philosophy of Aristotle was used by participants in debates to express their ideas. The Christological issue among the Lutherans, the predestinarian disputes among the Reformed, and the debate between the two over the Lord's Supper encouraged precise definition of doctrine. The neo-Aristotelianism of the theologians was part of a general trend in post-Reformation Europe to return to Aristotle. Popular in such southern European schools as Padua, Italy, and Coimbra, Portugal, Aristotelianism spread to the Protestant universities of Germany by the late sixteenth century. Early in the seventeenth century, a movement called Protestant Orthodoxy developed. Among the outstanding Lutheran leaders of this Age of Orthodoxy were Johann Gerhard (1582–1637), Johann Konrad Dannhauer (1603–66), Abraham Calov (1612–86), and Johann Andreas Quenstedt (1617–88). Their Reformed counterparts included Johannes Wolleb (1586–1629), Johann Heinrich Alsted (1588–1638), Gisbert Voet (1588–1676), and Francois Turrettini (1623–87).

Lutheran orthodoxy was not dead orthodoxy. It lived and flourished, as witness its useful productions. Johann Gerhard, outstanding Lutheran dogmatician, studied philosophy and medicine at Wittenberg. In 1605, he became lecturer at Jena, superintendent at Heldburg in 1606, general superintendent at Coburg in 1615, and professor of theology at Jena in 1616. His most famous work was *Loci theologici*. He also wrote polemical books, Bible commentaries, homiletical aids, and works on the Christian life.

Johann Konrad Dannhauer studied at Marburg, Altdorf, and Jena and was professor and pastor at Strasbourg. Famous for his preaching and teaching, Dannhauer found time to write over fifty works covering the entire scope of theology and including a series of polemical treatises against Roman Catholics, Calvinists, and Syncretists.

Abraham Calov, born in East Prussia, was educated at Koenigsberg and Rostock. He became pastor and teacher at Koenigsberg in 1637 and at Danzig in 1643 and professor at Wittenberg in 1650. Despite a busy life, he wrote more than most people read in a lifetime. His dozens of volumes, many numbering thousands of pages, cover the major topics of seventeenth-century theology and include twenty-eight works dealing with the syncretistic controversy. Perhaps his major achievements are *Biblia illustrata* (a commentary on the Bible) and *Systema locorum theologicorum* (a twelve-volume systematic theology).

Johann Andreas Quenstedt was a professor at Wittenberg. A man of quiet, kindly, irenic disposition, he wrote *Theologia didactico-polemica,* one of the greatest Lutheran theologies.

Prominent among Reformed scholars was Johannes Wolleb. He was born and educated in Basel, Switzerland, where he became a pastor and professor of Old Testament studies. His most famous of many works was the *Compendium theologiae Christianae.* Because of its sound theology and clear arrangement, it was used as a text in many Reformed universities.

Johann Heinrich Alsted, born at Ballersbach, near Herborn, Germany, was educated at Herborn. Remaining at his alma mater as professor, he wrote dozens of volumes that made him famous wherever the Reformed faith had secured a foothold in Europe. He attended the 1618–19 Synod of Dordrecht and supported its condemnation of Arminianism. The Thirty Years' War forced him to move to Transylvania, where he became professor in a new school that the Calvinist prince of that land had established. He remained there until his death. Alsted not only applied Aristotelian logic to theology in such works as *Theologia scholastica didactica* but also tried to unify all knowledge in *Encyclopaedia scientiarum omnium.* His approach was typical of many Protestant scholars who tried to put into a single work the whole range of knowledge—metaphysics, logic, geology, and the other sciences. Using a variant of scholasticism developed by Peter Ramus, Alsted wrote the *Encyclopedia septem tomis distincta*. These volumes were widely used throughout the academic world of the seventeenth century.

Gisbert Voet, a Dutch Calvinist, was educated at Leiden and later became a minister. His pastoral activity, which began in 1611, took him to places where Roman Catholicism and Arminianism were popular, thus providing him with opportunity to develop a polemical style. An industrious person, he taught Arabic, Syriac, logic, physics, metaphysics, and theology and preached eight times a week. His major work was completed at Utrecht, where he became professor of theology and Semitic languages in 1634. While serving in that post, he attacked Descartes, Cocceius, the Arminians, and any others who differed with him. One factor that led to such polemicism was his insistence on a life of devotion and strict morality. Voet's outlook is very similar to that of the Pietists, and his severe moralism led him to sympathize with the English Puritans. His major works include *Disputationes selectae theologicae*, *Desperata causa Papatus*, and *Exercitia et bibliotheca studiosi theologiae*.

Francois Turrettini was educated at Geneva, Leiden, Utrecht, Saumur, Montauban, and Nimes. He was pastor (from 1648) and professor (from 1653) at Geneva, where he fashioned a theology opposed to many seventeenth-century trends. Basing his study on Calvin's writings and the Canons of Dort, he wrote *Institutio theologiae elencticae*. Though discredited in the eighteenth century, it profoundly influenced American Presbyterians through the Princeton theology of Charles Hodge (1797–1878) and others.

The goal of Protestant Orthodoxy was to unify all theology and harmonize the remainder of knowledge with an understanding of God. It produced massive works, tightly outlined through many divisions and subdivisions and difficult for the twentieth-century mind to appreciate. The Age of Orthodoxy was to continue until the eighteenth century, when rationalism and Pietism superseded it. Orthodox theologians tried to present their views in standard form, in other words, as the doctrine of salvation and of the means for attaining salvation. Orthodox teaching relied on Aristotle and certain medieval logicians for the nature of its arguments, but its basis was Scripture.

The central tenet of seventeenth-century orthodoxy emphasized the Bible as the fundamental presupposition of theology. Scripture was trusted as God's Word, and the external statement was not differentiated from the underlying meaning. Orthodoxy believed that God inspired the prophets and apostles to write the message they received from Him. The divine Word they communicated was preserved in Scripture without error; therefore the Bible is the infallible norm for Christians as well as the court of final appeal in all theological arguments. Orthodox theology taught that the Scripture is its own best interpreter and that difficult passages are to be interpreted with the aid of clear ones. Great emphasis was placed on the literal interpretation of Holy Writ, taking it in its ordinary and apparent sense.

As the discussion moved on to the doctrine of God, Lutherans were especially concerned with the way the divine and the human natures of Christ are united in one person. They debated how the natures affect one another, or how the divine and human attributes interact in Christ. As to creation, they held that God first made an unformed mass and completed creation in six days. Man was considered the crown of God's work, but man fell through sin. Because of the unity of the race, the corruption of sin passed from generation to generation. According to this explanation, without regeneration, humans are under the wrath of God and subject to both temporal and eternal punishment.

As Lutherans and Reformed defined the subject of evil and sin, they parted company. The Calvinist idea that God preordained and carried out evil according to His secret will (the basis for the teaching of double predestination) was rejected by the Lutherans, who held that God permits evil and that He sets limits to its exercise but is not responsible for it. Lutherans found comfort in the doctrine of single pre-destination (to salvation). The elect, they taught, are those whom God predestined to salvation; the reprobate are those of whom God foresees, but does not predestine, that they will not have saving faith at death.

Lutherans maintained that one could pass from spiritual death to life only through the operation of the Law and the Gospel. The Law is God's eternal and unchanging wisdom for righteous living. Summarized in the Ten Commandments, it demands acts of goodness as well as a pure heart. But man is unable to obey, so the Law's role is not to save but to condemn. Forgiveness comes only through Christ's redeeming love and sacrifice as proclaimed in the Gospel and is received in penitent faith. Evangelical teaching in the Age of Orthodoxy differed from that of medieval Christianity on the doctrine of repentance. Rather than stating with the Medieval Church that repentance (or penance) consists of contrition, confession, and absolu-tion, it held that repentance involves only contrition and faith. Contrition is the proper effect of the Law, which threatens, accuses, and condemns; faith is the proper effect of the Gospel, which comforts, edifies, and saves. By giving people an insight into sin and into the punishment of God, the Law drives a person to repentance. The Gospel brings forgiveness through Christ and comforts the believer. It was clear that works play no role in repentance. Good works, excluded from merit of salvation, were considered the fruits of faith. The deeds that the Christian performs were regarded as a means of glorifying God and helping one's neighbor.

Orthodoxy taught that the Sacraments (Baptism and the Lord's Supper) were the New Testament counterparts of circumcision and the Passover. Old Testament sacrifices were regarded as types of the coming Messiah. Baptism and the Lord's Supper applied God's promise of forgiveness to the individual. The invisible Church was believed to be the congregation of all saints and believers. The visible Church includes all who profess faith in the Gospel. Those who associated with Christ in only an external way will be separated from true believers on the Day of Judgment.

When that time comes, the world will be destroyed by fire, believers receiving eternal life and the wicked being cast into hell.

This summary applies to the major writers of the age, but as the seventeenth century unfolded, many details were elaborated and subtle shades of difference developed. It is important also to remember that there were several points of tension between Calvinists and Lutherans.

The Clergy. Doctrines were explained to the laity by pastors who were largely controlled by secular rulers. One of the unforeseen consequences of the Reformation was a reduction in the status and number of clergy in Protestant lands. In contrast to Roman Catholics and Anglicans, there were few aristocrats among the German Protestant clergy. Ministers were usually chosen from the lower classes and were looked down upon by the nobles. In the universities, the theological faculty was the only one open to the poor. Protestant clergymen produced under such circumstances had less polish and capacity for adjusting to higher society than their Roman Catholic counterparts. But what they lacked in sophistication and understanding of the world they made up for in book learning that sometimes bordered on pedantry. By the end of the seventeenth century, the typical parson had studied at a university and worked as a teacher or tutor before beginning his ministry. Village pastors had to supplement their income by such activities as farming, beekeeping, or brewing. At times, local nobles would hire pastors as grooms or tutors. City ministers were higher than the village pastors on the social scale, but the most favored members of the clergy were the court preachers and theological professors. Lutherans were especially respectful of the theological faculties, and out of this tradition grew the nineteenth-century belief in academic freedom for the universities of Germany.

Congregations served by these clergymen were passive. They had no rights, no organization, and little control over the pastor. Territorial rulers issued edicts for the church much as they would make laws for secular affairs. Every aspect of church life was controlled by the princes. They saw to it that the church had no bishop, synods, or other aspects of independent rule. Through his appointed consistory, the ruler controlled church finances, arranged discipline, and chose the clergy. Usually, the churches were under the direction of a general superintendent, and each diocese had a director to see that the regulations of the prince were observed. Visitations settled disputes, and reports were given to the ruler.

Princes controlled not only legal structure of the church but also doctrinal areas. Often, the ruler had little theological knowledge, and his intervention was hasty, thoughtless, and inconsistent. Territorial rulers became "Protestant popes" for their subjects. Various theoretical justifications were advanced that allowed a ruler to keep his power while giving the Church a measure of freedom. Johann Gerhard reasoned that the Church was divided into three groups: the clergy, the civil authority, and the rank and file of the laity. Each estate had its particular task in life. For example, the civil rulers were responsible for the government; the clergy were to punish, advise, and administer the Sacraments; the people were to follow the directions of the ruler and clergy. The power in such a system was the civil ruler who directed the other two groups. The prince was the divinely appointed guardian of the spiritual as well as of the material welfare of his subjects.

To further strengthen the ruler's position, arguments were often advanced that were based on treaties with Roman Catholic powers (for example, the Peace of Augsburg, 1555). These elaborate justifications stated that the rights formerly exercised by the hierarchy of the Roman Catholic Church had devolved on the civil rulers of the German Protestant states. Therefore, whatever the pope was able to do in former times, the princes could now do. Other writers went beyond the devolution argument, teaching that the pope and his representatives had usurped the original divine right of the prince. They held that civil rulers received their power directly from God and acted on His behalf.

But in either case, whether their authority came through the claims of the Roman Catholic Church or directly from God, the princes had absolute power in their own territories. Yet it was clear to the theologians that rulers were not bishops. The magistrates were not to preach and administer the Sacraments but to see that these duties were properly performed by appointed ministers. The pastors for their part were to support the prince and encourage a submissive attitude on the part of their parishioners. Princes were believed to be accountable to God alone for their sins. No clergyman would dare to exercise church discipline against a secular ruler since that would be regarded as a sign of disobedience.

The effect of princely control and scholastic theology on the preaching of the period was often unfortunate. The detailed scholarship so characteristic of the era carried over into the pulpit. Johann Benedikt Carpzov the elder (1607–57) said that there were one hundred different modes of preaching. Another said that there were twenty-six. Johann Gerhard advocated eleven styles of preaching: (1) grammatical, (2) logical, (3) rhetorical, (4) histrionic, (5) ecclesiastical, (6) historic, (7) esthetical, (8) scholastic, (9) elenctic, (10) mystical, and (11) heroic.

Another characteristic of sermons of the period was scholarly verbiage, which made them hard for the average person to grasp. Gerhard, who was a pastor while he was a professor, used Latin, Greek, and Hebrew in sermons because he felt that this lent added emphasis.

The orthodox clergy also included much sensational and imaginary material in their sermons. In an attempt to add interest to scholarly detail, the preachers used fables, stories, illustrations, strained metaphors, and strange images. Titles of sermons or sermon collections that indicate this include "Heaven's Kiss of Love," "Bitter Oranges and Sour Lemons," "Pale Fear and Green Hope in Sleepless Nights," "Splendid Poverty," "Salted Sugar," "Heaven in Hell," and "The Only-Begotten Twin." Carpzov delivered a yearlong series of sermons in which he compared the Lord to various workmen, including a well digger, a lantern maker, and a cloak maker. Another preacher drew a parallel between the devil and a vicious dog, showing how Satan bit Adam and then bit Christ in the leg and how Christ drove him back to his kennel in hell. On another occasion, the same preacher delivered a sermon comparing Christ to a chimney sweep and discussed the sweeper, the flue, and the broom.

Despite the style of scholarship, strained expression, and polemical approach, the clergy of the period could boast of many deeply spiritual colleagues who were conscientious in the care of souls. Gisbert Voet advised Christians how to lead a godly life. He prescribed prayer, fasts, vigils, and solitary devotion in the soul's war against the world, the flesh, and the devil. He included a chapter on "euthanasia, or the art of dying," and another on visitation of those who need consolation. Johann Heinrich Alsted wrote a detailed work on casuistry, in which cases of conscience are arranged in accordance with the articles of the Creed and the Ten Commandments. Calvinists showed a greater interest than Lutherans in church discipline. Lutherans practiced private confession on the basis of the Catechism and its form of absolution.

As the Age of Orthodoxy settled over the Protestant area of Europe, the Roman Catholic Church enjoyed renewal in France. After the Edict of Nantes (1598) had given Protestants legal and civil rights, the Huguenots (French Calvinistic Protestants) lost much of their zeal. A great revival of Catholicism corresponded with the Protestant decline. The healthy state of the Roman Catholic Church and clergy in France coincided with other areas of national achievement. The seventeenth century saw the golden age of French literature, with such writers as Pierre Corneille (1606–84), Molière (1622–73), Jean Baptiste Racine (1639–99), Jean de La Fontaine (1621–95), and François de La Rochefoucauld (1613–80). These geniuses encouraged the clergy to artistry in preaching and religious writing. The political and social atmosphere of the land also stimulated the ministers. Louis XIV delighted in hearing a minister preach who not only was eloquent but also passionately believed what he said. The clergy, encouraged by the king's attitude, hoped to make him a better person and through him reach the entire nation. The king's interest in religion made church attendance fashionable at court and aided the Church in its influence on French life.

The freedom given to the Huguenots also encouraged the Catholic clergy of France to greater faithfulness. For much of the century, the Roman Catholic Church could no longer depend on persecution to counter Protestantism but was forced to use preaching and a faithful, caring ministry to win people. A remarkable group of clergy rose to meet the Huguenot challenge, including François de Sales (1567–1622), Vincent de Paul (1580/81–1660), and Jacques-Bénigne Bossuet (1627–1704).

François de Sales was a Savoyard who was educated at Paris and Padua. Ordained in 1593, he did missionary work in a part of Savoy (an area in southeastern France and northwestern Italy) that was under the spiritual influence of the Genevan Calvinists. Achieving remarkable success in his ministry, he became bishop of Geneva in 1602. His loving, patient attitude coupled with his outstanding preaching made him a favorite with Henry IV of France. Not only was he an effective preacher, but he also did much religious writing. His popularity has been the inspiration for the founding of several religious orders.

Vincent de Paul was born in southwestern France and educated at Dax and Toulouse. He was ordained in 1600. In 1625, he founded the Lazarist Order, and in 1634 he helped found the Daughters (or Sisters) of Charity. Deeply spiritual and influenced by François de Sales, Vincent stressed the incarnation and man's total dependence on the merits of Christ.

Bossuet, born at Dijon, France, was educated at Paris and soon achieved fame for remarkable preaching. He was brilliant with a remarkable knowledge of the Bible, the Church Fathers, and the intellectual trends of the century. As bishop of Meaux, he was drawn up into the major religious conflicts of the day, which involved Protestant conversionism, Quietism, Jansenism, Gallicanism, and biblical criticism. He also found time to tutor the dauphin, serve as court preacher, and gain election to the French academy. Throughout a long and busy life, he managed to write several books and is still remembered for his vigorous defense of the divine right of kings.

Witchcraft and the Beginning of Science. The Age of Orthodoxy also saw the rise of modern science. Some writers refer to the era as the period of the scientific revolution and hold that it prepared Europe for global leadership in the nineteenth century. The first phase of this important intellectual change began about 1560. It was a time when old ideas were challenged by a new outlook. The second period began during the mid-seventeenth century and featured the work of Isaac Newton (c. 1642–1727). He replaced the theocentric outlook with a centerless secular one that has been the basis of the Western intellectual outlook ever since.

The idea that most sixteenth-century Christians accepted about the world had been inherited from the ancient Greeks. Elaborated by medieval scholars, this view taught that every being, according to its degree of perfection, had a place assigned in the universe. This great chain descended from God and the angels through the physically perfect stars, planets, sun, and moon to the four elements of the world (earth, air, fire, and water). The universe was believed to be geocentric, with the earth at the center, surrounded by circling planets and the fixed stars. Although at variance with twentieth-century cosmology, this view fits the observed phenomena. Christian theology seemed to receive support from the geocentric theory. Man was in the center of God's creation, where Christ had come to perform His saving ministry. The hierarchical structure of the universe assured man that God was in control. The sun's movement around the earth seemed to be verified by Joshua's command that the sun stand still (Joshua 10:12–13), by Ecclesiastes 1:5, and by several statements in the Psalms.

Historians have suggested that people at the time of the scientific revolution began to question the geocentric cosmology because they had more accurate measuring devices or had developed better mathematics or made a series of "fortunate guesses." Whatever the reason, early scientists did break down prevailing assumptions about the universe but could not immediately arrive at a new consensus. The most famous scientific pioneer was Nicolaus Copernicus (1473–1543). He assigned the central place in the universe to the sun and held that the rising and setting of the stars could be explained by the earth rotating on its axis. It has been thought that he developed the heliocentric theory to simplify his calculations. Despite his modifications, Copernicus retained much of the medieval system. Johannes Kepler (1571–1630) advocated more sweeping changes, which condemned the medieval view to oblivion. Kepler explained that the planets move in an elliptical rather than a circular fashion about the sun. Galileo Galilei (1564–1642), through the use of a telescope, provided many observations that tended to confirm the heliocentric theory.

The new science eventually destroyed the Aristotelian synthesis and caused those who wished to defend the older view to become more narrow and belligerent. In this connection, possibly as an offshoot of a combination of factors, belief in witches increased. In such an atmosphere, heretics and socially different people were regarded as servants of the devil. The period from about 1600 to about 1680 saw the high point of witchcraft in Europe. By the 1690s, the only major action against witches occurred in New England. During the years when witch trials were common, it was believed that thousands of women and some men made secret agreements with the devil and regularly attended sabbats. Travel to the sabbat assemblies was said to be supernatural, involving the use of flying broomsticks or winged goats. Those who attended these meetings worshiped the devil, who appeared either as a black-bearded man, a toad, or a goat. After listening to strange music and participating in revolting acts of homage, the witches engaged in sexual orgies with Satan and his servants. Often feasts of roast children, fricassee of bat, or exhumed corpses were held. When not attending these assemblies, the witches were expected to suckle familiar spirits in the form of bats, toads, or moles and to cause infertility in newlyweds, disease, and storms.

Evidence for the existence and behavior of witches was secured by torture. Though horrible torture might make a person confess anything, it seems that many in the seventeenth century believed they were witches. Most of those who confessed to witchcraft were cruelly executed.

Scholars in the Age of Orthodoxy included discussion of witchcraft in their works and even published encyclopedias on the subject. These works insisted that every detail of witchcraft was true and that all objections to the persecution of these emissaries of Satan must be stopped. Most writers on the subject believed that the number of witches was increasing and that the reason for such a sorry state was the leniency of judges. Undoubtedly, the struggle in Europe between Catholics and Protestants led to the renewed emphasis on witchcraft. Protestants were just as insistent as Catholics on the reality of witches.

But with the spread of belief in Newton's explanation of the world, interest in witchcraft declined. Newton provided a new synthesis after earlier scientists had destroyed the medieval worldview. As a professor at Cambridge University, he managed to construct a model of the universe and a way of reasoning that became acceptable to most people. His work is based on the universal law of gravity, which postulated that every particle attracts every other particle with a force that is proportional to the product of their masses and inversely proportional to the square of the distance between their centers. To arrive at this solution, he devised a new mathematical technique, infinitesimal calculus.

Newton published his findings in a massive Latin work entitled *Philosophiae Naturalis Principia Mathematica* (1687). The *Principia*, as the book is commonly known, demonstrated the law of gravity in relation to the planets and included the science of mechanics, defining force, momentum, and inertia with mathematical precision. After proposing the law of gravity, Newton showed that the pull of the moon and that of the sun caused tides, that the earth and the other planets are flattened at their poles, and that the path of the comets can be traced because they are under the sun's influence.

Newton established the methodology of much of modern science. Included in it are three principles: (1) Insistence on experimental observation. He was very suspicious of general ideas and felt that whenever possible they should be tested by experiments. (2) The law of simplicity. When there are several valid explanations for a phenomenon, the simplest one is to be accepted. (3) Extensive use of mathematics, expressing the universal law of gravity as a formula. The combination of experimental observation and mathematics has proven very successful for science.

Newton could use mathematics to a greater extent than his predecessors because of the progress made during the seventeenth century. In the year 1600, Roman numerals were still commonly used. Modern symbols for multiplication, division, and addition were not accepted. Much mathematical work was done in a literary form. A virtual explosion of mathematical knowledge changed all this by the year 1700. In rapid succession, decimals, logarithms, analytical geometry, laws of probability, and calculus were developed. Practically every philosopher or thinker had to be a mathematician.

Between 1630 and 1700, most educated Europeans came to accept the heliocentric viewpoint and the mathematical-mechanical description of the universe as Newton explained it. The emphasis on uniform law and rationality led to the decline of belief in witchcraft. Evil beings in league with the devil could not easily exist in a world run by Newtonian laws. A sample of the new way of thinking was the reaction of the judge at one of the last witchcraft trials in England. He dismissed the case with the sarcastic remark that there was no law against traveling between London and Oxford on a broomstick.

Hymns and Devotional Literature. The warm and vibrant faith of the Age of Orthodoxy is not always clearly evident to us in the theological works of the period. But the hymns and devotional literature of that time are different. Suffering and turmoil produced great poets and poignant expressions of the Christian faith. In many ways, this was the golden age of Lutheran hymnody, with such great writers as Philipp Nicolai, Johann Heermann, Johann von Rist, and Paul Gerhardt.

Philipp Nicolai (1556–1608) was a pastor and theologian in Westphalia. He lived through the dreadful experience of the plague. Though he buried thirteen hundred people within six months, he wrote the words and music of "Wake, Awake for Night Is Flying," so rich with Scripture and the assurance of God's care. Nicolai also wrote "How Brightly Beams the Morning Star." These two works are called, respectively, the King and the Queen of Chorales.

Johann Heermann (1585–1647) was a pastor at Koeben at the time of the Thirty Years' War. During his ministry, the city was almost destroyed by fire; it was sacked four times by Wallenstein's armies; and in 1631, it was visited by the plague. Heermann was forced to flee for his life several times. He also lost all his possessions. Yet it was during this period in 1630 that he wrote the beautiful hymn "O Dearest Jesus, What Law Hast Thou Broken." Other well-known hymns by Heermann include "Jesus, Grant That Balm and Healing"; "O God, Thou Faithful God"; and "O Christ, Our True and Only Light."

Johann von Rist (1607–67), a prolific writer, was made poet laureate in 1644 by Ferdinand III (1608–57; king of Hungary 1625–57; Holy Roman Emperor 1637–57). He suffered greatly in the Thirty Years' War when his home was plundered and his possessions seized. Yet he wrote 680 hymns, most of which speak comfort to those in trouble. His hymns include "Break Forth, O Beauteous Heavenly Light"; "Arise, Sons of the Kingdom"; and "O Living Bread from Heaven."

The leading hymnist of the period was Paul Gerhardt (1607–76). Born in Saxony, he served as a tutor for many years after his graduation. In 1657, he was appointed to a church in Berlin, where he became famous as a preacher. Urged by the ruler of Prussia, he became involved in discussions concerning union between Calvinists and Lutherans, but he refused to compromise the Lutheran position. His intransigence in this matter cost him his pulpit, and he was removed in 1666. For a while, he had no parish and was in a desperate situation, but in 1668, he became archdeacon at Luebben, where he remained until his death. His wife and four of his five children preceded him in death.

In the furnace of affliction, Gerhardt wrote 134 German and 14 Latin hymns—hymns that have a subjective mood based on his own experiences and that mirror personal misfortunes and the social calamities of his age. Gerhardt conquered his doubts through faith in God, based on the Lord's workings in nature, the Church, and Scripture. Deeply conscious of sin, he realized the forgiving power of the grace of God. Some of his better-known hymns include "O Sacred Head, Now Wounded"; "Evening and Morning"; "Jesus, Thy Boundless Love to Me"; and "O Lord, How Shall I Meet Thee."

In the Calvinistic areas of Europe there was not much hymn writing until the influence of Pietism was felt. For many years the Reformed totally rejected "hymns of human composure" and polyphonic composition. Instead, they used material versions of the 150 Psalms set to tunes. The Psalms were sung in unison and without the accompaniment of "popish instruments."

The deeply religious feelings of the Age of Orthodoxy can also be seen in devotional works. Such literature consists of edifying and popular presentation of the Christian faith for use by individuals and groups gathered informally for prayer and meditation. Many of these books were similar to such late medieval mystical works as *Imitation of Christ* by Thomas à Kempis. The Lutherans developed specialized prayer books for different occupations, for soldiers and travelers, and even for expectant mothers. They also had meditations and prayers designed to be read at certain times of the day. The most famous seventeenth-century devotional works were by Johann Arndt (or Arnd; 1555–1621)—*Books on True Christianity* and *Little Garden of Paradise*. Arndt was educated at Helmstedt, Wittenberg, Strasbourg, and Basel before he became a pastor and church administrator. His books emphasized mysticism in the interpretation of the Christian life by asserting that true belief is not enough to be a true Christian, but moral purification through righteous living is also necessary.

Other important devotional books of the period include Lewis Bayly (c. 1565–1631), *The Practice of Pietie*; Johann Gerhard, *Holy Meditations*; Johann Heermann, *Practice of Piety*; and Heinrich Mueller (1631–75), *Heaven's Kiss of Love*.

Baroque Art. At the same time (c. 1580–1750), a new form of expression, the baroque, replaced Renaissance classicism in many parts of Europe. The word *baroque* is derived from a Portuguese word that refers to irregularly shaped pearls. Like some other terms in art history, such as "gothic" and "impressionism," it was first used disparagingly. But many twentieth-century critics consider baroque a distinct, complex style with many admirable characteristics. Baroque artists tried to harmonize a number of styles. The result was art characterized by extravagance, decorativeness, and grandeur. A painting of the era featuring a group of figures is clear and natural, but the individuals cannot be visualized by themselves. The suggested movements of the bodies and the direction of the eyes blend together to provide a dramatic situation and create a whole that is greater than the sum of its parts. Similarly, painting, sculpture, and architecture combined to give a unity to the interiors of buildings. The earliest expression of this is found in Il Gesu, a Jesuit church in Rome. Inside the building, a painting on the ceiling (*The Worship of the Holy Name of Jesus*) is skillfully merged with the rest of the structure to create a breathtaking effect. The theatrical quality of baroque lent an impressive larger-than-life quality to its productions.

Rome was the center for the new style, which spread throughout Europe. Local areas often tempered the expressions of baroque, but it generally included lavishly ornamented buildings decorated with cherubs and angels, twisted and bent columns, and intricate designs in gold and marble. These structures included not only churches but also palaces and government buildings. The baroque style was carried throughout Europe by the Counter-Reformation.

Other art forms also reflected the baroque style. The musical achievement of the period is widely recognized. It ended the period of polyphonic music and introduced harmonic music. Two baroque composers, George Frideric Handel (1685–1759) and Johann Sebastian Bach (1685–1750), stand out from their colleagues because of their superb technical ability and musical genius. Handel was a Saxon who settled in England, where his patrons were George I (1660–1727; king of Great Britain and Ireland 1714–27) and George II (1683–1760; king of Great Britain and Ireland 1727–60). He wrote primarily for large public audiences. Even his religious compositions, such as *Messiah* and *Esther*, were intended for public performances in concert halls rather than in churches. He became England's national composer and was buried with honors in Westminster Abbey.

Bach's life was not very distinguished except for his music. Born into a large, musically inclined family, he fathered twenty children. Bach worked as organist and choir leader in the small towns and petty courts of Germany. If much of his life was routine, his interest in and mastery of music was extraordinary. He tried to hear the leading musicians of his day and copied virtually every piece of music he could find.

Bach's true vocation was neither entertaining nor teaching, but service to God. Deeply religious motives encouraged him to labor over the intricacies of such instruments as the harpsichord and to write music. The aim of such stately works as *Mass in B Minor* and the *Passion According to St. Matthew* was to achieve technical excellence coupled with great beauty and thus reflect something of the nature of God. To compose music was for Bach an act of faith, and to perform it was an act of worship.

Absolutist Princes. The forerunners of present day national states were the absolutist monarchies of the seventeenth and eighteenth centuries. Such absolutism was based on the idea that the king is chosen to rule by God and is responsible to God alone for his actions. The ruler was thought to be a divine agent on earth; consequently, it was considered wrong to question his orders. The king's power was to his state as God's will is to the universe.

ABSOLUTIST PRINCES		
	EVENTS	OUTCOMES
LOUIS XIV OF FRANCE (1638–1715)	"Sun King" assumed personal control of France, aided by Jean-Baptiste Colbert (1619–83). State revenues tripled under mercantilism. Acquired colonies. Funded Academies. Aligned with Catholicism. Fought numerous wars.	France became a model state to other rulers, though increasingly immoral. French became the general language of Europe. Louis oppressed Protestants as dissenters and drove over 200,000 out of the country.
PRUSSIAN RULERS: FREDERICK WILLIAM (1620–88), FREDERICK WILLIAM I (1688–1740), AND FREDERICK II (1712–86)	Severe, energetic rulers. Adopted mercantilism and expanded the military through a draft system. Expanded territory through war. Treated the church as a tool of government.	Prussia became a powerful, militaristic nation, dominating central Europe. Policies and wars proved costly and gave rise to later German nationalism.
PETER THE GREAT OF RUSSIA (1672–1725)	Westernized Russia, bringing it out of medieval, Asian isolation. Suppressed opposition. Used poll tax to expand government and conscription to expand western-style military. Negotiated trade. Put himself in charge of Russian Orthodox Church.	Russia became a leading world power but more oppressive to its people. "Old Believers" rejected changes to church practice. Numerous wars expanded territory at great cost.

The Puritan combined his faith with activities of secular life. Work was not believed to be outside the sphere of Christian concern. During the Middle Ages, the term "religious" had been applied to a priest or other full-time church worker, but to the Puritan, any vocation, be it that of merchant, lawyer, pastor, or homemaker, was a religious vocation. Dignity was given to all honorable callings.

During the struggle against the Stuart kings in the early seventeenth century, the Puritan position was adopted by the main group in Parliament. Deeply convinced that God is sovereign over human affairs, the Puritans were not afraid to question the power of the king. The opposition that they mounted led to the defeat and execution of Charles I, but they were not able to agree on the form that the new government should take. The various political and social solutions they offered left Oliver Cromwell (1599–1658) no choice but to establish a military dictatorship.

These disagreements could be detected in the Westminster Assembly (1643–53; met irregularly in its last years). The meeting was called to guide Parliament in its religious decisions. It issued the Westminster Confession, a classic statement of Presbyterianism. One of the major divisions in the assembly involved a split between the Independents (Congregationalists) and the Presbyterians. An Independent, John Owen (1616–83), became Cromwell's adviser on religious matters and championed a pluralistic settlement. Under Cromwell, churches were pastored by Presbyterians, Baptists, or Independents, and Jews were allowed to settle in England. But freedom of worship was not extended to Roman Catholics and Unitarians.

More radical Puritan sects developed, each seeking to establish its particular vision of the kingdom of God. A group called the Levellers gained many followers in the Parliamentary army. Interpreting liberty in Christ as including political democracy, they advocated universal male suffrage, freedom of religion, and equality before the law. Fearing mutiny, Cromwell suppressed them, but Leveller leaders such as John Lilburne (c. 1614–57) continued to agitate for their ideals.

The Puritan era saw widespread interest in the prophetic books of the Bible and their application to history. Many Protestant scholars revived the old theory of five monarchies in the Book of Daniel. This theory held that four major world empires— Babylonia (or Assyria), Persia, Greece, and Rome—would rule the world. During the last of these empires, the kingdom of God (the fifth monarchy) would come to earth as the millennium, or thousand-year reign of Christ on earth. Details of the coming age were supplied by careful studies of Revelation, the last book in the Bible. Earlier Protestant reformers, such as Calvin, had refused to discuss the Book of Revelation and regarded the calculation of the millennium as a waste of time. But by the seventeenth century, leading mathematicians and scholars discussed the end of the age. Joseph Scaliger (1540–1609) wrote a book on chronology that was used to calculate the time of Christ's final coming. John Napier (1550–1617), the Scotsman who invented logarithms, devoted his genius to apocalyptic speculation. And in the 1640s, many believed that the greatest discovery of the time was the interpretation of the number of the beast (666; Revelation 3:18) suggested by a fellow of Oxford University.

The Puritan Revolution, the overthrow of the Stuart kings, and the ferment that resulted added fuel to the fire of prophetic enthusiasm. The second coming of Christ and the establishment of His millennial kingdom gave meaning to the troubled times through which the land was passing.

Baptists taught that the Church of England could not be reformed and that it was necessary for true Christians to separate from the national church and form their own groups. These separatist bodies were to accept members who made a personal confession of faith in Jesus Christ and were baptized as believers. Some have tried to establish a link between the seventeenth-century Baptists and the Anabaptists, but the connection is tenuous at best. In 1609, a congregation of English refugees in Amsterdam led by John Smyth (perhaps c. 1570–1612) reorganized themselves along what they considered New Testament lines and were baptized with "believer's Baptism." In 1611/12, a part of this group under Thomas Helwys (c. 1550–c. 1616) returned to England and founded the first Baptist church at Spitalfields, now in London. They were called the General (Arminian) Baptists, and by 1644, they had forty-seven congregations.

Future growth came largely from another group, the Particular (Calvinistic) Baptists. The first of these churches came into existence 1638–40. Their antecedents are in a Separatist or Independent congregation organized in 1616 at Southwark, London, by Henry Jacob (1563–1624). His group held that believer's Baptism by immersion was the only valid practice. By 1644, there were seven congregations of Particular Baptists. Though Baptists emphasized the authority and autonomy of each congregation, they cooperated with one another to draft confessions of faith and to deal with common problems, such as raising funds for military needs during the Puritan Revolution. Because Baptists served with distinction in the Parliamentary Army and were staunch Protestants, Cromwell favored them when he was in power. With the restoration of Charles II, they became part of English dissent and as such lost their privileges. By that time, there were Baptist churches in America through the cooperation of Roger Williams.

While the mainstream of Puritanism moved in a path that involved a more systematized doctrine and church life, other groups stressed the importance of the mystical experience or inner light. One of the chief mystical inspirations was the work of Jakob Boehme (1575–1624), a German shoemaker. He wrote several mystical books in rather obscure and difficult terminology. He was also very critical of the Protestantism of his day because of its bibliolatry, doctrine of election, and notions of heaven.

One of Boehme's more important English followers was George Fox (1624–91). Reared in a strict Puritan atmosphere, Fox left home at nineteen to search for enlightenment. Three years later, he came to rely on the "Inner Light of the Living Christ." From that time on, he became a traveling minister who did not attend church, condemned religious controversy, and preached that truth is to be found in God's voice speaking directly to the soul. Fox has left a *Journal* of his experiences in which the influence of Boehme can be traced. The followers of Fox were called Friends or Quakers. They took as their central teaching the doctrine of the inner light, that is, that the power of the Holy Spirit is given to all people and is not limited by Scripture. Since each individual received the inner light, all persons were to be equal in the Church. Clergymen were unnecessary, for the Spirit would inspire those who should speak. They continued to make an important contribution in the twentieth century and were among the first to protest horrible prison conditions and slavery.

After the restoration of Charles II in 1660, Puritans were subjected to intense persecution, and the movement lost its force in England. By that time, there were thriving Puritan settlements in New England. The Puritans had come to the New World hoping to establish model communities with properly reformed churches so that the people of England would be able to see what God would do if His people obeyed Him. Under such leaders as John Winthrop (1588–1649) and John Cotton (1584–1652), the congregational tradition developed. It was established that church members must make a "declaration of their experience of a work of grace." Such a requirement made certain that the Church would be in the hands of the elect. In addition, only church members could vote or hold office in the government of the colony.

Puritans were not only interested in a just society, but they were also deeply committed to scholarship. John Bunyan (1628–88) and John Milton (1608–74) were Puritans. Arrested in 1660 during the great persecution, Bunyan spent several years in prison producing such literary masterpieces as *The Holy City* and *Pilgrim's Progress*. The latter work established him as one of the most influential religious writers of all time. In it, he traces with vivid imagination, in allegorical fashion, the journey of Christian from the City of Destruction to the Heavenly City. John Milton's two immortal works, *Paradise Lost* and *Paradise Regained*, deal with the fall and the redemption of mankind. He also wrote *Areopagitica*, a defense of freedom of the press, and *Samson Agonistes*, an allegory based on the life of Samson.

Catholic Mysticism and Jansenism. Under the leadership of Louis XIV, France became the dominant power in Europe in the seventeenth century. Its influence was felt not only in politics and economics but also in religion and the arts. The age was a time of renewal for the Roman Catholic Church, encouraged by its rise to a position of undisputed power in France. The improvement in the fortunes of French Catholicism had started before Louis came to the throne. During the last half of the sixteenth century, the land had been ravaged by brutal civil wars between Catholics and Protestants (Huguenots). By the beginning of the seventeenth century, the conflicts were settled and a period of impressive rebuilding began. Under leadership of such able government ministers as Cardinal Richelieu (1585–1642; cardinal 1622; chief minister of Louis XIII 1624–42), the power of the nobles was cut, and the Huguenots were reduced to submission. It was during the same period that the Roman Catholic Church experienced a revival in France.

As with most periods of ferment and achievement, the age of Catholic renewal produced controversy. There was a struggle over the connection of the French church with Rome as well as arguments involving Jansenism and a new type of mysticism called Quietism. The issue over the liberty of the French church was settled in favor of a firm allegiance to the pope.

Jansenists followed the teaching of Cornelius Jansen (1585–1638), a Flemish bishop. They contended that church ceremonies were obscuring the fact that a person can be saved only through God's love and grace operating on the heart. This love comes to those whom God chooses. Their rejection of free will and their emphasis on predestination were similar to Calvinism. Indeed, their enemies accused them of being "warmed-over Calvinists." The Jansenists insisted that they were not Protestants, but at the same time they condemned the moral laxity of Catholics and the overemphasis on free will in Catholic doctrine.

Jansenism was brought to France by Jean Du Vergier de Hauranne (1585–1643), abbot of St. Cyran, who won many influential people to his cause, including several members of the famous Arnauld family. A convent at Port Royal became a center of Jansenism. Perhaps the doctrinal teaching of the Jansenists could have been tolerated, but their independent turn of mind and the moral emphasis of their preaching drew them into a series of struggles with the Catholic Church and the French government. Besides encouraging purity and holy living among the clergy and people, they also wished to reduce the secular power of the church. They condemned the Jesuits for "laxist" teaching (e.g., granting absolution on too easy terms). Such laxness, they felt, encouraged immorality. Jansenists themselves led very strict, austere lives characterized by simplicity of worship and love for religious culture.

A group of clergymen and pious laymen who believed in Jansenism settled near Port Royal, dedicating themselves to lives of scholarship and contemplation. Among them was Blaise Pascal (1623–62), scientist and philosopher.

Louis XIV became involved in the Jansenist controversy. He was alarmed by the large number of influential people attracted to the belief, and he felt that the emphasis on a strict moral life was a condemnation of his own lifestyle. His Jesuit confessors encouraged him to ask the pope to denounce Jansenism. Clement XI (1649–1721; pope 1700–21) in 1713 condemned the group. The convent at Port Royal was suppressed in 1709 and destroyed in 1711.

By the end of the seventeenth century, more trouble appeared for the Roman Church in France because of a new mystical group. Quietists, as they were called, were inspired by the teaching of Miguel de Molinos (perhaps about 1628/40–1696), a Spanish priest who resided in Italy and presented his views in *Spiritual Guide*. Molinos proposed guidelines that would eventually lead to union with God. The Jesuits had him condemned and imprisoned. Despite opposition, Quietism spread to France, where its followers emphasized passive prayers as the main Christian activity. The leading French Quietist was Madame Guyon (1648–1717), a woman from an important family who energetically propagated her views and won many converts.

Her teaching, elaborated in *Short and Very Easy Method of Prayer*, emphasized single-minded contemplation of God whereby the soul loses all interest in its own fate. Even the truth of the Gospel paled to insignificance before "the torrent of the forces of God" to which an individual must yield. Bishop Bossuet (1627–1704; bishop of Meaux 1681) warned her to stop such teaching, and others accused her of being mentally unbalanced, but she persisted in presenting her ideas. She was repeatedly arrested and finally condemned by the pope and imprisoned.

The ferment and vigor found in the Roman Catholic Church in the seventeenth century could match developments in Protestantism. Jansenism parallels Puritanism, and Quietism is in certain respects similar to Pietism.

Pietism. The Peace of Westphalia, which ended the Thirty Years' War in 1648, allowed each ruler in Germany to choose one of three options as the faith of his subjects: Catholicism, Lutheranism, or Calvinism. Thus was confirmed the independence of a large number of principalities, in each of which the Church was dependent on the ruler. The prince was exempted from the discipline of the Church and was answerable to God alone. Pastors were treated as employees of the state, and the Church was regarded as a useful agency of public policy charged with the duty of teaching such attitudes as integrity, submission, loyalty, and obedience. In this era of stifling state-Church religion, Pietism emerged as a renewal of the evangelical fervor of the early Protestant reformers. The new religious outlook had its roots in mysticism, Puritanism, and Anabaptism.

Pietism may be defined as Bible-centered moralism that results in a personal conviction of sin and repentance. This leads to forgiveness through Christ, personal conversion, a life of holiness, concern for the needs of others, and an emotional experience in worship. Attempts to harmonize faith and reason and an intellectual emphasis were not of much concern to Pietists. For them, religion was not reserved for authorities and experts; it was something that had to do with a person's feeling and expressed itself in a pious life of service to others. Pietism insisted that believers manifest Christ in their daily lives. It was a reaction against formalistic creeds, and it made faith individualistic.

The two early Pietist leaders were Philipp Jakob Spener (1635–1705) and August Hermann Francke (1663–1727). Spener, called the Father of Pietism, grew up in Alsace and attended the University of Strasbourg. There, he studied philosophy, languages, history, and theology. His favorite teacher, Johann Konrad Dannhauer (1603–66), encouraged him to study Luther and helped him understand the evangelical teaching of the grace of God. Dannhauer also suggested that laypeople be more involved in the Church and that some aspects of theological study be undertaken in the vernacular rather than in Latin. Spener was a serious, ascetic, religiously minded student.

In 1659, Spener left Strasbourg and, according to the custom of the time, visited other universities to broaden his educational experience. In the course of his two-year academic journey, he went to Basel, Bern, Geneva, Lyon, Freiburg, and

Tuebingen. This tour made a lasting impression on him. While in Geneva, he fell under the influence of Jean de Labadie (1610–74), who was then at the height of his career. Labadie was a Reformed preacher who blended Jansenism with Calvinist piety to form a strong experiential, otherworldly, mystical faith that came to emphasize the importance of separation and small-group meetings. Spener enjoyed hearing him preach, and several years later, he had one of Labadie's tracts published in a German translation.

After returning to Strasbourg, Spener finished his degree, married, and became a teacher and a preacher. His goal was to be a professor, but in 1666, he accepted a call to be senior clergyman in Frankfurt. His duties included preaching at the city's main church, presiding over pastors meetings, ordaining new ministers, and inspecting the parishes. Many of the ministers under his charge were twice his age, but he managed the situation very capably. While in Frankfurt, he tried to secure greater lay involvement in the life of the Church, improved catechism classes, urged the authorities to enforce certain blue laws, and began an extensive correspondence with individuals throughout Germany. Later, he would be called "the spiritual counselor of all Germany." In 1670, he gathered in his home a group of people who were especially interested in a deeper Christian life. They discussed sermons, prayer life, the Bible, and various devotional books.

Spener was a prolific writer; the work that first gained his reputation and on which his fame rests is *Pia desideria* (*Pious Desires*). A Frankfurt printer wanted to publish a new edition of some of Johann Arndt's sermons and asked Spener to write the preface. Spener used the occasion to present his ideas for revival in the Church. Later, his remarks were issued as a separate book. The work made the following proposals for revival: (1) personal religion should be deepened by greater attention to a study of Scripture; (2) laymen must be more involved in the work of the Church; (3) Christians ought to be encouraged to practical works rather than spending all their time in dry theological debates; (4) in all theological disputes, a spirit of love must be shown, so that others can be won to Jesus Christ; (5) theological education should be improved with a special emphasis given to the moral and spiritual life of ministers; (6) preaching should be marked with conviction and fervor so that people might be converted. Despite opposition of many church leaders, Spener believed that, if his program were followed, the Church would be revived, the Jews converted, and the power of the papacy destroyed.

In 1686, Spener left Frankfurt for a position in Dresden. He hoped to have an influence on John George III (1647–91; elector of Saxony 1680–91). But the elector seldom attended church, and Spener found it necessary to condemn him for drunkenness. The friction between the two men caused Spener's stay to be rather short. During his Dresden years, he did meet August Hermann Francke (1663–1727), who was to become his successor as the leader of Pietism.

In 1691, Spener left Dresden and went to Berlin, where he served as inspector of churches and as a preacher at the Church of St. Nicholas. He remained there fourteen years. He was increasingly drawn into the controversies caused by the spread of Pietism. Something of the bitterness of these debates can be seen in the charge brought by the theological faculty of the University of Wittenberg that Pietists were guilty of 284 heresies. Spener was called a Rosicrucian, a Chiliast, a Quaker, and a fanatic. His last years were spent not only replying to strange comments such as these, but also in editing his correspondence and papers for publication. Much of this material provided ethical guidance for his followers in the form of answers to such questions as these: What is to be said about dreams, visions, and special revelation? May a Christian wear expensive jewelry with a good conscience? May he attend a dance or theater? May a Protestant marry a Roman Catholic? Can laymen administer Holy Communion? Can an unconverted pastor proclaim God's Word effectively? Busy with his Master's business until the last, Spener died hoping for a better day for the Church.

August Hermann Francke, Spener's chief disciple, was born in Luebeck and studied at Erfurt and Kiel. He taught at Leipzig, was pastor at Erfurt and Glaucha, and in 1692 became professor at Halle, where he spent the rest of his life.

Largely as a result of Francke's efforts, Halle became the international center of Pietism. Gifted with limitless energy, boundless enthusiasm, great organizational ability, and a flair for what later ages would call public relations, he created an amazing complex of institutions, including an orphanage, boarding schools, Latin school, publishing house, pharmacy, and Bible institute.

Francke was also the dominant figure on the Halle theological faculty for many years. From this position, he inspired many students to serve God as foreign missionaries in such distant areas of the world as America and India. The Lutheran Church in the United States owes much of its growth to these Pietist missionaries.

Pietism was spread throughout Germany and Scandinavia by graduates of Halle, the publications of such men as Spener, and personal contacts. Many beautiful hymns were written by Pietists to express their faith. A notable area of enthusiasm for Pietism was Wuerttemberg, where Johann Albrecht Bengel (1687–1752) became its leader. Deeply influenced by Pietist professors at the University of Tuebingen, Bengel studied the works of Spener and Francke and spent some time in 1713 at Halle. He was an unusual Pietist because of his great dedication to scholarship. From 1713 to 1741, he taught at a seminary in Denkendorf and wrote widely in the field of biblical exegesis. In 1742, he became a high official at Herbrechtingen and in 1749 at Alpirsbach and influenced many pastors to become Pietists. One of Bengel's works, *Gnomon Novi Testamenti*, was especially popular.

Moravians and Brethren. Though Pietism began as a reform movement within the established Church, several separatist bodies sprang from it. One of these was the Church of the Brethren; another was the Moravian Church. The Brethren began at Schwarzenau, Germany, in 1708, when eight people under leadership of Alexander Mack (1679–1735) were rebaptized by triple immersion. Mack was influenced by radical Pietism and was convinced that the New Testament required separate groups of believers rather than a state church. He had settled in one of the few areas of Germany where religious dissenters could practice their beliefs. This was the tiny county of Wittgenstein, northeast of Frankfurt, in the hill country between the Eder and the Lahn Rivers. The count who ruled the area risked the policy of toleration because of personal conviction and the need for settlers. By the time the legal machinery of the Holy Roman Empire dealt with them, most of the dissenters had left for the Netherlands. The early Brethren in Wittgenstein restored what they felt were apostolic practices. These included Baptism by triple immersion face forward, the love feast (consisting of a meal, the Eucharist, and foot washing), anointing of the sick with oil, laying on of hands for Christian service, congregational church government, and opposition to war, oaths, and worldly clothes.

The Brethren won many converts, and churches were established in Switzerland, the Palatinate, and Altona. In most places, they were subject to intense persecution.

Their plight in Europe led the Brethren to consider migration to America. William Penn had traveled in Germany, encouraging sectarians to come to his colony. His agents distributed tracts and booklets that made Pennsylvania seem like an attractive place to settle. In 1719, many Brethren left Europe and came to Germantown, near Philadelphia. Another group migrated in 1729 under Mack's leadership. By 1735, most Brethren were living in the New World. Those who remained in Europe joined such Anabaptist groups as the Mennonites or died out. The Brethren (or Dunkards, Dunkers, or Tunkers; from the German for "immerse") became a permanent part of American life.

The Moravians, led by Nikolaus Ludwig von Zinzendorf (1700–60), also developed from radical Pietism. Born into a Pietist noble family (he was Spener's godson), Zinzendorf was reared by his maternal grandparents and an unmarried aunt. His grandmother was especially influential in forming his deep piety. She was a gifted person who could read the Bible in the original Hebrew and Greek and participate in the most profound theological discussions. Between the ages of ten and sixteen, Zinzendorf attended Francke's preparatory school at Halle. Then he enrolled at the University of Wittenberg for legal study. His relatives insisted on this, though he wanted to be a minister. His social status as a noble would not permit him to become a clergyman. In 1721, after graduation, he took a position as a counselor at the court of the king of Saxony. About that time, he received an inheritance, which he used to buy an estate. Frustrated by his inability to become a minister, he felt that he might serve God by directing the religious life of the tenants. A short time later, a group of Protestant refugees settled on his property.

These settlers were the remnants of the Old Moravian Hussite Church, who were driven from their land by persecution. Under leadership of Zinzendorf, they founded a village called Hernnhut (which may be translated either "on watch for the Lord" or "watched over by the Lord"), where they tried to return to apostolic practices. These included the rites of foot washing, the kiss of peace, and the casting of lots. They also worked out the peculiar Moravian practices, such as intense community religious life encouraged by daily services; division of the community into choir groups based on age, marital status, and sex; religious education; and an active program of missions, especially to the oppressed black slaves in the West Indies and to people of preliterate cultures. The emphasis was on a monastic type of life with the unmarried separated by sex and children reared in child-care centers. Every effort was made to encourage a communitarian approach, with common occupations attended by instrumental and vocal music.

The views of Zinzendorf were not entirely reflected at Herrnhut. The Moravians were convinced separatists, whereas he wished to remain a Lutheran. He showed a tolerance toward other creeds and even devised a plan for the reunion of the Protestant, Roman Catholic, and Eastern Orthodox Churches. He was also interested in some rather strange doctrines and mystical practices.

Some accused Zinzendorf of deviation from orthodoxy, but his views were examined and approved in 1734. Yet in 1736, he was banished from Saxony. Exiled for eleven years, he traveled widely and preached his Pietist ideas wherever he went.

Even before his exile, he had been interested in preaching the Gospel in faraway places; he inspired the Moravians to send missionaries to the West Indies (1732), Greenland (1733), and Georgia (1735). A Moravian mission founded in London was to be a decisive influence in the life of John Wesley.

In 1747, Zinzendorf was allowed to return to Herrnhut, where, with the exception of some time spent working with the Church in England, he remained until his death.

Methodists. Religious life in England reached a low point in the early eighteenth century. On every hand, there was profanity, inhumanity, and gross political corruption. The lower class was ignorant and depraved. Harsh laws demanded that people be executed for petty crimes. In the midst of such discouraging circumstances, the populace turned to drink for solace. Churches were poorly attended, public worship was formal and lifeless, and sermons were vague moral discourses that seldom mentioned the Gospel of Christ.

Methodism grew under the leadership of two Wesley brothers, John (1703–91) and Charles (1707/08–1788). Their father was a pastor, and their mother, Susannah, was a remarkable woman. She not only bore nineteen children (John was the fifteenth, Charles the eighteenth), but she also closely supervised their educational and religious development. The Wesley brothers attended Oxford University, where they established a religious club. Their group met for Bible study, frequent observance of Communion, and fasting. Their strict piety caused the other students to call them "the Holy Club," "Bible Moths," and "Methodists." The name *Methodist* was to become an honorable title for their movement.

One would have expected that John Wesley would have taught or preached and become an important person in the Anglican Church. Such did not prove to be the case. For a man of his temperament, it was not enough to be decent and competent. Christianity had to mean more than that to him. He believed that faith ought to be a vital and living experience, yet he knew that for him it consisted of a formal orthodoxy. His problem was clear: How could he trade his dead faith for a living experience with God? To find the solution, he multiplied good works, increased his asceticism, and gave his life to serve as a missionary to the American Indians.

John Wesley spent the years from 1735 to 1738 as a missionary in the colony of Georgia, but his work met with little success. While traveling to America in 1735, he met some Moravians who witnessed to him about their faith in Christ. Their assurance of salvation made a profound impression on Wesley. When he returned to England, he worshiped with them for a time and later visited Herrnhut. At a prayer meeting in London on May 24, 1738, he received assurance of his own salvation as he listened to a reading of Luther's preface to Romans.

As a result, John Wesley reacted against the moralistic rationalism of the Anglican Church. One of his Oxford friends, George Whitefield (1714–70), had broken with the Anglican system and was preaching to miners in the fields near Bristol. Wesley struggled with his conscience for a time, but by 1739, he, too, was preaching in the fields. During the last half of his life, he preached over 40,000 sermons and journeyed over 250,000 miles, mostly on horseback. Some historians have credited the Wesleyan revival with saving England from a violent upheaval similar to the French Revolution.

Preaching in the streets and fields often aroused violent opposition. Wesley meant only good for the poor miners, sailors, and factory workers to whom he preached, yet they frequently tried to assault him. He was the center of dozens of riots, many instigated by a local pastor. Some of his assistants were badly hurt, some even killed. Wesley had an iron will and could stare down a drunken mob. He was small, 5 feet 6 inches tall and weighing 120 pounds, but his absolute fearlessness and complete confidence in God carried him through situations that would have unnerved most others. He even seemed to thrive on adversity.

Wesley preached justification by faith, the new birth, and Christian perfection (sanctification). His teaching of perfection, the ethical transformation of the believer, seemed to indicate to his enemies a kind of works-righteousness or self-delusion. Wesley denied both of these allegations, but he did not find it an easy doctrine to explain. He drew his teaching from certain mystical writers, such as William Law (1686–1761), Thomas à Kempis (c. 1379/80–1471), and Jeremy Taylor (1613–67). Though he insisted that a Christian could be holy in this world, he did not mean that he would be free of all wrongdoing.

As a loyal Anglican, Wesley had no intention of establishing a new church. His special mission was to preach the Gospel to people unreached by the Church and to provide for their spiritual nurture and discipline. Following the example of the Moravians, he gathered followers into bands, classes, and societies. The first of these was established at Bristol in 1739. At these meetings, members judged each others' spiritual lives and studied to deepen their Christian knowledge. Wesley selected laymen who would be able to help him preach the Gospel to the masses. In 1744, the lay preachers met at a conference (which later became annual) to receive instruction and assignment of their area of work. Wesley was not fond of the idea of lay pastors at first, but he later gave it his warm support. Areas of ministry, called circuits, were established. After one or two years, ministers were moved to different circuits. In this form, Methodism spread throughout the British Isles. The early history of the movement is characterized by its gradual separation, despite Wesley's reluctance, from the Anglican Church.

Charles Wesley became the sweet singer of Methodism and wrote thousands of hymns, including "Jesus, Lover of My Soul"; "Love Divine, All Loves Excelling"; "Oh, for a Thousand Tongues to Sing"; and "Christ the Lord Is Risen Today."

Within the Church of England, the Wesleyan revival strengthened the Evangelicals. They were Calvinists who stressed conversion, strict morals, simplicity of worship, and a life of service to others. Prominent Evangelicals included John Newton (1725–1807), William Wilberforce (1759–1833), and Hannah More (1745–1833).

A more famous early advocate of Sunday School was Robert Raikes (1735–1811), a newspaper publisher greatly concerned for the well-being of children. He organized schools to give religious and moral training to poor young people on the only day on which they did not work. The students were taught to read the Bible; often, instructions were given also in arithmetic. The Sunday School was an important step in the development of popular education.

The Methodist revival affected not only the Church of England but stirred also the nonconformist churches, which included such groups as the Baptists, Congregationalists, and Presbyterians, descendants of the Puritans. One nonconformist, John Howard (c. 1726–90), was involved in improving prison conditions in England. Others joined the Wesleyans in attempts to stop gambling, dueling, cruel sports, child labor, drunkenness, and pornography.

The late eighteenth century also saw the rise of the modern missionary movement. In 1792, the Baptist Missionary Society was organized through the efforts of William Carey (1761–1834), a self-educated teacher, shoemaker, and pastor. He went to India as a missionary in 1793. Other organizations established for worldwide missions included the London Missionary Society (1795), the Scottish Missionary Society (1796), and the Church Missionary Society (1799). Associations were also formed for distributing Bibles and Christian literature.

The Methodist and Evangelical revival changed the course of history in England. Humanitarian reform, cooperation with industrialization, and the desire to win the lost to Christ gave the English the ability to lead Western Europe in its global expansion.

The Great Awakening in America. During the early modern era, the English settled in North America, fought several wars to maintain their control, and finally lost the richest part of the continent to the newly independent colonies in America. By the end of the third generation, perception was that the thirteen English colonies had reached a low ebb in culture and religion. The Church of England, officially established in half of the colonies, had little influence outside of Maryland and Virginia. In Virginia, only about 5 percent of the people were church members. New Englanders seemed to have a greater interest in religion, but the conviction that had been the basis of Puritan power had perhaps waned. For centuries, no group of Western European people had been so little exposed to Christian teaching and institutions.

The colonies were reinvigorated spiritually by the "Great Awakening," a religious movement that lasted in America from c. 1725 to c. 1750. It was a mass conversion of people through evangelistic preaching. The movement began in New Jersey among the Dutch Reformed churches with the ministry of Theodorus Jacobus Frelinghuysen (1691–1747). Encouraged by what he saw in the Reformed congregations, a Presbyterian, Gilbert Tennent (1703–64), began evangelistic preaching among the Scots-Irish. Stressing the need for a personal decision for Christ rather than the mere outward observance of religious ceremonies, his work persuaded many New Jersey Presbyterians.

In 1734–35, the Great Awakening came to Massachusetts through the preaching of Jonathan Edwards the Elder (1703–58), one of the most brilliant individuals America has produced. Edwards was the son of a Congregational minister. After graduating from Yale, he became pastor of the Congregational church in Northampton, Massachusetts. He had a keen and penetrating mind with a mystical bent and profound religious convictions. Preaching slowly and distinctly with great feeling, he made his listeners aware of the consequences of sin and the horrors of hell. In 1734–35 and again in 1740–43, waves of a religious awakening swept over his community and hundreds professed faith in Jesus Christ. Edwards wrestled with a long-established principle of his grandfather, Solomon Stoddard (1643–1729), that moral people, though unconverted, may partake of Communion. After long and earnest controversy over this practice, which he opposed, he was forced from his pastorate in 1749. He moved to an American Indian ministry at Stockbridge and later became president of Princeton College.

George Whitefield (1714–70) linked the regional movements of the Spirit into the Great Awakening. Born in Gloucester, he attended Oxford University, where he was closely associated with the Wesleys. In 1735, he was converted and began his preaching ministry. He had a loud, clear voice and could speak with dramatic intensity. His preaching moved thousands, including so worldly a person as Benjamin Franklin (1706–90). He followed the Wesleys to Georgia in 1738. Later, he made six other visits to the colonies. His ministry took him from Georgia to Massachusetts, and he preached to Congregationalists, Anglicans, Presbyterians, Reformed, Methodists, Baptists, Lutherans, and Quakers. Other evangelists followed his example and preached wherever they could get an audience.

Many criticized the Awakening. Some condemned the excitement and emotional disturbances of the meetings, offensive features of which included convulsions, laughing, screaming, visions, and trances. Some preachers deliberately encouraged these activities. Many revivalists had harsh words for those who would not join in the meetings.

Support of the revival became a test of faith. This attitude led to divisions in the Church. The Presbyterians and the Congregationalists split into the "New Lights" and the "Old Lights." The New Lights favored the revivals.

Despite its faults, the Great Awakening did much to help the future nation. It led to the founding of churches, increased the seriousness of rank-and-file church members, and caused a new commitment to missions, which were mainly to American Indians. Prominent among those interested in winning American Indians was a prospective son-in-law of Jonathan Edwards, David Brainerd (1718–47), who died before his marriage and whose journals became a popular devotional book. The condition of blacks was also brought to the attention of Christians by the Awakening. From 1714 to 1760, the number of black slaves in America increased from 58,850 to 310,000. There were few slaves in the north because they were economically impractical. But in the South, where many workers were needed on the large indigo, rice, and tobacco plantations, slavery developed into a major institution. Blacks as well as whites were converted during the Great Awakening. Most Christian churches did not speak out against slavery, but Quakers and Mennonites did. One of the main advocates of better treatment of blacks was a Quaker, John Woolman (1720–72). He tried to reconcile American Indians with whites and worked to improve the status of blacks through the abolition of the slave trade.

The Great Awakening also made a great contribution to education. Among the numerous academies and colleges that were established as a result of the revival, the best known are the University of Pennsylvania, Rutgers, Brown, Princeton, and Dartmouth. Of equal importance was a new mood of understanding that developed between denominations. This more open attitude contributed to the spirit of toleration in the United States, and it provided for an evangelical consensus that still influences the nation.

PIETIST THEOLOGY AND ITS INFLUENCE ON CULTURE

The Pietists did not present their views in a systematic fashion, as did the major orthodox theologians of the seventeenth century. But the main Pietist beliefs can be summarized from the writings of Philipp Jakob Spener and August Francke, who were especially interested in the reform of the Church. For reform, it was felt that each Christian must have a personal relationship with God. To win others to their ideas, they did not elaborate on theological categories but emphasized a life of purity that would demonstrate the power of Christ.

The Pietists' desire to simplify religion led to a spirit of tolerance and religious freedom. Because human beings are finite and limited and theological knowledge is not precise, latitude must be given to dissenters. Spener felt it best not to insist on uniformity beyond certain basic teachings. His position was summarized in the following statement: "In necessary things, unity; in things not necessary, liberty; in all things, love."

The Pietists agreed with the orthodox that the invisible Church consists of all who truly follow Christ, and they regarded the visible Church as part of the invisible. They tended, however, to emphasize the invisible more than the visible Church. The radical Pietist Gottfried Arnold (1666–1714) took their teaching to such an extreme that he wrote a book focusing on the invisible (nonorthodox) Church. The work, the *Impartial History of Heresy and the Church*, tried to view heretics from their own writings rather than from the charges of their opponents. He claimed to see more truth in some heresy than in the official Church theology. So long as the pious remained part of the actual visible Church, Pietists emphasized the invisible group. When a congregation seemed to live up to their ideals, they stressed the visible community, as the Anabaptists had done.

Spener and Francke were orthodox in their view of the Sacraments, but their emphasis on the individual's response to salvation tended to change traditional views. They held to infant Baptism, but they stressed the possibility of losing the new birth unless one lived in obedience to God. Spener taught that unbaptized children of Christians, Jews, and Turks would not suffer damnation. The Pietists' stress on the subjective side of salvation led many to disregard infant Baptism and emphasize a later conversion experience.

Another change that Pietism brought to the view of the Church was an interest in apostolic times. The way to revive Christianity, they believed, was to restore the Early Church. The first step in this direction was to have godly ministers. The pastor was to be the shepherd of the flock and not just another official. To do this, he should be well trained, lead a holy life, and preach in a clear and forceful manner. The Church also needed a greater involvement on the part of laymen if apostolic power was to return. Pietists reemphasized Luther's teaching of the priesthood of all believers. To encourage lay participation, they tried to break down the distinction between clergy and laity. They also desired a more democratic church polity. In the age of orthodoxy, social class distinctions were extremely important. For example, it was considered a disgrace for an upper-class child to be baptized in the same water as a worker's infant. Pietists reacted against such things; at their meetings, servants and masters would sit together in equal fellowship. Spener objected to the way the churches were to reinforce the attitudes of secular society. His ideal was a Presbyterian form of church government, with congregations hiring their own pastor and both clergy and laymen serving on the governing boards of the church.

The small-group meetings that Spener began in Frankfurt also had a place in the restoration of the primitive Church. These developed from catechism classes and met on Mondays and Thursdays at Spener's home during the years 1670–82. At these gatherings, sermons, Bible texts, and devotional works were discussed, and prayers were offered. These meetings were not supposed to take the place of regular worship services. Several members withdrew from the church because of them, and Spener became suspicious of the practice. He wanted to remain with the official Church and reform it from within rather than separating from it.

Pietism stressed the authority of the Bible. Spener firmly believed that Scripture is the verbally inspired Word of God. But he parted company with the orthodox theologians in his insistence that Scripture was supreme over creeds and doctrinal statements. Both Spener and Francke felt that creeds had led people to read the Bible in a narrow way. Too many Christians searched the Scriptures to find texts to prove their theological presuppositions.

Pietists also differed from the orthodox in emphasizing the practical purpose of Bible study. Scripture was given, they held, for the cultivation of a devotional life rather than as a textbook from which to draw doctrines. The Bible was to be read for encouragement, warning, and consolation. The Holy Spirit was believed to be necessary for a proper understanding of God's Word. Without Him, one merely read the cold and dry written word of a book. It was the Spirit that gave life and enlightened the mind of the believer. Spener taught that Christians who pray, meditate, and lead a holy life will understand the deep meaning of the Scripture.

EMPHASES IN PIETISM	
SALVATION AND SOCIETY	Salvation must be demonstrated by a holy life, including a "born again" experience. Christians related to society without absorbing its values.
EDUCATION AND CHARITY	Four types of schools at Halle, Germany: (1) Paedagogium for sons of nobles; (2) Latin school for professional and merchant families; (3) German school for trade workers and housewives; (4) free school for the poor. Curricula applied to life. Support for orphans, widows, and the sick.
FOREIGN MISSIONS	Danish-Halle Mission sends Ziegenbalg and Pluetschau to India. They emphasize education in God's Word, translation, knowledge of culture, personal conversion, and training of indigenous church leaders. Their missionary letters inspired others, especially in England.
HYMNS AND DEVOTIONS	Joachim Neander (1650–80) wrote the first Reformed hymns, ending their practice of singing only Psalms. Lutheran J. A. Freylinghausen (1670–1739) and Moravian Nicolaus Zinzendorf (1700–60) extended the hymn tradition in their churches. Spener wrote *Pia Desideria*, a classic devotional of the movement.
PIETISM AND THE PRINCES	Pietism moved princes to open orphanages and improve schools. E.g., Frederick William I of Prussia issued a decree that led to thousands of new schools.

The back-to-the-Bible emphasis of Pietism led to a renewal of expository preaching, taking a text from Holy Scripture and carefully explaining its meaning. Lay people were urged to study the Bible on their own. Universities were encouraged to offer courses in biblical theology. Those who were able should master Greek and Hebrew, the languages of the Bible, so they could study it in the original tongues and thus deepen their understanding. Such advice led to a renewed emphasis on philology (word studies), which had characterized the approach of the early Protestant reformers. These studies tended to clash with the philosophical (Aristotelian) emphasis of the orthodox theologians.

Finally, Pietists emphasized the New Testament. Spener believed, of course, that all Scripture was given by inspiration of God, but he placed the New Testament above the Old. The New Testament as the highest stage of God's revelation to man and the fulfillment of the Old commanded the Pietists' attention.

ENLIGHTENMENT, REVOLUTION, AND CHRISTIANITY

The development of modern science led to many changes in the intellectual outlook of the eighteenth century. The new approach, called the Enlightenment, grew from the leadership of individuals who wished to apply the ideas of Isaac Newton (1642–1727) to religion and society. The leaders of this movement were brilliant Frenchmen called philosophers, or philosophes. The attitudes of the philosophes spread to other lands and included such writers as Benjamin Franklin (1706–90), Thomas Jefferson (1743–1826), Joseph Priestley (1733–1804), and David Hume (1711–76). As exponents of the scientific worldview, they used many literary forms and wrote in such brilliant style that they made even the most dry and abstract subjects interesting.

The most famous philosophe was François-Marie Arouet, who took the name Voltaire (1694–1778). Born to a middle class family of moderate wealth, as a young man, he offended a noble by some of his writings and was forced to flee to England. He enjoyed freedom of expression there and also became acquainted with the ideas of Newton and John Locke (1632–1704). Convinced that the world was a great machine run by natural laws, he devoted the rest of his life to demonstrating this to others. He returned to France and wrote essays, dramas, novels, and poetry to spread his teaching. Because his work threatened traditional religion, he found it necessary to live just across the border in Switzerland. Though he was the friend of aristocrats, princes, and kings, he never abandoned his views of social justice for all men based on the laws of nature and nature's god (natural theology).

Another important philosophe, Denis Diderot (1713–84), tried to publicize the new scientific outlook through a great encyclopedia. This work, which appeared in twenty-eight volumes between the years 1751 and 1772, was more than a mere collection of facts. It declared that man could improve himself if he replaced faith with reason as his guiding principle. Such teaching constituted a threat to every form of established authority. Because of this, the earlier volumes of the work were suppressed, but by the time the last one appeared, the *Encyclopedia* had triumphed over intolerance and could be openly distributed. Diderot was determined to make useful knowledge widely available. He assured the high quality of his work by securing articles from over 130 experts and writers, a veritable Who's Who of eighteenth-century talent that included Voltaire, Rousseau (1712–78), and the famous mathematician Jean Le Rond d'Alembert (c. 1717–83). A unique feature of the *Encyclopedia* was its eleven volumes of illustrations. The three thousand pages of pictures had a tremendous impact. Many of them helped doctors and scientists. The industrial diagrams showed craftsmen how to do everything from making rope to weaving lace step-by-step. The work also contained implied criticisms of existing ideas and institutions. The article on the goddess Juno criticized the cult of the Virgin Mary, the article on salt discussed the injustice to the poor of taxes on necessities, and the article on Geneva condemned the French government.

The religious view expounded by the philosophes was deism, an outlook similar to what would today be called Unitarianism. Deism had been elaborated during the seventeenth century. In some respects, it was a resumption of the religious humanism of Renaissance men like Desiderius Erasmus (c. 1466–1536) and Thomas More (1478–1535). In contrast to the view of the Reformation that regarded natural man and his culture as basically evil, the humanists were optimistic about man and the world. Many seventeenth- and eighteenth-century writers adopted the humanists' outlook and tried to establish a religion that would be a base for the entire range of cultural activities. They believed in an ethical god and were moved to reverence and worship by the order of nature and the capacity of man. These ideas were opposed to orthodox Christian teachings about salvation and the Holy Scriptures, but these men did not at first attack Christianity. They rather tried to work within the Church, trying to liberalize theology and to redirect the energies of Christians. The earliest expression of deism is *De veritate* (*On the Truth*), by Edward Herbert, better known as Baron Herbert of Cherbury (1583–1648).

During the first half of the eighteenth century in England, deist and orthodox theologians debated over miracles and the Old Testament prophecies of Christ. The Deists lost the battle. The defenders of Christianity demonstrated a vitality in their faith not found in natural religion freed of revelation. Upon closer scrutiny, deism turned out to be a collection of ideas rather than a living faith. David Hume's *Dialogues on Natural Religion* pointed out that the deists assumed everything that needed to be proved and logically had no better case than orthodox theology. The real choice was between Christianity and skepticism.

While the debate died out in England, it was renewed with vigor elsewhere. The chief spokesman for French rationalism was Voltaire. Advocates of deism could also be found in Germany. Hermann Samuel Reimarus (1694–1768) defended natural religion and rejected miracles. He believed that the miraculous element was introduced into Scripture because of the fanaticism and deceit of the biblical writers. The great miracle of revelation, according to Reimarus, is the world, and in nature one can find God, morality, and immortality.

The American Revolution. The first new state founded on principles of the Enlightenment was begun in America. The revolution that led to the American Republic grew from a series of conflicts between the English and the French during the seventeenth and eighteenth centuries. These wars (sometimes called the Second Hundred Years' War) involved not only Europe but also the colonial world. They resulted in the triumph of the British in North America and India. The American colonies had contributed little in either men or money to the victory. The war had been won by British soldiers and taxes. When peace came, the English decided that the colonies should make a greater contribution to defense costs. The efforts of the British government to collect taxes for this purpose led to the alienation of the colonists and to the War of Independence.

Religion also helped to bring on the crisis. Many colonial pastors supported the resistance to Britain. With few exceptions, the Baptists, Congregationalists, and Presbyterians were ardent champions of the revolution. Efforts of Anglicans to establish a diocese in the colonies frightened many colonial ministers. A series of joint meetings of Congregationalists and Presbyterians made it clear that to them episcopacy was the ecclesiastical tool of absolute government. Government, they taught, was based on a compact, or contract, between the ruler and the citizens. Many Anglicans, especially those in southern colonies, joined in the protest against an American bishop. In fact, two-thirds of the signers of the Declaration of Independence were members of the Church of England.

But other sincere colonial Christians opposed the revolution. These included Anglicans in New England and in the middle colonies as well as Methodists. John Wesley wrote very critically of the revolution, and many members of his church followed these views. He believed that the revival that had spread in America was stifled by materialism, which caused the revolution. Also, Wesley agreed with the Lutheran teaching of the duty of passive resistance to constituted authority. Another group that opposed the conflict was composed of pacifists, such as the Quakers, the Church of the Brethren, the Moravians, and the Mennonites. During the fighting, these peace churches were misunderstood and persecuted by both sides.

In September 1774, the First Continental Congress met in Philadelphia and challenged Parliament's right to control the colonies. Shortly before a second meeting of the Congress, a skirmish between the Massachusetts militia and the British army at Lexington Green and Concord Bridge (April 19, 1775) opened the hostilities. The colonists felt they were defending their rights as free people. In their challenge to Parliament and the English king, they took the first steps in the direction of both republicanism and the equality of man. The philosophes' ideas were taking root in the new world. As relations with the English deteriorated and as the need for European allies became apparent, the Declaration of Independence was adopted by the Continental Congress (July 4, 1776). With French aid and under leadership of General George Washington, the fighting began to turn in the colonists' favor. In 1781, a sizable force of French infantry and a French fleet cooperating with the Americans enabled Washington to force Britain's largest army in America to surrender at Yorktown. In the Treaty of Paris (1783), Britain recognized the independence of the colonies.

The instability of the new nation under the Articles of Confederation worried the more wealthy classes, who felt the need for a stronger central government. Their concern led to the Constitutional Convention, which met in Philadelphia in 1787. Out of this meeting came the American Constitution, which went into effect in 1789, creating a federal republic, with certain powers reserved to the states and others given to the central government. The states under this system were more than administrative units of a central bureaucracy. The Constitution also utilized Montesquieu's idea of the separation of powers into the legislative, executive, and judicial branches, with checks and balances built into the governmental mechanism. The judiciary was unique in its power to interpret the constitutionality of the action of the states and the Congress. George Washington (1732–99), a respected leader of high moral standards, was the first president of the Republic (1789–97).

The Constitution forbade the use of religious tests for office holders and guaranteed that there would be no established religion. It reflects the movement for religious liberty that had prevailed in Virginia. Just before national independence, James Madison (1751–1836) and Thomas Jefferson (1743–1826) had led a campaign, supported by Presbyterians and Baptists, that had resulted in religious freedom in the colony. The middle colonies had already adopted the same solution. In New England, the established Congregationalism held on for a generation after independence, but it also gave way before the rationalism of the Enlightenment and the revivalist churches. The United States of America began its history with a religious life shaped by a free church Protestant denominationalism.

The American Revolution has had a profound effect on other peoples. During the eighteenth century, the establishment of an independent republic in America was widely interpreted by Europeans as proving that the ideas of the philosophes could be put into practice. The United States demonstrated that it was possible for a people to set up a government based on the rights of the individual.

The French Revolution. The ideas of the Enlightenment that were given concrete form by the American Revolution provided a model of freedom for Europeans. Frenchmen who had fought in the War of Independence, and the French financial crisis brought on by the expense of supporting the Americans, contributed to the outbreak of the French Revolution. This movement, which was an attempt to realize in Europe many of the achievements of the American government, was to have a greater impact on history than the American Revolution. It brought more social and economic changes and influenced a larger portion of the globe. It also marked the triumph of the middle class (bourgeoisie) and the awakening of the common man, a phenomenon that civilization is still struggling with.

The gross inefficiency of the French government of the eighteenth century (the *ancien régime*) was another reason for the upheaval. Although France was the center of philosophe thought, it had never been ruled by an enlightened despot. Its social and governmental organization was based on aristocratic privilege, with the population divided into three "estates," or orders, each of which had different legal rights. The first estate was the clergy. The second was the nobility. The third, which included everyone else, had some twenty million peasants and four million artisans and middle class out of a total French population of less than twenty-five million. The first two estates, only 2 percent of the population, owned 35 percent of the land and were exempt from taxation. The tax burden was borne by the third estate and fell most heavily on the peasants, who made up 80 percent of the population. Economic factors were not as important in the alienation of the middle class from the government because many of them were improving their lot, but they resented the social advantages of the nobility and the exclusion of the bourgeoisie from the better positions in the army, the church, and the bureaucracy. The middle class wanted political power and social standing to match their economic gains.

The Revolution, which came as a reaction to this inefficient and unjust system, began in 1787 as an aristocratic movement, but it became progressively more radical until a reaction set in under Napoleon (1769–1821). The French government had been centralized under the king during the seventeenth century, and noble governors had been replaced by the royal bureaucracy. When Louis XVI (1754–93; king of France 1774–92) found himself in financial difficulties because of heavy expenses in support of the American Revolution, the nobles tried to regain power. In 1787, when the government tried to levy a uniform property tax, regardless of the social status of the owner, the aristocrats demanded that the national parliament, the Estates-General, be assembled. The group had not met since 1614, but the nobles insisted that such a sweeping tax change could not be made without the consent of the entire nation through its representative assembly. The king finally agreed that the Estates-General convene in 1789. The nobles assumed that they could control the body, but they were wrong. The meeting unleashed a revolutionary storm that destroyed the ruling institutions of France.

The monarchy was powerless, but other nobles, determined to regain their lost privileges and property, secured foreign aid against the new government. There was also a party within the National Assembly that wanted war in order to establish revolutionary regimes in other countries. Conflict began in 1792, with Austria and Prussia fighting France. At first, the French were defeated, but they later recovered and drove back the Austrian-Prussian forces. The war led to the dethroning of the king and to the election of a National Convention by universal male suffrage. In 1793, Britain, Holland, and Spain joined the war against France, but by 1795, all enemy armies were defeated by the revolutionary troops. A draft army, inspired by love of country and led by able young generals who had risen from the ranks, proved successful.

The pressure of war led the National Convention to become more radical. The Committee of Public Safety became the dominant force in the government. This group managed the fighting, encouraged the people to heroic action, conducted foreign policy, and ruthlessly crushed opposition through the Reign of Terror. Thousands charged with treason or other offenses against the government were guillotined. The king (Louis XVI) and queen were guillotined in 1793; then, the terror got out of control. One after another of the revolutionary leaders were executed. The terror frightened the middle class. They were also worried about the growing radicalism of the common people, who demanded government regulations of prices and wages, a more just distribution of land, and a social security system. The lower classes had to be brought under control so that the bourgeois gains of the revolution could be kept. This was done first by a Directory of five (1795) and then by Napoleon (1799).

Napoleon Bonaparte was a Corsican-born artillery officer who became an extremely successful leader of the revolutionary armies. He overthrew the Directory and governed France as First Consul (1799–1804) and then as Emperor (1804–14). Napoleon introduced many domestic reforms that had the effect of making the revolutionary changes permanent. He also made war with most of Europe. This caused a nationalistic reaction among the other states against France. Napoleon's domestic policies have much in common with the moves made by the enlightened despots of the eighteenth century. He tried to rationalize the French government by codifying laws, centralizing the administration, setting up a national school system, and reaching an agreement with the papacy on church-state relations in France. Napoleon was sympathetic with religion and wanted to establish tolerance among rival faiths. Wherever he extended his control, the Inquisition was abolished and religious freedom was given to minorities. Most French people welcomed the Napoleonic settlement after years of revolutionary turmoil. But Napoleon's more positive achievements were eclipsed by his war record. His military genius enabled him to extend his control over much of Europe. Napoleon's rule was progressive, but it was a foreign rule imposed by force. The people of Europe were becoming nationalistic, and their nationalism came as a result of resistance to the French. This explains the armed revolt in Spain that weakened French strength and the growing opposition in Germany. In 1812, when Napoleon invaded Russia, the people of all classes united to resist him. Russian military strength, combined with the bitter winter, led to the defeat of his Grand Army. Forced to retreat to France, Napoleon abdicated and was exiled to the island of Elba in 1814. He returned to France in 1815 and tried to lead his people to victory but was defeated at Waterloo and exiled again. Napoleon was defeated by the very forces he encouraged.

Christianity in a Revolutionary Age. The French Revolution and the forces it unleashed constituted a serious threat for most forms of Christianity. The early stages of the upheaval were accomplished with the cooperation of the lower clergy (i.e., the parish priests). These men broke with the upper class, who held the high posts in the ecclesiastical system, and voted with the third estate. The National Assembly showed its respect for these priests by paying their salaries though church taxes, and land holdings were abolished. The lower clergy favored the new arrangement because they were given higher salaries. In 1790, the Assembly passed the Civil Constitution of the Clergy, which completely subordinated the Church to the state. When certain clergymen protested, a resolution was passed stating that all ministers had to take an oath to obey the constitution. Many clergy refused. The pope declared that all who swore allegiance to the French government were heretical and gave them forty days to recant. Earlier, the papacy had condemned the Declaration of the Rights of Man and of the Citizen and had officially aligned Roman Catholicism with absolutism and aristocracy.

In 1792, France was attacked by Prussia and Austria. In the desperate struggle that followed, many Frenchmen came to feel that Pius VI (1717–99; pope 1775–99) was the moving spirit behind the enemy coalition. Action was taken against priests who would not support the revolutionary cause, and they were given fifteen days to emigrate. Many were robbed, beaten, and lynched, but about forty thousand managed to escape. They became for the most part propagandists against the French government. The National Convention, which came to power in 1792, had a favorable attitude toward religion and in 1793 proclaimed religious liberty. But an uprising, led by antirevolutionary clergy, changed the Convention's attitude. This led to a great persecution of the Church and the establishment of a religion of reason (in reality, a worship of the state) in France.

A civil religion had been developing in the land since the early days of the Revolution. In 1790, Bastille Day (July 14) was celebrated throughout France in a very religious fashion. An oath was taken to the country, often around an altar in the open air, generally preceded by a Catholic religious service. The Christian holidays were de-emphasized, and special observances were held to honor nature or pagan symbols. By 1793, Christianity was equated with counterrevolution, and the Committee of Public Safety recommended the elimination of all vestiges of the faith, including Sundays and saints days. Christianity was replaced by the "Cult of Reason." Churches were converted into "Temples of Reason." The Virgin and the saints were replaced by revolutionary heroes, such as Rousseau and Voltaire. The new religious movement was inaugurated by the famous ceremony at Notre Dame in Paris, where the statue of the Virgin was replaced by an actress to whom hymns were sung. Some two thousand towns turned their churches into temples of reason, and many rural parishes followed the example. Foreign countries charged the revolutionary government with being antireligious, so it tried to meet their criticisms by officially sanctioning the worship of a supreme being. The new religion was introduced in June 1794 at a formal ceremony modeled after the Mass.

A revised calendar was introduced to replace the old Church Year. September 22, 1792, the day of the establishment of the Republic, was designated as the beginning of Year 1. The year was divided into twelve months of thirty days, with each of the months named for seasonal characteristics. Every tenth day was to be a time of rest. In 1806, when Napoleon abandoned the new calendar, few regretted his move. Additional actions taken against the Church at the time the calendar was changed included the suspension of the payment of clerical salaries and a prohibition against priests serving as teachers in the schools. A system of public schools organized throughout France became the center for inculcating civil religion.

Under the Directory (1795–99), there was more religious liberty, and with the rise of Napoleon to power (1799–1814), conditions improved noticeably for the Church.

Napoleon had several reasons for desiring better relations with the Roman Catholic Church. These included his convictions that France was fundamentally Catholic, that reconciliation with the Church would help him achieve his plans, and that people require the authority of revealed religion to achieve happiness. He arranged the 1801 Concordat with the papacy, which recognized Roman Catholicism in France and provided that the clergy would be paid by the state. The Organic Articles of 1802, attached to the Concordat without papal consent, declared that Napoleon could act as he saw fit for the advancement of France. The pope protested in vain the addition of this statement. In 1804, Pius VII (1742–1823; pope 1800–23) assisted at Napoleon's coronation, but later, when he refused to cooperate, the pontiff was deported to France and imprisoned. The pope responded by excommunicating Napoleon.

The struggle between the revolutionary forces and the Christian faith had profound implications for the future. Nationalist religion was to be a major challenge to Christianity in the modern age. Until the Enlightenment and the revolutionary era, people had not thought in terms of the nation. The growth of vernacular languages, the breakup of the Catholic Church into national churches, and the development of dynastic states prepared the way for the new ideology.

These developments caused patriotism to compete with the Church for the loyalty of the masses. The total demands of the modern state proved difficult to reconcile with obedience to God. Even in the American republic, where the government never took the radical antireligious position found in France, nationalism has tended to become a rival to Christianity or to distort the Christian message. An early example of this is in the work of Timothy Dwight.

TIMOTHY DWIGHT (1752–1817) AND AMERICAN NATIONALISM	
BACKGROUND	Influential minister, scholar, and president of Yale (1795–1817); opposed the views of the philosophes and excesses of the French Revolution.
ANTI-CATHOLIC, ANTI-LODGE	The Roman Catholic Church opposed true Christianity, requiring reform. A new threat came with the lodges, which the philosophes had infiltrated.
KINGDOM OF GOD	Signs of a new age were prosperous foreign missions, Jewish citizenship, the antislavery movement, and decline of Islam. Revival and the American system of religion and political liberty were spreading throughout the world.

CHAPTER SIX

Christian Churches in Modern Times

CHANGES FROM 1800 TO
THE FIRST WORLD WAR

Louis XVI, king of France, was resplendent in his official garb made of gold cloth, with the blue sash of the Order of the Holy Ghost, as he brought up the procession marking the opening of the States General. It was May 4, 1789. There had been much clamor for this national assembly of representatives of the three estates of France in the hope that it might lead the nation to a solution of its many problems. The three estates were the clergy, the nobility, and the commoners. Representatives of each estate traditionally cast one vote as a block. Even in peaceful and untroubled times, the first two estates would vote against the third. And the years before 1800 were neither peaceful nor untroubled for France. Besides, because of the growth of the monarchy, the assembly had not met for 175 years.

When the assembly was finally convened in 1789, the problems of the nation were acute. The government was deeply in debt, the economy was in great difficulty, and widespread dissatisfaction among the people manifested itself in an attitude of rebellion against authority. France still had many traces of feudalism, though Louis XVI had abolished serfdom on crown lands in 1779. In the rest of France, it was abolished by the National Assembly in 1789. Though there was considerable social mobility by that time, the vestiges of feudalism were very frustrating. There were rents to be paid in money, labor, and kind. Commoners were obligated to grind their grain in their lord's mill, bake their bread in his ovens, and press their grapes in his winepress. Especially galling to the rural peasant were the crop damages that resulted from the lord's right to hunt on the peasants' land.

The system of taxes was irregular and often arbitrarily imposed, falling most heavily on the lower classes. The national government was deeply in debt because France had extended generous aid to the Americans in the American Revolution. In the intellectual spheres in France, there was a strong current of rationalism that undermined the basic assumptions of Christian theology and the powerful Roman Catholic Church. Rationalistic intellectuals were called philosophes, with men such as Voltaire prominent among these despisers of the Church. Voltaire's oft-repeated motto, "Crush the Beast" (that is, clerical fanaticism), found many a sympathetic ear and aroused much animosity. The higher clergy especially, drew widespread contempt. They were almost invariably drawn from the nobility and, as abbots and bishops, occupied the most lucrative positions, which were closed to the clergy rising from the ranks of the commoners. It was quite common that the higher clergy were publicly known as unbelievers. At one point, the king, not otherwise known for his conservative views in theology, when considering nominees for the position of bishop of Paris, remarked that at least this bishop ought to believe in God. The lower clergy, the parish priests, were of a different stripe. Though in most cases they were financially better off than craftsmen, laborers, and peasants, they were not wealthy and in general carried out their duties in a conscientious manner.

France had been regarded as queen of the nations of Europe. Its culture and civilization had long been the envy of all others. But now it faced a crisis. Since the days of the "Sun King," Louis XIV (1638–1715; king in his own right 1661–1715), France had been slipping. Louis XV was a weak and debauched ruler. But even without his example, French society could have attained its reputation as the modern Sodom. Louis XVI was weak and irresolute, too deeply mired in the problems of the government and of the society of France to understand their seriousness—much less to find solutions—even when threatened by the guillotine, which finally ended his life in January 1793.

With the demand, less than four years earlier, that the king convene the States General, the door to the French Revolution had already been opened a crack. Events moved at a steady pace through a quarter century that became a watershed of modern history. Once the violence of the French Revolution reached its height, the Church in France went into inexorable decline. Furthermore, the course of events set in motion by the French Revolution was soon to sever philosophical and theological moorings also in other countries of Europe.

In the opening procession of the 1789 meeting of the States General, Maximilien de Robespierre was among the representatives of the third estate, dutifully carrying a ceremonial candle symbolic of the expiring flicker of peace and harmony. Soon, he would represent a much more radical view in the Revolution, namely the Terror, which radicalized the Revolution in 1793 and 1794. Robespierre is credited with the enigmatic statement that without terror, virtue would remain powerless. He used the terror of the guillotine, which claimed forty thousand people in a few months. But by July 1794, Robespierre and his friends themselves fell prey to the guillotine in a violent reaction against excessive violence.

During these stormy years, the once-powerful Roman Catholic Church in France was crushed. It had survived intense struggles with the papacy. It was a loyal daughter of the papacy, but with its prerogatives as a French national church safeguarded. This proud Gallican Church had also been eminently successful in its tests of strength with the monarchy in France. From the time of Cardinals Richelieu and Mazarin early in the seventeenth century, the higher clergy were such effective diplomats and statesmen representing the national interests of France that the French monarchs could not have functioned without the support of the Gallican Church. It is true, however, that the French kings reserved the right to make all higher appointments in the Catholic hierarchy within France.

Even when the Christian foundations were gradually eroded in the eighteenth century by the deists and the philosophes, the outward power structure of the Church remained, based on privilege and on a great depth of economic resources, primarily land ownership. In the Revolution, this was all to be toppled in a few years, never to be rebuilt.

Less than 1 percent of the nearly twenty-five million people of France were Catholic clergy, comprising the first estate, or order of society. The Roman Catholic Church, through the various orders of regular clergy and through the dioceses, owned great wealth in France.

The Government and the Church. We look now at the internal problems of the French government that destroyed itself and the Church in the Revolution. In the National Assembly, Talleyrand, bishop of Autun, proposed on October 10, 1789, that imminent government bankruptcy could be averted by takeover of the church properties. After long, intense debate, this was done. Clergy were then paid by the state. This almost instantaneous loss of all ecclesiastical income was soon followed by other legislation that was increasingly detrimental to the Church. The regular orders were suppressed, dioceses were rearranged, and a new constitution for the Church was drawn up; debated in the Assembly in May, June, and July 1790; and incorporated into the new national constitution. This secularized the Church, including the election of bishops and appointment of other clergy. The pope was disgusted at this "Gallican pestilence," but Louis XVI, unimpressed, promulgated the Civil Constitution of the Clergy, which made the clergy subject to civil election. Next, the Assembly declared that all clergy employed by the state take an oath of loyalty to the new state constitution, in which the Civil Constitution was embodied, or lose their posts and their salaries. In Spring 1791, the pope issued a forthright denunciation of the Civil Constitution, whereupon the French seized papal territories within the borders of France, including Avignon. This severed relations with the papacy. Only a few bishops and about one-third of the parish priests signed the new constitution. For about a year, the Assembly tolerated nonconforming clergy, but by mid-1791, it began to crack down.

Religious persecutions followed, growing more intense with the French declaration of war against Austria in April 1792 and in the confusion that resulted from the collapse of the French throne in August. Many were killed by various cruel means. Over thirty thousand fled the country. Those clergy and members of religious orders who were willing to be subservient to the government were urged to break their vows of celibacy and marry. This symbolic step would signify a break with the Roman Catholic Church. The new radical government known as the National Convention, which in September 1792 displaced the National Assembly, launched an all-out policy of extermination against the Church and introduced an anti-Christian ersatz religion—a form of deism that made much of its adherence to the belief in a supreme being created after the image of man. A law passed in October 1793 introduced a new calendar that eliminated Sunday, and with it, presumably, all church festivals.

Each month was divided into periods of ten days, with the tenth a day of rest. In Paris, the bishops and some of the clergy were forced to resign, and in the Cathedral of Notre Dame, a woman was enthroned as the Goddess Reason. It was reported that only 150 parishes in France still celebrated regular Mass.

Napoleon. An easing of the internal revolutionary fervor in France did not help the restoration of the government or the Church much since the country was embroiled in serious international war by the mid-1790s. Signally successful in the French invasion of Italy was Napoleon Bonaparte, a young captain of artillery. When Britain, Austria, Russia, Naples, and Sweden formed a new coalition against France, the government of France, known as the Directory, was in danger of collapse. Napoleon seized power, saved the revolutionary government from total collapse, and escalated the international war. In France, there was a growing feeling that the nation had a messianic mission—that it was divinely appointed to save the world from feudalism and to enlighten the world in the new ideology of liberty, equality, and fraternity. Napoleon arrived in Paris from his military expedition in Egypt in October 1799. The turn of the century, therefore, marks a critical point in French church history. Napoleon was himself not enamored of Christianity, but he saw it as a useful control device for the people, and he was a realist and saw the papacy as a significant moral power in the world. Napoleon therefore legitimized the Church in France, provided it remained subservient to the power of the state. He also established a concordat with Pius VII (pope 1800–23), which was signed in July 1801.

By that time, the Church in Italy had sustained some severe shocks from the French Revolution, which left the papacy only a very shaky base from which to respond to developments in France. Napoleon had invaded the Papal States in central Italy in 1796, and a hard settlement was imposed on the papacy. In February 1798, a French army occupied Rome, and the pope was deposed as secular ruler, though permitted to continue his spiritual functions. Pope Pius VI (pope 1775–99), ill and eighty, had sought refuge outside of Rome but was considered a prisoner of the French Republic and died in southern France on August 29, 1799.

As master of Italy, Napoleon set up puppet governments in the form of several republics, in which church properties were despoiled and the clergy subdued under the new secular power. The next pope, Pius VII, had a much more difficult experience under the secular power. Napoleon had himself crowned king of Italy, then escalated his rank to that of emperor, and by 1809 annexed the Papal States to his empire. Since Pius VII did not agree to Napoleon's demands, the pope was taken to France as a prisoner. His adamant refusal to perform the functions expected of him, especially the consecration of new bishops who would presumably be more subservient to the French civil authority, exasperated the French emperor. Only the ultimate defeat of Napoleon freed the papacy from this very difficult situation.

At the zenith of his power, Napoleon occupied the whole heartland of the Continent. This occupation turned out to be a traumatic experience for the churches everywhere, but especially for Roman Catholicism in areas like the Austrian Nether-lands (the later Belgium) and the Catholic territories of Germany.

The conquest of Napoleon shook the churches to the very foundations. Because of Napoleon's handling of the pope, the prestige of the pope as a prince of this world and as final authority in moral and spiritual matters was lastingly undermined. The secular and anti-Christian ideology of the French Revolution—liberty, equality, fraternity—engendered ersatz religion even in the most devoted Roman Catholic countries as well as in Protestantism. With the rising tide of nationalism, to a large degree triggered by the French Revolution, as coagulant, this anti-Christian triple ideology was to plague Roman Catholic and Protestant countries alike.

With the defeat of Napoleon, the dominant theme in the power politics of Europe was restoration of legitimate rulers. Despite the ostensibly Christian objectives of the most influential rulers in Europe who tried to put the pieces together again, the churches could not be restored to the prewar condition. Czar Alexander of Russia verbalized the Christian emphasis and objectives of the leaders of the restoration in the document forming the Holy Alliance with Frederick William III, king of Prussia, and Francis, emperor of Austria. But no matter how piously the document was phrased, the Christian emphasis was a facade, and it only compromised an already sorely tried and seriously endangered Christianity to the purposes of international power politics. For a while, however, the Christian emphasis looked real, and the longer it did, the louder became the hue and cry from the secular, anti-Christian left about the falseness of the churches. This is part of the legacy of the Restoration, which followed the French Revolution and left its mark on all of the nineteenth century.

Secularization. The defeat of Napoleon and the restoration of legitimate monarchy in France by the victorious allies, principally England, Austria, Prussia, and Russia at the Congress of Vienna in 1814 and 1815, could by no means reverse the trend in secularization of the church in France and elsewhere. Neither did the conservative restoration, backed by all the power of Europe, succeed in stopping the continuous revolution in thought and theology.

Structurally, there were those who hoped to be able to restore the previous status. The "ultras" tried to turn back the clock, to restore the Church as a rich organization in a Christian state. But there were crosscurrents in France that made any kind of unified church policy quite impossible.

In 1814, the Quadruple Alliance of Britain, Russia, Austria, and Prussia could not envision the possibility of anyone ruling a nation who was not of royal birth. Therefore one of the main themes of the Restoration was the preservation of "legitimacy." Legitimate rulers had to be restored to power throughout Europe. In France, Louis XVII, son of the executed king, had died in prison, so Louis XVI's brother was elevated to the throne as Louis XVIII. He was required to grant a political charter to somewhat liberalize the government of France, in contrast to the absolute monarchy of former times. And he was expected to reign as a Christian monarch, a role he tried to carry out despite his own personal lack of religious enthusiasm and conviction. His task was difficult. Even within the ranks of the Roman Catholic members, some were loyal to the papacy and were labeled ultramontanists, but even some among them were liberal in the political and ideological sense. Others were Gallican, some were skeptics, and still others were downright hostile to both the Church and the government.

Social Trends. France became the home of radical new social philosophies that were strongly antichurch and materialistic. Claude Henri de Rouvroy, comte de Saint-Simon (1760–1825), is one of the earliest pioneers of Continental socialism, an intellectual and social trend that proved to be intensely anti-Christian. Saint-Simon advocated the building of the new society on the basis of science and industry. He appealed to the governments of Europe to undertake large-scale industrial enterprises so as to improve society. This kind of social planning he made into a new religion. Some of his followers even imitated polity and liturgy from Christianity to enhance their new religion of Saint-Simonianism. Saint-Simon and some other early French socialists were not taken seriously. But this was the avant-garde of more serious anti-Christian social theory to come, which was to produce a climate very unfavorable for the churches. The fact that Karl Marx studied the French socialists and learned significant points of his theory from them when he was in exile in Paris illustrates the widespread radical influence that emanated from France in the nineteenth century. This radical ideology became another provocative factor that moved the Roman Catholic papacy to the reactionary right extreme.

The more immediate danger, however, came from other sources. First of all, the defeat of Napoleon and the Restoration had brought renewed opportunities for papal intervention in the affairs of the Church in France. There was a revival of papal prestige, if not power, which, in the confusion of secularist ideologies like nationalism, socialism, and materialism, served to increase the self-delusion of the curia about its own influence and power. This led the papacy to try to roll back the tide of history, and that in turn discredited the papacy in the eyes of the world. Furthermore, because of circumstances, the Church in France adopted a policy of cooperation with the French government that proved catastrophic. The French had a penchant for tolerating abuse from a government that promised national glory and prestige. After the Revolution, France stood before the world stripped of honor and glory. The Church allowed itself to be used in the hope of recapturing some French glory.

The charter of 1814 had reestablished the Roman Catholic Church as the official religion of the state, provided there be liberty for other persuasions. The Concordat of 1817 was to eliminate the unfavorable strictures on the Catholic Church in France. A new wave of ultramontanism became evident among French thinkers. The Swiss scholar Karl Ludwig von Haller had written a book in 1816 in which he tried to reawaken awareness of the need for authority of the Church as well as of the state. In France, the vicomte de Bonald held similar views, advocating an alliance of the Church and the state and asserting that absolute government was the best in both spheres.

Joseph Marie de Maistre, a Roman Catholic layman and diplomat, also supported such ideas. Sovereignty, he said, came from God alone; since it is based on the will of God, it is entirely fitting that kings should submit to spiritual authority as embodied in the papacy. He claimed that rebellions originated with Protestants and Jansenists. His book on the power and primacy of the pope, *Du pape*, marks a milestone in the conservative reaction.

Louis XVIII died September 16, 1824, and his brother succeeded him as Charles X. In this decade, the government policy was increasingly favorable to the Church. Churchmen may have been more optimistic than reality warranted when Charles X granted indemnity for land confiscated during the Revolution to those who fled France (émigrés)—a move probably motivated as much by the desire to stabilize land values as to recompense losses. As long as émigrés had any kind of claim, others refused to buy confiscated land from the government, and this depressed the land values. But the crosscurrents in theology were reflected in those who warned against clerical domination over the government, against the feared resumption of the Inquisition, and against Jesuit intrigue. During this period, at least, the church in France was able to rebuild its ministry by training new recruits.

In 1830, however, another, less violent revolution shook France. The result was that Charles X was deposed and the "citizen king," Louis Philippe, was enthroned. The new government brought with it a period of almost twenty years—till the next revolution in 1848—of strongly anticlerical policy.

At the critical juncture several influential men in France tried to strike a compromise between conservative Catholicism and the new concept of greater political and social freedom. François René de Chateaubriand was the first of the French thinkers who, influenced by the romanticism of Jean-Jacques Rousseau, tried to find a new stance. In his book on the genius of Christianity, he used the subjective and sentimental argument to prove the viability of Catholicism, which was the only Christian tradition he could accept within his definition of "Christianity." Because of the genius of Catholicism, the arts and the culture of Europe had been much benefited, he asserted. A contemporary also somewhat under the influence of romanticism was Hugues Félicité Robert de Lamennais (1782–1854). He made it a special objective of his studies to find the religious foundation for society and concluded that it must be found in a common conviction of man. Since the highest appreciation for truth derives from the Church, the Church should be freed from state influence. These men were ultramontanists, but they were also enamored of a romantic appreciation for liberty. After the revolution of 1830, they began to advocate this dual stance. Their position, however, got them into difficulty with the papacy. Lamennais and several of his friends went to Rome to lay their platform before Gregory XVI. The pope's total rejection of the motto for the new France, namely, "God and liberty," was enunciated in the encyclical *Mirari vos*, issued August 15, 1832. This document warned against the errors embodied in the attempt to embrace aspects of the new liberalism. It sounded the death knell of the hope of Lamennais and other Frenchmen to combine Catholicism and liberalism. It denied the suggestion that the Church needed regeneration and reform; it rejected the validity of freedom of conscience and of the press and denounced any suggestion that the Church should ally itself with the new liberalism. The significance of this was that, in the French attempt to find a viable separation of the Church from the state, the papacy took an ever more radical-right extremist position that grew to fruition by about 1870. However, even though the reign of Louis Philippe (1830–48; also called July Monarchy because of the events of July 27–29, 1830, which brought it to power) saw the decline of the French attempt to combine Catholicism with liberalism, Catholicism in France seemed to be finding new vigor among the masses in the revival of the various religious orders for both men and women, in the founding of a new lay order (the Society of St. Vincent de Paul), and in a new missionary spirit focused especially on Asia. In the meantime, other midcentury developments in France and its world role detracted very seriously from the possibility of French Catholicism becoming a positive and constructive force in the world.

PROTESTANTISM IN GERMANY IN THE NINETEENTH CENTURY

France was the most influential nation in Europe before the French Revolution, and the Roman Catholic Church in France was the most prestigious church in any nation of the world. But Germany, crushed and trampled under the heels of the conquering French armies, was to rise after the Napoleonic defeat as the most important nation for new intellectual and cultural developments, which were destined to leave a lasting mark on the theology of both Catholics and Protestants. In fact, Germany, with her universities and their important departments of philosophy and theology, can be pictured as the helmsman, giving direction to the theological development of Christianity in the nineteenth and twentieth centuries.

Influence of the French Revolution. Before the French Revolution, Germany was an aggregate of some three hundred feudal and semifeudal dukedoms and principalities that were loosely presided over by the Hapsburg emperors, who held Austria as their family territories. According to the earlier medieval tradition of decentralization, the succession to the throne in this Holy Roman Empire was by election. When an emperor died, a seven-man board of electors, consisting of four secular princes and three princes of the church, would meet and elect a successor. At the time of the Reformation, however, the Hapsburgs in Austria had managed to get a monopoly on the throne, and they perpetuated this line of rulers until the empire crumbled.

Long before the Hapsburgs lost control, the electors of Brandenburg, in northern Germany, were able to put together a new power base that increasingly challenged the Hapsburg monopoly. In the seventeenth century, the House of Hohenzollern in Brandenburg managed to acquire feudal suzerainty over part of Prussia, with the kings of Poland as overlords. In the eighteenth century, the electors of Brandenburg, by means of astute participation in various wars and by shrewd diplomacy, emerged as kings in Prussia. From there on, this ruling house gained more and more territory until it finally displaced the Austrian Hapsburgs as the main German power, became the center of the new German Empire in the 1860s, and smashed both Austrian and French power in the 1860s and 1870s, only to be destroyed in turn as an entity in World War I.

But a hundred years earlier, this rising power, as well as the rest of Germany, came perilously close to being destroyed by Napoleon. In the first decade of the nineteenth century, Napoleon overran all of Germany. The Hapsburg power toppled, and the Prussian king sued for peace. Napoleon indulged in his favorite pastime of rearranging the conquered territories, even as he did in Italy and the rest of Western Continental Europe.

The French Revolution had held out to the Germans the hope of sweeping out the vestiges of feudalism and of modernizing the land. Many Germans had looked forward to the invading French as their rescuers from their premodern bondage. But the harsh realities of military invasion and Napoleon's dealings with the defeated German territories soon disillusioned the Germans and provoked strong reaction.

Napoleon ruthlessly reshuffled German territories. Two basic presuppositions with which Napoleon approached the problem of dealing with a conquered Germany were (1) reducing the power of Austria and Prussia and (2) accomplishing this by combining some of the lesser states and by elevating some of them to kingdoms. Saxony came in for special attention because of its strategic location between Hapsburg lands in Austria to the south and Prussia to the north. Furthermore, Saxony was by far the most important of the states that Napoleon made into a kingdom, with Bavaria a close second.

Even before the Reformation, Saxon lands were divided by the Wettin family into Ernestine and Albertine Saxony. By the eighteenth century, much of Saxony plus other neighboring territories had been unified under an aggressive archduke, Frederick Augustus I of the Albertine line, elector of Saxony 1694–1733, known also as Augustus the Strong (king of Poland under the name Augustus II; 1697–1704, 1709–33). In his furious ambition to enhance his position, he espoused Roman Catholicism at the expense of his Lutheran heritage. This put him in much better favor with the Catholic Hapsburgs, who were his feudal suzerain overlords. With their support, he became king of Poland. As a result of his driving ambition and of the uncertainties of the power politics he played with his three more powerful neighbors to the north and east—Prussia, Sweden, and Russia—constant wars drained the resources of Saxony, alienated the Polish people, and made life miserable for almost everyone under his influence.

After the Napoleonic Wars, the society and economy of Saxony lay prostrate. The populace was dislocated and disillusioned. The Saxons who were now under Prussian rule carried along a bagful of resentments and problems that made it very difficult for the Prussian kings to carry out an effective administration in those new territories, especially in church affairs.

Saxony was not the only territory to be reshuffled after Napoleon. The rearrangement of German territories effected by Napoleon ran contrary to the principle of legitimacy (the restoration of legitimate rulers everywhere), but the clear need for the German states to do something to overcome the old feudal divisions was so strong that the basic state system as devised by Napoleon was permitted to continue after Vienna. This gave Germany fewer than thirty kingdoms, dukedoms, and other lesser territories—the whole included in the German Confederation, a loose structure set up as a substitute for the almost defunct German empire under the Hapsburgs.

All these developments caused a traumatic shock in varying degrees for all of Germany, not only in the political and economic sphere but also in the intellectual and theological life of Germany. The intellectual changes, in fact, proved to be of great significance, for they brought with them new emphasis in German theology that soon affected churches not only in Germany but throughout the world.

The Enlightenment. One of the most significant eighteenth-century intellectual threads woven into the theology of modern Germany, albeit in modified nineteenth-century form, is the Enlightenment, or *Aufklaerung*. Germany by no means had a monopoly on the Enlightenment, nor was it born in Germany. Englishmen, such as Thomas Hobbes (1588–1679), and French philosophers, such as René Descartes (1596–1650), preceded the earliest significant German rationalists.

To a certain extent, Gottfried Wilhelm Leibniz (1646–1716), one of the earliest important German rationalists, was indebted to Descartes and possibly to the English deists. All his life, Leibniz tried to reconcile reason and revelation, albeit not too successfully. But several other major outside influences on Leibniz are evident, and he in turn exerted a significant influence especially on later French rationalists such as Voltaire. One of the main non-European influences on Leibniz was the Chinese philosopher Chu Hsi (1130–1200) and his neo-Confucianism, with which Leibniz became familiar through the writings of Jesuit missionaries in China. But there is also a strong indigenous strain in Leibniz and other German rationalists.

If it is true, as Peter Reill asserts, that the early rationalists tried to rescue revealed religion from annihilation by showing that religion was reasonable, it is equally true that this emphasis soon began to undermine the certainty of the origins of the Scriptures in divine revelation. This view by no means challenges the claim for considerable positive achievement for the Enlightenment made by Friedrich Uhlhorn, a prominent historian of Lutheranism in Germany. He credits the Enlightenment with helping to remove German superstitions, such as belief in witchcraft, which prevailed among Christians even through the eighteenth century. He also asserts that the influence of the Enlightenment is to be credited with removing much of the coarseness in German culture.

RATIONALISM'S INFLUENCE ON CHRISTIANITY		
	EVENTS	OUTCOMES
GOTTHOLD EPHRAIM LESSING (1729–81)	Assumed progress of civilization from primitive to total autonomy of man. Published Reimarus's papers holding that the Gospels were not truly historical.	Man can progress until he no longer needs God. Publications undermined Christian belief in reliability of Scripture.
JOHANN HERDER (1744–1803)	Influenced Sturm und Drang movement from rationalism toward romanticism. Studied socialization of human beings, language, and poetry.	Transitional thinker from Enlightenment to romanticism. Study of poetic forms led to form criticism; ideas of historical development led to historical criticism in biblical studies.
IMMANUEL KANT (1724–1804)	Used reason in attempt to salvage Christianity. Held that the mind has a priori functions and categories. Personal morality is intuitive.	Concluded that natural, moral religion consisted of moral duties as divine commands. Influenced romantic interest in intuition.
FRIEDRICH HEGEL (1770–1831)	God's act of creating something other than Himself set in motion a dialectical process between God and man. Mankind strives for reunion with God as Absolute.	Thesis versus antithesis leads to synthesis, which would describe world history and thought. Such a process would culminate in higher and better attainment with Christianity as the current highest development.
FRIEDRICH ERNST SCHLEIERMACHER (1768–1834)	Would reconcile rationalism with confessional theology. Held that feeling of dependence on transcendent Being was essence of religion.	Sacrificed essence of Christian theology to make it more acceptable to rationalists. Lacked certainty about core Christian teachings.
FERDINAND CHRISTIAN BAUR (1792–1860)	Tuebingen school of theology drawn from above thinkers. Baur held that Petrine theology versus Pauline theology led to catholic theology.	Taught history of dogma in which theology develops. Views of biblical canon changed; historical critical method became preferred approach to Bible. Began quest for historical Jesus.
CHRISTIAN KONRAD VON HOFMANN (1810–77)	Erlangen school of theology sought to retain biblical theology and accommodate rationalistic theology.	Heilsgeschichte (salvation history); God reveals Himself through great events rather than written word. Theology confirmed by experience, not proof texts.

The Quest for the Historical Jesus. Related to this general trend, though usually given a different label, is the quest for the historical Jesus. Since it was assumed by the rationalists that the Gospel narratives about the life and work of Christ were not reliable, it was alleged that critical historical scholarship had to be brought to bear on the problem to find out what could be accepted as authentic. This type of scholarship was going on before Baur taught at Tuebingen, but the Tuebingen school provided new impetus for this study. One of Baur's students, David Friedrich Strauss (1808–74), devoted himself to this research and made one of the most provocative studies to come out of mid-nineteenth-century German theology. In 1835, while his mentor Baur was still in his own formative stage, Strauss wrote a two-volume *Life of Jesus (Leben Jesu)*, which shook the theological world to its foundations. Albert Schweitzer (1875–1965), famous scholar and medical missionary in Africa, wrote the history of the whole movement known as the quest for the historical Jesus.

Strauss's book left churches and theologians disturbed and uncertain as to what in the Gospels could be believed because he introduced the concept of myth for many events in the biblical narrative. The miracles, for example the casting out of evil spirits and the raising of the dead, he held to be impossible. But we should not assume that by myth he means simply a human fabrication deliberately concocted. Rather, in his terminology, myth means the imprecise and inadequate human way of verbalizing some transcendental truth that is beyond our comprehension. In his book, Strauss argues, with rationalist prejudice, that miracles are impossible. The theologian must approach his task without prejudices, he says, and thus dare not presuppose miracles. Strauss states that if anyone finds this unchristian, he will say that he finds them unscientific. What was basic to this view of myth is the Hegelian assertion that religion indeed presented truth, but not in the final absolute form of pure philosophical concepts, only in the incomplete and inadequate form of "representation," for which Hegel and the theologians use the German term *Vorstellung*. The nineteenth-century theologians like Strauss then used the term *myth* to designate those older and antiquated sagas of ancient people who expressed things and events not as they actually were or happened, but only as best as they could with their limitations of understanding.

In a later reworking of his study on the life of Jesus, Strauss adhered to his radical views. In another major study on Christian doctrine, he considered it a priori that the body of Christian doctrine had been demolished by critical biblical studies. He is typical of the radical scholars who question all points of Scripture doctrine and regard them as the creation of the later Church. In his radical position, Strauss was not always the most popular intellectual of his day; not many agreed with him. But he opened up possibilities of biblical criticism. Others who followed him, such as Ludwig Feuerbach (1804–72), became even more radical and insisted that God had not created the human race as Scripture stated—man had created the notion of God in his own mind. It was therefore alleged that man, in believing the Christian doctrines of God, sin, and grace, was actually alienating himself from his own basic nature and ascribing to God the noble attributes that were really his own. Marx and other militant materialists could then say that man, by insisting on obedience to and worship of God, was actually debasing himself because he was deliberately continuing his enslavement to the product of his own imagination.

Pietism and Confessional Awakening. In the swirl of German intellectual and religious life, one other highly significant trend developed in the decades after the Napoleonic Wars. Some Lutherans, especially in Saxony, in the Prussian province of Saxony, in Silesia (a territory conquered by Prussia in the eighteenth century at the expense of the Austrian Hapsburgs), and in Pomerania (also subjected to Prussian rule in modern times in several annexations, primarily from Sweden) came to the realization that religious life was quite sterile. There were also spontaneous awakenings in unrelated areas and different church bodies. Some of these movements had their roots in German Pietism. Much of this antedates 1800, and thus a brief mention must suffice. A typical example of this type, and quite a noteworthy churchman in the Reformed Church, is Johann Heinrich Jung-Stilling (1740–1817), teacher, economist, mystic, poet, and physician. In his youth, he came under the influence of Pietism, and as an adult, he associated with men like Johann Caspar Lavater (1741–1801), who, like Jung-Stilling, was captivated by the Enlightenment, but who also stressed inner feeling and religious sentimentality. The trauma of the French Revolution gave movements like this a sharp apocalyptic emphasis, especially in the Rhineland. There was an intense concern with the anticipated end of the world and the final coming of Christ. Because of physical upheavals and the spiritual disturbances of the wars, a great unrest developed, with Germans migrating eastward to Russia and others trying to get to Palestine, there to await the manifestation of the heavenly kingdom. This type of emigration is not associated with other nineteenth-century German emigrations, for example, to Australia and America.

The movement described above was based primarily on the southern German kingdom of Wuerttemberg, where there never was a growth of confessional Lutheranism. But there was a similar awakening also among the committed Reformed in Germany territories. In the territories of the lower Rhine, a Reformed theologian named Gottfried Daniel Krummacher (1774–1837) became the acknowledged leader of a very influential Pietistic awakening movement that influenced also Prussia.

This type of Pietistic awakening eventually contributed the main thrust to the Protestant mission expansion of the nineteenth century. In west central and northern Germany, there were similar movements that moved beyond Pietism to a renewed emphasis on confessional theology. In contrast to the former, mostly in the Reformed churches, the confessional movements were mostly Lutheran. They reacted to the rationalism of the Enlightenment, the subjectivism of Pietism, and the emotionalism of romanticism. They developed a high level of conscious appreciation for traditional, confessional theology. Since appreciation for distinctive confessional theology was all but dead in Germany about 1800, this new emphasis is by its critics also called repristination theology. The confusion prevailing in the churches of Germany because of the wars and the mayhem evident in the field of theology (because of men like Baur, Strauss, and Feuerbach) provoked a strong reaction. Though many of the mediating theologians are often also classified as belonging to the awakening, most of the Lutherans involved in the awakening eventually occupied a more conservative confessional position than the mediating theologians or the Erlangen school. Another significant difference of the confessional awakening is that it put more emphasis on the congregation.

The state church system of Germany had a deleterious effect on the vitality of the Church, which both Pietists and confessionalists regretted. The German ruling nobility often did not have much feeling for the Church. Many of the nobility were unbelievers. Yet, in the golden age of orthodoxy, the theologians often stressed the divine institution of government authority. There was little proclamation of God's impending judgment. As more and more criticism was generated against the German nobility and against the outdated feudal system that legalized their prerogatives, the Church also came under suspicion for trying to legitimize the nobility and their power. But the Pietistic reaction and the rationalism for which Pietism so often prepared the way contributed to a decline of the Church in Germany. There are sources that tell of a very small percentage of people attending church, though officially, under the territorial system in vogue since the Reformation and basically confirmed in 1648 at the end of the Thirty Years' War in the Treaty of Westphalia, every citizen was a member of the church that his ruler established. The system of having the ruler's church as the official and only church of the realm did not work well for long. In Brandenburg (the later Prussia) the rulers adopted the Reformed faith, while their subjects were almost all Lutheran. In Saxony, as recounted above, the rulers became Roman Catholic. In other areas both of these churches were aggressive at the expense of subjects who held to different confessions. Ecclesiastical power politics only tended to turn the little man away from the church. The fact that there was no accountability built into the system contributed to the erosion. Pastors were paid by the state and by feudal grants and stipends even if none of their members came to church. It sometimes happened that on a Sunday not a single member would show up for services. The new speculative trends in theology only contributed to further alienation. Friedrich Paulsen, native of northwest Germany and later a famous professor of ethics at the University of Berlin, but no great admirer of the confessional awakening, in his youth saw the erosion of church life. In his autobiography he related that, by force of long habit, church attendance in his area of Germany continued for some decades after the erosion had set in, but the last third of the nineteenth century saw it all washed out.

The Consistories and Patronage. In German territories, the state church system had a deadening effect on the churches. Church affairs were managed by government consistories or boards of ecclesiastical affairs. In many territories, nobility had the right, called *Patronat*, to appoint the clergy. This management from above effectively froze out participation of the people in church affairs. Germans already made too much of ecclesiastical elitism. In early modern times, the clergy in Protestant Germany were all drawn from the nobility or gentry. With the French Revolution, however, the clergy ranks were open to everybody. This may be part of the reason why German church historians complained about the increasingly serious debasement of

German Lutheran clergy in the nineteenth century, saying that pastors had less and less culture, polish, and education. All this no doubt had a massive impact on the gradual deterioration of church life in Germany in the nineteenth century.

Prussian Churches. In Prussia, the "Lutheran Supreme Consistory" was reorganized in 1750 to consist of two presidents and seven councilors. The king appointed the minister of state and of war, Count von Dankelmann, as first president. Among the council members was at least one Reformed churchman, K. H. Sack. This board was charged with responsibility for training and examining pastors; for supervising the spiritual life of the Church, including the doctrine and practice of the churches; for appointing all pastors, teachers, and theological professors; for supervising all hospitals and homes for the poor; and for overseeing all finances in the royal churches and the ecclesiastical foundations.

Prussia was a rising power in Germany, and there the problems of the churches were most acute. One churchman laments the debasement of the churches there under the influence of rationalism, especially in the reign of Frederick II (Frederick the Great), king of Prussia 1740–86. The king himself took a snide view of the Church and of the clergy and derided those who thought otherwise. By that time, the Lutheran Church in Germany could almost be called a stinking corpse, according to one German churchman. Frederick, dedicated to his vain ambition to be the most enlightened ruler in Europe, seriously hurt the Church when he promulgated edicts that put strictures on church discipline. He personally denigrated the salutary Church custom of confession, and, to show everyone that he made the decisions, he appointed the notorious scoundrel Karl Friedrich Bahrdt (1741–92) as professor of theology at Halle.

With the Napoleonic Wars, too, the German government-controlled system of church affairs was more secularized. Typical of the period were departments of cultural and religious affairs that were to serve all citizens, even unbelievers. This was a radical departure from the former days, when in smaller territories there was religious homogeneity, with a benign ruler watching over church affairs.

It was in Prussian territories that the first serious opposition against deteriorated church conditions, counterfeit theology, and government control of church affairs erupted in the form of the confessional awakening. In the accounts of many who experienced the confessional awakening, it is obvious that they regarded rationalism as the chief enemy. They may not always have had enough perspective to analyze the chaotic conditions prevailing after the Napoleonic Wars as a major factor in the unrest that they experienced. They certainly must have felt, but possibly could not diagnose, causes of these deteriorating economic conditions. But Prussian territories were by no means the only places where awakenings took place.

German Awakenings. In the eighteenth century, the Moravian *Unitas Fratrum* in Saxony had experienced a revival of religious life and of the mission mandate that somewhat resembled the nineteenth-century movement. This was the first major European church movement not in the state churches and thus provided a sort of prototype for the nineteenth century. Moravians made very significant contributions to renewed church life and to missions already in the eighteenth century. In Wuerttemberg there was a Pietistic movement, mentioned above, that had its roots deep in the eighteenth century but could not come to full bloom till the dust of the Napoleonic Wars had settled. This movement provided a very powerful mission impulse that will receive more attention in a later chapter. In Bavaria, there was a revival that upgraded church life at home and contributed a significant mission thrust to overseas outreach of the Church. In this movement, Johann Konrad Wilhelm Loehe (1808–72) became one of the most significant Lutheran churchmen of the century, especially by supporting work in the United States. In Saxony the *Pilger aus Sachsen* appeared for the first time in 1845, one of the first religious periodicals in Germany that had a significant impact on the revival movements as well as on church life. Ludwig Harms (1808–65) in North Germany was an effective preacher and gave a powerful stimulus to the mission outreach when he founded the Hermannsburg Mission. Claus Harms (1778–1855) in Kiel was one of the first voices to be heard in this movement. In 1817, he issued Luther's Ninety-Five Theses together with ninety-five of his own against rationalism and the proposed Prussian Union of Lutherans and Reformed. Ernst Wilhelm Hengstenberg (1802–69), professor at the University of Berlin since 1828, became one of the leaders of the new orthodoxy in Lutheranism, though he found it possible to remain in the German union church, which many of the confessional Lutherans found quite unacceptable. Even earlier than the *Pilger aus Sachsen*, Hengstenberg produced a significant church paper called *Evangelische Kirchenzeitung*. Hengstenberg also wrote some very significant books on theology. But for some people, he was too doctrinaire and too supportive of the state power structure.

Hengstenberg is somewhat atypical in the religious awakenings because in him there is much less of the antigovernmental populist emphasis of many of these religious leaders. The attempt of German governments to bring about the union of Lutherans and Reformed was a crucial turn of events that produced much antigovernment reaction and provoked a sizable emigration from Germany exclusively for religious reasons. This has a long and involved history; only a few salient points can be related here.

Prussian Union. In some German lands like Prussia, where the kings were Reformed, a union of the two denominations was attempted even before the Napoleonic Wars. In 1817, the Prussian king once more took up this favorite project when he issued a royal directive that a union of the Lutheran and Reformed churches should be effected through joint worship services. To achieve this, he had a union agenda prepared, the use of which caused a furor especially where the Lutheran confessional revival had been unfolding. The king ordered the introduction of the new agenda in the military garrison church in Potsdam and urged its use throughout his realm.

The king was probably surprised that criticism of the agenda came first of all from the Reformed, who charged that it was tainted by Pietism and mysticism. The

Reformed did not appreciate the heavy emphasis on elaborate liturgical revival, which the king favored. The agenda was supposed to help restore salutary older customs, such as chanting, kneeling, and the use of candles. These things were considered Roman Catholic vestiges by many, especially the Reformed and the rationalists, and thus were highly unpopular. Lutherans, on the other hand, opposed the agenda for other reasons. It called for the breaking of bread in Communion, a Reformed custom, and Lutherans generally held it impossible to yield to Reformed practice on the grounds that it would imply yielding to Reformed doctrine also. The point in the agenda that provoked the sharpest criticism was the rubric of the distribution. Lutherans, believing in the real presence of the body and blood of Christ in the Sacrament, always used the words "This is My body. . . . This is My blood." The new agenda prescribed the rubric "Christ said, 'This is My body . . .'" Everybody could then put his or her own interpretation on what the words of Christ actually meant. This rubric drew forth the sharpest criticism from the growing numbers of confessional Lutherans, or Old Lutherans, as they were called by this time. In Silesia, where some of the sharpest criticism became evident, the Lutheran nonconformists were led by a prominent theologian and professor Johann Gottfried Scheibel. He and some of his adherents repeatedly petitioned the king to grant them separate Lutheran existence, but to no avail. After more than a decade of struggle with the king's church polity, Scheibel was forced out of office in 1832. Many of the Old Lutheran pastors were driven into exile or even imprisoned. The state controlled church life to the point that every individual was assigned to a particular congregation. If at times people attended a church other than their own in order to hear a confessional pastor or avoid a crassly rationalistic one, the police may have winked at such irregularities. But in 1834, a royal edict was proclaimed that prohibited religious services in private homes for more people than the immediate family. This law also restricted publication of religious tracts, prohibited the administration of ministerial acts by pastors suspended by the government or by laymen, and required all Protestants to send their children to the state school. When nonconformist confessional Lutherans insisted on having their own services, if need be in their private homes, they ran afoul of this new royal edict, and many were persecuted severely by the royal police in Prussian territories. This induced many confessional Lutherans to emigrate to Australia and America.

When Frederick William III died in 1840, conditions among German Protestants were in a sorry state. Some Old Lutherans had already left the country, and many others soon followed, providing a small but highly significant transplant of confessional Lutheranism that would be separated from the theology of European Protestantism for one hundred years.

Frederick William IV, king of Prussia 1840–61, was not as hard-nosed in religious affairs as his father had been. He freed the nonconformist Lutheran pastors from prison, and in 1841 a number of them met to organize the first Free Church, the General Synod of the Evangelical Church in Prussia, often called the Breslau Synod since its central board, or Oberkirchenkollegium, was located in Breslau in

Silesia. In 1845, the government formally approved this new church body. Many Lutherans, however, continued in the United Evangelical Church, organized in compliance with the king's desire to unite all Lutherans and Reformed in Prussia. The mediating Lutherans of course had little discomfort in this type of church, and even conservatives like Hengstenberg found it possible to stay in the Union Church. Many of the other German states followed basically the same pattern, with variations in the formal acceptance of confessions and differences in organizational detail.

In Prussia, district synods were introduced in 1843 and provincial synods in 1844. In 1846, a general synod met in Berlin, but it did not succeed in adopting a creed acceptable to all. Neither could it agree on the function of the Church in the area of social welfare, so this area of urgent need in the changing social conditions of Germany was relegated to the Inner Mission enterprise, a loosely organized ancillary organization founded by J. H. Wichern (1808–81). The unsuccessful revolution of 1848 brought about more government control in all areas of life, including church life, though eventually laymen were admitted in the provincial synods.

The Revolution of 1848. A widespread sociopolitical revolt, for the most part unsuccessful, rose against established governments in most of the nations of Continental Western Europe. In German territories, the revolt was directed against feudal vestiges in government and the bureaucratic regulations these governments established, designed to keep themselves in power and to control the restless youth groups and nationalist movements. A potent nationalism was developing in Germany that was crying for a united nation and that tried to get all the German territories together into one recognized state. This nationalist movement brought with it severe religious and theological deterioration. The German philosopher Fichte had already called for a German national church as the embodiment of the unity of German national culture. In 1813, Fichte called for the establishment of a religion in which all Germans could join—a state religion. He asserted that the kingdom of law and justice, furthered by human reason, and the kingdom of heaven, promised by Christianity, are really one and the same. Due to the wars of liberation, the influence of romanticism, and the nationalistic striving of the German people, biblical terms such as redemption, regeneration, and resurrection were given political overtones by German pastors. One pastor proclaimed Germany as the true visible Jerusalem. Nationalism became a new religion in Germany, and many Protestants joined the trend. There were many Lutherans who were convinced that it was a scriptural mandate to defend the authority of government at any cost, and the Revolution of 1848 furthered this kind of abject submission to government authority. There was actually a strong reactionary tendency in both government and church in Germany in the second half of the nineteenth century. Christian socialism was represented, for example, by J. H. Wichern (1808–81), F. von Bodelschwingh (1831–1910), Friedrich Naumann (1860–1919; his efforts failed repeatedly and his effectiveness was limited), and Adolf Stoecker (1835–1909; originated modern anti-Semitism on social and economic grounds). After the establishment of the new German Empire on the basis of Prussian power in 1866, the secularization process was carried further. When Chancellor Bismarck, chiefly in order to defuse social unrest, inaugurated his state social welfare program, the Church was quite effectively shoved to one side. There was, in fact, considerable sentiment and even scholarly opinion expressed that the German state would completely supplant the Church before very long. Richard Rothe, prominent theologian, even rationalized this according to the laws of the Hegelian dialectic. The deterioration of the indigenous church in Germany opened the way not only for increasing secularity, but also to the mission work of other churches and religious groups that showed more vigor than the German Church did.

Prospects for Lutheranism in Germany toward the end of the nineteenth century were, therefore, less than encouraging. The Reformed churches in Germany did not fare very much better because the new trends in theology produced more and more secularism among the Reformed and in the Union churches.

THE CHURCHES IN ENGLAND

Christianity in the British Isles had a rather distinctive development compared to that on the European Continent. At the time of the Reformation, Ireland remained predominantly Roman Catholic, while England, Wales, and Scotland became Protestant. Long before the latter three joined the United Kingdom early in the eighteenth century, the Reformation had run its course. A strongly anchored state church, Reformed in theology and Episcopal in polity, developed in England. In the seventeenth century, there was vigorous dissent against the Anglican Church (or Church of England) among the Separatists, nonconformists, and Presbyterians. After the English Revolution, the pendulum swung back somewhat in favor of the Anglican Church. Although the rigid laws against non-Anglicans were relaxed considerably in the last part of the seventeenth century and early years of the eighteenth century, the Anglican Church has remained the official church in Great Britain. In Scotland, the indigenous reform movement was strongly Presbyterian, and the persistent attempts of the Stuart kings (who also ruled England after the death of Queen Elizabeth in 1603) did not succeed in imposing Anglicanism on the resourceful Scots.

The Evangelicals. In the eighteenth century, the Anglican establishment was not able to meet the widespread human needs caused by the industrial revolution. The vacuum was filled by the revival movements led by men such as George Whitefield (1714–70) and John Wesley (1703–1791). Their followers are called Methodists because of their strict methods in self-discipline. When Wesley died in 1791, there were seventy thousand Methodists in Great Britain and Ireland and about sixty thousand in America, though they had not yet separated from the Anglican Church.

Methodism was related to the broader movement of the Evangelicals, most of whom remained in the Anglican Church. Because the Evangelicals encountered opposition in the Church of England, they formed small groups, the best known of which was located at Clapham, where John Venn was rector 1792–1813; his father,

Henry Venn, had been one of the earlier Evangelical leaders. William Wilberforce, one of the most active and outspoken Christian laymen of the time, was a member there; a member of Parliament, he is best remembered for spearheading the drive to abolish slavery. It is a very noteworthy achievement of these English Christians that they brought pressure to bear on Parliament to pass laws against slavery well before the American Civil War. Since by that time the British navy was dominant on the seas, it enforced also on other nations the British law against the transportation of slaves. This concern on the part of the Evangelicals for African slaves led directly to mission work in West Africa and in other unevangelized areas of the world.

Besides these groups of active Christians among Evangelicals and Methodists, there was another trend with an opposite viewpoint that opposed much in the life and doctrine of the Church. Unitarianism was the radical form of this tendency, which broke away from the Church already in the seventeenth century. Its adherents began by calling for an adjustment of doctrine to fit modern changes. The French Revolution put a temporary damper on this, but after 1815, this movement developed into a very influential school that was to gain worldwide prominence and that would exert a negative influence on Christianity especially in its mission outreach, as we shall see in a later chapter. Although some in this camp, such as William Paley (1743–1805), desired to defend Christianity against the more radical contemporaries, many in this school had no time or inclination for this type of defense. Some of these more radical thinkers are identified with the classical liberals, also known as classical economists, since most of them were extremely interested in economics. This interest in economics becomes the dominant secular theme in eighteenth-century England, which was subtly but totally at odds with Christian ethics. Economics, it was soon found, was intimately related to political power. Some of the most persistent critics of the Church used the new science of political economy as the secular base in an attempt to build a new society and a new world that, if not antagonistic to Christianity and the Church, would ignore the spiritual domain as if it did not exist.

For example, Jeremy Bentham (1748–1832) and others of the philosophical radicals emphasized that the test of value was utility. If anything succeeded in bringing the greatest happiness to the greatest number, it was good. This hedonistic value system ran contrary to the absolute biblical values of Christian ethics. Not only did Bentham use a completely humanistic base to develop a business ethic, but in *Introduction to the Principles of Morals and Legislation* (1789), he set forth the antiscriptural notion that it was only the avoidance of pain and the desire for pleasures that caused man to develop a system of law. Bentham did not stand alone in the development of utilitarianism, but he is one of the key leaders and one of the best-remembered of the school that had a devastating impact on Christianity and the churches.

Unitarianism. The antagonism of Bentham and other classical liberals against the Church is illustrated in the lives of men such as Thomas Robert Malthus, a clergyman and one of the significant writers in this school. Charles Darwin, a generation later, had studied theology in preparation for the ministry. James Mill, father of John

Stuart Mill and a friend and colleague of Bentham, was trained for the ministry in the Presbyterian Church but gradually passed through deism into unbelief.

Not only did many become apostate—the movement also swept many into Unitarianism. Joseph Priestley (1733–1804) is one of the best-known Unitarians. Many like him, lay and clergy, from the Independents as well as from Anglicanism, joined in aggressive Unitarian groups to propagandize the world. In 1813, Parliament repealed an old religious act that exacted a penalty for a denial of the Trinity. This induced many secret Unitarians to come out into the open. Presbyterianism was especially susceptible to "conversion." James Martineau (1805–1900), a Presbyterian pastor, is an example of those who were influenced by contemporary German biblical criticism. Harriet Martineau (1802–76), the former's sister and a prominent traveler and literary figure, even departed from Unitarianism to become a disciple of Auguste Comte. Although Unitarians in Britain were never more than a small minority, they had wide influence. The center of their influence was in Manchester, where they helped found the *Manchester Guardian* and Manchester University.

New Secularism and Relativism. If German theologians of the time destroyed the biblical foundations for theology, English radicals provided a substitute for it, namely the new secularism and relativism that begins with the presupposition of the autonomy of man. Other prominent intellectuals carried this development into the twentieth century. Noteworthy are men such as John Stuart Mill (1806–73), Charles Darwin (1809–82), and Herbert Spencer (1820–1903). Spencer is the father of the concept of evolution, which was applied by Darwin to the biological area. J. S. Mill was one of the most prominent humanistic reformers in Victorian England. All three proposed ideas that were studied all over the world, and their influence is immeasurable. Thomas Henry Huxley (1825–95), student and admirer of Darwin, vigorously propagated evolutionism in his writings. He described his own religious position as agnosticism, a word he coined to describe a person who did not know divine existence to be a fact.

The degree to which this radical trend also influenced Christianity in England is indicated by the radical theology published there in the nineteenth century. One of the most significant volumes was called *Essays and Reviews*, published in February 1860. This book shocked the Church, for the authors, among other things, suggested universalism as a real option and said that the biblical creation narrative was only myth. One of the essays, *The Education of the World*, reads like Lessing's *The Education of the Human Race* (1788), and may propose Auguste Comte's (1798–1857) notion of eras in history culminating with the modern age dominated by a science in which man no longer needs God. The longest essay was by Benjamin Jowett (1817–93), who was much influenced by the German philosophers, especially Hegel (1770–1831) and F. C. Baur (1792–1860).

This secular trend boded ill for British Christianity, and this secularism gained adherents from all churches. Jowett came from a long Evangelical tradition. However, among Evangelicals, as among Methodists and in other churches, there were signs that Christianity was not dead in nineteenth-century Britain. But these small pockets of vitality were not able to bring about a nationwide renewal of the Church. One reason might be because both Evangelicals and Methodists tended to separate themselves if they failed to leaven the lump of the whole population. But it is true that conditions were so poor, the theological trend so antiauthoritarian, and the churches so unable to reach the people in this great need that the revival of interest in Christianity and church life in these groups failed to swing the mass of people as such, though legally Britain was a Christian nation. By midcentury, it was estimated that only 6 percent of the working people attended church, and in some cities, it was as low as 2 percent.

Roger Lloyd takes up the nineteenth-century decline of Christianity and of the Church in England as a necessary background to the twentieth century. He cites in some detail four cases of conscientious clergymen working seriously in the vineyard. This proves, he asserts, that conditions were not as bad as they sometimes have been made out to be. Yet he describes in disturbing tones the deadness in the Anglican Church in the nineteenth century.

It is helpful to note that after the English Reformation, the Anglican Church had retained much of the hierarchical organizational structure except for acknowledgment of the pope as head of the Church. In the Anglican Church, the archbishop of Canterbury was the ranking ecclesiastical superior under the formal authority of the English sovereign. The administrative divisions are the provinces (York and Canterbury), each divided into dioceses with a bishop at the head. The dioceses are subdivided into parishes, which are grouped for certain administrative functions into deaneries. In the cities, the cathedral churches are governed by the cathedral chapters, which have a very long history of development. They emerged from the "college," or board of clergymen living together at a cathedral church and providing the services there. Cathedral chapters were headed by a dean, in more recent times also called a provost, and were staffed by canons and in certain cases also by prebendaries. In the parish, the functioning clergyman was called the vicar, rector, or curate, depending on the type of parish he occupied.

In Great Britain, there was a very close tie between the church and the state, and this is reflected in the position of bishops in the governmental structure. Of the English bishops, twenty-six always sit in the House of Lords. Five specific ones have regular seats, and the other twenty-one are filled as vacancies occur in the order of the seniority of consecration of all the other thirty-eight bishops (with the exception of the bishops of Sodor and Man). Bishops were required to spend more than half of each year in London. This would seem to conflict with their responsibilities as chief pastor in the dioceses.

Church and Society. The Methodist movement, as well as the emphases of the Evangelical reformers, pointed out that within the Church of England, there was no real concern with the common people in their everyday problems. The services and the liturgy of the Church of England were dull and lifeless. Few people came to church. Pluralities, the system under which bishops held a number of simultaneous offices, was one of the most widespread evils in the Church that showed the higher clergy as greedy in the eyes of the sorely disillusioned and alienated populace. An English newspaper in 1831 exposed part of this when it listed all the offices and positions held by a group of sixteen bishops: sixteen bishoprics, six deaneries, one chancellorship, three archdeaconries, two cathedral treasureships, eight cathedral prebends, twenty-one rectories, and four vicarages. In the cathedral chapters, Bentham saw only "nests of idlers." In many of them, the pursuit of wealth was the main concern, and cathedral libraries, in many cases the best libraries for miles around, were often locked up with nobody in the chapter knowing who had the key. The bishops also comprised the chief opposition in Parliament against reforms of all kinds. The more agitation there was for reform, the more the bishops resisted, so that Prime Minister Earl Grey in 1831 publicly admonished the House of Lords.

One very disturbing factor in England was that everyone, even members of the Independent churches, had to pay the government-imposed church rate for the benefit of the established church. This was not abrogated until 1868. Independents at times berated the Anglican clergy for this extortion on behalf of a church for which they had no appreciation.

Most Englishmen realized that there was something wrong in the spiritual life of the nation. The organized church was still and cold, and people were alienated from it. But what to reform, and how to reform it—those were questions on which there was violent disagreement. Even recent writers disagree radically in the analysis of the problems and the merits of the various solutions proposed at the time. For example, John R. H. Moormann, Lord Bishop of Ripon, says that the man who did most to set the very necessary reforms in the English Church in motion was Thomas Arnold (1795–1842). Yet it was Arnold who, as much as anybody, helped popularize the romanticism of Samuel Taylor Coleridge, which helped to destroy Christian theology. It was Arnold who advocated the view that the state and the Church have essentially the same function and that ideally the two could merge. He echoed Benthamite hedonism when he said that civil society, just like a religious organization, aims at the greatest happiness of man. He was therefore very close to Frederick Denison Maurice (1805–72), who made a name for himself at the newly founded University of London. Because of his keen interest in social problems, Maurice is sometimes accorded stature as a great churchman that his radical left-wing theology will not support.

In the otherwise staid Victorian age, some violent storms severely buffeted the churches. Queen Victoria, ruling from 1837 when King William IV died, lent a bit of romanticism as well as stability to the whole worldwide involvement of the British. She ascended the throne as a single woman not yet twenty with the world at her feet as Queen of the United Kingdom of Great Britain and Ireland. From 1876 on, she was also Empress of India, plus a dozen or so other honorifics attached to the royal incumbent. This was the heyday of the British Empire. Scientific and technological progress lent a false sense of unlimited material and economic security. This was the period of the *Pax Britannica*, the "British Peace."

The established church was suffering from hardening of the arteries. It spent its best energies in preserving the status quo and in criticizing the overly enthusiastic zeal of the Evangelicals. It was further crippled by the new theology being imported from the Continent. The Evangelicals also used up an enormous amount of energy combating this new theology. Thus, the secular segment of British political society, growing out of the background of the classical liberals, outdistanced the churchmen in concern for further reforms to alleviate the suffering of the poor in the industrial slums of England.

Chartism. By the later 1830s, it was evident that Chartism, arising apart from the churches and without real Christian motivation, was the dominant theme.

Chartism is the radical democratic movement in England from 1838 to 1850. It is the parallel to the revolutionary movements of 1848 on the Continent.

The Reform Bill of 1832 had greatly extended the franchise, but it covered mostly the middle classes. Radical leaders drew up further points or objectives for reform; this document was called the "People's Charter." The points covered consisted of equal electoral areas throughout the realm, universal suffrage, payment of Parliament members, no property qualifications, vote by ballot, and annual parliaments. Eventually, all but the last of these points were secured.

In various places, there were serious strikes and even violence on the part of the poor factory workers, whose conditions were unbelievably crushing. But lack of unity in the movement, the granting of some of the demands of the strikers, and possibly a difference of national temperament kept Chartism from becoming as explosive and violent as the revolution on the Continent. A projected nationwide strike in 1842 sent groups of workers around to all the factories, breaking the plugs out of factory boilers; the name "Plug Riots" is derived from this. These riots let the steam out of the boilers while also releasing the ire of the working classes. From then on, Chartism declined in fervor and support.

Despite increasing secularization in England, there were several movements that manifested themselves in religious and ecclesiastical dimensions, for example, a revival of interest in hymnody. Reginald Heber (1783–1826), an Anglican churchman who seemed akin to the Evangelicals, made a lasting contribution to worship through hymnody. At a time when congregational singing in English churches was in disrepute, Heber wrote many fine hymns, including "Holy, Holy, Holy, Lord God Almighty"; "Hosanna to the Living Lord"; and "From Greenland's Icy Mountains." His widow published some of his hymns in 1827. Another contributor to English hymnody was John Keble (1792–1866), many of whose hymns were published in 1827 in *The Christian Year*.

The Oxford Movement. There was also a group of churchmen in England who were opposed to the fashionable liberalism evident in many of the reformers. They were alarmed at the erosion of sound theology in the Church and repelled by the permissiveness of Broad Churchism. One of the leaders in this group, Edward Bouverie Pusey (1800–80), was aware that he worshiped a different God than Frederick Denison Maurice. Pusey and other scholars at Oxford University began to realize that the liberalism of their time had lost the doctrine of man as a sinful creature, of redemption through Christ, and of the real nature of the Church. They made conscious efforts to correct this deficient theology.

These Oxford critics were first known as Tractarians because they began to issue tracts or booklets as a means to communicate their concerns. Later, the movement was called the Oxford movement because it was centered in the university. It is one of the significant developments in nineteenth-century English Christianity.

In 1833, the first of the *Tracts for the Times* appeared. Just before that, a historic sermon was preached by John Keble, entitled *National Apostasy* (July 14, 1833). Evident in the initial step of this new movement was a distinct departure from much previous thought about the relationship of the church to the state. Keble strongly denounced Erastianism (control of the church by the state). This was also the theme that John Henry Newman soon picked up when he issued the first of the tracts. Keble's critical sermon was induced by the passage of the Irish Church Temporalities Act of 1833, which, as Keble interpreted it, suppressed ten bishoprics of the Established (Anglican) Church of Ireland. Keble reproved the flaccid churchmen, who were controlled by political power, for having sold out the English Church in Ireland. This emphasis evident in Keble at that time stressed the authenticity of the Anglican Church as the true church, which preserved the apostolic heritage, such as the Sacraments and apostolic succession, and which in its traditional liturgy preserved the bond with the Ancient Church. This emphasis on the bond with the Ancient Church was no doubt greatly amplified by the romanticist input of men like Samuel Taylor Coleridge (1772–1834), who had a great influence on Arnold, Maurice, John Henry Newman (1801–90), and others. Newman considered Coleridge one of the great precursors of the Oxford movement. The romanticism of Coleridge emphasized the organic nature of institutions like the Church. This gave a totally different perspective to the new view on the nature and polity of church power.

John Henry Newman was one of the most prominent men in the Oxford movement and wrote quite a number of the tracts. For quite a time, the position that was espoused and promulgated strongly emphasized the Church of England as a true branch of the apostolic Church. The Tractarians insisted that the nonconformists taught only a part of the truth and that Rome taught more than the truth. For some years, there were even rather direct criticisms of Rome expressed by participants in the Oxford movement. But a turning point came when Newman learned of the concept of development of Christian doctrine. He came to reason that the apostles had not elaborated on all the doctrines they had taught but that this was done gradually in the Roman Catholic tradition. By the time he wrote Tract 90, the last to be published, he could assert that the Thirty-Nine Articles—the main confession of the Anglican Church—were not inconsistent with Roman dogma. What the Anglican confession condemned, Newman asserted, was not Catholic doctrine as such, but the abuses of that doctrine. Thus Newman adopted a conciliatory stance to invocation of saints, to the teaching on purgatory, and to the whole Roman sacramental system. This last tract aroused a storm of criticism. This, and Newman's gradual shift to a very favorable view of Rome, moved him in 1845 to leave Anglicanism and join the Roman Catholic Church. Quite a number of others in the Oxford movement followed suit. Many held back, however, and Pusey felt hurt by Newman's move. This "return to Rome" is a mid-nineteenth-century phenomenon, manifestations of which one finds on the Continent as well as in America. But nowhere was it so dramatically and so forcefully carried out as in England. This also coincided with the papal reestablishment of the Roman Catholic presence in England after an interval of about four hundred years. All this brought with it a liturgical revival, reintroduction of more traditional vestments and liturgical appointments, and a revival of medieval customs such as the monastic life in the Anglican Church. Monastic communities for men as well as for women were established. Members engaged in missions and social welfare work. The Anglo-Catholic movement likewise had a heavy emphasis on social welfare work. All this no doubt provoked the Evangelicals to more vigor. People became more conscious of older practices of the Church, and this made certain reform measures possible.

The Roman Catholic hierarchy was reestablished in England in 1850. In 1851, the Parliament enacted the Ecclesiastical Titles Act, which prohibited Roman Catholic bishops from assuming territorial titles such as Anglican bishops had. But for the most part, the Catholic dioceses chose names and areas that did not coincide with existing Anglican dioceses. Westminster became the Catholic archdiocese with three provinces, Westminster, Liverpool, and Birmingham, and sixteen dioceses. But the Roman Catholic population in England remained small. In the mid-twentieth century, it was estimated at 3,227,000 members.

The Church in Ireland. The English view on the Irish Church problem in the nineteenth century mentioned above has been one of the most difficult problems for the British in modern times. One must remember that the Gaelic Irish have always been sensitive about their differences from the English. This was not lessened through the centuries as the British used one device or another to conquer and control the Irish. In Oliver Cromwell's time in the seventeenth century, the English had imposed a new Puritan landlord class on Ireland. By sheer weight of military conquest, the English simply confiscated much of the land they desired. But Ireland was not very docile, and there were always the French to lend a hand against their old enemies, the British. When the Stuart line of kings ended in 1688 in the Glorious Revolution, and William and Mary from Holland were invited by Parliament to rule England, the partisans of James II (called Jacobites) continued the agitation for revolution, with the aid of the French. But by the eighteenth century, when the Hanoverian line began to rule, Jacobite hopes began to fade.

The land tenure system in Ireland was the worst in Europe, and many Irish gentry abandoned the Emerald Isle to go to the Continent, perchance to find a position in the military service of some needy ruler. In the meantime, the poorer people were ruined by the heavy rents imposed in Ireland. There was little prospect for changing the system, since the government officials were responsible only to the government in London. However, toward the end of the eighteenth century, the strictures on Roman Catholics leasing or owning land were erased.

In the time of the French Revolution, the Irish began again to seek alliance with the French against the English, so the government came down hard on them. Tensions abounded in Ireland, but the government actually feared the Ulster Presbyterians more than it did the Roman Catholics in the south.

In 1800, a new arrangement was effected in the union of the United Kingdom and Ireland. Irish resistance was so strong, however, that Prime Minister William Pitt had to buy votes to get it passed by the Irish Parliament. But a vigorous popular movement continued in Ireland. In 1828, Daniel O'Connell stood for Parliament from one of the Irish counties and was elected despite the fact that the law in the United Kingdom stated no Roman Catholic could hold office. His election, in the context of the chronic tensions with Ireland, forced the British Parliament into the Emancipation Act of 1829, which lifted the strictures against Catholics.

In this persistent movement on the part of the Irish to gain more prerogatives at the expense of the British, people like Keble were very sensitive when the British Parliament began to face some aspects of reality in Ireland. The established church was the Anglican Church, which had all the rights and privileges. The Irish Church Temporalities Act of 1833, which provoked Keble's sermon of reproof, had tried to consolidate some of the bishoprics in the established church in Ireland.

In all of Ireland, there had been twenty-two bishoprics and 1,400 benefices, which served 850,000 Anglicans. Resentment and antagonism of the Roman Catholic majority was so intense that the Whigs, with Roman Catholic support, passed the Temporalities Act—the logical sequel to the Catholic Emancipation Act of 1829. In view of the overwhelming preponderance of Catholics, there was further need to trim the Anglican sails. The census of 1861 showed that of a population of 5,798,967, only 693,357 were in the established church, whereas 4,505,265 were Catholics. In 1869, Gladstone sponsored the Act of Disestablishment, which became law January 1, 1871.

But Ireland continued to be a problem for the British. When World War I broke out, the Irish again were intriguing with the enemies of Britain. After the war a new arrangement was effected, and in 1921, the Irish Free State was recognized, which was to have the same status in the British Empire as any dominion. The Irish kept on working toward a greater measure of autonomy, for it galled them to take the oath of allegiance to the British crown. By the 1940s they had worked out complete independence, and on December 21, 1948, the British Sovereign's ceremonial function of accrediting foreign diplomats for Ireland was transferred to the president of Ireland, Sean O'Kelly.

Northern Ireland was another matter. This tortured land had the choice of going along with the south in the Irish Free State after World War I, but chose not to do so. But there was never really any period when conditions were peacefully settled. The religious mix may explain most of the tensions, for the 1951 census showed that in Northern Ireland there were 471,460 Roman Catholics, 410,215 Presbyterians, 353,245 Church of Ireland members, 66,639 Methodists, and 69,362 people adhering to other churches.

Changes during the Twentieth Century. As the churches of England entered the period of the World Wars, the pattern presented many hues. There had been some very serious attempts to revive Christianity and its influence in society and even in world affairs. Some of the finest achievements of Christians in these areas were made by the British. But the attempts to revive the Church were so diverse and mutually antagonistic that friction wasted much of the reform energies. The Oxford movement, for example, was irreconcilably opposed to the Evangelical movement, and Anglicanism was unable to accept the Evangelicals, just as the liberals were unable to accept the Romanizing trend in Oxford. Furthermore, too many Englishmen were so content basking in the enjoyment of British imperial achievements that they failed to take adequate stock of the cataclysmic changes that were dumped on them in the World Wars. The twentieth-century catastrophes overwhelmed Great Britain just at the time when they were making daring new experiments in the sociopolitical sphere and when the Liberal Party, which at least stood for secular and humanistic reforms, was squeezed nearly to death by the new Labor Party.

The Anglican Church is still the established church, but it has lost much ground numerically. There has been massive secularization.

CONTINENTAL CHURCHES IN NINETEENTH-CENTURY EUROPE

So far, we have surveyed France, Germany, England, and the most significant Christian churches in them. But we need to take a broader look at the overall situation of the churches in other parts of Europe also. In modern times, Western Christianity was the most aggressive. For better or for worse, it was assumed to be setting the standards for world Christianity. We need, therefore, to accord it attention proportionate with its influence.

Roman Catholic Influence. France, as pointed out above, was predominantly Roman Catholic. Italy, Spain, Portugal, and Austria were also predominantly Roman Catholic. Italy, of course, was part of the heartland of the Roman Catholic Church. From early times, Rome was the residence of the popes. Two factors need special emphasis in this connection. From medieval times, the popes had acquired a major portion of central Italy as their own territory, which they ruled as secular rulers. This ecclesiastical dominance over a secular state reflected the papal doctrine of the two swords, or two powers, the spiritual and the temporal: the first controlled by the popes, the second exercised by the secular rulers who were to be subservient to the directives and the will of the papacy. In the practical world of politics, the popes often had to apply devious intrigues and even naked force to attain their objectives and to maintain their position and influence. In modern times, however, they seldom attained their ideal. With the rise of the modern states, papal power was even more overshadowed and frustrated.

As stated above, in France, the theory of Gallicanism had always advocated holding even papal ecclesiastical power at arm's length. And as far as the secular power of the papacy is concerned, the French had learned to show a great distaste for this—in fact, they shunned it like the plague. With the rise of Napoleon, the political dominated the ecclesiastical, and the popes fought for survival. When French armies invaded Rome the second time in February 1798, the pope was summarily deposed as a secular ruler, and the art treasures of the Vatican were plundered. In the several Italian republics that Napoleon set up, the wealth of the churches was used to prosecute the war and enhance secular power. At that time, the outlook for the Roman Catholic Church in Italy was bleak indeed. Pius VI, the aged pontiff, died in disgrace August 29, 1799. The prospects for his successor, Pius VII, at first looked no more promising. The election and the coronation of the new pope could not even be held in Rome. But when the Roman Republic collapsed due to French reverses, the pope was able to enter Rome. Before long, the pope reached a working agreement, called a concordat, with the French emperor, but the emperor held all the high cards and preserved for the secular government the prerogative to nominate all bishops and through them to control the whole hierarchy down to the parish priests. Accepting such a submissive role did not preserve the pope from further humiliation at the hands of Napoleon. The adamant attitude of the pope provoked Napoleon in 1808 to occupy Rome once more; soon thereafter, the Papal States were annexed to the French empire. Before Napoleon's fall, Pius VII had to endure many further indignities and insults. But after Napoleon's deposition and exile, the Papal States were restored. However, the glory had departed, and it was but half a century until the rising tide of nationalism in Italy once more challenged the power of the pope as a secular ruler.

But at a critical time before that, Ercole Consalvi (1757–1824) served as papal secretary of state. Consalvi was the chief engineer in negotiating the restoration of the Papal States in 1815, and he led the way in revising their administrative polity. This resulted in the promulgation of a *motu proprio* by Pius VII that served as a sort of constitution for the Papal States. This reduced some of the previous privileges of the elite, and laymen were given some role in the government. Some provision was also made for improvement of agriculture, police service, and other social programs.

Before we look at the complete loss of the Papal States, however, we need to put some other Roman Catholic countries into proper perspective.

A SURVEY OF CHURCHES FROM WEST TO EAST	
SPAIN	Government opposed French Revolution. France conquered Spain; persecuted clergy. Liberal movement developed, preserved the monarchy, secularized church property, outlawed the Inquisition. In 1820 half of monasteries closed; clergy fled the country. Struggle for the throne. 1876 constitution recognized Roman Catholicism but allowed toleration for others.
FRENCH PROTES- TANTS	French Revolution brought tolerance for Protestants but they were supervised by the state. English Methodism spread revival, leading to mission societies and YMCA. Alsace-Lorraine was ceded to Germany (1870), which included nearly all French-speaking Lutherans. French Reformed split into three different groups.
BELGIUM	Changed hands between Holland, Spain, and Austria. Protestant Dutch king became heavy-handed with Roman Catholics. Catholics, allied with liberals, rebelled against Dutch (1830) to found Belgium with freedom of worship.
HOLLAND	Reformed survived the Spanish Inquisition. Later divided by Rationalism, Confessionalism, and Pietism. After Napoleon, Dutch churches were state churches, but freedom of religion and worship were in constitution. Department of religious affairs supervised all Protestants.
NORWAY	Lutherans. United to Denmark until 1814, then ruled by Sweden. Bonds with Sweden dissolved in 1905. Pontopiddan produced a catechism; Hauge brought Pietistic revival. Gisle Johnson revitalized churches; Inner Mission (1855). Emphasis on lay involvement.
SWEDEN	Lutheran state church. Retained bishops. Influenced by German rationalism. Aulen and Nygren led to Motivforschung school, emphasizing dogmatic theology. Leaders in Lutheran World Federation. Rosenius developed Swedish Mission Covenant; pietistic. Members began leaving state church to form Free Churches. Temperance movement.
FINLAND	Lutherans. Governed by the Swedes. In 1809 Sweden ceded Finland to Russia. The Finns resisted Russian influence. Briefly independent after 1917 Russian Revolution. Like Swedes, influenced by both Rationalism and Pietism. State church remained Lutheran.
DENMARK	Lutheran state church influenced by rationalism and other movements. All citizens required to be baptized and confirmed. Peasants emancipated in 1788; private ownership of land. Mynster (1775–1854) went through changing religious views and influenced countrymen. Grundtvig (1783–1872) emphasized the Apostles' Creed as most important, above the Bible. Taught antinomian views.
ITALY	Politically divided in the 1850s. In 1861 Victor Emmanuel, king of Sardinia, became king of Italy, though French troops remained in Rome. When they left in 1870, Italian nationalists surrounded the Vatican, which reacted by establishing the doctrine of papal infallibility. The new Italian government established the Law of Guarantees for the papacy.

A SURVEY OF CHURCHES FROM WEST TO EAST	
AUSTRIA	Roman Catholic. Suppressed Protestants. Emperor Joseph II (1741–90) issued decree of toleration. Views at odds with Rome. Austria gained Italian territories. Revolution of 1848 caused government to make concessions to the Rome, which exercised increasing influence, though Protestants also received new freedoms.
POLAND	Mostly Roman Catholic. Divided among Russia, Prussia, and Austria at end of eighteenth century.
BAVARIA	Roman Catholic. Concordat with papacy in 1817. Revolution of 1848 caused some clergy to seek democratic reforms, marriage for priests, and selection of priests by congregations. Papacy intervened to appoint Ketteler as bishop (1850) and affirm traditional views, though Ketteler and August Reichensperger addressed social problems too.
PRUSSIA	Protestant rulers; Catholic minority. Tensions over appointment of bishops and Roman Catholic influences.
EASTERN EUROPEAN COUNTRIES AND TERRITORIES	Estonia and Latvia, Lutheran. Lithuania, Roman Catholic. Balkans were largely Eastern Orthodox with western churches represented; tensions with Muslim Turks. Serbs rebelled against Turks; Serbian Church granted autonomy in 1831. Greece revolted against Turks in 1820s. Patriarch and 30,000 others murdered. Greek Parliament declared Greek Church autonomous. Reconciled to Constantinople in 1863. Bulgaria sought freedom from Turks and from Constantinople; gained in 1878. Romanians did likewise in 1859.
RUSSIA	Orthodox since AD 1000. Czarist government came to dominate church matters. Division of Old Believers in seventeenth century due to dispute over ritual. Church resisted Peter the Great's westernization. Unrest in nineteenth century; Napoleonic invasion. After Napoleon's defeat, Czar gained influence in western affairs. Heroic devotion of Serafim of Sarov (1759–1832) inspired people. German philosophy influenced Chernyshevsky (1828–89), who urged reforms. Moscow viewed as third/new Rome up to Revolution of 1917.

Challenges in the Nineteenth Century. Once the French Revolution had been put down and Napoleon exiled, the nineteenth century seemed to be an era of peace. But the revolution had not been defused. The complex drives in human society searching for freedom and recognition were not squelched, but only suppressed. Though no war erupted involving all major European powers, such as typified the eighteenth century, there were some rather sharp political and military earthquakes. The Revolution of 1848 has been alluded to a number of times. It was, for the most part, a failure. People did not succeed in obtaining their full objectives, though in many cases, limited partial goals were reached. For example, Hungarians fought tooth and nail for freedom from the Hapsburgs and lost, but before long, the Hapsburgs were compelled to make a modicum of concessions and set up the dual monarchy of Austria-Hungary. In Germany, the national aspirations of the people had been frustrated and most hopes remained unfulfilled in 1848, but the people obtained some lesser concessions. Through it all, the unification of Germany, which was one of the major objectives of the revolutionaries, proceeded. This was not in a democratic but in an autocratic manner, when the Hohenzollern rulers of Prussia managed to scramble to the top of the political heap, largely with the aid of Chancellor Bismarck, and became German emperors. Many Germans, repelled by Prussian high-handed approaches in church affairs, were very antagonistic to the emperors. This was a major factor in the restless situation in German Protestant churches in the nineteenth century.

Each of the developments mentioned above had a domino effect, some of them even on distant parts of the world. The Revolution of 1848, for example—really a series of revolts in France, Germany, Italy, and Austria—produced an enormously vigorous anti-Christian movement in Europe, especially forceful in Germany. In France, it was sublimated to nationalistic chauvinism and imperialism. In Britain, no revolution took place, but the basic ingredients for it had nonetheless been present. Though not in quite as explosive a mix as in other countries, the anti-Christian reaction was visible also, though accompanied by less advocacy of violence than on the Continent.

The unification of the German empire under Prussia had the same domino effect. Prussia had to defeat Austria as the leading political and military power in central Europe. This they achieved in the Seven Weeks' War in 1866. Austria had controlled most of northern Italy. Now that hold was broken, and the Italian unification movement was made possible. This in turn played havoc with the Roman Catholic Church, which then provoked the most reactionary theological response from Rome. This culminated in a very hard line against all new "isms" and in the dogma of papal infallibility.

The Italian Revolution of 1848 and the Italian unification movement of the 1860s severely rocked Italy, which had been divided into many separate states without even a pro forma nominal empire, such as existed in Germany. The northern part of Italy was annexed by Austria, and some other states in Italy were also controlled by the Austrians. In the south, almost half of the Italian peninsula plus the island of Sicily comprised the Kingdom of the Two Sicilies. North of that was the main center portion, the Papal States. In the northwest, the main territory was the Kingdom of Piedmont. When the tide of revolution swept over Europe in 1848, it also affected Italy. One party, called neo-Guelfs, was headed by a priest who called for a coalition of the pope and Piedmont to enable Italy to free itself from the Germans and Austrians. Another party, headed by Mazzini, called for the unification of all of Italy as a secular, nonecclesiastical state. When the actual revolt broke out in January 1848, King Charles Albert of the Piedmont, Pope Pius IX, and others made minor liberalizing concessions; this aroused unwarranted expectations for more reforms. But the Hapsburgs were already involved in putting down the revolt and drew in France on their side to help squelch it. Though Pius IX declared that he was equally concerned with all people and withdrew his troops from the fighting against the Austrians and the French, the political and secular involvement of the pope smacked too much of medieval times when the papacy claimed to wield both swords. The Austrians put down the uprising by July 1848. But in November, the radicals in Rome rose in revolt again, and the pope had to flee for his life.

DEVELOPMENT OF MODERN THEOLOGY

In the nineteenth and twentieth centuries, the German-speaking regions of Europe raised up the most influential theologians, as will be evident in this chapter. A number of factors contribute to this dominance of German thinkers in theology. Germans were a more populous people in central Europe, dwelling from Switzerland in the south and west to East Prussia (Lithuania) in the north and east. The nations where the Germans lived offered university training and economic developments that allowed for advanced theological study and publication. Germany was likewise the homeland of the largest Protestant denominational family (Lutherans) as well as a great number of Roman Catholic, Reformed, and also Anabaptist Christians. All these circumstances guaranteed close interaction between the different western Christian traditions, whose dialogues affected fellow churchmen more broadly in Europe and around the world, especially when great numbers of Germans emigrated from their homelands to North America, South America, Australia, and Russia.

The dominance of German thinkers in theology is less likely to continue in the future. While the churches of Western Europe are experiencing decline, churches of the southern hemisphere are experiencing remarkable growth. The English, Spanish, and Chinese languages are increasingly used for international business, which means that far more Christians are studying and using those languages than German. It is not yet possible to determine who the next most influential theologians will be and where they will arise. But Germany's dominance in the nineteenth and twentieth centuries is likely to wane.

Søren Kierkegaard. Søren Kierkegaard (1813–55) was a Danish theologian who departed from traditional confessional Lutheranism to develop a unique theology. His lack of popularity in his own country in his own lifetime would indicate that he get hardly a mention in any modern church history. But troubled souls rediscovered and popularized him early in the twentieth century.

Kierkegaard grew up in Copenhagen, where his whole family belonged to the congregation of which Jakob Peter Mynster was pastor. Kierkegaard was capable of extreme emotions—from severe melancholy to great merriment. He was somewhat of a confidant of his father, who himself had experienced extremes in his own life and had come from abject loneliness in utter poverty to affluence and comfort, retiring at forty.

At one time, Kierkegaard's father divulged to the son a serious transgression that weighed on him, and, as a result, the son suffered a traumatic experience. Soon thereafter, a number of the Kierkegaard children and their mother died, and the father was plunged into deep depression. The son gave himself over to such reckless dissipation that he lived in agonizing remorse ever after. In the midst of this, he discovered

INFLUENTIAL FIGURES IN MODERN THEOLOGY		
	EVENTS	OUTCOMES
SØREN KIERKEG-AARD (1813–55)	Danish theologian, reared under Pastor J. P. Mynster. Subject to extremes in emotion. Father's failings troubled him. Refused to commune at state church; troubled by failure of organized Christianity.	Little regarded during his life, now regarded as founder of existentialism due to his influential writings. Stressed need to choose between Christ and the world; takes "leap of faith."
ALBRECHT RITSCHL (1822–89)	Professor at Goettingen. Reacted against materialism and philosophical trends. Emphasized the will and the practical and ethical dimensions of religion. Historical Jesus as prototype.	Focused on justification, reconciliation, and love. Love would bring about the kingdom of God. His approach became known as culture-Protestantism.
ADOLPH HARNACK (1851–1930)	Admired Ritschl. Wrote impressive history of dogma, fulfilling aspirations of Tuebingen school. Gospel must be stripped of dogmatic accretions to reach the pure faith.	Wrote widely read *What is Christianity?* (1900). Jesus was not the Gospel but its messenger—without miracles, revelation, or redemption.
ERNST TROELTSCH (1865–1923)	Studied under Ritschl. Investigated social teachings of Christians (churches, sects, and mystics). Lutheran Church underdeveloped; Calvinism more developed.	Christianity developed from its social and cultural setting; represented the highest development in religion for Westerners.

great joy when he came to realize that God is love, after all. While he was enjoying an emotional recovery, he resumed the study of theology and became engaged to be married. But suddenly, he relapsed into despair and broke off the engagement. When he died in 1855, he refused the Lord's Supper from a pastor of the state church, since he denounced this church as the enemy of real Christianity.

The despair, pessimism, emotional subjectivism, and enormous self-preoccupation of Kierkegaard were all traits with which later generations of Christians could empathize since they, too, became troubled by the failure of organized Christianity to provide meaningful answers to the world's ills. Kierkegaard's admirers later made these traits the main ingredients of existentialism. (This philosophical school focuses on the individual's experience of existence rather than objective analysis. It includes themes of freedom, choice, human frailty, and responsibility toward others who share human existence.) Kierkegaard was crowned posthumously as the founder of the existentialist school. He wrote prodigiously. His best-known work is probably *Either/Or* (1843), in which he stresses that each individual is confronted with the necessity of making a choice between Christ and the world. If one chooses a life of pleasure, Kierkegaard could say from personal experience, he or she will be haunted by despair or dread (angst, as he expressed it in *The Concept of Dread*; 1844). A person torn by this predicament must make the decision to take the "leap to faith." But this is a purely subjectivistic experience. One critic of Kierkegaard's thought, Hannah Arendt, no great proponent of confessional Christianity, finds the leap as she understands it—a leap from doubt into a vacuum—meaningless, simply injecting subjectivistic irrationalism into religion.

But there is an emphasis in Kierkegaard that must be taken seriously, namely his criticism of the organized church. There was no doubt a powerful provocation for this caustic criticism. The organized, official church, Kierkegaard felt, was anti-Christian. As much as this criticism needed to be made, coming from an erratic man with extremes of emotions, the criticism was rejected as coming from a madman. It was rejected until the mad, irrational twentieth century, when kindred spirits viewed Kierkegaard as a new leader in Christian thought. But as much as organized Christianity deserved this criticism, the criticism suffers weaknesses, because it is radically individualistic. It is only in community, people upholding and supporting one another—Christians call it koinonia—that the glaring deficiencies of organized religion can be countered.

German Movements. In the English context, we noted in previous chapters how aggressively the politicoeconomic philosophy of laissez-faire and of individual competition imposed itself on English thought, so much so that this became a religion for some people. Worse yet, Christians who by choice wanted to stay in the Church and maintain their Christian heritage adopted this kind of secularist philosophy and confused it with biblical theology and divine revelation, to the point that they could not distinguish the two.

And we surveyed the situation in Germany, with special emphasis on early nineteenth-century theological developments that brought about a new environment in which the churches had to find a new viable existence. In the case of Germany, as in France, it is important to keep the political situation in mind. It is human nature to react against such situations, and this interaction often gives rise to new directions and new emphases in the intellectual and the religious areas. In Germany, for example, we noted that philosophers of the idealist school, such as Kant and Hegel, were alarmed at the rational thought that had drifted in from England and France and flourished also in their own country. This had raised questions even about the existence of God and had challenged the very foundations of the Christian faith. The idealist philosophers, to put it simply, tried to rescue the existence of God. Kant had been probably less sanguine about the success of their enterprise, but he had emphasized that even though the very nature of man may preclude the possibility of knowing God as He really is, man has the moral imperative to live according to the commonly accepted ethical norms. Hegel was more ephemeral, explaining that God did indeed exist, for He was primary reality by very definition; God was pure idea, in which the material realities of the created world first were generated.

But this kind of speculative defense for the existence of God and the certainty of the Christian faith really did God and His Church a disservice, because it left people with the notion that we would have a certain hold on God if we contained Him in the limits of the activity of the human mind.

For some Germans, this was altogether too abstruse and too cerebral. They preferred to emphasize that religion had another dimension: that of the heart, of human feelings and emotions. The romanticist school, under leadership of men such as Herder, caused further questions in the teachings of the churches. In one way or another, Herder foreshadowed most of the ingredients of modern theology. Schleiermacher further advanced the importance of subjective feeling in religion when he stressed that religion was basically man's feeling of dependence on a transcendence. It is very significant that Schleiermacher, like Herder before him, speaks much more often of religion than of Christian theology. They did not deliberately despise the word *theology* and its content, but their thinking had become so subjectivistic that they no longer thought as much about the revealed body of divine truth (theology) as of man's efforts to search for God in his own way (religion). This already was a significant shift in attitude. It was Paul Lagarde who in 1873 insisted that theology should be changed into a science of religion. But he was at first a lone voice calling for this romantic shift. When comparative religion became more influential, it carried the day. This shift from "theology" to "religion" is also due to the growing aversion against systematic theology and dogmatics. This was partly because many scholars had come to the conclusion that dogma had developed in history and was not embedded and contained in the revealed Word of God. This shift was partly to be in opposition against any kind of authority advanced by the new theology.

There were significant developments in the terminology that the professional teachers in Germany used. They taught religion, like Schleiermacher, or religious philosophy, like Hegel, rather than theology. The concept of development (*Entwicklung*) takes on an ever greater significance. Herder had been interested in the phenomenon of the development of religious ideas in human society. Hegel constantly used the term to express the process of the world spirit reaching upward to its source, God, in ever more effective ways. Thus, he viewed the whole gamut of the development of human intellectual and religious life. In medieval times, men were less advanced and needed more of the sensate supports that they found in the Medieval Church. Man in modern times was able to dispense with those crutches and stand firmly in a purely intellectual religion, like Protestantism. In the same line of reasoning, Hegel could expound his claim that philosophy was a higher exercise than religion because it was a further development in the progression of the world spirit away from the sensate to the pure ideal.

This concept of development underlies the notion that human history generally has been a steady progression to higher levels of human attainment. The idea of progress, in fact, is built into the theory of evolution as one of its most essential ingredients.

The notion of progress as a necessary phenomenon in human history soon became the core of some new systems of thought, especially in the purely secular or non-Christian domain. For example, Auguste Comte (1798–1857), a French thinker, remembered especially as the father of the science of sociology, pictured the whole of human history as consisting of three eras. The first was the theological, in which men still thought there were gods of which man had to stand in fear. The second was the metaphysical, in which philosophy was dominant. The transition to this era, Comte thought, was seen already in the Greek philosophers, such as Socrates, who lived in a society that accepted the notion of gods, but who themselves seriously questioned those religious notions on the basis of philosophy. The third era was the era of science. That was the era which Comte thought he himself was bringing in more fully in modern Europe. When science once took over, man could safely discard the old notions of deities. He could also supersede his reliance on speculative philosophy.

Once this supposition was more fully applied to the study of religion, a whole new school developed, the history of religion school, or, as the Germans called it, the *Religionsgeschichtliche Schule*. This school of thought accepted an assortment of presuppositions of previous thinkers: the rationalist charge that the Scriptures were unreliable accounts, the emphasis on religion versus revealed theology, the idea of progress in human history, and the claims of modern science. Out of this, they wove a pattern of thought according to which the people in ancient times simply did not have the capacity to explain religious phenomena because their own weltanschauung, or cosmology, was prescientific. The strange phenomena that they could not understand they then explained as supernatural. These imprecise verbalizations then comprise what we call myth. The term *myth* had been used by both secular and religious writers, but Johann Gottfried Eichhorn (1752–1827) and Johann Philipp Gabler (1753–1826) first applied it in their critical study of the Old Testament. Eichhorn's *Introduction to the Old Testament* (1783) is a significant turning point. When Gabler, a decade later, edited Eichhorn's *Urgeschichte*, he precipitated a real cleavage between the theology of the Church as based on the revealed Word of God and scientific enlightenment, as he proposed it, to clear up the problem of myth in the Bible. Eichhorn explained myth as the sagas of the ancient world expressed in the limited thought-form and language of that time.

Gabler states that if the development of the human understanding progresses step by step, then divine revelation must go the same course. Divine revelation indeed did reveal many a truth that the human genius would have discovered by itself eventually. But when these were revealed, it was only in the form that was suitable for the time. Thus, one can understand the different religious systems of the world. Truth itself is eternal, but the form in which it comes to us is constantly changing. This separation of the truth itself and the form in which it comes is a real Kantianism. One of the very subtle but significant semantic shifts that Eichhorn gave to his students was that he no longer took "revelation" to mean what it used to mean, namely, God showing forth and uncovering some aspect of the divine mystery of salvation to prophets or apostles for the purpose of proclaiming it to God's people for their understanding and also for the purpose of recording this knowledge for future generations. Eichhorn took the word to refer to the process of enlightenment of the human understanding. In general, every idea man has really comes from God,

Eichhorn asserted. But when man attains a particularly brilliant insight, he thinks it is special revelation from God.

As Hans-Joachim Kraus puts it, all adherents of the history of religion school hold that revelation is a phenomenon that is manifest in most religions and is provided to explain the causes of cultic, mythical, and moral ideas ordered by a deity.

The view of myth in non-Christian religions is what produced the chief appeal for the history of religion school. Others soon picked up this intriguing speculation from Eichhorn. The first organized attempt to pursue this further was made at the University of Goettingen. Wilhelm Wrede (1859–1906), Wilhelm Bousset (1865–1920), and Herman Gunkel (1862–1932) became famous for their part in this enterprise. This first materialized as an identifiable school of thought and theology in the last years of the nineteenth century. But the main pieces were already scattered about a century earlier, and many individuals added their little building blocks to the structure.

The *Syllabus of Errors*. Changes that affected Protestant thinkers likewise affected Roman Catholic thinkers. This concerned more conservative church leaders. For Pope Pius IX, his confrontations with Italian revolutionaries such as Mazzina and Garibaldi and his observations of other countries brought him to the conclusion that he had to develop a strong stance. Aggressive papal pronouncements were not unheard of; in 1854 he had established the dogma of the immaculate conception by papal pronouncement. On December 8, 1864, the tenth anniversary of the dogma, he issued the encyclical *Quanta cura*. This was accompanied by a document soon to become famous, the *Syllabus of Errors*. The nature of this document was unusual. It consisted of a summary and digest of papal statements in various earlier documents. The syllabus did not carry the signature of the pope, but the nature of it was definitely official.

The syllabus first denounced and rejected gross departures from biblical theology, such as pantheism, nationalism, and coarse rationalism. Even Protestants could sympathize with this part. Then some of the more subtle problems of the day were taken up. The Church's duty to pass judgment on secular philosophies was emphasized. The idea that papal decrees could impede the free progress of knowledge was rejected. The validity of Scholasticism was reaffirmed. The syllabus rejected the idea that there should be freedom of religion, and it denied the possibility that men might find salvation in any other church. It denounced in one breath Socialism, Communism, secret societies, and Bible societies as "pests" that must be avoided.

A hundred years and more after the syllabus was issued, many people even in the Roman Catholic Church wish it had never seen the light of day. Many "issues" condemned in it were fearsome specters (like Communism). But these very movements showed that there was something radically wrong in human society that they tried to counter. Pius IX perhaps did not understand that modern yearning for freedom was provoked in part by authoritarianism, of which the Roman Catholic Church was seen to be a part. Man needs authority, especially in religion and ethics. But authority can be arbitrarily abused. Critics of the *Syllabus* concluded that what Pius IX prescribed for the cure was more of the disease that had caused the symptoms in the first place.

Vatican I. Once the papacy was on a determined reactionary course, and once the provocations that put it on this course became ever more raucous, there was no turning back. Vatican Council I was convened under Pius IX. When one remembers that, according to the Roman Catholic authorities on their own councils, this was only the twentieth council in nineteen centuries and that since the Council of Trent in the sixteenth century no other council had been called, the significance of Vatican I becomes clear.

The council convened on the Feast of the Immaculate Conception, December 8, 1869, just fifteen years after the promulgation of the dogma. The council continued through the fall of 1870, the very time when French power collapsed, Rome was occupied by unfriendly troops, and German superiority in Europe was forcefully reiterated. The *Constitution on the Church* reaffirmed the primacy of Peter and the bishops of Rome as his successors. Then followed the conclusion that all faithful Christians in the world must concur with the Roman Catholics that the Roman Catholic Church, with the pope as its head, has power over all other churches. This idea included the assertion of papal infallibility when the *Constitution* stated that the see of Peter had remained free of error and that it was a divinely revealed truth that the pope when speaking ex cathedra, that is, when speaking officially as pastor and teacher and when he defines a doctrine, is in possession of divine infallibility.

This question of infallibility provoked serious dissent among the bishops of the Roman Catholic Church attending the council. There were 744 bishops enrolled at the peak attendance. A preliminary vote indicated that about three-quarters would vote in favor of the decree, eighty-eight were strongly opposed to it, and sixty-two approved, but with reservations. Most of those who were opposed, however, absented themselves when the official vote was taken, and thus the majority in favor looked overwhelming. It was significant that the pope introduced all decrees to be dealt with, whereas in Roman Catholic tradition, the council introduced decrees. Thus collegiality was out of style; papal autocracy was undisguised. This drew serious criticism, resulting in a split in the Roman Catholic Church, for it led to the formation of the Old Catholic Church. The bishops who most seriously opposed papal infallibility were French and German. One top German Roman Catholic scholar and bishop, Karl Josef von Hefele (1809–93), hesitated to publish the decree in his diocese and did not do so until April 1871. Sharp dissent came also from Johann Ignaz von Doellinger (1799–1890), a top scholar and churchman at the University of Munich. Under a pseudonym, he had issued a serious criticism of infallibility before the council had convened. Doellinger was excommunicated by his archbishop after the recessing of the council when he declined to accept the dogma of infallibility.

The Old Catholic movement in Germany conducted an organizing meeting August 27, 1870, under the leadership of Doellinger. Mostly professors from Roman

Catholic universities were in attendance. Later, 1,359 laymen met and stated that they did not accept the decree concerning the absolute power and infallibility of the pope. Within a few years, the theologians and laymen got together and established the Old Catholic Church, recognized officially by the German imperial government in 1873. A bishop was elected by the church and consecrated by the Jansenist bishop of Deventer (Holland). The *Kulturkampf*—the fight for cultural dominance in Germany—provided sympathy and support for the Old Catholic Movement. The Old Catholic Church adhered to much of Roman Catholic theology, except that it opposed the papal dogma of 1870 and generally eased some of the strict controls and the clericalism of the Roman Catholic Church. For example, auricular confession was made voluntary and laymen again received a part of the administration of church affairs. Pastors also were again chosen by the congregations.

The hard line of Vatican I and long-smoldering tensions between the Roman Catholics and the German government touched off the *Kulturkampf.* This struggle with the Roman Catholics is the one engagement that Bismarck, the Iron Chancellor, lost. The struggle was building up since Vatican I, and in 1873, Rudolph Virchow applied the term *Kulturkampf* to it. Though the precise meaning was challenged, the purpose was clear. Bismarck intended to take political countermeasures against the political results of the papal dogma of infallibility.

There was also the problem of the concern that Catholics in the new German empire would use obstructionist tactics against the government. Much of the concern dealt with Polish Catholics in the German Empire. Bismarck was also concerned that the aggressive stance of the papacy would make the incorporation of southern German states difficult.

Earlier, allegations surfaced that Roman Catholics in positions of power, including some Jesuits, had been pulling political strings ever since Prussia defeated Austria in 1866, which action had resulted in very unfavorable chain reactions for the papacy in Italy. Influential Roman Catholics were urging France to avenge the insult and smite Germany. French policy at that time was very aggressively imperialistic, and the French government might use religious causes for its own purposes. But German military victory in the Franco-Prussian War upset French plans. German leadership then lashed back against the Roman Catholic influence. First of all, the political authorities tried to prevent the official proclamation of the decree of papal infallibility. The German government also tried to force Roman Catholic bishops to keep the Old Catholics in the schools. Besides, Bismarck was concerned about the internal influence of the Roman Catholic Center Party in domestic politics. Until 1870, he tried to work with this party, but opposition from the staunchly Catholic Poles living in Posen and Prussia against Prussian state policy turned Bismarck against the Center Party and against the Roman Catholic Church. Within the Center Party were many radical Catholics and ultramontanists, whom Bismarck considered a most immediate threat. By royal decree on July 8, 1871, the Catholic section of the Ministry of Religious Affairs was abolished on the grounds that it was meddling in the Polish question. Later in 1871, a law was passed prohibiting clergy from discussing political questions from the pulpit. In 1872, the German government began the process of bringing all church schools under the direct control of the government department of education. But the Center Party was gaining in political influence.

In May 1872, the pope rejected the ambassador whom Bismarck was going to appoint to the curia, Gustav Cardinal Hohenlohe, a prominent German churchman who was a thorn in the side of the pope and a friend of Doellinger. This action moved Bismarck to ban the Jesuits and several other orders from Germany. Several times, Pius IX issued very tart denunciations of Bismarck. In 1873, the German government changed its constitution to provide for state control over the education of the clergy and over their appointment and dismissal. Then the May Laws were enacted, which comprise the crescendo of the whole movement. These spelled out government control of the education, examination, and certification of the clergy, the right of the state to veto any unacceptable clergy appointments, and the superiority of the civil courts over those of the church.

But Roman Catholics were making headway in the political area, and Bismarck saw that he could not win a long, drawn-out showdown with the Catholic Church. The Catholics whom he had imprisoned were considered martyrs. Even the non-Catholic Prussian Conservatives, mostly Lutherans, began to look askance at the harsh measures taken by the government. Thus, before the decade was over, Bismarck had to back down, and the *Kulturkampf* came to an inglorious end.

In Switzerland also there was a protest movement in opposition to Vatican I called the Christian Catholic Church of Switzerland. In Austria, a similar movement began with five priests in 1880 after years of government opposition. This grew to about sixty clergy by 1900, with over sixteen thousand members.

In America, the Independent (Polish) Catholic Church, a similar development, numbered twenty-two priests and eighty thousand members in 1902. Some other Roman Catholic splinter groups could also be called Old Catholic.

Liberal Catholicism. Some historians date the beginning of liberal Catholicism to Lamennais's *Des progrès de la Révolution et de la guerre contre l'Église* (1829) and the attempt of Lamennais and his friends Lacordaire (1802–61) and Montalembert (1810–70) to identify with the revolution of 1830 under the motto "God and liberty." The papal encyclical *Mirari vos*, mentioned in chapter 38, condemned this position. Liberals were again put down in the 1860s by the *Syllabus of Errors*. When Pius IX prepared to convene Vatican I, liberal Catholics rejoiced because they thought the pope wanted to correct the bad impression he had made with the *Syllabus of Errors*. They were utterly surprised to find that the opposite was the case.

Despite the heavy reaction in the theology of Vatican I, the liberals were not dead. They worked at the broadening of the education laws in France, and a law of 1875 made possible the establishment of Catholic universities. The Institute Catholique in Paris turned out to be a key institution for liberal Roman Catholic theology, which in its later French form is labeled as modernism. But it must be noted that liberal Roman Catholic theology called modernism is not the same as liberal theology in the Protestant tradition. There are similarities, but the reader is advised to note the differences as these are unfolded below.

Catholic liberalism developed in Germany before it did in France and England. A Catholic school of theology existed at the University of Tuebingen since 1817, with J. A. Moehler (1796–1838) the most important theologian. This school was very similar to the Schleiermacher school in Protestantism, though some Roman Catholic theologians felt that Schleiermacher's doctrine of revelation left no room for a unique, historical revelation in Christ. This Roman Catholic theology approved of Lessing and his notion of a continuous process of revelation in the maturation of the human race. This German school of liberal Roman Catholic theology probably did not influence later Frenchmen very much for various reasons. Before the middle of the century, already Doellinger and the University of Munich began to overshadow Tuebingen. Doellinger, however, is known as an opponent of ultramontanism rather than as a liberal. When Doellinger organized a congress of Roman Catholic scholars at Munich in 1863, it seemed as if liberalism would become an integral part of this antiultramontanism, since Doellinger took a position that was very critical of Roman Catholic Scholastic theology.

Doellinger's ideas were also transmitted to England through a student at Marburg, John Emerich Edward Dahlberg, otherwise known as Sir John Acton (1834–1902), the later Lord Acton, famous historian and scholar. Acton defended free scientific research and historical criticism. He held, however, that there was a difference between the infallible defined dogmas of the Church and the rest of the Church's teachings, which were in a state of change. Acton explained that in the Roman Catholic Church, faith rested on the living tradition of the Church, whereas Protestantism had tried to shift the foundations to the infallibility of the Scriptures, which now posed an insuperable difficulty for Protestants.

These earlier Roman Catholic liberals may not have had a direct influence on the movement known as modernism in France. The Frenchman Alfred Loisy (1857–1940) was a pioneer in this. After preparing for the priesthood, he studied biblical criticism at the Institute Catholique in Paris under Louis Duchesne (1843–1922), the famous historian. Later he also studied under Ernest Renan (1823–92) at the College de France. Renan had written a derogatory life of Christ. In 1890, Loisy became a professor at the Institute Catholique. When Renan died in 1892, the head of the Institute Catholique, Maurice Le Sage d'Hauteroche d'Hulst, wrote a fairly favorable obituary article calling for a frank discussion of "the biblical problem." The conservatives in the Roman Catholic Church were very alarmed, and in November 1893, the encyclical *Providentissimus Deus* was issued, which denounced biblical criticism. In unrelated action by the curia, Loisy was demoted, but not destroyed. A few years later he issued *L'Evangile et l'Église,* basically a critique of Harnack's *Das Wesen des Christentums.* Loisy's position was much more church-oriented than Harnack's liberal theology, but Loisy called for a different kind of Gospel exegesis as well as a reform of the polity of the Church. Thus, his views precipitated a severe crisis in Roman Catholicism. Although Loisy tried to deflect the criticism against his critical scholarship in a later volume, he posited two kinds of truth, that of church dogma and that of the judgment of faith. Before the end of 1903, five of Loisy's books were put on the Index of Forbidden Books. When Loisy was threatened with excommunication, he issued an equivocal retraction, which, however, failed to satisfy the curia. It is quite possible that the papacy would have taken more direct action sooner if the matter of the disestablishment of the French Church had not preoccupied it.

The tensions in France on political and religious questions were building up at the turn of the century. In the 1890s in the Dreyfus affair, the intrigues of the clerical party, in league with the military generals, became generally evident. They stood for superpatriotism, or one could say chauvinism, which would have excluded all Jews, Protestants, and liberals from France. This hard line came to be called nationalism. When the fabricated and forged charges against Dreyfus were exposed, the colonel who had drawn them up for the General Staff committed suicide in prison. The moderates in France were convinced that the Roman Catholic regular clergy were trying to set up an ultramontane government in France. In retaliation, the government began to move against the religious associations and enacted the law for freedom of association in 1902. The chagrined monks were hoping to get the curia to bring about a rupture with France. When the relatively moderate Pope Leo XIII died and the uncompromising Pius X became pope, a crisis was precipitated. President Loubet of France visited the king of Italy in April 1904. The pope protested this in a public critique that the French considered quite insulting. The Socialist Party in Parliament thereupon demanded reprisals against the pope. This hurried along the disestablishment of the Roman Catholic Church in France, enacted into law in 1905. The pope took this as an insult and called on all good Catholics in France to consider this law null and void. Obviously, while these tensions were unfolding, the curia was prevented from looking after the problem of French modernists.

If the pope thought the French problem would go away if it were ignored long enough, he did not count on the Roman Catholics in England also developing problems at the same time. There, the Jesuit George Tyrrell (1861–1909) as well as Baron von Huegel became involved with the Roman Catholic hierarchy in similar questions. Von Huegel has been dubbed the lay bishop of modernism, but he was not as controversial as some of the clergy leaders were.

On July 3, 1907, the decree *Lamentabili* was issued by the Roman curia against the modernist errors, and on March 8, 1908, Loisy was excommunicated. The pope listed sixty-five propositions, most of them directed against Loisy, a few of them against Tyrrell, covering questions such as the Church's authority in biblical interpretation, inspiration of the Bible, historicity of the Gospels, divine revelation, and various aspects of Christology. On September 8, 1907, the pope issued the encyclical *Pascendi*, which tried further to summarize and identify what the previous decree had simply labeled as "errors." In this encyclical, modernism was labeled as the synthesis of all heresies. It also prescribed disciplinary measures to be observed in the training of the clergy and in censorship of works of theology intended for publication.

A short time after that, Pius X issued the *motu proprio Sacrorum antistitum*, usually called the Oath against Modernism, required of all clergy and professors in the Roman Catholic Church at their ordination or installation. This oath requires candidates for positions to reaffirm the official Roman Catholic position on points of dogma challenged by the modernists, and it includes the formal acceptance of *Lamentabili* and *Pascendi*, with special emphasis on their rejection of the difference between dogma and history.

In France, modernism was pretty well smothered by the strong papal interdiction. Loisy was excommunicated in 1908. Tyrrell had issued caustic criticisms of the papal action and was excommunicated already in 1907, but was not secularized. In all, about thirty priests left the Church in the modernist controversy. But the Roman Catholic Church was not cleansed. This new theology was soon to manifest itself again.

Historical Criticism. Having surveyed major thinkers and events in Roman Catholicism and Protestantism, it will be helpful to look more closely at two particular schools of thought and offer some critique based on subsequent studies. In Protestant circles, there were no church-wide heresy suppression mechanisms such as the papacy commanded, and thus the new theology could develop more rapidly. If one were to try to find the overarching descriptive for modern theology under which most of its aspects could be subsumed, it would be the term *historical criticism*. Although the history of religion school is usually not considered an integral part of this, it was definitely ancillary to it. But there is much more to it than that.

If we consider first of all the word *criticism*, we can see what one main emphasis of the new theology was. Literary criticism is considered to be a chief part of historical criticism. This is the discipline that critically examines the text of the sacred writings in order to determine which part may be authentic and which may not be so.

One needs to distinguish carefully here between lower criticism and higher criticism. Lower criticism was always practiced by serious theologians, especially in modern times when study of the manuscripts of the books of the Bible was begun through the work of Reformation era scholars like Erasmus and Reuchlin. Scholars of that time accepted implicitly the internal claim of the Scriptures that they consisted of revelation that God had given to the prophets and apostles and that this revelation was written down for posterity by those prophets and by those apostles under the inspiration of the Holy Spirit. Since the original documents written by them were no longer extant, it was necessary for scholars critically to examine the copies in order to ascertain which were most likely the most identical with the originals. This exercise was called lower criticism.

However, when scholars began to use their critical judgment as to what parts of the ancient manuscripts they were willing to accept as being of prophetic and apostolic authorship, the new discipline of higher criticism was born. Eichhorn used the term to describe what he was doing. When he tried by means of literary criticism to prune away from the Old Testament record what he considered unauthentic, he was practicing higher criticism. Scholars used semantics, etymology, and other linguistic disciplines to engage in higher criticism. One avenue of their studies led to the conclusion that the Old Testament books of Moses were of multiple authorship since different terms are used for God, and for other reasons. Thus there were *J* sections using Jahweh, *E* sections using Elohim, and there were also sections obviously edited by a redactor, which they called *D* section for Deuteronomist, and priestly sections were *P*. These methods of criticism involved much speculation and were subject to the changing interests of the scholars.

Literary criticism is still emphasized, but the twentieth-century Bible critics have found it somewhat inadequate because it did not pay attention to further facets of Bible criticism that scholars discovered more recently. These are chiefly the form or genre of the ancient literature, and the way they thought it was transmitted when it was allegedly in oral form. This latter aspect presupposed that all ancient literature was transmitted orally for a long time and was written only long after its composition. This latter discipline is known as redaction criticism. Form criticism came first, with the basic aspects first formulated by Herman Gunkel in his book *Schoepfung und Chaos in Urzeit*, published in 1895. Gunkel's work was partly based on pioneer work in historical criticism that Julius Wellhausen (1844–1918) had done. Redaction criticism was launched by Gerhard von Rad in mid-twentieth century. Hans Conzelmann's treatise on the Gospel of Luke (1954 in German) applies redaction criticism principles to New Testament studies. Willi Marxsen, in *Der Evangelist Markus* (1956), had proposed the term *Redaktionsgeschichte*. This came to be translated conventionally in English as redaction criticism, and it sought to study how ancient documents were edited. These studies had radically altered the problem of hermeneutics—the interpretation of Scripture—as well as the problem of the canon. With the new assumptions taken for granted, modern man simply understood the divine revelation of God's plan of salvation in a way that differed greatly from earlier Christians.

Some critics emphasized oral transmission of biblical accounts over many generations. The stress on the oral transmission of the content of the biblical books overlooks the internal evidence that the prophets wrote down very soon after receiving God's revelation what they had proclaimed orally. In the Old Testament, for example, Moses repeatedly received the command to write down the revelation. There is, furthermore, no better example than that of Jeremiah to show how a prophet had preached over a long period of years and had his sermons recorded immediately by a scribe. In the New Testament, the Letter to the Galatians shows the case of an apostle who wrote down, obviously very soon, what he had preached.

Higher critics at first asserted that the assumption of an early written revelation of God's Word was invalid because man in ancient times could not write. When archaeology demonstrated that this presumption of the scholars was not true, they shifted arguments without adjusting their earlier conclusions that were based on faulty history.

Some ancient literature was transmitted orally—Chinese literature, for example, and certain types of African literature. The whole thrust of the form critics and of the redaction critics, however, had been on the changes that had allegedly taken place in the oral transmission of biblical accounts. Apart from the point that specialists in the history of secular literature have been making to the effect that oral transmission stressed precise memorization of the material to be preserved, there is the very significant study by Birger Gerhardsson, *Memory and Manuscripts*, which shows that, among the ancient Israelites, the ability to memorize verbatim the sayings of the early teachers was requisite even to be considered a student in the school of the scribes, who saw to the transmission of the ancient tradition.

These new aspects of historical criticism, form criticism, and redaction criticism rejected the former assumption that one was dealing with ancient documents that were revealed by God and had been written down by prophets and apostles under inspiration of the Holy Spirit. As related above, the very possibility of revelation and inspiration were rejected first. With that presupposition, scholars went back to work on the text and began to sharply criticize it. This, of course, also struck at the conviction of Christians through the ages that the Early Church, for example, had regarded the manuscripts collected into the canon of the New Testament as written by apostles. They had seen them for that very reason as the Word of God and therefore worthy to be included in the Bible. Once that certainty was questioned, the whole problem of interpretation became an open issue. In most recent times, there are new philosophical and psychological concepts that further complicate this area of theology, as will be shown below.

The most popular label of modern theology, historical criticism, must also be examined as to the implication of the word *historical*. The historical investigations of the text of the Bible and of biblical backgrounds received a tremendous inducement from the Renaissance and the Enlightenment. Much of this was very salutary. No self-respecting theologian today, even in the confessional and conservative tradition, would want to ignore the progress and contributions of modern scholarship particularly in this area. Issues arose, however, when rationalistic scholars put the biblical text to the test of human reason. They thought the historicity of events recorded in the Bible could not be proven to their satisfaction.

The emphasis on the need of historical verification of the content of the Scripture helped to develop historicism. There was also much input from non-biblical secular studies. Historicism is actually the culmination of the science of history as it was developed by modern scholars. Since this science of history was put into use in testing the trustworthiness of the Bible and its content, this is a most significant development—and also a very disruptive one—in the history of modern theology. Historicism is a label that was later imposed on various aspects of a trend in the study and writing of history, but there is no general agreement among scholars as to what aspects and what emphases can be included under this label. It is used in purely secular history, but it is also applied to biblical history and church history. There is little debate that historicism meant the interpretation and evaluation of the Bible and of Christianity in terms of the process of their development. This means that ideas, customs, and conventions of men, society, and cultures are historically conditioned. It means that ideas are only reflections of the prevailing historical condition.

One of the basic tenets of historicism is that everything is historically conditioned, even God. A real adherent of the historicocritical theology can therefore agree that in ancient times, people properly worshiped God as described in the Bible, but by modern times He has changed. This view also makes possible the acceptance of the books of the Bible as valid in their time. It makes possible the acceptance of the confessions of the churches as documents properly and validly expressing a position for a prevailing historical situation (*Tendenzschriften*).

Comparative Religion. In the eyes of many, historicism validated comparative religion. It made possible the process theology of the twentieth century, the idea that there is no given, only a process of development, not only in theology but in all areas of existence. Historicism also made possible later twentieth-century movements in theology such as the "death of God" theology.

In the mid-twentieth century, Christian scholars were often confronted with disclaimers against comparative religion. Many scholars avow that it is no longer accepted by most scholars, and thus its views are no longer a problem for us today. However, if a careful investigation is made of the historical development of later twentieth-century theology, it becomes evident that many of the claims of comparative religion are still with us and in fact are embedded in the most fundamental presuppositions in religious studies today.

There is no fault in the study of non-Christian religions as such. One needs to conduct this type of study to understand non-Western cultures and civilizations. One must conduct studies like this to understand the complex problems involved in cross-cultural mission outreach. For too long, conservative Christians have been simplistic and obscurantist in ignoring those challenging areas of study. Thus the Christian witness to peoples of other cultures was made more difficult. However, these facts do not support the common claim that all religions contain some divine revelation and divine truth that can lead toward salvation—an idea that comparative religion has popularized and that is widespread also among nominal Christian scholars today.

One of the results of the claims of the history of religion school is universalism, the belief that everyone can be saved in their own way in any of the many world religions. This idea is quite popular among many Christians. Related to this modern universalism is the concept of anonymous Christians hidden in non-Christian religions. Karl Rahner (1904–84), the German Roman Catholic theologian, has given great impetus to the thought that serious believers in non-Christian religions will be saved in their own way, making it unnecessary for Christians to want to convert them to Christianity.

These various trends in modern theology became mutually supportive. One trend fed on the "progress" made in another area. In comparative religion and in the quest for the historical Jesus, this is especially evident.

The history of religion school formed just before the opening of the twentieth century. Herman Gunkel, mentioned earlier, is typical of this school. He put some of the key tenets in a very succinct way. He said that one must get rid of the idea that in ancient times mankind obtained religious good only through Judaism. He asserted that the seed of divine revelation fell also on other religious fields. In ancient times, in fact, there were religious ideas and insights that the writers of both Testaments borrowed from other religions. He held that the sacred writers collected materials that had been extant in oral form long before their time, even in other religions.

CHRISTIAN CHURCHES IN THE AMERICAS AND AUSTRALIA

The history of Christian churches in the Americas and Australia must be seen in its relationship to the history of Europe and its churches. Christianity was introduced to America by the first European explorers and colonialists in three major movements. First came the Spanish Catholics, who claimed the West Indies, South America, Middle America (including Mexico), and the southern part of what is now the United States. By the mid-1500s, the Spanish had staked out their claims, had begun their shameless exploitations of the land and the people, and had begun to transplant Roman Catholicism in a way that too often made the Church an integral part of the imperialistic invasion. Conversions happened to the point that nominally made the whole population Roman Catholic, but this was often conquest by force. In South America, the one exception to Spanish rule was the area that the Portuguese occupied and colonized, now essentially eastern Brazil. Portuguese colonial policy was somewhat less harsh than that of the Spanish. But they also colonized, and they also transplanted the Roman Catholic Church.

About one hundred years after the beginning of the Spanish colonization, the French, mostly Catholics, began to show an interest in North America, particularly the St. Lawrence River and the Great Lakes basin. Not to be outdone, at about the same time in the early 1600s, Protestants from England began to colonize the middle Atlantic seaboard. All three Christian and cultural traditions—Spanish Catholic, French Catholic, and English Protestant—had their own characteristics. Despite the crudity and cruelty with which the Spanish made converts, both the Roman Catholic Church and the Spanish language became deeply embedded in the life of the people, if not always in their hearts. The French had a much gentler and more open approach to the American Indians. But they also had a zeal for planting the Church, and though they did not succeed in building a long-lasting empire in America, as the Spanish did, their cultural and religious input made a lasting impression.

The French made a fair attempt at possessing and holding the northeast and central part of America, namely the St. Lawrence River, the Great Lakes basin, and the Mississippi valley. They held Canada as a royal domain. In 1699, they established a fort at Biloxi Bay; they founded New Orleans in 1718. In 1753, they settled in on the site where Pittsburgh now stands. In the French and Indian War, the French suffered a setback as they turned Louisiana over to Spain to keep it from falling into English hands. But in the Napoleonic Wars, the French took it back. In 1803, they sold Louisiana to the United States. In 1763, at the Treaty of Paris, they had to surrender Canada to the British. French culture and Roman Catholicism were implanted in Quebec, but the rest of the new world north of the Spanish holdings was now open to English and Protestant exploitations and expansion.

The English Protestants used a different approach. Though Anglicanism was the official religion in England, there were many dissenters, so the English transmitted various religious trends to America. Anglicanism was represented in Virginia, with all its Erastian features fully visible, and nonconformists such as the Puritans were expelled from the colony. Representatives of Puritan nonconformism settled in Massachusetts early in the seventeenth century. In the early American colonies, there were a few non-English atypical cases, such as the Lutheran Swedes on the Delaware, the Reformed Dutch in New Amsterdam, and various religious traditions in William Penn's colony, including Quakers, Lutherans, Moravians, the German Reformed, left-wing German sects, and English Catholics. But the Dutch were defeated in a war and relieved of their American territory, and Sweden was culturally overwhelmed. These all were to add a little variety to the mix by the time the English colonies gained independence.

Colonial America. Several factors must be borne in mind to enable one to understand the religious situation in America in 1800, the point at which this present study begins. First, there was more than a century and a half of history—including church history—before the American Revolution. Second, during this time the original religious orientations in the various colonies had gone through considerable changes. The original English colonists, whether in Virginia or Massachusetts, were Calvinists, though on church polity they differed vehemently—the Anglicans in Virginia holding to episcopacy, state churchism, and generally a high church view. These were the points to which the nonconformists in Massachusetts objected. Episcopacy was too Romish, so they adhered to a congregational polity. And they had turned the old Erastian arrangement (that the state dominate the church) upside down. They had established the principle that the church controls the state. Thus there was no tolerance in Massachusetts for any religious deviance. Baptists were expelled. Quakers were persecuted. Romanists would have been unthinkable there. The Baptists were instrumental in breaking down this intolerance. The American Constitution provided for separation of church and state, but in New England it took a while before they were separated.

DENOMINATIONS IN EARLY AMERICA	
ANGLICANS	Strongest in Virginia. Tories/British Loyalists. Lost ground after the Revolution due to political ties with England. Protestant Episcopal Church founded (1793). Parliament consecrated an American bishop.
BAPTISTS	Colonial Baptists challenged the Puritans and grew. Established Philadelphia Bible Association (1707), which established Brown University.
CONGREGA-TIONALISTS	Puritans who avoided central administrative organizations in the church. One of the largest groups before the Revolution; with Presbyterians, c. 40% of population. Their theology was susceptible to change.
LUTHERANS AND MORAVIANS	Palatines and Salzburgers emigrated in the 1700s. German immigration centered on Pennsylvania. Muehlenberg organized Ministerium (1748).
METHODISTS	Wesley, as an Anglican, opposed the Revolution. Methodists recruited lay preachers. Grew rapidly during and after the Revolution due to circuit riders. Attracted immigrants from different backgrounds.
PRESBYTERIANS AND REFORMED	Established Presbytery of Philadelphia (1706). Grew rapidly from Scotch-Irish immigrants to become one of the largest groups. German Reformed arrived as distinct group.
QUAKERS	Treated poorly in Massachusetts. Helped found Pennsylvania. Fifth-largest group before Revolution.
ROMAN CATHOLICS	Before Revolution, less than one in a thousand of the population. English, Irish, and German Catholics disunited. Faced anti-Catholic sentiment due to nondemocratic ways. French arrived after French Revolution. Founded St. Mary's Seminary (1791). St. Mary's Cathedral, Philadelphia, and others were lay-run (1808 schism). Carroll (1735–1815) was first bishop at Baltimore. Became archbishop in 1808. Huge growth by 1850 due to Irish immigrants.
UNITARIANS	Reaction against Calvinism. Favored universalism. American Unitarian Association founded (1825). Many Congregational churches joined.

Religious Awakenings in America. In the eighteenth century, only a minority of Americans belonged to Christian churches, though most homes probably had Bibles. As the nineteenth century opened, a distinct new aspect of American churches was the change evident in the Calvinist tradition, which included a number of churches. The Great Awakening of the eighteenth century was probably the catalyst that precipitated the development of what was called the New England theology. Leaders in this were Jonathan Edwards (1703–58) and two of his disciples, Joseph Bellamy (1719–90) and Samuel Hopkins (1721–1803). Edwards was an outstanding and gifted Congregationalist and a graduate of Yale. As an earnest young pastor in

Massachusetts, he was distraught by the undisciplined youth and by the inroads of Arminian theology. His preaching met with response, and Edwards became one of the chief engineers of the Great Awakening of the middle of the eighteenth century. This helped to revitalize the churches, though it did not completely reverse the decline of church membership, and it stimulated church-sponsored higher education and missions.

This new surge in spiritual life is usually called "Evangelicalism." This trend tended to depart from hard-line Calvinism. In the readjustment that followed, Edwards and his followers were called "Consistent Calvinists." They wanted to establish the doctrine that man was saved only by God's grace. This reaffirmation was a thrust against deism, already quite popular at that time. Deism rejected the possibility of original sin and the certainty of eternal punishment. It is not altogether clear why those who took up a middle position between the New England theology and deism, such as Ezra Stiles (1727–95), were called Old Calvinists. They failed to appreciate the fine differences between the theologies of the day.

At the opening of the nineteenth century, the Second Awakening was beginning, induced by revivalistic preaching in a number of places almost simultaneously. Several preliminary revivals preceded the one in Logan County, Kentucky, in 1800. There, some missionary preachers conducted camp meetings. Frontier farm families came in their wagons to camp out for days, absorbing religion and receiving catharsis for their sins. These camp-meeting revivals soon were held up and down the frontier. They were marked by uninhibited emotionalism.

James McGready, a Presbyterian pastor in Logan County from 1796 on, initiated these revivals. Peter Cartwright (1785–1872), a Methodist circuit rider who worked that area also before he followed the frontier further west to Illinois and Missouri, records some fascinating observations in his *Autobiography*, mentioning that this area in Kentucky was known as Rogues' Harbor because of thieves and desperadoes who had sought anonymity there. The Cane Ridge revival in Bourbon County, Kentucky, in 1801 also made history. It was estimated that 10,000–25,000 attended that revival.

Although the Kentucky revival began in the Presbyterian Church, Baptist and Methodist churches made the most gains as a result. The Presbyterians lost some ground because they could not abide the apparent disorder of such revival activity. The numerical success of mass conversions also raised the question of ordaining new pastors to care for the many converts. Methodists and Baptists did not insist on high educational achievement for ministers. This put them into tension with Presbyterians and other comparatively conservative denominations. Despite tremendous growth of membership, schisms developed as a result of the revivals. The first was the "New Light" schism, precipitated by Barton W. Stone (1772–1844) in 1803. Stone was born in Maryland, had studied under a Presbyterian minister, and was ordained into the Presbyterian ministry. He had some reservations about the Calvinistic doctrine of unconditional election. He and some friends established an independent presbytery in Kentucky, and when the revivals began, they tried to overcome denominational differences by forming a union of Christians without creedal distinctions. They designated themselves "Christian" and took the Bible as their only creed. Several similar groups sprang up in other places. One was organized by Thomas Campbell (1763–1854), a Presbyterian minister, and his son Alexander (1788–1866). It was within a few years after the Cane Ridge revival that Campbell came to Pennsylvania from Scotland. He was soon followed by his son. They organized a church as a corrective to the Presbyterians. One of the issues at stake was infant Baptism, which the Campbells regarded as wrong. They had a Baptist minister baptize them and their families by immersion, but they did not remain Baptists. They organized their own church, the Disciples of Christ. Later, the followers of Stone and the Campbellites merged.

As a result of the question of ordaining only partly prepared men to the ministry, the Presbyterians suffered other losses. In Cumberland County, Kentucky, the pastors in the Cumberland Presbytery were disciplined by the Synod of Kentucky for ordaining insufficiently prepared men. The revivalist members of the presbytery then formed the Cumberland Presbyterian Church (1810). Other fractures hurt the Presbyterians, but the Methodists thrived on the camp meetings, and in about a decade they had a virtual monopoly on the movement.

A movement related to the revival was that spearheaded by Charles G. Finney (1792–1875), a Presbyterian lawyer in Adams, New York. In the North, the revival movement was kept in check by the organized churches. Even when there were special meetings and services, they were controlled and carried on in the context of the local congregations and under control of the pastors of those churches. Finney related that in 1821 he had a "conversion experience," and thereafter he went out with zeal for the Lord. He studied theology under a Presbyterian pastor and was sent out as a traveling missionary. He began in the Mohawk Valley in 1825 and spoke to people earnestly and forcefully about basic spiritual values and about their salvation. Finney became the pioneer evangelist who adapted the revival to the urban environment. The tactics he used came to be known as "new measures," which were debated and denounced in church papers and theological journals of the nineteenth century. New measures involved a sharp confrontation with the person to be converted and emotional pressure to achieve a breakdown of resistance that would culminate in the person stepping forward to the "anxious bench" and making public confession of sin. Since such meetings included men and women, often ran for many hours, and involved women in individual public confession and prayer, this "domesticated" revival approach attracted much attention throughout the United States. The new measures were applied also in traditional denominations, including Lutheran and Dutch Reformed.

American Unitarianism. The eighteenth century saw the influx of deism and its rationalism and materialism from England and France. Added to that was the influence of German liberal thought. Besides, the works of Dutch theologian Jacob

Arminius (1560–1609) gained popularity in America. Arminius held that man was not totally corrupt, that man could by his own determination move closer to God, and that Calvinistic concepts of limited grace and dual predestination were untenable. This mix of ideas was a theology that made a deep impression on American churches. Its most significant and radical form eventually was Unitarianism, which did much to emasculate Christianity in America.

Unitarianism professed high regard for the Bible and for Jesus but superimposed human reason on everything. It had a fierce feud with New England Calvinism for some decades. The term "Unitarian" was accepted by most members of the movement by 1819, but some still preferred "liberal," even in the 1830s. Unitarians were antisectarian. The issue on which they were most concerned was not only the Trinity but also the doctrine of man. They held to a radical view of the perfectibility of man.

Transcendentalism. Channing can probably be called a transition figure from Unitarianism to Transcendentalism. But Theodore Parker (1810–60) spelled it out in his essay on this topic. The term *transcendentalism* was borrowed from Kant and other earlier philosophers, but there is new meaning in it as it is used in the American school. Parker and others found the "sensationalism" of the deist philosophers to be a futile approach to the problem of reality. He opted for the view that there is in the human intellect or consciousness something that transcends the senses. Human beings have intuitions that transcend sense experience. In religion, he said, we have to admit that man has a religious faculty or nature. The idea of God exists a priori.

The American Transcendentalists, however, did not manage to raise themselves by their own bootstraps very far above the level from which they began in Unitarian rationalism. They attained only the level of the human heart. It was a mixture of romantic idealism that had no room for objectively revealed religion. When Emerson and others in 1836 founded the Transcendental Club in Boston as a countermovement to the Enlightenment, their motivating ideology by their own definition remained romantic idealism. Parker himself was enamored of liberal German theology of the time, including that of Friedrich Strauss. He went so far as to claim that Christianity did not even depend on the actual existence of Christ.

Mission Societies and the Westward Expansion. We have already mentioned how the revivals spread in Kentucky early in the nineteenth century. That was a time of new expansion in the history of the United States. People from the eastern states pushed westward through the Cumberland Gap. From Pennsylvania they came along the Ohio River, and further north through the Great Lakes, to possess the land that lay open before them. It was often the revival preacher who brought the only religion found on the frontier. Peter Cartwright, mentioned above, is one of the most fascinating examples. His *Autobiography* reflects a wide variety of experiences. Through his long years of work in Tennessee, Kentucky, and Illinois, he baptized possibly as many as twelve thousand people.

Much of the expansion of the churches on the frontier in the nineteenth century was through mission societies organized for this purpose. Some of the significant movements came out of New England Congregationalism. In 1798, the Congregational churches in Connecticut organized the Missionary Society of Connecticut. Their purpose was "to Christianize the heathen in North America." In 1809, the society had twenty-four missionaries in a field ranging from Vermont to Pennsylvania and Ohio. Soon other Congregational churches in other New England states had similar societies. Presbyterians did likewise. The two denominations then formed the Plan of Union in 1801 for cooperative mission efforts. Although the Plan of Union led more people among the new converts into the Presbyterian Church, by the 1830s the Presbyterians began to feel a bit uncomfortable in this cooperative structure because of the departure from strict Calvinism that they detected in the New England theology of their Congregationalist partners, and in 1837 the Plan of Union was terminated. However, four Presbyterian groups that were formed under the Plan established their own General Assembly and maintained cooperative mission work with the Congregationalists.

Under the cooperative arrangements of the Plan of Union, the American Home Mission Society was founded in 1826. This was one of the most significant events of that time. This missionary society sent out hundreds of workers before it was dissolved in 1861 in favor of denominational societies. They sent out "bands" or teams that organized schools and churches throughout the Midwest and West. Yale and Andover supplied much of the manpower. The first of these mission teams to attract attention was the Illinois Band. Asa Turner, one member, served as pastor in Quincy, Illinois, for a while, then went to Iowa, where he assisted in establishing a school that became Grinnell College. In 1857, a team of four from Andover went to Kansas. Others went to the Dakotas, and before the end of the century, a team of Yale men went to Washington State.

Other denominations, too, had their mission societies. In 1802, the Baptists in Boston formed the Massachusetts Baptist Missionary Society. Soon they sent missionaries out as far afield as Canada and Wisconsin. Their General Missionary Convention, called into being in 1817 to look especially after their foreign missions, also did domestic work. One of their leaders, and an outstanding worker, was John Mason Peck (1789–1858), originally a Connecticut Congregationalist. He went west to work and by 1817 was in St. Louis, preaching and gathering people into churches. Hundreds of missionary societies and thousands of interesting and picturesque pioneer missionaries are noted in the nineteenth-century annals of the churches.

Among all the religious enthusiasm that was generated in the revivalistic atmosphere, however, there was some deviation from the mainline denominations. One of the more startling developments was the Church of Jesus Christ of Latter-day Saints, founded in 1830 in Seneca County, New York, by Joseph Smith (1805–44). His area of New York had been swept by revivals conducted by itinerant Baptist and Methodist preachers. Smith's whole family had been touched by the emotionalism of the revivalist movement. He claimed to have had visions from God, in which it was revealed to him where there were hidden certain tablets recording the further will of God for man, and that he had found these tablets, a translation of which he issued as the Book of Mormon (1830). In 1832, Brigham Young, born, like Smith, in New England, joined the movement. Its religion included emphasis on optimism, self-improvement, and hard work. Under Smith's leadership, the Mormons moved west, feared, hated, and persecuted for their fanaticism and strange social customs, including polygamy. In Carthage, Illinois, Smith was killed when rioting occurred, but Young led many people to Utah (1846–47), where they set up a flourishing colony. Some of the Mormons who remained in the Midwest went to western Missouri under the leadership of Joseph Smith (1832–1914), son of the founder. This group was known as the Reorganized Church of Jesus Christ of Latter-day Saints but now is called Community of Christ.

As in Europe at that time, there was much millennial fervor in the air. There were confused and complex hopes for a utopian kingdom on earth, possibly initiated by the imminent return of Christ. One of the movements that grew out of this was led by William Miller (1782–1849), who was converted and became a Baptist preacher. From a detailed study of the apocalyptic passages of the Bible, he predicted that the second coming of Christ would take place in 1843. He began to lecture on his Adventism, and gained many followers, who were, of course, disappointed when 1843 came and went without the return of Christ. Setting a later date did not help. But a new denomination grew out of this—the Seventh-day Adventists, a church body vigorous in its mission outreach and doctrinaire in its internal discipline and ethical observances.

Somewhat related to this movement were developments in the latter part of the nineteenth century that spilled over into the twentieth century. The Free Methodist Church of Pekin, New York, established in 1860, declared that it was possible for people to achieve complete holiness. In 1881, the Church of God (Anderson, Indiana) was established with a similar emphasis on holiness. The Christian and Missionary Alliance, founded in 1887 by A. B. Simpson, a Presbyterian minister, was likewise similar. In 1895, a Methodist founded the Church of the Nazarene in California. As the twentieth century unfolded, these holiness groups grew in proportion to the increased reaction against the materialistic attitudes found in many mainline American churches.

Related to this reaction against secularism is the Pentecostal movement, which originated at the end of the nineteenth century with the work of R. G. Spurling and A. J. Tomlinson in Tennessee and North Carolina. The Church of God (Cleveland, Tennessee) is one of the most significant churches resulting from this. In 1914, the Assemblies of God was founded in Hot Springs, Arkansas; they also show very impressive growth in membership. A similar movement was organized by Aimee Semple McPherson (1890–1944). In 1923, she dedicated her Foursquare Gospel Tabernacle in Los Angeles.

Missions to American Blacks. The mission outreach powered by the revivals of the early nineteenth century also reached out to the non-European races in America.

Of course, there had been many blacks—including the free—who became Christians well before 1800. In northern cities, there were many blacks who lived in alleys between the main thoroughfares, where the white Americans lived. Before long there were social organizations for blacks who had thus congregated in the urban areas. One type of organization was the mutual-benefit society; another type was the Church. The former often came first. In Newport, Rhode Island, there was such a fraternity for mutual help, the African Union Society, organized in 1780. In 1807, it merged with the African Benevolent Society. This group then founded a school, and in 1824 it established a church for its members.

In most American churches, blacks were admitted to membership in white churches. But for services, they would have to sit in the "African corners" or "nigger pews" in the remote corners of the gallery. At times, white churches even had black pastors. John Chavis served as pastor of a white Presbyterian congregation in North Carolina until 1831, when state law prohibited blacks from preaching.

Before the end of the eighteenth century, discrimination was becoming more common even in Baptist and Methodist churches, where most black Christians congregated. This gave rise to separate church organizations for blacks. The first such church was the African Methodist Episcopal Church. Its first bishop was Richard Allen, a Methodist and former slave who had purchased his freedom after he had converted his master to Christianity. In Philadelphia, Allen attended St. George's Methodist church. His strong leadership talents did not find adequate outlet there, so he organized the Bethel African Methodist Episcopal Church in 1794.

In Baltimore, there were similar developments in the Methodist Church. Blacks had a separate chapel there for a while without making a break with the parent body. Finally, they set up a separate congregation with their own black pastor. Similar trends are evident in many other cities. In 1816, representatives of African Methodist churches in a number of states met in Philadelphia to form a "synod," with Richard Allen as bishop. In New York City, a similar program had arisen, with the result that black members founded their own church in 1801. In 1821, this group adopted the name African Methodist Episcopal Church Zion and elected James Varick (c. 1750–1828) as its first bishop.

Even during the American Revolution black Baptists had separate congregations in several southern states, and by 1820 there were a number of southern cities with black congregations. In the first decade of the nineteenth century, northern cities like Boston, New York, and Philadelphia saw the organization of black Baptist churches. But these generally remained affiliated with the parent body.

Somewhat related to the above is the abolitionist movement. In America, as in Great Britain, there were Christians who were thoroughly convinced that slavery was wrong and who began gradually in the early decades of the nineteenth century to crystallize their ideas. In the 1820s, this usually took a milder form than in the 1830s. In 1816, the American Colonization Society had been organized to resettle freed slaves in Africa. The British Society had resettled freedmen in West Africa, and thus the colony of Sierra Leone came into existence. The Americans established Liberia just east of Sierra Leone. Eventually many blacks were relocated there. But this movement did not really come to grips with the basic moral issue of slavery.

Sydney Ahlstrom has pointed out in *A Religious History of the American People* that the 1830s saw a revolutionary change comparable only to the radical change of attitude in American race relations of the 1960s. The 1830s mark the rise of violent northern antislavery sentiment that finally forced the issue in America, which was resolved in the blood bath of the Civil War.

The American Civil War. Once the Civil War erupted, the work of churches in America was seriously disrupted, especially in the border states and in those southern states where military activity took place. About a thousand Protestant pastors volunteered for chaplaincy duty, however, and it is estimated that thousands of troops were converted. But all this cannot counterbalance the bloodshed and suffering that demoralized the nation in those terrible years. Even if the 600,000 dead had had no relatives to mourn them, or the 400,000 maimed who survived had had no kin to weep with them, the war ripped at the inner gut life of the nation. Tragic, too, were the guerrilla activities that brought looting, rape, and murder to many places in the border states. But the real pathos was the inability of rational people, many motivated by Christian principles, to find a way to solve problems peaceably in the cause of liberty. The hatred that lived on after the war is evident in southern Presbyterian Robert Lewis Dabney (1820–98), who continued to propound the view after the war that abolitionists had deliberately provoked the war to revolutionize the government and feed their own spite. Henry Ward Beecher (1813–87; son of Lyman Beecher) advocated compassion for the defeated southerners but maintained that the southern scheming political leaders had provoked the war. Phillip Schaff (1819–93), German-born and bred as he was, was capable of less subjectivism and feelings of retribution and saw the war as a tragic purging of the sin of a nation. He saw the whole experience as preparing America for a greater role in the cause of human freedom.

When the dust settled after the Civil War, there were certain readjustments the nation and the churches had to make. In the North, many Protestants, who had been enticed by the Republicans and the radical antislavery position, became the mainstay of the radical Reconstructionists. Since the 1930s, historians have tended to review the historiography of Reconstruction and write a less harsh judgment of it, but the postwar period was a time of agonizing readjustment for many.

The homogenization of black churches in the South had its positive side. The church served as an agency of social control, especially in the rural South. The churches often supplied the inducement and the means for the first steps of education for the blacks. W. E. B. Du Bois (1868–1963), famous black sociologist, highlighted the significant function of the pastor in the black congregations. Some black clergy became quite influential. For example, Henry Turner (1834–1915), an ex-slave and first black captain in the United States Army, served in the South Carolina legislature after the war until blacks were expelled from this body in 1868. He was also a prominent churchman, serving as bishop in the African Methodist Episcopal Church.

Among the white churches, the Methodists were some of the first to shake off the apathy of the war and resume functioning like a church again. In 1866, the Southern Methodists surpassed the one million mark in membership. But they continued to be more successful in rural areas than in the cities. Southern Baptists, too, came back to life in the latter 1860s, though they continued to be plagued by many divisions.

Other challenges confronted churches in the postwar period too. Besides the problem of rebuilding the nation, there was the challenge of the many new immigrants from Europe. Protestants and Roman Catholics who worked in this fertile home mission field gained many of the immigrants. These immigrants supplied the labor for building railroads and for manning factories in expanding American cities and in the industrialization of postwar America. Before the century was over, American churchmen knew they were confronted with new problems, because urban work did not respond to the same outreaches as rural work had. Many of the well-established congregations of the mainline denominations were able to hang on until well into the twentieth century, but the trend is evident long before 1900. At that time, unfortunately, there were too few specialists who could diagnose the trends of the times and induce a shift of methodology for reaching people in the new sociological context. Churches therefore were drifting, driven by swirling currents of change. Many did not even bother to put their paddles in the water, because they felt that they were being moved along by some irresistible power.

Mission Work among American Indians. One area where this rudderless drifting of the churches after the Civil War made itself especially evident was in mission outreach to the American Indians. In the study of American Christianity, it would be comfortable if one could omit the story of the sad failure of the Christian missions to the American Indians. It is, no doubt, one of the saddest chapters of all Christian mission history. But it must be told. Unfortunately, careful researching and narration of this story may well be impossible. First of all, the assortment of churches and mission societies that have worked among American Indians is so diverse that thorough research into all the archives might take more than a lifetime. Furthermore, what is most important in this type of research is careful study not only of the original culture and civilization of the American Indians but also of their response to the Christian message. This poses a formidable difficulty for the historian in the case of people who had no recorded language and therefore no written historical records. One must go at this task aware of the limitations under which a study must be made.

None of the main European Christian traditions in America had ignored the American Indians. But mission outreach to them was seldom motivated by unfeigned love and hardly ever undertaken with adequate wisdom. When one reads the annals of the Spanish in America, it is seldom that one finds the likes of Bartolomé de Las Casas, the first Christian priest to be ordained in America. He made it his mission to help his fellow Spaniards stay honest, if not Christian, in their outreach to the American Indians. Pathos-filled stories in *The Jesuit Relations* tell of courage and consecration among the French. Among the Protestants, the English in Virginia and in Massachusetts were desirous of converting the heathen, but the culture shock, when European met American native, was often so violent that the American Indians did not even hear the Gospel the Europeans meant to communicate.

In the eighteenth century, the Moravians had one of the best records of success among American Indians, but the French and Indian War and the American Revolution played havoc with their efforts and their converts. Americans then already were willing to follow a policy that gave precedence to the prosecution of the war, even if lives of missionaries and their converts were jeopardized.

The major mission societies working among American Indians at the turn of the century, such as the American Board, the New York Missionary Society, and the Northern Missionary Society, all had seen their work suffer attrition, and they began to wonder whether the eastern American Indians should not be relocated further west, so that mission work could be carried on among them under more stable conditions. In 1820, Jedidiah Morse made a study of the American Indian tribes, and in his book published two years later as a report to the Secretary of War, he urged the policy of removal. In 1824, the Bureau of Indian Affairs was established. In 1849, Indian Affairs were put under the Department of the Interior. The annals and archives of various churches are replete with records of bravery and martyrdom, but often the missionary was a lone voice who saw how the American Indians were being maltreated and yet could do nothing about it because he could not muster the support of a whole church body to stand up against government American Indian agents or American Indian traders. Sometimes, missionaries themselves did not know what was going on.

As one surveys the history of nearly four centuries of Christian mission outreach to the American Indians, one must acknowledge that this was a badly bungled job on the part of Christians. The missionaries and the American settlers in general almost completely failed to understand the massive problems of cross-cultural mission outreach to a people so different in their social structure. The many who realize what the problem was and are trying to work in either social rehabilitation or in evangelism among American Indians find it very difficult to undo in short order the great damage that has been done to the American Indian.

Latin American Christianity. The story of the Church in Latin America comprises a special segment of history. Here is about one-seventh of the world, taken over by two small Iberian countries. At this early point in the modern era, a few premodern vessels armed with muzzle-loading cannons and several hundred warriors armed with swords, lances, and muzzle-loading blunderbusses were enough to conquer the thinly distributed population of indigenous peoples. Because of the ruthlessness of the conquest and the chauvinism of the Spanish, the demographic, linguistic, religious, and cultural displacement was massive. The Spanish had, furthermore, no genius for technology and for modernization, such as the Anglo-Saxons had. Thus, Latin America stagnated under Spanish rule not only sociologically but also economically. Religiously, too, the Spanish had little genius for transplanting a vibrant level of Christianity. Tension between the Roman curia and the kings of Spain and Portugal was also a significant factor in transplanting Christianity to the New World. Rome had granted the kings complete control over episcopal appointments, and through this prerogative had given the kings effective control over all church affairs and mission activities in the colonies. This was the *real patronato de las Indias*, in Portuguese called *padroado* ("patronage").

The first impact of the Spanish on the indigenous peoples was very authoritarian. The popes no doubt thought they could use the kings, and the kings thought they could use churchmen, and thus the Gospel had no free course. Religion became formalistic, at best, for the American Indians. The rule in the church was firmly in the hands of the Spanish clergy, of which there was an oversupply in most of the colonies most of the time. In the first century of the Spanish conquest, many adventurous priests came for material reasons. Because of various reasons, partly theological, partly a matter of church polity, partly ethnic chauvinism, the native peoples had no genius for developing an indigenous clergy, and thus the church was never truly indigenous in the Americas, even until modern times. But the Roman Catholic Church kept its monopoly of religious activity in Latin America, as in the home country, through the Inquisition. The ruthlessness of the Inquisition rivals that of the secret police of the harshest totalitarian regime of the twentieth century.

The social structure in the Spanish colonies reflected the Spanish genius also. The Spanish officials were for the most part European. They often bought their appointment from the king, with the certainty that they could recoup their investment in America in short order. This institutionalized graft and corruption in their government. People of Spanish (or European) descent born in America were called Creoles, and sometimes they could rise to significant official positions, occupying positions on city councils and other comparable posts. Creoles comprised most of the business class and professional men. Below them were those of mixed blood, called mestizos, and below them, the indigenous peoples, and below them, the slaves. In Spanish areas, the class structure was quite institutionalized, though it is true that in Portuguese Brazil this was not so much the case. The Portuguese had a lack of consciousness in respect to racial distinction that made the society of Brazil more homogeneous. The fact that Brazil was very thinly populated may also have been a factor in that difference.

The Church in Latin America blundered along through several centuries under the political umbrella of the Spanish and the Portuguese, until the French Revolution suddenly upset the whole system.

There was some intellectual and ideological input in Latin America from the Enlightenment that helped prepare the soil for revolution, but the practical end of it was political expediency and feasibility. When Napoleon invaded Spain early in the nineteenth century, this set off the independence movements in Latin America. Napoleon's act of conquest simply shook the Spanish colonies loose from control by the mother country.

In Mexico, the leader of the independence movement was a Roman Catholic priest, Miguel Hidalgo y Costilla (1753–1811). He had read the French philosophers and had been evicted from his parish because of his radical views. He raised the banner of revolution against Spain in September 1810. Mexico at that time had about 40,000 Spaniards, 1 million Creoles, 1.5 million people of mixed blood, and 3.5 million American Indians. Hidalgo was captured and shot the next year, but José Maria Morelos (1765–1815), one of the lieutenants and also a priest, carried on the revolution until he was also captured and executed. Mexico eventually was able to gain independence and cut loose from Spain, but the first few decades marked an uncertain course with counterrevolutions as regular as the phases of the moon. This did not do much for the Church in Mexico, though Roman Catholicism remained the official religion. The government, however, claimed the *patronado*. Two important individuals came to power, Benito Juárez (1806–72) and Sebastián Lerdo de Tejada (1825–89). The Juárez Laws of 1855 expelled the Jesuit order from Mexico and also terminated the immunity of the church courts. The next year, the Lerdo Laws required the church to give up all landed property that was not actually being used for church purposes. Other regulations terminated state support to the church in collecting tithes and regulated the fees of the clergy, requiring the clergy to serve the poor gratis. The new constitution of 1857 incorporated all this legislation.

While Juárez's government was working out its program, it ran into difficulties with foreign governments because it could not meet even the interest on foreign debt. Great Britain, France, and Spain then began to formulate plans for intervention. When Napoleon III of France, always open to any imperialistic adventure, saw that the United States was temporarily preoccupied with the Civil War, he took the lead and set up in Mexico the government of Maximilian, the brother of the Austrian Emperor Franz Joseph. Juárez and his liberals resisted. After the US Civil War was over, the United States made it plain to France that the French protectorate would not be permitted to continue in Mexico. Maximilian was soon toppled and was executed June 19, 1867. This was a victory for the liberals in Mexico. Juárez resumed the rule but died in 1872. Lerdo then served as president until he was overthrown by Porfirio Díaz (1830–1915), who was president until 1911. He was a Mason and only a nominal Roman Catholic, but under him the severe religious restrictions were somewhat relaxed.

In South America, two outstanding leaders of independence from Spain were Simón Bolívar (1783–1830) and José de San Martín (1778–1850). Bolívar was active in the north and west of South America, San Martín in the south (Argentina and Chile). Bolívar had been to Europe, where he had studied current philosophers like Rousseau, and when he returned to Venezuela he formed a creole junta and set up a government professing loyalty to Ferdinand VII, the Spanish king recently deposed by Napoleon. In 1811, Venezuela was declared independent, but the last opposition forces were not conquered until 1823. In 1819, Bolívar won a victory that freed Colombia (then called New Granada). Bolívar dreamed of uniting the states of the north and the west, but local interests frustrated him, and Peru, Colombia, and Ecuador emerged as separate nations. But in the meantime, San Martín had been defeating the Spanish forces in Argentina (1816) and Chile (1821).

The independence movements developed into extremely anti–Roman Catholic movements, with considerable religious apathy and anticlericalism also evident. Roman Catholicism survived but was relegated to an even less influential position in the public life of the new nations.

The Portuguese colony of Brazil followed a slightly different road to independence. In 1808, the Portuguese monarchy moved its whole government to Brazil to escape Napoleon's armies. In 1815, after the Napoleonic Wars, the king returned to Portugal, but Brazil was granted a special status in the Portuguese Empire comparable to dominion status in the British Empire. In 1822, when the royal government tried to reassert its authority over Brazil, the son of King John, Prince Pedro, declared the Brazilian colony independent from Portugal. Pedro was crowned emperor. In 1831, however, he abdicated in favor of his five-year-old son and returned to Portugal. Pedro II proved an intelligent ruler, honest and conscientious, but a bit too liberal to suit the Roman Catholic hierarchy. Probably his own liberal leaning fostered the growth of sentiment for a republic. In 1889, the emperor abdicated in favor of the new republican government.

In the Latin American independence developments in the nineteenth century, one of the serious points of tension was between the higher clergy, who were all Spanish, and the lower clergy, who were composed of Creoles or mestizos. Many priests were active in public affairs. In some cases, this put them into contact with liberal political ideas that affected their theology.

Protestantism in Latin America was slow in coming, since the Roman Catholics had a jealously guarded monopoly. But with the nineteenth-century independence movement, some cracks appeared in the walls of control. In some countries, the Roman Catholics remained the established church; in others, Catholicism was the preferred religion; and in certain places, there was at times even some toleration for Protestants.

Protestant pioneer James Thomson represented the British and Foreign Bible Society to promote Lancastrian schools in Latin America. He worked in the Caribbean and in Mexico, Argentina, Chile, and Peru in the 1820s. The American Bible Society distributed Bibles by the 1830s. The American Board explored parts of Latin America, but it did not seem a propitious time to begin Protestant work. William Taylor (1821–1902) was a globe-trotting American Methodist evangelist who did much to open the door for Protestantism when he arrived on the scene in 1877. He tried to set up self-supporting missions undergirded with income from schools to be staffed by missionaries from the United States, and he enlisted workers for Peru, Bolivia, and Brazil. Before the end of the nineteenth century, the YMCA also opened work in Brazil. In the quarter century before World War I, a number of Protestant mission societies and denominations, chiefly from the United States, managed to open work in various Latin American countries, including the small countries of Central America. One factor that helped advance the cause of Protestantism was immigration from Europe. Brazil and Argentina, for example, with vast land resources and very small populations, opened their borders to the immigrants. But it was not until the twentieth century that Protestantism really took root and grew in Latin America.

Today, the majority of Latin America's population is affiliated with the Roman Catholic Church, though this ranges from very active (as in Mexico and Colombia) to in name only (as in Cuba). Thus in the decades after World War II, the Vatican has sought to revitalize the Roman Catholic Church by sending thousands of priests and religious women from Europe to Latin America. Vatican II (1962–65) also revitalized the church, especially after Latin American bishops met in Medellin in 1968 and translated the documents into their context. The laity was now reading the Bible for themselves and attending classes emphasizing personal growth and service to the church and society. By 2000, the number of priests had increased more than 70 percent. However, the Medellin Conference also brought forth the controversial liberation theology that would be so attractive to the poor and the oppressed in Latin American countries.

In countries such as Ecuador and Bolivia, the Roman Catholic Church is challenged by the indigenous religious movement that seeks political recognition for tribal groups. This discontent over civil rights status became especially apparent when indigenous peoples opposed the fifth centenary of Columbus's first journey to America. Such "celebrations" are largely spurned by priests, missionaries, and anthropologists. The Roman Catholic Church also has to contend with African-based religions that made their way in the 1950s from Brazil to urban centers in Uruguay and Argentina. One well-known African-based religion is voodoo, which began to function more openly after the 1986 fall of Haiti's leader Jean-Claude Devalier. Voodoo identified with the cultural life adhered to by Haitian blacks who survived as slaves.

Thus within Roman Catholicism many sociologists have pointed to a strand of hybrid belief systems called syncretism, which combines official church teachings with non-Christian beliefs from within the indigenous culture or that have been imported from the African populations. The Virgin of Guadalupe in Mexico is evidence of the former, and the voodoo practices in Haiti are evidence of the latter. In Latin America, the phenomenon of folk Christianity is prevalent.

Christian Churches in Canada. As noted above, the French first tried to colonize the northern part of the North American continent, but they were displaced by the English in the eighteenth-century wars. After the War of the Spanish Succession in 1713, the English got Acadia, which they renamed New Scotland, or Nova Scotia; then in the Treaty of Paris (1763), after the Seven Years' War, the French surrendered the rest of Canada. Colonization got a boost when many loyalists left the thirteen colonies for Canada at the time of the American Revolution. At first the Maritime Provinces (Nova Scotia, New Brunswick, and Prince Edward Island) and Quebec were separated from Ontario, but a Union Act of 1840 tried to join Ontario and Quebec. Lord Durham, the special high commissioner, had expressed the hope that the French Canadians and the English in these provinces would cease to be "two nations warring in the bosom of a single state." But they continued warring even after the Union Act.

In the British North America Act of 1867, Canadian provinces were joined under one administration. This was the first federal union in the British Empire. In the decades after that, the British began to pay more attention to the rest of Canada. Government continued to be expanded and reorganized. In 1886, the Canadian Pacific Railway was completed, tying the whole country together. Since the major settling of the country came late compared to Canada's southern neighbor, the various theological developments narrated for the United States have no relevance for Canada. But this does not mean that Christianity was not important to Canadians. Canada became one of the most Christian nations in the world. The relative proportion of Christian church members in the total population of Canada just before World War I was reported to be 95 percent, considerably higher than in the United States. Roman Catholicism also was relatively much stronger than in the United States, due to the early French influx. Later, there was also a heavy immigration of Irish that helped the total Roman Catholic population grow. Most numerous Protestants were Scotch-Irish Presbyterians and Anglicans. Methodists had experienced a relative decline at the turn of the century. Furthermore, Canada did not have the variety of radical sects found in the United States in the nineteenth century.

Many immigrants in the nineteenth century were Irish Roman Catholics. By World War I, over one million Canadians—one-seventh of the population—were Irish. By far, the majority of them were Roman Catholics. The French Roman Catholics did not always fully appreciate their cousins from the Emerald Isle.

The Anglican Church was the most favored among the Protestants because it was the official church. But because of this, it was handicapped in reaching the immigrants and the lower classes. Its clergy were too few and too formalistic to become ready missionaries on the frontiers of British North America. Growth from within was also difficult, though Canadian Anglicans had an episcopacy by 1815. Consequently, many of the Protestant gains were made by Presbyterians, Baptists, Methodists, and Quakers. North European immigrants also brought the Lutheran Church to Canada, served in many cases by traveling missionaries from the United States. The Quakers had come in from England and from the United States by the early nineteenth century. Baptists from England and the United States sent workers and funds to support missions on the Canadian frontier in the eighteenth and nineteenth century. Methodist influence likewise came chiefly from the United States. Furthermore, the Protestant missionary societies, such as the Society for the Propagation of the Faith, the Society for Promoting Christian Knowledge, and the Church Missionary Society, carried on programs of expansion that also reached the Indians and Eskimos of Canada. In the beginning of the period of the global wars in the twentieth century, Canada still had a vast frontier left in the north and west, reflected in the stance of the churches.

Australia and New Zealand. Australia, though geographically far removed from Canada, has an affinity with it within the Commonwealth of Nations. Australia is somewhat smaller than Canada. Very early in the colonial period, European explorers had been interested in Pacific land south of the equator. Captain James Cook reached both New Zealand and Australia. Soon the English government decided to deport convicts to Australia. It must be kept in mind that English law at that time was exceedingly harsh against insolvent paupers. In 1787, the first group of convicts was sent, with a contingent of prison guards and a governor to keep them under discipline. The Napoleonic Wars made it impossible for the British government to follow through on the convict colony concept, though more convicts were sent out. Early in the nineteenth century, the vast areas of Australia were further explored by the English. The white population soon dominated the aborigines. In 1850, each of the various states was granted responsible government by act of Parliament, and on January 1, 1901, the Commonwealth of Australia was established, but the population was only about seven million.

The Anglican Church was introduced to Australia through the chaplains who came with the first contingent of convicts. Samuel Marsden (1765–1858) was the first outstanding Anglican pioneer, arriving a few years after the first convicts. He called attention to New Zealand also. Through support of the English mission societies, the work of the Church was furthered. At first, it was to be administered by the Bishop of Calcutta, but in 1836 William Grant Broughton (1788–1853) was named Bishop of Australia. By the end of the nineteenth century, this single diocese had been divided into about half a dozen. In the nineteenth century, English and Scottish Presbyterianism were also introduced. Soon Methodists, Baptists, and Congregationalists also arrived. In the mid-nineteenth century, some German Lutherans also came, but Lutheranism did not gain prominence in the strongly Anglican and English sod of Australia. Through Irish Catholics, the Roman Catholic Church was introduced into Australia.

New Zealand had been the object of English mission societies that began work among the aborigines early in the nineteenth century. By midcentury, Anglicans and Scottish Presbyterians had planted colonies of Europeans there. But the population remained small, about one million at the end of the nineteenth century. Because of the English origins, early in the twentieth century the Church of England claimed almost half of all Christians in New Zealand, though Presbyterians, Methodists, Baptists, and the Roman Catholic Church were also represented.

In the later twentieth century, New Zealand and Australia remained quite distinctive in their culture and their ethnic composition because they are basically

Western in every aspect, though geographically more closely associated with the Asian part of the world than with the Western.

The Social Gospel. In American churches, a major movement known as the Social Gospel emerged in the latter part of the nineteenth century and early in the twentieth century. Many factors fed this development. There were strong proponents who made this their ideology, and there were also strong opponents of the movement. It was a controversial issue with broad implications, and it therefore deserves careful attention.

By the mid-nineteenth century, French and English social thinkers led Americans to similar concerns. The New England departure from strict Calvinism provided favorable ground for such ideas. There was also in the American intellectual air the strong millenarian trend mentioned above. By the middle of the century, this made for a utopianism in American thinking that convinced people that an ideal commonwealth could be established on earth. There may even have been churchmen in the nineteenth century who remembered a seventeenth-century prediction that America would be a very special city of God set on a hill.

In *Revivalism and Social Reform in Mid-Nineteenth-Century America*, Timothy L. Smith traces this preoccupation with social reform to the nineteenth-century revivals rather than to the liberal theology of the early nineteenth century, as many other historians have done. He advances some cogent arguments, but his point is only partly proven.

The liberal theology of Albrecht Ritschl and Adolf Harnack provided some input for the Social Gospel Movement. Unitarianism in America placed strong emphasis on the goodness of man. The evolutionary philosophy of the nineteenth century had an unlimited optimism and confidence in the progress that man could achieve through science. The midcentury millennial preoccupation also made a contribution. This and the trend to secularism induced men to abandon the otherworldly hope and shift to the hope of the kingdom of God here and now. One dimension of the hope for a better society in America was expressed by Edward Bellamy (1850–98), whose novel *Looking Backward* (1888) looked forward to radical social changes and gained him a reputation far beyond his merits. Henry George (1839–97) was even more of a theorist. His *Progress and Poverty* (1879) claimed that the basic problem with the American socioeconomic system was the private appropriation of the increasing land values, and therefore he proposed a surefire cure for this: the single tax on land.

The first prominent protagonist for the Social Gospel was Washington Gladden (1836–1918), a Congregationalist pastor who had a decidedly liberal leaning. As a pastor in industrial towns, he was immersed in the stark reality of social problems. In books such as *Social Salvation* (1902), he called on churches to concern themselves with social injustice. Walter Rauschenbusch (1861–1918) was also a very significant advocate of the Social Gospel. His father was August Rauschenbusch, an immigrant from Germany who abandoned his Lutheran heritage in favor of Baptist membership because he felt the Lutherans were too unconcerned with contemporary problems. He became a professor in the Baptist seminary in Rochester, New York. Walter was educated there and then served as pastor of a German Baptist church in a slum section of New York City. There, he was immersed in the reality of social problems. Later, as professor at the Rochester seminary, he wrote *Christianity and the Social Crisis* (1907). His book *Christianizing the Social Order* (1912) was frank and forthright in his challenge of the laissez-faire, individualistic capitalist system in America. In his book *Social Principles of Jesus* (1916), he scored the system of private property in America so severely he made even the petite bourgeoisie wince with pain. In his attempt to undergird his social theory with a theology, he produced *A Theology for the Social Gospel* (1917), in which he propounded major revisions of biblical theology so forthrightly that conservative theologians were repelled. Rauschenbusch gave up biblical Christology, rejected the concept of sin as defined by total individual depravity, and advocated a new view of the kingdom of God.

Among Roman Catholics in America there were also signs that their attitudes to social questions were undergoing some modification in the latter decades of the nineteenth century and early in the twentieth century. John Ireland (1838–1918), archbishop of St. Paul, and James Cardinal Gibbons (1834–1921), archbishop of Baltimore, were pioneers in leading the Catholic Church to a more favorable stance to the US system. In the 1890s, they ran into much opposition within the Roman Catholic hierarchy, and they caused many a raised eyebrow between the United States and Rome. The change is also evident in Leo XIII's encyclical *Rerumnovarum* (1891), which gave evidence of more concern with social problems than any other papal pronouncement of the nineteenth century. When Archbishop Ireland addressed a gathering in Milwaukee just before the opening of World War I, he chose for his topic "Catholicism and Americanism" and appealed to Leo XIII for support for the new view that the Roman Catholic Church could coexist with the American state. This new stance in the Roman Catholic Church was institutionalized in the Catholic University of America, Washington DC, founded 1889 and headed by John J. Keane, a leader of "Americanism." But neither in the faculty nor in the Roman Catholic clergy in America was there total unanimity in those early years on the new problems and their newly proposed solutions. This was evident not only in the social issues but also in education. A feature of the social activist program was strong advocacy of state-sponsored education not only as a means of social improvement but also as a way of homogenizing the whole American population. Conservative churches such as the Lutherans, who, besides the Roman Catholics, were the only major denomination with parochial schools, opposed this tendency very strongly. When the Bennett Law was proposed in Wisconsin in 1889, it was primarily the Lutherans who defeated it at the polls. Catholics were theoretically on the side of the Lutherans, but Ireland shocked some of his own compatriots when he suggested that parochial schools might be unnecessary. It is evident, therefore, that at the end of the century a major change was underway in the Roman Catholic Church's attitude toward the whole sociopolitical situation in America. In the twentieth century, this tendency toward a comfortable coexistence came to a much fuller bloom.

Asian and African Expansion of Christianity

In modern times, Christianity has been considered a Western cultural phenomenon in its outreach to Asian and African peoples. In premodern times, many attempts had been made to propagate Christianity among non-Western peoples. The Spanish and Portuguese in their colonial outreach shortly after 1500 provide a major example. In the nineteenth century, there were even more aggressive waves of Western expansionism. The expansion of Christianity in the nineteenth century is closely associated with European imperial expansion. In the period of the World Wars, a very violent reaction occurred against imperialism that also affected the churches unfavorably.

In Catholic circles, the modern expansion of Christianity was often closely controlled by the Catholic monarchs, like those of Spain and Portugal. There were Roman Catholic orders of clergy (called the regular clergy because they worked under the regulations of monastic orders) that served in foreign missions, but they were most often under royal control. In Protestant churches, we see a similar polity. Almost all European nations had a state church. Calvinistic Anglicanism was official in England. Lutheranism was the official church in Scandinavia and in some of the German principalities. Among Protestant nations, however, state churches were for the most part disinterested in mission expansion early in the modern period. Exceptions to this pattern can be found in the attitude of the Swedish and Danish kings, who in certain cases promoted Lutheran missions. For example, under the sponsorship of the Danish kings, Lutheran missionaries were sent to India early in the 1700s to initiate the first Protestant mission enterprise there.

One of the chief structures through which European nations, especially the Protestant ones, carried on their overseas commerce until far into the nineteenth century was the chartered company. Spanish kings had direct royal control over their colonial enterprises, but in England, for example, the East India company was chartered by Queen Elizabeth to exploit relations with India. This is one of the best-known of the corporations chartered by a government for colonial purposes, but it is only one of hundreds like it. The French, Dutch, and other nations operated the same way. These chartered companies jumped into the pool of world competition before international law had been definitely formulated. There was no common, formal, and a priori recognition of national sovereignty at that time. Generally, the principle held that might was right. The chartered companies generally were granted the right to maintain their armies and navies and to use them against foreign powers. They could and did make war and negotiate treaties. Since these chartered companies were interested in making money through commercial enterprise, their policy specified that changing the social and cultural situation of the people they were about to fleece should be avoided. Companies such as the East India Company therefore maintained a strongly worded policy against permitting missionaries into the territories they controlled. Its opposition to any mission enterprise was once more verbalized in 1793.

But there were Christians in many countries who felt very keenly the obligations of the Great Commission, that Christians had the obligation to go into all the world and to evangelize all nations. Since the state churches were often immobile and paralyzed with bureaucracy and politics, motivated Christians organized special societies to carry out mission work. But it was not an easy task. When William Carey, an English cobbler who was trying to stimulate his fellow Christians to get serious about beginning mission work in India, made a plea to a Baptist ministers' conference, emphasizing that the Great Commission was obligatory on every generation, the chairman denounced Carey as a miserable enthusiast. The conference endorsed the chairman's viewpoint. Carey then became instrumental in organizing the Baptist Missionary Society in 1792. This is one of those societies that at the threshold of the nineteenth century mark an important turning point in the world outreach of Western Christendom. The London Missionary Society, founded 1795, is also significant among the hundreds of such societies. It was interdenominational, but the society did not succeed in overcoming the problem of denominational differences in mission fields. Another significant English society is the Church Mission Society, basically Episcopalian, but fairly broad church in its polity.

In Germany, the *Deutsche Christentumsgesellschaft* was organized in 1778, but the Napoleonic Wars prevented much activity during the first years. In 1815, the Basel Missionary Society was organized out of this movement. It had affiliates in many other German cities and sent missionaries to the Midwest American frontier and to Asian and African countries. This missionary society and its affiliates produced some of the most consecrated pioneers in the history of Christianity. At a time when there was very little prevention against tropical diseases such as malaria and yellow fever, these missionaries went out willingly to new areas of the world, such as tropical Africa, where they knew that life expectancy for Europeans was only a few years. This missionary movement, centering especially in the German kingdom of Wuerttemberg, was especially significant also because, at first, it supplied many missionaries for the British missionary societies, which had difficulty recruiting their own nationals.

Another continental mission outreach was sponsored by the Moravians, or the Unitas Fratrum. Its first burst of mission activity came in the eighteenth century, but early in the nineteenth century, the Moravians were still going strong. Some of the most dedicated missionaries in the annals of the Christian Church have been Moravians. Moravians were outstanding not only for their zeal but also for innovative approaches in mission methods. They did not make the mistake of many mission societies in sending out a few individual missionaries who with their families were to establish centers of Christian witness in strange lands and foreign (and sometimes unfriendly) cultures all by themselves. Moravians sent out teams, often eight to ten workers together, members of which could uphold and strengthen one another in their difficult assignments.

MISSION DEVELOPMENTS	
INDIA	William Carey arrived in 1793. By 1800 India controlled by British East India Company. Founded Christian chapels, sent chaplains such as Henry Martyn (1805). Am. Board of Commissioners for Foreign Mission (1810), mostly Congregational. Send Scudder (1819) to Ceylon. Presbyterians in Punjab by 1830s.
CHINA	Early Roman Catholic missionary efforts by Spanish and Portuguese. Due to controversies, emperors sent them out in the eighteenth century. British forced entry in 1842 due to opium wars. British and French missionaries reentered. J. Hudson Taylor founded China Inland Mission. Anti-Christian reactions in 1860s. Wars hampered mission activity: Boxer Uprising, Revolution of 1911, emergence of communists in 1921. Missionary activity halted in 1951–52.
JAPAN	Jesuits had early success. By 1600 revolution changed everything. Tokugawa rulers banned Christianity. Hundreds of thousands were executed. Closed until nineteenth century. Commodore Perry forced treaty on Japan in 1854, which reopened country to trade and mission. Christianity remained illegal but there were converts by 1859. By 1890s more than 25,000 Christians. Suffered during WWII but survived.
RUSSIA	1917 Revolution turned against Orthodox Church. In 1922 government confiscated church treasures. A pro-Bolshevik church formed but did not gain popular support. Antireligious restrictions eased during WWII but retuned after the war.
AFRICA	Portuguese brought Catholicism to sub-Saharan Africa. Dutch and English introduced Protestantism before 1800. English and American Evangelicals established West African colonies to resettle freed slaves, most of whom were Baptist. After the British seized the Cape, the London Missionary Society entered South Africa. Robert Moffatt (1795–1883) and David Livingstone (1813–73) were famous missionaries to Africa. Imperialist occupation intensified after 1870. After WWII, Africans sought independence. The churches played a significant role in the independence movement.

CHAPTER SEVEN

The Spread of Global Christianity

MISSION AND MESSAGE FROM THE WORLD WAR ERA TO THE PRESENT

Mission played an important role in the movements that developed in the twentieth century. During World Wars I and II, the Christian churches were catapulted into an era of new challenges and new opportunities such as they had never encountered before. The nineteenth century foreshadowed some of the changes, but there were not many who read the signs of the times correctly. The Roman Catholic Church in Europe especially was in the eye of the storm when World War I broke out.

But no people and no nation was immune from the wars. The significant aspect of world history in the twentieth century is that World Wars I and II are really connected as parts of one massive upheaval of global dimensions, and they affected the whole world. It is not possible to write the history of these wars in one volume. It is even harder to summarize it in a short section of Church history. The sheer mass of material and the utter complexity of it is probably the reason few Christian scholars really analyze the massive changes that have overtaken the churches and the world in this period.

World War I left the central European nations prostrate in abject defeat. This provoked World War II. The wars escalated the waste of natural and human resources to the point where humanity became desensitized to thinking about the 140,000 people killed in Hiroshima with one bomb. This and the enormous tension and animosities that lived on after the wars make it impossible for Christians to make any kind of stewardship evaluation on the question of wasted resources provoked by the wars and many other related questions. The aftermath of World War II especially brought with it a widespread anti-imperialism movement that, in turn, reacted on Christian missions. This marks a reversal in the position that churches hold on a worldwide basis and is more revolutionary than anything since the time of Emperor Constantine in AD 300, as far as churches are concerned.

Fundamentalists. At Princeton under Charles Hodge (1797–1878), his son Archibald Alexander Hodge (1823–86), and Benjamin Warfield (1851–1921), a strong reaction developed in defense of the Scriptures as the inspired Word of God and the basis of the theological enterprise. Also from the Moody Bible Institute in Chicago, a conservative influence emanated that sponsored Bible conferences to muster support for the conservative view of Scriptures. The Niagara Bible Conference of 1895 drew up a list of doctrines considered most fundamental, emphasizing especially (1) verbal inerrancy of the Bible, (2) the virgin birth, (3) the substitutionary atonement of Christ, (4) the physical resurrection of Christ, and (5) the bodily return of Christ for judgment. A longer list of essential doctrines had been drawn up in 1878, but this was simplified by some of the fundamentalists in the 1890s. Later, this was expanded. A conference in Philadelphia in 1919 added some other essential points of doctrine such as the Trinity, the doctrine of sin, regeneration by the Holy Spirit, and resurrection and everlasting existence of both the saved and the lost. But in fundamentalist shorthand, the five points are considered as being the most fundamental of the fundamentals. The points of doctrine enunciated indicate also which were the significant doctrines that the liberals had been challenging or rejecting. These points soon came to be known as the "fundamentals," and those adhering to them were known as fundamentalists. This view was deliberately sponsored as the opposite pole of theological liberalism. One of the strong emphases of this conservative school of theology was dispensationalism, an emphasis on the successive dispensations or eras of history that God had marked out, ending with the last era, the millennium, or thousand-year reign of Christ on earth.

The dispensationalist theology tended to be strongly Calvinistic; therefore, the fundamentalist movement had little appeal either to Arminians or to Lutherans. But the fundamentalists received massive publicity because they had several wealthy businessmen supporting their public relations program. Through a special fund established by several laymen, *The Fundamentals*, booklets on the fundamental theological issues of the day, were published beginning in 1910. The content consisted of somewhat fewer than a hundred essays authored by many scholars from various denominations. Their orientation was, however, in the Bible school tradition rather than based in the seminary tradition. The fundamentalist movement had a touch of anti-intellectualism in its first years. This is understandable when one realizes that they took exception to the liberal theology ensconced in the seminaries and universities. To counter this, the Bible School or Bible College Movement was launched by fundamentalists. Moody Bible Institute in Chicago (opened in 1889) and Winona Bible School of Theology were among their first schools.

The Ecumenical Movement. During World War I, the popularity of the fundamentalists decreased; a second movement arose that would come to dominate the story of the Church in the twentieth century. An important international missionary conference had been held in Edinburgh in 1910, which, by emphasizing ecumenism in missions, confronted fundamentalists with a difficult challenge. This really marks the beginning of a countermove called the Ecumenical Movement.

The Ecumenical Movement in its full orchestration began early in the twentieth century, though it had a long prelude in the nineteenth century. The motivation for ecumenism may not be exactly identifiable with liberal theology, but in the thinking of many churchmen, especially among the opponents of ecumenism, the two were closely associated. This contributed to growing polarization of churches and of churchmen between the fundamentalists and the liberal ecumenists—a mark of twentieth-century world Christianity with a very deleterious effect on Christian witness in the world. The 1910 Edinburgh Mission Conference played the opening strain of this ecumenical symphony. Although there had been earlier meetings with a similar objective to overcome the denominational fracturing of Christian churches in the world, Edinburgh was the first time that there was a truly global scope to the participation as well as to the program and objectives of such a conference.

Attempts to overcome the multifarious organizational fracturing in Protestantism began well back in the nineteenth century. The organizing principle was sometimes national, as in the case, for example, of the *Deutscher Evangelischer Kirchentag* (German Evangelical Church Diet), the first meeting of which convened in 1848. In Germany, the *Allgemeine evangelisch-lutherische Konferenz* met the first time in 1868. This was the forerunner of the Lutheran World Convention, first convened in 1923, and of the Lutheran World Federation, organized in 1947.

In England, the Evangelical Alliance was formed in 1846. Its participants were individuals instead of churches. This also had German support, and the convention of 1857 was held in Berlin. The meeting in Paris in 1855 had given impetus to the founding of the World Alliance of Young Men's Christian Associations. The first Young Men's Christian Association had been organized in 1844 in London. But youth organizations on the Continent antedate that by decades. In the last decades of the nineteenth century, the World Student Movement grew tremendously, and by 1895, the World Student Christian Federation was a flourishing organization. Similar to this, and possibly more important, was the Student Volunteer Movement, launched in the 1880s. A number of conferences had been held, but continuity was achieved only in 1888 when a permanent executive committee, with John R. Mott as chairman, was established. Christian students all over the world participated in this and fixed their objective as "the evangelization of the world in our generation."

Conferences of foreign missionaries and of churchmen from mission churches, such as India and China, were also being held throughout much of the latter nineteenth century. Each type of these conferences tried to overcome the disunity among Protestant churches on the basis of some principle, either national, denominational, by age groups, or by type of ministry sponsored.

The 1910 Edinburgh Missionary Conference was important because it was the first such conference that was not limited to age groups, denominations (that is, Protestant), or nations, but was truly worldwide. It had an especially strong world mission thrust. This is significant because many Christian churches, even before the Reformation, had tended to be restricted and limited by their national environment. In the post-Reformation era, it has certainly been one of the glaring shortcomings especially of Protestant churches that they suffer from national chauvinism. This nationalism dominated Christianity in the period of World War I. But the 1910 conference had not been without effect. It established a Continuation Committee as well as other committees to foster Christian unity and to undertake a more careful study of the work on the mission fields. As a result of the conference, *The International Review of Missions* was founded 1912 by the Continuation Committee. The study of missions sponsored by the conference was highly important because the science of missiology was in its infancy, and a scientific analysis of the work that churches had been doing in the mission fields was something very new for the time. Strangely enough, the conference did not make provisions for a careful study of the conditions of the old, well-established churches, the sending churches, in the Western nations. The outbreak of World War I suspended the activity planned and projected by this conference in 1910. As soon as the war was over, the objectives spelled out were implemented. In 1921, the Continuation Committee became the International Missionary Council by change of name. The International Missionary Council had already been suggested by Gustav Warneck in 1888. Warneck was an early pioneer in Europe for the new science of missiology. Furthermore, the committee on Mission Survey and Occupation initiated a major survey of the missionary situation in China, which was published in 1922.

The Edinburgh Conference had also induced the formation of a China Continuation Committee in 1913, which not only sponsored the missiological study mentioned above but also was instrumental in getting the National Christian Council organized in China in 1922. Out of this was formed the Church of Christ in China. But this union failed to bring unity to the Protestant churches in China. The China Inland Mission, mostly comprised of more conservative missionaries than the National Christian Council, did not join. Neither did the Anglicans, Lutherans, Methodists, and most Baptists. The churches that joined were mostly the Presbyterians and the Congregationalists. They claimed to have one-fourth of the Protestants in China.

One concern of the ecumenical movement was the impediment of denominations in worldwide Christian witness. But the problem with the ecumenical outreach was that it was based on liberal theology, which left many confessional Christians dissatisfied. At the 1925 Life and Work Conference, where Bishop Soederblom was influential, one participant stated that the work of the Church was the social duty to complete God's creation, namely to effect the humanization of humanity. Soederblom expressed concern about the problem that denominationalism was causing. Samuel Simon Schmucker, another Lutheran not generally known as a conservative, had emphasized earlier that one important bond of union among early Christians was mutual respect of their acts of discipline. This was flagrantly violated by nineteenth- and twentieth-century Christian churches, as is evident from the fact that churches generally accepted people who were under church discipline in other churches, without making many inquiries or asking many questions. The ecumenists criticized such disregard on the part of some churches for disciplinary action of other churches. Those whom the ecumenists criticized did not pay adequate attention.

But the problem with the liberal ecumenical movement was that there was no biblical theology to serve as a real foundation for this ecclesiastical League of Nations. The whole movement was to a large degree a hobby of enterprising and ambitious churchmen rather than an involvement of the churches and the people at the grass roots. As one observer points out, the ecumenical movement was top-heavy; it could be described as being all head, with no body. The local congregations should have been the key to it, but they were almost invariably bypassed.

It was this kind of deficiency in the ecumenical movement that caused such a sharp polarity, and this worldwide polarity between liberal ecumenicals and the conservatives, which did so much to weaken the Christian witness in modern times, was especially acute in China. The Chinese polarity, in fact, tended to exacerbate this tension in America. Thus the China mission served as a sounding board that amplified the discordant witness of the Christian churches in the West in the twentieth century. In the China mission, there no doubt had been a considerable difference of emphasis for some time between conservative Protestants and the liberals. This dates back well before 1900. But once the ecumenical drive began trying to herd all missionaries into one corral, the conservatives had to make a conscious reassessment of where they stood.

The Chinese Communist Party was organized in 1921. In this and many other ways, there was evident a radicalization of the Chinese Revolution. The liberal Christians saw things that were favorable in this, whereas the conservatives were invariably on the other side in their views. They favored the conservative governments—when there was any identifiable government in China at all—and the warlords, who were almost all labeled as "reactionaries" by the Marxists.

The widening split between the two polarities among the missionaries in China was running its course at first without Western churchmen being fully aware of it. But in 1917, Augustus H. Strong, prominent Northern Baptist scholar and past president of Rochester Theological Seminary, made a tour of the Far East. He was shocked at the radical nature of the liberal theology he encountered in Asia and ran up danger signals when he got back. He gained some thoughtful attention in his own church body, but world opinion was going the other way, which made Strong's witness difficult. The year after Strong was in China, for example, a coalition of Chinese universities and scholars sponsored John Dewey and Bertrand Russell in China to help them find a handle for getting their revolution on the right track. Dewey with his pragmatism came in a poor second to the radical proposals of Russell. But apart from this, men of world renown had nothing but contempt for conservative biblical theology. When Strong warned that the liberal danger was so acute that it was not only a matter of the China mission, but that Baptists had to reform or die, his church listened. In May 1920, some 150 Northern Baptist leaders issued a call for a caucus on the Fundamentals of the Faith. A Baptist church paper, the *Watchman Examiner*, picked up the emphasis on the fundamentals; it not only became a household word but a much more controversial issue than it had before. The fundamentalists in the Northern Baptist convention continued their program of witnessing to their convictions by meeting in conjunction with the annual sessions of the Northern Baptist Convention. As an agency for their witness, they formed the Baptist Bible Union. They also continued to point out that the seminaries in the Northern Baptist

Convention were teaching modernism. Among the Baptists this issue eventually resulted in a number of splits. In 1933, several score churches withdrew and formed the General Association of Regular Baptists, which established several theological seminaries and eventually comprised some four hundred congregations. In 1943, the Conservative Baptist Foreign Mission Society was organized by those who were concerned about "modernism" in the American Baptist Foreign Mission Society. Furthermore, in 1947, the Conservative Baptist Association of America was formed by other churches that were displeased with the theology of the Northern Baptist Convention.

Sydney Ahlstrom has pointed out that modernism or liberalism and fundamentalism are "mirror" phenomena of each other and often exacerbate each other. This was probably true among the Baptists but much more so among the Presbyterians. Shortly after Dr. Strong, the Baptist, had been in China and brought back distressing reports about the liberalism of missionaries there, William Henry Griffith Thomas, an Episcopalian clergyman, had visited China. Early in 1921, he addressed a group of Presbyterians in Philadelphia and indicted some Presbyterian missionaries in China as promulgators of higher criticism and modernism. This touched off a long period of tensions in the Presbyterian Church that had some very radical aftereffects. In the Presbyterian Church, the problem was exacerbated by the fact that Harry Emerson Fosdick (1878–1969), well-known pulpit orator and liberal churchman, had also visited China and reported very differently from Dr. Strong and Dr. Thomas. A pastor in the Presbyterian communion by the name of J. Gresham Machen (1881–1937) soon came to the fore among the critics of "modernism" in Presbyterian circles. Machen's book, *Christianity and Liberalism* (1923), is still considered a typical critique of the liberal position of that time and an important landmark in fundamentalism. Machen asserted that liberalism was not simply a harmless variant of Christianity but that it was a totally different dimension. The debate in Presbyterian circles became so acute that a minority withdrew and established Westminster Seminary in Philadelphia, organized a separate foreign missions board, and established the Orthodox Presbyterian Church. As was the case with many right-wing separation groups, this one soon split on the issue of millennialism.

While the neoorthodox were trying to get their own corrective to liberalism recognized, the fundamentalists kept on with their line of attack, and still the liberals sailed on. Some observers feel that by the 1930s, fundamentalism had spent its energies and was no longer a force in American Protestantism. But it was by no means dead. In the mission fields at least, it was very much alive, and even on the domestic scene, it showed some vigor in the 1930s and 1940s. It is true that the liberals with their emphasis on social concerns made the newspapers much more often. Their startling reports of the achievements of the Chinese Communists in the Yenan area in northwest China sounded as if a veritable paradise had already been inaugurated. In the United States, the Roosevelt New Deal also appealed to liberals. During the Great Depression, conservatives had to lie low because they themselves often had to rely on government agencies that they really did not approve. The liberals—political and theological—made such flagrantly favorable propaganda for Stalin's Russia, even during the notorious purges of 1936, that some Americans were driven into the arms of the fundamentalists by the sheer exuberance of the liberals toward socialism and Marxism.

When the United States was drawn into World War II and President Roosevelt persuaded the American nation that the USSR must be bailed out, the liberals had their day, but the fundamentalists were not dead even then, only discredited.

In the meantime in 1942, while the war was raging, the National Association of Evangelicals was formed, partly as a counteraction against the liberal National Council of Churches (NCC), the successor of the Federal Council of Churches, which had been founded in 1908. Twenty-five million Protestants had not affiliated with the NCC despite Reinhold Niebuhr's considered statement that it was the crowning achievement of the liberals. The National Association of Evangelicals organized many of those dissatisfied with the liberal view into a vigorous new alliance. They toned down the old strident cry of the fundamentalists, replaced the name with "evangelical," and tried consciously to appear less anti-intellectual. These evangelicals launched some very successful programs of worldwide significance, like Youth for Christ. Among the early mainstays of the Evangelicals were the Assemblies of God and the Church of God (Cleveland, Tennessee). But the new Evangelicals were not able to pull along all the fundamentalists. Some declined to join the march to new horizons.

According to Hans Küng, a mark of the twentieth century, particularly of the post–World War II period, is the emerging ecumenical paradigm. Indeed, an overview of the twentieth century and the beginning of the twenty-first century has shown the strong ecumenical character of Christianity in which alliances have been forged between denominations and other Christian organizations. Various agendas (theological or confessional) and political interests stand behind such fellowship declarations and alliances. It is important to look at some developments within Christianity over the course of the decades after World War II.

The World Council of Churches, or the Ecumenical/Conciliar Movement. Although the ecumenical movement is larger than the World Council of Churches (WCC), it is strongly associated with this international ecumenical Christian community headquartered in Geneva, Switzerland. The legacy of the WCC reaches back to the great World Missionary Conference in Edinburgh in 1910, but it is debatable whether the organization continues the legacy of Edinburgh. The conference at Edinburgh represented all Christians; at that time, the path to division had not been laid. However, after World War II, the Christian world has undergone often-turbulent change.

The WCC was formed August 23, 1948, when 147 church bodies assembled in Amsterdam. Intentions to organize had been voiced already in 1937 when the two parent organizations, the Faith and Order Movement and the Life and Work

Movement, merged. Subsequent mergers took place in 1961 when the International Missionary Council (IMC; now called WCC-CWME; see below) was added and in 1971 when the World Council of Christian Education, which had its roots in the eighteenth-century Sunday School movement, joined the WCC. The WCC also created new commissions: the Commissions on Faith and Order and on Life and Work.

The WCC unites 349 Christian church bodies from more than one hundred countries on all continents. Its members include most of the Orthodox churches; numerous Protestant churches, including the Anglican Communion, some Baptists, many Lutherans, Methodists, and Reformed; a broad sampling of united and independent churches and some Pentecostal churches; and some Old Catholic churches. Since Vatican II, the Roman Catholic Church has opened its ties with the WCC and, though not a member, holds an observer status and cooperates with it on joint ventures.

A noticeable feature of the WCC is its broad ecumenical spirit. The WCC is fully intent on realizing complete unity in faith and fellowship among all its member churches. It intentionally pursues a conciliatory character and excludes or seeks to overcome controversial theological issues that may be divisive for member churches. It also takes a very nonconfrontational approach to non-Christians, proposing dialogue rather than evangelism and conversion. Over the years, the Faith and Order Commission of the WCC has worked to establish consensus in doctrine and practice. For example, at its 1982 plenary commission meeting in Lima, Peru, the Faith and Order Commission adopted arguably its most widely distributed and studied ecumenical document: *Baptism, Eucharist and Ministry.* This "Lima text," as it came to be known, explores the growing agreement—and remaining differences—in fundamental areas of the member churches' faith and life.

When it comes to social issues, the WCC is known to readily address them, including Communism, free-market capitalism, imperialism, and industrial oppression. As a result, the WCC's position is challenged by conservative and fundamental Christians who take issue with both its open ecumenism and aggressive stance on social issues.

The WCC meets officially in an assembly every seven or eight years, at which delegates from member churches elect a Central Committee that governs between assemblies. Various committees and commissions answer to the Central Committee and its staff. At the 1948 meeting in Amsterdam, important theologians and world leaders were present, including Swiss theologian Karl Barth (1886–1968), known for his multivolume *Church Dogmatics*; U.S. theologian Reinhold Niebuhr (1892–1971) of Union Theological Seminary; and John Foster Dulles (1888–1959), who served as U.S. secretary of state under President Dwight D. Eisenhower. Subsequent general assemblies were held at Evanston, Illinois (1954); New Delhi, India (1961); Uppsala, Sweden (1968); Nairobi, Kenya (1975); Vancouver, Canada (1983); Canberra, Australia (1991); Harare, Zimbabwe (1998); Porto Alegre, Brazil (2006); and Busan, Republic of Korea (2013). The position of general secretary of the WCC has been held by Willem A. Visser 't Hooft (1948–66), Eugene Carson Blake (1966–72), Philip A. Potter (1972–84), Emilio Castro (1985–92), Konrad Raiser (1993–2003), Samuel Kobia (2004–9), and Olav Fykse Tveit (2010–).

The WCC plans her mission and consultation through the Commission of World Mission and Evangelism (CWME), which was founded in 1921 as the International Missionary Council (IMC) but was merged into the WCC in 1961. At the IMC conference held at Willingen, Germany, in 1952, the widely used term *missio Dei* ("mission of God") was introduced. Missiologists such as Karl Hartenstein (1894–1952) and Georg Vicedom (1903–74) served as formative figures in the post-World War II promotion of *missio Dei*. Although Vicedom is known for many ethnological and missiological treatments, he is best known for popularizing the *missio Dei* concept in 1958 with the book *Missio Dei.*

The merging of the IMC into the WCC raised concerns with many who noted that the direction of the IMC would change. Indeed, in the years after New Delhi (1961), the Church-centered missionary framework, still affirmed at Willingen in 1952, was steadily displaced by the concept of the world as the locus of God's mission. The new direction was concisely summarized in the phrase "The world sets the [church's] agenda."

At the WCC Fourth Assembly in Uppsala (1968), this shift away from the Church's central place in God's mission was affirmed. Consequently, Christ's person and His redemption was reinterpreted as inaugurating a comprehensive "shalom" for the world. The Dutch missiologist Johannes Christian Hoekendijk (1912–75)—and, to a lesser degree, Hans Jochen Margull (1925–82) and Ernst Lange (1927–74)—is often touted as the theologian who insisted in the 1960s on the use of the term "shalom" for a broader, holistic concept of salvation against an ecclesiocentric concept of mission. Terms such as "peace" and "righteousness" that had been associated with the Church were now found comprehensively in the social and political context of the world and enacted there for all people. An additional report from the U.S. delegation brought the term "humanization," which then was affirmed at Uppsala. The concerns for this shift were expressed by Donald McGavran's question: "Will Uppsala betray the two billion?" In 1972 at the newly formed CWME conference in Bangkok, the term "salvation" was under discussion, and for the first time, the term "liberation" became the dominant motif, thus underscoring the shift of understanding God's mission to the world.

The 1960s and early 1970s were turbulent years for the WCC because its shift brought tension and separation within its membership. An outcome of this shift was the formation of the Lausanne Movement, a conservative movement that was and is strongly influenced and shaped by American Evangelicalism and its prominent theologians.

The Nazis and the Churches. The Roman Catholic Church, as stated above, was in the eye of the storm especially in the European theater. This put Roman Catholic leadership in a very awkward position. Critics have viewed the decisions of that time unfavorably, but it is important to have a fuller understanding of the circumstances. Pius X died August 20, 1914, only a few weeks after the political tensions exploded into military violence. Despite the war, in short order, those cardinals present elected Benedict XV (pope 1914–22). The pope pleaded with the belligerents for peace but was drowned out by the roar of the guns. After the war, the Catholic Church had new opportunities in France and Italy and in the newly created countries, like Poland, Lithuania, and Czechoslovakia. The Vatican was able to reestablish with France the diplomatic relations that had been severed in 1905, when France disestablished the church—a move that the pope had not acknowledged. The establishment of diplomatic relations with the Vatican by Great Britain, Holland, and Portugal lent a deceptive appearance of prosperity to papal world influence.

Pius XI (pope 1922–39) sailed stormier seas, for he inherited the full blast of the reaction against the crushing aftereffects of the war. In Italy, Benito Mussolini (1883–1945) marched on Rome with his blackshirted partisans in 1922 and intimidated the king. Mussolini was made prime minister and used this position to launch himself as Il Duce. He and Pope Pius managed to effect a standoff. Eventually, they signed treaties, one of which specified a payment of one million dollars to the pope as compensation for loss of revenue. The secular power surrendered any claim to patronage but agreed to continue to pay the salaries of all bishops and priests. This looked promising for the papacy. But in a few years, Italian forces invaded Ethiopia, provoking condemnation and sanction from the League of Nations against Italy. This put the pope into a very difficult position; he did not care to speak out against this naked aggression because his faithful clergy and members in Italy joined in the victory celebrations.

But this was not the last opportunity the papacy had to stand up unequivocally against evil and aggression. In Germany, Hitler was coming to power in 1933. On January 30, he became chancellor, and in March, he issued a policy statement to the effect that he would work for peaceful relationships with the Church. Five days after that, the German bishops, assembled in the Fulda Bishops Conference, withdrew their earlier prohibitions against membership in the Nazi party on the part of Roman Catholic Church members and admonished the faithful to loyalty and obedience to the new regime. On July 20, 1933, the pope concluded a concordat with Hitler that was supposed to assure freedom of function in the religious domain for the Roman Catholic Church in Germany. Article 32 of this agreement gave Hitler one of the most important concessions that he desired—the assurance that priests would stay out of politics. After the war was over, an astute Roman Catholic archbishop admitted publicly that the concordat had deceived the Roman Catholics and, in fact, the whole world. However, the archbishop himself had said that the concordat was proof that the two totalitarian powers could find agreement if their domains were kept mutually separated.

At that time in the rise of the Nazis, the government was trying to get control of the Protestant churches and was paying scant attention to the Roman Catholic

334 / THE SPREAD OF GLOBAL CHRISTIANITY

Church. By 1935, the government turned its attention to the Roman Catholics also, and the 1933 concordat was disregarded by the government. In 1937, the pope issued a reproof in the encyclical *Mit brennender Sorge* and also reproved Mussolini in the encyclical *Non abbiamo bisogno*. The German encyclical was read from all Roman Catholic pulpits in Germany on Palm Sunday, March 21. It condemned the extravagance of the Nazis but did not condemn totalitarianism in principle. The voice of the Church in moral and ethical questions was ignored. The position of the Roman Catholics was somewhat ambivalent, to say the least, and the concordat made it seem that the Church actually condoned Hitler.

Early in 1939, a new Roman Catholic paper was launched in Frankfurt called *Der neue Wille*, which sponsored friendlier relations with the German Nazis. This paper praised Hitler as the builder of a great new German nation and called on bishops to recognize Hitler's plans for a positive new European social order. When Hitler started the European phase of World War II with the invasion of Poland in September 1939, the Roman Catholic bishops put out a pastoral letter urging Roman Catholics to do their duty to their nation and their Führer.

Limitations of space allow reference only to the pitiful destruction of churches in Europe in World War II—not so much the buildings but rather the moral and spiritual fiber of the people. Thoroughly secular and violent ideologies took complete control of people and nations, so that Christians destroyed one another on a wholesale basis. That has scarred the sensitivities of people to this day. Non-Western Christians took offense when they saw how "Christian" nations tried to destroy one another. One cannot say to what extent the wars damaged modern man and church work on a worldwide basis.

The periods of World War I and II did much to destroy the foundation of all the churches. This can be clearly seen in the situation in Germany. Theologians began to promote a theology of "orders of creation" in the 1930s, justifying a prominent place for Germany in the world order. This mind-set of course has a large dose of racism for its rationale. This theology implied a sort of primal revelation from God that took precedence over the Scriptures. The Christian Nationalist Movement, called *Deutsche Christen*, used this theology to justify its fanaticism of *Blut und Boden* ("blood and soil"). They appealed—improperly—to Martin Luther's doctrine of the two kingdoms to justify German statism. The Confessing Church was organized in 1933 under the leadership of Martin Niemoeller (1892–1984) in adherence to the ancient creeds and the Barmen Theses, with emphasis on basic Lutheran confessions.

Missions. The great international councils, successors of Edinburgh 1910, had only widened the gap between liberals and Evangelicals in North America. In 1928, the International Mission Council met in Jerusalem. By that time, the great liberal leaders, such as John R. Mott, realized that the Christian Church faced a powerful and ruthless enemy in materialism. They suggested that all Christians join in offering the hand of fellowship to the other religions of the world to combat this common enemy. This general theme was reflected also in a major study of the world mission of the Church that appeared in the early 1930s.

This thorough restudy of the world mission task of the Christian churches begun in 1930 was financed mostly by John D. Rockefeller Jr. The study was called the Laymen's Foreign Mission Inquiry. In 1931–32, a committee visited various mission fields in Asia, producing two stages of reports. The fact-finding committee was chaired by William Ernest Hocking (1873–1966), prominent American intellectual and professor of philosophy at Harvard. This mission inquiry seriously questioned whether Christian missions could serve any purpose other than social and educational uplift. The theology on which this was based was the new liberal theology, which we have examined earlier. Archibald G. Baker held that religion was only a phase of the cultural development of a people, thus there was only limited applicability of the mission challenge.

There were serious challenges to this position from the neoorthodox as well as from the fundamentalists and evangelicals. A prominent Dutch scholar, Hendrik Kraemer (1888–1965), was commissioned to make a study for the committee of the International Missionary Council for the conference in Madras in 1938. This report served as a partial corrective, but the neoorthodoxy of Kraemer could satisfy neither the evangelicals nor the confessional Christians. The polarity between the liberals and the conservatives increased to the breaking point. World War II intervened, but it did not succeed in covering over the polarity. Unfortunately, the right-wing radicals issued such strident criticism that the cause of the conservatives was jeopardized. One crucial point of difference was that the right-wing conservatives came to emphasize more and more forcefully that the Church as an organization should have no part in social and political action, but that it was a sphere only for the individual. The conservatives felt quite hostile to the liberals for making the Church the agency of revolutionary change.

Another significant international church council was convened in 1947 at Whitby, Ontario, Canada. There was much that was positive and laudatory in the attitude of the Western churches toward the younger churches in the developing nations. But the positive tone of this new approach to facing world responsibility was soon dampened by unfortunate developments in the cold war. China was still open, but the revolution boded ill for the future. The Korean War broke out within a few years of this council.

The World Council of Churches was launched in 1948. The next international mission conference after that was held in 1952 at Willingen, Germany. Under the shadow of the World Council of Churches, this conference bogged down in debates on the proper theological foundation of the Church's world mission.

In the conference conducted in Ghana in 1957–58, the question was raised why there should be separate world mission conferences at all. There was evidence that participants thought that the day of the mission societies was over and that the Church itself was the mission. When the world Christian community was preparing for the 1961 conference at New Delhi, India, which was significant because it was a joint conference of the World Council of Churches and of the International

Missionary Conference, a significant book was published, namely, *The Theology of the Christian Mission*. For the critical scholar, of course, it is imperative to study all ideas, including those with which he or she disagrees. Thus for scholars, a book like this is necessary. But it is to be feared that this book was received as a positive contribution to supply alternatives as to what message the Christian witness should disseminate in the world. And to the degree that it was taken this way, it institutionalized liberal theology in world Christianity, especially in the mission witness throughout the world.

Evangelicalism and the Lausanne Movement. Another movement that runs parallel to the Conciliar Movement, or the WCC, is the Lausanne Movement, which owes its beginning to Billy Graham (1918–), prominent in United States evangelism circles since the 1940s. Under Graham's vision and guidance, all evangelicals united around theological principles such as Christ's uniqueness and the infallibility of Scripture, a unity that included the common task of evangelization of the world. The Congress of Lausanne was preceded by a world congress on evangelism in Berlin in 1966 at which twelve hundred delegates attended from more than one hundred countries. At this conference, concerns for the direction and lack of theological content of the WCC were also raised. In 1970, the prominent evangelical-Lutheran German missiologist Peter Beyerhaus (1929–) published with others the Frankfurt Declaration. The last of its seven affirmations pointed out the problem with the WCC-CWME direction, namely, that it pursued a utopianism at the expense of Christ's second coming and His enactment of the heavenly kingdom.

The Lausanne Conference or Congress was held in July 1974 in Switzerland. Approximately 2,700 participants and guests from over 150 nations gathered. In addition to Graham, the conference included Samuel Escobar (1934–), Francis Schaeffer (1912–84), Malcolm Muggeridge (1903–90), and John Stott (1921–2011). At his plenary address, leading missiologist Ralph Winter (1924–2009) introduced the term "unreached people groups," which again underscored the strong commitment of the Evangelical Movement to missions in contradistinction to the WCC, which in 1972 in Bangkok called for a moratorium on foreign missions. The term "unreached people groups" pointed to thousands who remained without a single Christian witness. Thereby, the Lausanne Movement underscored the focus on cross-cultural evangelization as the primary task of the Church. To that end, it relied for many years on the findings of theologians teaching at Fuller Theological Seminary, including Winter, who was named by *Time* in 2005 as one of the world's leading twenty-five Evangelical theologians. Also at Fuller was Donald McGavran (1897–1990), a former missionary to India who founded and led the Church Growth Movement within Evangelicalism for many years.

One of the major undertakings of the 1974 Congress was the development of the *Lausanne Covenant*. Drafted in large part by a committee chaired by Stott, the covenant articulates the movement's Christian convictions, such as the authority and power of the Bible, the uniqueness of Christ as the only Savior and the universality of His death and resurrection, a commitment to evangelism and its relationship to culture and social responsibility. To this day, the *Lausanne Covenant* serves as a basis for unity and a call to global evangelization. It set the stage for the formulation of further documents by the Lausanne Movement, such as the *Pasadena Statement on the Homogenous Unit Principle* (1977), the *Willowbank Report on Gospel and Culture* (1978), and the *Glen Eyrie Report on Muslim Evangelization* (1978).

Since 1974, dozens of Lausanne-related global, regional, and topical conferences have been convened all over the world. Global gatherings include the Consultation on World Evangelization (Pattaya 1980), Conference of Young Leaders (Singapore 1987), International Congress on World Evangelization (Lausanne II; Manila 1989), the Forum for World Evangelization (Pattaya 2004), the Younger Leaders Gathering (Kuala Lumpur 2006), and Lausanne III (Cape Town, South Africa 2010). The goal of Cape Town 2010 was to restimulate the spirit of Lausanne represented in the Lausanne Covenant: to promote unity, humbleness in service, and a call to action for global evangelization. More than four thousand leaders from nearly two hundred countries attended this gathering.

The Lausanne Movement represents Evangelicalism, which in turn is an umbrella organization that embraces members from all denominations ranging from the Southern Baptists to the Anglican Communion. Pentecostalism and charismatic communities are also associated with Evangelicalism. Although it is often perceived as identical to fundamentalism, Evangelicalism shares with fundamentalists only a conservative stance on theology and social issues. Very strong in North America, Evangelicalism embraces communities all over the world. Founded in London in 1951, the World Evangelical Alliance has member churches from 128 nations. Also, over one hundred international organizations participate in the alliance to create a broad association of more than 420 million Christians. Aside from its strong commitment to conservative Christian principles, Evangelicalism also takes a conservative stance on social and cultural issues, rejecting same-sex marriage, abortion, and embryonic stem cell research.

There is a somewhat post-Evangelical trend taking place within the movement that is largely the result of emergent church leaders such as Rick Warren (1954–) and Brian McLaren (1956–). Warren and McLaren wish to expand Evangelicalism's agenda to embrace an active ecclesiology against overt individualism and social issues such as poverty, combating AIDS in the Third World, and protecting the environment. Conservative leaders such as David Hesselgrave and James Dobson (1936–) have become outspoken critics of the trend, seeing in it a postmodern effect on conservative Evangelicalism and a move away from convictions espoused by the foremost leaders of conservative Evangelicalism, including Jerry Falwell (1933–2007), televangelist Pat Robertson (1930–), and Carl Henry (1913–2003). Henry served as the first editor-in-chief of *Christianity Today*, which was founded by Billy Graham to serve as a scholarly voice for Evangelical Christianity and as a challenge to the liberal *Christian Century*. The Church Growth Movement and its theology stood for decades as the recognized flagship of Evangelicalism, as will be discussed later. Since McGavran's death, the Church Growth Movement has diversified into various streams that extrapolate and develop classic principles of Church Growth as expressed in McGavran's magnum opus *Understanding Church Growth*.

Sadly, Evangelicalism is not immune to its own scandals. Just as the Roman Catholic Church struggles to assert credibility after numerous incidents of sexual misconduct by her priests, so, too, Evangelicalism has been shaken by scandal, such as the sexual misconduct of Ted Arthur Haggard (1956–), the founder and former pastor of the New Life Church in Colorado Springs, Colorado. His problems forced him to resign from his leadership role in the National Association of Evangelicals, which he had served from 2003 until November 2006. The association, headquartered in Washington DC and currently led by Leith Anderson, represents millions of people in more than forty-five thousand local churches from more than forty denominations.

Vatican II. If the polarity between revealed theology and humanistic theology is a major problem among Protestants, in the Roman Catholic Church there is a polarity equally as sharp. The Roman Catholic Church may seem like a monolith to outsiders. The strong emphasis on the central authority of the papacy in matters of doctrine and practice gave an aura of total unanimity. There were signs in modern centuries, however, that the unity was not as complete as it seemed. In the nineteenth century the papacy came down hard on new social and political ideas of freedom. The papacy suppressed the historicocritical approach in theology also with a strong hand up to about the period of World War II. The encyclical *Divino afflante Spiritu* was issued by Pius XII on September 30, 1943, on the fiftieth anniversary of *Providentissimus Deus*. This is considered by Roman Catholic scholars to be a turning point for their church. The encyclical summarized teachings of Leo XIII and other popes on the question of the inerrancy of the Bible and on the problems in this area arising from modern science and from historical criticism. In the second part of the encyclical, there is a strong emphasis on the need to use form criticism in Bible study. The encyclical pledges much greater freedom to Roman Catholic scholars in such endeavors. This encyclical is construed as having removed the strictures of the hierarchy on application of critical Bible studies. In a few years it was followed by another encyclical, *Humani generis*, issued by Pius XII on August 12, 1950. In the opening paragraphs, it was stated that evolutionism, existentialism, and historicism were contributing to the array of modern errors in theology. On the question of human evolution, the encyclical took up the question of the possibility of the evolution of human life from preexisting life, and it stated that such an opinion has not yet been proven. The pope asked in effect: "Even if there were preexisting life, would we not have to hold at least that at some point God intervened and infused a soul into an evolving pair of living beings and thus made them man?" The encyclical, however, rejects the possibility of polygenesis, the possibility of the descent of the human species from more than one pair of ancestors.

Catholic scholars have generally taken these encyclicals as opening a new permissive era in Roman Catholic theology, and indeed they did. Many modern Roman Catholic scholars, like Pierre Teilhard de Chardin (1881–1955), have departed from revealed theology as radically as the most radical Protestants have. Ironically, however, there is evident in the Roman Catholic Church also a real renaissance of Bible study, and there are Roman Catholic scholars as well as laymen who have a solid biblical faith. It defies rational explanation how this total polarity can exist in one church. But this much is certain: the monolithic nature of the Roman Catholic Church has been demolished. It behooves both Roman Catholics and Protestants to try to determine what this means for the modern church.

The changes in the Roman Catholic Church are reflected especially in the pontificate of Pope John XXIII and the council he convened, Vatican II. This council met from October 11, 1962, to December 8, 1965. It is a highly significant development in modern church history. It is interesting to note that the ecumenical movement had so preoccupied so many Protestant leaders all over the world, that when news was released that the pope was going to convene an ecumenical council, some Protestant church leaders were elated because they thought they were going to be invited to Rome to take part in consultation with the highest authorities in the Roman Catholic Church.

This Roman Catholic ecumenical council is so important that it deserves much more space than is available here. The first council to be called by the Vatican in nearly a century, it attracted much attention. The theology of Vatican II reflects the same polarity as all of Roman Catholic theology of the past several decades. One reads the theological formulations of Vatican II, called constitutions, with mixed reaction. There are many salutary emphases. There is, for example, an honest concern for sinful human beings. The *Church in the Modern World* is a constitution that restores some salutary emphases of biblical anthropology. The *Decree on the Apostolate of Lay People* accords the laity a more clearly expressed participation in the Body of Christ than any previous Roman Catholic document. In the light of the traditional clericalism in the Roman Catholic Church, this is especially significant. There is also a partial easing of the traditional Roman Catholic strictures against mixed marriages. Although the medieval doctrines of indulgences and of the treasury of merits are reiterated, there is an openness especially in the area of human concerns that became the entrée for new developments like liberation theology. But this council probably created more problems than it solved.

The new stance of Roman Catholic theology was not accepted unanimously in the Roman Catholic Church. One concession that many Protestants thought was long overdue was that the Mass could be said in the vernacular instead of Latin. Some concessions are taken farther than intended. This is evident in the wave of defections from the priesthood in the Roman Catholic Church in recent years, largely as a result of the inability of church authorities to hold the line on celibacy. Radical change is evident also in the training of the clergy. Many Roman Catholic seminaries have non-Catholics teaching theology. This is inviting disaster. Many seminaries have abandoned the old curriculum, and many theological students are unable to handle Latin, which was the traditional approach for laying the foundation of all other theological learning in the Roman Catholic priesthood.

One modern development in Roman Catholic theology, which was evident well before Vatican II and which became a major foundation stone for new emphases like liberation, is the change of interpretation on the medieval assertion that outside the Roman Catholic Church there is no salvation. This is a dogma that had been set forth officially as early as 1302 in the bull *Unam sanctam*. In modern times, this sounded too chauvinistic; therefore, more compromising Roman Catholic theologians have modified the inclusiveness—or exclusiveness—of this dogma. It is officially defined that salvation is possible outside the Roman Catholic Church. Does this sound like duplicity? Both conservative and liberal critics think so. One prominent scholar who took umbrage at this is Walter Kaufmann, famous Harvard philosopher. In *Faith of a Heretic*, he emphasizes that it was this duplicity in the Roman Catholic theological position that provoked him to leave the church and abandon Christianity.

The broadening of the parameters for salvation by some theologians is a significant change. The Vatican II Decree on the Missionary Activity of the Church only hinted at this expansion, but individuals, including popes, have carried it much farther, e.g., 1949 letter of Pius XII to Cardinal Cushing of Boston. The pope wrote that it was not necessary for people outside the Church to be incorporated into the Church, but what was required was a sincere desire or intention to obtain salvation, and this desire did not even have to be explicitly realized or expressed.

Another Roman Catholic writer explains this position by making a distinction between "outside the Church there is no salvation" and "outside of the Church there is no grace." The first statement is true, but the second is not thereby ruled out because there is the matter of *desiderium* or *propositum sacramenti*. This is the sacrament of desire, to which Roman Catholic theologians refer. This means simply that if a non-Christian has the desire to attain salvation and lives his life according to his best knowledge, this is accounted as adequate by God for him to be saved.

Hans Küng, a prominent Roman Catholic theologian, explains the possibility of such a major change in theology by making a distinction between dogma and theology. The first cannot change, but the latter does. Although dogma does not change, there is a further development of dogma, and even the unchangeable utterances of the highest authorities in the Church come to be seen in a better and more balanced way without really being falsified. This view is possible only if one holds to philosophical monism.

Karl Rahner, a German Roman Catholic theologian, has become a spokesman for the notion of salvation not only for non-Roman Catholics but for everybody who sincerely desires it. Rahner has, in fact, popularized the concept of anonymous Christians. He states that God can give His grace to people apart from the sacraments. If this notion was taken only one step farther, one would have universalism, the notion that all human beings are saved, regardless of what their faith or knowledge of God or of Jesus Christ may be. A similar trend in Roman Catholic theology is represented by Johannes Metz, who has written and edited a large number of recent Roman Catholic books on such issues.

RECENT INFLUENTIAL THEOLOGIANS	
PAUL TILLICH (1886–1965)	Protestant theologian. Christian revelation answers questions in modern culture such as man's estrangement, fear of "non-being," etc. Church is obligated to bridge people from modern culture to her message through a "method of correlation."
KARL BARTH (1886–1968)	Reformed; founder of neoorthodoxy. Sought God's self-revelation in Scripture. Brought Word-based theology back to European Protestantism, rejecting human-based liberal theology. Wrote Barmen Declaration to oppose German Christian movement.
DIETRICH BONHOEFFER (1906–45)	Lutheran neoorthodox theologian who opposed the Nazis. Leader at illegal Finkenwalde seminary. He emphasized Christology, practice of the faith (discipleship), and joined an undercover resistance movement that sought to assassinate Hitler. Executed by the Nazis.
REINHOLD NIEBUHR (1892–1971)	Reformed neoorthodox theologian turned socialist. Held that inadequate liberal theology and capitalism would prevent attainment of the kingdom of God on earth. Emphasized realism rather than idealism in addressing social concerns.
RUDOLF BULTMANN (1884–1976)	Lutheran professor turned existentialist. Modern scientific world view required reinterpretation of biblical theology, which was prescientific. Sought to demythologize the Bible to focus on how one experiences things in the present.
KARL RAHNER (1904–84)	Roman Catholic. "Anonymous Christians" adhere to other religions while unknowingly following Jesus Christ. They receive the grace of God without knowing it. Proposal based on God's graciousness and psychology. Cf. Papal statements *Lumen Gentium, Nostra Aetate,* and *Dominus Jesu.*
HANS URS VON BALTHASAR (1905–88)	Roman Catholic. Encouraged inter-Christian dialogue; influenced preparations for Vatican II. Used analogical theology to relate the Creator to His creation, which leads one to engage the world God made. God condescends in love. "Even if a unity of faith is not possible, a unity of love is," he wrote.
HANS KÜNG (1928–)	Roman Catholic. Global Ethos Project searching for common "world ethos." Peace between religions must be attained through dialogue about common elements.
ALVIN PLANTINGA (1932–)	Protestant theistic philosopher. Applies analytic philosophical methods to problems of God's existence, knowledge of God, and the existence of evil. God, who self-evidently exists, created the world with the potential for evil, but mankind is responsible for actual evil.

The doctrine of anonymous Christians contradicts the long-held Western Christian confession of the Athanasian Creed, which is an official confession for Roman Catholics as well as orthodox Protestant churches. The creed states that only those who worship the Holy Trinity and confess the incarnation, death, and resurrection of Jesus Christ can be saved. It remains to be seen whether Roman Catholic theologians will fully embrace the direction indicated by Vatican II, Küng, Rahner, and Metz or whether future Roman Catholic theologians will abide by the long-standing teaching of Western Christendom on this issue.

The Persistence of Liberal Theology. In the churches that had a loose polity, such as Congregationalists, doctrinal discipline would have been impossible even if desirable. In the Northern Presbyterian Church, however, a number of famous scholars were confronted with the issue of their liberal theology. Charles A. Briggs (1841–1913), Henry Preserved Smith (1847–1927), and Arthur Cushman McGiffert (1861–1933) were the most famous. Briggs was on the faculty of Union Theological Seminary (New York) when he publicly rejected the doctrine of verbal inspiration. When heresy charges were brought against him, the seminary shielded him from prosecution by his church. When Smith came to his defense, Smith was convicted of heresy by his presbytery. He left the Presbyterian Church to join the Congregationalists and secured a position at Union. When McGiffert was charged with heresy, he left the Presbyterian Church also to join the Congregationalists.

Neoorthodoxy and its denunciation of liberalism notwithstanding, liberal theology in America did not die out quickly. It was much too deeply embedded. Neoorthodoxy also did not offer an alternative to liberalism that was attractive to many who were dissatisfied with liberalism. The confessional churches saw in neoorthodoxy an uncomfortable similarity to socialism. This probably seemed a bigger barrier because many conservative American Christians, in the 1930s especially, thought that the individualistic competitive laissez-faire system of economics as first advocated by Adam Smith was an inseparable cultural adjunct to conservative Christianity. But overall, neoorthodoxy altered too many basic biblical doctrines to make it attractive to conservatives.

The persistent flourishing of liberalism in American churches continued into the twentieth century. It was deeply embedded in the academic tradition, first at Harvard, then ironically at Andover, first founded in opposition to Harvard liberalism, and before the turn of the century at the University of Chicago. But also Yale and Union Theological Seminary (New York) and even Baptist schools such as Rochester Theological Seminary became promoters of liberal theology. Twentieth-century man rejoiced at the fantastic progress he was making, also in the matter of adjusting theology to the new scientific understanding. At the same time, the outward religious establishment continued to flourish, while theology was reshaped and became less and less about God. The liberal view was energetically defended by men like Shailer Mathews (1863–1941) at the University of Chicago, especially in his *The Gospel and Modern Man* (1910) and his *The Faith of Modernism* (1924). George Burman Foster

(1858–1918), also at the University of Chicago, under the influence of the German theologians of the latter nineteenth century, was also a daring participant in pushing the Christian faith even beyond the liberal limits. While neoorthodoxy tried to serve as a corrective against liberalism, a major movement with small beginnings emerged already before the end of the nineteenth century. It tried to emphasize the fundamental doctrines of the Bible as a corrective against liberalism. This movement has therefore been called Fundamentalism.

CHRISTIANITY AFTER WORLD WAR II

This section is an update on the global status of Christianity after World War II. However, because of the sheer amount of material—much of it not yet recorded in printed literature but accessible only via online material—it is not an exhaustive historic presentation. Rather, it is a selection of a few events and people deemed important by the author for an understanding of Christianity today.

The reader should bear in mind the important concern underscoring this report, namely, that the spread of Christianity worldwide is severely challenged by other religions and volatile political powers and structures. That is the case even if the immediate context of the reader reflects little of these challenges. There is also the concern that Christianity—though a universal faith—has not reached many parts of the world. There are still many people without the message of their salvation through Jesus Christ.

A significant focus of Christianity after World War II has become the discussion of its proper relationship to other religions, particularly to Islam. The September 11, 2001, attack on the Twin Towers in New York City carried out by radical Muslims who belonged to the terrorist group al-Qaeda further strained the relationship. The attack has led to military action in Iraq and Afghanistan. And threats by a Christian pastor in Florida to burn the Qur'an on the ninth anniversary of September 11 sparked unrest in the remote area of Indian-ruled Kashmir, resulting in the death of sixteen Christians.

Christianity's Responses to Other Religions: A Case Study of Vatican II. For the past forty years, a dominant theme within Christianity has been the theological discussion of Christianity's relationship to other religions. These discussions were triggered by Vatican II (1962–65), a major event in the history of Christianity. The Second Vatican Council was summoned by Pope John XXIII in 1962 to update the beliefs and practices of the Roman Catholic Church. More than two thousand bishops attended the council, eight hundred of whom came from the younger churches of Asia, Africa, and Oceania.

The documents produced by this council affected more than the Roman Catholic Church—they impacted all of Christianity. *De Ecumenismo* extended an open hand to all non-Catholic churches, an offering that had not been seen previously. *Gaudium et Spes* (*The Church in the Modern World*) called for material assistance to developing nations and invited businesses to readily offer such assistance. It renounced nuclear war as "a crime against God." And it called for a clear mission to the world and a call to faith in the Lord and Master Jesus Christ. *Lumen Gentium (The Dogmatic Constitution of the Church)* presented the Roman Catholic Church in a far less monarchial and hierarchical manner and instead spoke of the Catholic Church as the "people of God" on pilgrimage, a church that is in communion with members who have been baptized in other denominations. This document also embraced adherents of other religions, including Jews and Muslims. Such statements appear duplicitous and in conflict with Western Christian confession and the need to profess Jesus Christ as the only Savior.

These statements would draw on earlier Jewish and Christian ideas about the Logos or God's Word/reason pervading human thought and preparing them for the Gospel. Yet they seem to take the ideas a step further by not actually requiring faith in Jesus Christ.

Medellin Conference (1968). A watershed event in the history of the Roman Catholic Church and for the entire Christian Church is the CELAM conference of Medellin (the Latin American Episcopal Conference). From August 24 to September 6, 1968, the Catholic bishops of Latin America met and purposefully sought to read the statements reached at Vatican II in light of the Latin American context. Among the many matters discussed at that conference, particularly noteworthy is the conference's decision to take a new approach toward the poor. Some of the conference's documents called for a "solidarity with the poor" (Poverty 10), which would be expressed in a radical new approach. In her five hundred years, the Roman Catholic Church had neglected this population group, but now the church would place her resources and personnel in the service of the urban and rural poor. Many priests and workers for the Roman Catholic Church chose to live among the poor. The decisions achieved at Medellin may also be understood as a "coming of age" for the Roman Catholic Church in Latin America, which until that point had followed closely the direction of the Roman Catholic Church in Europe, Spain, Rome, and Portugal. Although affirmed ten years later at the 1979 CELAM conference in Puebla Mexico (with the Puebla Document), Medellin's call for justice and solidarity with the poor—especially the theological consequence of the conference's decision, liberation theology—did not receive favorable responses everywhere in the Roman Catholic Church. For this reason, Medellin represents a turning point in the life of the Roman Catholic Church and for Christianity as the whole.

Liberation theology embraces the Medellin decision to address the massive and unjust poverty in Latin America. As a theological movement and practice, it received prominence in the 1970s and 1980s. In terms of theology, liberation theology rereads Scripture and the sayings of Christ from a Latin American context that reflects unjust economic, political, or social conditions. Moreover, it critically analyzes church practice and society's treatment of the poor. In response, many opponents of liberation theology have accused it of Marxist and communist tendencies.

Perhaps the most famous proponent of liberation theology is the Peruvian priest Gustavo Gutiérrez (1928–), who may arguably be regarded as the father of the movement because of his influence on the discussions at Medellin. He wrote *A Theology of Liberation* (1971), which defined the movement. Other well-known supporters of the movement include Leonardo Boff of Brazil, Jon Sobrino of El Salvador, and Juan Luis Segundo of Uruguay. Liberation theologians do follow their own specific interpretation of biblical texts, which is a hermeneutic guided by the circumstances of the context. Thus the mission of Jesus Christ is one of a social and political liberator, a political messiah (Luke 22:35–38; Matthew 26:51–52). Liberation theologians interpret events in Scripture such as the exodus and the institution of the Eucharist to address their current political concerns. Similarly, the Church and all incumbents of the hierarchy and power are called to act against poverty and the sins that cause it. Liberation theologians even believe there can be a call to arms, if necessary, to achieve Jesus Christ's mission of justice in this world. Here, liberation theology draws from Marx's concept of class struggle and revolution to underscore the process of liberation. It is precisely for the latter element in liberation theology that official Roman Catholic leaders (such as Pope John Paul II and Pope Benedict XVI [Joseph Ratzinger]) opposed it as ideological in its approach and one-sided in its interpretation of Scripture. For example, in 1984 and 1986, liberation theologians were admonished by the Vatican's Congregation for the Doctrine of the Faith, which was presided over by Joseph Ratzinger. Also in the 1990s, Ratzinger opposed and rejected features in liberation theology. He blocked liberationist priests, including Leonardo Boff, from serving as teachers of the Catholic Church. In other parts of the world, theologians who followed similar sentiments of liberation theology—such as Tissa Balasuriya in Sri Lanka and Sebastian Kappen, an Indian theologian— were also censured. Nonetheless, basic concerns and themes of liberation theology— among them the problem of injustice, rejection of violence, and emphasis on Christian responsibility for the poor and oppressed—were never dismissed by the official Roman Catholic leadership.

Pope Francis is Jorge Mario Bergoglio, former archbishop of Buenos Aires, Argentina, where poverty is a key concern. He is the first Jesuit to become pope and the first from the global south. Elected in 2013, Pope Francis displayed a welcome openness toward all, even impressing Cuban Communist leaders when he visited them in 2015. But he has concerned some Catholics with his comments about poverty and profit. As he makes his theological views and efforts clearer, it remains to be seen whether his high popularity will continue.

Some European Protestant theologians, among them Jürgen Moltmann and Frederick Herzog, have supported liberation theology and provided theological insight on that movement. Moltmann's book *Theology of Hope* put forward a theology of the cross that meant hope for the oppressed and poor not only in a spiritual sense but also in terms of finding in the cross inspiration for attaining relief from temporal, abject conditions.

American Civil Rights Movement. American ideas about liberation theology developed especially among African Americans. In the 1950s and 1960s the Civil Rights Movement became part of life in the United States and was largely associated with one of the foremost religious leaders of that period, Martin Luther King Jr. (1929–68). King was a young Baptist minister and theologian who since 1953 had served as full-time pastor of Dexter Avenue Baptist Church in Montgomery, Alabama. Montgomery became the site of civil unrest when on December 1, 1955, Rosa Parks refused to yield her seat to a white bus patron. Parks was arrested and a 381-day boycott of the bus system commenced. On November 13, 1956, the U.S. Supreme Court declared that the state and local laws of Alabama that enforced segregation on buses were unconstitutional.

King's contribution is significant as he worked to guarantee voting rights to the African American population in the United States and to address segregation and discrimination. King pursued a nonviolent, Christian vision of justice for the neighbor. To that end, the Selma-to-Montgomery march in 1965 can be viewed as the climax of the American Civil Rights Movement. March 7, 1965 ("Bloody Sunday"), saw six hundred marchers move through the streets. Police officers violently opposed them, using billy clubs and tear gas. On March 9, they marched again, but the participants turned back before leaving Selma. On March 21, they marched for five days and reached Montgomery, fifty-one miles away.

In the mid 1960s, King also took on other projects related to racial issues, including the Vietnam War and economic injustice. On April 4, 1968, King was assassinated in Memphis, Tennessee.

Western Christian churches struggled with issues of authority, fellowship, poverty, and power as much of Western society did in the post-war years, especially in the Americas. Also at this time, West would meet East again as the new global situation allowed Christians of the Eastern tradition to prosper in the West.

The Eastern Orthodox Church after World War II. "Eastern Orthodoxy" is an inclusive term for a large number of independent Orthodox churches. These often include ethnic identification as part of the name indicating where the church body originated: Greek, Russian, Serbian, Romanian, Ukrainian, Bulgarian, Antiochian, Albanian, Carpatho-Russian.

There are about four million Eastern Orthodox Christians in North America. Although most members are the result of immigration to the United States in the late nineteenth and early twentieth centuries from Greece, the Slavic lands of Eastern and Central Europe, and the Middle East, since the 2000s, significantly more growth in Eastern Orthodox churches has come through conversion rather than immigration. This demonstrates the increasingly visible force that is Eastern Orthodoxy within American religion.

In North America also, the term Eastern Orthodox is a generic term embracing a large family of more than thirteen church bodies. However, the two most significant church bodies to which at least three quarters of all Eastern Orthodox

Christians in the United States belong are the Greek Orthodox Archdiocese of North and South America and the Orthodox Church in America. The locations of Eastern Orthodox churches range from Florida, across Pennsylvania, to Kodiak, Alaska, where it became involved in mission to the native Alaskan people more than two hundred years ago.

For about one thousand years, from the time of the apostles until the new millennium, Christianity existed by and large as one church. In fact, the first seven ecumenical councils of the "undivided" Christian Church were held in Eastern territory:

AD 325   The First Council of Nicaea (present-day Iznik, Turkey)

AD 381   The First Council of Constantinople (present-day Istanbul, Turkey)

AD 431   The Council of Ephesus

AD 451   The Council of Chalcedon (present-day Kadiköy, Turkey)

AD 553   The Second Council of Constantinople

AD 680–681   The Third Council of Constantinople

AD 787   The Second Council of Nicaea

A number of events, such as the debate over the jurisdiction of Rome versus Constantinople and the discussion around the *filioque* ("and the Son") in the Nicene Creed, led to the divide between East and West. Thus the year 1054 marked the official schism between East and West when representatives of both churches, the Orthodox and Roman (Western) Church, exchanged official documents of separation. Particularly distressing to the East were the actions of the soldiers of the Fourth Crusade as they marched on Constantinople in 1204. The troops ransacked the city—which at the time was still Christian—both desecrating churches and forcing the use of the Latin rite. Against that backdrop, a significant post–World War II event occurred in 1964 when Pope Paul VI and Patriarch Athenagoras of Constantinople were mutually reconciled at Jerusalem. Denunciations (the *anathemas*) made against each other in 1054 by the churches of Rome and Constantinople were symbolically lifted or at least modified. A 1965 declaration evolved from this event. This rapprochement has been referred to as the "dialogue of love," signifying the following steps:

1.   It brought about a mutual revocation in 1965 of the anathemas of 1054.

2.   The relics of Sabbas the Sanctified (a common saint) were returned to Mar Saba.

3.   In 1999, Pope John Paul II accepted an invitation of Patriarch Teoctist of the Romanian Orthodox Church. This was the first time in a millennium that the pope visited an Orthodox country.

Although these gestures signifying the dialogue of love are a step in the right direction, effective theological talk on matters of dogma, the so-called "dialogue of truth," is a step that has not occurred. Property disputes in Russia and former Communist states have influenced joint theological meetings between representatives of the Roman Catholic Church and the Eastern Orthodox. However, theological debate will be necessary, given that differences exist on three major topics: (1) the Holy Trinity, specifically the disagreement over the *filioque*; (2) life after death, namely, the fact that the Roman Catholic Church affirms purgatory; and (3) the immaculate conception of Mary, which also is affirmed by the Roman Catholic Church. Differences in liturgical practices also exist and would require mediation, including the application of the water in Baptism (the Roman Catholic Church advocates sprinkling, while the Eastern Orthodox Church practices immersion); the reception of the Lord's Supper (Roman Catholics still advocate reception of the bread only); unction (anointing with oil), which in the Roman Catholic Church is typically applied to those in danger of death; the type of bread used in the Lord's Supper (the Roman Catholic Church uses unleavened, whereas the Eastern Orthodox Church uses only leavened bread).

Another significant event in the history of Eastern Orthodoxy occurred in 1970 when the patriarchate of Moscow permitted the Russian Orthodox (Greek Catholic) Church of North America (The Metropolia Church). That same year, at St. Tikhon's Monastery, South Canaan, Pennsylvania, a special council of leaders and laity renamed the church body The Orthodox Church in America (OCA).

The Bolshevik Revolution of 1917 not only ushered in Communist rule in the territory of Eastern Orthodoxy, but it also was a declaration of war on all forms of religion. For seven decades, Eastern Orthodoxy endured various forms of persecution, though the church found ways to survive. With the progressive collapse of Communism that began with the fall of the Iron Curtain in 1989, the Eastern Orthodox Church has experienced a dramatic revival. In Russia and most of the former Communist states, the church has established itself as an authoritative and influential institution.

The opening of borders that began in 1989 sparked interest in Eastern Orthodox churches concerning the situation of the Orthodox "diaspora" throughout the world and how unity among the various orthodox bodies could be initiated. In addition, ecumenical relations with other Christian denominations and with other religions have also begun. For North American Eastern Orthodox communities, the question of unity is significant. In 1994, at Ligonier, Pennsylvania, twenty-nine Orthodox bishops and leaders from many traditions met and declared interest in pursuing unity among the churches. Although most Orthodox church bodies seem to have been established along ethnic lines, unfortunately, no further steps toward essential unity in North America have been taken since 1994.

Gathering Data about Recent Developments. One major challenge in providing information on Christianity is how to gain access to facts that are truthful and correct. Admittedly, facts come from different sources and not all corroborate. Thus the following presentation relies on major sources that have been accepted as truthful and do indeed seem to corroborate with one another.

One way to present Christianity is by the number of current adherents. Such information would be available from a combination of census reports and population surveys. Some countries, such as France and the United States, by law do not provide census data that includes adherents of Christianity and religions. It is also difficult to gain exact information on countries such as China and Pakistan, where Christianity is growing but not yet officially supported. Some reports on certain regions may also contain degrees of biases toward Christianity, especially if there is a mandatory religion. In such cases, official government-provided statistics may not always be the best source. Then there is the question of how one should present the adherents to Christianity. Should they be those who actively practice it or who just adhere to it? There are a large number of people who self-identify with a specific religion but who are not religiously active. If, for example, asked to choose between Christianity and other religions, some would say they were Christians; if asked to choose between Christianity, other religions, or "not religious," they would say "not religious." This may make categorization difficult. Moreover, are we to consider only adults or to include children as well?

Statistics for rates of conversion are difficult to gather and often unreliable. Obtaining precise numbers is challenged by social taboos, such as the ban on apostasy in Islam or social and economical marginalization in India if someone's conversion becomes known. Arguably, for this reason, India has a large population of devotees (*bhakti*) to Jesus who remain unassociated with the Christian Church.

The above facts serve the purpose to point out the challenge statisticians have. This report, however, assumes that these concerns have been taken into consideration from those sources used to provide this overview.

Third World or *Two-Thirds* **Churches**. In the presentation of Christianity after World War II, the term "Third World" seems to dominate literature. This term has been used to designate those regions in Africa, Asia, Latin America, and the Pacific that were compared and contrasted with the Western capitalist and communist worlds, the First and Second Worlds. It seems that the term Third World initially harbored little negative connotations; those who belonged to it actively embraced it as a self-designation. However, today and for some time now, the term Third World is largely negative and used by outsiders—by those who belong to the Western world—in derogatory and discriminatory fashion for those considered to be inferior, underdeveloped, third-rate people. In fact, it became dominant among French intellectuals designating countries who opposed colonial powers and the Cold War nuclear threats of the First (capitalist) and Second (communist) Worlds. Now it has become a term pointing to common concerns among those nations: colonial past; poverty; and political, economic, and social ills.

The term "Two-Thirds World" is no better replacement. What was said of the Third World can just as well be said of the Two-Thirds World. In addition to the cultural, political, social, and economical distinctions associated with the terms Third World and Two-Thirds World, both also serve a geographic purpose. Since the changed situation after the fall of the iron curtain in 1989/90, new geographic regions with non-Christian populations, such as Central and Eastern Europe, were added.

It seems that the terms Third World and Two-Thirds Worlds have been used by those who do not belong to it in order to describe non-Christian and Christian populations in such regions. They also include young churches that have emerged from Western missionary work. In addition, these terms stand for a shared history in which these nations were exploited by Western countries and colonial domination and now have experienced some manner of independence since approximately the end of World War II. For example, India became independent in 1947, China in 1949, and many countries followed so that by 1980, the majority of countries in the world have received their independence. To this day, however, many nations are still searching for their own identity: political upheavals and tribal skirmishes demonstrate this fact and may in large part be traced to their colonial past.

Given these facts, it would seem logical to grant either of these terms only limited validity, and yet Third World seems a primary phrase to identify certain countries in the world. Although not all share a common colonial past, many do share poverty as a common trait—but this, too, is rapidly changing. In terms of economic expansion, Western countries now compete with the new economic powers of the so-called Third World countries. Moreover, Christian numbers in the Western world, One-Third World, are decreasing, while in marked contrast, Christianity is on the upsurge in Third World countries.

Finally, the terms Third World and Two-Thirds World tend to blur the distinctions among these countries, including economic, cultural, political, educational, and religious differences. Thus, while we use the terms, we should always bear in mind the above concerns. Today, scholars have begun to speak of the "Global South" as a way of describing this region in a more neutral way.

Christianity Compared to Other Religions. The population information discussed below is gleaned from a combination of census reports, random surveys (in countries where religion data is not collected in a census, for example, the United States or France), and self-reported attendance numbers. The following information is from Barrett's statistics in 2000, which reflect comparisons of Christianity with a selection of other religions and the regions in which they are located. By 2000, the world's population was more than six billion people. One should also note that many of these religions embrace numerous subgroups.

Christianity is the world's largest religion, with a little over two billion followers. Islam follows, with a little over one billion followers. Hinduism comprises less than 15 percent of the world's religious followers. Smaller groups, such as ethnoreligions

A FEW GLOBAL TRENDS AT A GLANCE	
UNREACHED PEOPLE	About two-thirds of the world population are non-Christians, concentrated between 10 degrees and 40 degrees north of the equator (the "10/40 Window"). But 95% of Christian missionaries are sent to Christianized areas.
POST-COLONIAL ERA AND "YOUNG" CHURCHES	Many Sub-Saharan and Asian Protestant church bodies are now independent from the Western churches that founded them. Since Vatican II, Catholic churches are developing services in their own languages and contexts.
POST-CHRISTIAN TRENDS IN THE WEST	Secularization and religious pluralism, which holds that the differences between religions are simply different perceptions of one truth, are increasing. Number of nominal Christians increasing. Many immigrants are non-Christians.
EASTERN EUROPE	Christianity declined rapidly under Communist rule (e.g., c. 70% of former East Germany professes no religion). Orthodox Church remains politically influential in Russia and some other post-Communist states. Western missionaries moved into the region where churches that survived Communism continued to exist, creating tensions.
THE URBAN WAVE	Urban growth in all areas except Europe and the United States, leading to megacities in Latin America, Africa, and Asia. Megachurches are developing, with weekly attendance of over two thousand.

(folk religions), Buddhism, and Chinese folk religions make up about 5–10 percent. The remaining groups are less than 1 percent: Shintoists, Sikhism, Judaism, Bahá'í Faith, and Jainism. There are about 150 million people who profess atheism, mostly in Europe and North America.

As stated above, Christianity represents the largest religious group, encompassing about 33 percent of the world's population of more than six billion people. As of 2000, the countries with the largest Christian population are as follows:

United States	235 million
Brazil	155 million
Mexico	95 million
China	89 million
Russia	84 million
Philippines	68 million
India	62 million
Germany	62 million
Nigeria	51 million
Congo-Zaire	49 million

By 2025, Germany will most likely drop out of the top ten and be replaced by Ethiopia, a nation that is experiencing phenomenal growth and that by 2025 is expected to have sixty-eight million Christians. A noticeable feature of these ten countries is that the majority are located in the so-called Third World.

The question that should be asked is whether Christianity is the fastest growing religion. That answer includes, of course, a number of aspects, such as strong regional growth, growth through immigration, growth through conversion, or growth through higher birthrate. Because of few conversions and low birthrates in many European countries, Christianity's growth is negatively impacted. By contrast, countries in which Islam or Hinduism predominates also seem to be populous and have high birthrates. European countries with significant immigrant populations from North Africa and Turkey see Islam on the rise because of higher birthrates in these communities compared with nonimmigrant groups.

Christianity has played a major role in addressing the rise in birthrates in many parts of the world, not unanimously, however. On June 29, 1968, Pope Paul VI issued *Humanae vitae*, an encyclical that forbids Roman Catholics from the use of artificial means of contraception. This is still considered to be the official Roman Catholic position. However, because of changing views on traditional sexual conventions, the ban on contraception is widely challenged by public figures in Roman Catholicism, including Hans Küng, and in Protestant Christianity.

In certain areas of the world, other religions besides Islam have stepped forward to compete. For example, in Australia, Buddhism is considered to be the fastest-growing religion in terms of percentage gain (from 200,000 to 358,000 adherents between 1996 and 2001, a 79.1 percent growth rate). In 2001, the American Religious Identification Survey (ARIS) reported a sharp increase in the number of Deists in the United States (717 percent growth since 1990). Is Deism then the fastest-growing religion in the United States, or is this a statistical or classification phenomenon? Only time will tell.

Global Shift. One further interesting observation is the change of Christianity's configuration worldwide. In 1900, the Christian population of Europe constituted about 68 percent of all Christians in the world; in North America, about 14 percent. In 1900, four out of five Christians lived in Europe or North America. Now, Christians in Europe have dwindled to 28 percent of the worldwide Christian population, and those in North America to 13 percent. By contrast, in 1900, Christians in Africa totaled 2 percent of all Christians worldwide. However, that percentage has risen to 18 percent. Likewise, in Asia, the population in 1900 was approximately 4 percent of the worldwide Christian total, but it has risen to 16 percent of the total today. Moreover, a glance at Latin America similarly presents a positive growth. In the period of 1900–2000, Christianity in Latin America rose from 11 percent to 24 percent of the total population.

We can thus safely say that Christianity's growth takes place outside the Western world. Christians in the Third World constitute about 58 percent of Christianity, and that growth will increase to about 80 percent by the end of the twenty-first century. Considering these facts, the twentieth century has shown rapid growth in Christianity on the continents of Africa, Asia, and South America. In Africa, the countries with the most Protestant Christians are Nigeria, the Republic of South Africa, and Congo. The fact that China, India, Indonesia, and Korea are the most Christian countries of Asia may be surprising, since India is predominantly Hindu, China is associated with Communism, and Indonesia has a predominantly Muslim population.

A close study of the decline of Christianity in the Western world and the rise of Christianity on the continents of Asia and Africa and in Latin America reveals some startling socioeconomic facts. Some have noticed that countries that post a decline in Christian population are wealthy, relatively peaceful, and emphasize sexual equality, whereas countries with a rapid growth of Christianity are less affluent and have less equality among the classes or between the genders. It seems that Christianity fades where there are better living conditions and increases where living conditions are poor. This phenomenon is evident also for Korea, which saw an increasing Christian population until the 1960s. But sharp economic growth brought economic affluence, social well-being, sexual equality—and a corresponding negative affect on the growth of Christianity in Korea.

Christian theological thinking, too, has been affected by this trend. Given the economic challenges of Third World countries and the struggles experienced by their people, including Christians, Western theologies have typically taken a preferential option for the poor. A significant shift among many Christian representatives occurred at the ecumenical World Council of Churches and its conferences, especially its 1968 conference in Uppsala and the 1973 gathering in Bangkok, where they reinterpreted the biblical message and the person of Christ to embrace a sociopolitical component. This shift toward a liberation theology and utopian ideal of creating a kingdom of God on earth rather than maintaining a traditional focus on the spiritual state and eternal destiny sent ripples through the Christian Protestant world.

Renewal Movements within Christianity. Christianity may attribute its growth in non-Western countries to Pentecostalism, or Renewal Movements. There are three major groups: classical Pentecostalism ("the First Wave"); the Charismatic Movement ("the Second Wave"), which has made inroads into mainline Protestant churches and Roman Catholicism; and the neocharismatics, or neo-Pentecostalism ("the Third Wave"). The latter two waves have taken place after World War II. As of 2002, the Renewal Movement is estimated to embrace about 523 million people, which makes up about 27.7 percent of organized global Christianity. Of the 523 million people, 65 million are Pentecostals, 175 million are charismatics, and 295 million are neocharismatics. Of those belonging to the renewal groups, only about 79 million live in North America, while the vast majority reside in Latin America (141 million), Asia (134 million), and Africa (126 million). The Third Wave, the neocharismatic group, signifies a more recent phenomenon of independent and post-nondenominational groups surfacing throughout the world. According to Barrett, in 2000, there were about 18,810 independent and indigenous churches and groups.

In the United States, Pentecostalism was associated with the poorer regions, particularly among Southern whites and blacks. For example, the Church of God in Christ (COGIC)—led by Bishop Charles Mason (1866–1961), who had received a Spirit baptism at Azusa in 1907—was by 2000 the largest American and Holiness Pentecostal church, with an estimated five million members. However, Pentecostalism has moved into the middle-class. The Assemblies of God, for example, joined the National Association of Evangelicals in 1942. By 2000, the Assemblies of God had two million members in the United States. By that time, Pentecostalism had grown among the Korean and Hispanic population, with the Hispanic population being the fastest growing Pentecostal group in the United States. About 20 percent of the Hispanic population in the United States are Pentecostal, which is about six million people.

The Charismatic Movement, or the Second Wave, features the discovery of spiritual gifts. In April 1960, Dennis Bennett (1917–1991), a priest at St. Mark's Episcopal Church in Van Nuys, California, announced to his congregation that he had spoken in tongues. He was asked to resign, but many point to this event as the beginning of the Charismatic Movement in mainline Protestant denominations, including the Episcopalians, Methodists, Reformed, Baptists, Lutherans, and Presbyterians. Lutheran pastor Larry Christenson (1928–), from San Pedro, California, claimed to have received a Spirit baptism while attending a Pentecostal gathering and was instrumental in bringing the Charismatic Movement to Great Britain and Germany in 1963. Within Roman Catholicism, the Charismatic Movement surfaced in 1967 when a group of teachers at Duquesne University spoke in tongues. They were influenced by two textbooks: David Wilkerson's *The Cross and the Switchblade* (1963) and John Sherrill's *They Speak with Other Tongues* (1964).

The foundation for the Second Wave, or Charismatic Movement, in the mainline churches had been laid prior to the 1960s by individuals such as Agnes Stanford, who wrote *The Healing Light* (1947), and by Pat Robertson (1930–). The latter theologian was a member of the Southern Baptist Convention, who through his 1959 purchase of a defunct television station launched the Christian Broadcasting Network in 1966. A third notable figure, Oral Roberts (1918–2009), launched a healing ministry in 1947 that began public broadcast in 1955. In 1965, Roberts established Oral Roberts University. Mention must also be made of David du Plessis (1905–87), an Assembly of God member, who had wide ecumenical impact on the Charismatic Movement through his dialogue with Roman Catholicism and through his lectures at theological seminaries such as Princeton, Yale, and Union.

In the 1970s and 1980s, independent Pentecostalism, or Third Wave, took a new approach to material wealth, abandoning the original classical Pentecostal ideals of austerity and denial of wealth. Although Oral Roberts and Jim Bakker already regarded wealth as a blessing from God, independent Pentecostal preachers such as

Kenneth Hagin Sr., his student Kenneth Copeland, and the black neo-Pentecostal preacher Fredric K. C. Price embraced the idea of prosperity and the ability for Christians to promote their own financial destiny provided they have faith. This "Word of Faith" movement in the United States—also known as "positive confession," the "faith message," the "prosperity gospel," or the "health and wealth movement"—became popular around the world, finding sympathizers among the younger urban generation. Preachers within this Third Wave are known to lead lavish lifestyles, which has attracted criticism from denominational Pentecostals. Many contemporary televangelists hold charismatic or Pentecostal viewpoints, such as belief in spiritual gifts, divine healing, miracles, and a prosperity gospel. Many are outside denominational Pentecostalism and conduct much of their ministries independently and with little accountability. In the twenty-first century, the televised church services of Joel Osteen's Lakewood Church in Houston, Texas, and Benny Hinn continue to attract large audiences—though not without public criticism and concerns over style and methods. In contrast, Robert Schuller's once dominant Crystal Cathedral in Garden Grove, California, went bankrupt in 2010 and was sold to the Roman Catholic Diocese. Crystal Cathedral Ministries could not sustain itself following inner conflict and the decline of the aging Schuller's involvement, providing a cautionary tale to other personality-based ministries. Schuller died in 2015.

In Scandinavia, Pentecostals are the largest church outside the Lutheran state churches. Until the 1960s, Stockholm's Filadelfia Church, associated with Lewi Pethrus (1884–1974), was the largest Pentecostal congregation. After 1948, many people from the West Indies emigrated to Great Britain, and with them came African Caribbean Spiritism, which showed remarkable growth in the 1960s. As did many other mainline English-speaking churches worldwide, the evangelical Anglicans in England embraced John Wimber's (1934–97) "power evangelism," a campaign of renewing established churches, which he started in Anaheim, California. With his first visit to Great Britain in 1982, Wimber taught the role of signs and wonders—especially healing—as an instrument of church growth. In France and Spain, about a quarter of the Roma (Gypsy) people are known to be Pentecostals, and Italy has the second-largest population of Pentecostals in Western Europe after Great Britain.

In Eastern Europe, the following statistics demonstrate Pentecostalism's success despite its history of severe persecution (it received religious freedom only in 1991). By 2000, Ukraine could count 780,000 members; Russia, 400,000 members; and Romania, 300,000 members.

In 1994, the Assemblies of God numbered more than four million members in Africa. South Africa especially boasts many prominent leaders, such as Nicholas Bhengu (1909–85) and the healing evangelist David du Plessis (mentioned earlier). The well-known German itinerant Pentecostal preacher Reinhard Bonnke, who began his ministry in Lesotho, attracts large crowds throughout Africa. From South Africa, especially through migrant workers, Pentecostalism spread to Zimbabwe. It is also strong in the Congo because of the independent Pentecostal missionary William Burton (1886–1971). From Kenya, it spread to Uganda in 1986, though it has been hampered by protracted civil war. Pentecostalism, whether through the Assemblies of God or any of its families, is a significant movement throughout West Africa in countries such as Ghana and Nigeria. One particular trait facilitating Pentecostalism's popularity is divine healing of the sick through the laying on of hands and often accompanying rituals.

It is estimated that 11 percent of Africa's population is charismatic, and the movement has entered many mainline churches, such as the Anglican, Methodist, and Lutheran communities. A noticeable feature of the Lutheran Church Mekane Yesus in Ethiopia is the infiltration of the Charismatic Movement, particularly in its exuberant worship life. Many African indigenous churches also have embraced Pentecostal traits, though these churches tend to be syncretistic because they also include occult practices, placing value on trances, healing power, spiritual warfare, and polygamy.

Pentecostalism is making great inroads in Asia. In India, the Assemblies of God and the Indian Pentecostal Church of God are the largest Pentecostal denominations with 750,000 adherents in 2000. Indonesia boasts the greatest Pentecostal expansion: between 1965 and 1971, during the "Indonesian Revival," more than two million Javanese became Christian. By 2000, there were between nine and twelve million Pentecostals and charismatics, which represents about 4–5 percent of the total population in a country that is 80 percent Muslim, and thus not always welcoming to Christian activities. The Philippines, too, boast a large number of Pentecostals, which is a challenge to the Roman Catholic Church.

In 1949, when Westerners had to leave mainland China, the Pentecostal community counted approximately five million adherents. In 2000, that number varied from 20 to 75 million among the unregistered house churches, which makes China the largest Pentecostal and charismatic community in Asia. But the community has developed in isolation from the rest of Christianity. By 2000, an estimated 10 percent of all Protestants in China were members of two Christian groups: the True Jesus Church, founded by Paul Wei in 1917 in Beijing, and the Jesus Family, founded by Jing Dianying at Mazhuang, Shandong, in 1927. All Christian churches in China seem to practice healing in some form, ranging from prayer for the sick to the laying on of hands by a specially gifted leader. This indicates a strong charismatic and Pentecostal influence on China's Protestant Christianity.

One further country known for its Pentecostal presence is Korea, particularly because of the ministry of David (Paul) Yonggi Cho (1936–). Fifteen years after beginning a small tent church in a Seoul slum in 1958, Yonggi Cho was celebrating worship in a ten-thousand-seat auditorium called Yoido Full Gospel Church (YFGC). By 1993, the YFGC reportedly has 700,000 members and 700 pastors, which makes it one of the largest Christian congregations in the world. Yonggi Cho's church represents the "cell church" strategy propagated and widely used in the

1990s in the Pentecostal and charismatic movements and supported by the writings of Ralph Neighbor Jr. Many churches in Korea are also charismatic in orientation, featuring all-night prayer meetings, exorcisms, prayer mountains, and healing services. A strong connection to traditional shamanism continues to permeate Korean churches.

Of the Latin American countries, Brazil has more Pentecostals than any other nation. Beginning in 1952, a second phase of activity arose in South America with twenty to thirty new Brazilian Pentecostal denominations. The three most important are Brazil for Christ Evangelical Pentecostal Church, God Is Love Pentecostal Church, and Foursquare Gospel Church. After 1975, a third Pentecostal movement took place, one that embraces prosperity. The largest church associated with this movement is the Universal Church of the Kingdom of God (UCKG), founded in 1977 in Rio de Janeiro by Edir Machedo. This church has become the fastest-growing church in Brazil with a thousand churches and more than a million members and a presence in more than fifty countries outside of Brazil. By 2000, the Assemblies of God was the largest non-Catholic church body in Latin and Central America, totaling about four million members.

The above description does not take into account many other Pentecostals arising all over Central and Latin America. Many Pentecostal churches independent from Assemblies of God have emerged and are growing continuously all over South America and the Caribbean. They often are aided by foreign mission. The Charismatic Movement has made strong inroads into mainline churches in Argentina, Brazil, Chile, and Colombia, thereby contributing to institutional weaknesses in the Roman Catholic Church.

Middle East. Many people are not well informed about the state of Christianity in the Middle East. First, Christians in the West assume that Islam has completely replaced Christianity in the Middle East. Second, Christians in the West think that Christianity in the Middle East is of recent origin through the work of missionaries. In fact, Christianity was born in the Middle East (recall Pentecost; Acts 2:6–12), and Christians have lived and continue to live in the countries of North Africa and Southwest Asia (Morocco, Algeria, Tunisia, Libya, Egypt, Sudan, Turkey, Iran, Iraq, Syria, Jordan, Lebanon, Israel, Palestine, Saudi Arabia, Oman, Yemen, Kuwait, and United Arab Emirates).

The denominations of the Middle East may be grouped under four church families: Eastern (Byzantine) Orthodox (who accepted the Council of Chalcedon formula of 451); Assyrian Church of the East (Nestorian) and Oriental Orthodox (who did not accept the Council of Chalcedon's formula in 451); Catholic churches of the Latin rite (Roman Catholic) and of the Eastern rite; and Protestant (Evangelical and Anglican). In May 1974, the first general assembly of the Middle East Council of Churches (MECC) was held in Nicosia, Cyprus. This council brought together three families: the Eastern Orthodox, Oriental Orthodox, and Evangelical (Protestant). After careful negotiation, the Catholic churches of the Middle East joined the council in 1990, though the council remains incomplete because the Ancient Assyrian Church of the East, strongly represented in Iraq, and a number of smaller Protestant churches are not yet full members.

Despite the fact that the Middle East is the birthplace of Christianity, today it is largely Muslim, and Christianity is regarded as a foreign element. Conversion to Christianity is considered disloyal and in many countries is forbidden by sharia law. For this reason, the Orthodox, Catholic, and Protestant churches are generally small and isolated. Together, they make up only 5 percent of the population in the Middle East. The North African region is 9 percent Christian, and Western Asia (Turkey, Syria, Iraq, etc.) is 7 percent Christian.

Since declaring independence in 1920, Syria has sought to respect all religions and practices greater tolerance toward Christianity than other nations of the region. Although Syria's constitution demands that its head of state be a Muslim, the government provides Christians the freedom to buy land and build churches and parsonages. Moreover, Christians are able to practice their faith openly, including broadcasting worship services on Syrian television. In Syria, relationships between the Muslim community and the churches are good. However, in 2011 that relationship began changing with the Arab Spring. A civil war broke out, and currently millions of Syrians have fled the country seeking shelter elsewhere.

In Turkey, the Christian population is a minute percentage of the total population: approximately 0.2 percent of the country's sixty million people. The Armenian Orthodox Church has remained relatively stable in Turkey, whereas large numbers of the Greek and Syriac Orthodox churches have left the country.

For the countries of the Persian Gulf region, reliable data for the Christian population is difficult to determine. Estimates place the Christian population between one and two million, the majority of whom are migrant workers from Asia. The local population of Christians is less than one thousand. In view of the fact that governments in the Persian Gulf rely on foreign labor, they have loosened to a degree their stance on Christian worship. The largest Christian population is in Saudi Arabia. However, little is known about the state of Christianity in that country except that worship is private and underground for all Christians. Dubai, Qatar, and Kuwait have Christian communities that span from Pentecostal movements to Catholic and Coptic Orthodox congregations. Nonetheless, strict rules regulate Christian presence and in particular their relationship to the non-Christian Muslim population.

Since approximately its independence in 1956, Sudan has been plagued by civil wars between the Muslim north and the animist/Christian south. In the south, between three and five million people have been displaced. Because of attempts by the military regimes to impose Arabic and Islamic rule in the south, foreign missionaries have been expelled, and nearly a million people have been displaced as refugees outside the country. Although Christianity suffers persecution, governmental attempts to produce an Islamic nation has led to an exponential growth among Christians in the 1990s. The traditional, historic churches such as the Eastern Orthodox family, the Coptic Orthodox Church, and the oriental family of churches are principally located in the northern part of the country among Muslim people. The Catholic and Evangelical families of churches, such as Anglican and Presbyterian, can be found in the south among believers in animist religions. Christianity is reported to make up 19 percent of the Sudanese population.

Cyprus is the only country in the Middle East where Christianity is in the majority. Christians make up about 80 percent of the total population, and about 98 percent of the Christians belong to the Church of Cyprus. In 1974, Turkey invaded the island of Cyprus and occupied the north region—about 37 percent of the country. In this region, many Christian churches have been robbed and desecrated by the majority Sunni Muslims.

The borders of Israel were established in 1948, and as Jews returned to the region, many Muslims and Christians left. Today, Israel has about 105,000 Christians.

In Egypt, Christianity, consisting mainly of the Coptic Orthodox Church, functions with government permission. It carries out its activities primarily in the open despite being in the midst of extremist Muslim groups such as the Muslim Brotherhood, which seeks to implement Islamic sharia law in all social, political, and legislative aspects of life.

The appearance of the Islamic State of Iraq and the Levant and the continued existence of other violent Muslim groups led to the martyrdom of numerous Christians in Iraq, Syria, Egypt, Nigeria, Kenya, and India in 2015. The Pew Research Center predicted that the number of Muslims could equal the number of Christians by 2050. Competition between Muslim and Christian communities could lead to further persecution or conflict.

North America. North America is considered a largely Christian continent. However, as in Europe, the decline of Christianity is obvious, especially evidenced by those who call themselves "Christian" yet do not attend worship. The 2008 American Religious Identification Survey (ARIS) indicated that growing population and immigration did not add to an increased membership for most denominations. Nearly all of them had a smaller number of adherents.

It is difficult to determine the future of Christianity in the United States. However, we do know that cultural challenges such as abortion, same-sex unions, the ordination of women, stem-cell research, and end-of-life issues—aided through increased secularization—affect Christianity on the whole. Despite this seemingly negative picture, North American Christianity reveals great vigor and interest in worldwide mission, spending vast resources on both personnel (often short-term missionaries) and literature.

Broadcasting is one area in which American Christianity has a worldwide presence. Beginning in the 1940s, southern fundamental churches made extensive use of public radio broadcasting. This radio and later television revivalism gave rise to televangelists such as Pat Robertson and Jim Bakker and now Joel Osteen and others too numerous to count.

The mastery of modern communication technology is also part of North American mainline Protestantism. For example, in 1930, Walter Maier (1893–1950), an ordained pastor of The Lutheran Church—Missouri Synod, began broadcasting *The Lutheran Hour* from the AM station KFUO, which is currently located at the Synod's headquarters in Kirkwood, Missouri. When Maier died in 1950, a strong public representative was lost not only for the Lutheran faith but also for conservative evangelicalism in North America.

In the post–World War II era of public broadcasting, media and public speaking, and crusade events in North America, Billy Graham (1918–) held the leading role for decades and may be considered the foremost Protestant evangelist of the twentieth century. He gained national prominence through a successful evangelistic crusade in Los Angeles in 1949. A number of initiatives enhanced his reputation, including founding the Billy Graham Evangelistic Association (BGEA) in 1950; conducting crusades around the world; establishing his own radio, film, and television ministries; and the publication of *Decision* magazine and many best-selling books. Graham has infused into American Evangelicalism a renewed vigor for world mission and global outreach. To enhance that vision, through BGEA, he organized the Berlin Congress on Evangelism (1966) and regional conferences in Asia, Latin America, Africa, Europe, and the United States. He also promoted and organized the International Congress on World Evangelization at Lausanne, Switzerland (1974), and became a proponent of the Lausanne Movement that came out of that gathering.

One important feature of North American Christianity is the growth of Pentecostalism. Prominent U.S. Pentecostals include Oral Roberts, pioneer televangelist, founder of Oral Roberts University, and a Pentecostal Holiness minister who became a Methodist in 1965; Jimmy Swaggart, popular televangelist, revivalist, and Assemblies of God minister; and Jim Bakker, Assemblies of God minister and with his wife, Tammy Faye, head of the *PTL Club*, a popular television ministry. In the 1980s, Bakker was sentenced to prison for financial mismanagement, and Swaggart was stripped of his ministerial credentials for consorting with a prostitute. Both, however, have returned to their ministry. Despite these setbacks, Pentecostal churches grew enormously from the 1970s into the 1990s. Pentecostalism united with Evangelicalism and engages actively in the Moral Majority and the Religious Right movements to legislate conservative family values.

Donald McGavran (1897–1990) is a key figure in North American Evangelicalism because of his efforts to imprint a missiological and theological legacy. David Allen Hubbard is reported to have said of McGavran: "He has been lauded, and he has been blasted, but he has not been ignored." McGavran is considered the founder of the worldwide Church Growth Movement. As a missionary in India (1937–54), he investigated the conditions under which churches grew. He concluded that congregations grow best where there is a sense of belonging and togetherness, what he called the "we-feeling." McGavran realized that much of his own work and that of other missionaries was accomplishing little toward the goal of world evangelization and growth. He saw the necessity for a well-reasoned mission theory that developed new concepts of mission strategy as well as methodologies that would result in the growth of the Church. Upon his return to the United States, and after a number of setbacks, he founded in 1961 the Institute of Church Growth at Northwest Christian College in Eugene, Oregon. In 1965, he moved to Pasadena, California, where he founded the School of World Mission at Fuller Theological Seminary. Here, he further developed the principles for church growth. In 1970, McGavran's famous work *Understanding Church Growth* was published.

Part of McGavran's insights rest on his negative view of the traditional "mission station" approach of the nineteenth and twentieth centuries. He felt that the Christianity that formed around a mission station actually lacked the qualities necessary for growth and multiplication. Converts were segregated or extracted from their former social relationships and found their only fellowship with other mission station Christians, which only served to create a new tribe, a new caste, a separate society. Converts in this situation limit evangelism because they feel they are better than family members who do not convert and they depend heavily on the mission station for employment and social services. Instead of reaching out, these Christians sometimes became reluctant to share their Christian faith with others because it may mean fewer resources and services for themselves.

Thus McGavran rejected concepts that focus solely on "individual conversion" to Christianity and replaced it with movements of whole tribes or "homogenous units." To become a Christian, no convert should be required to cross racial, social, or linguistic barriers. The underlying principle is that people *like* to be with those of their own race and class without crossing any barriers. Differences with other people should be used rather than broken down to make Christians. In this context, McGavran developed two stages of "Christianization": "discipling" and "perfecting." The first stage involves becoming a Christian, and the second involves growth in the Christian life. Only in the second stage should there be attempts toward breaking down prejudice.

Principles derived from McGavran have impacted North American Christianity and have been taken up and diversified further by his students, including Peter Wagner, Win Arn, John Wimber, Carl George, George Gallup, and George Barna. These principles are exhibited by market-driven churches such as Saddleback Community Church in Orange County, California, which is led by Rick Warren, a graduate of Fuller Theological Seminary, and Willow Creek Community Church in Chicago, which is led by Bill Hybels. The latter especially uses marketing approaches (focus groups, advertising, polling, etc.) to reach out to Baby Boomers.

In the late twentieth century, there also arose within Evangelicalism the "emergent" or "emerging church movement," which sees the church as one that embraces postmodern ideas and the sentiments of the younger generations. It is a movement that wishes to diffuse the influence of modernism in Western Christianity as well as the strong individualism of traditional Evangelicalism. While the movement is very diverse, many emergents display the following characteristics:

- Missional living. Christians should go out into the world to serve God rather than isolate themselves into communities of like-minded individuals.

- Narrative theology. Teaching should focus on narrative presentations of faith and the Bible rather than systematic theology or biblical reductionism.

- Christ-centeredness. While not neglecting the study of Scripture or the love of the Church, Christians should focus their lives on the worship and emulation of the person of Jesus.

Author and pastor Brian McLaren is the most recognizable North American advocate for the emergent church, though he considers himself to be merely one voice among many in the conversation. Emergent Christians are predominantly found in Western Europe, North America, and the South Pacific. Some attend churches that specifically identify themselves as emergent, while others contribute to the conversation from within existing denominations.

The Emerging Church uses a "seeker-friendly" approach that developed at Saddleback Church and Willow Creek Church during the 1990s. These churches drew seekers to them with marketing, whereas emergent churches use a similar strategy to draw people to Jesus. They urge all members to be missionaries. Worship experiences in emergent churches can be quite different than those in the Saddleback/Willow Creek communities.

The Emerging Church movement is closely related to the house church movement in China because both challenge traditional notions of how the Church should be organized. Not all house churches are as influenced by postmodern philosophy as the emerging church, but many emerging churches are also house churches.

Twenty-First Century Mission in a Globalized World. Christianity of today, particularly through her mission, shares an infrastructure and information stream throughout the global world. These benefits were unavailable in the nineteenth and early twentieth centuries in the preparation of missionaries. Thus, two aspects identify Christian mission in the twenty-first century. First, with the changing demographics of world Christian populations, complemented by immigration of non-Christian people into Western nations, the flow of missionaries from the West to the rest of the world is expected to reverse itself. Thousands of immigrants and ethnic minorities settling in Western countries present a harvest field for all churches to address. Unlike the traditional stream of missionaries leaving Western countries for Third World nations, the West, too, deserves a steady increase of missionaries. This raises the need to re-strategize missions from a single-stream to a dual-stream approach. Mission in a globalized world needs to change from a pre-global mind-set to one that openly embraces the Western world as a mission field as well.

Second, though the focus should still be on worldwide outreach, it must include a modified strategy. If Barrett and Johnson's statistics are true, Christianity's population in the near future will not exceeded 34 percent. Some sectors of the world's population still have no Christian presence, as the 10/40 Window seems to project. According to Barrett, churches have rarely deployed missionaries to areas where heavily non-Christian populations exist. The result is that Christian mission concentrates more than 99 percent of its efforts in countries where the local Christians themselves could take on missionary tasks. Barrett argues that instead churches and their societies should deploy missionaries proportionally to the non-Christian and unevangelized populations in certain countries he identifies as World C. Thus the number of missionaries present in World C would increase.

Christianity and mission face non-Christian opposition in many parts of the world. According to the *Evangelical Dictionary of World Missions*, martyrdom is and will be measured in the hundreds of thousands (p. 620).

One further change affecting mission has been the paradigm shift in most Protestant denominations from career to short-term volunteer missions. In this regard, global accessibility through information and infrastructure has enabled a broader participation of missionaries worldwide. Since this is a recent phenomenon, a truthful evaluation of the benefits of such wide Christian participation still has to be conducted.

Epilogue. Jesus Christ promised that "the gates of hell shall not prevail" against the Church (Matthew 16:18). We have seen in these pages how often the Church has endured hardship, yet also how she has prevailed by God's grace. In all circumstances, the promises of God have upheld and strengthened the Church. Knowing the past likewise allows Christians and congregations today to face the future more wisely and confidently.

As one ponders Christianity's future in the twenty-first century, one becomes aware also of its challenges as well as its opportunities. It is difficult to make a global statement on Christianity's future because so much is determined by the regional context. But let us close with some general descriptions of Christianity's future challenges and opportunities:

First, the human care and social need around the world will not abate. On the contrary, the disparity between wealthy and poor countries will increase even further. Christianity will find itself on both sides of this issue. Christians blessed with resources will remain active in social care ministries and provide care for basic human needs. What compounds poverty and social issues are also factors like wars, diseases, environmental disasters, water shortages, child labor, and urban slums, to name just a few.

Second, Christianity continues to face opposition. In Western countries, secularization is gnawing steadily at Christian convictions. In other parts of the world, especially in countries where Christian populations have to contend with majority religions, persecution or marginalization of Christians occurs daily. The threat of syncretism will also challenge biblical truth and clarity of the Christian message to the world. In view of this, the ministry of teaching and instruction (Matthew 28:18–20) is in particular need among those who become future leaders of churches.

These difficulties should not discourage Christians who remember the work of the Church from age to age. Opportunities also abound. Globalization has made the world more accessible to the Gospel. Christianity has the potential of bringing Christ to all nations, particularly to regions showing low percentages of Christians. It remains to be seen how Christians will assume their missionary role described in the Scriptures and voiced heavenward in daily prayers. From the shores of Galilee to the corners of the globe, there is every reason for bold action and certain hope.

Index

Numbers in parentheses represent dates for persons or events.